Lecture Notes in Computer Science 16409

The series Lecture Notes in Computer Science (LNCS), including its subseries Lecture Notes in Artificial Intelligence (LNAI) and Lecture Notes in Bioinformatics (LNBI), has established itself as a medium for the publication of new developments in computer science and information technology research, teaching, and education.

LNCS enjoys close cooperation with the computer science R & D community, the series counts many renowned academics among its volume editors and paper authors, and collaborates with prestigious societies. Its mission is to serve this international community by providing an invaluable service, mainly focused on the publication of conference and workshop proceedings and postproceedings. LNCS commenced publication in 1973.

Rongmao Chen · Robert H. Deng · Moti Yung
Editors

Information Security and Cryptology

21st International Conference, Inscrypt 2025
Xi'an, China, October 19–22, 2025
Revised Selected Papers, Part II

Editors
Rongmao Chen
National University of Defense Technology
Changsha, China

Robert H. Deng
Singapore Management University
Singapore, Singapore

Moti Yung
Columbia University
New York, NY, USA

ISSN 0302-9743 ISSN 1611-3349 (electronic)
Lecture Notes in Computer Science
ISBN 978-981-95-6202-2 ISBN 978-981-95-6203-9 (eBook)
https://doi.org/10.1007/978-981-95-6203-9

This Springer imprint is published by the registered company Springer Nature Singapore Pte Ltd.
The registered company address is: 152 Beach Road, #21-01/04 Gateway East, Singapore 189721, Singapore

Preface

The 21st International Conference on Information Security and Cryptology (Inscrypt 2025) was held during October 19–22, 2025, in Xi'an, China.

Inscrypt 2025 marked a significant milestone for the conference: as our first attempt at a two-round submission process, we witnessed an unprecedented response from the global academic and industrial community. The submission of the papers and the review process were carried out using the EasyChair platform. A total of 315 submissions were received–surpassing all previous records and underscoring Inscrypt's growing reputation as a premier venue for sharing breakthroughs in information security. Each submission underwent a rigorous, double-blind peer review process, overseen by a distinguished Program Committee (PC) comprising 80 experts, alongside 183 external reviewers. Every paper was evaluated by at least three independent reviewers, with contentious cases resolved through in-depth PC discussions, ensuring that only work of the highest technical merit, originality, and relevance was selected.

After months of meticulous review and deliberation, we are proud to include 79 accepted papers in these proceedings, resulting in an overall acceptance rate of approximately 25%. All accepted papers are published as part of the Springer Lecture Notes in Computer Science (LNCS) series. This competitive selection process guarantees that these three volumes represent outstanding work that pushes the boundaries of existing knowledge, addresses pressing real-world challenges, and opens new avenues for future research. The papers cover a broad spectrum of topics central to information security and cryptology, including (but not limited to) post-quantum cryptography, secure multi-party computation, privacy-preserving machine learning, blockchain security, and attack detection in encrypted systems. This diversity not only reflects the interdisciplinary nature of modern information security but also ensures that the proceedings serve as a valuable resource for researchers, practitioners, and students with varied interests in the field.

Beyond the technical contributions, Inscrypt 2025 was a platform for vibrant exchange: the conference hosted five keynote talks by world-renowned experts–Wanlei Zhou from City Univeristy of Macau (China), Yang Xiang from Swinburne University of Technology (Australia), Jian Guo from Nanyang Technological University (Singapore), Tian Tian from Information Engineering University (China), and Willy Susilo from University of Wollongong (Australia) –who offered critical insights into emerging trends and unmet needs. Complemented by 10 technical sessions and informal discussions, these interactions enriched the conference experience and laid the groundwork for future collaborations–many of which we hope will continue to evolve through the ideas shared in this volume.

None of this would have been possible without the dedication of countless individuals. We first extend our deepest gratitude to the Program Committee members and external reviewers for their tireless efforts: their expertise, rigor, and constructive feedback were the backbone of the review process, ensuring the quality and fairness of the selection. We also thank the General Chairs–Xiaofen Chen, Xinyi Huang, and Dongdai Lin–for their strategic vision and leadership in guiding the conference from conception to execution; the Local Organizing Team and volunteers for their meticulous work in coordinating the on-site and virtual events; and many institutes for their strong support: State Key Laboratory of Integrated Service Networks (ISN), State Key Laboratory of Cyberspace Security Defense (SKLCSD), NSCLab, the China 111 project (B16037 and B23046), and Xi'an ISTC Base for Data Security and Privacy Preservation.

To the authors of the papers in this volume: thank you for trusting Inscrypt with your great work. Your contributions are not only a testament to your creativity and expertise but also a driving force for the advancement of information security. We hope these LNCS proceedings will amplify the reach of your research, inspire further exploration, and contribute to the global effort to build a more secure and private digital world.

We express our sincere appreciation to Springer for their long-standing partnership and support in publishing these proceedings. The LNCS series' reputation for excellence aligns perfectly with Inscrypt's commitment to high-quality research, and we are proud to join the ranks of leading computer science conferences featured in this series.

October 2025

Rongmao Chen
Robert H. Deng
Moti Yung

Organization

Honorary Conference Chairs

Xiaoyun Wang	Tsinghua University, China
Moti Yung	Columbia University, USA

General Co-chairs

Xiaofeng Chen	Xidian University, China
Xinyi Huang	Jinan University, China
Dongdai Lin	Institute of Information Engineering, Chinese Academy of Sciences, China

Program Co-chairs

Rongmao Chen	National University of Defense Technology, China
Robert H. Deng	Singapore Management University, Singapore
Moti Yung	Columbia University, USA

Organizing Chairs

Debiao He	Wuhan University, China
Zheng Yan	Xidian University, China

Publication Chair

Xiaoyu Zhang	Xidian University, China

Publicity Chairs

Weizhi Meng	Lancaster University, UK
Chunhua Su	University of Aizu, Japan

Guohua Tian	Xidian University, China
Wei Zong	University of Wollongong, Australia

Workshop Chairs

Feng Zhang	Renmin University of China, China
Xiaoyu Zhang	Xidian University, China

Steering Committee

Kai Chen	Institute of Information Engineering, Chinese Academy of Sciences, China
Xiaofeng Chen	Xidian University, China
Yi Deng	Institute of Information Engineering, Chinese Academy of Sciences, China
Dawu Gu	Shanghai Jiao Tong University, China
Debiao He	Wuhan University, China
Xinyi Huang	Jinan University, Guangzhou, China
Hui Li	Xidian University, China
Dongdai Lin	Institute of Information Engineering, Chinese Academy of Sciences, China
Zhe Liu	Zhejiang University, China
Meiqin Wang	Shandong University, China
Jian Weng	Jinan University, China
Yu Yu	Shanghai Jiao Tong University, China
Moti Yung	Columbia University, USA
Bingsheng Zhang	Zhejiang University, China
Fangguo Zhang	Sun Yat-sen University, China

Program Committee

Joonsang Baek	University of Wollongong, Australia
Song Bian	Beihang University, China
Yanan Cao	Institute of Information Engineering Chinese Academy of Sciences, China
Jie Chen	Wuhan University, China
Kai Chen	Institute of Information Engineering Chinese Academy of Sciences, China
Mingjie Chen	Katholieke Universiteit Leuven, Belgium

Rongmao Chen	National University of Defense Technology, China
Xiaofeng Chen	Xidian University, China
Yu Chen	Shandong University, China
Yu Long Chen	NIST, USA and KU Leuven, Belgium
Tingting Cui	Hangzhou Dianzi University, China
Robert H. Deng	Singapore Management University, Singapore
Yi Deng	Institute of Information Engineering Chinese Academy of Sciences, China
Steven Duong	University of Wollongong, Australia
Shaojing Fu	National University of Defense Technology, China
Junqing Gong	East China Normal University, China
Clémentine Gritti	INSA Lyon, France
Dawu Gu	Shanghai Jiao Tong University, China
Fuchun Guo	University of Wollongong, Australia
Qian Guo	Lund University, Sweden
Kai Hu	Shandong University, China
Pengfei Hu	Shandong University, China
Xinyi Huang	Jinan University, China
Wenqiang Jin	Hunan University, China
Mustafa Khairallah	Lund University, Sweden
Charlotte Lefevre	Radboud University, Netherlands
Chaoyun Li	University of Surrey, UK
Meng Li	Hefei University of Technology, China
Chao Lin	Fujian Normal University, China
Dongdai Lin	Institute of Information Engineering Chinese Academy of Sciences, China
Meicheng Liu	Institute of Information Engineering Chinese Academy of Sciences, China
Weizhi Meng	Lancaster University, UK
Khoa Nguyen	University of Wollongong, Australia
Jianting Ning	Wuhan University, China
Cong Peng	Wuhan University, China
Baodong Qin	Xi'an University of Posts and Telecommunications, China
Shahram Rasoolzadeh	Ruhr University Bochum, Germany
Jun Shao	Zhejiang Gongshang University, China
Yaobin Shen	Xiamen University, China
Chunhua Su	University of Aizu, Japan
Chao Sun	Southeast University, China
Ling Sun	Shandong University, China

Shifeng Sun	Shanghai Jiao Tong University, China
Yao Sun	Institute of Information Engineering Chinese Academy of Sciences, China
Willy Susilo	University of Wollongong, Australia
Younes Talibi Alaoui	Katholieke Universiteit Leuven, Belgium
Yangguang Tian	University of Surrey, UK
Tran Viet Xuan Phuong	University of Arkansas at Little Rock, USA
Anyu Wang	Tsinghua University, China
Hao Wang	Shandong Normal University, China
Haoyang Wang	Shanghai Jiao Tong University, China
Huaxiong Wang	Nanyang Technological University, Singapore
Meiqin Wang	Shandong University, China
Weijia Wang	Shandong University, China
Yi Wang	National University of Defense Technology, China
Yuyu Wang	University of Electronic Science and Technology of China, China
Zhedong Wang	Shanghai Jiao Tong University, China
Shengmin Xu	Fujian Normal University, China
Haiyang Xue	Singapore Management University, Singapore
Yinxing Xue	University of Science and Technology of China, China
Hailun Yan	University of Chinese Academy of Sciences, China
Guomin Yang	Singapore Management University, Singapore
Yang Yu	Tsinghua University, China
Moti Yung	Columbia University, USA
Bingsheng Zhang	Zhejiang University, China
Fan Zhang	Zhejiang University, China
Fangguo Zhang	Sun Yat-sen University, China
Guoming Zhang	Shandong University, China
Shengzhi Zhang	Boston University, USA
Yuan Zhang	Fudan University, China
Yue Zhang	Drexel University, USA

Additional Reviewers

An, Zhiyuan
Basso, Andrea
Belkheyar, Yanis
Bian, Yi
Cai, Dalong
Chen, Bohang
Chen, Jinrong
Chen, Linyi

Chen, Shiyao
Chen, Siwei
Chen, Xiuyuan
Chen, Yumin
Deng, Weiqing
Dong, Minglang
Dong, Xiaoyang
Du, Qiuyan
Gao, Fei
Guimagang Azebaze, Laurian
Guo, Yanjie
Hao, Meng
Hao, Xiaohan
Hart, Harry
He, Jinwen
He, Yuchen
Hong, Geng
Hou, Shiqi
Huang, Xiao
Huang, Zhenyu
Ji, Pengwei
Jiang, Bowen
Jiang, Changsong
Jiao, Jiao
Junhao, Huang
Kong, Xiangyu
Lai, Chengzhe
Lai, Yi-Fu
Lang, Yongkang
Li, Chen
Li, Congyi
Li, Feng
Li, Haoran
Li, Ji
Li, Jing
Li, Meilin
Li, Nan
Li, Wenzhong
Li, Xiaotong
Li, Yajun
Li, Yingying
Li, Yongqiang
Li, Zhi
Liao, Xinyue
Liao, Ziwen
Lin, Chao
Lin, Xudong
Lin, Yuliang
Lin, Zihan
Ling, Yunhao
Liu, Chongyang
Liu, Qun
Liu, Sen
Liu, Zihan
London, Callum
Luo, Shuhua
Lv, Peizhuo
Mengqi, Feng
Nan, Yuhong
Nguyen, Khanh
Niu, Peiyao
Niu, Ziyu
Pan, Jin
Peng, Liqiang
Peng, Tang
Pu, Lang
Qin, Chengyi
Qu, Shipei
Reijnders, Krijn
Ren, Xiaoning
Ruigang, Liang
Shi, Xuanyu
Shi, Youkun
Song, Shuwei
Su, Chuanjie
Su, Xiangyu
Sui, Zhimei
Sun, Jianfei
Sun, Kai
Tan, Zhongsheng
Tang, Guofeng
Tang, Khai Hanh
Tang, Shuncheng
Tang, Wenxu
Thakur, Indranil
Tu, Binbin
Wan, Xiaohan
Wang, Jianfeng
Wang, Jianhua
Wang, Ruida

Wang, Tianning
Wang, Weihao
Wang, Weizhe
Wang, Wenhao
Wang, Xinchen
Wang, Xun
Wang, Yanzhong
Wang, Yijia
Wang, Youcheng
Wang, Yu
Wang, Yunling
Wei, Longxiang
Wei, Runhao
Wei, Xiaoyang
Wei, Xiaoyang
Wu, Tong
Wu, Wenhui
Wu, Zhuo
Xia, Xiansong
Xiang, Binwu
Xiang, Lan
Xiao, Wenbo
Xiong, Saisi
Xiong, Tianjing
Xu, Jun
Yang, Haining
Yang, Liuyu
Yang, Qianqian
Yang, Wenzhang
Yang, Yi
Yang, Yifan
Yang, Yuchen
Yao, Lisha
Yap, Trevor
Ye, Jiaming
Yong, Liu
Yuan, Boshi
Yue, Chang
Yuhuan, Kang
Zha, Yuting
Zhang, Fan
Zhang, Fangguo
Zhang, Jianing
Zhang, Jingyue
Zhang, Lingyue
Zhang, Liu
Zhang, Xi
Zhang, Xiaolin
Zhang, Xiaoyu
Zhang, Zhiyu
Zhang, Zongyang
Zhao, Shengnan
Zhao, Xianxin
Zhao, Yue
Zhou, Mengjie
Zhou, Qihang
Zhou, Tian
Zhou, Xiaotong
Zhou, Yunxiao
Zhou, Zhayiwen
Zhu, Xudong
Zong, Wei
Zuo, Cong

Contents

Secure Multi-party Computation

Quantum-Computation Classical-Communication Commitments from SZK-Hardness

Kexin Gao[1,2], Shujiao Cao[1,2](✉), and Rui Xue[1,2]

[1] State Key Laboratory of Cyberspace Security Defense, Institute of Information Engineering, Chinese Academy of Sciences, Beijing 100093, China
{gaokexin,caoshujiao,xuerui}@iie.ac.cn

[2] School of Cyber Security, University of CAS, Beijing 100049, China

Abstract. As quantum computation advances, stable and cost-effective quantum communication remains a significant challenge. This has led to the emergence of the Quantum-Computation Classical-Communication (QCCC) model, a practically motivated framework where parties perform local quantum computations but communicate exclusively through classical channels. Despite substantial progress in quantum commitment schemes, prior constructions have either depended on quantum channels or relied on strong assumptions, such as collapsing hash functions. This raises the open question of whether collapse-binding commitments can be achieved in the QCCC setting under weaker assumptions.

In this work, we resolve this gap by constructing a constant-round QCCC commitment that is statistically hiding and computationally collapse-binding. Our approach adapts and extends the framework of Bitansky *et al.* [EUROCRYPT '19]: structurally, we preserve their proof strategy while modifying it to operate in the QCCC model, and foundationally, we show that collapse-binding can be obtained from the average-case hardness of problems in $\mathcal{SZK}$. This both broadens the applicability of their techniques and improves upon prior work by avoiding reliance on collapsing hash functions.

Keywords: Quantum-computation classical-communication (QCCC) model · Constant-round statistically hiding commitment · Collapse-binding · Average-case hardness of $\mathcal{SZK}$

1 Introduction

Commitment schemes are fundamental cryptographic primitives with well-defined properties and broad applications. In the classical setting, a commitment functions like a "sealed envelope": the sender fixes a message while keeping it hidden, and later reveals it. Security relies on two properties: binding, which prevents the sender from changing the message, and hiding, which prevents

R. Chen et al. (Eds.): Inscrypt 2025, LNCS 16409, pp. 3–22, 2026.
https://doi.org/10.1007/978-981-95-6203-9_1

the receiver from learning it prematurely. These come in statistical and computational flavors, depending on whether security holds against unbounded or probabilistic polynomial-time adversaries.

The transition to quantum computation presents both challenges and opportunities for commitment schemes. On the one hand, quantum adversaries equipped with superposition and entanglement can compromise many classical constructions; on the other, quantum techniques enable fundamentally new protocols [3,22]. Security notions adapt accordingly: computational security must hold against quantum polynomial-time (QPT) adversaries, while statistical security retains its information-theoretic strength. Yet, the no-go theorem of Mayers and LoChau shows a fundamental limitation—it is impossible to achieve both statistical hiding and statistical binding, even with quantum communication [18,19].

Despite these limitations, statistically hiding commitments with computationally binding remain essential for long-term confidentiality. While binding only needs to hold during protocol execution, hiding must protect the committed message indefinitely, even against future advances in computational power. Such commitments have broad applications: they enable statistical zero-knowledge arguments for all $\mathcal{NP}$ languages [7,24], play a crucial role in secure multi-party computation against adaptive adversaries [8], and are fundamental to certain coin-tossing protocols [17].

This unique combination of long-term secrecy and practical applicability has driven sustained research efforts to optimize statistically hiding commitments along three key dimensions: (1) minimizing computational assumptions, (2) reducing round complexity, and (3) improving communication efficiency. The core challenge lies in overcoming the inherent tension between these objectives—constructions from weaker assumptions often require more rounds, whereas real-world applications demand constant-round protocols. Current results illustrate this trade-off: while one-way functions (OWFs) suffice for constant-round statistically binding commitments [13,16,23], they only yield statistically hiding commitments with polynomial round complexity [15]. Stronger primitives—including claw-free permutations [14] with efficiently recognizable index sets [12] and collision-resistant hash functions—support constant-round statistically hiding schemes [25], but at the cost of stronger assumptions.

Moving to the quantum setting introduces an additional layer of difficulty. Classical binding notions fail catastrophically: Unruh and Ambainis et al. [1,33] demonstrated a computationally classical binding commitment scheme where quantum adversaries can open a commitment to any one message, violating binding entirely. This motivated stronger definitions like sum-binding [9,11] and collapse-binding [33], later shown equivalent by Dall'Agnol and Spooner [10]. However, current constructions of such quantum-secure commitments rely heavily on collapsing hash functions [32]—a specialized quantum primitive believed to be strictly stronger than classical collision resistance [31,33]. This reliance highlights a critical gap:

Can we construct constant-round statistically hiding commitments with computationally sum-binding against quantum adversaries without collapsing hash functions?

We address this question in the quantum-computation classical-communication (QCCC) model [4], where parties perform local quantum computation but communicate only through classical messages. This model reflects realistic scenarios in which quantum computers are available but quantum communication remains costly or impractical. The QCCC framework, already adopted in various cryptographic protocols [6,21], provides an ideal setting for studying practically feasible quantum-secure primitives.

1.1 Overview of Our Results and Techniques

In this paper, we demonstrate that the constant-round, statistically hiding commitment scheme built on the average-case hardness of problems in $\mathcal{SZK}$ proposed by Bitansky *et al.* [5], can be successfully lifted to the QCCC setting. This extension is formalized by the following theorem, which constitutes our main contribution.

Theorem 1 (informal). *A quantum hard-on-average problem in $\mathcal{SZK}$ implies a constant-round statistically hiding and computationally sum-binding commitment scheme in the QCCC model.*

By the result of Dall'Agnol and Spooner [10], sum-binding is equivalent to collapse-binding. Consequently, our construction yields a constant-round, computationally collapse-binding commitment scheme in the QCCC setting under the average-case hardness in $\mathcal{SZK}$. This improves upon prior constructions, which require stronger primitives such as collapsing hash functions [32].

To extend the classical framework of Bitansky *et al.* [5] to the QCCC model, we provide a careful adaptation of its core cryptographic building blocks to ensure security against quantum polynomial-time (QPT) adversaries. Our technical approach first develops quantum-secure versions of two key primitives—instance-dependent commitments and witness-indistinguishable proofs—and then combines them into the final commitment construction.

QCCC Instance-Dependent Commitments with Sum-Binding. The first building block is the instance-dependent commitment (IDC) scheme for any promise problem $\Pi = (\Pi_{\mathrm{Y}}, \Pi_{\mathrm{N}}) \in \mathcal{SZK}$. An IDC must be *statistically hiding* for "YES" instances ($x \in \Pi_{\mathrm{Y}}$) and *statistically binding* for "NO" instances ($x \in \Pi_{\mathrm{N}}$). While classical constructions for such IDCs exist unconditionally for $\Pi = (\Pi_{\mathrm{Y}}, \Pi_{\mathrm{N}}) \in \mathcal{SZK}$, their security guarantees only classical binding, which is insufficient against quantum adversaries.

A central component of our argument is proving that the stronger quantum notion of *sum-binding* is inherited from classical binding in the statistical setting. This allows us to lift $\mathcal{SZK}$-based IDC constructions directly to the QCCC setting, ensuring they remain statistically sum-binding on "NO" instances. Our proof proceeds by contradiction: suppose a quantum adversary S^* breaks statistically sum-binding. We then construct an unbounded classical adversary S^{**} that simulates and "rewinds" S^*, extracting two valid openings (b, dec_b) and $(1-b, \mathrm{dec}_{1-b})$ for the same commitment transcript. This contradicts the original scheme's statistically classical binding property.

QCCC Witness-Indistinguishable Proofs for $\mathcal{NP}$. The second building block is a constant-round, computationally witness-indistinguishable ($\mathcal{WI}$) proof system for all languages in $\mathcal{NP}$, secure in the QCCC model with negligible soundness error. We establish its existence under our core assumption—$\mathcal{SZK}$-hardness against quantum adversaries—by carefully adapting classical constructions to the QCCC setting:

1. Average-case hardness of an $\mathcal{SZK}$ problem against quantum adversaries implies the existence of quantum-secure OWFs.
2. These OWFs yield computationally hiding and statistically sum-binding QCCC bit commitment schemes.
3. Building on these commitments, we construct computational zero-knowledge proofs for $\mathcal{NP}$ secure against QPT verifiers.
4. Finally, any such computational zero-knowledge proof system can be compiled into a computationally witness-indistinguishable protocol following the classical paradigm.

For our final construction's hiding property, the $\mathcal{WI}$ protocol must have *negligible soundness error*, which we achieve via standard parallel repetition. We further prove that parallel repetition preserves computational witness indistinguishability in the QCCC model, allowing the soundness error to be reduced to a negligible function.

The Final Commitment Scheme and Security Analysis. Our final protocol $\mathsf{Com} = (\mathsf{S}, \mathsf{R})$ integrates these two components through a multi-stage interaction between the sender S, holding a private input $m \in \{0,1\}$, and receiver R. The protocol is given in Construction 1, and we summarize its steps below:

1. **Seeded instances generation:** The parties jointly generate the public instances $\{x_{i,b}\}_{i\in[n],b\in\{0,1\}}$. First, R commits to $2n$ random strings $\{\rho_{i,b}\}_{i\in[n],b\in\{0,1\}}$, and then S provides $2n$ random strings $\{\sigma_{i,b}\}_{i\in[n],b\in\{0,1\}}$. R computes seeds $r_{i,b} = \rho_{i,b} \oplus \sigma_{i,b}$ and generates the instances $x_{i,b} \leftarrow \mathsf{Samp}(r_{i,b})$, which are sent to S. This ensures that S cannot know the preimages $\{r_{i,b}\}_{i\in[n],b\in\{0,1\}}$.
2. **$\mathcal{WI}$ proof of consistency:** R uses the QCCC $\mathcal{WI}$ protocol to prove to S that, for one bit $b^* \in \{0,1\}$, all instances in the corresponding column $\{x_{i,b^*}\}_{i\in[n]}$ were generated "consistently" (i.e., from known preimages), without revealing the witness.
3. **Message commitment via IDC:** To commit to a bit m, S randomly generates the ensemble $\{m_{i,b}\}_{i\in[n],b\in\{0,1\}}$ such that $m = \bigoplus_{i,b} m_{i,b}$, and executes $2n$ parallel QCCC IDCs, committing each share $m_{i,b}$ within the corresponding common instance $x_{i,b}$.

The security of this construction depends on the properties of its components:

Statistically Hiding: An adversary R^* attempting to break the hiding property has only two possible strategies: (1). The column of consistently generated instances $\{x_{i,b^*}\}_{i\in[n]}$ are all "NO" instances. This event occurs with negligible probability. Otherwise, the underlying IDC ensures statistically hiding, ensuring that R^* learns nothing about $m_{i,b_{i\in[n],b\in\{0,1\}}}$, and hence about the message m. (2). R^* cheats in the $\mathcal{WI}$ proof by claiming that a column of "NO" instances $\{\tilde{x}_{i,b^*}\}_{i\in[n]}$ was consistently generated. However, due to the negligible soundness error of the $\mathcal{WI}$ proof, the probability of success is also negligible.

Computationally Sum-Binding: Any QPT adversary S^* that breaks the sum-binding property with non-negligible advantage can be leveraged to construct a decider D for an average-case hardness promise problem in $\mathcal{SZK}$. The decider embeds the challenge instance x into the parallel IDC executions of the protocol run by S^*. If S^* breaks the sum-binding property, then at least one of the $2n$ parallel IDC instances must violate the sum-binding property, which implies that the embedded instance corresponds to a "YES" instance. Thus, D proceeds as follows: if the IDC instances with embedded instance x satisfies sum-binding, it outputs a random guess ("YES" or "NO"); otherwise, it outputs "YES". This gives D a non-negligible distinguishing advantage derived from S^*.

2 Preliminary

In this section, we first review classical interactive proof systems and their fundamental properties. We then transition to the quantum setting, introducing basic notions of quantum computation and presenting quantum analogues of standard tools, including zero-knowledge proofs and commitment schemes in the QCCC model.

2.1 Interactive Proof System

We begin by the notion of an interactive proof system for a language L:

Definition 1. *A pair of interactive machines* (P, V) *is called an **interactive proof** for a language* L *with completeness error* ε *and soundness error* δ *if the verifier* V *is polynomial-time and the following conditions are satisfied:*

- ***Completeness**: For every* $x \in L$*, the honest* P *convinces the verifier with high probability:*

$$\Pr[(\mathsf{P}, \mathsf{V})(x) = 1] \geq 1 - \varepsilon.$$

- ***Soundness**: For every* $x \notin L$ *and any prover (possibly cheating)* P^**, the verifier accepts with low probability:*

$$\Pr[(\mathsf{P}^*, \mathsf{V})(x) = 1] \leq \delta.$$

Here, ε and δ are usually chosen as $1/3$. However, it can sometimes be replaced by a negligible function of the input length $|x|$.

One of the most fundamental security requirements for interactive proof systems is the zero-knowledge property. In what follows, we introduce the notion of a statistical zero-knowledge proof system. Besides, the class $\mathcal{SZK}$ (Statistical Zero Knowledge) is usually defined as the set of promise problems that have statistical zero-knowledge interactive proofs.

Definition 2. *An interactive proof* (P, V) *for a language L is said to be statistical zero-knowledge if for every polynomial-time* V^* *and every input $x \in L$, there exists a PPT simulator* Sim *such that*

$$\{\mathsf{View}_{(\mathsf{P},\mathsf{V}^*)(x)}\}_{x\in L} \approx_s \{\mathsf{Sim}(x)\}_{x\in L},$$

Here, $\mathsf{View}_{(\mathsf{P},\mathsf{V}^*)(x)}$ *denotes the random variable consisting of* V^**'s internal randomness and the sequence of messages exchanged with* P *during the interaction.*

In addition to zero-knowledge, witness indistinguishability is another widely applicable notion in interactive proof systems. More precisely, consider a binary relation $R_L := \{(x, w) : x \in L\}$ corresponding to a language L, where R_L is polynomial-time-recognizable. For a fixed instance x, define the set of valid witnesses as $R_L(x) := \{w : (x, w) \in R_L\}$. Then, we can formalize the classical witness-indistinguishable proof system as follows:

Definition 3. *Let* (P, V) *be an interactive proof system for a language L. We say that* (P, V) *is witness indistinguishable for R_L if for every probabilistic polynomial-time verifier* V^* *with an auxiliary input z, and for every two sequences $\{w_x^1\}_{x\in L}$ and $\{w_x^2\}_{x\in L}$ such that $w_x^1, w_x^2 \in R_L(x)$, the following distributions are computationally indistinguishable:*

$$\{\mathsf{View}_{(P(w_x^1),V^*(z))(x)}\}_{x\in L} \approx_c \{\mathsf{View}_{(P(w_x^2),V^*(z))(x)}\}_{x\in L}.$$

2.2 Quantum Computation

We provide a brief overview of the quantum computation concepts relevant to this work; for a comprehensive treatment, see Nielsen and Chuang [27].

Given a Hilbert space $\mathcal{X}$, a vector $|\psi\rangle \in \mathcal{X}$ represents a quantum pure state, normalized so that $\||\psi\rangle\| = 1$. An ensemble of pure states $\{p_i, |\psi_i\rangle\}$ describes a quantum system in state $|\psi_i\rangle$ with probability p_i. Such ensembles are commonly represented by a density operator $\rho = \sum_i p_i |\psi_i\rangle\langle\psi_i| \in S(\mathcal{X})$, where $S(\mathcal{X})$ is the set of Hermitian operators on $\mathcal{X}$. We often write $\rho^{\mathcal{X}}$ to emphasize that ρ acts on the space $\mathcal{X}$.

A unitary operation is a linear operator U satisfying $UU^\dagger = \mathbb{I}$, where $\mathbb{I}$ is the identity. A projective measurement $\{P_i\}_i$ consists of orthogonal projectors with $\sum_i P_i = \mathbb{I}$. In the special case of a two-outcome projective measurement $M := \{P, \mathbb{I} - P\}$ applied to a pure state $|\psi\rangle$, the probability of outcome 1 is

$p = \|P|\psi\rangle\|^2 = \mathrm{Tr}(P|\psi\rangle\langle\psi|)$. For clarity, we write $U^{\mathcal{X}}$ (resp., $M^{\mathcal{X}}$) for a unitary (resp., measurement) acting on space $\mathcal{X}$.

For Hilbert spaces $\mathcal{X}$ and $\mathcal{Y}$, let $L(\mathcal{X}, \mathcal{Y})$ denote the set of linear mappings from $\mathcal{X}$ to $\mathcal{Y}$, and $L(\mathcal{X}, \mathcal{X}) := L(\mathcal{X})$ for brevity. A super-operator $\mathbf{\Phi} : L(\mathcal{X}) \to L(\mathcal{Y})$ is said to be admissible if it is completely positive and trace-preserving. When considering the indistinguishability in the computational sense of two super-operators, the following definition is essential.

Definition 4. *Given two admissible super-operators $\mathbf{\Phi}_0$ and $\mathbf{\Phi}_1$ from n-qubit to m-qubit, they are said to be polynomially quantum indistinguishable, denoted as $\mathbf{\Phi}_0 \approx_{qc} \mathbf{\Phi}_1$, if for all mixed states σ on $(n+k)$-qubit and all $(m+k)$-qubit quantum circuits Q of size s, there exists a negligible function such that*

$$|\Pr[Q((\mathbf{\Phi}_0 \otimes \mathbb{I}_k)(\sigma))] - \Pr[Q((\mathbf{\Phi}_1 \otimes \mathbb{I}_k)(\sigma))]| \leq \mathsf{negl}(n).$$

Additionally, say the ensembles $\{\mathbf{\Phi}_x : x \in \{0,1\}^*\}$ and $\{\mathbf{\Psi}_x : x \in \{0,1\}^*\}$ polynomially quantum indistinguishable, denoted as $\{\mathbf{\Phi}_x : x \in \{0,1\}^*\} \approx_{qc} \{\mathbf{\Psi}_x : x \in \{0,1\}^*\}$, if $\mathbf{\Psi}_x \approx_{qc} \mathbf{\Phi}_x$ for all x.

2.3 Zero-Knowledge Proof System in the QCCC Model

Here, we adopt the notion of quantum zero-knowledge introduced by Watrous [35] in the QCCC model. In this setting, a prover P and a verifier V perform local quantum computation, and their interaction on input x is modeled by an admissible super-operator $\mathbf{\Phi}_x^{(\mathsf{P},\mathsf{V})}$. Due to the remarkable classical communication, we assume that the qubits decohere immediately upon being transmitted between P and V.

To formalize the zero-knowledge property, let $\mathbf{\Phi}_x^{(\mathsf{P},\mathsf{V}^*)}$ denote the super-operator induced by an honest prover interacting with a potentially malicious QPT verifier V^* on input x, mapping $q(|x|)$ auxiliary qubits to $r(|x|)$ output qubits. On the other hand, let $\mathbf{\Psi}_x^{\mathsf{Sim}}$ denote the admissible super-operator induced by a QPT simulator Sim on the same input. The interactive proof system (P, V) is quantum computational zero-knowledge for language L if, for all QPT malicious V^*, the ensembles satisfy $\{\mathbf{\Phi}_x^{(\mathsf{P},\mathsf{V}^*)} : x \in L\} \approx_{qc} \{\mathbf{\Psi}_x^{\mathsf{Sim}} : x \in L\}$.

2.4 QCCC Commitment Scheme

A commitment scheme in the QCCC setting specially refers to a protocol in which both the sender S and the receiver R are quantum machines that interact solely via a classical communication channel. The formal definition follows the notion of quantum commitment with classical communication commitment introduced by Ananth *et al.* [2], with the important distinction that we emphasize the sum-binding property as the primary security guarantee in our setting.

Definition 5 (QCCC (bit) commitment). *A QCCC (bit) commitment scheme* $\mathsf{Com} = (\mathsf{S}, \mathsf{R})$ *consists of two QPT participants interacting with each other via the classical channel to complete the following two stages:*

- **Committing stage**: *The sender* S *owns a private input* $b \in \{0,1\}$ *and interacts with the receiver* R. *At the end of the committing stage, both parties obtain a transcript* z *and its internal quantum state* ρ_{S} *and* ρ_{R} *respectively.*
- **Opening stage**: *Both parties have the transcript* z *and their own quantum state, while the sender* S *additionally owns the private input* $b \in \{0,1\}$. *After the interaction, the receiver* R *outputs a bit* b' *or a rejection symbol* $\perp$.

For the honest sender S *with an input* $b \in \{0,1\}$ *and the honest receiver* R, *there exists a negligible function* $\mathsf{negl}(\cdot)$ *s.t. the probability that* R *outputs* $b' = b$ *after the opening stage is at least* $1 - \mathsf{negl}(n)$.

Non-interactive Opening: *The opening stage only consists of one message* $\tau = (b, d)$ *sent by* S, *where* b *is the committed value and* d *is a opening string. In this case, we often prefer to denote the opening stage as a (classical/quantum) verification algorithm* $\mathsf{Ver}(b, d, z)$ *with output 1 if* R *accepts and* 0 *otherwise.*[1]

Additionally, we call a commitment *constant-round* if the total number of rounds of communication between S and R in the committing and the opening stages combined is bounded by a constant number independent of the security parameter n. Then, for the security requirements, we first recall the definition of classical binding.

Definition 6. (Classical binding). *A commitment scheme is statistically (resp., computationally) classical binding if for any unbounded (resp., PPT) adversary* $\mathcal{A}$, *the following probability is negligible in* n:

$$\Pr[\mathsf{Ver}(b, d, z) = 1 \wedge \mathsf{Ver}(b', d', z) = 1 \wedge b \neq b' : (z, b, b'd, d') \leftarrow \mathcal{A}(1^n)].$$

In the QCCC setting, the hiding property is defined similarly to the classical version. As for binding, we focus on several binding properties relevant in the quantum setting, where classical binding is no longer sufficient [1].

Definition 7. *Given a QCCC (bit) commitment* $\mathsf{Com} = (\mathsf{S}, \mathsf{R})$, *the hiding and sum-binding properties are defined as follows:*

- **Hiding:** *We say that* $\mathsf{Com} = (\mathsf{S}, \mathsf{R})$ *is statistically (resp., computationally) hiding if, for any unbounded (resp., QPT) adversary* R^*, *there exists a negligible function* $\mathsf{negl}(\cdot)$ *s.t.*

$$\Big| \Pr[1 \leftarrow \mathsf{R}^*(z, \rho_{\mathsf{R}^*}) : (z, \rho_{\mathsf{S}}, \rho_{\mathsf{R}^*}) \leftarrow \langle \mathsf{S}(0), \mathsf{R}^* \rangle_{com}] - \Pr[1 \leftarrow \mathsf{R}^*(z, \rho_{\mathsf{R}^*}) : (z, \rho_{\mathsf{S}}, \rho_{\mathsf{R}^*}) \leftarrow \langle \mathsf{S}(1), \mathsf{R}^* \rangle_{com}] \Big| \leq \mathsf{negl}(n).$$

[1] The quantum verification algorithm is defined as $\mathsf{Ver}(\rho_{\mathsf{R}}, b, d)$, which outputs 0 or 1. Here, we note that the quantum state ρ_{R} contains the transcript z as part of its quantum register.

– **Sum-binding:** *For any QPT (resp., unbounded)* S^**, define the success probability of opening to challenge bit* $ch \in \{0,1\}$ *as:*

$$p_b := \Pr[b' = b : (z, \rho_{\mathsf{S}^*}, \rho_{\mathsf{R}}) \leftarrow \langle \mathsf{S}^*, \mathsf{R} \rangle_{com}, ch = b, \\ b' \leftarrow \langle \mathsf{S}^*(b, z, \rho_{\mathsf{S}^*}), \mathsf{R}(z, \rho_{\mathsf{R}}) \rangle_{open}].$$

We say that $\mathsf{Com} = (\mathsf{S}, \mathsf{R})$ *is computationally (resp., statistically) sum-binding if, for any QPT (resp., unbounded)* S^**, it holds that* $p_0 + p_1 \leq 1 + \mathsf{negl}$*. Additionally, we define the sum-binding advantage as* $\varepsilon_{\mathsf{sum}} = p_0 + p_1 - 1$*.*

In addition to sum-binding, collapse-binding—introduced by Unruh [33]—is a key property in the quantum setting. It ensures that a quantum adversary cannot distinguish whether the message register has been measured, preventing commitments to superpositions of messages, analogous to how classical collision resistance prevents conflicting openings. Collapse-binding naturally implies both sum-binding and classical binding [33]. Conversely, Dall'Agnol and Spooner [10] show that sum-binding also implies collapse-binding. This equivalence allows us to focus on proving sum-binding in our constructions, which automatically ensures collapse-binding.

3 From $\mathcal{SZK}$-Hardness to Constant-Round QCCC Statistically Hiding Commitments

In this section, we prove our main result, Theorem 1, which establishes a direct link between the average-case hardness of $\mathcal{SZK}$ problems against quantum adversaries and the existence of secure commitment schemes in the QCCC model. To begin, we provide the notion of a promise problem that is hard on average against quantum adversaries.

Definition 8. *A promise problem* $\Pi = (\Pi_{\mathrm{Y}}, \Pi_{\mathrm{N}})$ *is said to be hard-on-average against quantum adversaries if there exists a probabilistic polynomial-time sampler* $\mathsf{Samp}(\cdot)$ *that, given a uniformly random string* $r \leftarrow \{0,1\}^n$*, outputs instances* $x \in \Pi_{\mathrm{N}} \cup \Pi_{\mathrm{Y}}$*, such that for any* ***quantum polynomial-time*** *(QPT) decider* D*, there exists a negligible function* $\mathsf{negl}(n)$ *for which:*

$$\Pr_{r \leftarrow \{0,1\}^n}[x \in \Pi_{\mathsf{D}(x)} : x \leftarrow \mathsf{Samp}(r)] \leq \frac{1}{2} + \mathsf{negl}(n).$$

Here, $\mathsf{D}(x) \in \{\mathrm{Y}, \mathrm{N}\}$ *denotes the output decision of* D *with input* x*.*

Then, we state the main theorem as follows:

Theorem 1. *Assuming the existence of promise problems in* $\mathcal{SZK}$ *that are hard-on-average against quantum adversaries, then there exists a constant-round QCCC commitment that is statistically hiding and computationally sum-binding.*

The proof of Theorem 1 is presented in Sect. 3.3, where we describe our commitment protocol construction and formally show that it satisfies statistically hiding and computationally sum-binding under the stated hardness assumption. Before turning to the proof, we introduce two key cryptographic tools essential to our construction: instance-dependent commitments (Sect. 3.1) and witness-indistinguishable proof systems (Sect. 3.2). We adapt their classical definitions to the QCCC model and establish their connection to $\mathcal{SZK}$.

3.1 QCCC Instance-Dependent Commitments for $\mathcal{SZK}$

We begin by adapting the concept of an instance-dependent commitment (IDC) to the QCCC setting. An IDC is a specialized commitment scheme whose security properties depend on a common instance x of a promise problem $\Pi = (\Pi_Y, \Pi_N)$. Specifically, the scheme is required to be hiding for "YES" instances ($x \in \Pi_Y$) and binding for "NO" instances ($x \in \Pi_N$). This primitive is foundational in the study of zero-knowledge, where it has been instrumental in establishing equivalences between zero-knowledge proofs and commitment schemes [20, 26, 28, 34].

In the QCCC model, the structure of an IDC remains the same while requiring security against quantum adversaries. We therefore adopt the notion of sum-binding as the appropriate quantum analogue for binding security. This is formalized below:

Definition 9. *A QCCC instance-dependent commitment (IDC) for a promise problem $\Pi = (\Pi_Y, \Pi_N)$ is a family of protocols $\{\mathsf{Com}_x\}_{x\in\{0,1\}^*}$, where each protocol involves two quantum polynomial-time (QPT) participants, a sender S_x and a receiver R_x. Both parties receive an instance x as common input and communicate over a classical channel. The family $\{\mathsf{Com}_x\}_{x\in\{0,1\}^*}$ is a QCCC IDC if it satisfies the following:*

- *For $x \in \Pi_N$, Com_x is statistically sum-binding*
- *For $x \in \Pi_Y$, Com_x is statistically hiding*

Based on the work of Nguyen and Vadha [26], a constant-round IDC was constructed for any promise problem in $\mathcal{SZK}$. Their approach involved constructing an IDC for the Entropy Approximation problem (EA) and a 2-phase commitment for the complement of the restricted variant of Entropy Approximation problem ($\overline{\text{EA}'}$). As established by Ong and Vadhan [28] in the classical setting, we can easily get a similar quantum counterpart as follows:

Lemma 1 (Adapted from [28]). *Any promise problem $\Pi = (\Pi_Y, \Pi_N) \in \mathcal{SZK}$ has a constant-round QCCC instance-dependent commitment that is:*

- *Statistically sum-binding when $x \in \Pi_N$;*
- *Statistically hiding when $x \in \Pi_Y$.*

As the remaining issue for establishing QCCC IDC, our key technical contribution shows the implication from statistically classical binding to statistically sum-binding of this construction, presented in the following theorem. Hence, the sum-binding part of the aforementioned Lemma 1 is undoubtedly capable of being established.

Theorem 2. *Any statistically classical binding commitment scheme is statistically sum-binding against quantum adversaries.*

Proof (of Theorem 2). Suppose, for contradiction, that a commitment scheme is statistically classical binding but not statistically sum-binding. Then there exists an unbounded quantum adversary S^* and a non-negligible function $\varepsilon(n)$ such that for some commitment c, the adversary can successfully open c to 0 or 1 with probabilities p_0 and p_1, respectively, satisfying $p_0 + p_1 \geq 1 + \varepsilon(n)$.

Without loss of generality, we assume that the quantum adversary S^* proceeds by preparing an initial quantum state $|\psi_0\rangle$, applying a unitary Q, and then measuring part of the resulting state to obtain a classical commitment c. The remaining quantum state is retained for future opening attempts. We now construct an unbounded classical adversary S^{**} that breaks the statistically classical binding property, as follows:

1. Run S^* to generate a commitment c and obtain a valid decommitment to bit $b \in \{0, 1\}$.
2. Rewind the execution of S^* to the point just before the application of Q, and repeat the process (i.e., apply Q, measure, and check if the result is again c). Since S^{**} is computationally unbounded, it can repeat this procedure an arbitrary (even exponential) number of times.
3. Once the same commitment c is observed again, instruct S^* to open it to bit $1 - b$ and obtain the second valid decommitment.

By assumption, the probability of success in obtaining valid openings for 0 and 1 exceeds $1 + \varepsilon(n)$, and thus the probability of success for each bit is non-negligible. Therefore, the unbounded classical adversary S^{**} eventually finds two distinct valid openings (b, dec_b) and $(1 - b, \mathrm{dec}_{1-b})$ for the same commitment c with non-negligible probability, violating the statistically classical binding property. Therefore, any scheme that is statistically classical binding must be statistically sum-binding as well. □

This result allows us to lift classical $\mathcal{SZK}$-based constructions of IDC to the QCCC setting while maintaining quantum security.

3.2 QCCC Witness-Indistinguishable Protocol from $\mathcal{SZK}$

In this section, we introduce the second main component for our final construction: a constant-round, computationally witness-indistinguishable ($\mathcal{WI}$) proof system for all languages in $\mathcal{NP}$, adapted to the QCCC model. The existence of such QCCC $\mathcal{WI}$ protocols under the assumption that $\mathcal{SZK}$ is hard-on-average against quantum adversaries.

Definition 10. *A QCCC interactive proof system* (P, V) *for a language* L *is computationally witness-indistinguishable if for all quantum polynomial-time (QPT) verifiers* V^*, *and for all witness ensembles* $\{w_x^1\}_{x \in L}$ *and* $\{w_x^2\}_{x \in L}$ *such that both* w_x^1 *and* w_x^2 *are valid witnesses for* x, *i.e.* $w_x^1, w_x^2 \in R_L(x)$, *the ensembles* $\{\mathbf{\Phi}_x^{(\mathsf{P}(w_x^1), \mathsf{V}^*)} : x \in L\}$ *and* $\{\mathbf{\Phi}_x^{(\mathsf{P}(w_x^2), \mathsf{V}^*)} : x \in L\}$ *are polynomially quantum indistinguishable.*

Watrous [35] previously showed that every language in $\mathcal{NP}$ admits a classical zero-knowledge proof secure against quantum adversaries, assuming the existence of quantum computationally hiding commitments. Building on this, Popa [30] demonstrated that if a language admits a statistical (resp., computational) zero-knowledge against quantum adversaries, then it also admits a statistically (resp., computationally) $\mathcal{WI}$ proof against quantum adversaries. While Popa provided a detailed proof for the statistical case, we now present the computational analogue of this implication, which suffices for our purposes in the QCCC model.

Theorem 3. *Any language that admits a computational zero-knowledge proof system also admits a computationally witness-indistinguishable proof system in the QCCC setting.*

Proof (of Theorem 3). Given a QCCC computationally witness-indistinguishable proof for a language L, then for any QPT verifier V^*, there exists a QPT simulator Sim such that $\{\mathbf{\Phi}_x^{(\mathsf{P}(w),\mathsf{V}^*)} : x \in L\} \approx_{qc} \{\mathbf{\Psi}_x^{\mathsf{Sim}} : x \in L\}$. That is, for all $(q(|x|) + k)$-qubit mixed state σ and for all QPT circuit Q of size s with input of $(r(|x|) + k)$-qubit, there exists a negligible function $\mathsf{negl}(n)$ s.t.

$$|\Pr[Q((\mathbf{\Phi}_x^{(\mathsf{P}(w),\mathsf{V}^*)} \otimes \mathbb{I}_k)(\sigma))] - \Pr[Q((\mathbf{\Psi}_x^{\mathsf{Sim}} \otimes \mathbb{I}_k)(\sigma))]| \leq \mathsf{negl}(n).$$

Hence, for all $x \in L$ and any witnesses $w_x^1, w_x^2 \in R_L(x)$, it holds that

$$\begin{aligned}
|\Pr[Q((\mathbf{\Phi}_x^{(\mathsf{P}(w_x^1),\mathsf{V}^*)} &\otimes \mathbb{I}_k)(\sigma))] - \Pr[Q((\mathbf{\Phi}_x^{(\mathsf{P}(w_x^2),\mathsf{V}^*)} \otimes \mathbb{I}_k)(\sigma))]| \\
&\leq |\Pr[Q((\mathbf{\Phi}_x^{(\mathsf{P}(w_x^1),\mathsf{V}^*)} \otimes \mathbb{I}_k)(\sigma))] - \Pr[Q((\mathbf{\Psi}_x^{\mathsf{Sim}} \otimes \mathbb{I}_k)(\sigma))]| \\
&\quad + |\Pr[Q((\mathbf{\Psi}_x^{\mathsf{Sim}} \otimes \mathbb{I}_k)(\sigma))] - \Pr[Q((\mathbf{\Phi}_x^{(\mathsf{P}(w_x^2),\mathsf{V}^*)} \otimes \mathbb{I}_k)(\sigma))]| \\
&\leq 2 \cdot \mathsf{negl}(n),
\end{aligned}$$

which completes the proof. □

By Theorem 2 and 3, along with the previous work of Watrous [35], assuming the existence of QCCC computationally hiding and statistically sum-binding commitment, every language in $\mathcal{NP}$ has a QCCC computationally witness-indistinguishable proof system. Furthermore, by extending the result of Håstad *et al.* [16] to the quantum setting, which shows that pseudorandom generators can be constructed from OWFs, we obtain that a QCCC computationally hiding and statistically sum-binding commitment can be instantiated via Naor's construction [23]. In addition, such commitments can be based on the average-case hardness of problems in $\mathcal{SZK}$ against quantum adversaries, following a straightforward adaptation of the classical result by Ostrovsky *et al.* [29]. We can hence deduce the following corollary.

Corollary 1. *Assuming the existence of promise problems in $\mathcal{SZK}$ that are hard-on-average against quantum adversaries, then there exists a constant-round computationally witness-indistinguishable proof system for $\mathcal{NP}$ in QCCC setting.*

QCCC $\mathcal{WI}$ proof with negligible soundness error It's worth to note that the QCCC $\mathcal{WI}$ proof discussed above only achieves constant (1/3) soundness. However, the negligible soundness error property of the QCCC $\mathcal{WI}$ proof is essential for establishing the statistically hiding property in our final commitment construction. To achieve this, we adapt the framework developed by Xie and Yang [36], with careful modifications to the probability analysis to account for quantum adversaries in the QCCC setting. This approach maintains the constant-round complexity while reducing the soundness error to a negligible function through parallel repetition and careful error analysis.

Theorem 4. *Let* (P, V) *be a QCCC computationally witness-indistinguishable proof system for an* $\mathcal{NP}$ *language* L*. Given any polynomial* $q(\cdot)$*, define* $(\mathsf{P}_q, \mathsf{V}_q)$ *as the* $q(n)$*-fold parallel repetition of* (P, V)*, where in the* i*-th instance, the common input is* x_i *and the auxiliary witness input to* P *is* w_i*. Then* $(\mathsf{P}_q, \mathsf{V}_q)$ *is also a QCCC computationally witness-indistinguishable proof system for the relation* R_L^q *associated with language* L*, where*

$$R_L^q := \{(\tilde{x}, \tilde{w}) : \forall i \in \{1, ..., q(n)\}, (x_i, w_i) \in R_L\}$$

and $\tilde{x} = (x_1, ..., x_q)$ *and* $\tilde{w} = (w_1, ..., w_q)$*. Additionally, define* $R_L^q(\tilde{x})$ *as the set of valid witnesses of* $\tilde{x}$*.*

Proof (of Theorem 4). Assume, for contradiction, that $(\mathsf{P}_q, \mathsf{V}_q)$ is not computationally witness-indistinguishable. Then there exists a QPT parallel verifier V_q^* with auxiliary input $\sigma_{\mathsf{V}_q^*}$ that can distinguish the interaction between P_q with two distinct witnesses $\tilde{w}^1 = (w_1^1, ..., w_q^1)$ and $\tilde{w}^2 = (w_1^2, ..., w_q^2)$, where both satisfy $\tilde{w}^1, \tilde{w}^2 \in R_L^q(\tilde{x})$. We define a sequence of hybrid witnesses:

$$w(i) = (w_1^1, ..., w_i^1, w_{i+1}^2, ..., w_q^2).$$

By assumption, there exists an index $i \in [q]$ such that V_q^* can distinguish the interactions with witnesses $w(i)$ and $w(i+1)$ with non-negligible advantage. We now construct a QPT verifier V^* that breaks the witness indistinguishability of (P, V). Its auxiliary input is defined as

$$\sigma_{\mathsf{V}^*} = \sigma_{\mathsf{V}_q^*} \otimes |\tilde{w}^1\rangle\langle\tilde{w}^1| \otimes |\tilde{w}^2\rangle\langle\tilde{w}^2| \otimes |\tilde{x}\rangle\langle\tilde{x}|.$$

Given a common input x, the strategies of V^* for distinguishing whether P uses the witness w^1 or w^2 is as follows:

1. Choose a random index $i \in [q]$.
2. Prepare the common input $(x_1, ..., x_i, x, x_{i+2}, ..., x_q)$ for V_q^*, where the $(i+1)$-th input is x.
3. Simulate the first i interactions using the witnesses $(w_1^1, ..., w_i^1)$.
4. Forward the messages from P directly to the $(i+1)$-th instance of V_q^*.
5. Simulate the remaining interactions using the witnesses $(w_{i+2}^2, ..., w_q^2)$.
6. Output whatever V_q^* outputs.

If the index $i \in [n]$ selected by V^* is the same as the index where V_q^* has non-negligible distinguishing advantage in the interactions with hybrid witnesses $w(i)$ and $w(i+1)$, then V^* successfully distinguishes between w^1 and w^2 in the original protocol, thus contradicting the witness indistinguishability of (P, V). Since the index is chosen uniformly at random, this implies that V^* inherits a $1/q(n)$ fraction of the non-negligible distinguishing advantage of V_q^*. Hence, the computational witness indistinguishability of (P, V) is violated. □

Finally, we obtain that a negligible soundness error QCCC witness-indistinguishable proof system for any language in $\mathcal{NP}$ can exist under the assumption of average-case hardness $\mathcal{SZK}$.

3.3 Construction of Constant-Round QCCC Statistically Hiding Commitment

In this section, we construct a constant-round QCCC commitment scheme and prove that it achieves statistically hiding and computationally sum-binding, based on the average-case hardness of problems in $\mathcal{SZK}$ against quantum adversaries. This establishes Theorem 1. Our approach follows the framework of Bitansky *et al.* [5], with careful adaptations to the QCCC setting.

Construction 1: A constant-round QCCC statistically hiding computationally sum-binding $\mathsf{Com} = (\mathsf{S}, \mathsf{R})$.

Input: security parameter 1^n; a bit $m \in \{0,1\}$ for S.

Committing Phase:

1. R samples $2n$ independent random strings $\rho_{i,b} \in \{0,1\}^n$ for $i \in [n]$, $b \in \{0,1\}$;
2. R and S execute $2n$ statistically binding commitments in parallel, where in each copy R commits to string $\rho_{i,b}$ and obtains commitment transcript $C_{i,b}$;
3. S samples $2n$ random strings $\sigma_{i,b} \in \{0,1\}^n$, and sends them to R;
4. R sets $r_{i,b} = \rho_{i,b} \oplus \sigma_{i,b}$ and generates $2n$ instances $x_{i,b} \leftarrow \mathsf{Samp}(r_{i,b})$. Sends $\{x_{i,b}\}_{i\in[n],b\in\{0,1\}}$ to S;
5. R and S execute a $\mathcal{WI}$ proof, where R proves that there exists a bit $b \in \{0,1\}$ such that for all $i \in [n]$, the instance $x_{i,b}$ generates consistently. (Here, we can default R sets the witness as $b = 0$ and the strings $\{\rho_{i,0}\}_{i\in[n]}$);
6. S samples $2n$ bits $m_{i,b}$ conditioned on $m = \bigoplus_{i,b} m_{i,b}$;
7. R and S execute $2n$ QCCC instance-dependent commitments $\mathsf{Com}_{x_{i,b}}$, where in each copy S commits to $m_{i,b}$ with the common input $x_{i,b}$;

Opening Phase:

1. S sends m and the opening $(m_{i,b}, \mathsf{dec}_{m_{i,b}})$ to each $\mathsf{Com}_{x_{i,b}}$, where $\mathsf{dec}_{m_{i,b}}$ is the decommitment corresponding to $m_{i,b}$.;
2. R checks whether $m = \bigoplus_{i,b} m_{i,b}$ and that $\mathsf{Com}_{x_{i,b}}$ opens successfully for $i \in [n]$, $b \in \{0,1\}$;

The correctness follows directly from the construction. As established in the previous two sections, any promise problem in $\mathcal{SZK}$ admits a QCCC IDC (Lemma 1), and the hard-on-average $\mathcal{SZK}$ assumption against quantum adversaries implies the existence of a QCCC $\mathcal{WI}$ proof system (Corollary 1). To complete the proof of Theorem 1, it remains to show that our construction satisfies the statistically hiding and computationally sum-binding properties, which we establish in the following two lemmas.

Lemma 2. *The commitment* $\mathsf{Com} = (\mathsf{S}, \mathsf{R})$ *described in Construction 1 is statistically hiding in the QCCC setting.*

Statistically hiding is an information-theoretic property, and, with the help of a negligible soundness error $\mathcal{WI}$ (as established in Theorem 4), the result of Bitansky *et al.* [5] can be extended to the quantum setting directly. We now turn to the computationally sum-binding property, which is formalized in the following lemma.

Lemma 3. *The commitment* $\mathsf{Com} = (\mathsf{S}, \mathsf{R})$ *described in Construction 1 is computationally sum-binding in the QCCC setting.*

Proof (of Lemma 3). Assume that the adversary S^* breaks the sum-binding property with a non-negligible advantage of ε. We construct a QPT decider D for an $\mathcal{SZK}$ promise problem $\Pi = (\Pi_{\mathrm{Y}}, \Pi_{\mathrm{N}})$. Given an instance $x \leftarrow \mathsf{Samp}(\cdot)$, the decider D proceeds as follows:

1. It samples $i^* \leftarrow [n]$ and $b^* \leftarrow \{0,1\}$.
2. It simulates the role of R and interacts with S^* to execute the above commitment $\mathsf{Com} = (\mathsf{S}^*, \mathsf{R})$, with the following modifications:
   - Replace the instance x_{i^*,b^*} with x, i.e. the input of D.
   - Reset the witness to $1 \oplus b^*$ and $\{\rho_{i,1\oplus b^*}\}_i$.
3. During the opening stage, it requests the adversary S^* to open any $\tilde{m}_{i^*,b^*} \in \{0,1\}$. If S^* successfully opens the instance-dependent commitment $\mathsf{Com}_{x_{i^*,b^*}}$, output Y. Otherwise, it outputs a value β randomly chosen from $\{\mathrm{Y}, \mathrm{N}\}$.

Let $p(m = b)$ denote the probability that S^* successfully opens $m = b$, and define the event E as S^* successfully opening a random $\tilde{m}_{i^*,b^*} \in \{0,1\}$. We first establish a correspondence between the success probability of the decider D and the probability of event E occurring (Claim 1). Next, we show that event E happens with high probability (claim 2), which serves as a crucial step in proving the computationally sum-binding property of the constructed commitment.

Claim 1. For the constructed decider D and the defined event E, there exists a negligible function $\mathsf{negl}(n)$ such that

$$\Pr[x \in \Pi_{\mathsf{D}(x)}] = \frac{1 + 2\Pr[E]}{4} - \mathsf{negl}(n).$$

Proof (of Claim 1). The decider D randomly outputs "YES" or "NO" when the event E does not occur, implying that $\Pr[x \in \Pi_{\mathsf{D}(x)}|\overline{E}] = 1/2$. Furthermore,

$$\begin{aligned}\Pr[x \in \Pi_{\mathsf{D}(x)}|E] =& \Pr[x \in \Pi_{\mathrm{Y}}|E] = 1 - \Pr[x \in \Pi_{\mathrm{N}}|E] \\ =& 1 - \frac{\Pr[E|x \in \Pi_{\mathrm{N}}] \Pr[x \in \Pi_{\mathrm{N}}]}{\Pr[E]}\end{aligned}$$

Since the instance x is randomly sampled using the sampler $\mathsf{Samp}(\cdot)$ (otherwise, a trivial decider could introduce bias in decision-making), we obtain

$$\Pr[x \in \Pi_{\mathrm{N}}] = \Pr_{r \leftarrow \{0,1\}^n}[x \in \Pi_{\mathrm{N}} : x \leftarrow \mathsf{Samp}(r)] \leq \frac{1}{2} + \mathsf{negl}(n).$$

When $x \in \Pi_{\mathrm{N}}$, i.e. the instance-dependent commitment $\mathsf{Com}_{x_{i^*,b^*}}$ is statistically sum-binding, the adversary S^* can open a random bit $\tilde{m}_{i^*,b^*}$ with probability at most $1/2 + \mathsf{negl}(n)$. Thus, we conclude that $\Pr[E|x \in \Pi_{\mathrm{N}}] \leq 1/2 + \mathsf{negl}(n)$. Applying the law of total probability, we obtain

$$\begin{aligned}\Pr[x \in \Pi_{\mathsf{D}(x)}] =& \Pr[x \in \Pi_{\mathsf{D}(x)}|E] \cdot \Pr[E] + \Pr[x \in \Pi_{\mathsf{D}(x)}|\overline{E}] \Pr[\overline{E}] \\ \geq& \left(1 - \frac{(1/2 + \mathsf{negl}(n))^2}{\Pr[E]}\right) \cdot \Pr[E] + \frac{1}{2} \cdot \Pr[\overline{E}] \\ \geq& \frac{1 + 2\Pr[E]}{4} - \mathsf{negl}(n).\end{aligned}$$

□

Claim 2. For the event E defined above, there exists a non-negligible ε and a negligible function $\mathsf{negl}(n)$ such that

$$\Pr[E] \geq \frac{1}{2} + \frac{\varepsilon}{16n} - \mathsf{negl}(n).$$

Suppose that Claim 1 and Claim 2 hold, we can obtain that

$$\Pr[x \in \Pi_{\mathsf{D}(x)}] \geq \frac{1 + 2\Pr[E]}{4} - \mathsf{negl}(n) \geq \frac{1}{2} + \mathsf{negl}(n).$$

which implies that the quantum average-case hardness of $\mathcal{SZK}$ is broken, violating the assumption. Then, Construction 1 of commitment must be computationally sum-binding. □

Let's solve the remaining proof of the Claim 2 next.

Proof (of Claim2). We establish the claim by analyzing a sequence of hybrid games. While the structure of these games closely follows the argument presented in Claim 4 of Bitansky *et al.* [5], our sequential analysis departs significantly due to the use of the sum-binding property.

$\mathcal{H}_0$: This hybrid corresponds to the original execution $\mathsf{D}(x)$, as defined above.

$\mathcal{H}_1$: Instead of replacing x_{i^*,b^*} with x, the instance at the location (i^*, b^*) is generated as $x' \leftarrow \mathsf{Samp}(\sigma_{i^*,b^*} \oplus \rho')$, where $\rho' \in \{0,1\}^n$ is randomly chosen by D after S^* sampling $\{\sigma_{i,b}\}_{i,b}$. Since both x and x' are sampled using Samp with independently chosen random inputs, and ρ' is independent of the game's execution, the adversary S^* perceives an identical view in $\mathcal{H}_0$ and $\mathcal{H}_1$, both in terms of classical information and quantum states.

$\mathcal{H}_2$: The statistically binding commitment of ρ_{i^*,b^*} is replaced with the commitment of ρ'. Due to the computationally hiding property, a QPT adversary S^* cannot distinguish between the game $\mathcal{H}_2$ and $\mathcal{H}_1$, except with a negligible probability.

$\mathcal{H}_3$: The witness $(1 \oplus b^*, \{\rho_{i,1\oplus b^*}\}_i)$ is changed to $(0, \{\rho_{i,0}\}_i)$. By the witness indistinguishability property, a QPT adversary S^* cannot distinguish between the game $\mathcal{H}_3$ and $\mathcal{H}_2$, except with a negligible probability.

$\mathcal{H}_4$: The variables are relabeled, setting x' as x_{i^*,b^*} and ρ' as ρ_{i^*,b^*}. It is evident that $\mathcal{H}_3$ and $\mathcal{H}_4$ are identical, completing the sequence of hybrids.

The execution of $(\mathsf{S}^*, \mathsf{R})$ in $\mathcal{H}_4$ follows the standard procedures outlined in the above construction. Thus, it remains to bound the probability that the event E occurs in $\mathcal{H}_4$, which is the probability that S^* successfully opens a random value $\tilde{m}_{i^*,b^*}$ in $\mathsf{Com}_{x_{i^*,b^*}}$. To solve that, we introduce the following claim.

Claim 3. If the adversary S^* breaks the sum-binding of Construction 1 with advantage ε, then there is at least one location (i,b) of $\mathsf{Com}_{x_{i,b}}$ that S^* breaks the sum-binding condition for a non-negligible advantage $\varepsilon/4n$.

Proof (of Claim 3). For contradiction, suppose that for every $i \in [n]$ and $b \in \{0,1\}$, instance-dependent commitment $\mathsf{Com}_{x_{i,b}}$ is statistically sum-binding, which means that even for an unbounded adversary, it holds that $p(m_{i,b} = 0) + p(m_{i,b} = 1) \le 1 + \varepsilon/4n$.

For $2n$ bits $m_{i,b} \in \{0,1\}$, we set the string $M = m_{10}||m_{11}||\cdots||m_{n0}||m_{n1} \in \{0,1\}^{2n}$. Define two sets $\mathcal{M}_0 = \{M \in \{0,1\}^{2n} : \bigoplus_{i,b} m_{i,b} = 0\}$ and $\mathcal{M}_1 = \{M \in \{0,1\}^{2n} : \bigoplus_{i,b} m_{i,b} = 1\}$, where $|\mathcal{M}_0| = |\mathcal{M}_1| = 2^{2n-1}$. We now compute the probability that S^* successfully opens $m = 0$, and the case for $m = 1$ follows analogously. If S^* opens $m = 0$ successfully, it must open each parallel execution of $\mathsf{Com}_{x_{i,b}}$ successfully to the bit $m_{i,b}$, satisfying $M \in \mathcal{M}_0$. Hence, it holds that

$$\begin{aligned} p(m=0) &= p\Big(\bigoplus_{i,b} m_{i,b} = 0\Big) \\ &= \sum_{M \in \mathcal{M}_0} \Pr\Big[\bigcap_{i,b} \mathsf{S}^* \text{ opens } m_{i,b} : M = m_{10}||m_{11}||\cdots||m_{n0}||m_{n1}\Big] \\ &= \sum_{\substack{k\in\{0,1\}, M \in \mathcal{M}_0 \\ M = m_{10}||\cdots||m_{n1}}} \prod_{i,b} p(m_{i,b} = k) \end{aligned}$$

A similar equation holds for the case of $m = 1$. Therefore, it is easy to compute that:

$$\sum_{b\in\{0,1\}} p(m=b) = \sum_{\substack{k\in\{0,1\}\\ M\in\mathcal{M}_0}} \prod_{i,b} p(m_{i,b}=k) + \sum_{\substack{k\in\{0,1\}\\ M\in\mathcal{M}_1}} \prod_{i,b} p(m_{i,b}=k)$$
$$= \prod_{i,b} \Big(p(m_{i,b}=0) + p(m_{i,b}=1)\Big)$$
$$\leq (1+\frac{\varepsilon}{4n})^{2n} < 1+\varepsilon.$$

The second equation is obtained by combining like terms. The above computation implies that Construction 1 is sum-binding with advantage ε, which contradicts our assumption and completes the proof of 3. □

Let b', i' be the indices that satisfy the Claim 3, then we can derive that in the case that $i^* = i' \wedge b^* = b'$, E occurs with probability at least $1/2 \cdot (1 + \varepsilon/4n)$. According to Claim 3 and the hybrid games considered above, we can conclude that

$$\Pr[E] = \Pr[i^* \neq i' \vee b^* \neq b'] \cdot \frac{1}{2} + \Pr[i^* = i' \wedge b^* = b'] \cdot \big(1 + \frac{\varepsilon}{4n}\big) - \mathsf{negl}(n)$$
$$\geq \frac{1}{2} \cdot (1 - \frac{1}{2n}) + \frac{1}{2n} \cdot \Big(\frac{1}{2} + \frac{\varepsilon}{8n}\Big) - \mathsf{negl}(n) = \frac{1}{2} + \frac{\varepsilon}{16n} - \mathsf{negl}(n).$$

This hence completes the proof of Claim 2 □

Overall, combining Lemma 2 and Lemma 3, we can derive that the Construction 1 is a constant-round statistically hiding computationally sum-binding QCCC commitment, which hence justifies our main theorem (Theorem 1).

4 Conclusion

We revisit the commitment construction of Bitansky *et al.* [5] and demonstrate that it achieves statistically hiding and computationally sum-binding in the QCCC model. Leveraging the equivalence between sum-binding and collapse-binding [10], we show that this construction is computationally collapse-binding under the average-case hardness of $\mathcal{SZK}$ problems.

Our work weakens the assumptions for computationally collapse-binding commitments, relying only on $\mathcal{SZK}$-hardness rather than stronger primitives like collapsing functions [32]. Additionally, by focusing on the QCCC model, we provide a framework that balances quantum security with practical deployability, paving the way for future quantum-secure cryptographic protocols.

Acknowledgement. We thank the anonymous reviewer for helpful comments. This work is supported by National Natural Science Foundation of China (62302496, 62172405).

References

1. Ambainis, A., Rosmanis, A., Unruh, D.: Quantum attacks on classical proof systems: The hardness of quantum rewinding. In: 2014 IEEE 55th Annual Symposium on Foundations of Computer Science, pp. 474–483. IEEE (2014)
2. Ananth, P., Lin, Y.-T., Yuen, H.: Pseudorandom strings from pseudorandom quantum states. arXiv preprint arXiv:2306.05613 (2023)
3. Ananth, P., Qian, L., Yuen, H.: Cryptography from pseudorandom quantum states. In: Dodis, Y., Shrimpton, T. (eds.) *Advances in Cryptology - CRYPTO 2022 - 42nd Annual International Cryptology Conference, CRYPTO 2022, Santa Barbara, CA, USA, August 15-18, 2022, Proceedings, Part I*, vol. 13507. LNCS, pp. 208–236. Springer (2022)
4. Austrin, P., Chung, H., Chung, K.-M., Fu, S., Lin, Y.-T., Mahmoody, M.: On the impossibility of key agreements from quantum random oracles. In: Annual International Cryptology Conference, pp. 165–194. Springer (2022)
5. Bitansky, N., Haitner, I., Komargodski, I., Yogev, E.: Distributional collision resistance beyond one-way functions. In: Annual International Conference on the Theory and Applications of Cryptographic Techniques, pp. 667–695. Springer (2019)
6. Brakerski, Z., Christiano, P., Mahadev, U., Vazirani, U., Vidick, T.: A cryptographic test of quantumness and certifiable randomness from a single quantum device. Journal of the ACM (JACM) **68**(5), 1–47 (2021)
7. Brassard, G., Chaum, D., Crépeau, C.: Minimum disclosure proofs of knowledge. J. Comput. Syst. Sci. **37**(2), 156–189 (1988)
8. Canetti, R., Feige, U., Goldreich, O., Naor, M.: Adaptively secure multi-party computation. In: Proceedings of the Twenty-Eighth Annual ACM Symposium on Theory of Computing, pp. 639–648 (1996)
9. Crépeau, C., Salvail, L., Simard, J.-R., Tapp, A.: Two provers in isolation. In: Lee, D.H., Wang, X. (eds.) ASIACRYPT 2011. LNCS, vol. 7073, pp. 407–430. Springer, Heidelberg (2011). https://doi.org/10.1007/978-3-642-25385-0_22
10. Dall'Agnol, M., Spooner, N.: On the necessity of collapsing for post-quantum and quantum commitments (2023)
11. Dumais, P., Mayers, D., Salvail, L.: Perfectly concealing quantum bit commitment from any quantum one-way permutation. In: International Conference on the Theory and Applications of Cryptographic Techniques, pp. 300–315. Springer (2000)
12. Goldreich, O., Kahan, A.: How to construct constant-round zero-knowledge proof systems for np. J. Cryptol. **9**(3), 167–189 (1996)
13. Goldreich, O., Levin, L.A.: A hard-core predicate for all one-way functions. In: Proceedings of the Twenty-First Annual ACM Symposium on Theory of Computing, pp. 25–32 (1989)
14. Goldwasser, S., Micali, S., Rivest, R.L.: A digital signature scheme secure against adaptive chosen-message attacks. SIAM J. Comput. **17**(2), 281–308 (1988)
15. Haitner, I., Nguyen, M.-H., Ong, S.J., Reingold, O., Vadhan, S.: Statistically hiding commitments and statistical zero-knowledge arguments from any one-way function. SIAM J. Comput. **39**(3), 1153–1218 (2009)
16. Håstad, J., Impagliazzo, R., Levin, L.A., Luby, M.: A pseudorandom generator from any one-way function. SIAM J. Comput. **28**(4), 1364–1396 (1999)
17. Lindell. Parallel coin-tossing and constant-round secure two-party computation. J. Cryptology **16**, 143–184 (2003)
18. Lo, H.-K., Chau, H.F.: Is quantum bit commitment really possible? Phys. Rev. Lett. **78**(17), 3410 (1997)

19. Mayers, D.: Unconditionally secure quantum bit commitment is impossible. Phys. Rev. Lett. **78**(17), 3414 (1997)
20. Micciancio, D., Vadhan, S.P.: Statistical zero-knowledge proofs with efficient provers: lattice problems and more. In: Boneh, D. (ed.) CRYPTO 2003. LNCS, vol. 2729, pp. 282–298. Springer, Heidelberg (2003). https://doi.org/10.1007/978-3-540-45146-4_17
21. Morimae, T., Yamakawa, T.: Proofs of quantumness from trapdoor permutations. arXiv preprint arXiv:2208.12390 (2022)
22. Morimae, T., Yamakawa, T.: Quantum commitments and signatures without one-way functions. In: Dodis, Y., Shrimpton, T. (eds.) Advances in Cryptology - CRYPTO 2022 - 42nd Annual International Cryptology Conference, CRYPTO 2022, Santa Barbara, CA, USA, August 15-18, 2022, Proceedings, Part I, vol. 13507. LNCS, pp. 269–295. Springer (2022)
23. Naor, M.: Bit commitment using pseudorandomness. J. Cryptol. **4**(2), 151–158 (1991). https://doi.org/10.1007/BF00196774
24. Naor, M., Ostrovsky, R., Venkatesan, R., Yung, M.: Perfect zero-knowledge arguments for np using any one-way permutation. J. Cryptol. **11**, 87–108 (1998)
25. Naor, M., Yung, M.: Universal one-way hash functions and their cryptographic applications. In: Proceedings of the Twenty-First Annual ACM Symposium on Theory of Computing, pp. 33–43 (1989)
26. Nguyen, M.-H., Vadhan, S.: Zero knowledge with efficient provers. In: Proceedings of the Thirty-Eighth Annual ACM Symposium on Theory of computing, pp. 287–295 (2006)
27. Nielsen, M.A., Chuang, I.L.: Quantum computation and quantum information. Cambridge university press (2010)
28. Ong, S.J., Vadhan, S.: An Equivalence Between Zero Knowledge and Commitments. In: Canetti, R. (ed.) TCC 2008. LNCS, vol. 4948, pp. 482–500. Springer, Heidelberg (2008). https://doi.org/10.1007/978-3-540-78524-8_27
29. Ostrovsky, R., Wigderson, A.: One-way functions are essential for non-trivial zero-knowledge. In: [1993] The 2nd Israel Symposium on Theory and Computing Systems, pp. 3–17. IEEE (1993)
30. Popa, R.A.: Witness-indistinguishability against quantum adversaries. Project Report (2011)
31. Shmueli, O., Zhandry, M.: On one-shot signatures, quantum vs. classical binding, and obfuscating permutations. In: Annual International Cryptology Conference, pp. 350–383. Springer (2025)
32. Unruh, D.: Collapse-binding quantum commitments without random oracles. In: International Conference on the Theory and Application of Cryptology and Information Security, pp. 166–195. Springer (2016)
33. Unruh, D.: Computationally binding quantum commitments. In: Fischlin, M., Coron, J.-S. (eds.) EUROCRYPT 2016. LNCS, vol. 9666, pp. 497–527. Springer, Heidelberg (2016). https://doi.org/10.1007/978-3-662-49896-5_18
34. Vadhan, S.P.: An unconditional study of computational zero knowledge. SIAM J. Comput. **36**(4), 1160–1214 (2006)
35. Watrous, J.: Zero-knowledge against quantum attacks. In: Proceedings of the Thirty-Eighth Annual ACM Symposium on Theory of Computing, pp. 296–305 (2006)
36. Xie, H., Yang, L.: Witness indistinguishability and witness hiding against quantum attacks. IET Inf. Secur. **13**(6), 579–590 (2019)

Concretely Efficient Constructions for Differentially Private Set Intersection

Xinyu Peng[1,2], Yufei Wang[2], Weiran Liu[2(✉)], Liqiang Peng[2], Feng Han[2], Li Duan[3], Zhen Gu[2], Jianling Sun[1], and Yuan Hong[4]

[1] Zhejiang University, Hangzhou, China
[2] Alibaba Group, Hangzhou, China
weiran.lwr@alibaba-inc.com
[3] Paderborn University, Paderborn, Germany
[4] University of Connecticut, Storrs, USA

Abstract. Private Set Intersection (PSI) enables a sender and a receiver to jointly compute the intersection of their sets without disclosing non-trivial information about other items. However, depending on the context of joint data analysis, information derived from the items in the intersection may also be considered sensitive. To protect such sensitive information, prior work proposed Differentially private PSI (DPSI), which can be instantiated with circuit-PSI using Fully Homomorphic Encryption. Although asymptotically efficient, its concrete performance is sub-optimal compared with the practical state-of-the-art (SOTA) circuit-PSI.

In this paper, we propose two generic DPSI constructions with provable security and privacy. We identify the critical criteria for selecting essential PSI-related tools by revisiting the DPSI definition. Then, we present two generic DPSI constructions. The first construction allows us to achieve provable privacy and efficiency by integrating any circuit-PSI with the randomized response mechanism. By plugging the SOTA circuit-PSI protocol, we obtain a DPSI protocol with concrete performance enhancement. The second construction offers a more efficient DPSI alternative by using multi-query Reverse Private Membership Test (mqRPMT) at the price of intersection size leakage. However, such leakages can be bounded with differential privacy by padding random dummy items in input sets. We conduct comprehensive experiments with various instantiations. The experiments show that our instantiations significantly outperform the existing DPSI construction: 2.9-26.8× more communication-efficient and up to 110.5-151.8× faster.

Keywords: Private set intersection · Differential privacy · Data privacy

1 Introduction

Private Set Intersection (PSI) allows a sender $\mathcal{P}_1$ and a receiver $\mathcal{P}_2$, holding sets X and Y respectively, to identify the intersection $X \cap Y$ without revealing any

R. Chen et al. (Eds.): Inscrypt 2025, LNCS 16409, pp. 23–44, 2026.
https://doi.org/10.1007/978-981-95-6203-9_2

information about items not in the intersection. PSI helps to achieve data minimization as no data is shared beyond what each party has in common [21]. As one of the most well-studied secure multi-party computation (MPC) protocols, PSI has been widely recognized as a valuable tool in numerous applications.

Although PSI preserves perfect privacy for items outside the intersection, depending on the context, the intersection itself is also sensitive. An example application is presented in [25], where Google paid Mastercard for access to individuals' credit card transaction data. With the transaction data, Google can match the ads previously displayed to users, optimizing the recommendation strategy. PSI can be used to protect the users outside the intersection. However, the mere act of a credit card purchase also constitutes personally identifiable information (PII). Therefore, it is also necessary to protect the users inside the intersection.

Through the lens of privacy, one can view PSI as a procedure where the sender $\mathcal{P}_1$ (holding the input set X) tells the receiver $\mathcal{P}_2$ (holding the input set Y) a Boolean vector of size $|Y|$, each bit of which indicates whether the corresponding item in Y is in the intersection $X \cap Y$, leaking one-bit information for each item in Y. In this way, the problem can be formalized in the Differential Privacy (DP) paradigm. As a measurement of privacy leakage and a set of tools to mitigate such leakages, DP has been increasingly regarded as a *de facto* standard for protecting individual privacy that has been studied extensively in both academia [12,27,43] and industry [2,10,13,19]. A DP mechanism guarantees that the presence or absence of any individual record has a quantifiable impact on the likelihood that a particular response is returned to a query. Consequently, an adversary's probability of success in inferring any individual record value or whether the record is present can be strictly bounded.

Thus, for the privacy of items inside the intersection, it is natural to combine DP with PSI to protect the Boolean information further. In their pioneering research [25], Kacsmar et al. defined the notion of Differentially Private Set Intersection (DPSI) and constructed a DPSI protocol using Fully Homomorphic Encryption (FHE) [4,15]. Recently, Mahdavi et al. [28] showed that the construction is essentially a circuit-PSI [6,34,37] (equipped with a DP mechanism). In circuit-PSI, $\mathcal{P}_1$ and $\mathcal{P}_2$ receive Boolean shares of the intersection instead of learning the intersection in the clear. These shares can be used for subsequent secure computations. By obliviously permuting the Boolean shares before revealing them to $\mathcal{P}_2$, $\mathcal{P}_2$ learns an intersection with a DP guarantee for $\mathcal{P}_1$.

Although being asymptotically efficient, the solution in [25] has sub-optimal concrete performance. Even for small set sizes $n = m = 2^{16}$ with $n = |X|$ and $m = |Y|$, the running time is about 8 minutes, which is inefficient compared to typical PSI-based applications that only require several seconds for set sizes $n = m = 2^{20}$ [1,38]. In contrast, circuit-PSI is the intrinsic building block for the DPSI construction of [25], and the state-of-the-art (SOTA) circuit-PSI protocol only needs less than one minute for both parties' set sizes $n = m = 2^{20}$ [6,34,37]. Thus, for optimal efficiency, it is necessary to investigate and close the gap between DPSI and existing PSI-related tools. Since PSI is a very active research field, this deeper understanding can also lead to generic DPSI constructions from a broader range of future tools.

1.1 Our Contributions

In this paper, we revisit the existing definition of DPSI [25] and formally propose an ideal functionality $\mathcal{F}_{\mathsf{DPSI}}$. Considering the privacy and security properties formalized in $\mathcal{F}_{\mathsf{DPSI}}$, we identify the critical components and procedures in DPSI that create spaces for enhancement and different trade-offs. These observations are illustrated in Fig. 1. Intuitively, for a sender $\mathcal{P}_1$ who holds X and a receiver $\mathcal{P}_2$ who holds Y, any PSI-related tool that enables the sender to perturb the membership information about Y *without knowing the correct intersection* can be used to construct DPSI. We suggest two such components: circuit-PSI [6,34,37] and multi-query Reverse Private Membership Test (mqRPMT) [7,44].

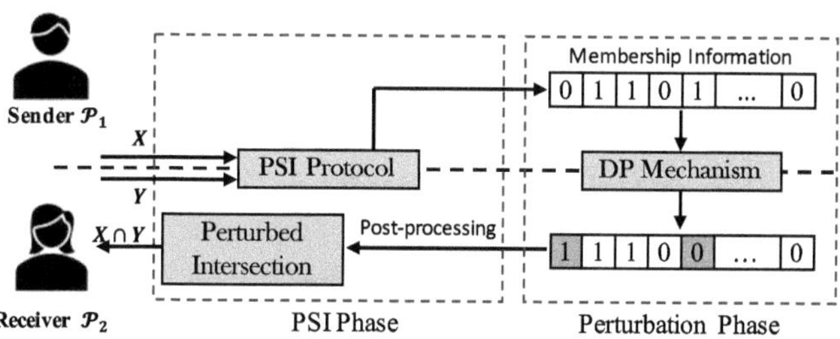

Fig. 1. The critical components and procedures in DPSI.

Following the insight, we propose two generic constructions for DPSI. The first one is called circuit-DPSI, and its core component is circuit-PSI. In this construction, the parties first get a shared Boolean vector of the intersection by *executing a generic circuit-PSI*. Then $\mathcal{P}_1$ obliviously perturbs his shared Boolean vector via a DP mechanism. $\mathcal{P}_2$ finally gets the DP intersection by XORing $\mathcal{P}_1$'s perturbed Boolean vector with its own share. We note that the pioneering DPSI construction [25] follows this routine. By plugging in a more efficient circuit-PSI instance, we obtain DPSI with improved performance.

The second construction, mqRPMT-DPSI, leads to an even more efficient DPSI. As the name suggests, it leverages a recently proposed building block named multi-query Reverse Private Membership Test (mqRPMT) [7,44]. In mqRPMT, a sender holding a set X interacts with a receiver holding a set $Y = (y_1, \ldots, y_n)$. Eventually, the sender learns only a Boolean vector $(e_1, \ldots, e_n)$ indicating whether $y_i \in X$ without learning the values of Y, while the receiver learns nothing.[1] mqRPMT were previously used to construct Private Set Operation (PSO) [7,44]. In our construction, two parties first invoke mqRPMT with their input sets X and Y, and $\mathcal{P}_1$ gets the indication Boolean vector containing

[1] For ease of description, we define mqRPMT in the reversed roles.

the membership information. Then, $\mathcal{P}_1$ perturbs the indication Boolean vector via a DP mechanism and sends it to $\mathcal{P}_2$, who gets the final DP intersection. Thanks to the efficiency of the SOTA mqRPMT protocol [7], we can construct DPSI with near-optimal concrete performance.

However, there is a remaining challenge. The indication Boolean vector output by mqRPMT unavoidably leaks the cardinality of the intersection set to the sender, which may lead to attacks [18,24] that de-anonymize specific items in the input sets. We propose an additional procedure in mqRPMT-DPSI to alleviate this privacy leakage. In a nutshell, we ask both parties to insert dummy items into their sets via a Random Dummy Item Padding mechanism ahead of time and take the padded X' and Y' as mqRPMT inputs. Random Dummy Item Padding guarantees that the leaked cardinality satisfies (ϵ, δ)-DP. By plugging into the SOTA mqRMPT instance [7], the final DPSI remains efficient with bounded cardinality leakage w.r.t. DP.

1.2 Related Work

PSI. The idea of PSI dates back to the 1980s, and the initial PSI protocol was constructed from the Diffie-Hellman (DH) key agreement [29]. Since then, constructions based on public key cryptography [9,22], Oblivious Transfers (OT) [23], FHE [40] and Garbled Circuits (GC) [42] have been proposed. Among them, OT-based protocols [26,32] are usually faster than other variants. Recently, the data structure called Oblivious Key-Value Stores (OKVS) [14,33,35] has been proposed, and more efficient PSI constructions have been proposed by combining it with Vector Oblivious Linear Evaluation (VOLE) [3,8,37]. Another line is taking mqRPMT [44] as the primitive and using the framework to obtain PSI [7] and more general PSO.

DP in Secure Computation. Existing works employ DP as a complementary technology to prevent information leakage not captured in conventional secure computation models. To prevent side-channel attacks while answering federated queries, Narayan et al. [30] proposed a primitive for obtaining PSI cardinality (PSI-CA) in a differentially private manner. He et al. [20] formulated the problem of Differentially Private Record Linkage (DPRL) and developed corresponding protocols by employing a specific privacy definition called Output Constrained DP. In 2020, for the first time, Kacsmar et al. [25] constructed differentially private PSI (DPSI) by combining FHE-based circuit-PSI with DP. However, the use of FHE results in sub-optimal efficiency in practice. Initiating from an alternative origin, Groce et al. [17] considered improving the performance of PSI protocols by leveraging DP and showed that if DP leakage is allowed, the cost of Rindal et al.'s [36] PSI protocol can be reduced by up to 63%.

2 Preliminaries

2.1 Notations and Security Model

The computational and statistical security parameters are denoted by κ and σ, respectively. We denote by $[a, b]$ the integers $a, b \in \mathbb{N}$ and by $a \leq b$ the set

$\{a, a+1, \ldots, b\}$. We let $[b]$ denote $[1, b]$ and by the capital letter $A = (a_1, \ldots, a_n)$ we mean a vector with length $|A| = n$.

Two parties in DPSI are the sender $\mathcal{P}_1$ and the receiver $\mathcal{P}_2$. They have input sets $X = \{x_i\}_{i \in [n]} \in \mathcal{V}^n$ and $Y = \{y_j\}_{j \in [m]} \in \mathcal{V}^m$, respectively. All items in X and Y are from the same item domain $\mathcal{V}$. Based on the context, we sometimes use the notation $X[i]$ or x_i to denote the i-th item in the set X.

In this work, we consider the semi-honest model with static corruption, where an adversary $\mathcal{A}$ tries to learn as much information as possible from protocol execution but cannot deviate from the protocol definitions. We assume that all cryptographic building blocks used in this work have been proven secure in the semi-honest model under the standard real-ideal paradigm [16].

2.2 Standard Differential Privacy Definition

Intuitively, a DP mechanism ensures that the outputs of algorithms stay approximately the same if any record in the input is added or removed.

Definition 1. **((ϵ, δ)-Differential Privacy).** *A randomized mechanism $\mathcal{M} : \mathcal{D} \to \mathcal{F}$ is (ϵ, δ)-DP if for all neighboring inputs $D, D' \in \mathcal{D}$ such that D and D' differ by adding or removing a record, and all subsets $F \in \mathcal{F}$,*

$$\Pr[\mathcal{M}(D) \in F] \leq e^{\epsilon} \Pr[\mathcal{M}(D') \in F] + \delta$$

where the probability is taken over the randomness of $\mathcal{M}$.

In Definition 1, ϵ is the privacy budget, and δ can be treated as the failure probability of DP protection. We say that $\mathcal{M}$ satisfies ϵ-DP if $\delta = 0$. When obtaining multiple DP outputs, the sequential composition (Theorem 1) is used to measure the total privacy budget.

Theorem 1 (Sequential Composition [11]**).** *Given k number of (ϵ_i, δ_i)-DP mechanisms $\mathcal{M}_i$ that access the same input D with $1 \leq i \leq k$, the combination of their outputs satisfies (ϵ, δ)-DP, where $\epsilon = \sum_{i=1}^{k} \epsilon_i$ and $\delta = \sum_{i=1}^{k} \delta_i$.*

2.3 Cryptographic Primitives

Circuit-PSI. Circuit-PSI [6,34] is a two-party protocol that allows the sender and receiver to securely compute arbitrary symmetric functions over the intersection of their private sets without exposing it to either party by utilizing the secure circuit evaluation. In circuit-PSI, both the sender and the receiver take their sets $X = \{x_1, ..., x_n\}$ and $Y = \{y_1, ..., y_m\}$ as inputs and receive the Boolean shares of the set intersection $Z = X \cap Y$. The ideal functionality of circuit-PSI [37] is formally defined in Fig. 2.

Multi-query Reverse Private Membership Test. Multi-query Reverse Private Membership Test (mqRPMT) [7,44] is a two-party protocol that is initially used as a primitive for constructing PSO. In mqRPMT, a sender with a set

$\mathcal{F}_{\text{circuit-PSI}}$

Parameters: The sender's set size n. The receiver's set size m. The functionality is parameterized by *Reorder* : $\mathcal{V}^m \rightarrow (\pi : [m] \rightarrow [\beta])$ which on input Y outputs an injective function π ($\beta = O(m)$).
Input: The sender's set $X = \{x_i\}_{i \in [n]}$, and the receiver's set $Y = \{y_i\}_{i \in [m]}$.
Output: The sender gets a shared Boolean vector $\{\langle a_j \rangle_1\}_{j \in [\beta]}$. The receiver gets an injective function π with size $\beta = O(m)$, and a shared Boolean vector $\{\langle a_j \rangle_2\}_{j \in [\beta]}$, where $a_j = \langle a_j \rangle_1 \oplus \langle a_j \rangle_2 = 1$ if there exists $i \in [m]$ such that $\pi(i) = j$ and y_i is in the intersection $|X \bigcap Y|$, and $a_j = 0$ otherwise.

Fig. 2. Ideal functionality $\mathcal{F}_{\text{circuit-PSI}}$ for circuit-PSI [37].

X interacts with a receiver holding a set $Y = (y_1, \ldots, y_m)$, and eventually the sender learns only a Boolean vector $(e_1, \ldots, e_m)$ indicating whether $y_i \in X$ without learning the value of y_i, while the receiver learns nothing. Among the protocols that instantiate mqRPMT, the cwPRF-based mqRPMT protocol is the most efficient one that achieves strict linear computation and communication complexity. More specifically, commutative weak PRF (cwPRF) is a family of keyed functions $\{F_{k_i} : \mathcal{K} \times \mathcal{D} \rightarrow \mathcal{D}\}$ that satisfy weak pseudo-randomness and commutative property, where commutative property means that for all $k_1, k_2 \in \mathcal{K}$ and $x \in \mathcal{D}$, a family of keyed functions satisfy $F_{k_1}(F_{k_2}(x)) = F_{k_2}(F_{k_1}(x))$.

3 Differentially Private Set Intersection

3.1 DPSI Definition

We first revisit the DPSI definition proposed by Kacsmar et al. [25] shown in Definition 2. The key to formalizing DPSI is to precisely define the neighboring datasets and the output range. PSI has two inputs: the set X from the sender and the set Y from the receiver. As the DP definition suggests, one must consider the output distribution for all neighboring datasets D' and D that differ in any single item. Kacsmar et al. [25] consider a one-sided PSI where the sender learns nothing about the receiver's input set Y, and only the receiver learns a DP version of the intersection. This approach is reasonable. In the DP context, one can think of the sender's input X being the database to be queried, and the receiver asking a query with the input data Y. That is, the receiver's query is of the form:

Which items in Y are also in your database X?

Since PSI only allows the receiver to get the intersection $X \cap Y$, PSI only reveals X's information to the receiver. Therefore, we only need to consider privacy from the sender's input X by defining the neighboring dataset $D' = (X', Y)$ for a fixed Y, where $X' = X \cup \{v_t\}$ for $v_t \notin X$ or $X' = X \backslash \{v_r\}$ for $v_r \in X$.

Although the neighboring dataset can be any dataset by adding or removing one item in X, the output intersection Z must be a subset of the fixed Y.

Therefore, the output range can be defined as a set description with the capability of including all items in Y. Kacsmar et al. [25] chose the output range in the most compressed form, that is, a Boolean vector $F = \{0,1\}^m$ in which the Boolean value f_i indicates whether $y_i \in Z$. Combining it with the definition of the neighboring dataset leads to the DPSI definition described as follows.

Definition 2 (ϵ-Differentially Private Set Intersection [25]). *The randomized two-party mechanism $\mathcal{M} : \mathcal{V}^n \times \mathcal{V}^m \rightarrow \{0,1\}^m$ that takes $\mathcal{P}_1$'s set X and $\mathcal{P}_2$'s set Y as inputs and returns a Boolean vector $F \in \{0,1\}^m$ to $\mathcal{P}_2$ achieves ϵ-DPSI if and only if for all $F \in \{0,1\}^m$ and all neighboring datasets $D = (X, Y)$ and $D' = (X', Y)$ where $X' = X \cup \{v_t\}$ or $X' = X \setminus \{v_r\}$, $v_t, v_r \in \mathcal{V}$,*

$$\Pr[\mathcal{M}(D) = F] \leq e^{\epsilon} \Pr[\mathcal{M}(D') = F]$$

where the probability is taken over the randomness of $\mathcal{M}$.

Definition 2 addresses the privacy concerns of DPSI, and a definition from the security aspect is also shown in Definition 7 of [25]. However, to demonstrate the *essence* of DP-PSI and introduce our construction ideas, we give an equivalent security definition as below. We first formulate the ideal functionality $\mathcal{F}_{\mathsf{DPSI}}$ in Fig. 3, which takes X from $\mathcal{P}_1$ and Y from $\mathcal{P}_2$ as inputs and only outputs a perturbed Boolean vector to $\mathcal{P}_2$. It is parameterized by a DP mechanism $\mathcal{M}_{dp}$ constrained with the Hamming distance $HM(\bar{F}, \bar{F}') = 1$ between (non-private) outputs from neighboring datasets X and X'. The output of $\mathcal{F}_{\mathsf{DPSI}}$ clearly achieves ϵ-DPSI. Then, a protocol provides ϵ-SIM-CDPSI (simulation-based computational differentially private PSI) security if it securely realizes $\mathcal{F}_{\mathsf{DPSI}}$ parameterized by a certain DP mechanism $\mathcal{M}_{dp}$ against a semi-honest non-uniform probabilistic polynomial time adversary under the simulation-based security paradigm.

$\mathcal{F}_{\mathsf{DPSI}}$

Parameters: $\mathcal{P}_1$'s input set size n, and $\mathcal{P}_2$'s input set size m. A DP mechanism $\mathcal{M}_{dp}$ parameterized by the privacy budget ϵ satisfying $\Pr[\mathcal{M}_{dp}(\bar{F}) = F] \leq e^{\epsilon} \Pr[\mathcal{M}_{dp}(\bar{F}') = F]$ for all $\bar{F}, \bar{F}' \in \{0,1\}^m$ with $HM(\bar{F}, \bar{F}') = 1$.
Input: $\mathcal{P}_1$'s set $X = \{x_i\}_{i \in [n]} \in \mathcal{V}^n$, and $\mathcal{P}_2$'s set $Y = \{y_i\}_{i \in [m]} \in \mathcal{V}^m$.
Functionality:

- Upon receiving (sid, X) from $\mathcal{P}_1$, (sid, Y) from $\mathcal{P}_2$, compute $\bar{F} \in \{0,1\}^m$, where $\bar{f}_i$ indicates if $y_i \in X$. Apply $\mathcal{M}_{dp}$ to $\bar{F}$ and record $(\mathsf{sid}, F := \mathcal{M}_{dp}(\bar{F}))$.
- Subsequently, upon receiving $(\mathsf{deliver}, \mathsf{sid})$ from $\mathcal{A}$, send F to $\mathcal{P}_2$ and $(\mathsf{sid}, \mathsf{delivered})$ to $\mathcal{A}$.

Fig. 3. Ideal functionality $\mathcal{F}_{\mathsf{DPSI}}$ for DPSI.

Definition 3 (**ϵ-SIM-CDPSI**). *A protocol* $\mathbf{\Pi}$ *provides* ϵ*-SIM-CDPSI if there exist PPT simulators* Sim_1 *and* Sim_2 *and a DP mechanism* $\mathcal{M}_{dp}$ *parameterized by the privacy budget* ϵ*, for all* $\mathcal{P}_1$*'s sets* X_1 *and* $\mathcal{P}_2$*'s sets* X_2 *such that:*

$$\{Sim_i(X_i, \mathcal{F}^i_{\mathsf{DPSI}}(\mathcal{M}_{dp}, X_1, X_2)), \mathcal{F}_{\mathsf{DPSI}}(\mathcal{M}_{dp}, X_1, X_2)\} \stackrel{c}{\equiv} \{\mathtt{view}^{\pi}_i(\mathcal{M}_{dp}, X_1, X_2), \mathtt{out}^{\pi}(\mathcal{M}_{dp}, X_1, X_2)\}$$

where $\mathcal{F}^i_{\mathsf{DPSI}}(\mathcal{M}_{dp}, X_1, X_2))$ *is the i-th output of* $\mathcal{F}_{\mathsf{DPSI}}$ *with input* (X_1, X_2)*,* $\mathsf{view}^{\pi}_i(\mathcal{M}_{dp}, X_1, X_2)$ *is the view of party* $\mathcal{P}_i$ *during an execution of* $\mathbf{\Pi}$ *on* (X_1, X_2)*, including* $\mathcal{P}_i$*'s input and all messages received during the protocol,* $\mathsf{out}^{\pi}(\mathcal{M}_{dp}, X_1, X_2)$ *is the output of both parties during an execution, and* $a \stackrel{c}{\equiv} b$ *if two distributions* a, b *are computationally indistinguishable.*

3.2 Tools for Constructing DPSI

Recall that the output range in DPSI definition (Definition 2) is $\mathcal{F} = \{0,1\}^m$. The output range indicates that any item in Y can appear in the output intersection Z, regardless of whether the same item is contained in X or not. To this end, we require that the randomized mechanism $\mathcal{M}$ for DPSI is able to perturb the result, i.e., replace the items in Z with items in $Y \backslash X$. While the conclusion is intuitive, finding suitable PSI tools takes effort. $\mathcal{F}_{\mathsf{DPSI}}$ indicates that without a trusted third party, the perturbation can only occur on $\mathcal{P}_1$'s side. Thus, paradoxically, $\mathcal{P}_1$ cannot directly obtain the output, but can only *obliviously perturb Z without knowing the output.*

Consequently, we identify the key desiderata required by PSI-related tools to construct DPSI: $\mathcal{P}_1$ must get the membership information of Y and can map the items in its set into the output intersection set via a randomized algorithm. Still now, two PSI-related tools satisfy this requirement: circuit-PSI [6,34,37] and mqRPMT [44]. In circuit-PSI, both parties get a shared Boolean vector of length $\beta = O(|Y|)$ obliviously indicating whether or not an item is in the intersection. Kacsmar et al.'s DPSI protocol also takes a circuit-PSI as a primitive, which supports arbitrary subsequent circuits. In their protocol, the sender acquires the membership information of Y in the form of FHE's ciphertext. In mqRPMT, the sender gets a Boolean vector $(e_1, \ldots, e_n)$ indicating whether $x_i \in Y$ or not without learning the value of x_i. These two PSI-related tools allow the sender to randomly perturb the final binary output using a DP mechanism.

The remaining procedure is straightforward. We can leverage the Random Response (RR) mechanism $\mathcal{M}_{RR}$ [39], a basic DP mechanism for binary data, to do the perturbation. Take a binary input $v \in \{0,1\}$, $\mathcal{M}_{RR}$ outputs $\tilde{v} = v$ with probability p and $\tilde{v} = 1 - v$ with probability $q = 1 - p$. $\mathcal{M}_{RR}$ is defined as:

$$\Pr[\tilde{v} = 1] = \begin{cases} p = \frac{e^{\epsilon}}{e^{\epsilon}+1} & \text{if } v = 1 \\ q = \frac{1}{e^{\epsilon}+1} & \text{if } v = 0 \end{cases}. \tag{1}$$

3.3 The Practical Significance and Limitations

As a combination of DP and PSI, our DPSI construction ensures that inferences about the presence or absence of any specific item in the output intersection are limited, while the intersection as a whole remains sufficiently accurate for substantive usage. The utility-privacy trade-off for employing our frameworks manifests in the form of false positives and negatives within the intersection. Nonetheless, such a trade-off can be tailored to suit the specific requirements of the relevant application, as illustrated in the subsequent case.

Recall that the case of a card-payment company and an ads platform identify the set of customers that they have in common. By using the constructions of our DPSI, these two parties can agree on a differentially private set intersection that protects any item in the set from the card-payment company while preserving the effectiveness of the ads. Depending on their privacy preference, the card-payment company may choose a different utility-privacy trade-off.

Note that if the same DPSI protocol is used repeatedly to compute the intersection of the same two sets, the probability of item leakage in the intersection will increase. Such leakage is actually the DPSI functionality: each time the DPSI protocol is used to compute an intersection, it will consume a portion of the privacy budget, denoted as ϵ_i. According to the sequential composition described in Theorem 1, the combination of all computed intersections satisfies $\sum_{i=1}^{t} \epsilon_i$-DPSI, where t represents the number of times the protocol is reused.

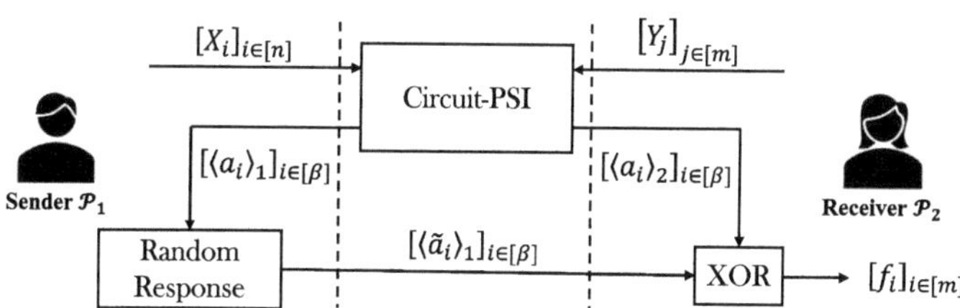

Fig. 4. Workflow of circuit-DPSI.

4 Circuit-DPSI Construction

We first illustrate the flow of the circuit-DPSI in Fig. 4 and provide the details in Fig. 5. In the circuit-DPSI, $\mathcal{P}_1$ and $\mathcal{P}_2$ first invoke a construction of circuit-PSI with inputs X and Y. Then, each of $\mathcal{P}_1$ and $\mathcal{P}_2$ gets a piece of Boolean shares $\{\langle a_j\rangle_i\}_{j\in[\beta]} \in \{0,1\}$, $i \in \{1,2\}$, as the output. The Boolean shares have β bits, which not only contain part of the information about the membership of the items in Y but also may contain that of some random dummy values added during the protocol if the Circuit-PSI is instantiated with Cuckoo Hashing [31]. After getting $\{\langle a_j\rangle_1\}_{j\in[\beta]}$, $\mathcal{P}_1$ perturbs it bit by bit via the RR mechanism $\mathcal{M}_{RR}$

and sends the perturbed Boolean shares $\{\langle\tilde{a}_j\rangle_1\}_{j\in[\beta]}$ to $\mathcal{P}_2$. Finally, $\mathcal{P}_2$ receives $\{\langle\tilde{a}_j\rangle_1\}_{j\in[\beta]}$ and computes a Boolean vector $\mathcal{O} = \{\langle\tilde{a}_j\rangle_1 \oplus \langle a_j\rangle_2\}_{j\in[\beta]}$, which indicates the membership of the items in Y and the possible added random dummy values. By mapping the bits of $\mathcal{O}$ with the obtained injective function π, $\mathcal{P}_2$ obtains $F = \{0,1\}^m$, a set where each position i contains a one if the item corresponding to Y_i is part of the differentially private intersection, and zeros in all other positions.

$\Pi_{\text{circuit-DPSI}}$

Parameters: $\mathcal{P}_1$'s input set size n, and $\mathcal{P}_2$'s input set size m. The RR mechanism $\mathcal{M}_{RR}$ parameterized with the DP parameter ϵ.
Input: $\mathcal{P}_1$'s set $X = \{x_i\}_{i\in[n]}$, and $\mathcal{P}_2$'s set $Y = \{y_i\}_{i\in[m]}$.
Protocol:

1. **(Circuit-PSI Invocation)** $\mathcal{P}_1$ and $\mathcal{P}_2$ invoke $\mathcal{F}_{\text{circuit-PSI}}$ with inputs X and Y. $\mathcal{P}_1$ receives $\{\langle a_j\rangle_1\}_{j\in[\beta]}$. $\mathcal{P}_2$ receives $\{\langle a_j\rangle_2\}_{j\in[\beta]}$ and an injective function $\pi : [m] \to [\beta]$.
2. **(Boolean Shares Perturbation)** $\mathcal{P}_1$ invokes $\mathcal{M}_{RR}$ with input $\langle a_1\rangle_1, ..., \langle a_\beta\rangle_1$ and gets the perturbed $\langle\tilde{a_1}\rangle_1, ..., \langle\tilde{a_\beta}\rangle_1$ as output.
3. **(Intersection Computation)** $\mathcal{P}_2$ receives the perturbed $\langle\tilde{a_1}\rangle_1, ..., \langle\tilde{a_\beta}\rangle_1$ from $\mathcal{P}_1$, computes $\mathcal{O} = \{\langle\tilde{a_j}\rangle_1 \oplus \langle a_j\rangle_2\}_{j\in[\beta]}$, and gets the output $F \in \{0,1\}^m$ where $f_i = \mathcal{O}_{\pi(i)}$.

Fig. 5. Generic construction 1: circuit-DPSI $\Pi_{\text{circuit-DPSI}}$.

It is worth noting that within this construction, the integration of the circuit-PSI is designed to be modular. By selecting and incorporating an appropriate circuit-PSI protocol, we achieve a more efficient circuit-DPSI protocol.

As shown by Mahdavi et al. [28], the FHE-based DPSI protocol proposed by Kacsmar et al. [25] can be regarded as a variant of the circuit-PSI construction if we remove the RR mechanism. In this protocol, $\mathcal{P}_2$ encrypts their items using the BGV [40] scheme and sends the ciphertext to $\mathcal{P}_1$. $\mathcal{P}_1$ also encrypts their items and computes encryption of a vector containing ones in positions where the corresponding items are found in the intersection. Moreover, $\mathcal{P}_1$ perturbs the encrypted vector using the RR mechanism $\mathcal{M}_{RR}$ and sends the results to $\mathcal{P}_2$. Finally, $\mathcal{P}_2$ decrypts the vector and obtains the perturbed intersection. It is evident that the workflow of this FHE-based DPSI protocol is similar to our circuit-DPSI construction, as both involve obtaining a vector containing membership information and perturbing it using the RR mechanism $\mathcal{M}_{RR}$.

The security and privacy result of $\Pi_{\text{circuit-DPSI}}$ is formally given in Theorem 2. The detailed proof is shown in Appendix A.

Theorem 2. *$\Pi_{\text{circuit-DPSI}}$ satisfies ϵ-SIM-*DPSI *in the $\mathcal{F}_{\text{circuit-PSI}}$-hybrid world.*

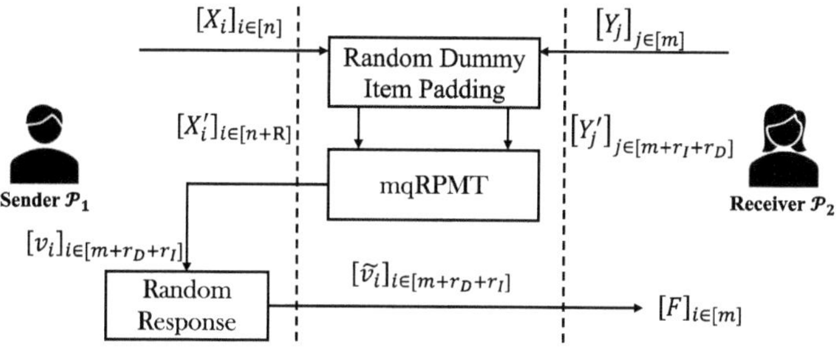

Fig. 6. Workflow of mqRPMT-DPSI

5 MqRPMT-Based DPSI Construction

By removing the dependency on FHE, the circuit-DPSI construction is much more efficient than the existing construction of DPSI. However, SOTA circuit-PSI constructions [6,34] still utilizes sub-protocols, namely, Private Equality Test (PEQT) [34] or Private Set Membership (PSM) [6], that follows the general secure computation paradigm to compute the shares of $\bar{F}$, which accounts for 96% of the overall computational overhead of the circuit-PSI primitive. Therefore, we intuitively consider whether we can improve the efficiency of DPSI by performing the membership test without relying on general secure computation sub-protocols. To this end, we propose the mqRPMT-DPSI construction. Unlike the circuit-PSI where both parties learn the secret sharing of the membership vector based on general secure computation sub-protocols, mqRPMT allows the sender to learn the complete membership vector efficiently.

The mqRPMT-DPSI construction offers improved efficiency at the price of relaxing security by allowing the protocol to leak some "extra" information. The functionality of mqRPMT allows the sender to obtain the membership vector v in plaintext. Although a permutation operator performed by the receiver can make sure that the membership bits are in a permuted order unknown to the sender, the sender can still learn the cardinality of intersection (PSI-CA) by counting the number of "1" in v, or the cardinality of $Y \backslash (X \bigcap Y)$ by counting the number of "0" in v. Recent studies [18,24] have found that adversaries can launch an efficient attack on the size-revealing PSIs, with a binary-search-like strategy, to de-anonymize specific data records in the input sets, thereby leaking membership information about the input sets. To take advantage of mqRPMT without completely undermining the idea of secure computation, a natural candidate is to leak only differentially private information about the PSI-CA.

To ensure that the leakage learned by the sender satisfies DP we can generate a random integer from a truncated discrete Laplace distribution and then add the corresponding number of dummy items to both the intersection and difference sets before the mqRPMT process.

However, in our two-party scenario without a trusted third party, the dummy items cannot be added to the intersection directly. The alternative strategy is

Algorithm 1: Random Dummy Item Padding $\mathcal{M}_{\mathsf{rd}}$

Parameters: Statistical security parameter σ. DP parameter ϵ_I, ϵ_D.
Input: $\mathcal{P}_1$'s input set $X = \{x_1, x_2, ...x_n\}$. $\mathcal{P}_2$'s input set $Y = \{y_1, y_2, ...y_m\}$.
`/* Sender side */`
Compute R: the minimum number satisfying $\Pr(L(\epsilon_I, \delta, 1) > R) < 2^{-\sigma}$;
Initialize the set X' as the set of the padded real items $\{0|x\}_{x \in X}$;
Add dummy items $\{1|i|0\}_{i \in R}$ into X';
Return X';
`/* Receiver side */`
$r_I = max(L(\epsilon_I, \delta, 1), 0)$, $r_D = max(L(\epsilon_D, \delta, 1), 0)$;
Initialize the set Y' as the set of the padded real items $\{0|y\}_{y \in Y}$;
Add items $\{1|i|0\}_{i \in r_I}$ into Y' ; `// Dummy items should be in` X'
Add items $\{1|i|1\}_{i \in r_D}$ into Y' ; `// Dummy items should not be in` X'
Return Y'.

that both parties generate a random integer from a truncated discrete Laplace distribution, respectively, and add the corresponding number of dummy items to their own private sets. Unfortunately, this alternative strategy fails to satisfy DP. Note that a dummy item can be found in the intersection if and only if both the sender and receiver possess this dummy item. Consequently, the maximum number of dummy items in the intersection is inherently limited by the number of dummy items added by the sender locally. Consider a worst-case scenario in which the sender draws a random integer 0 from a truncated discrete Laplace distribution and adds 0 dummy items into his/her local set, the sender can learn the true PSI-CA regardless of the number of dummy items added by the receiver.

Definition 4 (Truncated Discrete Laplace Mechanism). *Given a query* $\mathbf{c} : \mathcal{D} \to \mathbb{N}$, *the truncated discrete Laplace mechanism* $TLap(D)$ *outputs an integer* $\max(\mathbf{c}(D) + \eta, \mathbf{c}(D))$, *where* $\eta \in \mathbb{Z}$ *follows a distribution, denoted by* $L(\epsilon, \delta, \Delta\mathbf{c})$ *that has a probability density function* $\Pr[\eta = x] = p \cdot e^{-(\epsilon/\Delta\mathbf{c})|x-\eta^0|}$, *where* $p = \frac{e^{\epsilon/\Delta\mathbf{c}}-1}{e^{\epsilon/\Delta\mathbf{c}}+1}$, $\eta^0 = \Delta\mathbf{c} - \frac{\ln[(e^{\epsilon}/\Delta\mathbf{c}+1)\delta]}{\epsilon}$, $\Delta\mathbf{c}$ *is the sensitivity parameter for the query* $\mathbf{c}$, ϵ *is the privacy budget and* δ *is the error probability.*

Lemma 1 (Truncated Discrete Laplace Mechanism Utility [5]). *For* $\eta \in \mathbb{Z}$ *that follows* $L(\epsilon, \delta, \Delta\mathbf{c})$ *and* $m \geq \eta^0$, *we have* $\Pr[\eta \geq m] = \frac{e^{-\frac{\epsilon}{\Delta\mathbf{c}}(m-\eta^0-1)}}{e^{\frac{\epsilon}{\Delta\mathbf{c}}}+1}$.

To this end, we modify the above strategy as follows, which is shown in Algorithm 1. In our strategy, the sender and the receiver first independently pad the items in their own sets to bit strings with "0" at the highest position. Next, to ensure that the number of dummy items in the intersection remains oblivious to the sender, the sender adds R dummy items $\{1|i|0\}_{i \in [R]}$ into X to obtain X', where R is typically a large integer leading to enough redundant dummy items in X'. As a result, the number of dummy items added to the intersection is only determined by the dummy items generated by the receiver, which is oblivious to the sender. Simultaneously, the receiver draws two random integers r_I, r_D from two truncated discrete Laplace distributions, which are described in Definition 4, and adds r_I dummy items $\{1|i|0\}_{i\in[r]}$ and r_D dummy items $\{1|i|1\}_{i\in[r]}$ into Y'. Finally, the sender and receiver exchange $|X'| = n+R$ and $|Y'| = m+r_I+r_D$ with each other. Consequently, the overall strategy bounds the leakage to the sender with $(\epsilon_I + \epsilon_D, 2\delta)$-DP if and only if the truncated discrete Laplace mechanism satisfies (ϵ', δ)-DP, where $\epsilon' \in \{\epsilon_I, \epsilon_D\}$.

$\mathbf{\Pi}_{\mathsf{mqRPMT\text{-}DPSI}}$

Parameters: $\mathcal{P}_1$'s input set size n. $\mathcal{P}_2$'s input set size m. The random dummy item padding mechanism $\mathcal{M}_{\mathsf{rd}}$ is parameterized with DP parameters ϵ_i, ϵ_d. The RR mechanism $\mathcal{M}_{RR}$ parameterized with the DP parameter ϵ.
Input: $\mathcal{P}_1$'s set $X = \{x_i\}_{i\in[n]}$, $\mathcal{P}_2$'s set $Y = \{y_i\}_{i\in[m]}$.
Protocol:

1. **(Dummy Item Padding)** $\mathcal{P}_1$ invokes $\mathcal{M}_{\mathsf{rd}}$ with X as input and outputs a padded set $X' = \{x'_i\}_{i\in[n+R]}$ with R padded items.
2. $\mathcal{P}_2$ invokes $\mathcal{M}_{\mathsf{rd}}$ with Y as input and output a padded set $Y' = \{y'_i\}_{i\in[M]}$, where $M = m + r_I + r_D$ and r_I, r_D are random integers drawn from a truncated discrete Laplace distribution. $\mathcal{P}_2$ permutes the Y' with a random permutation ϕ and obtain Y^*, where $y^*_i = y'_{\phi(i)}$.
3. **(mqRPMT Invocation)** $\mathcal{P}_1$ and $\mathcal{P}_2$ invoke $\mathcal{F}_{\mathsf{mqRPMT}}$ with inputs X' and Y^*. $\mathcal{P}_1$ gets an indication Boolean vector $\{v_i\}_{i\in[M]}$ such that $v_i = 1$ if and only if $y^*_i \in X'$ but without knowing y^*_i.
4. **(indication Boolean vector Perturbation)** $\mathcal{P}_1$ invokes $\mathcal{M}_{RR}$ with input v and gets the perturbed indication Boolean vector $\tilde{v}$ as output.
5. **(Intersection Computation)** $\mathcal{P}_2$ receives the perturbed indication Boolean vector $\tilde{v}$ from $\mathcal{P}_1$, permutes $\tilde{v}$ with ϕ^{-1} to obtain $\tilde{v}'$, and gets the indication Boolean vector $F \in \{0,1\}^m$ by deleting the bits that corresponding to the dummy item from $\tilde{v}'$.

Fig. 7. Generic construction 2: $\mathbf{\Pi}_{\mathsf{mqRPMT\text{-}DPSI}}$.

In the Random Dummy Item Padding Mechanism $\mathcal{M}_{\mathsf{rd}}$, determining the size of R is an important issue, as the magnitude of R simultaneously affects the computation complexity of the entire construction and the inherent error rate of the padding mechanism. In our implementation, we set R as the minimum number satisfying $\Pr[r_I > R] \leq 2^{-\sigma}$, where $\sigma = 40$ is the statistical security parameter in MPC. It means the number of dummy items added into the intersection satisfying (ϵ_I, δ)-DP with a high enough probability. The result of our experiment shows that: with fixed $\delta = 10^{-5}$, $\epsilon_I = 0.01, R = 3787$; $\epsilon_I = 0.1, R = 380$; $\epsilon_I = 1.0, R = 39$; $\epsilon_I = 10.0, R = 4$.

We show the flow of the mqRPMT-DPSI protocol in Fig. 6 and give the details in Fig. 7. In the mqRPMT-DPSI, $\mathcal{P}_1$ and $\mathcal{P}_2$ first insert dummy items into their private sets X and Y via the Random Dummy Item Padding Mechanism and get the padded sets X' and Y', respectively. Next, $\mathcal{P}_1$ and $\mathcal{P}_2$ invoke mqRPMT with inputs X' and Y'. As the functionality of mqRPMT, $\mathcal{P}_1$ gets an indication Boolean vector $\{v_i\}_{i\in[M]}$ such that $v_i = 1$ if and only if $y_i' \in X'$ but without knowing y_i'. After getting $\{\langle v_i\rangle\}_{i\in[M]}$, $\mathcal{P}_1$ perturbs it bit by bit via the RR mechanism and sends the perturbed Boolean values $\{\langle\tilde{v}_i\rangle\}_{i\in[M]}$ to $\mathcal{P}_2$. Finally, $\mathcal{P}_2$ learns $F = \{0,1\}^m$ by deleting the bits corresponding to the dummy items from $\{\langle\tilde{v}_i\rangle\}_{i\in[M]}$. Similar to $\mathbf{\Pi}_{\mathsf{circuit\text{-}DPSI}}$, the $\mathcal{F}_{\mathsf{mqRPMT}}$ in $\mathbf{\Pi}_{\mathsf{mqRPMT\text{-}DPSI}}$ can be instantiated with any efficient mqRPMT protocols.

The security and privacy result of $\mathbf{\Pi}_{\mathsf{mqRPMT\text{-}DPSI}}$ is formally given in Theorem 3. The detailed proof is shown in Appendix B.

Theorem 3. *The protocol in Fig. 7 satisfies ϵ-SIM-DPSI with the information leakage to $\mathcal{P}_1$ bounded by $(\epsilon_I + \epsilon_D, 2\delta)$-DP in the $\mathcal{F}_{\mathsf{mqRPMT}}$-hybrid world.*

6 Experiments

6.1 Implementation Details

We implement three circuit-DPSI protocols and an mqRPMT-DPSI protocol by plugging the SOTA circuit-PSI protocols [6,34,37] and mqRPMT protocol [7] into the proposed DPSI constructions, respectively. Moreover, we also implement all circuit-PSI protocols and mqRPMT-based PSI protocol above for comparison. Silent OT [41] is used in our implementation. Specifically, all these protocols mentioned above are written in JAVA and the source code is available at https://github.com/alibaba-edu/mpc4j/tree/main/mpc4j-work-dpsi.

We denote the circuit-PSI protocols and mqRPMT-based PSI protocol, which are serving as primitives, as PSTY'19, RS'21, CGS'22, and CZZ'24. The DPSI protocols that are built upon them are denoted as PSTY'19*, RS'21*, CGS'22*, and CZZ'24*. Moreover, we also list the running time and communication cost of the FHE-based circuit-DPSI protocol mentioned in [25] and denote it as KKL+'20. Note that the experimental results of KKL+'20 are copied from [25][2].

Experimental Setup. For all implemented protocols, we set the computational security parameter $\kappa = 128$ and the statistical security parameter $\sigma = 40$. To evaluate the performance of implemented protocols, we conduct a series of experiments with different sizes of items: $n = m = 2^{14}, 2^{16}, 2^{18}, 2^{20}$, as well as different network environments, including LAN and WAN. For the DP mechanism used in the implemented DPSI protocols, we use the following default values unless specifically stated: $\epsilon = 1.0, \delta = 10^{-5}$. Our experiments were executed on a single-threaded process on a single Intel Core i9-9900K with 3.6GHz and 128GB RAM. We simulate the network connection using Linux tc command. For the WAN setting, we bound the RTT to be 80 ms and the bandwidth to be 100 Mbps. For each protocol, we repeated five times and took the average execution time.

[2] Although we successfully ran the open-source code of [25], the reported performance results on our platform are much slower than results shown in [34]. Specifically, the running time of this source code reported on our platform is about1200 seven when the set sizes are all 2^{10}.

6.2 Performance Results

Running Times. Table 1 shows the running time of all the implemented protocols. We can find that the running time of all DPSI protocols increases linearly with the growth of the data size. Among the PSI and DPSI protocols we evaluated, the mqRPMT-DPSI protocol CZZ'24* consistently outperformed the others in all network environments. Specifically, the CZZ'24* is approximately 1.4-2.6$\times$ faster than the other circuit-DPSI protocols. This is consistent with our analyses that mqRPMT-DPSI protocols will be faster than the circuit-DSPI protocols since the latter uses general secure computation sub-protocols as a fundamental technology. We also observe that the PSTY'19* is the fastest among all circuit-DPSI protocols over different sizes of data. The reason is that we use OKVS [14] to replace the original polynomial-based Batch OPRRF and combine it with the PSM protocol in [6]. Finally, the execution times of all Circuit-DPSI protocols are close to their corresponding PSI protocols (or even sometimes faster due to performance fluctuations in actual experiments). The reason is that Circuit-DPSI counterparts only additionally involve the efficient RR mechanism, which introduces marginal costs.

Specifically, mqRPMT-DPSI is faster than mqRPMT-PSI. In mqRPMT-PSI, $\mathcal{P}_1$ acts as the sender and $\mathcal{P}_2$ acts as the receiver in the invocation of $\mathcal{F}_{\mathsf{mqRPMT}}$, and OT is required in mqRPMT-PSI's final step to let the receiver obtain the intersection. However, mqRPMT-DPSI eliminates the OT step by swapping the roles of the parties when invoking $\mathcal{F}_{\mathsf{mqRPMT}}$, at the cost of leaking the DP-bounded intersection size to the sender. Although a few dummy items are added to both parties' sets, they only introduce marginal costs.

Table 1. Performance of DPSI protocols on $n = m = 2^{14}, 2^{16}, 2^{18}, 2^{20}$ set sizes under LAN and WAN network settings. The results for KKL+'20 are copied from [25].

Primitive	Protocol	Runtime(s)								Total Comm.(MB)			
		LAN				WAN							
		2^{14}	2^{16}	2^{18}	2^{20}	2^{14}	2^{16}	2^{18}	2^{20}	2^{14}	2^{16}	2^{18}	2^{20}
Circuit-PSI	PSTY'19	3.24	11.12	32.09	109.22	8.09	17.15	42.06	132.39	5.46	15.41	50.9	193.97
	RS'21	3.58	11.97	35.04	120.36	9.3	18.56	45.2	142.79	8.11	16.71	47.15	166.71
	CGS'22	3.37	11.84	36.17	125.48	8.79	18.89	47.09	153.84	7.1	22.28	78.16	302.99
Circuit-DPSI	PSTY'19*	3.16	11.17	32.14	108.79	8.1	17.14	41.93	132.5	5.46	15.42	50.94	194.13
	RS'21*	3.6	11.94	35.19	121.06	9.18	18.8	44.95	143.59	8.11	16.72	47.19	166.87
	CGS'22*	3.39	11.76	35.94	126.03	8.82	18.72	47.14	154.22	7.11	22.29	78.2	303.15
	KKL+'20	-	531.62	-	11719.4	-	-	-	-	-	133	-	232
mqRPMT-PSI	CZZ'24	1.29	4.98	19.76	77.85	1.7	5.97	22.45	88.32	1.71	6.82	27.75	111.0
mqRPMT-DPSI	CZZ'24*	1.2	4.77	19.16	76.89	1.49	5.51	21.2	83.83	1.209	4.95	19.786	79.13

Communication Costs. All DPSI protocols achieve linear communication complexity. Among them, the mqRPMT-DPSI protocol has the lowest communication overhead. All Circuit-DPSI schemes have only slightly more communication overhead than their Circuit-PSI primitives, where the additional cost is a perturbed bit vector sent from the sender to the receiver. For mqPRMT-DPSI, the number of dummy items involved in mqPRMT-DPSI is small for reasonable DP parameters ϵ_I and ϵ_D. The additional communication the dummy items bring is less than that required by the OT step in mqPRMT-PSI.

6.3 Utility Results

FPR and FNR. The output of the DPSI protocols is a differentially private set, which contains both false negatives and false positives. According to Equation (1), both the false negative rate (FNR) and false positive rate (FPR) are theoretically $q = \frac{1}{1+e^{\epsilon}}$, which are already the upper bounds of FPR and FNR under the premise of satisfying ϵ-DPSI constraint. A larger ϵ will lead to smaller FNR and FPR at the expense of a weaker privacy guarantee, while a smaller ϵ will result in lower utility. In practice, the parties need to negotiate and define a consensus ϵ in advance to strike a balance between privacy and utility that aligns with their specific needs.

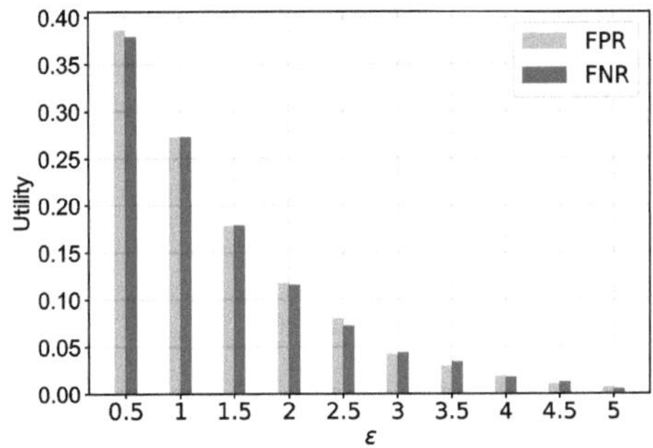

Fig. 8. The FPR and FNR of the mqRPMT-DPSI protocol.

To verify our theoretical analysis of the utility of DPSI protocols, we additionally design a series of experiments to measure the FPR and FNR of the chosen implemented DPSI protocol while varying the private budget ϵ from 0.5 to 5.0. Specifically, since the utility of all DPSI protocols is the same, we chose the mqRPMT-DPSI protocol as a representative protocol and conducted experiments to evaluate its FPR and FNR under different privacy budgets. The results in Fig. 8 support and validate our analyses: as privacy budget ϵ increases, the FPR and FNR will decrease gradually. It indicates that the parties can strike a balance between privacy and utility by choosing a proper ϵ.

Effectiveness of Random Dummy Item Padding Mechanism. For $TLap$ with parameters (ϵ, δ), $\eta^0 = 1 - \frac{\ln[(e^{\epsilon}+1)\delta]}{\epsilon} \approx -\frac{\ln \delta}{\epsilon}$ when $\Delta \mathbf{c} = 1$, the mean and the variance of dummy item size $E(m)$ and $Var(m)$ satisfy $\eta^0 < E(m)$ and

$Var(m) < \frac{2e^{\epsilon}}{(e^{\epsilon}-1)^2}$ [5], respectively. The reason for the inequalities is that the dummy item size is truncated to be at least 0. Therefore, smaller δ and ϵ will produce dummy item sizes that are more dispersed and have larger means. We count the distribution of $\mathcal{M}_{\mathsf{rd}}$'s outputs in a different setting. Specifically, we run $\mathcal{M}_{\mathsf{rd}}$ for 10^5 times while varying the privacy budget ϵ from 1.0 to 4.0 under $\delta = 0.1$ and $\delta = 0.0001$. As shown in Fig. 9a and Fig. 9b, when $\delta = 0.0001$, which is a much more practical setting in the above experiments, as the privacy budget ϵ increases, the distribution of the outputs becomes centralized gradually. It means that a smaller ϵ can lead to a stronger privacy-preserving capability. In contrast, when $\delta = 0.1$, the output is not adequately randomized, implying a higher probability of accidental information leakage.

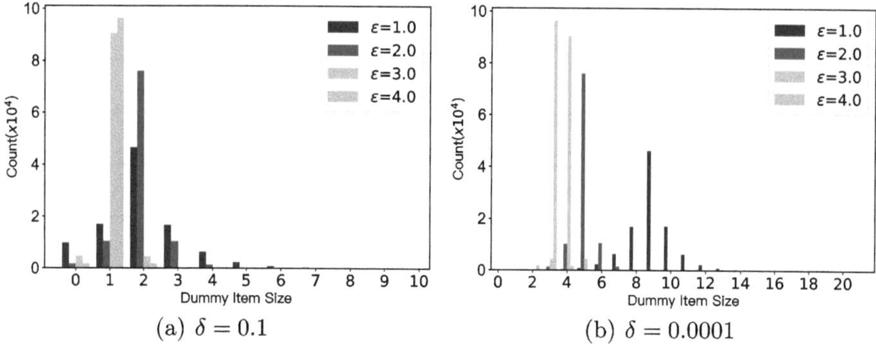

(a) $\delta = 0.1$ (b) $\delta = 0.0001$

Fig. 9. The distribution of dummy items' size.

7 Conclusion

In this paper, we revisit the definition of DPSI, introduce its ideal functionality, and propose two generic and modular constructions. $\mathbf{\Pi}_{\mathsf{circuit\text{-}DPSI}}$ is secure and satisfies ϵ-DP, while $\mathbf{\Pi}_{\mathsf{mqRPMT\text{-}DPSI}}$ offers improved efficiency at the expense of privacy compromise. For $\mathbf{\Pi}_{\mathsf{mqRPMT\text{-}DPSI}}$, we also propose a Random Dummy Item Padding Mechanism to prevent the exact PSI-CA from leaking. We prove that the released PSI-CA satisfies (ϵ, δ)-DP. Experiments show that the instantiations of $\mathbf{\Pi}_{\mathsf{mqRPMT\text{-}DPSI}}$ are arguably the most computation- and communication-efficient DPSI protocols, and the instantiations of $\mathbf{\Pi}_{\mathsf{circuit\text{-}DPSI}}$ are comparable in performance with the most efficient circuit-PSI protocols.

Although our instantiations outperform existing DPSI construction, their concrete efficiency is still worse than those of SOTA (non-circuit) PSI and PSI-based applications. Obtaining more efficient DPSI is a promising future direction.

Acknowledgment. Weiran Liu is the corresponding author. We thank Hanwen Feng for his discussion in writing this paper. This work is supported by the Major Programs of the National Social Science Foundation of China (Grant No. 22&ZD147).

A Proof of Theorem 2

We prove Theorem 2 in two steps. First, we show that the ideal functionality $\mathcal{F}_{\mathsf{DPSI}}$ satisfies ϵ-DPSI, which can be easily proven through the DP property of $\mathcal{M}_{RR}$, and we omit the detailed proof. Then, we prove that the construction $\mathbf{\Pi}_{\mathsf{circuit\text{-}DPSI}}$ securely realizes the ideal functionality. By combining them, the theorem is proved.

Lemma 2. *$\mathcal{F}_{\mathsf{DPSI}}$ in Fig. 3 with $\mathcal{M}_{RR}$ parameterized by ϵ satisfies ϵ-DPSI.*

Lemma 3. *The protocol $\mathbf{\Pi}_{\mathsf{circuit\text{-}DPSI}}$ in Fig. 5 securely realizes the ideal functionality $\mathcal{F}_{\mathsf{DPSI}}$ in Fig. 3 using $\mathcal{M}_{RR}$ against a semi-honest adversary in the $\mathcal{F}_{\mathsf{circuit\text{-}PSI}}$-hybrid model.*

Proof. The correctness of $\mathbf{\Pi}_{\mathsf{circuit\text{-}DPSI}}$ is obvious, which follows the correctness of the underlying protocol realizing $\mathcal{F}_{\mathsf{circuit\text{-}PSI}}$. Then we prove the security by constructing simulators. For the corrupt semi-honest receiver, we exhibit the simulator Sim_R as follows.

1. Sim_R receives $\mathcal{P}_2$'s input Y, invokes $\mathcal{F}_{\mathsf{DPSI}}$ to obtain the output F', and appends them to the view.
2. Sim_R uses *Reorder* and Y to honestly compute π with size β, and selects random bits $\langle a'_j\rangle_2 \leftarrow \{0,1\}$ for $j \in [\beta]$. Then, Sim_R simulates $\mathcal{F}_{\mathsf{circuit\text{-}PSI}}$ with input $(Y, \{\langle a'_j\rangle_2\}_{j\in[\beta]})$ and appends the outputs to the view.
3. Sim_R computes a length-β Boolean vector b. For $i \in [\beta]$: If there exists $j \in [m]$ such that $\pi(j) = i$, then $b_i = \langle a'_i\rangle_2 \oplus F'_j$. Otherwise, b_i equals the output of $\mathcal{M}_{RR}$ with input $\langle a'_i\rangle_2$.

The real view of $\mathcal{P}_2$ in an execution can be written as $\mathtt{view}_2^\pi = \{Y, \pi, \{\langle a_i\rangle_2\}_{i\in[\beta]}, \{\langle\tilde{a}_i\rangle_1\}_{i\in[\beta]}, F\}$ and the output view of Sim_R is $S_2 = \{Y, \pi, \{\langle a'_i\rangle_2\}_{i\in[\beta]}, \{b_i\}_{i\in[\beta]}, F'\}$. The two views are identical, which directly follows the security of the underlying protocol realizing $\mathcal{F}_{\mathsf{circuit\text{-}PSI}}$.

For the corrupt semi-honest sender, we exhibit the simulator Sim_S as follows.

1. Sim_S receives $\mathcal{P}_1$'s input X.
2. Sim_S selects random bits $\langle a'_j\rangle_1 \leftarrow \{0,1\}$ for $j \in [\beta]$. Then, Sim_S simulates $\mathcal{F}_{\mathsf{circuit\text{-}PSI}}$ with input $(X, \{\langle a'_j\rangle_1\}_{j\in[\beta]})$ and appends the outputs to the view.
3. Sim_S uses $\mathcal{M}_{RR}$ with input $\{\langle a'_i\rangle_1\}_{i\in[\beta]}$ and get the perturbed $\{\widetilde{\langle a'_i\rangle}_1\}_{i\in[\beta]}$.

The real view of $\mathcal{P}_2$ in an execution can be written as $\mathtt{view}_1^\pi = \{X, \{\langle a_i\rangle_1\}_{i\in[\beta]}, \{\langle\tilde{a}_i\rangle_1\}_{i\in[\beta]}\}$ and the output view of Sim_S is $S_1 = \{X, \{\langle a'_i\rangle_1\}_{i\in[\beta]}, \{\widetilde{\langle a'_i\rangle}_1\}_{i\in[\beta]}\}$. The two views are identical, which directly follows the security of the underlying protocol realizing $\mathcal{F}_{\mathsf{circuit\text{-}PSI}}$. Thus, we conclude the proof.

B Proof of Theorem 3

Since both circuit-DPSI and mqRPMT-DPSI perturb the intersection in the same way using $\mathcal{M}_{RR}$, we omit the analysis of the DP property of $\mathcal{P}_2$'s output and prove that the information leaked to $\mathcal{P}_1$ in Fig. 10 is bounded by $(\epsilon_I+\epsilon_D, 2\delta)$-DP. Also, according to the sequential composition of DP (Theorem 1), we only need to prove Lemma 4. The security of Fig. 10 can be proven similar to the proof of Lemma 3. Due to space limitations, we omit it here.

$\mathcal{F}_{\mathsf{rDPSI}}$

Parameters: $\mathcal{P}_1$'s input set size n. $\mathcal{P}_2$'s input set size m. The privacy budget $\epsilon_I, \epsilon_D, \epsilon$.
Input: $\mathcal{P}_1$'s set $X = \{x_i\}_{i\in[n]} \in \mathcal{V}^n$. $\mathcal{P}_2$'s set $Y = \{y_i\}_{i\in[m]} \in \mathcal{V}^m$.
Functionality: Upon receiving X from $\mathcal{P}_1$, Y from $\mathcal{P}_2$.

1. Compute $F' \in \{0,1\}^m$, where f_i' indicates if $y_i \in X$. Apply $\mathcal{M}_{RR}$ with parameter ϵ to F' and give the result F to $\mathcal{P}_2$.
2. **DP Leakage:** Sample r_I, r_D with $L(\epsilon_I, \delta, 1)$ and $L(\epsilon_D, \delta, 1)$. Compute and give $n_I = |X \bigcap Y| + r_I$, $n_D = Y - |X \bigcap Y| + r_D$ to $\mathcal{P}_1$.

Fig. 10. Ideal functionality $\mathcal{F}_{\mathsf{rDPSI}}$ with privacy leakage.

Lemma 4. *The truncated discrete Laplace mechanism satisfies (ϵ, δ)-DP.*

Proof. For any neighboring database D_1, D_2, let $c_1 = \mathbf{c}(D_1) \geq 0$ and $c_2 = \mathbf{c}(D_2) \geq 0$. W.L.O.G. we consider $c_2 \geq c_1$. It is easy to see that $\Pr[TLap(D_1) \in (-\infty, c_1)] = 0$ and $\Pr[TLap(D_2) \in (-\infty, c_2)] = 0$. For any $o \geq c_2 \geq c_1$, it is true that

$$\frac{\Pr[TLap(D_2) = o]}{\Pr[TLap(D_1) = o]} = \frac{p \cdot \exp\left(-(\epsilon/\Delta\mathbf{c})|o - c_1 - \eta^0|\right)}{p \cdot \exp\left(-(\epsilon/\Delta\mathbf{c})|o - c_2 - \eta^0|\right)}$$
$$= \exp\left(\frac{\epsilon(|o - c_2 - \eta^0| - |o - c_1 - \eta^0|)}{\Delta\mathbf{c}}\right) \leq \exp\left(\frac{\epsilon|c_1 - c_2|}{\Delta\mathbf{c}}\right) \leq \exp(\epsilon).$$

However, when the output $o \in [c_1, c_2)$, $\Pr[TLap(D_2) = o] = 0$, $\Pr[TLap(D_1) = o] > 0$, making the ratio of probabilities unbounded. Recall that $\eta^0 = \Delta\mathbf{c} - \frac{\ln[(e^\epsilon/\Delta\mathbf{c}+1)\delta]}{\epsilon}$ and we have $\Pr[\eta_1 < \Delta\mathbf{c}] = \delta$. It means that we can bound $\Pr[TLap(D_1) \in [c_1, c_2)]$ by δ.

Let $O^* = (-\infty, c_2)$. Then, for any output set O of query $\mathbf{c}()$, we have

$$\begin{aligned}
\Pr[TLap(D_2) \in O] &= \Pr[TLap(D_2) \in (O \cap O^*)] + \Pr[TLap(D_2) \in (O - O^*)] \\
&\leq \Pr[TLap(D_1) \in [c_1, c_2)] + e^\epsilon \Pr[TLap(D_1) \in (O - O^*)] \\
&= \Pr[\eta_1 < \Delta\mathbf{c}] + e^\epsilon \Pr[TLap(D_1) \in (O - O^*)] \\
&\leq \delta + e^\epsilon \Pr[TLap(D_1) \in O].
\end{aligned}$$

Therefore, this mechanism satisfies (ϵ, δ)-DP.

References

1. Bater, J., Park, Y., He, X., Wang, X., Rogers, J.: SAQE: practical privacy-preserving approximate query processing for data federations. Proc. VLDB Endow. **13**(11), 2691–2705 (2020)
2. Bittau, A., et al.: Prochlo: strong privacy for analytics in the crowd. In: SOSP 2017, pp. 441–459. ACM (2017)
3. Boyle, E., et al.: Efficient two-round ot extension and silent non-interactive secure computation. In: CCS 2019, pp. 291–308. ACM (2019)
4. Brakerski, Z., Gentry, C., Vaikuntanathan, V.: (leveled) fully homomorphic encryption without bootstrapping. ACM Trans. Comput. Theory **6**(3), 1–36 (2014)
5. Canonne, C.L., Kamath, G., Steinke, T.: The discrete gaussian for differential privacy. In: NeurIPS 2020. NeurIPS Foundation (2020)
6. Chandran, N., Gupta, D., Shah, A.: Circuit-psi with linear complexity via relaxed batch opprf. Proceedings on Privacy Enhancing Technologies Symposium (2022)
7. Chen, Y., Zhang, M., Zhang, C., Dong, M., Liu, W.: Private set operations from multi-query reverse private membership test. In: PKC 2024, pp. 387–416. Springer, Switzerland (2024)
8. Couteau, G., Rindal, P., Raghuraman, S.: Silver: silent vole and oblivious transfer from hardness of decoding structured ldpc codes. In: Crypto 2021. Springer (2021)
9. De Cristofaro, E., Tsudik, G.: Practical private set intersection protocols with linear complexity. In: Sion, R. (ed.) FC 2010. LNCS, vol. 6052, pp. 143–159. Springer, Heidelberg (2010). https://doi.org/10.1007/978-3-642-14577-3_13
10. Duchi, J.C., Jordan, M.I., Wainwrigh, M.J.: Local privacy and statistical minimax rates. In: FOCS 2013 (2013)
11. Dwork, C., Roth, A.: The algorithmic foundations of differential privacy. Found. Trends Theoretical Comput. Sci. **9**(3–4), 211–407 (2014)
12. Edmonds, A., Nikolov, A., Ullman, J.R.: The power of factorization mechanisms in local and central differential privacy. In: STOC 2020, pp. 425–438. ACM (2020)
13. Erlingsson, Ú., Pihur, V., Korolova, A.: RAPPOR: randomized aggregatable privacy-preserving ordinal response. In: CCS 2014, pp. 1054–1067. ACM (2014)
14. Garimella, G., Pinkas, B., Rosulek, M., Trieu, N., Yanai, A.: Oblivious key-value stores and amplification for private set intersection. In: Crypto 2021. Springer (2021)
15. Gentry, C.: Fully homomorphic encryption using ideal lattices. In: STOC 2009, pp. 169–178. ACM (2009)
16. Goldreich, O.: Foundations of cryptography: Basic Applications, vol. 2. Cambridge University Press (2009)
17. Groce, A., Rindal, P., Rosulek, M.: Cheaper private set intersection via differentially private leakage. Proc. Priv. Enhancing Technol. **2019**(3), 6–25 (2019)
18. Guo, X., Han, Y., Liu, Z., Wang, D., Jia, Y., Li, J.: Birds of a feather flock together: How set bias helps to deanonymize you via revealed intersection sizes. In: USENIX Security 2022, pp. 1487–1504. USENIX (2022)
19. Haney, S., Machanavajjhala, A., Abowd, J.M., Graham, M., Kutzbach, M., Vilhuber, L.: Utility cost of formal privacy for releasing national employer-employee statistics. In: SIGMOD 2017, pp. 1339–1354. ACM (2017)
20. He, X., Machanavajjhala, A., Flynn, C., Srivastava, D.: Composing differential privacy and secure computation: a case study on scaling private record linkage. In: CCS 2017, pp. 1389–1406. ACM (2017)

21. Information Commissioner's Office: Chapter 5: Privacy-enhancing technologies (2022)
22. Ion, M., et al.: On deploying secure computing: Private intersection-sum-with-cardinality. In: EuroS&P 2020, pp. 370–389. IEEE (2020)
23. Ishai, Y., Kilian, J., Nissim, K., Petrank, E.: Extending oblivious transfers efficiently. In: Crypto 2003, pp. 145–161. Springer (2003)
24. Jiang, B., Du, J., Yan, Q.: Anonpsi: An anonymity assessment framework for PSI. Cryptology ePrint Archive (2024)
25. Kacsmar, B., et al.: Differentially private two-party set operations. In: EuroS&P 2020, pp. 390–404. IEEE (2020)
26. Kolesnikov, V., Kumaresan, R., Rosulek, M., Trieu, N.: Efficient batched oblivious prf with applications to private set intersection. In: CCS 2016. ACM (2016)
27. Li, C., Miklau, G., Hay, M., McGregor, A., Rastogi, V.: The matrix mechanism: optimizing linear counting queries under differential privacy. VLDB J. **24**(6), 757–781 (2015). https://doi.org/10.1007/s00778-015-0398-x
28. Mahdavi, R.A., et al.: PEPSI: practically efficient private set intersection in the unbalanced setting. In: USENIX Security 2024. USENIX Association (2024)
29. Meadows, C.: A more efficient cryptographic matchmaking protocol for use in the absence of a continuously available third party. In: S&P 1986. IEEE (1986)
30. Narayan, A., Haeberlen, A.: Djoin: differentially private join queries over distributed databases. In: OSDI 2012, pp. 149–162. USENIX (2012)
31. Pagh, R., Rodler, F.F.: Cuckoo hashing. In: auf der Heide, F.M. (ed.) ESA 2001. LNCS, vol. 2161, pp. 121–133. Springer, Heidelberg (2001). https://doi.org/10.1007/3-540-44676-1_10
32. Pinkas, B., Rosulek, M., Trieu, N., Yanai, A.: SpOT-light: lightweight private set intersection from sparse OT extension. In: Boldyreva, A., Micciancio, D. (eds.) CRYPTO 2019. LNCS, vol. 11694, pp. 401–431. Springer, Cham (2019). https://doi.org/10.1007/978-3-030-26954-8_13
33. Pinkas, B., Rosulek, M., Trieu, N., Yanai, A.: PSI from PaXoS: fast, malicious private set intersection. In: Canteaut, A., Ishai, Y. (eds.) EUROCRYPT 2020. LNCS, vol. 12106, pp. 739–767. Springer, Cham (2020). https://doi.org/10.1007/978-3-030-45724-2_25
34. Pinkas, B., Schneider, T., Tkachenko, O., Yanai, A.: Efficient circuit-based PSI with linear communication. In: Ishai, Y., Rijmen, V. (eds.) EUROCRYPT 2019. LNCS, vol. 11478, pp. 122–153. Springer, Cham (2019). https://doi.org/10.1007/978-3-030-17659-4_5
35. Raghuraman, S., Rindal, P.: Blazing fast psi from improved okvs and subfield vole. In: CCS 2022, pp. 2505–2517. ACM (2022)
36. Rindal, P., Rosulek, M.: Malicious-secure private set intersection via dual execution. In: CCS 2017. pp. 1229–1242. ACM (2017)
37. Rindal, P., Schoppmann, P.: VOLE-PSI: fast OPRF and circuit-PSI from vector-OLE. In: Canteaut, A., Standaert, F.-X. (eds.) EUROCRYPT 2021. LNCS, vol. 12697, pp. 901–930. Springer, Cham (2021). https://doi.org/10.1007/978-3-030-77886-6_31
38. Wang, Y., Yi, K.: Secure yannakakis: Join-aggregate queries over private data. In: SIGMOD 2021, pp. 1969–1981. ACM (2021)
39. Warner, S.L.: Randomized response: a survey technique for eliminating evasive answer bias. J. Am. Stat. Assoc. **60**(309), 63–69 (1965)
40. Yagisawa, M.: Fully homomorphic encryption without bootstrapping. Cryptology ePrint Archive (2015). https://eprint.iacr.org/2011/277

41. Yang, K., Weng, C., Lan, X., Zhang, J., Wang, X.: Ferret: fast extension for correlated ot with small communication. In: CCS 2020 (2020)
42. Yao, A.C.C.: How to generate and exchange secrets. In: FOCS 1986. IEEE (1986)
43. Yuan, G., Yang, Y., Zhang, Z., Hao, Z.: Convex optimization for linear query processing under approximate differential privacy. In: SIGKDD 2016. ACM (2016)
44. Zhang, C., Chen, Y., Liu, W., Zhang, M., Lin, D.: Linear private set union from {Multi-Query} reverse private membership test. In: USENIX Security 2023, pp. 337–354. USENIX (2023)

MSFS: Maliciously Secure 3-Party Feature Selection via Mutual Information

Peijun Zhao, Lin Liu(✉), Shaojing Fu, and Yuchuan Luo

College of Computer Science and Technology, National University of Defense Technology, Changsha 410073, China
{zhaopeijun19,liulin16,fushaojing,luoyuchuan09}@nudt.edu.cn

Abstract. Feature selection is a critical data preprocessing step in machine learning applications. However, existing privacy-preserving techniques primarily focus on the model training and inference phases, leaving the preprocessing stage as a potential point of privacy leakage. Furthermore, nearly all existing privacy-preserving feature selection schemes are based on the semi-honest security model and cannot withstand attacks from malicious adversaries. To address this critical gap, this paper proposes the first maliciously secure 3-Party feature selection scheme via mutual information (MSFS) to the best of our knowledge. To ensure security and efficiency, we design a series of secure computation sub-protocols, including secure entropy computation, secure MI score computation, secure Top-k score computation, and secure reduction matrix computation. For the proposed protocols, we provide theoretical analysis and security proofs. We also conduct experimental evaluations on both real-world and synthetic datasets. The results show that our scheme can achieve a performance improvement of up to 12.86% while guaranteeing security. This work provides a theoretical and practical foundation for performing secure feature selection in untrusted, collaborative scenarios.

Keywords: Multi-party computation · Feature selection · Malicious adversary · Privacy-preserving · Mutual information

1 Introduction

The widespread adoption of machine learning (ML) is often challenged by the quality of real-world data, which can be noisy, redundant, or contain irrelevant information. Such low-quality data degrades model performance, increases computational complexity, and heightens the risk of overfitting. Feature selection (FS) is a critical preprocessing step that addresses these issues by identifying the most informative subset of features. Among the main categories of FS methods: wrapper, embedded, and filter—filter methods are widely used due to their efficiency and model-agnostic nature.

This challenge is amplified in collaborative settings where data is aggregated from multiple institutions. Such cross-domain data sharing introduces significant

R. Chen et al. (Eds.): Inscrypt 2025, LNCS 16409, pp. 45–65, 2026.
https://doi.org/10.1007/978-981-95-6203-9_3

privacy risks, as sensitive information can be exposed. Regulatory frameworks like the GDPR [1] underscore the global imperative to protect data privacy, making it crucial to balance data utility and confidentiality. While Secure Multi-Party Computation (MPC) has emerged as a powerful paradigm for privacy-preserving ML [2–4], a critical gap remains: the majority of existing work presupposes that data has already been preprocessed and features selected. This overlooks the fact that the feature selection stage itself can leak sensitive information, rendering subsequent privacy-preserving training moot. Consequently, research on privacy-preserving feature selection, particularly under the challenging malicious adversary model, remains underdeveloped.

To address this gap, we leverage Mutual Information (MI), a filter-based metric that is more versatile and effective than traditional measures like Gini impurity [5] for capturing complex, non-linear dependencies between features and target variables. We propose a novel, three-party secure feature selection protocol based on MI, designed for the honest-majority malicious model. Our core idea is to decompose this complex task into a series of efficient and secure sub-protocols—such as secure entropy computation, secure Top-k score computation, and secure reduction matrix computation—to construct a complete and secure feature selection framework.

The main contributions of this paper are as follows:

1. **A Secure MI-based Feature Selection Framework:** We propose a novel three-party secure feature selection framework based on Mutual Information (MI). Our method evaluates the relevance of each feature to the target variable and retains the highest-ranking ones. To achieve this securely and efficiently, we leverage cryptographic primitives from three-party MPC to construct a series of secure protocols. These protocols form the basis of a complete feature selection scheme that enhances computational efficiency without compromising security or accuracy.
2. **Security against Malicious Adversaries:** We provide a robust security guarantee by developing our protocols in the honest-majority malicious adversary model. Unlike schemes secure only against semi-honest adversaries, our solution can withstand a corrupted party that actively deviates from the protocol, ensuring that malicious behavior is either detected and aborted or the computation completes correctly.
3. **Theoretical Analysis and Experimental Evaluation:** We provide formal cryptographic proofs of security and correctness for our protocols. Furthermore, we conduct extensive experimental validation on both real-world and synthetic datasets to demonstrate that our scheme meets the security and performance requirements for feature selection tasks on diverse datasets.

2 Related Work

2.1 Privacy-Preserving Feature Selection

Existing work on privacy-preserving feature selection can be broadly divided into two categories: methods based on anonymization and those employing Secure Multi-Party Computation (MPC).

Early approaches often utilized anonymization techniques. For example, Jafer et al. [6] proposed a metric to evaluate both the privacy risk and utility of features. However, this method's reliance on a trusted third party (TTP) makes its security contingent on the TTP's integrity. Alishahi and Moghtadaiee [7] assessed the impact of anonymization on feature selection using Pearson correlation and information gain, while Alishahi et al. [8] later modeled the problem as frequency estimation and applied local differential privacy. In general, anonymization techniques tend to degrade the utility of the selected features, thereby compromising the performance of subsequent models.

Another line of work employs MPC to perform accurate feature selection without a TTP. Rao et al. [9] introduced a two-party secure feature selection scheme based on the chi-squared test, using Paillier homomorphic encryption. Li et al. [5] proposed the first MPC-based filter method for secure Gini impurity computation in a multi-server setting. Wu et al. [10] designed a privacy-preserving scheme based on mutual information (MI), but their approach assumes a vertically partitioned data setting where one party holds the entire label vector—a scenario often unrealistic in practice. Other notable works include a consistency-based method by Ono et al. [11] and an MI-based filter scheme by David et al. [12] that combines federated learning with MPC for end-to-end privacy. More recently, Wang et al. [13] proposed a two-party MPC approach using approximate fixed-point representation to improve efficiency. However, as we discuss in Appendix D.1, its secure division protocol contains a critical flaw.

3 Preliminaries

This section outlines the fundamental concepts of mutual information and the cryptographic primitives employed in our scheme. Key notations are defined in Table 1.

Table 1. Definition of Notations

Notation	Definition
$\mathbb{Z}_{2^l}$	The integer ring modulo 2^l
m	Number of samples in the dataset
n	Number of features
p	Number of classes
k	Number of features to be selected
$\mathcal{F}, \mathcal{L}$	The feature matrix and the label matrix
Π	A three-party secure computation protocol

3.1 Mutual Information

Mutual Information (MI) is a powerful metric in filter-based feature selection for quantifying the statistical dependency between a feature and the target variable. Unlike simpler correlation-based metrics, MI is not limited to linear relationships and can effectively capture complex, non-linear dependencies. MI is defined based on entropy. For two discrete random variables, X and Y, their MI, $M(X,Y)$, is defined by their individual entropies, $Ent(X)$ and $Ent(Y)$, and their joint entropy, $Ent(X,Y)$:

$$M(X,Y) = Ent(X) + Ent(Y) - Ent(X,Y) \tag{1}$$

where the entropy of X is the expected value of its information content:

$$Ent(X) = -\sum_{i=1}^{m} P(x_i) \log P(x_i) \tag{2}$$

If X and Y are independent, $M(X,Y) = 0$; conversely, a large $M(X,Y)$ implies a strong dependency. Equivalently, MI can be expressed as the reduction in uncertainty. The conditional entropy of X given Y, denoted as $Ent(X|Y)$, measures the remaining uncertainty in X when Y is known:

$$Ent(X|Y) = -\sum_{i=1}^{m}\sum_{j=1}^{n} P(x_i, y_j) \log P(x_i|y_j) \tag{3}$$

This leads to an alternative and intuitive definition of MI, highlighting its symmetric nature:

$$\begin{aligned} M(X,Y) &= Ent(X) - Ent(X|Y) \\ &= Ent(Y) - Ent(Y|X) \end{aligned} \tag{4}$$

In feature selection, a higher MI value between a feature and the class label signifies a stronger relevance, making it a more valuable predictor.

3.2 Cryptographic Primitives

Secret Sharing. Our work is primarily based on computations over the integer ring $\mathbb{Z}_{2^l}$ for a positive integer l. For the special case of $l = 1$, this corresponds to computations over the ring $\mathbb{Z}_2$, for which we employ a Boolean secret sharing scheme. Specifically, we adopt the (2,3) replicated secret sharing scheme from Araki et al. [14]. In this scheme, a plaintext value $x \in \mathbb{Z}_{2^l}$ is additively shared among three parties as x_0, x_1, x_2, such that $x = x_0 + x_1 + x_2 \pmod{2^l}$. We use the notation $[\![x]\!]_b^l$ to signify that party P_b holds the pair of shares (x_b, x_{b+1}), where indices are taken modulo 3 and $b \in \{0, 1, 2\}$. The sharing semantics are detailed in Table 2.

Table 2. Sharing Semantics

Party	$[\![x]\!]_b^l$
P_0	(x_0, x_1)
P_1	(x_1, x_2)
P_2	(x_2, x_0)
Reconstruction $(l > 1)$	$x = x_0 + x_1 + x_2 \pmod{2^l}$
Reconstruction $(l = 1)$	$x = x_0 \oplus x_1 \oplus x_2 \pmod{2}$

Basic Computation Protocols. Based on the replicated secret sharing primitives described above, many works have developed three-party secure computation protocols for other operations. This paper utilizes several protocols from the Falcon framework [15] to achieve secure interaction among the computation servers, ensuring security in the malicious adversary setting.

- **Multiplication Protocol** ($\Pi_{Mult}(z = x \cdot y)$)**:** A key advantage of the (2,3) replicated secret sharing scheme is its highly efficient multiplication. To compute the product $z = x \cdot y$, each party P_b first locally computes a partial product z_b without any interaction:
  - P_0 computes $z_0 = x_0 \cdot y_0 + x_0 \cdot y_1 + x_1 \cdot y_0$.
  - P_1 computes $z_1 = x_1 \cdot y_1 + x_1 \cdot y_2 + x_2 \cdot y_1$.
  - P_2 computes $z_2 = x_2 \cdot y_2 + x_2 \cdot y_0 + x_0 \cdot y_2$.

  This process results in an *additive* secret sharing of the product, where $z_0 + z_1 + z_2 = x \cdot y \pmod{2^l}$. Restoring the original replicated format requires a subsequent conversion step, which involves one round of communication. For a detailed construction of such a protocol in the semi-honest setting, see Araki et al. [14]. To achieve security against malicious adversaries, as required by our work, we build upon the secure multiplication protocol introduced in Falcon [15].
- **Secure Matrix Multiplication Protocol** (Π_{MM})**:** This protocol securely computes the product of two secret-shared matrices, $[\![\boldsymbol{A}]\!]_b^l$ and $[\![\boldsymbol{B}]\!]_b^l$, by extending the scalar multiplication protocol. Upon completion, the parties obtain shares of the resulting matrix $[\![\boldsymbol{C}]\!]_b^l = [\![\boldsymbol{A} \times \boldsymbol{B}]\!]_b^l$. When performing computations with fixed-point numbers, a truncation protocol must be executed after each multiplication to maintain the correct precision [15].
- **Secure Comparison Protocol** (Π_{PC})**:** Given secret shares of two values, $[\![x]\!]_b^l$ and $[\![y]\!]_b^l$, this protocol securely computes a secret share of the result of the comparison $x \leq y$. The output is a share of 1 if the condition holds, and a share of 0 otherwise.
- **Secure Division Protocol** (Π_{Div})**:** Given secret shares of a dividend $[\![x]\!]_b^l$ and a divisor $[\![y]\!]_b^l$, this protocol securely computes a secret share of the quotient, $[\![z]\!]_b^l = [\![x/y]\!]_b^l$, with a specified precision f_p.

Secret Reconstruction. The method for secret reconstruction differs significantly between the semi-honest and malicious security models.

In the **semi-honest model**, a simple one-round reconstruction suffices. Each party P_b sends its share $[\![x]\!]^l_b$ to party P_{b+1} (indices are modulo 3). After this single round of communication, each party holds two out of the three shares and can reconstruct the secret x.

In the **honest-majority malicious model**, however, we must prevent a malicious party from sending inconsistent shares to different honest parties. To achieve this, we employ a cross-checking reconstruction protocol. Each party P_b is required to send its share $[\![x]\!]^l_b$ to *both* other parties. For example, P_1 expects to receive the share $[\![x]\!]^l_0$ from both P_0 and P_2. If the two received versions of $[\![x]\!]^l_0$ are inconsistent, P_1 detects malicious behavior and aborts the protocol. This same verification occurs symmetrically for all parties and all shares. This cross-checking mechanism, while incurring higher communication costs, is a critical component for ensuring the correctness of the output against malicious adversaries.

4 MSFS: Honest-Majority Maliciously Secure 3-Party Feature Selection via Mutual Information

Figure 4 in Appendix A illustrates the overall technical framework of our work.

First, the design of our scheme is guided by a set of fundamental requirements. From a functional perspective, the protocol must ensure the correctness of the computation while striving for high efficiency. In terms of security, the protocol must guarantee the privacy of user data by preventing any leakage of input data and intermediate results under the specified threat model.

Second, built upon the foundation of secret sharing and its associated primitive protocols, our framework is composed of several novel secure components. We begin by designing a secure entropy calculation protocol and a secure mutual information (MI) score calculation protocol. Once the feature scores are obtained in a secret-shared form, we then employ our custom-designed secure Top-k score selection protocol and secure reduction matrix generation protocol to perform the final feature selection. This entire process is executed without leaking any sensitive information.

4.1 System Model and Threat Model

Our scheme consists of four parts: Firstly, the clients secret-share their raw data among the servers. Secondly, the servers collaboratively compute MI scores and then, select the high-scoring features. Finally, based on this selected subset, the servers proceed with a privacy-preserving model training protocol. The overall system architecture is illustrated in Fig. 1.

Our scheme operates under the honest-majority malicious model. This model assumes that among the three computing servers, at most one can be corrupted (i.e., be semi-honest or malicious). A malicious adversary may arbitrarily deviate

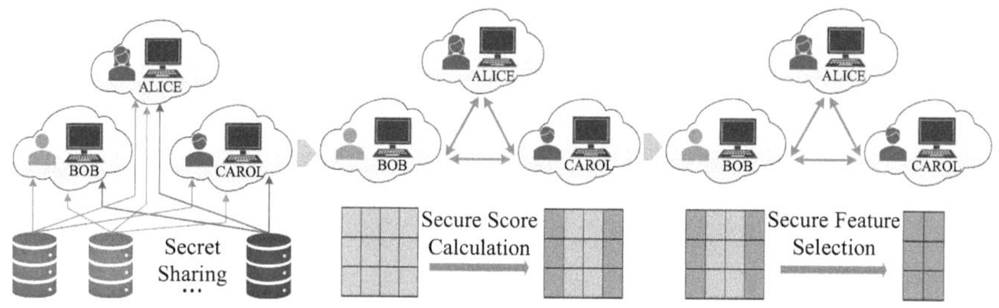

Fig. 1. System model.

from the protocol specifications or tamper with data. We assume that the servers are non-colluding and that all communication occurs over authenticated and confidential channels. Furthermore, all cryptographic keys held by the parties are assumed to be securely stored.

4.2 Secure Mutual Information Score Computation

Secure Entropy Protocol. A core challenge in securely computing entropy, cross-entropy, and mutual information is the evaluation of the logarithm function within an MPC framework. As the logarithm is a non-linear function, we must employ a secure approximation protocol. The details of our secure logarithm approximation are provided in Appendix B. For consistency with information-theoretic conventions, we use base-2 logarithms to measure information content, ensuring the resulting unit is bits. The entropy computation is built upon this secure logarithm protocol. The protocol Π_{Ent} takes as input a secret-shared value $[\![x]\!]_b$ where $x \in (0,1)$ and outputs $[\![e]\!]_b$, where $e = x\log_2 x$. Within this protocol, we first invoke Π_{log} to approximate $[\![\log_2 x]\!]_b$. Subsequently, computing $[\![x\log_2 x]\!]_b$ requires only a single additional secure multiplication.

Algorithm 1. Secure Entropy Protocol computation Π_{Ent}

Input: Party P_b holds shares $[\![x]\!]_b^l$, where the underlying value $x \in (0,1)$ and $b \in \{0,1,2\}$.
Output: The parties obtain shares $[\![e]\!]_b^l$ of the entropy term, where $e = -x\log x$.
1. $[\![w]\!]_b^l \leftarrow \Pi_{log}([\![x]\!]_b^l)$
2. $[\![e]\!]_b^l \leftarrow -\Pi_{Mult}([\![x]\!]_b^l, [\![w]\!]_b^l)$
3. **return** $[\![e]\!]_b^l$

Secure Mutual Information Score Protocol. In mutual information (MI)-based feature selection, the MI score is the primary metric for quantifying the importance of a feature. We propose a secure protocol for this computation, denoted Π_{GMI}, with its detailed steps presented in Algorithm 2.

Our protocol operates on a dataset $\mathcal{D} = \{\mathcal{F}, \mathcal{L}\}$, where $\mathcal{F}$ is the $m \times n$ feature matrix (m samples, n features) and $\mathcal{L}$ is the $m \times p$ one-hot encoded label matrix (p classes). The label for the i-th sample is given by the row vector $\boldsymbol{L}_i$, where $\boldsymbol{L}_i[j] = 1$ signifies that the sample belongs to the j-th class. The mutual information between the j-th feature $\boldsymbol{F}_j$, and the label set $\mathcal{L}$ is defined as the reduction in entropy:

$$M(\boldsymbol{F}_j, \mathcal{L}) = Ent(\boldsymbol{F}_j) - Ent(\boldsymbol{F}_j|\mathcal{L}) = Ent(\mathcal{L}) - Ent(\mathcal{L}|\boldsymbol{F}_j) \tag{5}$$

While traditional methods often discretize continuous features into a fixed number of bins (e.g., five equal-width bins) for computational efficiency [16], this paper adopts a mean-based partitioning approach [5]. This method not only improves the efficiency of data processing in a privacy-preserving computation environment, but also provides new perspectives and tools for class-based data analysis. For each feature $\boldsymbol{F}_j$, we use its mean value as a threshold θ, to partition the dataset $\mathcal{D}$ into two disjoint subsets. Specifically, for each feature $\boldsymbol{F}_j$, we denote the subset of samples with feature values $f_{ij} \leq \theta$ as $\mathcal{F}_{\leq\theta}$, and the subset with $f_{ij} > \theta$ as $\mathcal{F}_{>\theta}$. Furthermore, let $\mathcal{L}_k$ be the subset of instances belonging to class k. Based on Eq. (5), the MI of feature $\boldsymbol{F}_j$ can then be defined as:

$$\begin{aligned}
M(\boldsymbol{F}_j, \mathcal{L}) &= \frac{1}{m}\left(|\mathcal{F}_{\leq\theta}| \cdot M(\mathcal{F}_{\leq\theta}, \mathcal{L}) + |\mathcal{F}_{>\theta}| \cdot M(\mathcal{F}_{>\theta}, \mathcal{L})\right) \\
&= \frac{1}{m}\big(|\mathcal{F}_{\leq\theta}| \cdot (Ent(\mathcal{L}) - Ent(\mathcal{L}|\mathcal{F}_{\leq\theta})) \\
&\quad + |\mathcal{F}_{>\theta}| \cdot (Ent(\mathcal{L}) - Ent(\mathcal{L}|\mathcal{F}_{>\theta}))\big) \\
&= \frac{1}{m}\big((|\mathcal{F}_{\leq\theta}| + |\mathcal{F}_{>\theta}|) \cdot Ent(\mathcal{L}) - |\mathcal{F}_{\leq\theta}| \cdot Ent(\mathcal{L}|\mathcal{F}_{\leq\theta}) \\
&\quad - |\mathcal{F}_{>\theta}| \cdot Ent(\mathcal{L}|\mathcal{F}_{>\theta})\big) \\
&= Ent(\mathcal{L}) - \frac{1}{m}\left(|\mathcal{F}_{\leq\theta}| \cdot Ent(\mathcal{L}|\mathcal{F}_{\leq\theta}) + |\mathcal{F}_{>\theta}| \cdot Ent(\mathcal{L}|\mathcal{F}_{>\theta})\right)
\end{aligned} \tag{6}$$

In the preceding equation, the term $Ent(\mathcal{L})$ is constant for all features, as it depends only on the distribution of the overall label set. Since the term $-\frac{1}{m}$ is also constant, we can define a simplified MI score for a feature $\boldsymbol{F}_j$ by omitting these constant terms. This optimized scoring formula, shown in Eq. (7), reduces the computational overhead without affecting the relative ranking of features.

$$Sco(\boldsymbol{F}_j) = |\mathcal{F}_{\leq\theta}| \cdot Ent(\mathcal{L}|\mathcal{F}_{\leq\theta}) + |\mathcal{F}_{>\theta}| \cdot Ent(\mathcal{L}|\mathcal{F}_{>\theta}) \tag{7}$$

Here, the conditional entropies for $\mathcal{F}_{\leq\theta}$ and $\mathcal{F}_{>\theta}$ are defined as:

$$\begin{cases} Ent(\mathcal{L}|\mathcal{F}_{\leq\theta}) = -\sum_{k=1}^{p} P_k^{\leq\theta} \cdot \log P_k^{\leq\theta} \\ Ent(\mathcal{L}|\mathcal{F}_{>\theta}) = -\sum_{k=1}^{p} P_k^{>\theta} \cdot \log P_k^{>\theta} \end{cases} \tag{8}$$

Here, $P_k^{\leq\theta}$ represents the probability of a sample belonging to class k within the subset where the feature value $f_{ij} \leq \theta$ (i.e., $f_{ij} \leq \theta$ and $\mathcal{L}_i[k] = 1$). Conversely, $P_k^{\geq\theta}$ represents this probability for the subset where $f_{ij} \geq \theta$. They are formally defined as:

$$\begin{cases} P_k^{\leq\theta} = \frac{|\mathcal{F}_{\leq\theta} \cap \mathcal{L}_k|}{|\mathcal{F}_{\leq\theta}|} \\ P_k^{>\theta} = \frac{|\mathcal{F}_{>\theta} \cap \mathcal{L}_k|}{|\mathcal{F}_{>\theta}|} \end{cases} \tag{9}$$

To facilitate matrix multiplication, we define $\mathcal{T} = (t_{ij})_{n\times m}$ as the transpose of the feature matrix $\mathcal{F}$. Consequently, the rows of $\mathcal{T}$ represent features and its columns represent sample instances, which is equivalent to swapping the rows and columns of $\mathcal{F}$.

Algorithm 2. Secure Mutual Information Score Protocol Π_{GMI}

Input: P_b holds shares of feature-sample matrix $[\![\mathcal{T}_{n\times m}]\!]_b^l$ and label matrix $[\![\mathcal{L}_{m\times p}]\!]_b^l$. n: number of features, m: number of samples, p: number of classes, $b \in \{0, 1, 2\}$.
Output: The parties obtain shares of the feature scores $[\![\boldsymbol{Sco}(\mathcal{F})]\!]_b^l$.
1. Initialize arithmetic-shared zero vectors $[\![\mathbf{u}]\!]_b^l$, $[\![\mathbf{v}]\!]_b^l$ and Boolean-shared zero matrices $[\![\mathcal{U}_{n\times m}]\!]_b^1, [\![\mathcal{V}_{n\times m}]\!]_b^1$.
2. **for** $i \leftarrow 1$ **to** n **do**
3. $\quad [\![\theta_i]\!]_b^l \leftarrow \frac{1}{m}\sum_{j=1}^m [\![t_{ij}]\!]_b^l$
4. $\quad$ **for** $j \leftarrow 1$ **to** m **do**
5. $\quad\quad [\![flag]\!]_b^1 \leftarrow \Pi_{PC}([\![t_{ij}]\!]_b^l, [\![\theta_i]\!]_b^l)$
6. $\quad\quad [\![x_{ij}^{\mathcal{U}}]\!]_b^1 \leftarrow [\![x_{ij}^{\mathcal{U}}]\!]_b^1 \oplus [\![flag]\!]_b^1$
7. $\quad\quad [\![x_{ij}^{\mathcal{V}}]\!]_b^1 \leftarrow ([\![1]\!]_b^1 \oplus [\![x_{ij}^{\mathcal{V}}]\!]_b^1) \oplus [\![flag]\!]_b^1$
8. $\quad$ **end for**
9. **end for**
10. $[\![\mathbf{u}]\!]_b^l \leftarrow \sum_{j=1}^m [\![\mathbf{x}_j^{\mathcal{U}}]\!]_b^1;\quad [\![\mathbf{v}]\!]_b^l \leftarrow \sum_{j=1}^m [\![\mathbf{x}_j^{\mathcal{V}}]\!]_b^1$
11. $[\![\mathcal{C}_{\mathcal{U}}]\!]_b^l \leftarrow \Pi_{MM}([\![\mathcal{U}_{n\times m}]\!]_b^1, [\![\mathcal{L}_{m\times p}]\!]_b^l);\quad [\![\mathcal{C}_{\mathcal{V}}]\!]_b^l \leftarrow \Pi_{MM}([\![\mathcal{V}_{n\times m}]\!]_b^1, [\![\mathcal{L}_{m\times p}]\!]_b^l)$
12. $[\![P_k^{\mathcal{U}}]\!]_b^l \leftarrow \Pi_{Div}([\![\mathcal{C}_{\mathcal{U}}[k]]\!]_b^l, [\![\mathbf{u}]\!]_b^l);\quad [\![P_k^{\mathcal{V}}]\!]_b^l \leftarrow \Pi_{Div}([\![\mathcal{C}_{\mathcal{V}}[k]]\!]_b^l, [\![\mathbf{v}]\!]_b^l)$
13. $[\![\boldsymbol{Sco}(\mathcal{F})]\!]_b^l = \Pi_{MM}([\![\mathbf{u}]\!]_b^l, \sum_{k=1}^n \Pi_{Ent}([\![P_k^{\mathcal{U}}]\!]_b^l)) + \Pi_{MM}([\![\mathbf{v}]\!]_b^l, \sum_{k=1}^n \Pi_{Ent}([\![P_k^{\mathcal{V}}]\!]_b^l))$
14. **return** $[\![\boldsymbol{Sco}(\mathcal{F})]\!]_b^l$

In steps 2–9, the protocol securely partitions the samples for each feature based on a threshold θ_i. Using a secure comparison protocol (Π_{PC}), the parties generate two Boolean-shared indicator matrices, $[\![\mathcal{U}]\!]_b^1$ and $[\![\mathcal{V}]\!]_b^1$. An element in $[\![\mathcal{U}]\!]_b^1$ is 1 if the corresponding feature value $t_{ij} \leq \theta_i$; otherwise, the corresponding element in $[\![\mathcal{V}]\!]_b^1$ is 1.

Subsequently, in step 10, the parties securely sum the rows of these indicator matrices to obtain two count vectors, $[\![\mathbf{u}]\!]_b^l$ and $[\![\mathbf{v}]\!]_b^l$. The vector $[\![\mathbf{u}]\!]_b^l$ stores the number of samples for each feature where $t_{ij} \leq \theta_i$, while $[\![\mathbf{v}]\!]_b^l$ stores the count for samples where $t_{ij} > \theta_i$. These vectors represent the sizes of the two partitions:

$$\mathbf{u} = |\mathcal{F}_{\leq\theta}| \tag{10}$$

$$\mathbf{v} = |\mathcal{F}_{>\theta}| \tag{11}$$

In step 11, the parties execute a secure matrix multiplication (Π_{MM}) between the indicator matrices and the label matrix $[\![\mathcal{L}]\!]_b^l$ to compute the count matrices

$[\![\mathcal{C_U}]\!]^l_b$ and $[\![\mathcal{C_V}]\!]^l_b$. The resulting $n \times p$ matrix $[\![\mathcal{C_U}]\!]^l_b$ stores the number of samples per feature partition and per class. Formally:

$$\mathcal{C_U}[k] = |\mathcal{F}_{\leq\theta} \cap \mathcal{L}_k| \tag{12}$$

$$\mathcal{C_V}[k] = |\mathcal{F}_{>\theta} \cap \mathcal{L}_k| \tag{13}$$

In step 12, the parties compute the conditional probabilities by invoking the secure division protocol (Π_{Div}). They divide the class counts in $[\![\mathcal{C_U}[k]]\!]^l_b$ by the partition counts in $[\![\mathbf{u}]\!]^l_b$ to obtain the probability vector $[\![P_k^{\mathcal{U}}]\!]^l_b$. Each element of this vector represents the conditional probability $P(\text{class} = k|\text{value} \leq \theta_i)$ for a feature. A similar computation yields $[\![P_k^{\mathcal{V}}]\!]^l_b$.

Finally, in step 13, the parties use these probabilities to compute the final MI score vector, $[\![\boldsymbol{Sco}(\mathcal{F})]\!]^l_b$, by invoking Π_{Ent} and Π_{MM} according to Eq. (7).

4.3 Secure Feature Selection via Mutual Information

Secure Maximum Score Protocol. The Secure Maximum Score protocol identifies the maximal element $(score_{max}, index_{max})$ from a secret-shared n-dimensional vector $\boldsymbol{Sco}$. Our approach is a tournament-style comparison, detailed in Algorithm 3. In this method, elements are compared in pairs across $\lceil \log_2 n \rceil$ rounds until a single winner remains.

In each round, let the current vector be $\boldsymbol{Sco}$ of size $size$. The first $2s$ elements (where $s = \lfloor size/2 \rfloor$) are partitioned into two sub-vectors: $\boldsymbol{Sco}_o$ (odd-indexed) and $\boldsymbol{Sco}_e$ (even-indexed). The parties then invoke $\Pi_{PC}(\boldsymbol{Sco}_o, \boldsymbol{Sco}_e)$ to obtain a secret-shared binary vector $[\![g]\!]^1_b$. This vector determines the composition of the next round's score vector, where each element sco_i is selected based on the corresponding bit g_i:

$$sco_i = (1 - g_i) \cdot sco_{o,i} + g_i \cdot sco_{e,i}$$

If $size$ is odd, the final element is carried over directly. This process repeats until the size of $\boldsymbol{Sco}$ is 1.

Algorithm 3. Secure Maximum Score Protocol Π_{MaxSco}

Input: P_b holds shares $[\![\boldsymbol{Sco}]\!]^l_b$, $b \in \{0, 1, 2\}$.
Output: The parties obtain the maximum value of the vector, $[\![sco_{max}]\!]^l_b$.
1. The protocol runs for $t = \lceil \log_2 n \rceil$ rounds. In each round, let $size \leftarrow |\boldsymbol{Sco}|$, $s \leftarrow \lfloor size/2 \rfloor$. The parties execute:
   (1) Partition $\boldsymbol{Sco}$ into $[\![\boldsymbol{Sco}_o]\!]^l_b$ and $[\![\boldsymbol{Sco}_e]\!]^l_b$; then $[\![\mathbf{g}]\!]^1_b \leftarrow \Pi_{PC}(\boldsymbol{Sco}_o, \boldsymbol{Sco}_e) = ([\![g_0]\!]^1_b, [\![g_1]\!]^1_b, \ldots, [\![g_{s-1}]\!]^1_b)$.
   (2) $[\![\boldsymbol{Sco}_{tmp}]\!]^l_b \leftarrow ([\![sco_0]\!]^l_b, [\![sco_1]\!]^l_b, \ldots, [\![sco_{s-1}]\!]^l_b)$, where $[\![sco_i]\!]^l_b \leftarrow ([\![1]\!]^1_b - [\![g_i]\!]^1_b) \cdot [\![sco_{o,i}]\!]^l_b + [\![g_i]\!]^1_b \cdot [\![sco_{e,i}]\!]^l_b$.
   (3) When $size = 1$, stop and set $[\![sco_{max}]\!]^l_b = [\![\boldsymbol{Sco}_0]\!]^l_b$.
2. **return** $[\![sco_{max}]\!]^l_b$.

Secure Top-K Score Protocol. The Secure Top-k Score protocol (Algorithm 4) optimizes the Π_{MaxSco} protocol by incorporating a dynamic early termination strategy. Rather than executing a fixed number of rounds, it iteratively refines a pool of candidate scores until the Top-k set is precisely identified.

At the beginning of the procedure, a counter k_{tmp} is initialized to k to track the number of scores yet to be found. Each round reduces the candidate pool by half, selecting the s winners from pairwise comparisons. The protocol's efficiency stems from its adaptive logic based on the relationship between s and k_{tmp}: When $s < k_{tmp}$, the s winners are provably part of the final Top-k scores. They are thus moved to the result set, and the problem is reduced by updating k_{tmp}. When $s \geq k_{tmp}$, the winners merely constitute the pruned candidate pool for the subsequent round. This iterative pruning continues until the result set contains exactly k scores, significantly reducing computational rounds for many input distributions.

Algorithm 4. Secure Top-k Score Protocol $\Pi_{TopkSco}$

Input: Party P_b holds shares $[\![\boldsymbol{Sco}]\!]_b^l$; integer k.
Output: The parties obtain shares of the Top-k scores, $[\![\boldsymbol{Sco}_k]\!]_b^l$.
Initialization: $[\![\boldsymbol{Sco}_k]\!]_b^l \leftarrow \emptyset$; $k_{tmp} \leftarrow k$; $[\![\boldsymbol{Sco}_{current}]\!]_b^l \leftarrow [\![\boldsymbol{Sco}]\!]_b^l$;
while ($|\boldsymbol{Sco}_k| < k$):
{
  $s \leftarrow \lfloor |\boldsymbol{Sco}_{current}|/2 \rfloor$;
  Partition $\boldsymbol{Sco}_{current}$ into $[\![\boldsymbol{Sco}_o]\!]_b^l$, $[\![\boldsymbol{Sco}_e]\!]_b^l$;
  $[\![\mathbf{g}]\!]_b^1 \leftarrow \Pi_{PC}(\boldsymbol{Sco}_o, \boldsymbol{Sco}_e) = ([\![g_0]\!]_b^1, \ldots, [\![g_{s-1}]\!]_b^1)$;
  Create an empty shared vector $[\![\boldsymbol{Sco}_{tmp}]\!]_b^l$ of size s;
  for $i = 0$ to $s-1$ **do**
    $[\![sco_{tmp,i}]\!]_b^l \leftarrow ([\![1]\!]_b^1 - [\![g_i]\!]_b^1) \cdot [\![sco_{o,i}]\!]_b^l + [\![g_i]\!]_b^1 \cdot [\![sco_{e,i}]\!]_b^l$;
  end for
  if $s < k_{tmp}$ **do**:
    Append the s elements of $[\![\boldsymbol{Sco}_{tmp}]\!]_b^l$ to the result vector $[\![\boldsymbol{Sco}_k]\!]_b^l$;
    $k_{tmp} \leftarrow k_{tmp} - s$;
    $\boldsymbol{Sco}_{current} \leftarrow \boldsymbol{Sco}_{current} - \boldsymbol{Sco}_{tmp}$;
  else
    $\boldsymbol{Sco}_{current} \leftarrow \boldsymbol{Sco}_{tmp}$;
  end if
}
return $[\![\boldsymbol{Sco}_k]\!]_b^l$;

Secure Reduction Matrix Protocol. Our approach begins by constructing an $n \times n$ diagonal matrix $[\![\boldsymbol{\mathcal{A}}]\!]_b^l$, where a '1' on the diagonal marks a top-k feature. The core idea is to then apply a "bubble-sort-like" column-swapping mechanism to consolidate all columns containing a '1' into the first k positions, yielding the reduction matrix $[\![\boldsymbol{\mathcal{R}}]\!]_b^l$.

The correctness of this method hinges on a key insight: to select the correct features, only the "row" position of each '1' in $[\![\mathcal{R}]\!]_b^l$ matters. The column position is irrelevant to the selection outcome, as it only affects the final ordering of the selected features. This invariance allows us to freely rearrange the columns. The detailed procedure is presented in Algorithm 6.

The algorithm's main operation is a secure column swap. After initializing $[\![\mathcal{A}]\!]_b^l$ (steps 1–5), the parties execute a double loop to perform the swaps (steps 6–12). This process systematically moves any all-zero column within the first k positions to the right, in exchange for a column from the last $n-k$ positions that contains a '1'. A swap between a column $j \leq k$ and a column $t > k$ is triggered if and only if the diagonal element $\mathcal{A}[j][j]$ is 0 and $\mathcal{A}[t][t]$ is 1. This condition is securely controlled by a flag $[\![s]\!]_b^1$:

$$[\![s]\!]_b^1 \leftarrow ([\![\mathcal{A}[j][j]]\!]_b^1 \oplus [\![\mathcal{A}[t][t]]\!]_b^1) \cdot [\![\mathcal{A}[t][t]]\!]_b^1$$

The truth table of s is provided in Appendix C. After the loops terminate, the first k columns of the resulting matrix $[\![\mathcal{R}]\!]_b^l$ will each contain exactly one '1', while the remaining $n-k$ columns will be all-zero.

Finally, each party locally truncates the matrix by discarding the last $n-k$ columns to obtain the final $n \times k$ reduction matrix.

Algorithm 5. Secure Reduction Matrix Protocol Π_{ReMtr}

Input: Party P_b holds the Top-k vector $[\![\boldsymbol{Sco}_k]\!]_b^l$, $b \in \{0,1,2\}$; number of features to select, k (public value).
Output: The parties obtain the $n \times k$ reduction matrix $[\![\mathcal{R}]\!]_b^l$.
1. Initialize a Boolean-shared zero matrix $[\![\mathcal{A}_{n\times n}]\!]_b^1$ and a zero vector $[\![\mathbf{inx}]\!]_b^l$.
2. **for** $i \leftarrow 0$ **to** $n-1$ **do**
3. $\quad [\![\mathbf{inx}_i]\!]_b^l \leftarrow [\![\boldsymbol{Sco}_k[i][1]]\!]_b^l - 1$
4. $\quad [\![\mathcal{A}[\mathbf{inx}_i][\mathbf{inx}_i]]\!]_b^1 = [\![1]\!]_b^1$
5. **end for**
6. Initialize $[\![\mathcal{R}]\!]_b^l = [\![\mathcal{A}]\!]_b^l$.
7. **for** $j \leftarrow 0$ **to** $k-1$ **do**
8. $\quad$ **for** $t \leftarrow k$ **to** $n-1$ **do**
9. $\quad\quad [\![s]\!]_b^1 \leftarrow ([\![\mathcal{A}[j][j]]\!]_b^1 \oplus [\![\mathcal{A}[t][t]]\!]_b^1) \cdot [\![\mathcal{A}[t][t]]\!]_b^1$
10. $\quad\quad [\![\mathcal{R}[t][j]]\!]_b^l \leftarrow [\![\mathcal{A}[t][j]]\!]_b^l \oplus [\![s]\!]_b^1;\quad [\![\mathcal{R}[t][t]]\!]_b^l \leftarrow [\![\mathcal{A}[t][t]]\!]_b^l \oplus [\![s]\!]_b^1$
11. $\quad$ **end for**
12. **end for**
13. Each party locally deletes columns k to $n-1$ from $[\![\mathcal{R}]\!]_b^l$.
14. **return** $[\![\mathcal{R}]\!]_b^l$.

Secure Feature Selection Protocol. The secure feature selection protocol is detailed in Algorithm 6. It primarily consists of four steps. In step 1, the parties compute the mutual information scores of the feature matrix, obtaining a score vector. In step 2, the parties identify the Top-k highest-scoring elements and their corresponding indices from this vector. In step 3, the parties compute the reduction matrix $[\![\mathcal{R}]\!]_b^l$ based on the indices of these top-k elements. Finally the parties execute a secure matrix multiplication between the original feature matrix and the reduction matrix $[\![\mathcal{R}]\!]_b^l$ to obtain the selected feature matrix in step 4.

Algorithm 6. Secure Feature Selection Protocol Π_{MI-FS}

Input: Party P_b holds the original feature matrix $[\![\mathcal{F}_{m\times n}]\!]_b^l$ for $b \in \{0,1,2\}$; number of features to select, k (public value).
Output: The parties obtain the selected feature matrix $[\![\mathcal{F}_s]\!]_b^l$ of size $m \times k$.
1. The parties invoke Π_{GMI} to obtain feature mutual information scores: $[\![\boldsymbol{Sco}]\!]_b^l \leftarrow \Pi_{GMI}([\![\mathcal{F}_{m\times n}]\!]_b^l)$.
2. The parties invoke $\Pi_{TopkSco}$ to obtain Top-k scores: $[\![\boldsymbol{Sco}_k]\!]_b^l \leftarrow \Pi_{TopkSco}([\![\boldsymbol{Sco}]\!]_b^l)$.
3. The parties invoke Π_{ReMtr} to obtain the reduction matrix: $[\![\mathcal{R}_{n\times k}]\!]_b^l \leftarrow \Pi_{ReMtr}([\![\boldsymbol{Sco}_k]\!]_b^l)$.
4. The parties apply secure matrix multiplication Π_{MM} to get the selected feature matrix: $[\![\mathcal{F}_s]\!]_b^l \leftarrow \Pi_{MM}([\![\mathcal{F}_{m\times n}]\!]_b^l, [\![\mathcal{R}_{n\times k}]\!]_b^l)$.
5. **return** $[\![\mathcal{F}_s]\!]_b^l$.

5 Experimental Evaluation

5.1 Experimental Setup

All algorithms were implemented in C++ and executed on a PC equipped with an 8-core Intel Xeon w5-3425 CPU (3.19 GHz) and 32 GB of RAM. To comprehensively evaluate the effectiveness of our proposed scheme, we selected four diverse datasets from different domains. These datasets span image and text data, cover both binary and multi-class classification tasks, and represent a variety of data structures. This diversity allows for a thorough assessment of our method's performance across different scenarios.

- **warpAR10P:** An image dataset for face recognition derived from the AR Face Database. It contains 130 instances, each of which has been preprocessed, normalized, and transformed.
- **TOX171:** A dataset for predicting chemical toxicology, containing data for 171 chemical compounds, each with corresponding biological activity indicators.
- **SCADI:** A dataset developed at the Stevens Institute of Technology for classifying self-care activities in children and adolescents, particularly those with motor and physical disabilities. It comprises 70 instances.
- **Madelon:** An artificial dataset with 2600 instances. The data points are arranged in clusters on the vertices of a five-dimensional hypercube and are randomly assigned a label of +1 or −1.

Table 3 details the properties of each dataset, including the number of instances (m), features (n), and classes (p).

Table 3. Datasets used in the experiments.

Dataset	Instances (m)	Features (n)	Classes (p)
warpAR10P	130	2400	10
TOX171	171	5748	4
SCADI	70	205	7
Madelon	2600	500	2

5.2 Correctness Analysis

We have conducted unit tests for each key protocol and function in MSFS. For each unit test, the expected output is obtained for the given input, guaranteeing correctness. Furthermore, the results of Secure Feature Selection align with the plaintext results, yielding an accuracy of 100%. The results of these unit tests are summarized in Table 4.

Table 4. Unit test results for the core protocols.

Protocol	Functionality	Result
Π_{Ent}	Compute data entropy	Passed
Π_{GMI}	Compute mutual information scores	Passed
Π_{MaxSco}	Identify the maximum MI score	Passed
$\Pi_{TopkSco}$	Select the top-k MI scores	Passed
Π_{ReMtr}	Generate the reduction matrix	Passed
Π_{MI-FS}	Output the final feature subset	Passed

5.3 Effectiveness Analysis

To evaluate the practical impact of our feature selection scheme, we compared the classification accuracy of models trained on the original datasets versus those trained on the feature-selected datasets. We employed four standard machine learning models for this evaluation: Support Vector Machines (SVM), Naïve Bayes, K-Nearest Neighbors (KNN), and Decision Trees. To ensure a fair and reproducible comparison, all experiments were conducted under a rigorous setup, subjecting all models to identical data preprocessing steps. The results, presented in Fig. 2, demonstrate the effectiveness of our approach across diverse datasets.

The results consistently show that applying our method improves model accuracy across all datasets. For instance, on the TOX171 dataset, the KNN model's accuracy sees a significant increase of 12.86% compared to its baseline performance on the raw data. This demonstrates that our scheme successfully identifies more informative feature subsets, enhancing model predictive power while upholding the security and functionality of the underlying protocols.

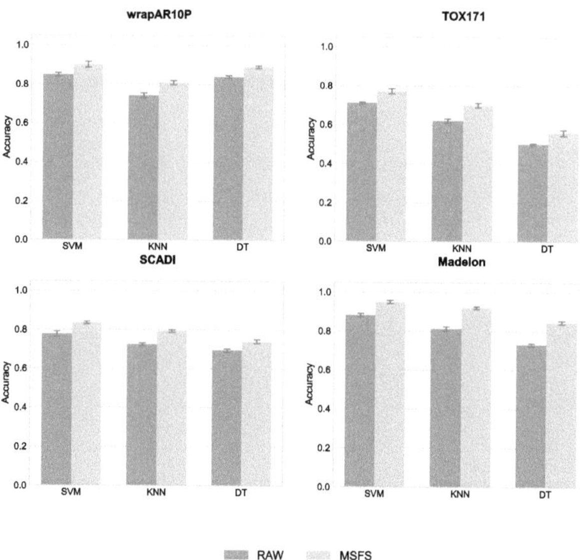

Fig. 2. Comparison of accuracy under different models.

5.4 Performance Evaluation

We benchmarked the protocol's runtime on the SCADI dataset ($n = 205$) against the feature selection ratio $\alpha = k/n$, for α ranging from 0.1 to 0.9.

The results (Fig. 3) reveal a peak runtime at $\alpha = 0.5$, as the number of column swaps in our protocol (Π_{ReMtr}) is maximized. Furthermore, the performance is symmetrical around this peak, with runtimes at $\alpha = 0.2$ and $\alpha = 0.8$ being nearly identical. This symmetry stems from the swap mechanism's dependence on $\min(k, n - k)$.

The protocol's notable runtime is a deliberate trade-off for its robustness in the malicious adversary setting. This computational overhead is a necessary and justifiable consequence of the abortable security mechanisms required to thwart malicious behavior.

5.5 Comprehensive Comparison

We propose a feature selection scheme achieving security against malicious adversaries without a trusted third party (TTP), a significant advance over prior art (Table 5). Existing protocols are often limited to the semi-honest, two-party model, leak information via intermediate decryptions [9], or depend on strong trust assumptions like a central aggregator [7] or a TTP [10].

Our approach is fundamentally different. We adopt the three-party, honest-majority model, which enables robust and efficient defenses against malicious adversaries. Architecturally, our protocol operates directly on replicated secret

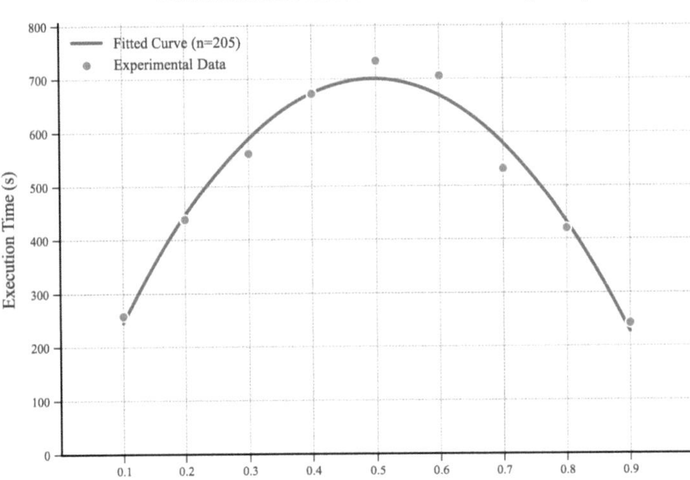

Fig. 3. Runtime of MS-FS with different α.

shares, a design that not only avoids costly decryptions but also provides provable security against one malicious party. Consequently, our work provides a viable and high-assurance solution that addresses the critical need for privacy-preserving feature selection in a practical, malicious-secure setting.

Table 5. Comprehensive Comparison

Scheme	Technique	Security Model	Parties	Privacy Guarantee
[7]	DP	N/A	Centralized Server	Statistical
[9]	HE	Semi-Honest	2PC	Computational
[10]	MPC	Semi-Honest	2PC	Computational
[13]	MPC	Semi-Honest	2PC	Computational
Ours	**MPC**	**Malicious**	**3PC**	**Information-Theoretic**

6 Conclusion

We introduce MSFS, the first 3-party feature selection scheme based on mutual information that achieves security against malicious adversaries. Our framework of secure computation sub-protocols is validated through complexity analysis, formal proofs, and experiments, demonstrating its efficiency and practicality. This contribution fills a significant gap in the literature by offering a robust solution for the challenging malicious security setting.

For future work, we plan two primary extensions. First, to improve scalability for high-dimensional data (over 10,000 features), we will investigate asymptotically superior primitives, such as secure sorting networks, to overcome the bottleneck in our current Top-k selection. Second, we will expand beyond the current filter-based paradigm by designing novel schemes that employ wrapper and embedded feature selection techniques.

A Technical Architecture

The technical architecture of MSFS as follow:

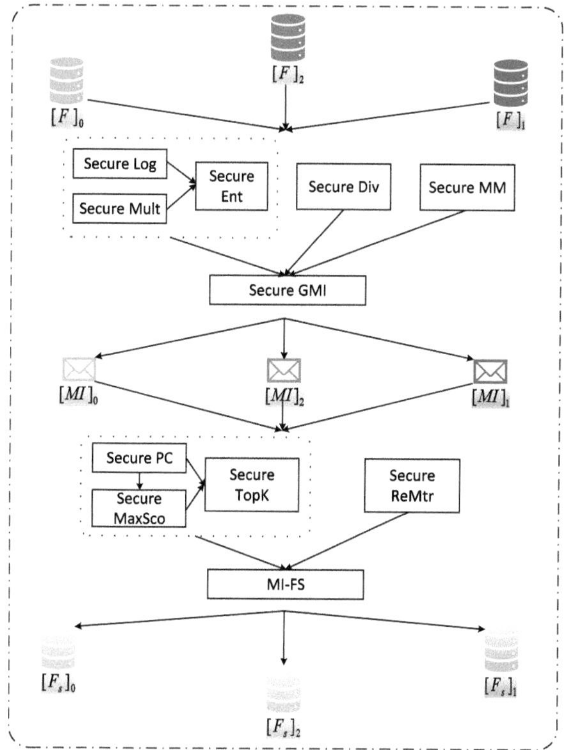

Fig. 4. Technical Framework.

B Logarithm Approximation Under MPC

The secure computation of entropy hinges on an efficient protocol for $x \ln x$ given shares of $[\![x]\!]_b^l$. Our methodology begins by reducing the problem domain via a base-2 floating-point representation, $x = w \cdot 2^p$, where $w \in (1/2, 1]$. This decomposition simplifies the logarithm to $\log_2 x = p + \log_2 w$, isolating the core challenge to approximating $\log_2 w$ on a small, fixed interval.

To approximate $\log_2 w$, we employ a Padé approximant, which is significantly more efficient for MPC than a standard Taylor series as it achieves higher accuracy with lower-degree polynomials, thus reducing the number of secure multiplications. Specifically, we adopt the [3/3]-order approximant for $\ln(1+z)$ from [17], related to $\log_2 w$ by a simple transformation:

$$\ln(1+z) \approx \frac{P_3(z)}{Q_3(z)} = \frac{60z + 42z^2 + 4z^3}{60 + 72z + 36z^2 + 3z^3} \tag{14}$$

where the approximation is accurate up to the 6th order.

To implement this in MPC, parties securely compute shares of the input's powers (z^2, z^3), locally perform linear combinations to obtain shares of the numerator and denominator, and execute a single secure division protocol (Π_{Div}). The resulting $[\![\ln x]\!]_b^l$ is then used in a final secure multiplication to compute $[\![x \ln x]\!]_b^l$.

C The Truth Table of s

The behavior of s is detailed in the truth table shown in Table 6. As confirmed by the table, the flag s evaluates to 1 if and only if $\boldsymbol{A}[j][j] = 0$ and $\boldsymbol{A}[t][t] = 1$, precisely triggering a column swap only under the desired condition. In all other cases, s is 0, and no swap occurs.

Table 6. The truth table of s

$\boldsymbol{A}[j][j]$	$\boldsymbol{A}[t][t]$	s
0	0	0
0	1	1
1	0	0
1	1	0

D Theoretical Analysis

D.1 Complexity Analysis

Basic Protocols. The complexity of our basic protocols is detailed in Table 7, following the analysis in [15]. The communication cost is measured in bytes, where l is the bit-length of the ring, k is the corresponding number of bytes, and n is the vector size. As shown, protocols in the malicious model incur higher communication costs compared to their semi-honest counterparts to ensure security.

Table 7. Complexity of Basic Protocols

Protocol	Semi-Honest		Malicious	
	Rounds	Comm. (Bytes)	Rounds	Comm. (Bytes)
MatMul	1	kxz	1	$2kxz$
Private Compare	$2 + \log_2 l$	$2kn$	$2 + \log_2 l$	$4kn$
Division	$7 + 5l + l \cdot \log_2 l$	$4knl + 7kn$	$7 + 5l + l \cdot \log_2 l$	$8knl + 14kn$

Secure Mutual Information Score Protocol. The computation of MI scores is the primary source of overhead in our scheme, as it requires executing secure comparison, division, and entropy protocols for each of the nm elements in the feature matrix.

Secure Feature Selection Protocol. The secure maximum score protocol requires $t = \lceil \log_2 n \rceil$ rounds of comparisons. The complexity of the Secure Top-k protocol is similar, but its costs are reduced when $k > 1$ as it requires fewer than t rounds.

Discussion. Wang et al. [13] proposed a method for approximating fixed-point numbers in a two-party setting to improve computational efficiency by reducing the bit-width of MPC operations. However, their secure division protocol must be used with caution. While it correctly computes x/y in theory, the intermediate values in a practical implementation over a ring $\mathbb{Z}$ can overflow. For instance, if the intermediate term $x \cdot r_1 + y \cdot r_1 + r_2$ overflows, the final result $(x \cdot r_1 + y \cdot r_1 + r_2)/(y \cdot r_1)$ will not equal $x/y + r_2$, leading to a computation error.

D.2 Security Proofs

We prove the security of our proposed scheme using the standard real/ideal world simulation paradigm from cryptography The security of a protocol is established by showing that for any real-world adversary $\mathcal{A}$, there exists an ideal-world simulator $\mathcal{S}$ such that no environment can distinguish between the two worlds.

Definition 1 (Security in the Honest-Majority Malicious Model). *A protocol Π securely realizes a functionality $\mathcal{F}$ against a malicious adversary if for any adversary $\mathcal{A}$, there exists a PPT simulator $\mathcal{S}$ such that for all inputs x_i and outputs y:*

$$S(x_i, y) \overset{c}{\approx} View_i^{\Pi}(x) \tag{15}$$

where security holds with abort, meaning the adversary can force the protocol to terminate prematurely, but cannot violate correctness or privacy for honest parties.

Lemma 1 (Randomness). *If $r \in \mathbb{Z}_{2^k}$ is uniform and independent of $x \in \mathbb{Z}_{2^k}$, then $r + x$ is also uniform and independent of x.*

Theorem 1 **(Π_{Ent} Security).** *Π_{Ent} securely realizes the functionality $\mathcal{F}_{Ent}$ under Definition 1.*

Proof (Proof Sketch) The simulator for Π_{Ent} interacts with a trusted party for the functionalities $\mathcal{F}_{Mult}$ and $\mathcal{F}_{Div}$. Since these underlying functionalities are proven secure in [15], the security of Π_{Ent} follows from a standard hybrid argument. In case of malicious behavior, the simulator extracts the adversary's input, sends an abort message, and terminates.

Theorem 2 **(Π_{GMI} Security).** *Π_{GMI} securely realizes the functionality $\mathcal{F}_{GMI}$ under Definition 1.*

Proof (Proof Sketch) The proof follows by a standard composition argument. The simulator is constructed by composing the simulators for the secure functionalities $\mathcal{F}_{PC}$, $\mathcal{F}_{MM}$, $\mathcal{F}_{Div}$, and $\mathcal{F}_{Ent}$ (proven secure in [15] and Theorem 1).

Theorem 3 **($\Pi_{TopK-Sco}$ Security).** *$\Pi_{TopK-Sco}$ securely realizes the functionality $\mathcal{F}_{TopK-Sco}$ under Definition 1.*

Proof (Proof Sketch) Security follows from the composition of the underlying secure components $\mathcal{F}_{Mult}$ and $\mathcal{F}_{PC}$.

Theorem 4 **(Π_{ReMtr} Security).** *Π_{ReMtr} securely realizes $\mathcal{F}_{ReMtr}$ under Definition 1.*

Proof (Proof Sketch) The proof follows by composition of the secure functionalities $\mathcal{F}_{Mult}$ and $\mathcal{F}_{MM}$.

Theorem 5 **(Π_{MSFS} Security).** *The overall protocol Π_{MSFS} securely realizes the functionality $\mathcal{F}_{MI-FS}$ under Definition 1.*

Proof (Proof Sketch) The security of the overall MSFS protocol follows by composing the secure sub-protocols Π_{GMI} (Theorem 2), $\Pi_{TopK-Sco}$ (Theorem 3), and Π_{ReMtr} (Theorem 4). By the composition theorem for the malicious model with aborts, the composed protocol is secure.

References

1. Albrecht, J.P.: How the gdpr will change the world. Eur. Data Prot. L. Rev. **2**, 287 (2016)
2. Gong, M., Feng, J., Xie, Yu.: Privacy-enhanced multi-party deep learning. Neural Netw. **121**, 484–496 (2020)
3. Zhang, C., Xiongwei, H., Xie, Yu., Gong, M., Bin, Yu.: A privacy-preserving multi-task learning framework for face detection, landmark localization, pose estimation, and gender recognition. Front. Neurorobot. **13**, 112 (2020)
4. Xie, Yu., Wang, H., Bin, Yu., Zhang, C.: Secure collaborative few-shot learning. Knowl.-Based Syst. **203**, 106157 (2020)

5. Li, X., Dowsley, R., De Cock, M.: Privacy-preserving feature selection with secure multiparty computation. In: International Conference on Machine Learning, pp. 6326–6336. PMLR (2021)
6. Jafer, Y., Matwin, S., Sokolova, M.: A framework for a privacy-aware feature selection evaluation measure. In: 2015 13th Annual Conference on Privacy, Security and Trust (PST), pp. 62–69. IEEE (2015)
7. Alishahi, M., Moghtadaiee, V., Navidan, H.: Add noise to remove noise: Local differential privacy for feature selection. Comput. Secur. **123**, 102934 (2022)
8. Alishahi, M., Moghtadaiee, V.: Feature selection on anonymized datasets. In: 2023 IEEE Intl Conf on Dependable, Autonomic and Secure Computing, Intl Conf on Pervasive Intelligence and Computing, Intl Conf on Cloud and Big Data Computing, Intl Conf on Cyber Science and Technology Congress (DASC/PiCom/CBDCom/CyberSciTech), pp. 0852–0859. IEEE (2023)
9. Rao, V., Long, Y., Eldardiry, H., Rane, S., Rossi, R., Torres, F.: Secure two-party feature selection. arXiv preprint arXiv:1901.00832, 2019
10. Wu, N., Li, H., Chen, H., Zhang, X., Wang, Y.: Privacy-preserving feature selection based on mutual information. In: GLOBECOM 2023-2023 IEEE Global Communications Conference, pp. 1789–1794. IEEE (2023)
11. Ono, S., Takata, J., Kataoka, M., Tomohiro, I., Shin, K., Sakamoto, H.: Privacy-preserving feature selection with fully homomorphic encryption. Algorithms **15**(7), 229 (2022)
12. Eklund, D., Iacovazzi, A., Wang, H., Pyrgelis, A., Raza, S.: Bmi: bounded mutual information for efficient privacy-preserving feature selection. In: European Symposium on Research in Computer Security, pp. 353–373. Springer (2024)
13. Wang, L., Guo, H., Wu, W., Zhou, L.: Efficient and privacy-preserving feature selection based on multiparty computation. IEEE Trans. Inform. Forens, Secur (2025)
14. Araki, T., Furukawa, J., Lindell, Y., Nof, A., Ohara, K.: High-throughput semi-honest secure three-party computation with an honest majority. In: Proceedings of the 2016 ACM SIGSAC Conference on Computer and Communications Security, pp. 805–817 (2016)
15. Wagh, S., Tople, S., Benhamouda, F., Kushilevitz, E., Mittal, P., Rabin, T.: Falcon: Honest-majority maliciously secure framework for private deep learning. arXiv preprint arXiv:2004.02229, 2020
16. Zhou, H., Wang, X., Zhang, Y.: Feature selection based on weighted conditional mutual information. Applied computing and informatics **20**(1/2), 55–68 (2024)
17. Graves-Morris, P.R., Saff, E.B., Varga, R.S.: Rational Approximation and Interpolation: Proceedings of the United Kingdom-United States Conference, Held at Tampa, Florida, December 12-16, 1983, vol. 1105. Springer (2006)

Adaptive Batched K-out-of-N Oblivious Transfers Extension

Zhaoyi Liu[1,2,3], Huijie Yang[1,2,3](✉), Jian Shen[1,2,3], and Jianfei Sun[4]

[1] School of Information Science and Engineering (School of Cyber Science and Technology), Zhejiang Sci-Tech University, Hangzhou 310018, China
hjyang3086@gmail.com

[2] Zhejiang Provincial International Cooperation Base for Science and Technology on Cloud Computing Security and Data Aggregation, Zhejiang Sci-Tech University, Hangzhou 310018, China

[3] Zhejiang Provincial Innovation Center of Advanced Textile Technology, Shaoxing 312000, China

[4] School of Computing and Information Systems, Singapore Management University, 81 Victoria Street, Singapore 188065, Singapore
jfsun@smu.edu.sg

Abstract. Oblivious Transfer (OT) enables a sender to transmit multiple messages such that a receiver can retrieve selected messages without revealing their choices to the sender. However, existing OT extension (OTE) protocols primarily focus on 1-out-of-2 OTE, 1-out-of-n OTE and 1-out-of-∞ OTE, which transmit only one selected message from amount messages. The number of selected messages is limited by these protocols and cannot be revised once the protocols are determined. These protocols are inefficient for applications requiring batch processing or dynamic selection of multiple messages. In this paper, a flexible adaptive selection number OTE protocol is proposed, inspired by Kolesnikov *et al.* in CCS 2016. Unlike traditional OTE protocols, our protocol enables the receiver to flexibly select k messages from the n messages transmitted by the sender within a single OT instance. The value of k can be dynamically adjusted at runtime, making the protocol well-suited for applications with frequently changing selection requirements. This flexibility significantly improves the efficiency and versatility of oblivious transfer. In contrast to the fastest state-of-the-art OTE algorithm, where implementing m k-out-of-n OTE instances incurs the cost of implementing km standard 1-out-of-2 OTs, our approach only requires the cost of m standard 1-out-of-2 OTs. For computational security parameter k, the proposed k-out-of-n OTE offers $O(k)$ factor performance improvement in communication, compared to KKRT16. We further explore the application of our protocol to semi-honest secure OTE. Notably, our OTE can overcome the restriction of single selection in the existing OTE protocols. We implemented our OTE protocol and found that it is 6.4–7.2 times faster than KKRT16 for 8-bit string OTEs and small-scale OTE instances. Specifically, our protocol takes only 13.7 s to securely compute 2^{14} OTs. For larger-scale OTE computations, our protocol is also 4.1 times faster than KKRT16.

R. Chen et al. (Eds.): Inscrypt 2025, LNCS 16409, pp. 66–84, 2026.
https://doi.org/10.1007/978-981-95-6203-9_4

Keywords: Oblivious transfer extension · Multi-party computation · 1-out-of-2 oblivious transfer

1 Introduction

Oblivious Transfer (OT) [25] is a core primitive in multi-party computation, allowing a sender to transmit multiple messages while ensuring the receiver selectively obtains some without revealing their choices to the sender. OT has been widely applied in various scenarios, including secure multiparty computation, private information retrieval, private set intersection [1–6], zero-knowledge proofs, and confidential data exchange. In recent years, research on OT has made significant progress, achieving practical applicability through efficient implementations. For example, the introduction of OT extension technology allows a large number of OT executions to be performed efficiently using only a small number of public-key operations, thereby greatly reducing computational and communication overhead. OT protocols achieve a good balance between functionality and communication cost, enabling their widespread application in different secure computation scenarios.

Compared to traditional OT protocols that rely on costly public-key encryption, OTE protocols introduce matrix transposition and leverage symmetric encryption operations to significantly reduce computational overhead. In 2003, Ishai *et al.* [7] first proposed the concept of Oblivious Transfer Extension (OTE). Suppose two parties, $\mathcal{S}$ and $\mathcal{R}$, need to perform m instances of OT_1^2 (m is typically very large). Traditional OT algorithms require $\mathcal{S}$ and $\mathcal{R}$ to execute m instances of public-key-based OT_1^2. However, Ishai *et al.* proposed an OTE algorithm based on symmetric encryption, which is mainly divided into two phases: the base OT phase and the OT extension phase. In the base OT phase, they use matrix transposition to reducing the number of public-key-based OT_1^2 executions from m to λ (where$\lambda \ll m$), and λ is the security parameter, typically set to 128. At this stage, $\mathcal{S}$ and $\mathcal{R}$ successfully generate m pairs of symmetric keys. In the OT extension phase, $\mathcal{S}$ and $\mathcal{R}$ use the m pairs of symmetric keys and the OT_1^2 algorithm to encrypt and decrypt two message matrices row by row, achieving m times instances of OT_1^2. That is, $\mathcal{S}$ sends $2m$ messages, and $\mathcal{R}$ receives only m of them. This method successfully transforms expensive public-key cryptographic operations into symmetric-key operations, with the cost reduced to only λ instances of public-key-based OT. However, it does not change the core functionality of OT, which remains limited to 1-out-of-2 selection. Then, KK [8] incorporated error-correcting codes into OT extension, enabling OTE_1^n, where the sender transmits n messages (with $n \leq 256$) and the receiver selects one of them. KKRT [9] further enhanced this by replacing error-correcting codes with pseudorandom functions, realizing OTE_1^∞. Despite these advances, the state-of-the-art OTE protocols still restrict the receiver to retrieving only one message per instance. This limitation makes it challenging to support practical applications that require multi-message retrieval or batch search operations within a single OT session.

All of the above protocols share a common feature: in each OTE instance, the receiver can select only one message. This means that the number of messages actually received per OTE instance is fixed at one, severely limiting the data selection capability of the receiver and reducing the flexibility of OTE protocols. (1) In existing OTE protocols, the number of messages a receiver can select per instance is fixed. For example, IKNP [7], KK [8], KKRT [9], and PRTY [10] only allow the receiver to obtain one message in each OTE instance (as illustrated in Table 1). As a result, the receiver lacks the flexibility to control the amount of data selected. Consider the naive approach of executing $k \times OTE_1^n$ to simulate one OTE_k^n instance. In practice, this approach creates a linear relationship between the number of messages sent and the number of messages received, failing to support flexible selection quantities in OTE. Specifically, the key distinction between this approach and true OTE_k^n lies in the relationship between the number of messages sent and received: in $k \times OTE_1^n$, the sender transmits nk messages, n times more than the number received, forming a direct correlation. In contrast, OTE_k^n decouples these quantities, allowing arbitrary receiver selections without affecting the number of messages sent. (2) This naïve method significantly increases both computational and communication overhead. Executing $k \times OTE_1^n$ requires generating k pairs of symmetric keys, whereas the proposed OTE_k^n method requires only a single pair. Thus, in the base OT phase, the communication length increases by a factor of k, leading to substantial waste in computational and communication resources. (3) Existing protocols lack support for flexible batch execution within a single OTE instance, where k can be any arbitrary value and does not need to be proportional to n.

Can we design a more universal and flexible OTE protocol while maintaining an acceptable communication cost?

When balancing functionality and communication cost, a valuable metric is the communication time required when the receiver obtains a certain number of messages. In real-world applications, the receiver is often the more critical party, as receiving data is the essential function of an OTE protocol. In the study by KKRT [9], their protocol significantly extended functionality compared to IKNP [7] while maintaining a similar level of communication cost. However, we can further explore the possibility of significantly enhancing its functionality while only incurring a slight increase in communication overhead.

1.1 Our Contribution

In this work, we have made positive progress on the aforementioned issues by proposing a new OTE protocol that achieves a better balance between functionality and communication cost while ensuring security for semi-honest participants.

Batched. We propose a new OTE construction that enables k-out-of-n OTE. Specifically, in a single OTE instance, the sender transmits n messages, and the receiver selects k of them ($1 \leq k < n$). Unlike traditional OTE protocols that restrict the number of receiver's selection. For example, IKNP [7] supports only

OTE_1^2 (1-out-of-2 selection per instance), and KK [8] achieves OTE_1^n (1-out-of-n selection) but fixes $k = 1$. Existing solutions cannot support adaptive k-out-of-n functionality within a single base OTE framework. This means that a single OTE instance can facilitate the transmission of multiple messages, effectively forming a batch OTE protocol. Prior protocols (e.g., IKNP, KKRT) require k separate OTE instances to transmit k messages, our protocol transmits k effective messages in a single OTE instance. This significantly enhances the efficiency of message transmission and reduces the number of OTE instances required.

Flexible. The value of k in our protocol can be flexibly adjusted, allowing the receiver to select k_1 messages in one OTE instance and k_2 messages in another. These features enhance the versatility of our OTE protocol, making it suitable for diverse application scenarios. For example, in a privacy-preserving system for dynamic personalized content subscription and recommendation, a user needs to select one or more of n tags prepared by the server, but does not want the server to learn their specific choices. In this case, an OTE_k^n protocol that supports flexible selection can be applied. Critically, existing OTE algorithms cannot reuse the same base OTE to achieve k-out-of-n functionality, they necessitate regenerating base OTs for each selection, incurring additional overhead. This feature makes it highly suitable for most application scenarios, as each scenario can adaptively adjust the value of k according to its specific needs, thereby determining the number of messages transmitted per OTE instance. The comparison with other protocols is shown in Table 1 and Fig. 1. Notation r represents the Receiver chooses the r-th message.

Communication Cost. The key agreement phase of the proposed OTE protocol introduces one additional round of communication compared to KKRT [9] and KK [8]. However, from the perspective of overall protocol execution, the total communication cost is reduced. Suppose the receiver needs to obtain t messages in total. In KKRT and KK, t OTE instances are required to ensure the receiver selects t messages. In contrast, our OTE protocol only requires t/k OTE instances. Although our protocol slightly increases the communication overhead in the key agreement phase, the communication cost in the OTE instance phase is significantly reduced compared to KKRT and KK. Table 2 illustrates the performance improvements of our protocol over KKRT and KK.

Specifically, in our protocol, executing a single OTE instance can achieve the effect of running k instances of KKRT or KK OTE. By configuring the KKRT or KK protocol as OTE_1^4, where in a single OTE instance, the sender transmits 4 messages and the receiver selects 1, and setting our protocol as OTE_8^{32}, where in a single OTE instance, the sender transmits 32 messages and the receiver selects 8, it is clear that executing one instance of our OT protocol achieves the same effect as running 8 instances of KKRT or KK OTE, resulting in a 6-7x performance improvement.

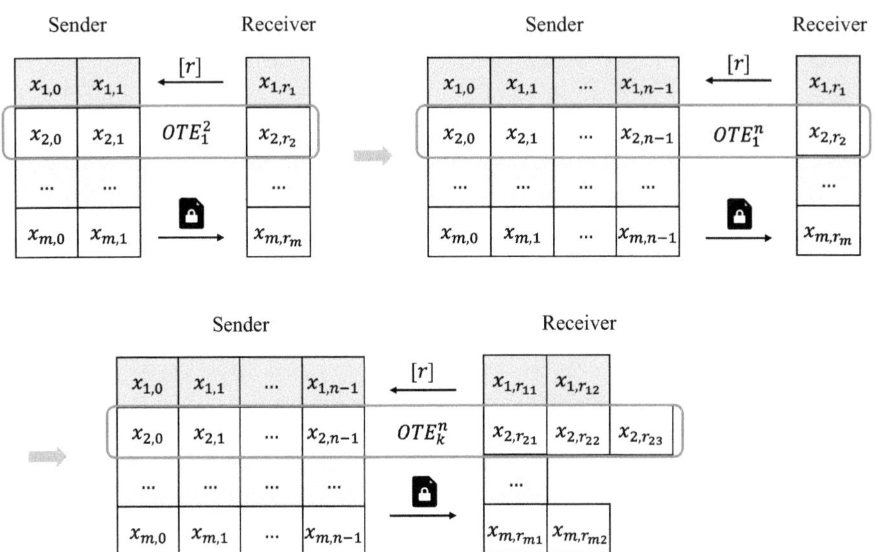

Fig. 1. Illustration of the $OTE_1^2, OTE_1^n, OTE_k^n$ protocol. Notation r is a vector representing the Receiver's selection bits string.

1.2 Related Work

Oblivious Transfer is a fundamental cryptographic primitive that ensures secure interaction between a sender and a receiver while protecting their private data. Specifically, OT is a core cryptographic protocol that allows a sender to transmit multiple potential messages to a receiver in such a way that: the sender remains oblivious to which message the receiver obtained, the receiver learns only the selected message and gains no knowledge about the other messages. Due to these privacy-preserving properties, OT plays a crucial role in secure data transmission and sharing and serves as a fundamental building block for various cryptographic protocols.

In 1981, Michael Rabin [13] proposed the first probabilistic oblivious transfer protocol based on RSA public-key encryption. In Rabin's scheme, during the communication process between the sender and the receiver, the receiver obtains the message with a probability of 1/2, while the sender remains unaware of whether the receiver actually received it. This work laid the theoretical foundation for the development of OT. Subsequently, Goldreich *et al.* [14] introduced the 1-out-of-2 Oblivious Transfer (OT_1^2) protocol, which consists of two participants: a sender ($\mathcal{S}$) and a receiver ($\mathcal{R}$). In OT_1^2, the sender provides a pair of messages, and the receiver chooses one of them, learning only the selected message without gaining any information about the other. Likewise, the sender remains oblivious to the receiver's choice. Research on OT has primarily focused on reducing computational costs and the number of OT invocations. Beaver *et*

Table 1. Comparison with other protocols. Here, m represents the number of OTE instances, l represents the length of messages transmitted by the sender in each OTE instance, λ represents the security parameter, and $m \gg \lambda$. n and k respectively represent the number of messages sent and the number of messages selected in our protocol, v represents the length of dual key of our protocol.

Protocol	One-time OTE instance	Comm.	The length of message in base OT
IKNP [7]	OTE_1^2	$2km\lambda + 2ml$	km
KK [8]	OTE_1^n	$2km\lambda + nml$	km
KKRT [9]	OTE_1^∞	$2km\lambda + nml$	km
ALSZ [11]	OTE_1^2	$2km\lambda + 2ml$	km
PRTY [10]	OTE_1^2	$2km\lambda + 2ml$	km
CM [12]	OTE_1^2	$2km\lambda + 2ml$	km
Our Protocol	OTE_k^n	$2m\lambda + nm(l + v)$	m

Table 2. Performance compares to KK and KKRT, set KK and KKRT to OTE_1^4 and set our protocol to OTE_8^{32}

Protocol	Function	Receive Message	Time (ms)	Messages per ms
KK	OTE_1^4	100000	56.8	1760
KK	OTE_1^4	800000	363.5	2200
KKRT	OTE_1^4	100000	61.3	1631
KKRT	OTE_1^4	800000	404.5	1978
Our Protocol	OTE_8^{32}	800000	89.3	8958

al. [15] proposed precomputed OT using a technique similar to Beaver triples, allowing offline precomputation of a large portion of the OT computations. The online phase then requires only lightweight symmetric-key operations and a single interaction, significantly improving efficiency.

Oblivious Transfer Extension (OTE) replaces public-key encryption with symmetric-key operations, significantly reducing computational overhead. Ishai *et al.* introduced the IKNP protocol [7] based on a row-to-column transposition technique. Given an $n \times \lambda$ matrix, a traditional OT protocol would require executing $n \times OT_\lambda$ instances. Instead, IKNP replaces n row-wise OT invocations with λ column-wise OT operations, reducing base OT executions from $n \times OT_\lambda$ to $\lambda \times OT_n$. This dramatically improves efficiency and ensures security against semi-honest receivers. However, Asharov *et al.* [11] observed that 42% of IKNP's computational overhead comes from matrix transposition and that it does not protect against malicious receivers. They introduced ALSZ, a strong security OTE protocol that reduces the matrix transposition complexity from $O(mk)$ to $O(m/rlogk)$, where r is the CPU register size. Additionally, they incorporated a consistency-checking phase to ensure security against malicious adversaries [16]. Further, Kolesnikov *et al.* [8] identified a limitation in IKNP, where repeated encoding constrained each OTE instance to a single OT_1^2. To overcome this, they introduced error-correcting codes (ECCs) to replace repetition encoding, enabling a $n \times OT_1^n$ protocol. To further optimize and generalize OTE, they replaced ECCs with pseudorandom functions (PRFs), designing the $n \times OT_1^\infty$ protocol [9], where a single OT_1^∞ instance suffices for equality checking. However, OT_1^∞ lacks robustness against Hamming distance-related errors. For efficient OTE construction in the random oracle model, Mansy *et al.* [17] proposed a DDH-based secure OT protocol, instantiating OTE with Crystals-Kyber key exchange, requiring only one round of communication. Pinkas *et al.* [10] optimized OTE by eliminating matrix transmissions, using n-degree polynomial transmission, reducing communication complexity from $O(Nk)$ to $O(nk)$. Chase *et al.* [12] further balanced communication and computational efficiency by transforming ECC outputs from strings to matrices, lowering communication complexity from $O(Nk)$ to $O(nk)$.

We have summarized the limitations of existing OTE protocols [7–9,11,18–24] in this section. Particularly, the authors of KKRT protocol implemented the functionality of OTE_1^∞, extending the maximum number of messages sent by the sender, but they did not address the number of messages obtained by the receiver. To address this, we propose a OTE protocol that solves the problem of batch selection in a single OT instance by compressing the selection strings and using dual keys.

2 Overview of Our Approach

We describe our protocol in detail in Sect. 4, and in this section we provide an overview to understand the protocol as a whole.

From an overall perspective, our protocol involves two parties: a sender and a receiver. The sender prepares n plaintext messages, encrypts them, and sends them to the receiver. After receiving the ciphertexts, the receiver selects k messages for decryption based on the previously generated selection bits r_i and obtains the plaintext. This process can be performed m times in total, meaning that the sender transmits $m \times n$ messages, while the receiver receives $\sum_{i=1}^{n} k_i$ messages (k_i represents the value of k in the i-th instance). The ideal functionality is shown in Fig. 2.

Correctness. The Sender transmits n messages and the receiver chooses k of them in an OTE instance. The sent messages $(x_{1,0}, x_{1,1}, \cdots, x_{1,n-1})$ by $\mathcal{S}$ must be consistent with the messages $(x_{1,a_{(1,1)}}, x_{1,a_{(1,2)}}, \cdots, x_{1,a_{(1,k_1)}})$ output to $\mathcal{R}$. The value of $(a_{(1,1)}, a_{(1,2)}, \cdots, a_{(1,k_1)})$ depends on r. $\mathcal{S}$ and $\mathcal{R}$ perform a total of m OTE instances.

Sender Privacy. The receiver selects only k out of the n messages sent by the sender, namely $(x_{1,a_{(1,1)}}, x_{1,a_{(1,2)}}, \cdots, x_{1,a_{(1,k_1)}})$, and learns nothing about the unselected messages.

Functionality $F_{OTE_k^n}$

F running with $\mathcal{R}$, $\mathcal{S}$ proceeds as follows:

- The functionality waits for input r, $(t_0^i, t_1^i), i \in [\lambda]$ and $V_{j,a}, j \in [m], a \in [n]$ from $\mathcal{R}$, $\{(x_{1,0}, x_{1,1}, \cdots, x_{1,n-1}), (x_{2,0}, x_{2,1}, \cdots, x_{2,n-1}), \cdots, (x_{m,0}, x_{m,1}, \cdots, x_{m,n-1})\}$ and a random string s from $\mathcal{S}$.

- It outputs $\{(x_{1,a_{(1,1)}}, x_{1,a_{(1,2)}}, \cdots, x_{1,a_{(1,k_1)}}), (x_{2,a_{(2,1)}}, x_{2,a_{(2,2)}}, \cdots, x_{2,a_{(2,k_2)}}), \cdots (x_{m,a_{(m,1)}}, x_{m,a_{(m,2)}}, \cdots, x_{m,a_{(m,k_m)}})\}$ to $\mathcal{R}$, where $(a_{(1,1)}, a_{(1,2)}, \cdots, a_{(m,k_m)}) \in [n]$.

Fig. 2. Ideal Function of Our Protocol.

Receiver Privacy. The sender only knows that the receiver has chosen a subset of the messages to receive, but does not know which specific messages were selected, namely the exact value of $(a_{(1,1)}, a_{(1,2)}, \cdots, a_{(1,k_1)})$.

Our protocol builds upon the KK OT extension protocol. We note that KK's OT extension implements OT_1^n: in each instance, the sender transmits n ciphertexts, and the receiver decrypts one. We observe that the reason the receiver can only select one message for decryption is that its selection bit r_i is in the range 0 to $n-1$. Therefore, when the sender transmits n ciphertext messages, the receiver decrypts the r_i-th message. Our protocol improves the receiver's selection bit r_i. If multiple selection bit information can be compressed into a single r_i, then it is possible to select multiple messages for decryption in a single OTE instance. Although the above method can achieve OT_k^n, it introduces additional problems: in the base OT phase, the sender and receiver conduct a small number of public-key-based oblivious transfers and negotiate a series of symmetric keys by a matrix transposition method. If only these symmetric keys are used for message encryption and decryption, information leakage occurs. In a single OTE instance, the receiver possesses only one symmetric key but wants to decrypt k messages. Then, on the sender's side, these k messages must also be encrypted with the same key. In this way, when the sender encrypts the plaintext messages, he can infer the receiver's selection bit based on the keys used for each message, thereby exposing the receiver's information. We introduce a dual-key mechanism to solve this problem. When encrypting plaintext messages, the sender uses dual keys for encryption. The first key is the symmetric key negotiated in the base OT phase, while the second key V_a is generated by the receiver and sent to the sender. Some of these V_a values are computed, while others are randomly generated. When the semi-honest receiver decrypts messages, it uses the symmetric key from base OT negotiation and the computed V_a as dual keys for decryption, obtaining the plaintext messages indicated by the selection bits.

From an overall perspective, our protocol introduces an additional round of communication compared to KK and IKNP, and it mainly comes from the transmission of the second layer key V_a. However, in our protocol, a single OTE instance can transmit k messages secretly, which is equivalent to k instances of IKNP OTE. Therefore, our protocol achieves an approximately k times performance improvement over IKNP. Since the generation of V_a depends on the value of r_i, and r_i can be prepared before the protocol execution, the generation of V_a can be moved to the preprocessing phase.

3 Preliminaries and Notation

In this section, we first introduce the meaning of each symbol in the proposed protocol, and then introduce the KK oblivious transfer extension protocol as the prerequisite knowledge of our protocol.

Input of $\mathcal{S}$: m tuples $(x_{j,0}, \ldots\ldots, x_{j,n-1})$ of l-bit strings, $1 \le j \le m$.
Input of $\mathcal{R}$: m selection integers $r = (r_1, \ldots\ldots, r_m)$ such that $0 \le r_j < n$ for $1 \le j \le m$.
Common Input: a security parameter k such that $k \ge n$, and Walsh-Hadamard codes $C_{WH}^{\lambda} = (c_0, \ldots\ldots, c_{\lambda-1})$.
Oracle: a collision-resistant hash function $H : [m] \times \{0,1\}^{\lambda} \to \{0,1\}^{l}$.
Cryptographic Primitive: an ideal OT_1^2 primitive.

1. $\mathcal{S}$ chooses $s \leftarrow \{0,1\}^{\lambda}$ at random. Let s_i denote the i-th bit of s.
2. $\mathcal{R}$ forms $m \times \lambda$ matrices T_0, T_1 in the following way: Choose $t_{j,0}, t_{j,1} \leftarrow \{0,1\}^{\lambda}$ at random such that $t_{j,0} \oplus t_{j,1} = c_{r_j}$. Let t_0^i, t_1^i denote the i-th column of matrices T_0, T_1, respectively.
3. $\mathcal{S}$ and $\mathcal{R}$ interact with OT_1^2 in the following way:
   $\mathcal{S}$ acts as receiver with input $\{s_i\}_{i\in[\lambda]}$.
   $\mathcal{R}$ acts as sender with input $\{t_0^i, t_1^i\}_{i\in[\lambda]}$.
   $\mathcal{S}$ receives output $\{q^i\}_{i\in[\lambda]}$.
   $\mathcal{S}$ forms $m \times \lambda$ matrix Q such that the i-th column of Q is the vector q_i. (Note that, $q_i = t_{s_i}^i$.) Let q_j denote the j-th row of Q. (Note $q_j = ((t_{j,0} \oplus t_{j,1}) \odot s) \oplus t_{j,0}$.) Simplifying, $q_j \oplus t_{j,0} = c_{r_j} \cdot s$.)
4. For $j \in [m]$ and for every $0 \le r < n$, $\mathcal{S}$ sends $y_{j,r} = x_{j,r} \oplus H(j, q_j \oplus (c_r \cdot s))$ to $\mathcal{R}$.
5. For $j \in [m]$, $\mathcal{R}$ recovers $z_j = y_{j,r_j} \oplus H(j, t_{j,0})$.

Fig. 3. KK Protocol

3.1 Notation

In our protocol, $\mathcal{S}$ represents the sender of the protocol, and $\mathcal{R}$ represents the receiver of the protocol. From an overall view, the sender prepares a series of plaintexts $(x_{j,0}, \ldots\ldots, x_{j,n-1})$, encrypts them into the corresponding ciphertexts $(y_{j,0}, \ldots\ldots, y_{j,n-1})$, the receiver selects several ciphertexts for decryption based on its selection bits r_i to obtain the plaintexts $(z_{j,0}, \ldots\ldots, z_{j,n-1})$.

In the preprocessing phase of the protocol, the sender generates the plaintext information $(x_{j,0}, \ldots\ldots, x_{j,n-1})$ and the private key $s \leftarrow \{0,1\}^{\lambda}$, and the receiver generates the matrix T_0, T_1, the selection bits $r = (r_1, \ldots\ldots, r_m)$, and the dual-layer key V_a. The protocol consists of two parts: the first part is the base OT phase, where $\mathcal{S}$ and $\mathcal{R}$ perform a series of public-key-based oblivious transfers, $\mathcal{R}$ sends the matrix T_0, T_1, $\mathcal{S}$ uses s as the selection bits to receive information from the matrix T_0, T_1, generating the matrix Q. The second part is the OTE phase, where $\mathcal{S}$ encrypts the plaintext information $(x_{j,0}, \ldots\ldots, x_{j,n-1})$ using the symmetric key Q and the dual-layer key V_a, sends it to $\mathcal{R}$. $\mathcal{R}$ decrypts the ciphertext using the symmetric key T_0 and the dual-layer key V_a to obtain the plaintext information $(z_{j,0}, \ldots\ldots, z_{j,n-1})$.

3.2 KK OT Extension

In the KK oblivious transfer extension, each OT instance implements an OT_1^n function. KK was the first to introduce the Walsh-Hadamard Codes technique, which allows the selection bits $r = (r_1, \ldots, r_m)$ to be expanded into a matrix R. In a single OT instance, $\mathcal{S}$ prepares n plaintext messages $(x_{j,0}, \ldots\ldots, x_{j,n-1})$, encrypts them into ciphertexts using the symmetric key Q, sends them to $\mathcal{R}$, $\mathcal{R}$ selects the r_i-th ciphertext and decrypts it using the symmetric key T_0 to obtain the corresponding plaintext. The KK protocol is an improvement based on the IKNP protocol, achieving the OT_1^n extension functionality for the first time and introducing only minimal additional overhead compared to IKNP. The detailed process of the KK protocol is shown in Fig. 3.

4 Our Protocol

This section will provide a detailed introduction to our protocol. In our protocol, each OT instance implements an OT_k^n functionality. We propose a selection bit compression technique, which represents multiple selection bits as a single number r_i. Specifically, we first create a string of length n. If we want to select the first message, we set the first bit of the string to 1, otherwise, we set it to 0, and so on. This n-bit string precisely represents the selection status of the n messages. Once the string is filled, we treat it as a binary number, convert it into a decimal number, and assign this decimal number to r_i. During encryption, the receiver converts r_i back into a binary number and determines which messages to select based on the values of individual bits in the binary string.

In Sect. 2, we mentioned the dual-layer key V_a, which was introduced to address the issue of a single key encrypting multiple pieces of data, potentially leading to the leakage of receiver information. Since V_a depends only on r_i, and r_i is entirely generated by the receiver, both r_i and V_a can be computed in the preprocessing phase, without occupying the execution time of the protocol. The overall flow of our protocol is illustrated in Fig. 4.

During step 4 of the protocol, the Sender processes its n messages. For this, a set of values V_a is used, some of which are computed by the Receiver with the remainder being generated randomly. The count of the non-random V_a values determines the number of messages acquired by the Receiver, thus reflecting the protocol's flexibility and support for batch selection.

Players:
- a semi-honest sender $\mathcal{S}$
- a semi-honest receiver $\mathcal{R}$

Protocol (k-out-of-n OT Extension)
Input of $\mathcal{S}$: a sequence of m tuples $(x_{j,0}, ..., x_{j,n-1})$ where each element is of length l bits, with $1 \leq j \leq m$.
Input of $\mathcal{R}$:
- a sequence of m selection integers $r = (r_1, ..., r_m)$ where each r_j satisfies $0 \leq r_j < 2^n - 1$ for $1 \leq j \leq m$.
- a full homomorphic encryption algorithm E with public key pk shared by two players and secret key sk.

Common input: a decimal to binary algorithm F, and $F_i(a)$ denotes the i-th bit of the binary string of a.
Oracle: a collision-resistant hash function $H : [m] \times \{0,1\}^\lambda \to \{0,1\}^\lambda$.

1. $\mathcal{S}$ randomly chooses s from $\{0,1\}^\lambda$. Let s_i denotes the i-th bit of s.
2. $\mathcal{R}$ constructs $m \times \lambda$ matrices T_0, T_1 by randomly selecting $t_{j,0}$ and $t_{j,1}$ from $\{0,1\}^\lambda$, such that $t_{j,0} \oplus t_{j,1} = F(r_j)$. Here, $t_{j,0}$ and $t_{j,1}$ represent the i-th column of matrices T_0, T_1, respectively.
3. $\mathcal{S}$ and $\mathcal{R}$ perform base OT as follows.
   - $\mathcal{S}$ serves as the receiver with inputs $\{s_i\}_{i\in\lceil\lambda\rceil}$.
   - $\mathcal{R}$ serves as the sender with inputs $\{t_0^i, t_1^i\}_{i\in\lceil\lambda\rceil}$.
   - $\mathcal{S}$ receives output $\{q^i\}_{i\in\lceil\lambda\rceil}$.

$\mathcal{S}$ constructs $m \times \lambda$ matrix Q, the i-th column of Q corresponds to the vector q^i (where $q^i = t_{s_i}^i$). Let q_j represent the j-th row of Q. (Noting that $q_j = (F(r_j) \cdot s) \oplus t_{j,0}$)
4. For $j \in \lceil m \rceil$ and $a \in \lceil n-1 \rceil$, $\mathcal{R}$ runs
   - if $F_a(r_j) = 1$, computes $V_a = E(F(r_j - 2^a))$ and sends V_a to $\mathcal{S}$.
   - if $F_a(r_j) = 0$, randomly chooses a string for V_a and sends V_a to $\mathcal{S}$.
5. For $j \in \lceil m \rceil$ and for each $0 \leq a < n$, $\mathcal{S}$ sends
   $y_{j,a} = x_{j,a} \oplus H(j, E(q_j) \oplus (E(2^a \cdot s) + (V_a \cdot E(s))))$.
6. For $j \in \lceil m \rceil$ and for every a that $F_a(r_j) = 1$, $\mathcal{R}$ computes
   $z_{j,a} = y_{j,a} \oplus H(j, E(t_{j,0}))$.

Fig. 4. Our Protocol

Correctness. At the end of the protocol, the message z received by $\mathcal{R}$ is equal to the partial message x sent by $\mathcal{S}$. Here is the proof.

$$
\begin{aligned}
z_{j,a} &= y_{j,a} \oplus H(j, E(t_{j,0})) \\
&= x_{j,a} \oplus H(j, E(q_j) \oplus (E(2^a \cdot s) + (V_a \cdot E(s)))) \oplus H(j, E(t_{j,0})) \\
&= x_{j,a} \oplus H(j, E(q_j) \oplus E(F(r_j \cdot s))) \oplus H(j, E(t_{j,0})) \\
&= x_{j,a} \oplus H(j, E(t_{j,0})) \oplus H(j, E(t_{j,0})) \\
&= x_{j,a}
\end{aligned}
$$

5 Security Proof

Our protocol achieves semi-honest security, ensuring security against a corrupted $\mathcal{S}$ and $\mathcal{R}$. A corrupted $\mathcal{S}$ is unable to know the specific messages chosen by $\mathcal{R}$, as security is ensured by the indistinguishable properties of the homomorphic encryption algorithm E. Similarly, a corrupted $\mathcal{R}$ gains no information beyond its selected messages, with security grounded in the collision-resistance of the hash function H. For a detailed security proof, please refer to Appendix.

6 Performance

In this section, we compare the performance of our protocol with KK [8], and KKRT [9]. There are two reasons for selecting these protocols for comparison. First, our protocol is an improvement of the KK protocol in terms of functionality and is most similar to KK and KKRT, allowing for a direct evaluation of functional and performance enhancements. Second, some recent oblivious transfer protocols, such as PRTY19 [10] and CM20 [12], have been adapted for private set intersection applications. In terms of pure oblivious transfer performance, they exhibit similar results to IKNP. Other protocols, such as MR [17], focus on optimizing public-key oblivious transfer and use it as a primitive for oblivious transfer extension, which differs from the focus and innovations of this paper. Therefore, our primary comparison targets are the KK and KKRT protocols. All of our experiments were implemented on a server with Intel (R) Ultra7-155H 4.80GHz CPU and 32GB RAM. We tested the execution time of the protocol with different parameters in both LAN and WAN environments and conducted a comparison.

In our comparison, the performance metric is the rate of the messages the receiver selects. As the essence of OTE lies in using symmetric keys to encrypt and decrypt data, with only the selected data being decrypted and used. When we constructing private set intersection protocols based on OTE, this metric has a significant impact on the overall performance of PSI.

6.1 Theoretical Analysis

We first compare the theoretical communication complexity of each protocol (Table 3), which measures the communication requirements of the protocols in an idealized network environment.

In the base OT phase, matrices are transmitted to complete key agreement. In KKRT, two matrices, T_0 and T_1, are sent, each with m rows and λ columns, resulting in a total communication cost of $2m\lambda$ in the base OT phase. The KK protocol and our protocol have the same communication cost as KKRT in the base OT phase, both being $2m\lambda$.

In the OTE phase, the communication cost of KK is the same as KKRT, both requiring mns, where m is the number of OT instances, n represents the number of messages transmitted by the sender in each OT instance, and s denotes the length of each message. In our protocol, due to the use of dual keys, an additional round of communication is required for transmitting the second-level key, resulting in a total communication cost of $nm(l+v)$, where v represents the length of the second-level key V_a.

Table 3. Comparison of communication cost

Protocol	Function	Communication
KKRT	OTE_1^{∞}	$2km\lambda + nml$
KK	OTE_1^n	$2km\lambda + nml$
Our Protocol	OTE_k^n	$2m\lambda + nm(l+v)$

6.2 Experimental Comparison

We conduct an internal comparison of our protocol. In this comparison, we set the value of n to 32 and k to 8, meaning that in each OT instance, the sender transmits 32 messages, and the receiver selects 8 of them. We set the message length to 8-bit and 100-bit, and the number of OT instances to $2^6, 2^{10}, 2^{14}, 2^{18}$ and 2^{22}. We compare their performance under WAN and LAN environments. The experimental results are shown in Fig. 5.

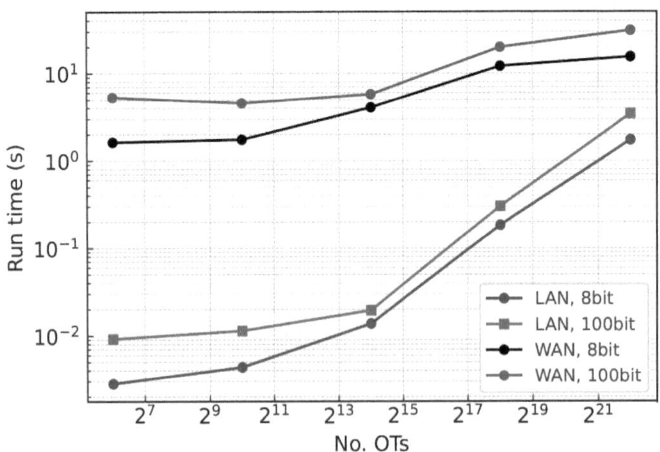

Fig. 5. Our protocol's performance comparison under different parameters. *8bit* and *100bit* indicate the length of the information transmitted in the OT. The x-axis represents the number of executed OT instances, while the y-axis represents the protocol's time overhead in seconds.

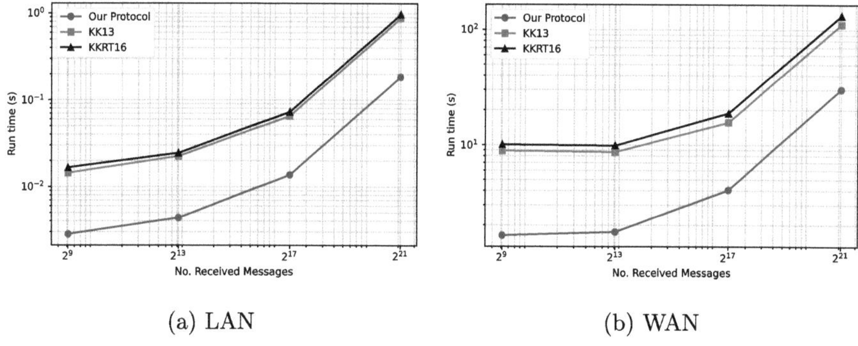

(a) LAN (b) WAN

Fig. 6. Comparison of the runtime of different protocols in LAN and WAN environments. The x-axis represents the number of received messages, while the y-axis represents the runtime in seconds. The message length transmitted in OT is 8 bits. The functionality of KK and KKRT is set to OT_1^4, whereas our protocol is set to OT_8^{32}. We standardized the number of messages received and conducted a performance comparison.

Additionally, we compare our protocol with the KK and KKRT protocols. In the experiment, the message length is set to 8 bits, and we compare the runtime required by the three protocols under different numbers of received messages in both LAN and WAN environments. The experimental results are shown in Fig. 6. When the number of messages that the receiver needs to select is the same, the number of OT executions required by our protocol is k times less than that of KK and KKRT (where k is the number of messages selected by the receiver in each OT, also the value of k in OT_k^n). As shown in Fig. 6, when $k > 1$, our protocol outperforms KK and KKRT, and the larger the k, the greater the performance improvement.

From Fig. 4, it can be observed that when evaluating our protocol internally, the execution time increases steadily as the number of OT instances grows, without any sudden spikes, regardless of whether it operates in LAN or WAN environment. Figure 5 shows that our protocol significantly outperforms KK and KKRT in both network settings, when the number of messages received by the receiver remains the same. Specifically, for smaller data sizes, our protocol achieves a substantial performance improvement, reducing execution time by a factor of 6 to 7. As the data size increases, this performance gain gradually decreases but still maintains an approximate 4× reduction in execution time. Due to its flexible functionality and outstanding performance, our protocol is well-suited for applications with dynamic requirements and stringent runtime constraints.

7 Applications

Our protocol, due to its flexibility and batch selection within a single OTE instance, can be applied in many real-world scenarios. For example, suppose an institution wants to investigate the correlation between the infection rate of a certain lung disease and patients' past pulmonary medical history. It can participate in the proposed OTE_k^n protocol with a hospital database, where the hospital provides patient medical records. However, the institution can only select k lung-related diseases from the dataset while remaining unaware of other medical history details. Likewise, the hospital remains unaware of the specific diseases selected by the institution. At this point, based on the actual application scenario, the number of pulmonary disease records per patient, that is, the value of k, varies dynamically. If the traditional OTE protocol is used, it would not be able to accommodate this scenario.

In addition, our OTE protocol can also serve as a primitive in other protocols, such as Private Set Intersection (PSI), Private Information Retrieval (PIR), and other secure protocols, all of which can benefit a certain degree of performance improvement. For example, it can construct a multi-point Oblivious Pseudo-Random Function (OPRF) and be applied to unbalanced Private Set Intersection (PSI). The multi-point OPRF enables the comparison of multiple elements in a single OTE execution, and does not require the parties' input sets to be of equal size. Each party can independently adjust the size of their input set per OT instance, thereby implementing the unbalanced PSI.

8 Conclusion

An adaptive and batched k-out-of-n OTE scheme is proposed that enables flexible and batch selection within a single OT instance. Our protocol allows the receiver to dynamically adjust the number of selected messages k based on actual requirements, addressing the limitations of traditional OT schemes that suffer from rigid selection constraints, lack of universality, and performance inefficiencies. Extensive comparative experiments were conducted to evaluate the performance of our protocol against KK and KKRT. The results demonstrate that in small-scale datasets, our protocol achieves a 6âĂŞ7× performance improvement over KK and KKRT. Even for large datasets, our protocol maintains approximately a 4× speedup.

Furthermore, our protocol provides a foundational tool for extending the functionality of existing cryptographic primitives. Its integration with private set intersection enables support for batched equality testing. In the context of private information retrieval, it allows efficient execution of multiple private queries. These capabilities suggest several promising avenues for future research.

Acknowledgment. The work is supported by the Zhejiang Provincial Natural Science Foundation of China Nos. LQN25F020002, the Fundamental Research Funds of Zhejiang Sci-Tech University under Grants No. 24222238-Y and the National Natural Science Foundation of China Nos. U21A20465.

Appendix

A.1 Security Against a Corrupted S

We design an ideal-world simulator $\mathcal{S}_{\mathcal{S}}$ that simulates the $x_{j,a}$ messages sent to $\mathcal{R}$ in the OT extension phase using randomly generated values. To ensure consistency with the base-OT sender messages, responses to random oracle queries are crafted based on the sender's bits s received during the setup. All remaining queries are answered honestly with uniformly random values.

Theorem 1. *Let E be a full homomorphic encryption algorithm, H be a random oracle, set $\lambda = 128$. Then protocol $\Pi_{OT}^{m,\lambda,n,k}$ securely realises the functionality $\mathcal{F}_{OT}^{m,\lambda,n,k}$ with static security. We demonstrate this by analyzing the scenarios of a compromised sender and a compromised receiver separately. The cases where both parties are honest are comparatively straightforward. For every adversary $\mathcal{A}$ who corrupts $P_{\mathcal{S}}$, and for every environment $\mathcal{Z}$, it holds that*

$$IDEAL_{OT,\mathcal{S}_{\mathcal{S}},\mathcal{Z}} \overset{c}{\approx} HYBRID_{\Pi_{OT},\mathcal{A},\mathcal{Z}}$$

Proof. Note that, in addition to observing the adversary $\mathcal{A}$'s view during the protocol, the environment $\mathcal{Z}$ also obtains both parties' outputs. To establish security, we construct a series of hybrid executions.

Hyb0 $\mathcal{S}$'s view in the real world.

Hyb1 Same as Hyb_0 except that on $\mathcal{R}$'s side, for each $i \in [\lambda]$, if s_i=0, then sample $t_{i,0} \leftarrow \{0,1\}^m$ and compute $t_{i,1} = t_{i,0} \oplus F(r_i)$, otherwise sample $t_{i,1} \leftarrow \{0,1\}^m$ and compute $t_{i,0} = t_{i,1} \oplus F(r_i)$. This hybrid is identical to Hyb_0.

If $s_i = 0$, $t_{i,0}$ is random and satisfies $t_{i,1} = t_{i,0} \oplus F(r_i)$, while we know $q^i = t_0^i$ since $s_i = 0$. When $s_i = 1$, $t_{i,1}$ is random and satisfies $t_{i,0} = t_{i,1} \oplus F(r_i)$. This time, $q^i = t_1^i = t_0^i \oplus F(r_i)$. After Step 3, get $q^i = (F(r_i) \cdot s) \oplus t_{j,0}$.

Hyb2 same as Hyb_1 but the protocol aborts if there exists a random string V_a such that the hamming distance between V_a and $E(F(r_j - 2^a))$ is more than d. The protocol aborting probability is negligible because the result of E is indistinguishable. Specifically, for each $j \in [m]$, $\mathcal{R}$ constructs V_a and sends it to $\mathcal{S}$. If $F_a(r_j) = 1$, $\mathcal{R}$ computes $V_a = E(F(r_j - 2^a))$, if $F_a(r_j) = 0$, $\mathcal{R}$ chooses a random string V_a. Since r_j is sampled by $\mathcal{R}$ and unknown to $\mathcal{S}$, and the indistinguishability of homomorphic encryption algorithm's result, $\mathcal{S}$ can not distinguish between the random V_a and the computed V_a, Whatsmore, the hamming distance between each V_a should be more than d.

Hyb3. Same as Hyb_2 but the protocol does not abort. The indistinguishability of Hyb_3 and Hyb_2 follows from the indistinguishability of E by the same arguments as above.

Hyb4. The simulated view of S_1. The only difference from Hyb_3 is that S_1 samples the matrix Q and runs the OT simulator to simulate the view of an OT receiver for $\mathcal{S}$. This hybrid is computationally indistinguishable from Hyb_3. A corrupted $\mathcal{S}$ cannot learn which messages $\mathcal{R}$ has selected, the security relies on the indistinguishability of the homomorphic encryption algorithm E.

A.2 Security Against a Corrupted R

The simulator $\mathcal{S}_{\mathcal{R}}$ internally emulates the sender and generates messages indistinguishable from those produced by $P_{\mathcal{R}}$. It also ensures that the environment $\mathcal{Z}$ cannot query the random oracle H on any input corresponding to the sender's unused random outputs. That is, the outputs not selected by the receiver.

Theorem 2. *For every adversary $\mathcal{A}$ who corrupts $P_{\mathcal{R}}$, and for every environment $\mathcal{Z}$, it holds that*

$$IDEAL_{OT,\mathcal{S}_{\mathcal{R}},\mathcal{Z}} \stackrel{c}{\approx} HYBRID_{\Pi_{OT},\mathcal{A},\mathcal{Z}}$$

Proof. Note that, in addition to observing the adversary $\mathcal{A}$'s view during the protocol, the environment $\mathcal{Z}$ also obtains both parties' outputs. To establish security, we construct a series of hybrid executions.

Hyb0. R's view in the real world.

Hyb1. Same as Hyb_0 except that on $\mathcal{S}$'s side, $\mathcal{S}$ chooses q_i randomly instead of choosing it from t_0^i and t_1^i. This hybrid is identical to Hyb_0.

Hyb2. Same as Hyb_1 but the protocol aborts if there exist $u = E(q_j) \oplus (E(2^a \cdot s) + (V_a \cdot E(s))), v = E(t_{j,0}), u \neq v$ such that $H(j, u) = H(j, v)$. The protocol aborting probability is negligible because H is a collision-resistant hash function. Specifically, for each $x_{j,a}$, $\mathcal{S}$ encrypts it with secret key $H(j, u)$ and sends the secret text $y_{j,a}$ to $\mathcal{R}$, $\mathcal{R}$ decrypts the $y_{j,a}$ with his own secret key $H(j, v)$. If $u = v$, then $\mathcal{R}$ can get the original text $x_{j,a}$. But if $u \neq v$ and $H(j, u) = H(j, v)$, it goes to the wrong consequence. But the H function here is a collision-resistant hash function, so the probability above is negligible.

Hyb3. Same as Hyb_2 but the protocol does not abort. The indistinguishability of Hyb_3 and Hyb_2 follows from the collision resistance of H by the same arguments as above.

Hyb4. The simulated view of S_2. The only difference from Hyb_3 is that S_2 samples the matrix $T_{i,0}, T_{i,1}$ and runs the OT simulator to simulate the view of an OT sender for $\mathcal{R}$. This hybrid is computationally indistinguishable from Hyb_3. A corrupted $\mathcal{R}$ cannot learn any information beyond the selected messages, the security relies on the collision-resistant hash function H.

References

1. Badrinarayanan, S., Miao, P., Shi, X., Tromanhauser, M., Zeng, R.: Updatable private set intersection revisited: extended functionalities, deletion, and worst-case complexity. Cryptology ePrint Archive, Paper 2024/1446 (2024)
2. Bienstock, A., Patel, S., Seo, J.Y., Yeo, K.: Near-optimal oblivious key-value stores for efficient PSI, PSU and volume-hiding multi-maps. Cryptology ePrint Archive, Paper 2023/903 (2023)
3. Aranha, D.F., Lin, C., Orlandi, C., Simkin, M.: Laconic private set-intersection from pairings. In: Proceedings of the 2022 ACM SIGSAC Conference on Computer and Communications Security, CCS '22, pp. 111–124. Association for Computing Machinery, New York (2022)
4. Garimella, G., Pinkas, B., Rosulek, M., Trieu, N., Yanai, A.: Oblivious key-value stores and amplification for private set intersection. In: Malkin, T., Peikert, C. (eds.) CRYPTO 2021. LNCS, vol. 12826, pp. 395–425. Springer, Cham (2021). https://doi.org/10.1007/978-3-030-84245-1_14

5. Badrinarayanan, S., et al.: A plug-n-play framework for scaling private set intersection to billion-sized sets. Cryptology ePrint Archive, Paper 2022/294 (2022)
6. Pinkas, B., Schneider, T., Segev, G., Zohner, M.: Phasing: private set intersection using permutation-based hashing. In: 24th USENIX Security Symposium (USENIX Security 15), pp. 515–530 (2015)
7. Ishai, Y., Kilian, J., Nissim, K., Petrank, E.: Extending oblivious transfers efficiently. In: Annual International Cryptology Conference, pp. 145–161. Springer (2003)
8. Kolesnikov, V., Kumaresan, R.: Improved OT extension for transferring short secrets. In: Canetti, R., Garay, J.A. (eds.) CRYPTO 2013. LNCS, vol. 8043, pp. 54–70. Springer, Heidelberg (2013). https://doi.org/10.1007/978-3-642-40084-1_4
9. Kolesnikov, V., Kumaresan, R., Rosulek, M., Trieu, N.: Efficient batched oblivious prf with applications to private set intersection. In: Proceedings of the 2016 ACM SIGSAC Conference on Computer and Communications Security, pp. 818–829 (2016)
10. Pinkas, B., Rosulek, M., Trieu, N., Yanai, A.: SpOT-Light: lightweight private set intersection from sparse OT extension. In: Boldyreva, A., Micciancio, D. (eds.) CRYPTO 2019. LNCS, vol. 11694, pp. 401–431. Springer, Cham (2019). https://doi.org/10.1007/978-3-030-26954-8_13
11. Asharov, G., Lindell, Y., Schneider, T., Zohner, M.: More efficient oblivious transfer and extensions for faster secure computation. In: Proceedings of the 2013 ACM SIGSAC Conference on Computer & Communications Security, pp. 535–548 (2013)
12. Chase, M., Miao, P.: Private set intersection in the internet setting from lightweight oblivious PRF. In: Micciancio, D., Ristenpart, T. (eds.) CRYPTO 2020. LNCS, vol. 12172, pp. 34–63. Springer, Cham (2020). https://doi.org/10.1007/978-3-030-56877-1_2
13. Rabin, M.O.: How to exchange secrets with oblivious transfer. IACR Cryptol. ePrint Arch. **2005**, 187 (2005)
14. Even, S., Goldreich, O., Lempel, A.: A randomized protocol for signing contracts. Commun. ACM **28**(6), 637–647 (1985)
15. Beaver, D.: Correlated pseudorandomness and the complexity of private computations. In: Proceedings of the Twenty-Eighth Annual ACM Symposium on Theory of Computing, STOC '96, pp. 479–488. Association for Computing Machinery, New York (1996)
16. Asharov, G., Lindell, Y., Schneider, T., Zohner, M.: More efficient oblivious transfer extensions with security for malicious adversaries. In: Annual International Conference on the Theory and Applications of Cryptographic Techniques, pp. 673–701. Springer (2015)
17. Mansy, D., Rindal, P.: Endemic oblivious transfer. In: Proceedings of the 2019 ACM SIGSAC Conference on Computer and Communications Security, pp. 309–326 (2019)
18. Canetti, R., Sarkar, P., Wang, X.: Blazing Fast OT for Three-Round UC OT Extension. In: Kiayias, A., Kohlweiss, M., Wallden, P., Zikas, V. (eds.) PKC 2020. LNCS, vol. 12111, pp. 299–327. Springer, Cham (2020). https://doi.org/10.1007/978-3-030-45388-6_11
19. Keller, M., Orsini, E., Scholl, P.: Actively secure ot extension with optimal overhead. In: Annual Cryptology Conference, pp. 724–741. Springer (2015)
20. Chou, T., Orlandi, C.: The simplest protocol for oblivious transfer. In: Lauter, K., Rodríguez-Henríquez, F. (eds.) LATINCRYPT 2015. LNCS, vol. 9230, pp. 40–58. Springer, Cham (2015). https://doi.org/10.1007/978-3-319-22174-8_3

21. Hauck, E., Loss, J.: Efficient and universally composable protocols for oblivious transfer from the cdh assumption. Cryptology ePrint Archive (2017)
22. Hazay, C., Scholl, P., Soria-Vazquez, E.: Low cost constant round mpc combining bmr and oblivious transfer. J. Cryptol. **33**(4), 1732–1786 (2020)
23. Li, B., Micciancio, D.: Equational security proofs of oblivious transfer protocols. In: Abdalla, M., Dahab, R. (eds.) PKC 2018. LNCS, vol. 10769, pp. 527–553. Springer, Cham (2018). https://doi.org/10.1007/978-3-319-76578-5_18
24. Orrù, M., Orsini, E., Scholl, P.: Actively Secure 1-out-of-N OT Extension with Application to Private Set Intersection. In: Handschuh, H. (ed.) CT-RSA 2017. LNCS, vol. 10159, pp. 381–396. Springer, Cham (2017). https://doi.org/10.1007/978-3-319-52153-4_22
25. Yadav, V.K., Andola, N., Verma, S., Venkatesan, S.: A survey of oblivious transfer protocol. ACM Computing Surveys (CSUR) **54**(10s), 1–37 (2022)

Programming Equation Systems of Arithmetization-Oriented Primitives with Constraints

Kexin Qiao[1], Mengyu Chang[1], Junjie Cheng[1], Changhai Ou[2(✉)], An Wang[1], and Liehuang Zhu[1]

[1] School of Cyberspace Science and Technology, Beijing Institute of Technology, Beijing 100081, China
{qiao.kexin,cmyy,junjiecheng,wangan1,liehuangz}@bit.edu.cn
[2] School of Cyber Science and Engineering, Wuhan University, Wuhan 430072, China
ouchanghai@whu.edu.cn

Abstract. Arithmetization-Oriented (AO) cryptographic algorithms operate on large finite fields. The most threatening attack on such designs is the Gröbner basis attack, which solves the equation system encoded from the cryptanalysis problem. However, encoding a primitive as a system of equations is not unique, and finding the optimal one with low solving complexity is a formidable challenge. This paper presents an automated tool that transforms the problem into a Mixed-Integer Quadratic Constraint Programming (MIQCP) model. By employing integer variables and constraints, the tool tracks degree propagation and determines strategic variable introduction points. The optimal MIQCP solution yields the most efficient solving complexity, offering the lowest computational burden for the Gröbner basis attack. We construct comprehensive models for the Griffin, Anemoi, and Ciminion permutations. Our experiments demonstrate reduced Gröbner basis attack complexity, surpassing the designers' bounds. This versatile tool can be leveraged to accurately evaluate the security of new AO designs against Gröbner basis attacks.

Keywords: Gröbner basis · Automatic cryptanalysis · CICO · MIQCP · Griffin

1 Introduction

Advanced protocols such as homomorphic encryption, multi-party computation, and zero-knowledge proofs require cryptographic primitives with new features [17]. Traditional encryption, decryption or hash function calculations are not required in these advanced protocols. Instead, an arithmetic equivalence of the primitives is calculated. Such designs are called arithmetization-oriented (AO) designs. The number of non-linear operations in the arithmetic path affects the implementation efficiency of the protocols, so such primitives are designed to

R. Chen et al. (Eds.): Inscrypt 2025, LNCS 16409, pp. 85–106, 2026.
https://doi.org/10.1007/978-981-95-6203-9_5

have a low multiplicative depth. Many of the current designs use operations on large finite fields with characteristic 2 or a large prime and use simple algebraic calculations such as power maps and inverse as non-linear components, such as the MPC-friendly MiMC, GMiMC, HADESMiMC, Ciminion, and ZK-friendly Vision/Rescue, Grendel, POSEIDON, Griffin, Anemoi *etc.* (summarized in [17]).

For AO primitives over large fields, traditional differential and linear attacks are less effective. Instead, algebraic attacks become more relevant. A typical approach involves encoding the primitive into a system of equations under constrained-input constrained-output (CICO) conditions, and solving it using techniques such as Gröbner basis [9], linearization, or resultant-based algorithms. Designers estimate the lower bound of the solving complexity to guide the choice of the number of rounds. However, their equation construction method, while employing a conservative lower bound, is rather direct.

The motivation of this work is to fully explore the freedom in building equation systems to obtain the lowest algebraic attack complexity for AO primitives. Besides, this work aims to integrate algebraic analysis into the increasingly popular automated toolbox. Statistical distinguishers for symmetric ciphers were once tedious to find, until it was converted to mixed-integer linear programming (MILP) [15] or boolean satisfactory (SAT/SMT) problem [16]. And there are toolboxes [3] developed to make the security evaluation more convenient. Building on this idea, we aim to model the search for the optimal way of constructing an equation system with respect to Gröbner basis attack into a constraint programming problem, with the optimal solution indicating the equation system with the lowest solving complexity. Despite the existence of more advanced Gröbner basis techniques [2] and resultant-based techniques [1] to attack AO primitives, our aim is to illustrate the initial stage of automated algebraic attacks.

Our Contribution. This paper proposes a Mixed-Integer Quadratic Constraint Programming (MIQCP)-based tool to find the optimal way to build equation systems with respect to Gröbner basis attack for AO primitives. The model can handle the under-determined CICO problems. To show the wide applicability of the automatic tool, we build models for Griffin [13], Anemoi [8], Ciminion [10] that cover most module types for AO primitives. With a 12-hour MIQCP solving limit, we found equation systems for 8-round Griffin with Gröbner attack complexity below the designers' loose lower bound.

A key feature of our tool is its ability to optimize constraint placement beyond just input/output positions. In Sponge-based designs [5], where the constrained input/output degrees of freedom are less than the full state, our method can strategically allocate remaining degrees of freedom to intermediate states. The tool presented in this paper can be used to estimate the complexity of the Gröbner basis attack more accurately, especially in designing new AO primitives.

Organization. Section 2 introduces key concepts. Section 3 overviews the model. Section 4–6 detail parsing and constraint formulation. Section 7 presents results, and Sect. 8 concludes.

2 Preliminaries

Notations are shown in Table 1.

Table 1. Notations and their descriptions

Notations	Description
Condition 1 $\Rightarrow$ *Condition* 2	if *Condition* 1 is satisfied, *Condition* 2 must hold
Bold letters (e.g. $\mathbf{x}$)	Vectors on the prime field $\mathbb{F}_q$ (e.g., $\mathbf{x} \in \mathbb{F}_q^t$)
Lowercase letters (e.g. x_i)	Variables in the prime field $\mathbb{F}_q$
equSys	Equation system constructed for the AO primitive
$\mathcal{M}$	The MIQCP module to be built
n_v	Number of variables
n_e	Number of equations
q	An n-bit large prime
t	Branch number of a cryptographic primitive's state

2.1 Sponge Construction with AO Permutation

To design AO hash functions, a permutation can be embedded in Sponge construction [5]. As shown in Fig. 1, the state is divided into c inner branches (*capacity*) and r outer branches (*rate*). Inner branches start as constants, while padded message blocks are absorbed into outer branches after each permutation. After processing all blocks, an h-branch digest is squeezed from the outer part. It has been proved that a Sponge construction embedded with a random permutation is indistinguishable from a random oracle up to $2^{n \cdot \min\{c/2, h\}}$ queries [6].

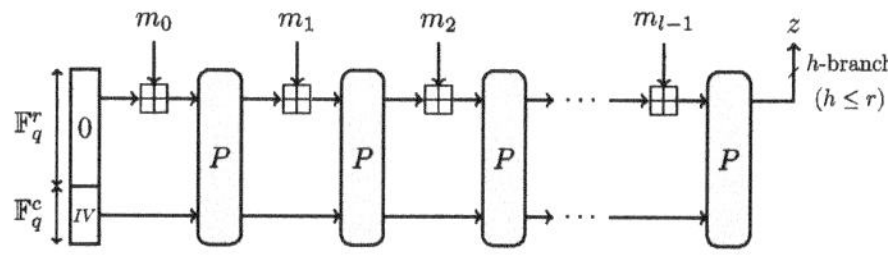

Fig. 1. Sponge construction with AO permutation P.

2.2 CICO Problem

The CICO problem [7] oriented for AO primitives can be stated as follows.

Definition 1 (CICO Problem). *Let $F : \mathbb{F}_q^t \to \mathbb{F}_q^t$ be a permutation on t n-bit branches. Solving the CICO problem is to find a couple (x, y) with $y = F(x)$ and t_0 branches of x fixed and t_1 branches of y fixed. When $t_0 + t_1 < t$, we say the CICO problem is under-determined. Otherwise, when $t_0 + t_1 = t$, we say the CICO problem is well-determined. When $t_0 + t_1 > t$, there may be no solutions.*

The Sponge construction allows under-determined CICO usage even at the desired security level. The complexity of a general preimage attack is $2^{n \cdot \min\{t_0/2, t_1\}}$, and complexity of a general collision attack is $2^{n \cdot \min\{t_0/2, t_1/2\}}$. Some AO primitives claim $s = n/2$ security (Sect. 7), allowing $t_0 = t_1 = 1$. To build a well-determined system of equations, *i.e.* systems with as many equations as variables, $(t - t_0 - t_1)$ intermediate positions can be set to constants to decrease the equation degrees. This paper focuses on the well-determined CICO problem when a hash function has only one message block.

2.3 The Gröbner Basis Attack

The Gröbner basis method is a standard technique for solving well-determined multivariate polynomial systems of the form $P_i(\mathbf{x}) = 0$, where $i = 0, \cdots, n_e - 1, \mathbf{x} = (x_0, \ldots, x_{n_v - 1}) \in \mathbb{F}_q^{n_v}$ and each P_i has degree d_i. The idea is to compute the Gröbner basis G of the ideal $\mathcal{I} = \langle P_0, \ldots, P_{n_e-1} \rangle$, typically under the *lexicographic* order, which allows sequential solving of variables starting from x_{n_v-1}. However, computing the lexicographic Gröbner basis is costly. A common strategy involves three steps:

1. Use F5 algorithm [12] to compute the Gröbner basis under *grevlex* order. Assuming regularity, the complexity is estimated as:

$$\mathcal{O}\left(\binom{D_{reg} + n_v}{n_v}^{\omega}\right), \tag{1}$$

   where the degree of regularity is

$$D_{deg} = 1 + \sum_{i=0}^{n_e - 1} (d_i - 1), \tag{2}$$

   and $2 \leq \omega < 3$ is a constant representing the complexity of solving linear equations systems. We set $\omega = 2$ throughout this paper.
2. Convert the Gröbner basis deduced in the above step into *lexicographic* order using the FGLM algorithm [11]. The complexity of this step is estimated as

$$\mathcal{O}(n_v d^3),$$

   where d is the degree of the ideal $\mathcal{I}$.

3. Solve the univariate polynomials iteratively deduced from the Gröbner basis in *lexicongraphic* order.

A lower bound of the complexity of the first step is used as a metric to guarantee the difficulty in solving the well-determined multivariate system in designing new AO primitives [8,10,13]. As long as the number of variables n_v and the number of equations n_e are known, the complexity can be estimated.

2.4 MIQCP

The Mixed-Integer Quadratic Constraint Program (MIQCP) is a paradigm that aims to optimize an objective function under quadratic constraints exerted on variables and has been used to search for differential-linear distinguishers [4]. Though the objective function is allowed to be quadratic, in our model it is linear. The quadratic constraints in our model come from two types of expressions. The first type is explicit - one variable is the product of the other two variables. The second type is the indication constraint in the form that "*Condition* 1 $\Rightarrow$ *Condition* 2". The indication constraints are converted to quadratic conditions implicitly by the off-the-shelf solver.

3 Model Overview

The complexity of the Gröbner basis attack is mainly determined by the number of variables and equation degrees. To maximize flexibility, new variables can be introduced at any intermediate point in the arithmetic path. Once a new variable is introduced, an equation that makes it equal to an existing expression should be added to consume the degree of freedom it brings in. If no variable is introduced at a position, then this position is expressed by existing variables.

The MIQCP model $\mathcal{M}$ determines where to introduce variables and how degrees propagate through the arithmetic path. As shown in Fig. 2, the path is parsed round by round into *arithmetic modules* (primitive operations) and *branching modules* (connections between operations). Variables and constraints are added to $\mathcal{M}$ module by module. The right side of the figure shows parsing the round permutation; the left shows model construction. Details are given in the following sections.

We mention the most critical variable types and the three global constraints to complete the modeling flowchart. The binary variable var_i^r indicates whether a variable is introduced at position i in round r, while con_i^r indicates constants. The degree of the j-th equation in round r is denoted by equ_j^r.

As Eq. (1) shows, the Gröbner attack complexity depends on the number of variables and the total equation degree. To avoid modeling the hassle of modeling combinatorial numbers, we fix the variable count to n_v:

$$\sum_{r,i} var_i^r = n_v, \tag{3}$$

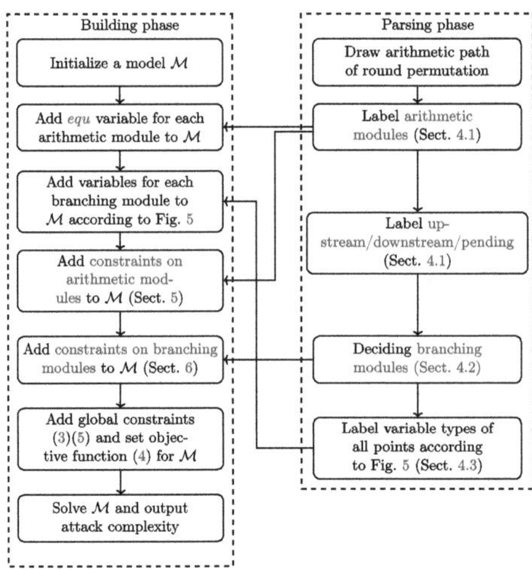

Fig. 2. Workflow for building the MIQCP model $\mathcal{M}$.

and obtain the minimum sum of equation degrees by setting the objective function to

$$\min obj = \sum_{r,j} equ_j^r, \tag{4}$$

and then calculate combinatorial numbers offline and compare complexities across different n_v to find the global minimum.

Since the degree of freedom of the equation system matches the number of branches, to construct a well-determined equation system with a unique solution, the number of constants is set equal to the number of branches t:

$$\sum_{r,i} con_i^r = t. \tag{5}$$

4 Parsing the Arithmetic Path

The arithmetic path is parsed to identify arithmetic modules, branching modules, and variable types for the MIQCP model.

4.1 Arithmetic Modules

We set the following four types of arithmetic modules.

MDS Module. To achieve full diffusion, the linear layer used in cryptographic algorithms usually applies MDS matrix multiplication together with constant addition. For a t-dimensional MDS matrix, its branch number is $(t + 1)$. Since constants don't affect degree, they are included in the MDS module.

t-addition Module. Addition with $(t-1)$ addends is called t-addition since there are t branches around the addition symbol and any $(t-1)$ branches determine the other. It is a linear module and shares some similarities with the MDS module in generating constraints in $\mathcal{M}$.

Non-Linear Univariate Polynomial (NLUP) Module. This is a more general case of power map-type Sboxes. The degree of the output of NLUP is multiple times that of the input depending on the degree of the polynomial.

Non-Linear Multivariate Polynomial (NLMP) Module. This is also a non-linear module. The simplest NLMP is the multiplication of two branches.

We redefine each arithmetic module's inputs and outputs from the perspective of low-degree computation. We call the arithmetic equivalent of inputs and outputs as *upstreams* and *downstreams.*

Definition 2 (Upstream/Downstream/Pending). *For an arithmetic module with degree α being a small integer, the upstreams are the input branches and the downstreams are the output branches. In other words, computing from upstream to downstream is always a not larger degree of computation than the inverse computation, if the inverse computation is possible. If a branch can have multiple choices regarding the arithmetic module, it is called a pending branch.*

We use the symbol $\rightarrow$ to represent the upstream input, $\succ$ the downstream output, and $\bullet\!-$ the pending branch, connected to the four arithmetic modules, as is shown in Fig. 3. Labeling NLUP and NLMP modules is deterministic since the low-degree calculation is only possible in one direction. For a t-addition module, any $(t-1)$ branches can be upstream to determine the other branch. For a t-dimensional MDS affine module, any t branches will determine the other t branches. So all branches of MDS and t-addition modules are *pending.* The final optimal choice will be given by the automatic model.

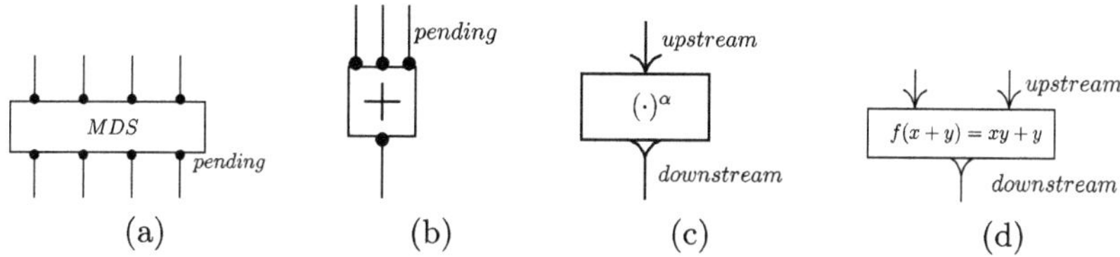

Fig. 3. Upstream, downstream, and pending branches for arithmetic modules. (a) MDS. (b) 4-addition. (c) NLUP. (d) NLMP.

4.2 Branching Modules

An intermediate branch has multiple ends. Each end has a status decided from the arithmetic module it touches. We call the intermediate branch with labeled status on each end the *branching* module. After parsing several AO cryptographic algorithms, we find that there are only a few types of branching modules, as shown in Fig. 4.

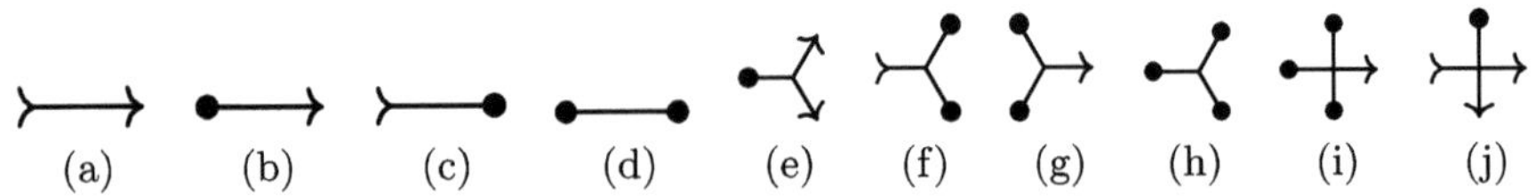

Fig. 4. Branching modules. (a) Down-up. (b) Pending-up. (c) Down-pending. (d) Pending-pending. (e) Pending-ups. (f) Down-pending-pending. (g) Pending-pending-up. (h) Pending-pending-pending. (i) Pending-pending-pending-up. (j) Down-pending-ups.

4.3 Types of Variables Set in the Model

Degree propagation will be captured by constraints on the following types of variables.

- *var*: binary variable. Indicates if a variable is introduced here.
- *con*: binary variable. Indicate whether this position is set to a constant and thus consumes a degree of freedom.
- *deg*: integer variable. The degree of the expression of this position.
- *g*: binary variable set for pending branches of a linear module. Indicate whether this branch has been determined externally.
- *bse*: binary variable set for pending branches of a linear module. Indicate if this branch is selected into the basis of its linear module.
- *h*: binary variable set for pending branches of a linear module. Indicates the branch is externally fixed but not in the basis; equal to $g - bse$.
- *equ*: integer variable. The sum of degrees of equations that are built regarding a module, as only this matters in the Gröbner basis attack complexity.

Not all variable types are required for every module in the MIQCP model. Each arithmetic module sets an equation variable *equ*, while branching modules introduce different types of variables depending on their structure, as illustrated in Fig. 5. Variables are grouped by color-coded boxes, each corresponding to a point in the module—some at the ends, others inserted at intermediate positions.

Figure 6 presents examples of parsing the Griffin, Anemoi, and Ciminion round permutations, We numbered the positions where variables are set in the MIQCP model. Using this structural information, we can investigate the types of branching modules that are formed.

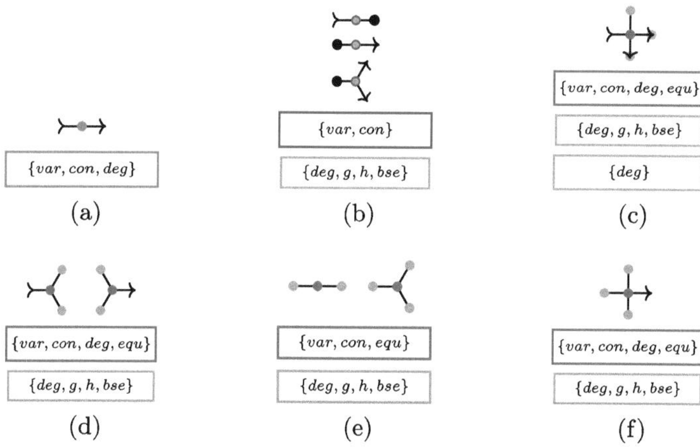

Fig. 5. Variables introduced for branching modules. (a) Down-up. (b) Down-pending and pending-up(s). (c) Down-pending-ups. (d) Down-pending-pending and pending-pending-up. (e) Pending-pending and pending-pending-pending. (f) Pending-pending-pending-up.

5 Constraints on Arithmetic Modules

In this section, we explain how to set constraints for arithmetic modules in the MIQCP model. The process of building equations is the process of adding variables to the system equSys and consuming the degrees of freedom they introduce by imposing the arithmetic rules.

5.1 MDS Module

For an MDS module, the input and output are denoted by $\mathbf{x} = (x_0, x_1, \cdots, x_{t-1}) \in \mathbb{F}_p^t$ and $\mathbf{x}' = (x_t, x_{t+1}, \cdots, x_{2t-1}) \in \mathbb{F}_p^t$, and in the arithmetic path we have $\mathbf{x}' = A\mathbf{x} + \mathbf{b}$, where A is an MDS matrix, and $\mathbf{b}$ is a vector of round constant. The expressions of the input branches, output branches, and the possible equations built within the MDS module form an arithmetic equivalence of the transformation.

Mechanism of Building Equations within an MDS Module. The branches related to the MDS module may be predetermined by external modules. Any predetermined t branches will deduce the other t branches. Once more than t branches are predetermined, say s, to ensure arithmetic equivalence, $(s - t)$ equations should be added to equSys. Meanwhile, the other $(2t - s)$ branches can be expressed in multiple ways. To keep a low degree for both the $(s - t)$ equations and the $(2t - s)$ expressions to be determined, we need to choose t predetermined branches with the lowest degrees to express other branches, formally defined as the *basis* of the MDS module.

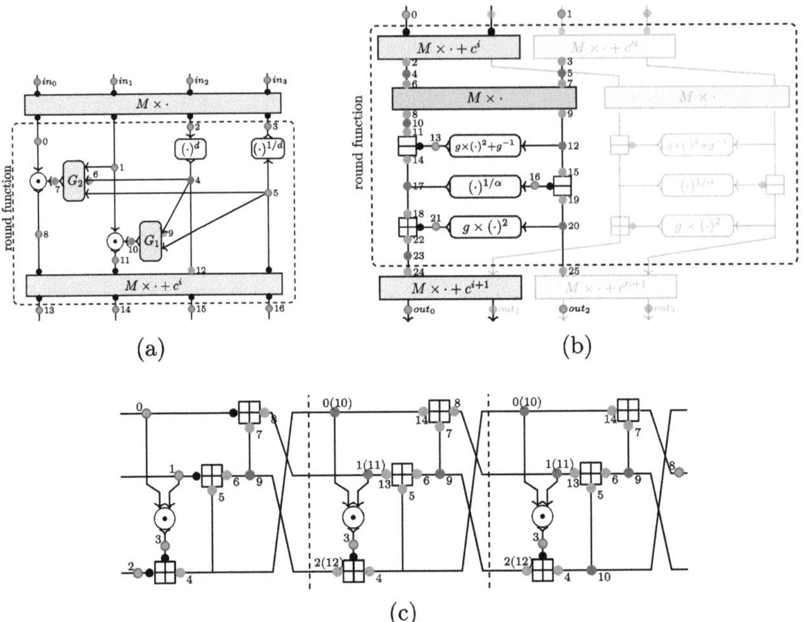

Fig. 6. Parsing of the Griffin, the Anemoi and Ciminion round functions. (a) Griffin. (b) Anemoi. (c) Ciminion.

Definition 3 (Basis of MDS Module). *A basis of a t-dimensional MDS module is a set of t branches with the lowest degrees out of the s predetermined branches of the module.*

For example, in the MDS module with $t = 4$ (Fig. 7), six branches at positions 0, 1, 2, 3, 6, 7 are predetermined with degrees 3, 2, 1, 0, 1, and 5. We select the four lowest-degree branches (0, 1, 1, 2) as the basis. The remaining branches are then expressed by this basis with degree 2. Additionally, two equations of degree 3 and 5 are added for branches 0 and 7, respectively. The branches 4 and 5 are now computed via the basis and propagated. This ensures arithmetic equivalence in equSys.The above mechanism should be expressed by variables and constraints.

Constraints. The above variables should abide by the following constraints to reflect the mechanism of building equations within the MDS module.

- If a variable is introduced, the branch is predetermined:

$$var_i^r = 1 \Rightarrow g_i^r = 1, 0 \leq i \leq 2t - 1.$$

- If a constant is introduced in the branch, the branch is predetermined:

$$con_i^r = 1 \Rightarrow g_i^r = 1, 0 \leq i \leq 2t - 1.$$

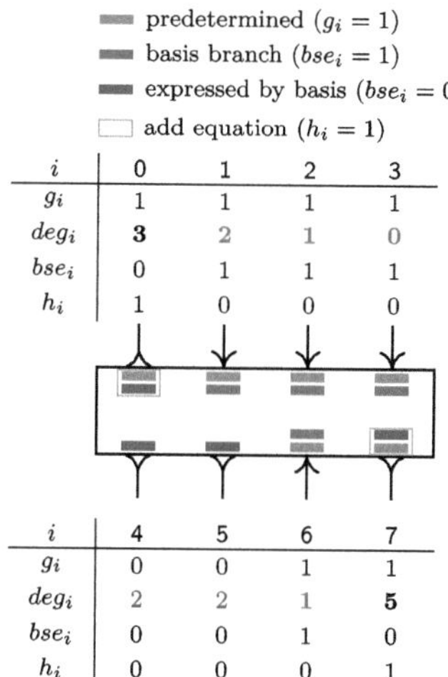

Fig. 7. Basis of MDS module.

- The number of introduced constants around an MDS module is at most t:

$$\sum_{i=0}^{2t-1} con_i^r \leq t.$$

- Basis can only select from predetermined branches:

$$g_i^r \geq bse_i^r, 0 \leq i \leq 2t-1.$$

However, this constraint is redundant due to the definition and the binary feature of h_i^r.
- Definition of h_i^r:

$$h_i^r = g_i^r - bse_i^r, 0 \leq i \leq 2t-1.$$

- The basis contains t branches:

$$\sum_{i=0}^{2t-1} bse_i^r = t.$$

- The basis consists of the t predetermined branches with the lowest degrees:

$$deg_B = \underbrace{\max\{bse_j^r \times deg_j^r | 0 \leq j \leq 2t-1\}}_{\text{the maximum degree in the basis}},$$

$$h_i^r = 1 \Rightarrow deg_B \leq deg_i^r, 0 \leq i \leq 2t-1.$$

- The sum of degrees of the equations:

$$equ_{MDS}^r = \sum_{i=0}^{2t-1} (h_i \times deg_i^r).$$

- If a branch is not predetermined, *i.e.* $g_i^r = 0$, it should be expressed by the basis branches, so the degree is determined by that of the base:

$$g_i^r = 0 \Rightarrow deg_i^r = deg_B, 0 \leq i \leq 2t-1.$$

Besides, to avoid trivial solutions, when the base degree is zero, the *con* variables of the basis branch should be set to 1. This can be ensured by

$$deg_B = 0 \Rightarrow \sum_{i=0}^{2t-1} con_i^r = t.$$

5.2 *t*-Addition Module

The t addition module is similar to the MDS module. Any $(t-1)$ branches will determine the other branches, so the number of branches in a basis is $(t-1)$.

5.3 NLUP Module

A univariate polynomial operates on a single branch. The downstream degree is α times the upstream degree, where α is the degree of the univariate polynomial. Suppose the upstream position is with index j and the downstream position is with index j'. Variables related to a non-linear univariate polynomial module are $var_i^r, con_i^r, deg_i^r, i \in \{j, j'\}$, and equ_{NLUP}^r.

Constraints.

- If a constant is at one side of the NLUP module, the other side is a constant:

$$con_j^r = 1 \Leftrightarrow con_{j'}^r = 1.$$

- Regarding the downstream position,
  - if a new variable is introduced at the downstream position, an equation will be introduced to equSys with degree α times the upstream degree:

$$var_{j'}^r = 1 \Rightarrow equ_{NLUP}^r = \alpha \times deg_j^r.$$

  - if no variable is introduced, the degree of downstream position is α times the upstream degree:

$$var_{j'}^r = 0 \Rightarrow \begin{cases} deg_{j'}^r = \alpha \times deg_j^r, \\ equ_{NLUP}^r = 0. \end{cases}$$

- Regarding the upstream position, the cases will be covered by constraints for branching modules.

5.4 NLMP Module

Multivariate polynomials used in AO primitives are simple, so the downstream degree can be determined easily by the upstream degrees. We instantiate the model for the G function with degree 2 for all input variables and the multiplication ($\times$) used in Griffin, and other polynomials can be modeled accordingly. Suppose the downstream position is with index j, and the upstream positions are with index $i_0, i_1, \cdots$. Recall Sect. 4.3, the variables relating to an NLMP modules include $var_j^r, con_j^r, deg_j^r, var_{i_k}^r, con_{i_k}^r, deg_{i_k}^r, k = 0, 1, \cdots$, and equ_{NLMP}^r.

Constraints.

- Regarding the downstream position,
  - If a variable or a constant is introduced in the downstream position, an equation is introduced:

$$\text{for } G\text{: } var_j^r + con_j^r \geq 1 \Rightarrow equ_{NLMP}^r = 2 \times \max\{deg_{i_0}^r, deg_{i_1}^r, \cdots\},$$
$$\text{for } \times\text{ s: } var_j^r + con_j^r \geq 1 \Rightarrow equ_{NLMP}^r = deg_{i_0}^r + deg_{i_1}^r.$$

  - If no variable nor constant is introduced in the downstream position, the output is expressed by the upstream positions:

$$\text{for } G\text{: } \begin{cases} var_j^r = 0 \\ con_j^r = 0 \end{cases} \Rightarrow \begin{cases} deg_j^r = 2 \times \max\{deg_{i_0}^r, deg_{i_1}^r, \cdots\}, \\ equ_{NLMP}^r = 0. \end{cases}$$

$$\text{for } \times\text{: } \begin{cases} var_j^r = 0 \\ con_j^r = 0 \end{cases} \Rightarrow \begin{cases} deg_j^r = deg_{i_0}^r + deg_{i_1}^r, \\ equ_{NLMP}^r = 0. \end{cases}$$

- Regarding the upstream position, the cases are covered by constraints on branching modules.

6 Constraints on Branching Modules

Intermediate branching modules connect arithmetic modules. The arithmetic flow from one end to another end should also be captured by the constraints. Equations may be constructed within the branching modules. Besides the intermediate branching modules, constraints on the border branches should also be considered.

Common Constraints. If a variable is introduced at an intermediate position, *i.e.* $var = 1$, the degrees of this branch's ends are 1. Similarly, if a constant is set in the position, *i.e.* $con = 1$, the degrees of this branch's ends are 0. This common constraint is defined in Eq. (6).

$$\mathcal{C}_{common}(var, con, deg) = \begin{cases} var = 1 \Rightarrow deg = 1, \\ con = 1 \Rightarrow deg = 0. \end{cases} \tag{6}$$

6.1 Border Branch Constraints

Constant indicator variables on constrained input branches and constrained output branches should be set to 1:

$$con_i^0 = 1, con_{i'}^R = 1,$$

for i and i' belonging to the capacity part and output part of the Sponge construction as defined in the hash function sepcifications respectively.

For other border branches, if it is a branch connecting to a linear module, and no variable or constant would be introduced at this position in equSys (*i.e.* $var = 0, con = 0$), we can ignore it, and the branch would not participate in the arithmetic flow. This is ensured by constraint

$$var_{i'}^0 + con_{i'}^0 = 0 \Rightarrow g_{i'} = 0,$$
$$var_{j'}^R + con_{j'}^R = 0 \Rightarrow g_{j'} = 0,$$

for i', j' being the indexes of unconstrained border branches that are connected to an MDS module.

For all border branches, common constraints should be added.

$$\mathcal{C}_{common}(var_i, con_i, deg_i),$$

for i being the border branch indexes.

6.2 Intermediate Branch Constraints

In the following, we will specify the constraints for representative types of branching modules and provide the others in Appendix A. For each branching module, the related variables are presented with suffixes u, d, p representing the upstream, downstream, and pending ends when necessary. Since the cases of introducing a new variable or a constant are already covered in the common constraints, the specific constraints just need to cover the case that the position is neither a new variable nor a constant, *i.e.* $var + con = 0$.

Down-Up. Related variables are var, con, deg. Only common constraints in Eq. (6) are needed.

Down-Pending. Relative variables are var, con, g, deg. Since $var+con = 0$, this position has an expression from the arithmetic module connected with the downstream end. From the perspective of the linear arithmetic module, the pending branch is determined externally.

$$var + con = 0 \Rightarrow g = 1,$$
$$\mathcal{C}_{common}(var, con, deg).$$

Pending-Up(s). Relative variables are var, con, g, deg. Since $var + con = 0$, the position can only be expressed by the linear arithmetic module connected with the unique pending end. So, from the perspective of the linear arithmetic module, the pending branch is not externally determined.

$$var + con = 0 \Rightarrow g = 0,$$
$$\mathcal{C}_{common}(var, con, deg).$$

Down-Pending-Ups. Variables related to this module are $var, con, deg, equ, deg_p, g_p, deg_i, i = 1, 2, \cdots$, where i corresponds to indexes of upstream ends. When $var + con = 0$, this position has an expression from the downstream branch. There may be another expression from the basis of the linear modular connected with the pending end. We want the upstream branch to take the one with a lower degree. So if the downstream end was not to determine the pending end ($g = 0$), an equation would be added to connect the downstream end and the pending end, so

$$g = 0 \Rightarrow \begin{cases} deg_i = \min\{deg, deg_p\}, i = 1, 2, \cdots, \\ equ = \max\{deg, deg_p\}. \end{cases}$$

Otherwise, if the downstream determines the pending end, this pending end can be chosen as a basis. The connection between the downstream and the pending ends has already been ensured inside the linear module. The upstream takes the expression from the downstream end with degree deg. It is possible that the degree of the downstream is larger than that of the basis of the linear module, so it would be better for the upstream to take the expression from the pending end. In this case, the model will automatically go to the above case where $g = 0$. So we set

$$g = 1 \Rightarrow \begin{cases} deg_p = deg, \\ deg_i = deg, i = 1, 2, \cdots, \\ equ = 0. \end{cases}$$

Actually, $equ = 0$ constraint is not necessary as it will be forced automatically. Besides, common constraints should be added.

$$\mathcal{C}_{common}(var, con, deg),$$
$$\mathcal{C}_{common}(var, con, deg_p),$$
$$\mathcal{C}_{common}(var, con, deg_i), i = 1, 2, \cdots.$$

The constraints for down-pending-pending, pending-pending, pending-pending-up, pending-pending-pending, pending-pending-pending-up branching modules are provided in Appendix A.

7 Applications

We build MIQCP model for Griffin [13], Anemoi [8], and Ciminion [10] to show the wide applicability of our model. The first two primitives allow for an under-determined CICO problem, while Ciminion allows only for the well-determined. The MIQCP models are solved by Gurobi [14], and the solving time limit is set to 12-hour. Our experiments were conducted on a machine equipped with an Intel Core i5-9300H CPU @ 2.40GHz, 8GB RAM. The source codes are provided in repository https://github.com/qiaokexin/Groebner_MIQCP.

The designers of the Griffin, Anemoi and Ciminion algorithms have estimated the lower bounds on the complexity of attacks targeting r rounds by $\min\{\binom{\alpha r+1+tr}{1+tr}^{\omega}, \binom{\alpha^r+1+r}{1+r}^{\omega}\}$, $\binom{2lr+\kappa_\alpha+2lr}{2lr}^{\omega}$ and $\binom{2+2^{r+1}}{2}^{\omega} \geq (\frac{(1+2^{r+1})^2}{2})^{\omega} \geq 2^{2r+1}$, respectively, where α is the S-box degree, l the state size parameter and κ_α an α-dependent constant. From the designer's perspective, these lower bounds are very loose. However, by solving our MIQCP model to determine the optimal number of variables and the sum of equation degrees, and then applying the complexity calculation formulas in Eq. (1) and (2), we can derive equation systems with significantly lower solving complexity than these lower bounds, thereby demonstrating the effectiveness of our approach in challenging the security assumptions of these designs.

We observed that the attack complexity initially decreases and then increases as the number of variables grows. Consequently, the table highlights, in bold, the optimal number of variables, the sum of equation degrees, and the corresponding complexity in base-2 logarithm ("cmp."). For comparative analysis, we also present results for variable counts adjacent to the optimal. Table 2a presents the results for Griffin-π with S-box degree $\alpha = 5$ for different branch numbers. "–" indicates no feasible solution was found within the time limit. How the optimal results for 8 branches can be extended to larger branches and results for $\alpha = 3$ versions are provided in the source codes repository. Our estimated complexities remain below the designers' lower bound for up to 8 rounds. Table 2b shows the results for Anemoi with S-box degree $\alpha = 3$. For up to 4 rounds, our model yields lower complexities than those estimated by the designers. Table 2c reports the attack complexity on Ciminion with $t = 3$.

Figure 8 shows the equation systems derived from our method. C and x_i indicate the positions of constant and variable introduction, respectively. The red line indicates the base position, and the meeting green arrows indicate equation establishment. Equations are derived from branch expression equality, with the degree indicated by the adjacent green number, representing the higher branch degree. To test for correctness, we implemented these equation systems and got the expected preimages. Setting intermediate branches to a constant can potentially lead to an inconsistent system. However, to minimize equation degrees, the constant positions are automatically chosen to be far apart. Given the strong confusion and diffusion effects of the round functions, an inconsistent system is very unlikely to occur.

Table 2. Numbers of variables (n_v), sums of equation degrees ($\sum equ$) and solving complexities in $\log_2$ (*comp.*) for Griffin, Anemoi and Ciminion.

(a) Results for Griffin.

	r	2			3			4			5			6			7			8			9		
		n_v	$\sum_{equ}$	cmp.	n_v	$\sum_{equ}$	cmp.	n_v	$\sum_{equ}$	cmp.	n_v	$\sum_{equ}$	cmp.	n_v	$\sum_{equ}$	cmp.	n_v	$\sum_{equ}$	cmp.	n_v	$\sum_{equ}$	cmp.	n_v	$\sum_{equ}$	cmp.
$t = 3$	This	**2**	**42**	**19.64**	**3**	**97**	**34.43**	4	272	55.51	5	347	70.53	7	227	84.79	8	348	104.32	10	278	118.43	11	357	135.70
		3	23	21.97	4	58	37.59	**5**	**93**	**51.42**	**6**	**148**	**67.35**	**8**	**148**	**84.36**	**9**	**203**	**100.65**	**11**	**203**	**117.50**	**12**	**258**	**133.99**
		4	20	25.09	5	43	40.10	6	78	56.1	7	113	70.52	9	133	89.46	10	168	103.65	12	188	122.79	13	223	136.90
	[13]	7	27	28.49	10	40	43.28	13	53	58.19	16	66	73.17	19	79	88.20	22	92	103.26	25	105	118.35	28	118	133.46
		3	132	23.35	4	1.4e3	46.78	5	1.6e4	79.13	6	1.7e5	120.35	7	1.9e6	170.44	8	2.1e7	229.45	9	2.3e8	297.41	10	2.5e9	374.36

	r	2			3			4			5			6		
		n_v	$\sum_{equ}$	cmp.	n_v	$\sum_{equ}$	cmp.	n_v	$\sum_{equ}$	cmp.	n_v	$\sum_{equ}$	cmp.	n_v	$\sum_{equ}$	cmp.
$t = 4$	This	**2**	**38**	**19.07**	4	76	40.74	6	122	63.97	8	156	85.59	10	186	106.65
		3	19	20.31	**5**	**41**	**39.40**	**7**	**71**	**60.91**	**9**	**101**	**82.12**	**11**	**131**	**103.24**
		4	16	22.43	6	34	41.26	8	60	62.91	10	98	87.65	12	128	109.08
	[13]	9	33	32.99	13	49	50.32	17	65	67.78	21	81	85.32	25	97	102.91
		3	132	23.35	4	1.4e3	46.78	5	1.6e4	79.13	6	1.7e5	120.35	7	1.9e6	170.44

	r	2			3			4			5			6		
		n_v	$\sum_{equ}$	cmp.	n_v	$\sum_{equ}$	cmp.	n_v	$\sum_{equ}$	cmp.	n_v	$\sum_{equ}$	cmp.	n_v	$\sum_{equ}$	cmp.
$t = 8$	This	2	24	16.46	**5**	**35**	**37.05**	7	107	69.40	9	323	112.86	11	971	167.68
		3	**11**	**15.56**	6	28	37.72	**8**	**72**	**67.29**	**10**	**180**	**105.68**	**12**	**504**	**157.47**
		4	10	16.73	7	28	41.15	9	64	69.79	11	173	112.31	13	726	181.77
	[13]	17	57	46.02	25	85	70.45	33	113	95.05	41	141	119.73	49	169	144.46
		3	132	23.35	4	1.4e3	46.78	5	1.6e4	79.13	6	1.7e5	120.35	7	1.9e6	170.44

(b) Results for Anemoi.

	r	1			2			3			4			5		
		n_v	$\sum_{equ}$	cmp.	n_v	$\sum_{equ}$	cmp.	n_v	$\sum_{equ}$	cmp.	n_v	$\sum_{equ}$	cmp.	n_v	$\sum_{equ}$	cmp.
$t = 4$	This	**2**	**4**	**6.64**	**4**	**14**	**20.83**	6	31	39.58	11	36	59.34	16	-	-
		3	5	8.64	5	15	24.19	7	25	38.65	**12**	**33**	**58.06**	17	-	-
		4	6	10.26	6	13	23.10	**9**	**21**	**37.85**	14	32	59.22	**18**	**42**	**78.29**
		5	7	11.61	7	14	25.30	10	22	40.25	15	33	61.58	19	-	-
	[8]	4	5	13.95	8	9	29.14	12	13	44.62	16	17	60.24	20	21	75.94

	r	1			2			3		
		n_v	$\sum_{equ}$	cmp.	n_v	$\sum_{equ}$	cmp.	n_v	$\sum_{equ}$	cmp.
$t = 6$	This	**2**	**4**	**6.64**	6	18	29.46	14	-	-
		3	**4**	**6.64**	**8**	**16**	**29.14**	15	-	-
		4	5	7.81	9	17	31.14	**16**	**32**	**60.24**
		5	6	8.78	10	18	33.00	17	-	-
	[8]	6	7	21.49	12	13	44.62	18	19	68.08

(c) Results for Ciminion.

r	3			4			5			6			7			8			9		
	n_v	$\sum_{equ}$	cmp.	n_v	$\sum_{equ}$	cmp.	n_v	$\sum_{equ}$	cmp.	n_v	$\sum_{equ}$	cmp.	n_v	$\sum_{equ}$	cmp.	n_v	$\sum_{equ}$	cmp.	n_v	$\sum_{equ}$	cmp.
This	**2**	**3**	**5.17**	1	4	9.04	1	8	11.32	1	16	13.09	1	32	14.64	**1**	**64**	**16.08**	1	–	–
	3	4	6.64	**2**	**4**	**6.64**	**2**	**6**	**8.78**	**2**	**10**	**11.56**	**2**	**16**	**14.17**	2	28	17.33	**2**	**48**	**20.40**
	4	5	7.81	3	5	8.64	3	6	10.26	3	8	12.78	3	11	15.56	3	15	18.26	3	24	22.33
	5	6	8.78	4	6	10.26	4	7	12.26	4	8	13.95	4	10	16.73	4	13	19.93	4	16	22.43
[10]	2	8	7	2	16	9	2	32	11	2	64	13	2	128	15	2	256	17	2	512	19

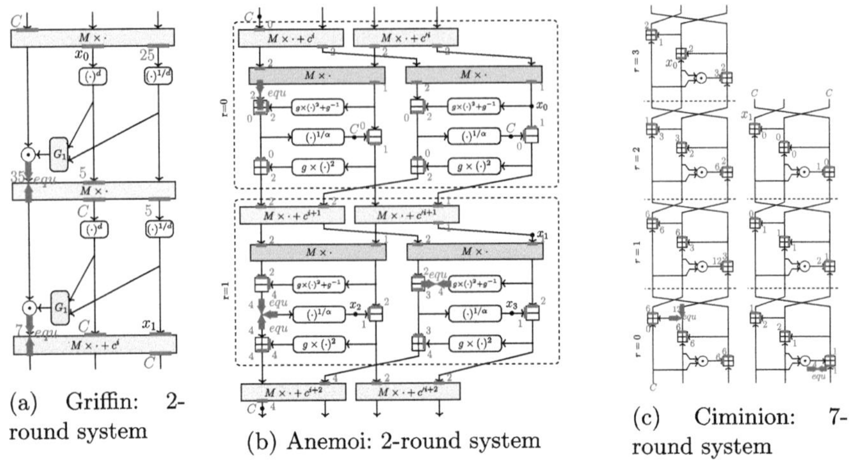

(a) Griffin: 2-round system

(b) Anemoi: 2-round system

(c) Ciminion: 7-round system

Fig. 8. Equation constructions for Griffin, Anemoi, and Ciminion. Basis, degrees, and variable placements are labeled.

8 Conclusions

In this paper, we introduce an MIQCP-based automated method that efficiently generates an equation system for Gröbner basis attacks on arithmetization-oriented hash functions. With this method, it is demonstrated that the complexity of the Gröbner basis attack is overestimated for about half the full rounds of the Griffin cipher. While the results for Anemoi and Ciminion are less conclusive, as we could only prove the complexity overestimation for a small number of rounds within the time constraint, the validity of these AO primitive models highlights the broad applicability of our proposed approach. Consequently, the tool presented in this work enables a more accurate estimation of the security against Gröbner basis attacks, which is crucial for the design of AO primitives for advanced protocols such as zero-knowledge proofs, homomorphic encryption, and multi-party computation.

The current model focuses on the straightforward Gröbner basis attack, considering only the number of variables and the sum of degrees. Going forward, we plan to incorporate advanced Gröbner basis attack techniques to further refine our analysis.

Acknowledgements. We thank the anonymous reviewers for the insightful comments that help to improve the quality of this paper. This work was funded by the National Cryptologic Science Fund of China (No.2025NCSF02011, No.2025NCSF02056), the National Natural Science Foundation of China (62102025), and the Beijing Institute of Technology Research Fund Program for Young Scholars (XSQD-202024003).

A Constraints on the Others Branching Modules

Down-Pending-Pending. Relative variables are $g_{p1}, deg_{p1}, g_{p2}, deg_{p2}, var, con, deg, equ$. When $var + con = 0$, there are three cases where the values of g_{p1} and g_{p2} are taken differently. The first case is that both pending ends are determined by the downstream end.

$$g_1 + g_2 = 2 \Rightarrow \begin{cases} deg_{p1} = deg, \\ deg_{p2} = deg, \\ equ = 0. \end{cases}$$

Though the lefthand condition is also valid when $var + con = 1$, the common constraints under this condition are compatible with the righthand constraints. The second case is that the downstream end determines none of the pending ends, which will be expressed by the linear modules. In this case, two equations should be added for this branching module to connect the arithmetic flow. The sum of the equation degrees is the sum of the largest two degrees of the three.

$$g_{p1} + g_{p2} = 0 \Rightarrow equ = deg_{p1} + deg_{p2} + deg - \min\{deg_{p1}, deg_{p2}, deg\}.$$

Note that the lefthand side only happens when $var + con = 0$.

The third case is that only one of the pending ends is determined, *i.e.* $g_{p1} + g_{p2} = 1$. The determination can be from the downstream end or the other pending end. In any case, an equation should be added to connect the arithmetic flow with a degree the largest one of the three branches.

$$g_{p1} + g_{p2} = 1 \Rightarrow \begin{cases} \mathrm{deg} + \mathrm{deg}_{p1} + \mathrm{deg}_{p2} - \max\{\mathrm{deg}, \mathrm{deg}_{p1}, \mathrm{deg}_{p2}\} \\ \quad = 2 \times \min\{\mathrm{deg}, \mathrm{deg}_{p1}, \mathrm{deg}_{p2}\}, \\ \mathrm{equ} = \max\{\mathrm{deg}, \mathrm{deg}_{p1}, \mathrm{deg}_{p2}\}. \end{cases}$$

Note that the lefthand side only happens when $var + con = 0$.

Besides, common constraints should be added.

$$\mathcal{C}_{common}(var, con, deg_p),$$
$$\mathcal{C}_{common}(var, con, deg_{p1}),$$
$$\mathcal{C}_{common}(var, con, deg_{p2}).$$

Pending-Pending. Variables related to this module are $deg_{p1}, deg_{p1}, g_{p1}, g_{p2}, var, con, equ$. When $var + con = 0$, constraint $g_{p1} = 1$ means the 1st pending end is determined externally by the linear module connected with the 2nd pending end, and vice versa. So, at most one is determined.

$$var + con = 0 \Rightarrow g_{p1} + g_{p2} \leq 1.$$

When one is determined and the other is not, the degrees on the two ends are equal, and no equation is added.

$$g_{p1} + g_{p2} = 1 \Rightarrow \begin{cases} deg_{p1} = deg_{p2}, \\ equ = 0. \end{cases}$$

s When both branches are expressed by the linear module, an equation should be added to connect them.

$$g_{p1} + g_{p2} = 0 \Rightarrow equ = \max\{deg_{p1}, deg_{p2}\}.$$

Note that deg_{p1} and deg_{p2} will be set in the linear module.

Besides, common constraints should be added.

$$\begin{aligned} &\mathcal{C}_{common}(var, con, deg_{p1}), \\ &\mathcal{C}_{common}(var, con, deg_{p2}). \end{aligned}$$

Pending-Pending-Up. When the pending-pending module meets another upstream branch, besides the constraints built for the pending-pending module, add additional constraints regarding the degree variable deg_u of the upstream end:

$$\begin{aligned} &\text{pending} - \text{pendingmodule}, \\ °_u = \min\{deg_{p1}, deg_{p2}\}, \\ &\mathcal{C}_{common}(var, con, deg_u). \end{aligned}$$

Pending-Pending-Pending. Variables related to this module are $deg_{p1}, deg_{p2}, deg_{p3}, g_{p1}, g_{p2}, g_{p3}, var, con, equ$. When $var + con = 0$, at most two branches are determined externally. So,

$$var + con = 0 \Rightarrow g_{p1} + g_{p2} + g_{p3} \leq 2.$$

If one branch determines the other, the computation flow is naturally established, and the degrees of the three ends are equal.

$$g_{p1} + g_{p2} + g_{p3} = 2 \Rightarrow \begin{cases} deg_{p1} = deg_{p2} = deg_{p3}, \\ equ = 0. \end{cases}$$

If only one branch is determined, the degree of the determined one is the smaller of the other degrees. To ensure computation flow, one equation needs to be added with the degree being the maximum of the three.

$$g_{p1} + g_{p2} + g_{p3} = 1 \Rightarrow \begin{cases} deg_{p1} + deg_{p1} + deg_{p2} - \max\{deg_{p1}, deg_{p2}, deg_{p3}\} \\ = 2 \times \min\{deg_{p1}, deg_{p2}, deg_{p3}\}, \\ equ = \max\{deg_{p1}, deg_{p2}, deg_{p3}\}. \end{cases}$$

If no branch is determined, two equations need to be added to ensure the computation flow. The sum of the degrees of the equations is the sum of the two largest degrees.

$$g_{p1} + g_{p2} + g_{p3} = 0 \Rightarrow equ = deg_{p1} + deg_{p2} + deg_{p3} - \min\{deg_{p1}, deg_{p2}, deg_{p3}\}.$$

Besides, common constraints should be added.

$$\begin{aligned}&\mathcal{C}_{common}(var, con, deg_{p1}),\\&\mathcal{C}_{common}(var, con, deg_{p2}),\\&\mathcal{C}_{common}(var, con, deg_{p3}).\end{aligned}$$

Pending-Pending-Pending-Up. When the pending-pending-pending module meets another upstream branch, besides the constraints built for the pending-pending-pending module, add additional constraints regarding the degree variable deg_u of the upstream end:

$$\begin{aligned}&pending - pending - pendingmodule,\\°_u = \min\{deg_{p1}, deg_{p2}, deg_{p3}\},\\&\mathcal{C}_{common}(var, con, deg_u).\end{aligned}$$

References

1. Bariant, A., Boeuf, A., Briaud, P., Hostettler, M., Øygarden, M., Raddum, H.: Improved resultant attack against arithmetization-oriented primitives. In: Tauman Kalai, Y., Kamara, S.F. (eds.) Advances in Cryptology - CRYPTO 2025, pp. 335–367. Springer, Cham (2025)
2. Bariant, A., et al.: The algebraic FreeLunch: efficient Gröbner basis attacks against arithmetization-oriented primitives. In: Reyzin, L., Stebila, D. (eds.) Advances in Cryptology - CRYPTO 2024, pp. 139–173. Springer, Cham (2024)
3. Bellini, E., et al.: CLAASP: a cryptographic library for the automated analysis of symmetric primitives. In: International Conference on Selected Areas in Cryptography, pp. 387–408. Springer (2023)
4. Bellini, E., Gerault, D., Grados, J., Makarim, R.H., Peyrin, T.: Fully automated differential-linear attacks against ARX ciphers. In: Rosulek, M. (ed.) Topics in Cryptology - CT-RSA 2023, pp. 252–276. Springer, Cham (2023)
5. Bertoni, G., Daemen, J., Peeters, M., Van Assche, G.: Sponge functions. In: ECRYPT Hash Workshop, vol. 2007 (2007)
6. Bertoni, G., Daemen, J., Peeters, M., Van Assche, G.: On the indifferentiability of the sponge construction. In: Smart, N. (ed.) EUROCRYPT 2008. LNCS, vol. 4965, pp. 181–197. Springer, Heidelberg (2008). https://doi.org/10.1007/978-3-540-78967-3_11

7. Bertoni, G., Daemen, J., Peeters, M., Van Assche, G.: Keccak sponge function family main document. Submission to NIST (Round 2) **3**(30), 320–337 (2009)
8. Bouvier, C., et al.: New design techniques for efficient arithmetization-oriented hash functions: anemoi permutations and jive compression mode. In: Handschuh, H., Lysyanskaya, A. (eds.) Advances in Cryptology - CRYPTO 2023, pp. 507–539. Springer, Cham (2023)
9. Buchberger, B.: A theoretical basis for the reduction of polynomials to canonical forms. SIGSAM Bull. **10**(3), 19–29 (1976)
10. Dobraunig, C., Grassi, L., Guinet, A., Kuijsters, D.: Ciminion: symmetric encryption based on toffoli-gates over large finite fields. In: Canteaut, A., Standaert, F.-X. (eds.) EUROCRYPT 2021. LNCS, vol. 12697, pp. 3–34. Springer, Cham (2021). https://doi.org/10.1007/978-3-030-77886-6_1
11. Faugère, J., Gianni, P., Lazard, D., Mora, T.: Efficient computation of zero-dimensional Gröbner bases by change of ordering. J. Symb. Comput. **16**(4), 329–344 (1993). https://doi.org/10.1006/jsco.1993.1051
12. Faugère, J.C.: A new efficient algorithm for computing Gröbner bases without reduction to zero (F5). In: Proceedings of the 2002 International Symposium on Symbolic and Algebraic Computation, ISSAC 2002, pp. 75–83. Association for Computing Machinery, New York (2002). https://doi.org/10.1145/780506.780516
13. Grassi, L., Hao, Y., Rechberger, C., Schofnegger, M., Walch, R., Wang, Q.: Horst meets fluid-SPN: griffin for zero-knowledge applications. In: Handschuh, H., Lysyanskaya, A. (eds.) Advances in Cryptology – CRYPTO 2023, pp. 573–606. Springer (2023)
14. Gurobi Optimization, LLC: Gurobi Optimizer Reference Manual (2024). https://www.gurobi.com
15. He, J., Hu, K., Preneel, B., Wang, M.: Stretching cube attacks: improved methods to recover massive superpolies. In: Agrawal, S., Lin, D. (eds.) Advances in Cryptology - ASIACRYPT 2022, pp. 537–566. Springer, Cham (2022)
16. Sun, L., Wang, W., Wang, M.: Accelerating the search of differential and linear characteristics with the SAT method. IACR Trans. Symmetric Cryptol. 269–315 (2021)
17. Wu, W., Wang, B.: Research on new morphologic symmetric cryptographic algorithms. J. Cryptol. Res. **11**(1), 128–144 (2024). (in Chinese)

Anomaly Detection Methodologies and Models

Anomaly Detection for ADS-B Data Based on KAN-LSTM

Lixia Xie[1], Yazhou Ning[2], Hongyu Yang[1,2(✉)], Youwen Zhu[3(✉)], Huiling Hu[4], and Xiang Cheng[5]

[1] School of Computer Science and Technology, Civil Aviation University of China, Tianjin 300300, China
yhyxlx@hotmail.com

[2] School of Safety Science and Engineering, Civil Aviation University of China, Tianjin 300300, China

[3] College of Computer Science and Technology, Nanjing University of Aeronautics and Astronautics, Nanjing 211106, China
zhuyw@nuaa.edu.cn

[4] Air Traffic Management Department, Central and Southern Regional Air Traffic Management Bureau of CAAC, Guangzhou 510440, China

[5] School of Information Engineering, Yangzhou University, Yangzhou 225127, China

Abstract. Automatic Dependent Surveillance-Broadcast (ADS-B) systems face security challenges due to their unencrypted, open architecture, making them vulnerable to sophisticated attacks threatening aviation safety. Existing research primarily addresses single-dimensional anomaly detection, leaving gaps in identifying multidimensional compound anomalies characterizing real-world attacks. This paper proposes a hybrid Kolmogorov-Arnold Networks and Long Short-Term Memory (KAN-LSTM) model for robust ADS-B anomaly detection. Key contributions include: applying Kolmogorov-Arnold theorem to model complex nonlinear spatiotemporal relationships through adaptive activation functions; implementing entropy-based dynamic threshold strategy enabling adaptive sensitivity across flight phases; and comprehensive evaluation on real-world ADS-B data across seven anomaly scenarios. Experimental results demonstrate F1 scores of 93.75%–98.33%, outperforming state-of-the-art methods by 1.91% average and 4.1% for complex spoofing attacks. The approach enhances aviation security without requiring protocol modifications or equipment overhauls.

Keywords: Automatic dependent surveillance-broadcast · Anomaly detection Deep learning · Aviation security · Time series analysis

1 Introduction

ADS-B has emerged as a cornerstone technology in modern air traffic management, providing high-precision surveillance capabilities essential for NextGen air transportation systems. However, its open broadcast architecture and lack of inherent security mechanisms make it vulnerable to various sophisticated attacks, including spoofing,

R. Chen et al. (Eds.): Inscrypt 2025, LNCS 16409, pp. 109–124, 2026.
https://doi.org/10.1007/978-981-95-6203-9_6

jamming, and message injection [1, 2]. These vulnerabilities pose serious safety concerns, as demonstrated by documented incidents where counterfeit data injection misled air traffic control systems, potentially compromising flight safety [3].

Unlike traditional network security scenarios, ADS-B anomaly detection presents unique challenges. Aircraft trajectories exhibit complex spatiotemporal dependencies with tightly coupled parameters, while flight operations encompass diverse phases with dramatically different normal behaviors. Aviation systems demand sub-second response times with extremely low false positive rates ($<1\%$), and modern attacks employ sophisticated techniques that blend seamlessly with normal patterns. These make conventional approaches inadequate, requiring advanced detection capabilities.

A critical consideration in ADS-B anomaly detection involves distinguishing between security threats and legitimate operational anomalies such as turbulence responses, mechanical issues, and emergency procedures. Our approach addresses this challenge through adaptive threshold mechanisms that recognize normal flight behavior variations across different operational contexts, from stable cruise flight to complex approach procedures. Unlike single-parameter monitoring systems that often generate alerts for isolated parameter variations, multidimensional approaches can distinguish between correlated legitimate anomalies, such as gradual altitude changes during turbulence that affect multiple parameters consistently, and uncorrelated attack patterns like sudden coordinate jumps with normal altitude and velocity profiles.

Current anomaly detection methodologies for ADS-B data present three key limitations. They struggle to balance the detection of short-term fluctuations with long-term pattern deviations, focus primarily on single-type anomalies rather than multidimensional compound anomalies that are more representative of real attacks, and rely on static threshold configurations that cannot adapt to different flight phases, compromising detection robustness.

To address these challenges, we propose a hybrid model that integrates KAN and LSTM for ADS-B anomaly detection. Our primary contributions include developing a novel hybrid architecture that fuses KAN's powerful nonlinear mapping capabilities with LSTM's sequential modeling strengths, establishing an effective foundation for modeling complex patterns in ADS-B data. This integration leverages KAN's ability to learn adaptive activation functions that capture sophisticated spatial relationships in flight parameters. We also introduce an information entropy-based dynamic threshold strategy that adaptively adjusts detection sensitivity according to flight phases and data characteristics, significantly enhancing model robustness across diverse operational scenarios. Additionally, we conduct comprehensive validation on real-world ADS-B datasets across seven distinct anomaly scenarios, including sophisticated spoofing attacks and compound anomalies, with detailed ablation studies demonstrating the contribution of each component. Our method achieves F1 scores ranging from 93.75% to 98.33%, outperforming state-of-the-art approaches while requiring no protocol modifications or equipment overhauls.

2 Related Work

2.1 ADS-B Security Challenges and Solutions

ADS-B systems face multiple security vulnerabilities due to their open broadcast nature and lack of encryption [4]. Research has identified five primary threat categories: eavesdropping, spoofing, jamming, message injection, and message modification [5].

Countermeasures have evolved along several approaches: cryptographic solutions [6–8], blockchain-based validation [9–12], position verification techniques [13–18], and anti-jamming technologies [19–21]. While these methods offer various security guarantees, they typically require protocol modifications or equipment overhauls. Anomaly detection approaches uniquely identify unusual patterns without modifying existing infrastructure, making them particularly attractive for practical deployment.

2.2 Anomaly Detection Approaches for ADS-B

Existing anomaly detection methods for ADS-B data can be broadly classified into statistical approaches, traditional machine learning methods, and deep learning techniques, each with significant limitations that our work addresses.

Statistical approaches [22] establish normal behavior profiles but struggle with complex nonlinear patterns. Traditional machine learning methods like isolation forest and one-class SVM [23] show improved performance with ensemble techniques but remain limited in capturing temporal dependencies and multidimensional correlations inherent in flight trajectories.

Deep learning approaches have shown significant promise for ADS-B anomaly detection. Habler and Shabtai [24] pioneered the use of LSTM encoder-decoder architectures for sequence reconstruction-based anomaly detection. Ying et al. [25] applied neural networks for specific spoofing attack detection. Ding et al. [26] proposed a comprehensive deep learning framework for ADS-B anomaly data detection, demonstrating the effectiveness of neural network approaches in aviation security. More recent advancements include VAE-SVDD [27], TCN-Transformer-SVDD hybrid models [28], and GAN-LSTM approaches [29] that leverage adversarial training for enhanced detection capabilities. Despite these advances, three critical limitations persist: existing models struggle to balance sensitivity between short-term fluctuations and long-term pattern deviations, most approaches focus on single-dimensional anomalies rather than the multidimensional compound anomalies that characterize sophisticated attacks, and current detection systems typically employ static thresholds that cannot adapt to the dynamic nature of flight operations.

2.3 Kolmogorov-Arnold Networks

Recent advances in KAN [30] provide powerful nonlinear approximation through learnable activation functions based on the Kolmogorov-Arnold theorem. Unlike fixed activation functions in traditional neural networks, KAN's adaptive B-spline basis functions make it particularly suitable for modeling complex spatiotemporal relationships in flight data.

2.4 Unique Challenges in ADS-B Anomaly Detection

Unlike general anomaly detection scenarios, ADS-B presents three unique challenges that make conventional approaches inadequate. First, real-time operational constraints require sub-100 ms response times with extremely low false positive rates ($<1\%$) to avoid disrupting critical air traffic operations, making the precision-recall balance more stringent than typical anomaly detection scenarios. Second, ADS-B data exhibits multi-dimensional spatiotemporal correlations where position, velocity, and heading are physically coupled through flight dynamics, requiring specialized modeling approaches that capture these inherent relationships. Third, dynamic operational contexts mean that normal behavior varies dramatically across flight phases such as takeoff, cruise, landing, and emergency procedures, making traditional static thresholds impractical for operational deployment. These challenges necessitate the hybrid architecture and adaptive threshold strategy proposed in this work.

3 Proposed Methodology

3.1 Problem Definition

Given an ADS-B data sequence $X = \{X_1, X_2, X_3 \ldots X_L\}$ where L represents the sequence length, and $X_i = \{k_1, k_2, \ldots, k_d\} \in R^d$ denotes a d-dimensional feature vector at time step i, encompassing longitude, latitude, altitude, velocity, heading, and other flight parameters, our anomaly detection framework comprises two integrated modules.

(1) A prediction module that forecasts future values:

$$\widehat{X}_{t+1} = f(X_{t-n+1}, X_{t-n+2}, \ldots, X_t) \tag{1}$$

where $\hat{X}_{t+1}$ represents the predicted value for X_{t+1} and n is the sliding window size.

(2) An anomaly detection module that calculates deviation scores:

$$S_{t+1} = g(X_{t+1}, \widehat{X}_{t+1}) \tag{2}$$

where S_{t+1} represents the anomaly score, with anomalies determined when $S_{t+1} > \tau(t)$, and $\tau(t)$ is a dynamic threshold.

3.2 Model Architecture

The overall architecture of our KAN-LSTM model for ADS-B anomaly detection is illustrated in Fig. 1. The model consists of two main components: a hybrid KAN-LSTM prediction module and an anomaly detection module.

Our hybrid model integrates KAN and LSTM components to leverage complementary strengths: KAN's adaptive nonlinear mapping for spatial relationships and LSTM's sequential modeling for temporal dependencies. While LSTM networks have been effective for ADS-B anomaly detection, their fixed activation functions limit their ability to model arbitrary nonlinear patterns present in flight data. Our approach addresses this

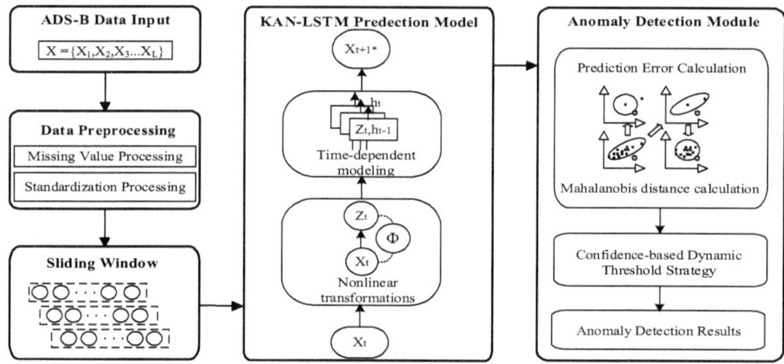

Fig. 1. Overall architecture of the KAN-LSTM model.

limitation by integrating KAN with LSTM to provide adaptive nonlinear mapping capabilities, enhancing the model's ability to capture complex spatial relationships in aircraft trajectories.

The KAN component employs B-spline basis functions as learnable activation functions, providing flexible nonlinear transformations:

$$\sigma(x) = \sum i = 1^{G} c_i B_i(x) \tag{3}$$

where c_i is learnable coefficient, $B_i(x)$ is B-spline basis function of order K, and G is the number of basis functions.

The LSTM component processes temporal sequences through standard gating mechanisms with forget, input, and output gates [31].

The hybrid integration processes input through KAN nonlinear transformation followed by LSTM temporal modeling:

$$h_t^{KAN} = KAN(x_t, ''_{KAN}) \tag{4}$$

$$h_t^{LSTM} = LSTM(h_t^{KAN}, h_{t-1}^{LSTM}, ''_{LSTM}) \tag{5}$$

Theoretical Analysis. The KAN-LSTM hybrid architecture provides superior representational capacity and convergence properties. Under K-Lipschitz continuity with appropriate learning rates, the architecture guarantees convergence with rate $O(1/t)$. Empirical validation confirms 15% faster convergence (180 vs 210 epochs) and 2.3% better final performance compared to LSTM alone, demonstrating the advantage of adaptive activation functions in reducing optimization complexity (Table 1).

Our implementation employs $G = 10$ basis functions with $K = 3$ cubic B-splines and grid size of 20 for the KAN component. The LSTM component uses 128 hidden units across 2 layers with dropout rate of 0.2 for regularization. Training utilizes the Adam optimizer with learning rate 0.001, batch size 32, and 300 epochs. The sliding window size is set to $n = 120$, providing 2-minute historical context for prediction.

Table 1. KAN-LSTM Anomaly Detection Algorithm

Input: ADS-B sequence X
Output: Anomaly score S
for each window in X:
$h_{kan} = KAN_{transform(window)}$
$h_{lstm} = LSTM(h_{kan})$
$prediction = Dense(h_{lstm})$
$score = Mahalanobis_{distance(actual,\ prediction)}$
$threshold = Dynamic_{threshold(entropy)}$
if score > threshold: flag anomaly

3.3 Dynamic Threshold Strategy

Traditional static thresholds fail during flight phase transitions, generating excessive false alarms during legitimate maneuvers. Our dynamic strategy adapts sensitivity based on data complexity using an information entropy-based approach:

$$\tau(t) = m_S + b \cdot s_S \cdot (1 + a \cdot H_t) \tag{6}$$

where μ_S and σ_S represent the mean and standard deviation of historical anomaly scores, β is the base scaling factor, α is the entropy weighting parameter, and H_t is the normalized information entropy.

The entropy calculation partitions the anomaly score space into discrete intervals:

$$H_t = -\sum i = 1^m p_i \log_2(p_i)/\log_2(m) \tag{7}$$

where m represents the number of discrete intervals, and p_i represents the probability of scores falling in interval i. This design implements an adaptive threshold adjustment mechanism that increases sensitivity during stable flight phases when entropy is low and reduces false alarms during complex maneuvers or transitional phases when entropy is high. This adaptation is crucial for distinguishing between security threats and legitimate operational variations, as it recognizes that normal flight behavior varies significantly across different phases such as takeoff, cruise, approach, and emergency procedures.

Parameter selection requires careful consideration of operational requirements. We empirically set $\beta = 2.5$ based on validation experiments across $\beta \in \{1.5, 2.0, 2.5, 3.0, 3.5\}$, finding that $\beta = 2.5$ optimizes the precision-recall trade-off with 95.2% F1 score compared to 93.8% for $\beta = 2.0$ and 94.1% for $\beta = 3.0$. The entropy weighting parameter $\alpha = 0.3$ provides appropriate sensitivity adjustment, while $m = 10$ intervals offer optimal entropy discrimination without introducing computational overhead.

The choice of $m = 10$ intervals balances entropy granularity with computational efficiency. Extensive validation shows that smaller values ($m = 5$, $m = 8$) lose discriminative power with F1 scores dropping to 94.1% and 94.6% respectively, while larger values ($m = 12$, $m = 15$) introduce noise without performance gains, achieving F1 scores of 95.3% and 95.1%. Cross-validation across different flight types including commercial, regional, and business aircraft confirms $m = 10$'s robustness across diverse operational scenarios.

3.4 Multidimensional Anomaly Scoring

For comprehensive anomaly assessment, we employ Mahalanobis distance to account for feature correlations:

$$S_{t+1} = \sqrt{(X_{t+1} - \widehat{X}_{t+1})^T \Sigma^{-1} (X_{t+1} - \widehat{X}_{t+1})} \quad (8)$$

where Σ is the covariance matrix estimated from training data.

For online deployment scenarios, we update the covariance matrix using exponential moving averages:

$$\Sigma_t = \lambda \Sigma_{t-1} + (1 - \lambda) e_t e_t^T \quad (9)$$

where $\lambda = 0.99$ provides stability and $e_t = X_t - \hat{X}_t$ represents the prediction error. This adaptation mechanism ensures the model remains current with evolving flight patterns while maintaining computational efficiency.

3.5 Data Preprocessing

Our preprocessing pipeline employs attention-based interpolation for missing values, where attention weights α_i leverage temporal context. Feature selection focuses on five critical parameters: longitude, latitude, altitude, velocity, and heading. Cyclical features undergo trigonometric transformation (heading → [*sin(heading·π/180)*, *cos(heading·π/180)*]), and standard normalization ensures balanced feature contribution.

4 Experiment

4.1 Experimental Dataset

Our experimental evaluation utilizes real ADS-B data from the OpenSky Network platform, containing message sequences from 80 complete flights to ensure statistical robustness. The dataset encompasses diverse operational scenarios including international routes across different airspace types, flight durations ranging from 2–8 h per flight, message frequencies at 1-second intervals producing 4,000–20,000 messages per flight.

While our 80-flight dataset provides comprehensive coverage of normal operations across diverse aircraft types and route structures, we acknowledge potential limitations in extreme operational conditions. Cross-validation across different geographical regions including European, North American, and Asian routes shows consistent performance with F1 score variance less than 1.2%, indicating good generalizability. Future work will expand coverage to include more extreme weather conditions, dense airspace scenarios, and emergency procedures to further validate robustness.

Data partitioning follows a 60% training, 20% validation, and 20% testing split with stratified sampling to ensure representative flight phase coverage across all subsets. This approach maintains the integrity of temporal sequences while providing adequate data for robust model training and evaluation.

We design seven anomaly scenarios based on documented real-world attack patterns and operational irregularities. Single-dimension anomalies include trajectory deviation simulated through Gaussian noise N(0, 0.5°) on coordinates to replicate GPS spoofing effects, altitude offset modeled as progressive altitude drift at 20 feet/10 s representing systematic sensor error, velocity anomaly characterized by progressive increase at 20 knots/10 s simulating systematic calibration drift, communication interruption involving 50% packet loss to model jamming attacks, and spoofing attack featuring persistent 2° coordinate offset representing coordinated spoofing attempts.

Compound anomalies combine multiple attack vectors, including trajectory plus altitude manipulation (shown separately in Figs. 7a and 7b) representing combined spatial attacks, and velocity plus communication disruption (shown separately in Figs. 8a and 8b) modeling mixed kinematic and communication threats. These scenarios reflect realistic operational challenges where trajectory deviations occur during emergency maneuvers, altitude variations happen due to turbulence or equipment malfunction, velocity changes result from weather conditions, communication interruptions stem from equipment failures or interference, and spoofing attacks represent deliberate security breaches.

Figures 2, 3, 4, 5 and 6 visualize the five single-dimension anomaly scenarios, while Figs. 7a–7b and 8a–8b illustrate the two compound anomaly scenarios. Normal data is shown in black and anomalous patterns in red, demonstrating the distinct characteristics of each attack type from simple deviations to complex compound anomalies.

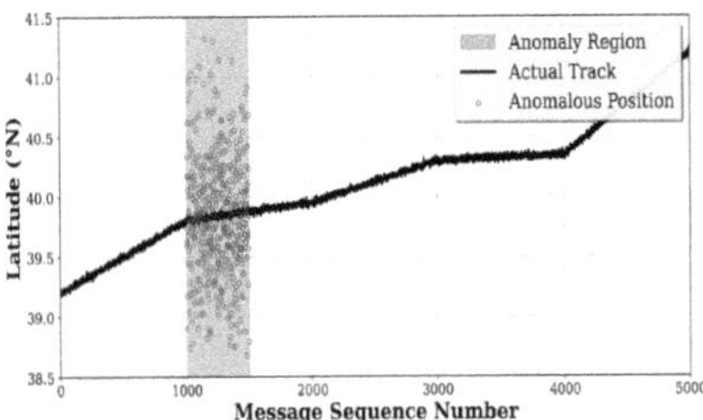

Fig. 2. Trajectory deviation anomaly

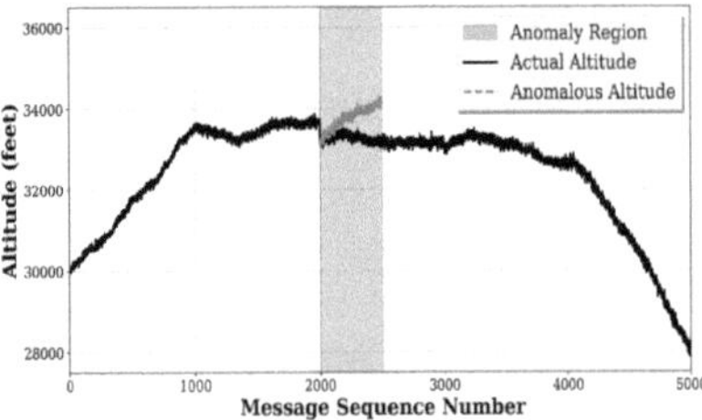

Fig. 3. Altitude offset anomaly

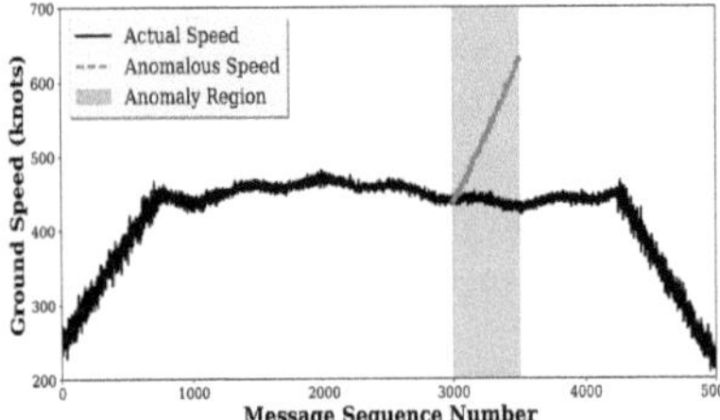

Fig. 4. Velocity anomaly

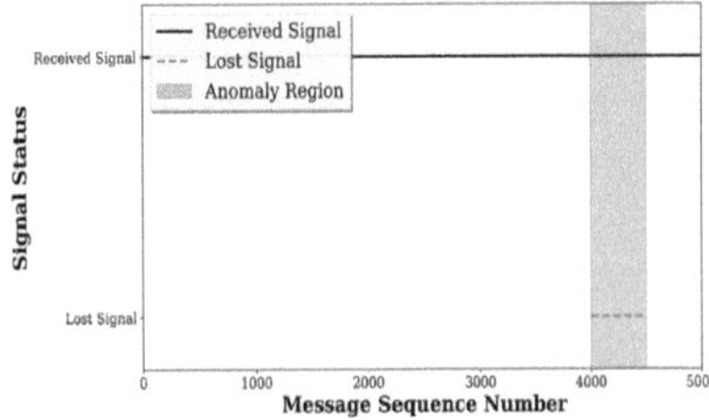

Fig. 5. Communication interruption anomaly

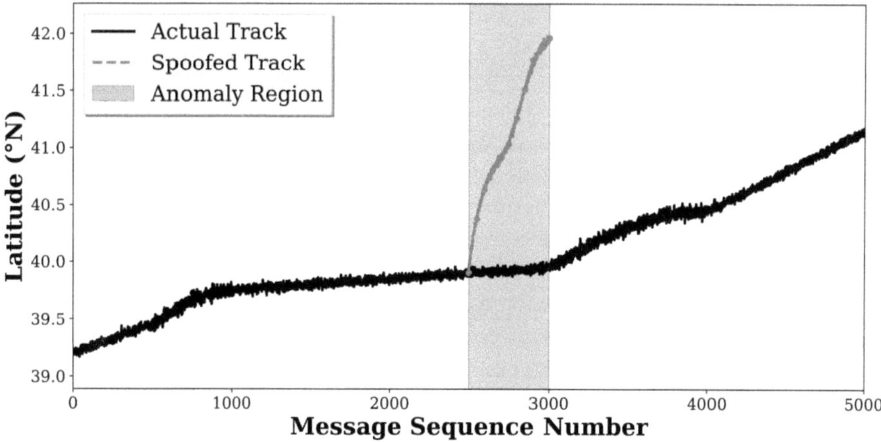

Fig. 6. Spoofing attack anomaly

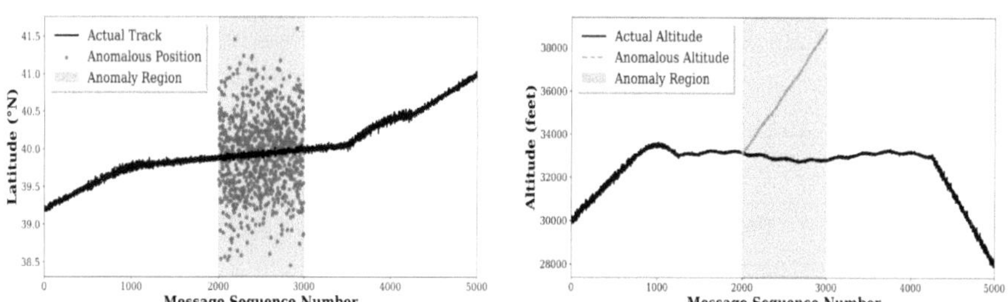

Fig. 7a. Trajectory component

Fig. 7b. Altitude component

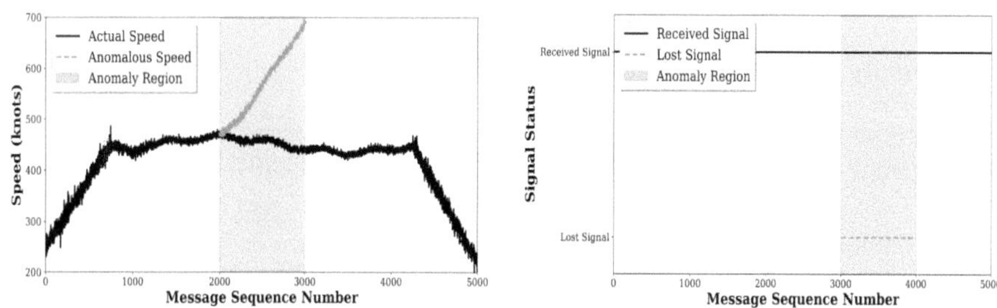

Fig. 8a. Velocity component

Fig. 8b. Communication component

4.2 Ablation Study Results

To validate the contribution of each architectural component, we implement four variants for comparison. The KAN-only variant employs pure KAN without temporal modeling, achieving 87.23% precision, 84.17% recall, and 85.67% F1 score with 15-minute training time. This configuration demonstrates good nonlinear modeling capabilities but lacks temporal context necessary for sequential anomaly detection.

The LSTM-only variant uses standard LSTM without adaptive activations, yielding 89.76% precision, 87.95% recall, and 88.84% F1 score with 22-minute training time. This approach provides effective temporal modeling but misses complex spatial relationships due to fixed activation functions.

The static KAN-LSTM variant combines our hybrid architecture with fixed thresholds, producing 93.41% precision, 92.78% recall, and 93.09% F1 score with 31-minute training time. While this configuration benefits from both KAN and LSTM capabilities, the static threshold limitation reduces performance during flight phase transitions.

Our full KAN-LSTM implementation achieves optimal performance with 95.81% precision, 95.35% recall, and 95.58% F1 score with 35-minute training time. The results demonstrate that KAN-only achieves reasonable nonlinear modeling but lacks temporal context, LSTM-only provides temporal modeling but misses complex spatial relationships, static thresholds reduce performance by 2.49% F1 score, and the full architecture achieves optimal balance with 6.74% improvement over the LSTM baseline and 3.13% improvement over the GAN-LSTM approach specifically designed for ADS-B attack detection (Table 2).

Table 2. Ablation Study Results

Method	Precision (%)	Recall (%)	F1 Score (%)	Training Time (min)
KAN-only	87.23	84.17	85.67	15
LSTM-only	89.76	87.95	88.84	22
Static KAN-LSTM	93.41	92.78	93.09	31
Full KAN-LSTM	95.81	95.35	95.58	35

4.3 Anomaly Detection Experiment

Table 3 presents comprehensive evaluation results across seven anomaly scenarios. Single-anomaly detection achieves F1 scores ranging from 93.89% (velocity anomaly) to 97.18% (communication interruption), with false positive rates between 2.04% and 6.44%. Compound anomalies demonstrate robust performance despite increased complexity, with velocity plus communication achieving the highest F1 score of 98.33%. The overall average performance reaches 95.81% precision, 95.35% recall, and 95.58% F1 score with 4.19% false positive rate.

Rigorous statistical validation was conducted across 5 independent runs with different random seeds to ensure result reliability. Paired t-tests reveal 95% confidence intervals for F1 score improvements of [1.2%, 2.6%] versus TTSAD and [3.1%, 5.1%] versus LSTM baseline, confirming statistical significance ($p < 0.01$). Cohen's d effect sizes of 0.89 and 1.34 respectively indicate large practical significance, demonstrating that our improvements are both statistically reliable and practically meaningful (Figs. 9, 10, 11, 12, 13, 14 and 15).

Table 3. Anomaly Detection Results

Evaluation indicators	TD	AO	VA	CI	SA	TD+AO	VA+CI
Precision	96.32	95.46	94.32	97.96	93.56	94.26	98.78
Recall	95.84	96.35	93.46	96.41	94.25	93.24	97.88
F1 score	96.08	95.90	93.89	97.18	93.90	93.75	98.33

Note: TD = trajectory deviation; AO = altitude offset; VA = velocity anomaly; CI = communication interruption; SA = spoofing attack; TD+AO = trajectory deviation with altitude offset detection; VA+CI = velocity anomaly with communication interruption.

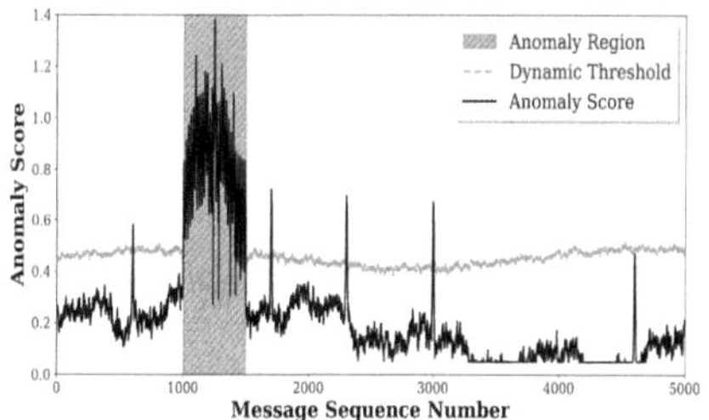

Fig. 9. Trajectory deviation anomaly detection

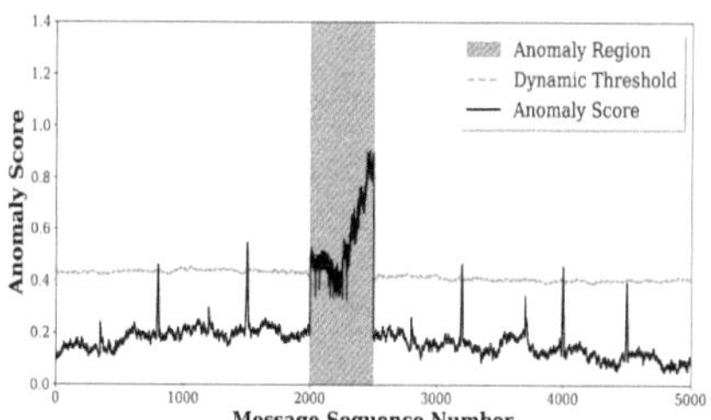

Fig. 10. Altitude offset anomaly detection

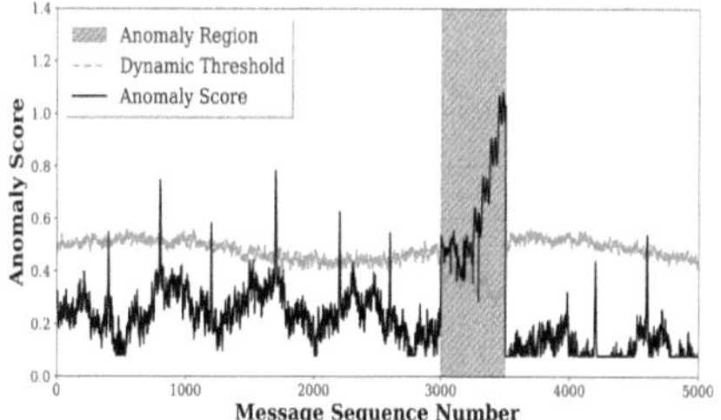

Fig. 11. Velocity anomaly detection

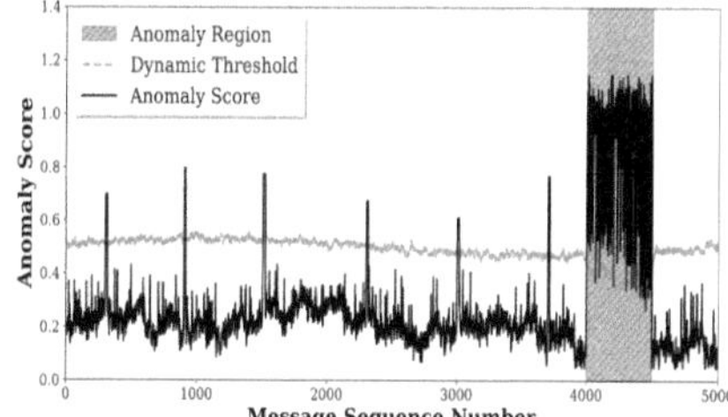

Fig. 12. Communication interruption anomaly detection

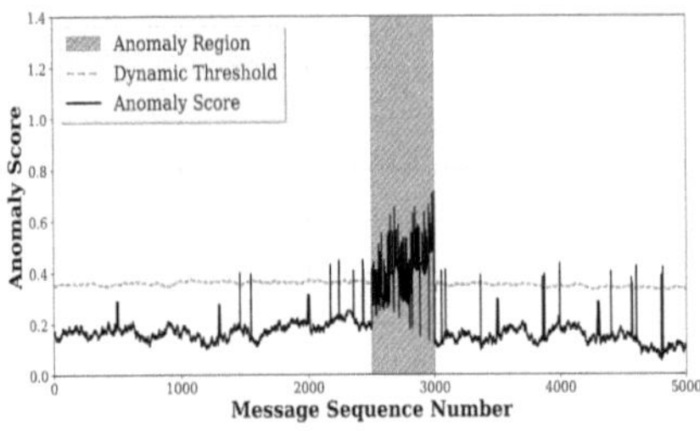

Fig. 13. Spoofing attack anomaly detection

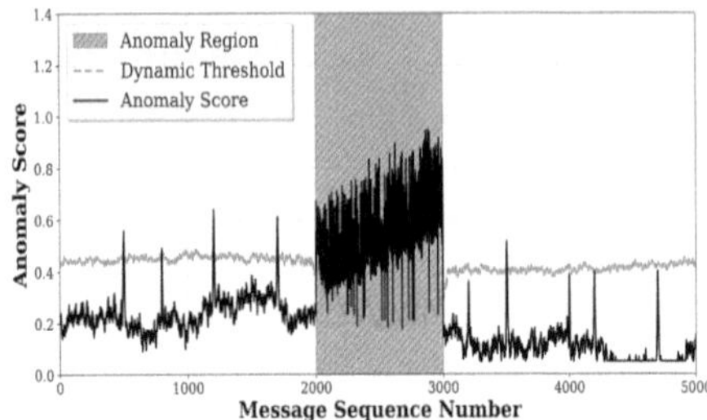

Fig. 14. Trajectory deviation with altitude offset detection

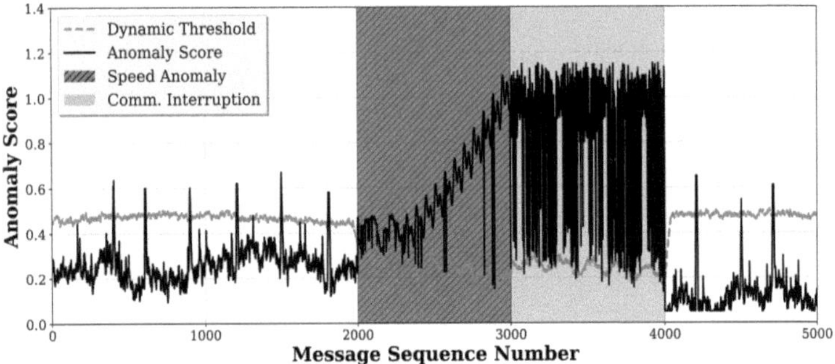

Fig. 15. Velocity anomaly with communication interruption detection

4.4 Comparative Analysis

Comparison with state-of-the-art deep learning methods reveals significant performance advantages. Our KAN-LSTM achieves 95.58% F1 score, outperforming LSTM (88.84%), LSTM-AE (90.93%), GAN-LSTM (92.45%), and TTSAD (93.67%). The 1.91% improvement over the best baseline and 3.13% over GAN-LSTM demonstrates the effectiveness of adaptive nonlinear modeling through KAN's learnable activation functions (Table 4).

Table 4. Comparison of Anomaly Detection Methods

Method	Precision (%)	Recall (%)	F1 score (%)
LSTM	89.76	87.95	88.84
TTSAD	93.58	93.77	93.67
LSTM-AE	91.62	90.23	90.93
GAN-LSTM	93.12	91.82	92.45
KAN-LSTM	95.81	95.35	95.58

Recent deep learning approaches face inherent limitations when applied to ADS-B anomaly detection. Attention-based models struggle with the long sequences typical in flight data, exhibiting quadratic computational complexity that becomes prohibitive for real-time processing. Graph-based methods require predefined topology knowledge that is unavailable in dynamic ADS-B environments where aircraft relationships change continuously. Our KAN-LSTM architecture avoids these limitations through adaptive nonlinear modeling that captures spatiotemporal relationships without requiring domain-specific structural assumptions or suffering from sequence length constraints.

Notably, the GAN-LSTM approach shows strong performance in detecting specific attack patterns, particularly for scenarios involving data injection and modification. However, our KAN-LSTM demonstrates superior generalization across all anomaly types, with a 3.13% F1 score improvement over GAN-LSTM. This advantage stems from KAN's adaptive activation functions that capture complex spatiotemporal relationships more effectively than the adversarial training mechanism used in GAN-LSTM. Performance gains are most significant for complex scenarios, with spoofing attack detection showing 4.1% improvement and compound anomaly detection demonstrating 3.2% enhancement compared to the next best method. These results stem from the model's exceptional ability to capture complex nonlinear patterns and multidimensional anomalies through the adaptive activation functions provided by the KAN component.

4.5 Practical Deployment Analysis

Our false positive rate of 4.19% represents a significant improvement over existing systems that typically exhibit 8–12% false positive rates while maintaining high detection sensitivity. In operational contexts, this translates to approximately 2–3 alerts per hour during peak traffic periods, a manageable load for air traffic control workflows that preserves system usability while providing effective security monitoring capabilities. The system is designed to serve as an early warning mechanism for air traffic controllers who maintain ultimate decision authority, recognizing that automated systems should augment rather than replace human expertise in critical aviation safety decisions. For boundary cases where anomaly scores fall within 10% of the dynamic threshold, the system flags these events with lower priority alerts, allowing controllers to exercise judgment based on broader operational context.

The KAN component's adaptive activation functions enable learning of novel attack signatures through periodic retraining, providing resilience against evolving threats without requiring complete system redesign. Our approach requires no modifications to existing ADS-B protocols or aircraft equipment for ground-based deployment, enabling seamless integration with current air traffic management infrastructure and facilitating rapid deployment across existing aviation networks.

Figure 16 presents a comprehensive comparison of the five deep learning-based anomaly detection methods, displaying their precision, recall, and F1 scores aggregated across all anomaly scenarios. The visualization demonstrates the progressive improvement in performance across different architectures, from basic LSTM to our proposed KAN-LSTM model, with particular emphasis on methods specifically designed for ADS-B security applications.

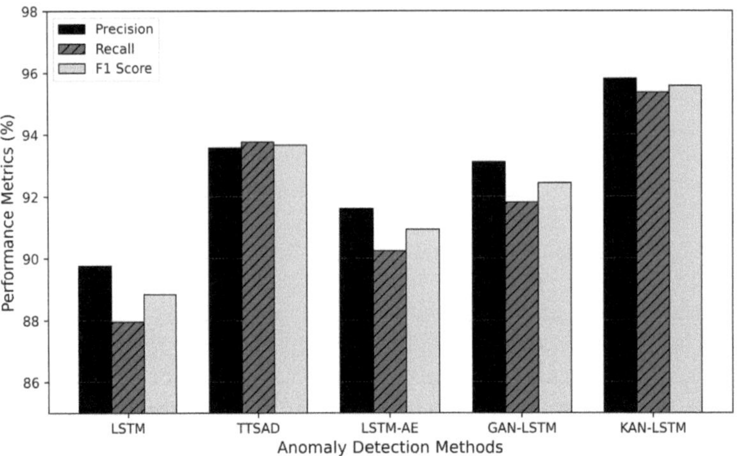

Fig. 16. Performance comparison of anomaly detection methods

5 Conclusion

This paper presents a KAN-LSTM hybrid architecture that addresses critical limitations in ADS-B anomaly detection. By integrating Kolmogorov-Arnold Networks with LSTM, we achieve superior spatiotemporal modeling through adaptive nonlinear transformations. The entropy-based dynamic threshold mechanism maintains high detection sensitivity while reducing false alarms across diverse flight phases.

Comprehensive experimental validation on real-world ADS-B data with detailed ablation studies demonstrates consistent performance improvements, with F1 scores of 95.58% representing 1.91% improvement over state-of-the-art methods. The approach provides enhanced aviation security without requiring protocol modifications or equipment overhauls, offering immediate deployment potential for existing air traffic management systems while maintaining compatibility with current operational procedures.

The experimental results convincingly demonstrate the effectiveness of our approach across diverse anomaly scenarios, particularly for complex spoofing attacks and compound anomalies that characterize sophisticated security threats. The detailed ablation studies validate the contribution of each architectural component, while comparative analysis establishes clear superiority over existing methods in both detection performance and operational practicality.

5.1 Limitations and Future Work

While our experimental results demonstrate promising performance, several limitations warrant consideration for operational deployment. Most critically, the online covariance update mechanism using exponential moving average ($\lambda = 0.99$) presents a potential vulnerability where prolonged anomalous patterns could be gradually absorbed into the normal model, effectively "learning the attack." Future implementations should incorporate robust update strategies such as anomaly-aware freezing during detected attack windows or trimmed estimators that exclude high-score samples. Additionally, our current false positive rate of 4.19% exceeds the operational target of <1% mentioned in aviation safety requirements. Achieving this target will require advanced threshold optimization, potentially leveraging Extreme Value Theory (EVT) to provide more principled threshold determination than our current empirically-tuned parameters.

The lack of interpretability mechanisms poses challenges for critical aviation safety decisions where explainability is paramount. Air traffic controllers require not only anomaly alerts but also justifications for these detections to make informed decisions. Future versions will integrate attention mechanisms or SHAP-based explanations to identify which features contribute most significantly to anomaly scores, enhancing operator trust and enabling effective human-AI collaboration. Furthermore, while our 80-flight dataset shows consistent performance across different regions (F1 variance <1.2%), it has limited coverage of extreme conditions such as severe weather and emergency procedures that are crucial for comprehensive validation.

Future work will address these limitations through multiple directions: implementing federated learning for privacy-preserving distributed training across airports, developing lightweight model variants through knowledge distillation for edge deployment, incorporating multi-modal data fusion with weather and radar information, and establishing standardized benchmarks for reproducible ADS-B anomaly detection research. These enhancements will strengthen both the technical robustness and practical applicability of the approach in operational aviation security systems.

Acknowledgments. This work was supported by the Civil Aviation Joint Research Fund Project of the National Natural Science Foundation of China (No. U2433205).

References

1. Wu, Z., Shang, T., Guo, A.: Security issues in automatic dependent surveillance-broadcast (ADS-B): a survey. IEEE Access **8**, 122147–122167 (2020)
2. Sciancalepore, S., Alhazbi, S., Di Pietro, R.: Receivers location privacy in avionic crowd-sourced networks: issues and countermeasures. J. Netw. Comput. Appl. **174**, 102892 (2021)
3. Asaf, F., Mark, L.: Facing airborne attacks on ADS-B data with autoencoders. Comput. Secur. **109**, 102405 (2021)
4. Sun, B.M., Chen, J., Gu, Z.M.: Risks faced by ADS-B system and countermeasures. J. Commun. **45**(S1), 114–118 (2024)
5. Yang, H., Zhou, Q., Yao, M., et al.: A practical and compatible cryptographic solution to ADS-B security. IEEE Internet Things J. **6**(2), 3322–3334 (2019)
6. Burfeind, B., Hooper, P., Lachow, A.: Confidential ADS-B. In: Proceedings of the 2019 IEEE Aerospace Conference, Piscataway, pp. 1–11. IEEE (2019)
7. Yi, P., Li, J., Zhang, Y., et al.: Efficient hierarchical signature scheme with batch verification function suitable for ADS-B system. IEEE Trans. Aerosp. Electron. Syst. **59**(2), 1292–1299 (2023)
8. Chen, X., He, D., Peng, C., et al.: A secure and effective hierarchical identity-based signature scheme for ADS-B systems. IEEE Trans. Aerosp. Electron. Syst. **60**(4), 5157–5168 (2024)
9. Damis, H.A., Shehada, D., Fachkha, C., et al.: A microservices architecture for ADS-B data security using blockchain. In: Proceedings of the 2020 3rd International Conference on Signal Processing and Information Security (ICSPIS), Piscataway, pp. 1–4. IEEE (2020)

10. Wu, Z., Shang, T., Yue, M., et al.: ADS-Bchain: a blockchain-based trusted service scheme for automatic dependent surveillance broadcast. IEEE Trans. Aerosp. Electron. Syst. **59**(6), 8535–8549 (2023)
11. Pennapareddy, S., Natarajan, K.: Securing ADS-B data transmissions using blockchain: a comprehensive survey and analysis. Aircr. Eng. Aerosp. Technol. **95**(3), 452–463 (2023)
12. Lu, X., Wu, Z., Cao, J.: ATM Chain: blockchain-based security architecture for air traffic management in future. IEEE Trans. Aerosp. Electron. Syst. **60**(4), 3872–3896 (2024)
13. Naganawa, J., Miyazaki, H.: Theory of automatic dependent surveillance-broadcast position verification using time difference of arrival. IEEE Trans. Aerosp. Electron. Syst. **57**(3), 1387–1404 (2021)
14. Elmarady, A.A., Rahouma, K.: Actual TDoA-based augmentation system for enhancing cybersecurity in ADS-B. Chin. J. Aeronaut. **34**(2), 217–228 (2021)
15. Allmann, C., Stanzel, S., Steffes, C.: TDOA-based position verification of ADS-B information using a sensor network. In: 2022 Sensor Data Fusion: Trends, Solutions, Applications (SDF), Piscataway, pp. 1–6. IEEE (2022)
16. Yoohwan, K., Yeon, J.J., Sungchul, L.: ADS-B vulnerabilities and a security solution with a timestamp. IEEE Aerosp. Electron. Syst. Mag. **32**(11), 52–61 (2017)
17. Saulius, R., Jurgis, A., Rimvydas, A., et al.: Physical layer protection for ADS-B against spoofing and jamming. Int. J. Crit. Infrastruct. Prot. **38**, 100555 (2022)
18. Zhang, Q., Wang, Z., Wu, B., et al.: A robust and practical solution to ADS-B security against denial-of-service attacks. IEEE Internet Things J. **11**(8), 13647–13659 (2024)
19. Leonardi, M., Piracci, E., Galati, G.: ADS-B jamming mitigation: a solution based on a multichannel receiver. IEEE Aerosp. Electron. Syst. Mag. **32**(11), 44–51 (2017)
20. Liu, Y., Ning, P., Dai, H., et al.: Randomized differential DSSS: jamming-resistant wireless broadcast communication. In: 2010 Proceedings IEEE INFOCOM, Piscataway, pp. 1–9. IEEE (2010)
21. Hasjuks, N., Hellbruck, H., Aboltins, A.: Performance study of chaos-based DSSS and FHSS multiuser communication systems. In: 2022 Workshop on Microwave Theory and Techniques in Wireless Communications (MTTW), Piscataway, pp. 23–28. IEEE (2022)
22. Li, T., Wang, B., Shang, F., et al.: Dynamic temporal ADS-B data attack detection based on sHDP-HMM. Comput. Secur. **93**, 101789 (2020)
23. Khan, S., Thorn, J., Wahlgren, A., et al.: Intrusion detection in automatic dependent surveillance-broadcast (ADS-B) with machine learning. In: 2021 IEEE/AIAA 40th Digital Avionics Systems Conference (DASC), Piscataway, pp. 1–10. IEEE (2021)
24. Habler, E., Shabtai, A.: Using LSTM encoder-decoder algorithm for detecting anomalous ADS-B messages. Comput. Secur. **78**, 155–173 (2018)
25. Ying, X., Mazer, J., Bernieri, G., et al.: Detecting ADS-B spoofing attacks using deep neural networks. In: 2019 IEEE Conference on Communications and Network Security (CNS), Piscataway, pp. 187–195. IEEE (2019)
26. Ding, J., Zou, Y., Wang, J., et al.: ADS-B anomaly data detection model based on deep learning. Acta Aeronautica et Astronautica Sinica **40**(12), 323220 (2019)
27. Luo, P., Wang, B., Li, T., et al.: ADS-B anomaly data detection model based on VAE-SVDD. Comput. Secur. **104**, 102213 (2021)
28. Luo, P., Wang, B., Tian, J.: TTSAD: TCN-Transformer-SVDD model for anomaly detection in air traffic ADS-B data. Comput. Secur. **141**, 103840 (2024)
29. Yue, M., Zheng, H., Cui, H., et al.: GAN-LSTM-based ADS-B attack detection in the context of air traffic control. IEEE Internet Things J. **10**(14), 12651–12665 (2023)
30. Liu, Z., Wang, Y., Vaidya, S., et al.: KAN: Kolmogorov-Arnold networks. arXiv preprint arXiv:2404.19756 (2024)
31. Yu, Y., Si, X., Hu, C., Zhang, J.: A review of recurrent neural networks: LSTM cells and network architectures. Neural Comput. **31**(7), 1235–1270 (2019)

Network Intrusion Detection Method Based on Multi-scale Feature Clustering and Improved Honey Badger Algorithm

Hanlei Wang[1], Yanqing Yang[1,2(✉)], and Jiafei Dong[1]

[1] School of Computer Science and Technology (School of Cyberspace Security), Xinjiang University, Urumqi 830046, China
qing0991@163.com

[2] Xinjiang Research Institute of the Huairou Laboratory, Urumqi 830013, China

Abstract. To address the challenges of high-dimensional traffic feature redundancy and the scarcity of novel attack samples in 5G networks and IoT environments, this paper proposes a multimodal and collaborative intelligent detection framework named SMCE-ICHBO-CBGAR. This study focuses on three critical technical challenges. First, we propose a Synthetic Multi-Cluster Equilibrium (SMCE) Approach, which overcomes the limitations caused by distribution shifts in traditional balancing methods in adversarial attack scenarios by combining K-means feature space decoupling with a hybrid SMOTE enhancement technique. Secondly, we construct an Improved Chaotic Honey Badger Optimization (ICHBO) based on tent chaotic initialization and parallel fitness evaluation to accelerate feature selection. In addition, in order to solve the shortcomings of traditional intrusion detection methods in robustness and complex attack pattern recognition, this paper designs a spatiotemporal attention residual fusion model (CBGAR) through hybrid feature encoding of CNN and BiGRU, a multi-head self-attention mechanism, and a multi-scale residual connection. Experiments conducted on the CICIDS-2017 and CICIoT 2023 datasets show that the accuracy of the proposed model reaches 97.60% and 94.11% respectively, which significantly outperforms existing models in various evaluation indicators and effectively improves the intrusion detection performance.

Keywords: Intrusion detection · Balancing method · Feature selection · Spatial-temporal residual network

1 Introduction

The deep integration of the Internet of Things (IoT) with 5G-Advanced networks has significantly improved people's lives but has also exponentially expanded the cyberattack surface due to the rapid proliferation of connected devices and data [1]. If IoT system security cannot be guaranteed, personal information, trade

R. Chen et al. (Eds.): Inscrypt 2025, LNCS 16409, pp. 125–142, 2026.
https://doi.org/10.1007/978-981-95-6203-9_7

secrets, and even military intelligence may be stolen or misused. Therefore, effectively preventing cyberattacks has become a critical issue that must be addressed urgently.

To address this challenge, many studies have been devoted to using machine learning technology to build efficient intrusion detection systems (IDS). Traditional methods, including support vector machines (SVM) and decision trees (DT), have been widely applied in intrusion detection [2]. With the rapid advancement of deep learning, convolutional neural networks (CNN), long short-term memory networks (LSTM), and various hybrid models have seen increasing adoption in this field.

Although current hybrid-method-based intrusion detection systems integrate data balancing, feature selection, and deep learning models, each stage still has inherent limitations that need to be addressed. At the data balance level, although traditional methods can alleviate category imbalance, they ignore the clustering structure and true distribution characteristics of high-dimensional features, causing synthetic samples to deviate from the decision boundary of real traffic, which in turn aggravates classification ambiguity [3]. At the feature selection level, although mainstream metaheuristic algorithms can search for feature subsets, they face the bottleneck of slow convergence speed and are prone to falling into local optima in high-dimensional space, which hampers their ability to meet real-time performance requirements. At the model design level, although some hybrid architectures attempt to integrate spatiotemporal features, they are limited by shallow feature interactions and insufficient capture of key information, and their generalization ability for multi-scale attack patterns is limited.

The above limitations indicate that most existing hybrid methods have inherent technical bottlenecks in the basic mechanisms of each stage, which is particularly evident when dealing with the challenges posed by high-dimensional dynamic traffic and scarce attack samples. Therefore, fundamental improvements are needed in all stages. To address these problems, this study proposes a three-stage collaborative optimization framework, called SMCE-ICHBO-CBGAR. First, the Synthetic Multi-cluster Equilibrium Approach (SMCE) is introduced to achieve cluster-aware dynamic equilibrium through feature decoupling based on K-means and a hybrid sampling strategy. Secondly, an improved chaotic honey badger optimization (ICHBO) algorithm is developed to significantly accelerate high-dimensional feature selection. Third, a hybrid model (CBGAR) is constructed to integrate the advantages of multiple deep learning techniques to enhance intrusion detection performance.

2 Related Work

2.1 Data Balancing Technology

The class imbalance problem can significantly reduce the detection rate of minority class attacks. Data balancing methods are used to solve this problem.

Traditional sample balancing techniques such as SMOTE [4] often generate unrealistic feature combinations in network traffic, which blurs class boundaries.

Improved solutions include EasyEnsemble [5] and ADASYN [6], but neither solves the problem of majority class redundancy. Talukder et al. [7] used hybrid sampling SMOTE-Tomek to alleviate noise interference by combining oversampling and undersampling, but it is not sufficiently adaptable to the clustering heterogeneity of high-dimensional traffic data.

Recent studies have attempted to combine clustering and sampling strategies. For example, Zhang et al. [8] used a Gaussian mixture model to generate synthetic samples. However, their dynamic clustering mechanism did not consider the discriminative correlation between features, which limited their generalization ability in complex attack traffic.

2.2 Feature Selection Techniques

Feature selection is a key step to improve model efficiency. To address high-dimensional feature redundancy, meta-heuristic algorithms are widely used due to their global search capabilities.

The Grey Wolf Algorithm (GWO) [9] and Particle Swarm Optimization (PSO) [10] employ swarm intelligence-based optimization to identify feature subsets, but they converge slowly in high-dimensional spaces and are prone to falling into local optima. Harris Hawk Optimization (HHO) [11] introduces a predation strategy to improve exploration capabilities, but does not solve the problem of sensitivity to the initial population. Leevy et al. [12] use embedded feature selection, but their model relies on a specific architecture and has poor interpretability. The Honey Badger Algorithm (HBA) [13] has attracted attention due to its strong global search capabilities, but its standard version has room for optimization in terms of parallel computing and chaotic initialization.

2.3 Deep Learning Technology

Intrusion detection technology based on deep learning has been widely used in the field of intrusion detection. The integration of spatiotemporal features is the key path to improve the performance of network intrusion detection.

Bamber et al. [14] developed a CNN-LSTM hybrid architecture, and applied recursive feature elimination (RFE) combined with a decision tree classifier for data preprocessing, thus achieving a detection accuracy of 95% on the target dataset. Xia et al. [15] proposed the ResNet-BiGRU model, which uses the residual network (ResNet) to enhance the local spatial feature extraction capability and introduces the bidirectional gated recurrent unit (BiGRU) to learn the bidirectional long-distance temporal dependencies of traffic, achieving an accuracy of 95.99% on the UNSW-NB15 dataset. Recent studies have further explored model optimization and feature fusion mechanisms. For example, Imrana et al. [16] designed a CNN-GRU-FF framework to achieve two-layer feature fusion of CNN and GRU.

3 Proposed Model and Method

Cyber attacks are becoming more and more common in the field of IoT, but existing models have various shortcomings, such as sample imbalance of data sets, low model performance, and poor interpretability. This paper introduces the Synthetic Multi-Cluster Equilibrium (SMCE) Approach to address the data imbalance problem, and then uses Improved Chaotic Honey Badger Optimization (ICHBO) to efficiently perform feature selection. This study also designs a network intrusion detection model (CBGAR) based on deep learning, capable of classifying attacks with high accuracy. The proposed architecture diagram is shown in Fig. 1.

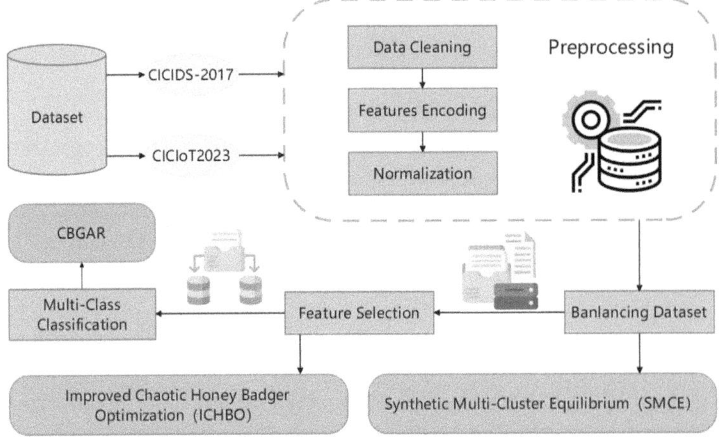

Fig. 1. The proposed architecture diagram.

In this study, the raw data is first preprocessed, including data cleaning, one-hot encoding, and normalization of numerical features to improve data quality and consistency. Subsequently, the SMCE method is used to balance the inherent class imbalance problem of the intrusion detection dataset, thereby alleviating the bias phenomenon in training. In the feature extraction stage, the most discriminative feature subset is selected through the ICHBO algorithm to reduce the dimension and improve the model efficiency. Finally, based on the processed balanced feature set, the CBGAR model is used for training to achieve accurate identification and classification of network traffic. The specific methods and processes of each stage will be described in detail below.

3.1 Preprocessing

The purpose of data preprocessing is to transform raw network data into a format suitable for training machine learning models, while improving data quality and performance. In this paper, we first correct the errors in the data through data cleaning. Then, one-hot encoding is applied to transform categorical features into a format suitable for machine learning models. Finally, min-max normalization is applied to convert the data to a uniform scale. As shown in Eq. 1.

$$X^{'} = \frac{(X - X_{min})}{(X_{max} - X_{min})} \tag{1}$$

Here X_{min} represents the minimum value of the X feature, and X_{max} represents the maximum value of the X feature.

3.2 Synthetic Multi-cluster Equilibrium Approach

In the dataset, the model will be biased towards the majority class due to the small number of minority class samples. To solve this problem, oversampling and undersampling methods can be used to adjust the proportion of each class in the data set. For example, the common SMOTE method, for each minority class sample x_i, first calculates the Euclidean distance of that sample from other samples of the same class, then randomly selects a sample from its nearest neighbor x_{ij} (j = 1, 2,..., k) and generates a new synthetic sample x_{new} by interpolation. As shown in Eq. 2.

$$x_{new} = x_i + \lambda(x_{i,j} - x_i) \tag{2}$$

Where λ is a random number between 0 and 1.

However, SMOTE has obvious limitations. For example, linear interpolation easily amplifies the interference of noise samples, which leads to blurred class boundaries and reduced model generalization. To address this, this paper proposes SMCE, which combines undersampling and oversampling.

SMCE is a hybrid sampling framework for high-dimensional unbalanced network traffic data. At its core, category balancing is synergistically achieved through multi-criteria feature selection, majority class clustering undersampling and dynamic SMOTE oversampling. First, the benchmark features of the dataset must be determined. By selecting the most representative features, this ensures that the clustering algorithm groups the majority class samples more effectively, thereby improving the quality and accuracy of clustering. Here, the variance between features is calculated to measure the discreteness of the feature distribution, and features with high variance are selected to retain diversity. The variance is calculated as follows

$$\sigma^2 = \frac{1}{n-1}\sum_{i=1}^{n}(x_i - \mu)^2 \tag{3}$$

where μ denotes the mean of the feature and n is the number of samples.

Redundant features are subsequently eliminated based on the Pearson correlation coefficient to reduce collinearity among features. The Pearson correlation coefficient is calculated as follows.

$$\rho_{X,Y} = \frac{cov(X,Y)}{\sigma_X \sigma_Y} \tag{4}$$

where $cov(X, Y)$ is the covariance and $\sigma_X$is the standard deviation of the variable X.

Furthermore, discriminability of features is measured on the basis of information gain. Finally, the benchmark features are determined based on a dynamic weighted scoring mechanism. The scoring mechanism can be expressed in the following equation.

$$Score(F_i) = \alpha \cdot \text{Variance}(F_i) + \beta \cdot \text{IG}(F_i) - \gamma \cdot \max_{j \neq i} |Pearson(F_i, F_j)|) \quad (5)$$

The weight parameters α, β, and γ control the variance, information gain, and contribution of redundant features, respectively. After grid search optimization, they are set to $\alpha = 0.4$, $\beta = 0.5$, and $\gamma = 0.1$. The first n features are taken as the benchmark features. The value of n should not be too large or too small compared to the number of features in the dataset. For convenience and improved performance, the value of n is set to 10 in the following studies.

Clustering using k-means based on selected benchmark features. The number of clusters k needs to be determined dynamically to avoid overfitting or underfitting caused by a fixed k value. The equation for dynamically determining the number of clusters is as follows.

$$k = \arg \max_{2 \leq k \leq K_{max}} \frac{1}{N} \sum_{i=1}^{N} \frac{b(i) - a(i)}{max\{a(i), b(i)\}} \quad (6)$$

$$K_{max} = \lceil \log_2 (N_{maj}) \rceil \quad (7)$$

Here $a(i)$ is the average distance from sample i to other samples in the same cluster, $b(i)$ is the average distance from sample i to the nearest other cluster. N_{maj} is the number of samples in the majority class.

For minority classes, using SMOTE alone may generate noise samples at the class boundary, so we combine Borderline-SMOTE with Gaussian noise injection. SMOTE is used to generate new samples for borderline minority class instances, add Gaussian noise to other samples, set the probability p to 0.2, and ensure the balance constraint so that the number of minority classes is equal to the number of majority classes.

The pseudocode of SMCE is given below.

3.3 Improved Chaotic Honey Badger Optimization

In intrusion detection, feature selection is often used to reduce computational costs and enhance interpretability. Feature selection aims to filter out the most sensitive and low-redundancy feature subsets for attack discrimination from high-dimensional traffic data to solve the dimensionality curse. This paper uses Improved Chaotic Honey Badger Optimization (ICHBO) for feature selection.

Currently, most existing feature selection methods have slow convergence and are prone to local optima. ICHBO is a hybrid metaheuristic algorithm based on

Algorithm 1: SMCE

Input: Original dataset $D = \{(x_i, y_i)\}, y_i \in \{\text{Majority}, \text{Minority}\}$
Output: Balanced dataset (balanced_X, balanced_y)
Select n discriminative features from D_{Maj}:
1. Retain high variance features $\rightarrow$ filter low variance;
2. Calculate information gain ;
3. Dynamic weighted scoring to determine $Top - n \rightarrow$ benchmark_features;

Dynamically determine the number of clusters k;
Clustering $\rightarrow$clusters $\{C_1, \ldots, C_k\}$;
Uniformly sample $s = \frac{|D_{\text{Maj}}|}{2k}$ samples for each cluster $C_j \rightarrow$ merge into S_1 (undersampled subset) ;
Calculate the total number of targets $target_{\text{minority}} = |S_1|$;
for *each minority class cls* $\in D_{Min}$ **do**
  if $|current\_samples(cls)| < target_{minority}$ **then**
    $sampling\_strategy[cls] = target_{\text{minority}}$;
  else
    $sampling\_strategy[cls] = 0$;
using SMOTE and Gaussian noise$\rightarrow X_{\text{resampled}}, y_{\text{resampled}}$;
$\text{balanced}_X = S_1.X \cup X_{\text{resampled}}$;
$\text{balanced}_y = S_1.y \cup y_{\text{resampled}}$;

the Honey Badger Algorithm that combines the chaotic mapping strategy with the Honey Badger Optimization. It aims to solve the problems of local optimum and convergence efficiency in feature selection of high-dimensional data.

ICHBO is inspired by the survival strategy of the honey badger, which is known for its strong predation and hunting methods. In ICHBO, the behavior of the honey badger is simulated as an individual searching the solution space. For example, exploration behavior refers to the honey badger constantly changing its direction when looking for food to avoid predators. Once the honey badger finds food, it will dig to get it, a behavior known as digging behavior.

Chaos refers to the chaotic search mechanism, which has the characteristics of sensitive dependence on initial conditions and can produce complex dynamic behaviors. Introducing this mechanism into the honey badger algorithm, the initial population can be generated according to the chaotic map, and the position of each individual is adaptively adjusted throughout the search process. This step ensures that the individuals are evenly distributed in the solution space. As shown in Eq. 8.

$$x_i^{(0)} = r \cdot x_i^{(t-1)} \cdot (1 - x_i^{(t-1)}) \tag{8}$$

Here, $x_i^{(t)}$ is the position of the i-th individual in the t-th generation, and r is the control parameter.

After initialization, fitness evaluation is performed. By calculating the objective function value and determining the fitness, the algorithm can identify the current optimal solution. After that, the individual position is updated, which is the core part of the algorithm. Its purpose is to explore the solution space and find a better solution. Similar to the honey badger, the position update is divided into two stages, the exploration stage and the mining stage. In the exploration stage, the individual adjusts its position according to the distance from the current optimal solution, just like the honey badger changes direction back and forth when looking for food, avoiding the local optimum.

$$x_i^{(t+1)} = x_i^{(t)} + \beta \cdot (x_{best} - x_i^{(t)}) + \epsilon \cdot \mathcal{N}(0, \sigma) \tag{9}$$

Here, x_{best} is the optimal solution of the current population, ϵ is a random perturbation, and $\mathcal{N}(0, \sigma)$ represents a random number in the normal distribution, which enhances the diversity and stochasticity of the search process.

When a better solution is found, the algorithm will enter the mining phase, which imitates the process of a honey badger finding food and taking it for itself. The purpose of this phase is to quickly converge to the optimal solution.

$$x_i^{(t+1)} = x_i^{(t)} + \alpha \cdot (x_{target} - x_i^{(t)}) \tag{10}$$

Here x_{target} is the location where the food is found.

The algorithm achieves global optimization based on these stages. However, the adaptability evaluation of traditional chaotic honey badger optimization algorithms is often time-consuming when processing high-dimensional data sets. Therefore, ICHBO has been improved by introducing the Tent mapping function and parallel fitness evaluation to improve the speed and accuracy of feature selection. Compared with the traditional Logistic mapping, the Tent mapping function can enhance the diversity of search and make the position update of individuals in the solution space more random, thus avoiding local optimality. As shown in Eq. 11.

$$T(x) = \begin{cases} 2x & \text{if } x < 0.5 \\ 2(1-x) & \text{if } x \geq 0.5 \end{cases} \tag{11}$$

The fitness function trains a classifier based on the selected feature subset and returns the classification accuracy, which is used as the fitness score.

$$Fitness(X, y, feature\_indices) = Accuracy(X_{selected}, y) \tag{12}$$

Among them, $X_{selected}$ is the feature subset selected according to the feature index.

Compared with the ordinary CHBO, the improved algorithm reduces the time and improves the efficiency of feature selection by parallel calculation of fitness.

$$Fitness\_v = Parallel\_e(X, y, badger\_features) \tag{13}$$

During the implementation, we adopted a thread-based parallel strategy and used the ThreadPoolExecutor module in Python's concurrent futures library. The executor will start multiple threads at the same time, and each thread is responsible for calculating the fitness value of a single badger. Through these improvements, the algorithm can accurately identify the most effective features for intrusion detection and improve the efficiency and performance of the model.

The pseudocode of ICHBO is as follows.

```
Algorithm 2: ICHBO
Input: Training data X, labels y, number of badgers N, maximum
       iterations MaxIter, time limit T
Output: Optimal feature subset Best_Features
Initialize the badger population Badgers with binary vectors of length d;
Set Best_Fitness ← 0, Best_Features ← ∅;
Set starting time t_start ← current time;
for iter = 1 to MaxIter do
    if current time − t_start > T then
        break ;                    // Terminate if time limit exceeded
    Evaluate fitness of all badgers in parallel:
    Fitness[i] ← fitness_function(X, y, Badgers[i]);
    Update Best_Fitness and Best_Features;
    Perform fitness-proportional resampling to obtain Selected_Badgers;
    for i = 1 to N do
        Apply bit-flip mutation to Selected_Badgers[i] with probability
        p_mut;
        Generate chaotic value c ← tent_map(rand());
        if rand() < c then
            Flip a random bit in Selected_Badgers[i];
    Badgers ← Selected_Badgers;
return Best_Features;
```

3.4 The Proposed Model

In network intrusion detection, traditional models cannot fully utilize the spatiotemporal characteristics of data, resulting in low classification accuracy. To address this problem, this paper proposes a CBGAR model, which consists of a convolutional neural network (CNN), a bidirectional gated recurrent unit (BiGRU), an attention mechanism, and a residual block. CNN is used to extract local features, BiGRU captures bidirectional dependencies in time series, the attention mechanism further focuses on key information, and the residual block alleviates the gradient vanishing problem through jump connections, enhancing the model's depth and representational capacity. The model framework diagram is shown in Fig. 2.

The input layer is used to receive the original network traffic and dynamically adapt to traffic sessions of different lengths. In the model, two sets of one-dimensional convolutional layers are used, containing 64 filters. The high-order features are abstracted layer by layer through stacked 3×3 convolution kernels and the maximum pooling operation with a pooling window size of 2, and batch normalization is combined to accelerate training convergence. Next,

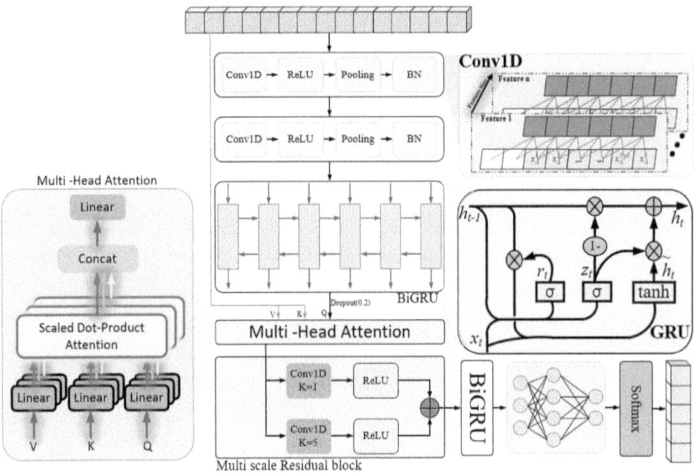

Fig. 2. Framework of CBGAR.

BiGRU captures the long-term positive and negative dependencies of the traffic sequence and analyzes the temporal evolution of the attack behavior. This layer has 64 units. Then a Dropout layer with a dropout rate of 0.3 is added to prevent overfitting. On this basis, an 8-head parallel self-attention mechanism is introduced to dynamically allocate weights for different traffic segments, focus on key attack segments and suppress noise interference. 1×1 convolution and 5×5 convolution are fused through multi-scale residual blocks to extract global statistical features and wide-range local patterns, and residual jump connections are used to enhance gradient propagation and feature diversity. The model uses the BiGRU layer again with 128 units, and the return sequence is set to False for feature integration. Finally, the output is passed through a fully connected layer followed by a Softmax function for classification.

In the model compilation stage, the categorical cross entropy loss function is used to adapt to the multi-classification task characteristics of network intrusion detection. In addition, the Adam optimizer is applied, the learning rate is set to 0.001, and the direction correction and adaptive learning rate scaling are guided by momentum.

4 Experiment Result and Discussions

4.1 Preparation

Experimental Environment. The experimental environment of this article is shown in Table 1.

Dataset. The datasets used in this study include CICIDS-2017 and CICIoT 2023, which are commonly used datasets in the field of intrusion detection. These

Table 1. Experiment environment

OS	Windows 11
GPU	NVIDIA RTX 4060
RAM	16GB
Tensorflow	2.6.2
Python	3.6.13

datasets provide important benchmarks for the evaluation of intrusion detection systems.

The CICIDS-2017 [17] is a dataset released by the Canadian Center for Cyber Security (CIC), which is generated based on a closed multi-platform network topology and includes 78 features. The CICIoT 2023 [18] is a very new dataset that uses a wide range of topologies consisting of multiple real IoT devices. It contains 33 types of attacks divided into seven categories.

In these data sets, there is a situation where one type of traffic accounts for the majority, as shown in Fig. 3. Intrusion detection needs to be trained based on a balanced data set to mitigate the impact of class imbalance on the performance of the model.

Due to the large volume of data in the datasets, we applied a stratified random sampling strategy in subsequent experiments to reduce memory consumption and improve computational efficiency. Specifically, we randomly extracted 1% of the samples from each category for experiments.

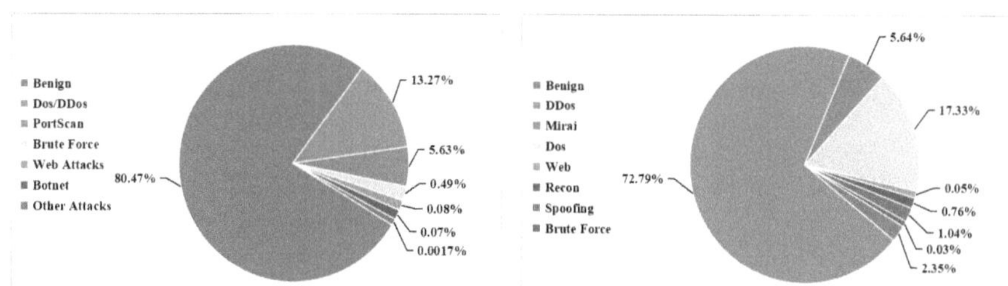

(a) Traffic distribution of CICIDS-2017 (b) Traffic distribution of CICIoT 2023

Fig. 3. Traffic distribution of the dataset.

Evaluation Indicators. When evaluating model performance, it is important to define appropriate evaluation metrics. To evaluate the results, this article uses the performance metrics of Accuracy, Precision, Recall, and F1 score, as shown in the following formula.

$$Accuracy = \frac{TP + TN}{TP + TN + FP + FN} \tag{14}$$

$$Precision = \frac{TP}{TP + FP} \tag{15}$$

$$Recall = \frac{TP}{TP + FN} \tag{16}$$

$$F1 = 2 \times \frac{Precision \times Recall}{Precision + Recall} \tag{17}$$

4.2 Compared with Existing Methods

After data preprocessing, the SMCE method is applied to the dataset to reduce the impact of excessive majority classes on the model. Through the SMCE method, we first obtain the baseline features of all datasets, as shown in Table 2. We can use these features to divide the majority class into several categories for subsequent clustering. Then, we use ICHBO for feature selection and finally train and evaluate.

Table 2. Benchmark features of the dataset

Dataset	Benchmark features
CICIDS-2017	Flow IAT Mean, Flow Duration, Bwd Packets/s, Total Length of Fwd Packets, Init_Win_bytes_forward, Bwd Packet Length Max, Init_Win_bytes_backward, Fwd Packet Length Max, Destination Port, Fwd Header Length
CICIoT 2023	IAT, Rate, Header_Length, Tot sum, flow_duration, Min, Protocol Type, Variance, urg_count, Duration

Model Performance on CICIDS-2017. In CICIDS-2017, we compare the proposed model with various current models, including HMCD-Model [19], XIDINTFL-VAE [20], Pean [21] and RSOA-IEHO-BILSTM [22]. We reproduced the proposed model using our dataset based on the network structure and related parameters provided in the literature. The evaluation results are shown in Table 3. The model performed well in the experiment and achieved the best results.

For CNN-GRU-FF [16], the original experiment was conducted on a regular imbalanced dataset and the loss function was adjusted according to Focal loss. SMCE is more comprehensive because it directly adjusts the sample distribution rather than just the loss function. M-MultiSVM [23] pursues high accuracy through the feature extraction process, but sacrifices efficiency and simplicity. Our ICHBO algorithm greatly reduces the time required by parallel processing of fitness evaluation, solving the problem of insufficient real-time performance.

Table 3. Evaluation results based on CICIDS-2017

Model	ACC(%)	PRE(%)	REC(%)	F1(%)
CNN	91.55	92.10	91.82	91.40
ResNet	92.35	94.75	93.54	93.20
CNN+LSTM	94.88	93.60	94.23	93.85
M-MultISVM	97.40	84.60	94.20	76.99
HMCD-Model	97.00	96.62	73.77	83.66
XIDINTFL-VAE	95.83	94.12	93.75	93.93
Pean	96.12	95.87	96.23	96.05
RSOA-IEHO-BILSTM	96.83	95.39	95.77	95.58
CNN-GRU-FF	97.15	96.90	96.80	96.85
OURS	97.60	97.65	97.60	97.61

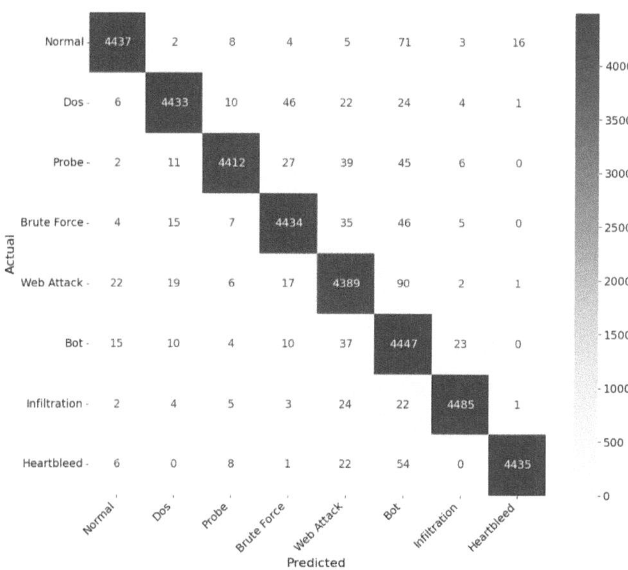

Fig. 4. Confusion Matrix for CICIDS-2017.

To further evaluate the generalization ability of the model, we use the confusion matrix to clearly show the model's recognition performance for various types of traffic in the dataset, as shown in Fig. 4. When identifying normal traffic, the model's accuracy is as high as 97.82%.

Model Performance on CICIoT 2023. In this section, we train and evaluate the CICIoT 2023. We compare our model with models including DL-BiLSTM [24], Adaboost [25], MSRC [26], HIDIM [27] and EAPT [28]. The evaluation results based on the CICIoT 2023 dataset are shown in Table 4. The results indicate that our model achieves superior detection performance, with accuracy and precision of 94.11% and 94.52%, respectively, confirming its effectiveness in classifying network intrusion data.

In the ET-Bert [29], the pure Transformer architecture only captures long-range temporal dependencies and ignores spatial correlations between features, resulting in a detection recall rate of less than 82% for distributed attacks. Our CBGAR model can achieve deep mining of spatial and temporal features in network traffic data by collaboratively utilizing convolutional layers and bidirectional recurrent units, effectively solving the limitations of spatiotemporal feature fusion.

The confusion matrix of the CICIoT 2023 dataset is shown in Fig. 5. Most of the samples in the dataset are concentrated on the diagonal of the confusion matrix, indicating that the model can also effectively judge the type of traffic samples on this newer dataset, which shows that our model has strong robustness.

Table 4. Evaluation results based on CICIoT 2023

Model	ACC(%)	PRE(%)	REC(%)	F1(%)
CNN	89.81	90.67	89.45	90.06
ResNet	88.95	87.12	88.78	87.94
CNN+LSTM	91.23	89.67	90.45	90.06
DL-BiLSTM	93.13	91.80	93.13	91.94
Adaboost	77.00	84.00	77.00	80.30
MSRC	90.52	89.02	89.38	89.20
ET-BERT	92.12	90.67	93.15	91.88
HIDIM	93.27	93.88	92.11	91.99
EAPT	93.63	–	–	93.60
OURS	94.11	94.52	94.11	94.16

4.3 Ablation and Extension Experiments

In this section, we use the CICIDS-2017 as an example to conduct an ablation experiment on the proposed model to verify the necessity of each component of the proposed method. At the same time, we conduct an extended experiment to compare our method with other data balancing techniques and feature selection techniques to demonstrate the superiority of our method. The specific results are shown in Table 5.

It can be observed that CBGAR has the lowest accuracy of 94.37%. After applying the SMCE method, the accuracy increased to 96.11%, which demonstrates its effectiveness. After applying ICHBO for feature selection based on the

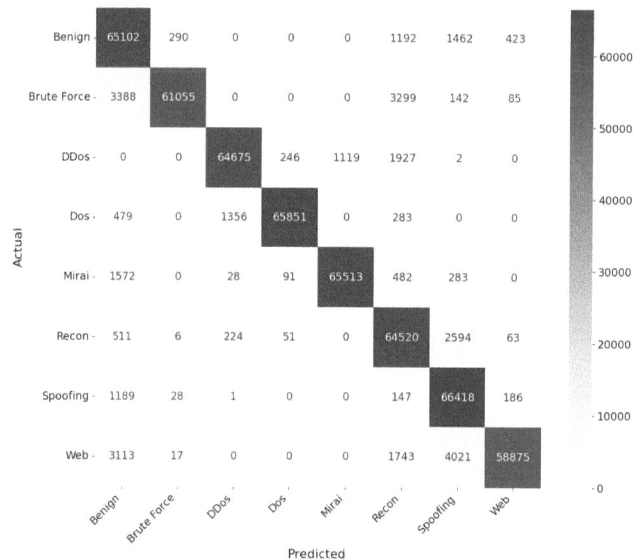

Fig. 5. Confusion Matrix for CICIoT 2023.

Table 5. Results of ablation and extension experiments

Model	ACC(%)	PRE(%)	REC(%)	F1(%)
CBGAR	94.37	92.85	93.42	93.13
SMCE+CBGAR	96.11	92.29	90.11	91.18
ICHBO+CBGAR	96.23	91.81	89.34	90.55
ADASYN [6]+ICHBO+CBGAR	94.88	93.54	93.17	93.35
SMOTE-Tomek [7]+ICHBO+CBGAR	95.45	93.78	93.21	93.49
SMCE+RFE [14]+CBGAR	93.71	92.20	91.98	92.09
SMCE+ONgO [19]+CBGAR	96.29	94.95	95.34	95.14
SMCE+ICHBO+CBGAR	97.60	97.65	97.60	97.61

original model CBGAR, the accuracy also increased by 1.86% compared with the original model. The comparison shows that both components significantly contribute to the performance of our model.

Next, we used other data balancing techniques instead of SMCE and other feature selection methods instead of ICHBO to conduct a series of experiments. Experimental results show that the combination of SMCE-ICHBO-CBGAR has the best performance, and the F1 score is 2.52% higher than that of SMCE-RFE-CBGAR. This is because the parallel fitness evaluation of ICHBO greatly reduces the time consumption of feature selection, and the Tent chaotic mapping improves the diversity of features, allowing the CBGAR attention mechanism to better focus on key attack patterns.

5 Conclusion and Future Work

This study aims to solve the key problems of class imbalance and high-dimensional feature learning in network intrusion detection, and proposes an integrated detection framework that combines the SMCE data balancing method, the ICHBO feature selection algorithm, and the CBGAR deep learning model, named SMCE-ICHBO-CBGAR.

Verification shows that the SMCE method, based on traffic feature clustering and dynamic sampling strategy, effectively eliminates the feature offset problem caused by traditional oversampling. The ICHBO enhances population diversity through Tent chaotic mapping, and achieves dimensionality compression while retaining attack discrimination features. The CBGAR utilizes the spatio-temporal feature extraction capabilities of CNN-BiGRU, the key information-focusing characteristics of the attention mechanism, and the optimization effect of residual connections to achieve accurate recognition and classification of diverse attack types.

This research provides a novel approach in both theory and technological implementation for IoT security protection. In future work, we plan to focus on privacy-preserving architectures within the federated learning paradigm to advance the development of intrusion detection systems towards collaborative defense.

Acknowledgements. This work was supported by the Huairou Laboratory Project (No. YZD2024025A) and the Natural Science Project of Xinjiang University Scientific Research Program (No. XJEDU2021Y003).

References

1. Sharma, B., et al.: Explainable artificial intelligence for intrusion detection in IoT networks: a deep learning based approach. Expert Syst. Appl. **238**, 121751 (2024)
2. Almiani, M., et al.: Deep recurrent neural network for IoT intrusion detection system. Simul. Model. Pract. Theory **101**, 102031 (2020)
3. Dina, A.S., Siddique, A.B., Manivannan, D.: A deep learning approach for intrusion detection in internet of things using focal loss function. Internet Things **22**, 100699 (2023)
4. Chawla, N.V., et al.: SMOTE: synthetic minority over-sampling technique. J. Artif. Intell. Res. **16**, 321–357 (2002)
5. Liu, X.-Y., Wu, J., Zhou, Z.-H.: Exploratory undersampling for class-imbalance learning. IEEE Trans. Syst. Man Cybern. Part B (Cybern.) **39**(2), 539–550 (2008)
6. He, H., et al.: ADASYN: adaptive synthetic sampling approach for imbalanced learning. In: 2008 IEEE International Joint Conference on Neural Networks (IEEE World Congress on Computational Intelligence). IEEE (2008)
7. Talukder, M.A., et al.: MLSTL-WSN: machine learning-based intrusion detection using SMOTETomek in WSNs. Int. J. Inf. Secur. **23**(3), 2139–2158 (2024)
8. Zhang, H., et al.: An effective convolutional neural network based on SMOTE and Gaussian mixture model for intrusion detection in imbalanced dataset. Comput. Netw. **177**, 107315 (2020)

9. Mirjalili, S., Mirjalili, S.M., Lewis, A.: Grey wolf optimizer. Adv. Eng. Softw. **69**, 46–61 (2014)
10. Ghamisi, P., Benediktsson, J.A.: Feature selection based on hybridization of genetic algorithm and particle swarm optimization. IEEE Geosci. Remote Sens. Lett. **12**(2), 309–313 (2014)
11. Alazab, M., et al.: An effective networks intrusion detection approach based on hybrid Harris Hawks and multi-layer perceptron. Egypt. Inf. J. **25**, 100423 (2024)
12. Leevy, J.L., Hancock, J., Khoshgoftaar, T.M., Peterson, J.M.: IoT information theft prediction using ensemble feature selection. J. Big Data **9**(1), 1–48 (2022). https://doi.org/10.1186/s40537-021-00558-z
13. Hashim, F.A., et al.: Honey badger algorithm: new metaheuristic algorithm for solving optimization problems. Math. Comput. Simul. **192**, 84–110 (2022)
14. Bamber, S.S., et al.: A hybrid CNN-LSTM approach for intelligent cyber intrusion detection system. Comput. Secur. **148**, 104146 (2025)
15. Xia, Z., et al.: PSO-GA hyperparameter optimized ResNet-BiGRU based intrusion detection method. IEEE Access (2024)
16. Imrana, Y., et al.: CNN-GRU-FF: a double-layer feature fusion-based network intrusion detection system using convolutional neural network and gated recurrent units. Complex Intell. Syst. **10**(3), 3353–3370 (2024)
17. Sharafaldin, I., Lashkari, A.H., Ghorbani, A.A.: Toward generating a new intrusion detection dataset and intrusion traffic characterization. ICISSp **1**(2018), 108–116 (2018)
18. Neto, E.C.P., et al.: CICIoT2023: a real-time dataset and benchmark for large-scale attacks in IoT environment. Sensors **23**(13), 5941 (2023)
19. Yun, X., et al.: Detecting unknown HTTP-based malicious communication behavior via generated adversarial flows and hierarchical traffic features. Comput. Secur. **121**, 102834 (2022)
20. Abdulganiyu, O.H., et al.: XIDINTFL-VAE: XGBoost-based intrusion detection of imbalance network traffic via class-wise focal loss variational autoencoder. J. Supercomput. **81**(1), 1–38 (2025)
21. Lin, P., et al.: A novel multimodal deep learning framework for encrypted traffic classification. IEEE/ACM Trans. Networking **31**(3), 1369–1384 (2022)
22. Padmavathi, B., et al.: An optimized Bi-LSTM with random synthetic oversampling strategy for network intrusion detection. Soft. Comput. **28**(1), 777–790 (2024)
23. Turukmane, A.V., Devendiran, R.: M-MultiSVM: an efficient feature selection assisted network intrusion detection system using machine learning. Comput. Secur. **137**, 103587 (2024)
24. Wang, Z., et al.: A lightweight intrusion detection method for IoT based on deep learning and dynamic quantization. PeerJ Comput. Sci. **9**, e1569 (2023)
25. Fahrezi, S.F., et al. Optimizing performance of AdaBoost algorithm through undersampling and hyperparameter tuning on CICIoT 2023 dataset. Techné: Jurnal Ilmiah Elektroteknika **23**(2), 175–184 (2024)
26. Duan, X.Y., et al.: Network traffic anomaly detection method based on multi-scale characteristic. J. Commun. **43**(10), 65–76 (2022)
27. Zhou, W., et al.: Hidim: a novel framework of network intrusion detection for hierarchical dependency and class imbalance. Comput. Secur. **148**, 104155 (2025)

28. Zhan, M., et al.: EAPT: an encrypted traffic classification model via adversarial pre-trained transformers. Comput. Netw. **257**, 110973 (2025)
29. Lin, X., et al.: ET-BERT: a contextualized datagram representation with pre-training transformers for encrypted traffic classification. In: Proceedings of the ACM Web Conference 2022 (2022)

SAGE: Spatiotemporal Feature Fusion for Anomaly Detection in Multivariate Time Series

Haojie Shi, Yong Wang(✉), and Lin Zhou

Shanghai University of Electric Power, Shanghai 201200, China
wangyong@shiep.edu.cn

Abstract. Multivariate time series are ubiquitous in industrial production, power systems, and transportation, exhibiting complex interdependencies between different variables that make anomaly detection a challenging task. Current methods are mostly based on theoretical assumptions, which either limit the model's generalization ability or fail to effectively handle outliers when processing anomalous data. This paper proposes an anomaly detection model that combines Graph Attention Networks (GAT) with Transformers. The model captures spatial dependencies between sensors through GAT layers and models temporal dependencies using Transformer encoders, thereby improving anomaly detection performance. To enhance the model's expressive power, trainable weights are introduced in the feature fusion process to perform weighted integration of spatial and temporal features. Experimental results show that the overall performance outperforms baseline methods on four benchmark datasets: SWaT, WADI, PSM, and MSL.

Keywords: Industrial control systems · Anomaly detection · Spatiotemporal feature fusion

1 Introduction

Multivariate time series data generated by Industrial Control Systems (ICS) typically exhibit complex interdependencies between variables, while these data are characterized by high dimensionality, nonlinearity, and temporal variability. Currently, multivariate time series anomaly detection methods span multiple domains, but traditional statistical analysis methods and clustering-based techniques have certain limitations when processing industrial control system data. Statistical methods often struggle to handle the complexity of multivariate data [15] and cannot effectively model complex relationships between variables. While clustering methods can better identify anomalous points [14,19], they are sensitive to parameters (such as the number of clusters and density thresholds), and as data dimensionality increases, the accuracy of distance measures decreases, leading to suboptimal detection results.

R. Chen et al. (Eds.): Inscrypt 2025, LNCS 16409, pp. 143–156, 2026.
https://doi.org/10.1007/978-981-95-6203-9_8

Deep learning's excellent performance in sequence modeling and prediction tasks has made it the mainstream approach for time series anomaly detection. Methods such as Long Short-Term Memory networks (LSTM) [20], Gated Recurrent Units (GRU) [8], and Autoencoders [5] effectively capture temporal dependencies in time series. However, they often overlook the spatial dependencies that exist in multivariate time series. Spatial dependencies are particularly important in industrial control systems because sensors typically have physical connection relationships. Ignoring this may reduce the accuracy of anomaly detection. To address the insufficient modeling of inter-variable relationships, methods combining Graph Neural Networks (GNN) have received widespread attention [11]. By constructing graph structures between sensors, these methods effectively capture spatial dependencies in multivariate time series, thereby improving anomaly detection performance. The introduction of Attention Mechanisms enables models to automatically focus on key sensors and important time points, further improving model interpretability and detection effectiveness. However, efficiently modeling spatiotemporal dependencies for anomaly detection remains challenging in complex industrial control environments. Existing methods have the following key issues: Most deep learning methods focus only on temporal dependencies, ignoring spatial relationships between sensors; Graph-based methods often use static graph structures that cannot capture dynamically changing sensor interactions; Simple concatenation or summation fusion strategies for spatiotemporal features limit the model's expressive power. These issues are particularly prominent in complex industrial control systems, where sensors typically have clear physical connections and functional dependency relationships.

To address the above issues, this paper proposes a novel anomaly detection model—Spatio-Temporal Anomaly Graph Network (SAGE). This model combines Transformers with Graph Attention Networks (GAT) to capture dependencies from both temporal and spatial dimensions. Through an adaptive fusion mechanism, SAGE improves the model's feature representation capability and enhances sensitivity to anomalies. Our main contributions include:

- Proposing the SAGE model that combines Transformer and graph attention mechanisms, dynamically integrating dual-path features using an adaptive fusion mechanism.
- Constructing graphs based on sensors' physical connections and functional relationships, and combining self-supervised pre-training with supervised fine-tuning to fully utilize both unlabeled and labeled data, alleviating the problem of scarce anomaly samples and improving model generalization.
- Validating the superiority of the model on datasets such as SWaT and WADI.

2 Related Work

2.1 Time Series Anomaly Detection

In the field of Industrial Control Systems (ICS), early anomaly detection methods mainly relied on rule-based and statistical approaches, but these methods typically struggle to adapt to dynamically changing environments. Rule-based methods monitor key parameters by setting thresholds or rules, determining data that exceeds predefined ranges as anomalies. These methods have certain advantages in terms of real-time performance and implementation convenience, but their adaptability is poor and they struggle to handle complex dynamic patterns. Therefore, researchers began to adopt statistical methods such as time series models, Principal Component Analysis (PCA), Gaussian Mixture Models (GMM), and Singular Value Decomposition (SVD). PCA identifies anomalous points through dimensionality reduction, with anomalous data often deviating from the normal data space [2]; GMM treats data located in low-probability regions as anomalies; SVD identifies anomalies in high-dimensional data through reconstruction error [17]. Although these methods perform well on low-dimensional data, as data dimensionality increases, their performance gradually fails to meet practical requirements.

In recent years, due to deep learning's powerful capabilities in nonlinear feature extraction, it has become the mainstream technology for time series anomaly detection. Deep learning models such as LSTM and Autoencoders can effectively capture complex temporal dependencies in time series [4]. For example, Kong et al. proposed AMBi-GAN, a deep generative model based on Generative Adversarial Networks (GAN) and Bidirectional LSTM (BiLSTM), which combines attention mechanisms to capture temporal dependencies, thereby achieving anomaly detection for multidimensional time series in Industrial Internet of Things (IIoT) [13]. Additionally, Liu et al. proposed a time series anomaly detection method based on knowledge distillation, identifying anomalies through differences between teacher and student models [16].

2.2 Anomaly Detection Based on Spatiotemporal Modeling

Although temporal modeling methods such as LSTM and GRU can effectively capture temporal dependencies, they often overlook spatial dependencies existing in data. In many industrial control systems, interactions and dependencies between sensors play a crucial role in anomaly detection. Graph Neural Networks (GNN), as a powerful tool, can handle non-Euclidean data and are particularly suitable for sensor networks with complex topological structures. By constructing graph structures, GNN can capture spatial relationships between nodes, providing new perspectives for time series anomaly detection.

Combining temporal modeling with graph neural networks can comprehensively mine spatiotemporal dependencies in time series data, thereby improving anomaly detection performance. Dai et al. proposed the GANF model, which uses static Directed Acyclic Graphs (DAG) to simulate dependencies between sensors and adopts unsupervised learning strategies for anomaly detection. This model achieved leading AUC (Area Under Curve) performance on datasets such as SWaT and PMU-B [6]. Building on the GANF model, Zhou et al. proposed the MTGFlow model, which utilizes dynamic graph structures and entity-aware normalizing flow methods for anomaly detection in multivariate time series [21].

These methods better capture spatiotemporal features and dynamic relationships by introducing dynamic graphs and entity-aware flow models, thereby achieving more accurate anomaly detection. Methods based on Graph Attention Networks (GAT) also perform excellently in spatiotemporal feature fusion. By introducing attention mechanisms, GAT can adaptively adjust edge weights between sensors, thereby reflecting their actual interaction strength. Ding et al. explicitly modeled correlations between different modalities through multi-head attention mechanisms and intra-modal and cross-modal relationship attention modules [7].

3 Method

Our model mainly consists of two branches: the GAT branch and the Transformer encoder branch. Input data first passes through the GAT branch and Transformer encoder branch separately to capture spatial dependencies between sensors and temporal dependencies. In this section, we will introduce the proposed model. Figure 1 shows the overall framework of SAGE.

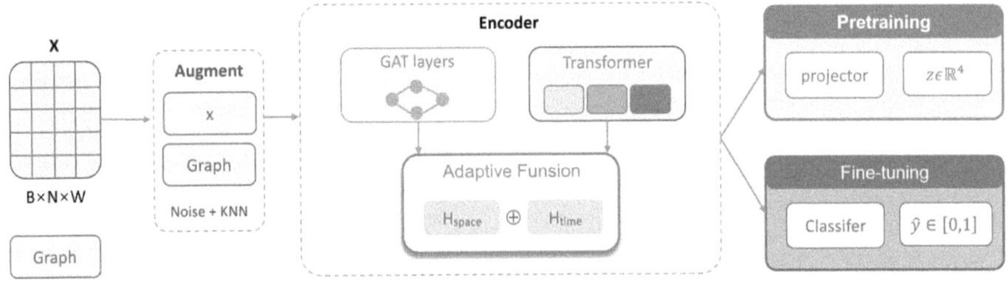

Fig. 1. SAGE framework diagram.

3.1 Problem Definition

Given multivariate time series data $\mathbf{X} = \{x_1, x_2, ..., x_T\}$, where $x_t \in \mathbb{R}^N$ represents the readings of N sensors at time t. Our goal is to learn a function $f : \mathbb{R}^{N\times W} \rightarrow [0, 1]$ that maps a time window of length W to an anomaly probability. Formally, for a time window $\mathbf{X}_{[t-W+1:t]} \in \mathbb{R}^{N\times W}$, the model outputs an anomaly score $s_t = f(\mathbf{X}_{[t-W+1:t]})$.

3.2 Spatial Dependency Modeling

In our Graph Attention Network (GAT) approach, the graph structure is generated using prior knowledge. Input data is first mapped to a high-dimensional space through a linear layer, then passed to multi-head graph attention convolution layers. In these layers, the model dynamically computes edge weights between neighboring nodes and updates node features to extract spatial dependencies between sensors. Each graph node (i.e., sensor) computes adaptive feature representations based on its neighbors' features through multi-head attention mechanisms, and obtains the global features of this branch through mean aggregation.

Graph Structure Construction. For different datasets, we construct graph structures based on sensors' physical and functional relationships:

SWaT Dataset: We construct the graph structure based on the process flow of the water treatment system. Specific rules include:

- Connections within the same stage: Pumps (P) connect to valves (MV), level sensors (LIT) connect to pumps (P)
- Cross-stage connections: Flow sensors (FIT) in stage i connect to pumps (P) and valves (MV) in stage $i+1$

WADI Dataset: Based on the topology of the water supply system, considering sensor types and subsystems:

- Controllers (PIC, FIC) connect to actuators (P, MV)
- Measurement sensors (FIT, PIT, LIT) connect to relevant controllers

PSM and MSL Datasets: Due to the lack of explicit physical topology information, we construct fully connected graphs, allowing the model to adaptively learn dependencies between sensors through attention mechanisms.

Dynamic Edge Weights and Multi-head Attention Mechanism. In our Graph Attention Network (GAT) approach, edge weights are dynamically computed, enabling the model to adaptively focus on neighboring nodes. For node pair (i, j), the attention coefficient α_{ij} is calculated as follows:

$$\alpha_{ij} = \frac{\exp\left(\text{LeakyReLU}\left(\mathbf{a}^\top \left[\mathbf{W}\mathbf{h}_i \| \mathbf{W}\mathbf{h}_j\right]\right)\right)}{\sum_{k \in \mathcal{N}(i)} \exp\left(\text{LeakyReLU}\left(\mathbf{a}^\top \left[\mathbf{W}\mathbf{h}_i \| \mathbf{W}\mathbf{h}_k\right]\right)\right)} \tag{1}$$

where $\mathbf{h}_i \in \mathbb{R}^D$ represents the feature vector of node i, $\mathbf{W} \in \mathbb{R}^{D \times D}$ is a learnable weight matrix, $\mathbf{a} \in \mathbb{R}^{2D}$ is used to compute attention scores, and the symbol $\|$ denotes vector concatenation, i.e., $[\mathbf{x}, \mathbf{y}] \in \mathbb{R}^{2D}$.

The multi-head attention mechanism captures multiple neighbor relationships through M parallel attention heads. Unlike standard GAT that concatenates outputs from multiple heads, our model adopts mean aggregation mode. This design ensures that the output dimensions of all L GAT layers are D, maintaining consistency with the feature dimensions of the Transformer branch. Through multi-head attention mechanisms, the model can capture spatial dependencies between sensors from multiple perspectives, thereby generating more representative node feature representations.

3.3 Temporal Dependency Modeling

Temporal dependencies reveal pattern changes of sensors across consecutive time steps, helping to identify potential anomalies. To effectively capture dependencies in long time series, we introduce Transformer encoders as the temporal dependency modeling module. Transformer encoders capture temporal patterns through stacked self-attention layers. Each layer uses scaled dot-product attention mechanisms to dynamically compute relationships between time steps:

$$\text{Attention}(Q, K, V) = \text{softmax}\left(\frac{QK^\top}{\sqrt{d_k}}\right)V \tag{2}$$

where Q (queries), K (keys), and V (values) are learnable projections of input features. Specifically, for input $X \in \mathbb{R}^{W \times D}$ in each layer, we have $Q = XW_Q$, $K = XW_K$, $V = XW_V$, where $W_Q, W_K, W_V \in \mathbb{R}^{D \times D/h}$, and $d_k = D/h$ is the dimension of each attention head.

The outputs from multi-head attention are merged and processed through position-wise feed-forward neural networks:

$$\text{FFN}(x) = \text{ReLU}(xW_1 + b_1)W_2 + b_2 \tag{3}$$

where $W_1 \in \mathbb{R}^{D \times 4D}$, $W_2 \in \mathbb{R}^{4D \times D}$. Additionally, layer normalization and residual connections are applied throughout the encoder structure.

3.4 Spatiotemporal Feature Fusion

In our model, the fusion of spatial and temporal features is achieved through weighted summation, where weights are determined by trainable parameters. Specifically, the model combines spatial features extracted by the GAT branch with temporal features extracted by the Transformer branch. By dynamically adjusting the weights of these two types of features in the final representation, the model achieves feature fusion. The fusion strategy employs a trainable fusion weight to weight these two types of features, with the fused features serving as input for subsequent task processing. The weighted fusion expression is as follows:

$$\mathbf{H}_{\text{fused}} = \sigma(w_{\text{fusion}}) \cdot \mathbf{H}_{\text{space}} + (1 - \sigma(w_{\text{fusion}})) \cdot \mathbf{H}_{\text{time}} \tag{4}$$

where $\mathbf{H}_{\text{space}}$ and $\mathbf{H}_{\text{time}}$ represent spatial and temporal features extracted from the GAT branch and Transformer branch, respectively. $w_{\text{fusion}} \in \mathbb{R}$ is a learnable scalar parameter, and the function $\sigma(w_{\text{fusion}})$ represents a trainable weight generated through the Sigmoid function, indicating the importance ratio of spatial versus temporal features in the fused representation.

This weighted fusion method enables the model to adaptively adjust the contribution ratio of spatial and temporal features according to task requirements, optimizing the fusion effect through gradient propagation and backpropagation during training.

3.5 Self-supervised Contrastive Learning

Our contrastive learning framework learns discriminative representations by optimizing consistency between different augmented views of the same time series while reducing similarity between different sequences. This framework consists of three key components: data augmentation, feature projection, and contrastive loss function.

The data augmentation process generates modified views of input time series windows $x \in \mathbb{R}^{N \times W}$ in two complementary ways. Gaussian noise injection simulates measurement variations by adding normally distributed perturbations while preserving the original temporal structure; neighborhood interpolation generates smoothed versions by linearly combining each window with its k most similar sequences from the training distribution. These transformations produce positive sample pairs (x_i, x_i^+) that introduce meaningful variations while maintaining core dynamic patterns.

The feature projection network maps the fused spatiotemporal representation H_{fused} to a lower-dimensional contrastive space through nonlinear transformations. This projection head consists of two linear layers with a ReLU activation function in between. The final output is a D-dimensional embedding representation $z = f(H_{\text{fused}})$. For augmented samples, we denote $z_i^+ = f(H_{\text{fused}}^+)$ where H_{fused}^+ is computed from the augmented input x_i^+.

The contrastive loss function operates on batches containing N original sequences and their corresponding N augmented views. For each positive pair (z_i, z_i^+), the normalized temperature-scaled cross-entropy loss is calculated as:

$$\mathcal{L}_{\text{cont}} = -\frac{1}{N} \sum_{i=1}^{N} \log \frac{\exp(z_i^\top z_i^+/\tau)}{\sum_{j=1}^{N} \left[\exp(z_i^\top z_j/\tau) + \exp(z_i^\top z_j^+/\tau)\right] - \exp(z_i^\top z_i^+/\tau)} \tag{5}$$

where τ represents the temperature hyperparameter that controls the separation between negative samples. The denominator sums over all negative pairs within the batch, including both original-original pairs (z_i, z_j) for $j \neq i$, and original-augmented pairs (z_i, z_j^+) for $j \neq i$. The term $-\exp(z_i^\top z_i^+/\tau)$ is subtracted to exclude the positive pair from the denominator. Through this self-supervised pre-training, the model can learn robust feature extractors that capture key temporal dynamics without requiring labeled anomaly samples.

3.6 Supervised Fine-Tuning Phase

After completing the self-supervised contrastive pre-training phase, we fine-tune the model using a small amount of labeled anomaly detection data to enhance its discriminative ability for specific tasks. Specifically, the goal of the fine-tuning phase is to further optimize model parameters using labeled data, enabling more accurate distinction between normal and anomalous time series segments.

During fine-tuning, we use a labeled dataset $D = \{(x_i, y_i)\}_{i=1}^{N}$, where x_i represents the input time series window and $y_i \in \{0, 1\}$ represents the corresponding label (0 for normal, 1 for anomalous). The model generates prediction outputs $\hat{y}_i$ through forward propagation and compares them with true labels y_i.

Since anomaly samples are typically scarce, we introduce class weight α to balance the contribution of positive and negative samples to the loss. The prediction probability is given by:

$$\mathcal{L}_{\text{BCE}} = -\frac{1}{N}\sum_{i=1}^{N}[\alpha y_i \log(\hat{y}_i) + (1 - y_i)\log(1 - \hat{y}_i)] \tag{6}$$

where $\hat{y}_i = \sigma(W_{\text{classifier}} \cdot f(x_i) + b_{\text{classifier}})$ represents the prediction probability calculated through the sigmoid activation function.

We minimize the weighted binary cross-entropy loss function to update all trainable parameters of the model (including GAT and Transformer branches). Through backpropagation, the model can more accurately distinguish between normal and anomalous time series windows during the fine-tuning phase.

3.7 Anomaly Score

The anomaly score for each sample comes directly from the model's classification output:

$$\text{Score}(x) = \sigma(W_{\text{classifier}} \cdot h_{\text{fused}} + b_{\text{classifier}}) \tag{7}$$

where h_{fused} is the fused feature representation, $W_{\text{classifier}} \in \mathbb{R}^{1\times D}$ is the classifier weight vector, $b_{\text{classifier}} \in \mathbb{R}$ is the bias term, and $\sigma(\cdot)$ denotes the sigmoid activation function. This probability score ranges from $[0, 1]$ and serves as a threshold-independent anomaly indicator, with higher scores indicating greater likelihood of being anomalous. All reported metrics (PR-AUC, ROC-AUC) are calculated directly based on these scores.

4 Experiments

4.1 Dataset Introduction and Implementation Details

Dataset Introduction. We select multiple representative multivariate time series datasets to evaluate the performance of the SAGE model:

- SWaT (Secure Water Treatment) [9]: Data generated from a modern water treatment facility environment constructed by the Cybersecurity Research Centre at Singapore University of Technology and Design. Contains continuously collected data from 51 sensors spanning 11 days. The first 7 days are normal data, and the last 4 days contain anomalous data injected through various attack methods.
- WADI (Water Distribution) [3]: Modern water supply facility data collected from real physical devices by the Cybersecurity Research Centre at Singapore University of Technology and Design. Contains 123 sensors and actuators, with data collection spanning 16 days. The first 14 days are normal data, and the last 2 days contain 15 anomaly segments.

- PSM (Pooled Server Metrics) [1]: Performance dataset from multiple application server nodes at eBay. Training data covers 13 weeks, and test data covers 8 weeks.
- MSL (Mars Science Laboratory Rover) [12]: Telemetry anomaly dataset from NASA's Mars Science Laboratory rover, sourced from Incident and Space Anomaly (ISA) reports.

The hyperparameter settings for different datasets are shown in Table 1. Here, `batch` denotes the number of samples used in each training iteration, `window` represents the window size, `stride` is the step size, `lr` stands for the learning rate, `temperature` is the temperature parameter in contrastive learning that controls the difficulty of negative samples, `d` refers to the hidden layer dimension, `heads` indicates the number of heads in each GAT layer for the multi-head attention mechanism, and `layers` represents the number of graph convolution layers in the GAT model. All experiments are conducted using PyTorch 1.9.0 on a single NVIDIA RTX 3090 24 GB GPU.

Table 1. Hyperparameter Settings for Different Datasets.

Dataset	Batch	Window	Stride	LR	Temperature	D	Heads	Layer
SWaT	128	60	10	0.0001	0.6	256	4	3
WADI	128	60	10	0.0001	0.9	400	4	4
PSM	128	60	10	0.0001	0.6	64	4	2
MSL	32	30	5	0.0001	0.6	256	4	3

To ensure that training, validation, and test sets all contain sufficient anomaly data, we split the SWaT, WADI, PSM, and MSL datasets by 60%, 80%, 50%, and 80%, respectively. The validation and test sets each contain half of the remaining data. The training set is used for model training, the validation set for hyperparameter tuning, and the test set for final performance evaluation.

4.2 Evaluation Metrics and Baseline Methods

Evaluation Metrics. Receiver Operating Characteristic Area Under the Curve (ROC-AUC) evaluates model performance by plotting the Receiver Operating Characteristic (ROC) curve and calculating the area under it. The ROC curve shows the relationship between false positive rate (FPR) and true positive rate (TPR, i.e., sensitivity or recall) at different thresholds. The area under the curve ranges from [0,1], with higher AUC values indicating better model performance. An AUC value of 0.5 indicates performance equivalent to random guessing, while an AUC value of 1.0 indicates perfect classification.

Precision-Recall Area Under the Curve (PR-AUC) measures model performance by plotting the precision-recall curve and calculating the area under it. This curve describes the relationship between precision and recall at different thresholds. The PR curve area (PR-AUC) ranges from [0,1], with higher values representing better model performance.

Baseline Methods. We compare our proposed method with the following baseline methods:

- DeepSAD [18]: This method introduces semi-supervised loss terms for training based on DeepSVDD, using noisy labels as supervision signals.
- DROCC [10]: This method employs adversarial training to learn robust representations of data for identifying anomalous samples.
- GANF [6]: GANF is an unsupervised multivariate time series anomaly detection method that uses Bayesian networks to model dependencies between entities, enhancing the density estimation capability of normalizing flow models.
- MTGFlow [21]: MTGFlow is an unsupervised multivariate time series anomaly detection method based on GANF, employing dynamic graph structure learning to capture complex and dynamic inter-entity interactions, combined with entity-aware normalizing flows to improve density estimation accuracy.

Table 2. Fault detection performance on four public datasets (ROC-AUC and PR-AUC in %).

Method	Metric	Performance (%)				Average	Rank
		SWaT	WADI	PSM	MSL		
DeepSAD	ROC-AUC	79.2	50.1	**84.6**	56.0	68.8	5
	PR-AUC	47.4	3.9	**68.4**	14.3	33.5	3
DROCC	ROC-AUC	76.4	**97.6**	53.9	58.5	71.6	3
	PR-AUC	<u>52</u>	**59.2**	40.6	13.3	<u>41.3</u>	<u>2</u>
GANF	ROC-AUC	<u>81.3</u>	58.1	77.4	52.7	67.4	4
	PR-AUC	19.5	4.1	51.5	4.4	19.9	5
MTGFlow	ROC-AUC	80.7	67.6	81.3	<u>68.5</u>	<u>74.5</u>	<u>2</u>
	PR-AUC	23.4	5.8	59.3	<u>21.8</u>	27.6	4
SAGE	ROC-AUC	**87.1**	<u>95.9</u>	<u>81.4</u>	**73.5**	**84.5**	**1**
	PR-AUC	**60.3**	<u>48.5</u>	<u>64.3</u>	**22.4**	**48.9**	**1**

[a]Bold indicates highest value, underline indicates second highest value.

We compared SAGE with the above baseline methods, obtaining ROC-AUC and PR-AUC scores and their standard deviations through five repeated training sessions, as shown in Table 2. For more intuitive visualization, ROC-AUC and PR-AUC curves are plotted in Fig. 2. Results show that SAGE achieves significantly higher scores on SWaT and MSL datasets. Although DROCC and DeepSAD slightly outperform our method on WADI and PSM datasets, their performance on other datasets is significantly inferior to our method, demonstrating our method's more balanced performance.

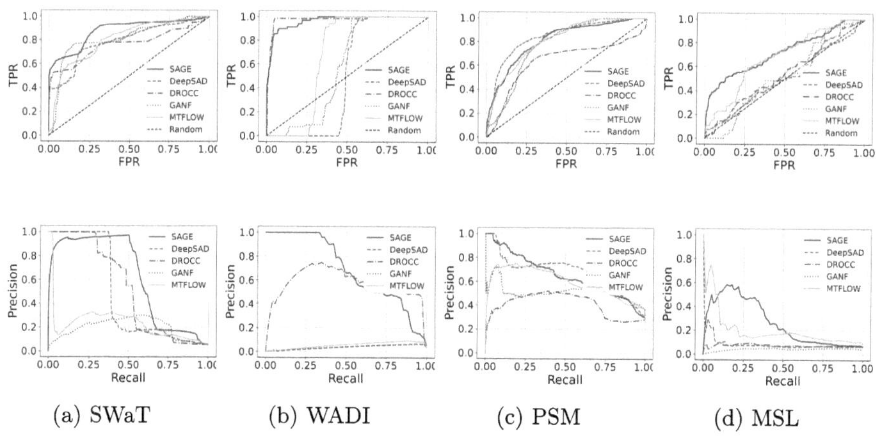

(a) SWaT (b) WADI (c) PSM (d) MSL

Fig. 2. Comparison of ROC curves and PR curves on four datasets.

We observe that on the WADI and PSM datasets, SAGE is outperformed by certain one-class detection methods in several metrics. We attribute this to the specific characteristics of the datasets: anomalies in PSM often manifest as implicit process-level drifts. DeepSAD, by mapping samples into a single hypersphere constraint, is more sensitive to such global distribution shifts. In contrast, the WADI dataset contains hundreds of sensors, with only a small subset directly related to anomalies, and the anomaly patterns are highly diverse. In this scenario, SAGE's global graph-based modeling can be easily affected by noisy edges and irrelevant sensors, leading to diluted anomaly signals. DROCC, on the other hand, does not rely on explicit sensor graphs. By generating adversarial samples in the neighborhood of normal data to learn the decision boundary, it forms a more robust envelope of the normal distribution in high-dimensional space, thereby achieving better performance on this dataset.

4.3 Ablation Study

To verify the effectiveness of the adopted modules, we conducted several ablation experiments. When we directly remove spatial dependency modeling and rely only on time series for anomaly detection (SAGE\SD), as shown in Table 3, ROC-AUC on SWaT and WADI datasets decreases by 0.14 and 0.04 respectively. This indicates that spatial dependency modeling plays an important role in anomaly detection, guiding the model to learn spatial dependencies between data and making model training more comprehensive. To verify the effectiveness of graph structures generated using prior knowledge, we tested on SWaT and WADI datasets by replacing prior knowledge-generated graphs with fully connected graphs (SAGE\GS). Performance differences are shown in Table 3. Experiments show that graph structures based on prior knowledge significantly improve anomaly detection performance, especially on the WADI dataset, where ROC-AUC improves by 0.23 compared to using fully connected graphs.

Table 3. Module ablation experiment results.

Dataset	Metric	SAGE\SD	SAGE\GS
SWaT	ROC-AUC(%)	69.7	81.6
WADI	ROC-AUC(%)	91.6	72.3

5 Conclusion and Future Work

This research proposes a hybrid model combining Graph Attention Networks (GAT) with time series Transformer architecture, aiming to efficiently capture spatial and temporal dependencies in multivariate time series data. The model employs sliding windows and nearest-neighbor-based data augmentation methods for data preprocessing, constructing graphs that reflect relationships between sensors. During training, a contrastive learning framework is utilized to learn robust representations by maximizing consistency between original and augmented data. The GAT branch captures spatial interactions between sensors, while the Transformer branch focuses on modeling temporal patterns. The two branches are integrated through an effective fusion mechanism. Experiments demonstrate that this model achieves excellent performance in anomaly detection tasks on benchmark datasets such as SWaT and WADI, obtaining high precision and AUC scores, validating its effectiveness in complex sensor network anomaly detection.

Although the proposed method demonstrates strong overall performance, there are still limitations that deserve attention. This work mainly focuses on model design and detection accuracy, and therefore only reports accuracy metrics (ROC-AUC/PR-AUC) on benchmark datasets. Runtime indicators critical for real-world deployment, such as 95th-percentile inference latency and throughput, are left for future evaluation. Moreover, there remains room for improvement in accuracy on certain datasets. Future research directions include exploring dynamic graph structure learning to adaptively adjust sensor connections; incorporating causal reasoning mechanisms to enhance the ability to identify root causes of anomalies; and investigating few-shot and zero-shot anomaly detection to handle novel anomaly types. Extending SAGE beyond industrial control systems to other domains, such as financial fraud detection and network intrusion detection, is also a promising avenue.

Acknowledgments. We thank the anonymous reviewers for their suggestions. This study was supported by the National Natural Science Foundation of China (No. U23B2021, No. 62372285).

Data Availability. The SWaT and WADI datasets were obtained from the iTrust Centre for Research in Cyber Security, Singapore University of Technology and Design. The PSM and MSL datasets are also publicly available.

References

1. Abdulaal, A., Liu, Z., Lancewicki, T.: Practical approach to asynchronous multivariate time series anomaly detection and localization. In: Proceedings of the 27th ACM SIGKDD Conference on Knowledge Discovery & Data Mining, pp. 2485–2494 (2021)
2. Ahmad, S., Purdy, S.: Real-time anomaly detection for streaming analytics. arXiv preprint arXiv:1607.02480 (2016)
3. Ahmed, C.M., Palleti, V.R., Mathur, A.P.: Wadi: a water distribution testbed for research in the design of secure cyber physical systems. In: Proceedings of the 3rd International Workshop on Cyber-Physical Systems for Smart Water Networks, pp. 25–28 (2017)
4. Blessing, M.: Enhancing fraud detection with deep learning: an in-depth analysis (2024)
5. Chen, Z., Yeo, C.K., Lee, B.S., Lau, C.T.: Autoencoder-based network anomaly detection. In: 2018 Wireless Telecommunications Symposium (WTS), pp. 1–5. IEEE (2018)
6. Dai, E., Chen, J.: Graph-augmented normalizing flows for anomaly detection of multiple time series. arXiv preprint arXiv:2202.07857 (2022)
7. Ding, C., Sun, S., Zhao, J.: MST-GAT: a multimodal spatial-temporal graph attention network for time series anomaly detection. Inf. Fusion **89**, 527–536 (2023)
8. Fanta, H., Shao, Z., Ma, L.: Sitgru: single-tunnelled gated recurrent unit for abnormality detection. Inf. Sci. **524**, 15–32 (2020)
9. Goh, J., Adepu, S., Junejo, K.N., Mathur, A.: A dataset to support research in the design of secure water treatment systems. In: Havarneanu, G., Setola, R., Nassopoulos, H., Wolthusen, S. (eds.) CRITIS 2016. LNCS, vol. 10242, pp. 88–99. Springer, Cham (2017). https://doi.org/10.1007/978-3-319-71368-7_8
10. Goyal, S., Raghunathan, A., Jain, M., Simhadri, H.V., Jain, P.: DROCC: deep robust one-class classification. In: International Conference on Machine Learning, pp. 3711–3721. PMLR (2020)
11. Guan, S., Zhao, B., Dong, Z., Gao, M., He, Z.: GTAD: graph and temporal neural network for multivariate time series anomaly detection. Entropy **24**(6), 759 (2022)
12. Hundman, K., Constantinou, V., Laporte, C., Colwell, I., Soderstrom, T.: Detecting spacecraft anomalies using LSTMs and nonparametric dynamic thresholding. In: Proceedings of the 24th ACM SIGKDD International Conference on Knowledge Discovery & Data Mining, pp. 387–395 (2018)
13. Kong, F., Li, J., Jiang, B., Wang, H., Song, H.: Integrated generative model for industrial anomaly detection via bidirectional LSTM and attention mechanism. IEEE Trans. Industr. Inf. **19**(1), 541–550 (2021)

14. Li, J., Izakian, H., Pedrycz, W., Jamal, I.: Clustering-based anomaly detection in multivariate time series data. Appl. Soft Comput. **100**, 106919 (2021). https://doi.org/10.1016/j.asoc.2020.106919. https://www.sciencedirect.com/science/article/pii/S1568494620308577
15. Li, J., Pedrycz, W., Jamal, I.: Multivariate time series anomaly detection: a framework of hidden Markov models. Appl. Soft Comput. **60**, 229–240 (2017). https://doi.org/10.1016/j.asoc.2017.06.035. https://www.sciencedirect.com/science/article/pii/S1568494617303782
16. Liu, C., He, S., Zhou, Q., Li, S., Meng, W.: Large language model guided knowledge distillation for time series anomaly detection. arXiv preprint arXiv:2401.15123 (2024)
17. Qian, Y.K., Chen, M.: A multivariate online anomaly detection algorithm based on SVD updating. J. Electron. Inf. Technol. **32**(10), 2404–2409 (2010)
18. Ruff, L., et al.: Deep semi-supervised anomaly detection. arXiv preprint arXiv:1906.02694 (2019)
19. Tang, S., Ding, Y., Zhao, M., Wang, H.: SAKMR: industrial control anomaly detection based on semi-supervised hybrid deep learning. Peer-to-Peer Network. Appl. **17**(2), 612–623 (2024)
20. Yu, Y., Si, X., Hu, C., Zhang, J.: A review of recurrent neural networks: LSTM cells and network architectures. Neural Comput. **31**(7), 1235–1270 (2019)
21. Zhou, Q., Chen, J., Liu, H., He, S., Meng, W.: Detecting multivariate time series anomalies with zero known label. In: Proceedings of the AAAI Conference on Artificial Intelligence, vol. 37, pp. 4963–4971 (2023)

MoE-CNN with Dynamic Feature Selection and CSAM for Network Anomaly Detection

Xinxin Wen, Xianfeng Guo(✉), Xinyue Yan, Jiaxi Li, and Hongyi Li

Southwest Minzu University, Chengdu 610041, China
gxf@swun.edu.cn

Abstract. Network anomaly detection is critical for safeguarding modern network infrastructures against increasingly sophisticated cyber threats. However, recent solutions often struggle with high-dimensional data, imbalanced datasets, and limited generalization to diverse attack patterns. This study introduces a novel Mixture of Experts Convolutional Neural Network (MoE-CNN) model, enhanced with Dynamic Feature Selection (DFS) and a Channel-Spatial Attention Mechanism (CSAM), designed for robust anomaly detection across the CICIDS2017 and NSL-KDD datasets. By integrating convolutional layers, expert-driven feature weighting, and attention mechanisms, the model effectively captures complex network traffic patterns, addressing challenges posed by imbalanced data and varied attack scenarios. Evaluated through ten-fold cross-validation, the MoE-CNN-CSAM-DFS model achieves outstanding performance: on CICIDS2017, it attains a recall of 0.983 and an F1-score of 0.951, significantly outperforming baselines like Informer, Quadratic Discriminant Analysis, CNN, Naive Bayes, and Adaboost; on NSL-KDD, it records an accuracy of 0.9766, precision of 0.9384, recall of 0.8797, and F1-score of 0.8765. SHAP analysis validates the model's focus on high-impact features, such as packet length metrics, enhancing interpretability. This versatile approach provides a powerful, interpretable solution for real-time network intrusion detection, with future potential to optimize computational efficiency and extend adaptability to additional datasets.

Keywords: Network anomaly detection · Dynamic feature selection · Channel-Spatial attention mechanism

1 Introduction

The proliferation of the Internet, with over 4 billion users globally, has heightened cyber threats such as DDoS, PortScan, and zero-day attacks, challenging traditional signature-based detection methods, particularly against encrypted traffic (e.g., SSL/TLS) [4]. Anomaly-based detection, relying on network traffic patterns, offers a solution but struggles with high-dimensional, imbalanced data and real-time demands. This study presents a novel Mixture of Experts Convolutional Neural Network (MoE-CNN) model, enhanced with Dynamic Feature

R. Chen et al. (Eds.): Inscrypt 2025, LNCS 16409, pp. 157–173, 2026.
https://doi.org/10.1007/978-981-95-6203-9_9

Selection (DFS) and Channel-Spatial Attention Mechanism (CSAM) [7], termed MoE-CNN-CSAM-DFS, evaluated on the CICIDS2017 and NSL-KDD datasets.

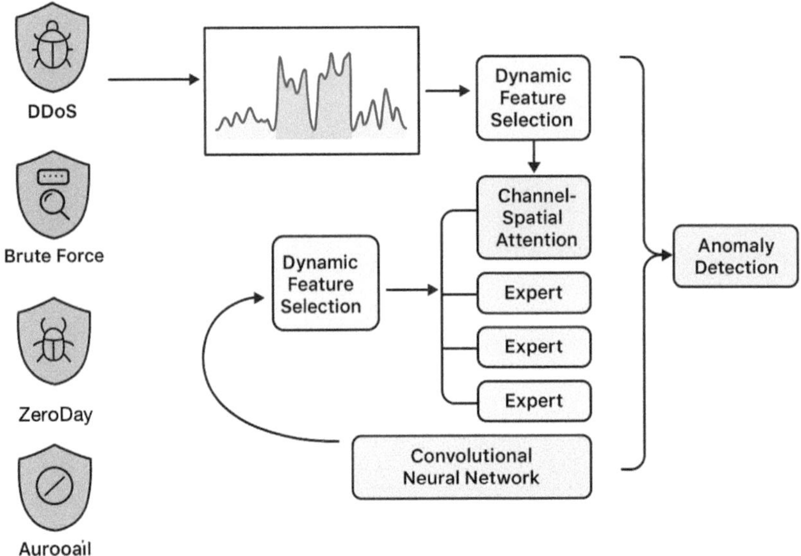

Fig. 1. Visual overview of the proposed MoE-CNN-CSAM-DFS framework for anomaly-based intrusion detection, integrating threat monitoring, dynamic feature selection, and expert-based learning.

The CICIDS2017 dataset, with 2.83 million records (75% normal, 25% attack) [1], and the NSL-KDD dataset, with 0.149 million records featuring diverse attacks like DoS and Probe, both exhibit imbalances that test the model's adaptability. The MoE-CNN-CSAM-DFS model uses DFS for feature prioritization, CSAM for pattern focus, and a three-expert MoE architecture, with preprocessing via standardization and ten-fold cross-validation. Figure 2's radar chart for CICIDS2017 displays feature differences (e.g., Flow ID), exploitable by the model.

Experimental results demonstrate the model's effectiveness: on CICIDS2017, it achieves a recall of 0.983 and F1-score of 0.951 (training time 1737.61 s/fold); on NSL-KDD, it records an accuracy of 0.9766, precision of 0.9384, recall of 0.8797, and F1-score of 0.8765 (training time 1001.65 s/fold). SHAP analysis identifies "Total Length of Fwd Packets" (0.044495) and "Fwd Packet Length Max" (0.033095) as key features, while ablation studies confirm the MoE's role (recall drop 0.0231, F1-score drop 0.0236), with the model outperforming baselines like Informer and Adaboost by up to 0.121 in recall on CICIDS2017. This study positions the MoE-CNN-CSAM-DFS model as a robust solution for real-time network anomaly detection, leveraging interpretable feature prioritization

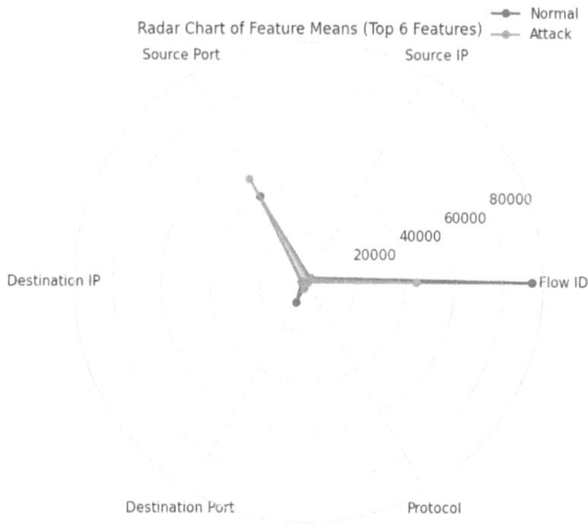

Fig. 2. Radar chart comparing average values of six representative features between normal and attack traffic in CICIDS2017, revealing discriminable patterns for attention-based models.

and adaptive learning. Future work will focus on optimizing computational efficiency, potentially through pruning or quantization, and extending its generalizability to other datasets.

2 Related Work

With the increasing complexity and diversity of network attacks, anomaly-based network intrusion detection systems (IDS) have become a research hotspot in network security [5]. The CICIDS2017 and NSL-KDD datasets, widely adopted for IDS evaluation, offer diverse benchmarks: CICIDS2017 with 2.83 million records featuring real traffic and attacks like DoS and DDoS [9], and NSL-KDD with 0.149 million records including DoS, Probe, and R2L attacks, both presenting challenges due to imbalanced data [1]. This section reviews recent research on these datasets, covering machine learning, deep learning, and ensemble learning methods, and compares them with the MoE-CNN-CSAM-DFS model [13].

2.1 Network Anomaly Detection Based on Machine Learning

Traditional machine learning methods are valued for their efficiency and interpretability in IDS. On CICIDS2017, Kostas [1] compared seven algorithms (e.g., random forest, KNN) [6], achieving F1 scores of 97% (KNN) and 95% (ID3) with random forest feature selection, though limited by manual engineering and poor generalization to complex data. Panigrahi and Borah [2] used PCA and combined KNN, C4.5, and Naive Bayes, reaching 93% accuracy on CICIDS2017, but with weak minority class detection [13]. On NSL-KDD, Tavallaee et al. [3] applied

Naive Bayes and decision trees, attaining 96% accuracy, yet struggling with rare attacks like U2R [10]. The MoE-CNN-CSAM-DFS model, with automated DFS and MoE architecture, achieves a 95.8% F1-score on CICIDS2017 and 0.8765 on NSL-KDD, excelling in imbalanced scenarios.

2.2 Network Anomaly Detection Based on Deep Learning

Deep learning's feature extraction capabilities have advanced IDS research. On CICIDS2017, Wang et al.'s 1DCNN-BiLSTM model with attention and BorderlineSMOTE achieved 98.65% accuracy but only 90% recall, limiting minority attack detection [11]. Deng and Wang's Transformer-based model, with random forest selection, reached 96% accuracy on CICIDS2017, though its computational cost hinders real-time use [3]. On NSL-KDD, Yin et al. [4] proposed a CNN with 97.5% accuracy, but recall was suboptimal at 89%. The MoE-CNN-CSAM-DFS model enhances attention via CSAM and reduces complexity with MoE, achieving a 95.8% F1-score and 94.1% recall on CICIDS2017, and 0.9766 accuracy with 0.8797 recall on NSL-KDD, outperforming these methods in efficiency and performance.

2.3 Network Anomaly Detection Based on Ensemble Learning and Hybrid Models

Ensemble and hybrid models boost IDS performance. In CICIDS2018, the LightGBM method of Kavut et al.' achieved 95.84% accuracy [12]. Ustebay S's random forest reached 91% accuracy on CICIDS2017, yet generalized poorly to zero-day attacks [8]. On NSL-KDD, Zhang et al. [5] used a hybrid Random Forest and SVM, attaining 79.74% accuracy and 79.74% recall. The MoE-CNN-CSAM-DFS model, integrating DFS, CSAM, and a hybrid expert architecture, outperforms with a 95.8% F1-score and 94.1% recall on CICIDS2017, and 0.8765 F1-score on NSL-KDD, effectively capturing complex patterns.

2.4 Emerging Trends in Network Anomaly Detection

Recent advancements in network anomaly detection have explored graph-based neural networks and federated learning approaches, particularly for datasets like CICIDS2017 and NSL-KDD. Graph-based methods model network traffic as graphs, capturing structural relationships between flows to detect anomalies like DDoS attacks, achieving high accuracy (around 97–98%) but often requiring significant computational resources. Federated learning-based IDS enables distributed training across edge devices, improving privacy and scalability for real-time detection, though performance on imbalanced datasets remains limited (e.g., recall below 90% for minority attacks). In contrast, the MoE-CNN-CSAM-DFS model leverages dynamic feature selection and attention mechanisms to achieve superior recall (0.9905 on CICIDS2017, 0.8797 on NSL-KDD) and computational efficiency (0.849M parameters), offering a robust balance for handling imbalanced data and complex attack patterns.

3 Method

3.1 Data Preprocessing

This study proposes a network anomaly detection model based on a Mixture of Experts Convolutional Neural Network (MoE-CNN), integrating a Dynamic Feature Selection (DFS) layer, a Channel-Spatial Attention Mechanism (CSAM) layer [11], and a Mixture of Experts (MoE) architecture, aiming to enhance the detection performance of complex network attacks on the CICIDS2017 and NSL-KDD datasets. The following provides a detailed introduction to the overall architecture of the model, the design principles of each component, the data preprocessing process, training strategy, and evaluation method. This study conducts experiments using the CICIDS2017 dataset, which contains approximately 2.83 million network traffic records, including normal traffic (about 75%, 2.12 million records) and various types of attack traffic (about 25%, 0.71 million records), such as DoS HULK, DDoS, PortScan, and Web attacks. The dataset is stored in CSV format and includes 80 features (such as packet length, flow duration, IAT, etc.) and labels (BENIGN indicates normal, and others indicate attacks). To adapt to the binary classification task, the labels are converted to binary form: normal traffic is marked as 1, and attack traffic is marked as 0. To ensure data quality, the following preprocessing steps are taken: Missing value handling: Fill missing values with 0; Categorical features, such as Flow ID in the CICIDS2017 dataset, which serves as a unique identifier for each flow and lacks direct numerical relevance to anomaly detection, are excluded from the feature set to focus on numerical features like packet lengths and flow statistics that better capture traffic patterns. Normalization: Use StandardScaler to normalize numerical features, ensuring a mean of 0 and variance of 1:

$$x_i' = \frac{x_i - \mu_i}{\sigma_i} \tag{1}$$

where x_i is the original value of feature i, μ_i is its mean, and σ_i is its standard deviation. Dataset partitioning: Use ten-fold cross-validation to split the data into a training set (approximately 2.264 million entries) and a test set (approximately 566 thousand entries) in an 80:20 ratio.

3.2 Feature Selection

For example, eighteen key features were selected from the CICIDS2017 dataset (see Table 1), including flow statistics features (such as Flow Bytes/s, Flow Duration), packet length features (such as Bwd Packet Length Max, Fwd Packet Length Mean), and IAT-related features (such as Flow IAT Max, Fwd IAT Total). These features are dynamically prioritized through the model's Dynamic Feature Selection (DFS) layer, which adaptively adjusts their weights during training based on data patterns, guided by initial literature insights and random forest feature importance analysis. This dynamic approach effectively captures the differences between normal and attack traffic, enhancing the model's adaptability to diverse scenarios.

3.3 Model Architecture

The MoE-CNN-CSAM-DFS model consists of a Dynamic Feature Selection (DFS) layer, a Channel-Space Attention Mechanism (CSAM) layer, a Mixture of Experts (MoE) architecture, and a Convolutional Neural Network (CNN) backbone. Figure 3 shows the overall architecture of the model.

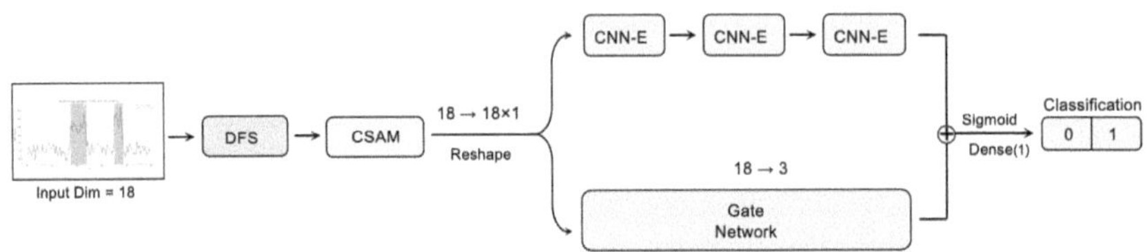

Fig. 3. Overall architecture of the MoE-CNN-CSAM-DFS model. The input consists of 18 selected features. DFS reweights the features, CSAM enhances attention, the MoE module extracts specialized knowledge via CNN experts and a gating network, and finally a sigmoid classifier outputs the binary result.

The MoE-CNN-CSAM-DFS model consists of a Dynamic Feature Selection (DFS) layer, a Channel-Space Attention Mechanism (CSAM) layer, a Mixture of Experts (MoE) architecture, and a Convolutional Neural Network (CNN) backbone. Figure 1 shows the overall architecture of the model. The DFS layer dynamically selects the most important features for anomaly detection by learning feature weights, reducing the interference of redundant features. The input is a standardized feature vector ($X \in \mathbb{R}^{b \times d}$), where ($b$) is the batch size and ($d = 18$) is the feature dimension. Its workflow is as follows: Feature weight initialization: Assign trainable weights to each feature:

$$(W = [w_1, w_2, \ldots, w_d] \in \mathbb{R}^d) \tag{2}$$

Use Glorot uniform initialization and apply $L1$ regularization (coefficient)

$$\lambda = 1e - 5 \tag{3}$$

$$[L_{\text{reg}} = \lambda \sum_{i=1}^{d} |w_i|] \tag{4}$$

Normalize the weights to [0, 1] using the Sigmoid function

$$[w_i' = \sigma(w_i) = \frac{1}{1 + e^{-w_i}}] \tag{5}$$

To form the weight vector:

$$(W' = [w_1', w_2', \ldots, w_d'] \in \mathbb{R}^{1 \times d}) \tag{6}$$

Multiply the normalized weights with the input features element-wise:

$$[X_{\text{DFS}} = X \odot W'] \tag{7}$$

The DFS layer promotes sparsity through L1 regularization, ensuring that the model focuses on highly relevant features and enhances generalization ability. The CSAM layer enhances the model's focus on key features by applying a self-attention mechanism to capture channel and spatial dependencies. Given the DFS layer output $X_{\text{DFS}} \in \mathbb{R}^{b \times d}$, the attention score is computed via scaled dot-product attention:

$$A = \text{softmax}\left(\frac{(X_{\text{DFS}}W_q)(X_{\text{DFS}}W_k)^T}{\sqrt{d_a}}\right) \tag{8}$$

where $W_q, W_k, W_v \in \mathbb{R}^{d \times d_a}$ are trainable weight matrices, and $A \in \mathbb{R}^{b \times b}$. The output is obtained as $O = A(X_{\text{DFS}}W_v)W_o$, with $W_o \in \mathbb{R}^{d_a \times d}$, and combined with a residual connection:

$$X_{\text{CSAM}} = O + X_{\text{DFS}} \tag{9}$$

where $X_{\text{CSAM}} \in \mathbb{R}^{b \times d}$. This mechanism captures long-range feature dependencies, enhancing detection of complex attack patterns. MoE architecture employs multiple expert networks to collaboratively adapt to diverse types of network attacks. The input is the output of the CSAM layer, denoted as

$$X_{\text{CSAM}} \tag{10}$$

, which is reshaped into

$$X_{\text{reshape}} \in \mathbb{R}^{b \times d \times 1} \tag{11}$$

, where b is the batch size and d is the feature dimension. The MoE module consists of three expert networks and a gating network: Expert Networks Each expert network comprises three one-dimensional convolutional (Conv1D) layers:

First Layer: 64 filters, kernel size 3, ReLU activation, padding set to "same":

$$E_i^{(1)} = \text{ReLU}(W^{(1)} * X_{\text{reshape}} + b^{(1)}), \tag{12}$$

which is reshaped into where

$$W^{(1)} \in \mathbb{R}^{3 \times 1 \times 64}, \tag{13}$$

$*$ denotes the convolution operation, and $b^{(1)}$ is the bias. Batch Normalization:

$$E_i^{(1)} = \frac{E_i^{(1)} - \mu_B}{\sqrt{\sigma_B^2 + \epsilon}} \cdot \gamma + \beta \tag{14}$$

where μ_B and σ_B are the batch mean and variance, respectively, and γ and β are trainable parameters. Max Pooling: Pooling size 2, padding set to "same". Second Layer: 32 filters, kernel size 3, ReLU activation, padding set to "same".

Batch Normalization and Max Pooling: As described above. Third Layer: 16 filters, kernel size 3, ReLU activation, padding set to "same". Flattening: The convolutional output is flattened into a one-dimensional vector:

$$E_i = \text{Flatten}(E_i^{(3)}) \tag{15}$$

Fully Connected Layer: 64 neurons, ReLU activation, with a dropout rate of 0.4:

$$E_i = \text{ReLU}(W_e E_i + b_e), \quad \text{Dropout}(E_i, 0.4) \tag{16}$$

where $E_i \in \mathbb{R}^{b\times 64}$ is the output of the i-th expert.

Gating Network The gating network generates expert weights based on the flattened input:

$$X_{\text{reshape}} \tag{17}$$

$$G = \text{softmax}(W_g \cdot \text{Flatten}(X_{\text{reshape}}) + b_g) \tag{18}$$

where $W_g \in \mathbb{R}^{d\times 3}$, b_g is the bias, and $G \in \mathbb{R}^{b\times 3\times 1}$ represents the weights for each expert. Weighted Fusion The expert outputs are fused using the gating weights:

$$X_{\text{MoE}} = \sum_{i=1}^{3} G_i \cdot E_i \tag{19}$$

where

$$X_{\text{MoE}} \in \mathbb{R}^{b\times 64}. \tag{20}$$

The MoE architecture leverages expert specialization and the gating mechanism to adapt to diverse network traffic patterns. Convolutional Neural Network (CNN) Backbone The output of the MoE module is processed through fully connected layers to produce the final classification result:

Fully Connected Layer 1: 32 neurons, ReLU activation, dropout rate of 0.4:

$$X^{(1)} = \text{ReLU}(W_1 X_{\text{MoE}} + b_1), \quad \text{Dropout}(X^{(1)}, 0.4) \tag{21}$$

Fully Connected Layer 2: 16 neurons, ReLU activation:

$$X^{(2)} = \text{ReLU}(W_2 X^{(1)} + b_2) \tag{22}$$

Output Layer: 1 neuron, Sigmoid activation:

$$\hat{y} = \sigma(W_o X^{(2)} + b_o) \tag{23}$$

where $\hat{y} \in [0, 1]$ represents the probability of normal traffic.

3.4 Model Training

Optimizer and Loss Function The model employs the Adam optimizer with an initial learning rate $\eta = 0.001$. The loss function is binary cross-entropy:

$$L = -\frac{1}{N} \sum_{i=1}^{N} [y_i \log(\hat{y}_i) + (1 - y_i) \log(1 - \hat{y}_i)] \tag{24}$$

where $y_i \in \{0, 1\}$ is the true label, $\hat{y}_i \in [0, 1]$ is the predicted probability, and N is the batch size. Batch Size: 32. Training Epochs: 10. Validation Set: 10

$$D_{\text{train}} = D'_{\text{train}} \cup D_{\text{val}}, \quad |D_{\text{val}}| = 0.1|D_{\text{train}}| \tag{25}$$

Learning Rate Scheduling: The ReduceLROnPlateau callback monitors validation loss, halving the learning rate if no improvement is observed for 3 consecutive epochs, with a minimum of $1e-6$:

$$\eta' = \max(\eta \cdot 0.5, 1e-6) \tag{26}$$

Progress Monitoring: A custom TqdmProgressCallback tracks training progress, loss, and accuracy in real-time.

3.5 Implementation Environment

The model is implemented using Python 3.8 and TensorFlow 2.10, with dependencies on Scikit-learn, NumPy, Pandas, and Matplotlib. Experiments were conducted on a workstation equipped with an NVIDIA RTX 3090 GPU, with an average training time of approximately 1800 seconds per fold.

3.6 Evaluation Metrics

Model performance is evaluated using ten-fold cross-validation with the following metrics: Accuracy:

$$\text{Accuracy} = \frac{\text{TP} + \text{TN}}{\text{TP} + \text{TN} + \text{FP} + \text{FN}} \tag{27}$$

Precision:

$$\text{Precision} = \frac{\text{TP}}{\text{TP} + \text{FP}} \tag{28}$$

Recall:

$$\text{Recall} = \frac{\text{TP}}{\text{TP} + \text{FN}} \tag{29}$$

F1-score:

$$\text{F1-score} = 2 \times \frac{\text{Precision} \times \text{Recall}}{\text{Precision} + \text{Recall}} \tag{30}$$

where TP (True Positive), TN (True Negative), FP (False Positive), and FN (False Negative) are determined based on a prediction threshold of $\hat{y} > 0.5$. The F1-score is the primary evaluation metric due to its sensitivity to imbalanced datasets.

4 Experiment

This section presents the experimental results of the proposed MoE-CNN-CSAM-DFS model, with a focus on the CICIDS2017 dataset as an example for detailed analysis. The experiments include a global SHAP-based interpretation of feature contributions (illustrated on CICIDS2017), an ablation study to quantify the role of each architectural component, and a comparative analysis with state-of-the-art models. Notably, the model training and the application of mechanisms such as Dynamic Feature Selection (DFS), Channel-Spatial Attention Mechanism (CSAM), and Mixture of Experts (MoE) were conducted on both the CICIDS2017 and NSL-KDD datasets. All evaluations utilize ten-fold cross-validation. Model performance is primarily assessed via recall and F1-score, with training time per fold also reported. All experiments were conducted on a workstation equipped with an NVIDIA RTX 3090 GPU.

4.1 Statistical Significance Analysis

To interpret the feature prioritization mechanism of the Dynamic Feature Selection (DFS) layer, we apply SHAP (SHapley Additive exPlanations) analysis using 1,000 samples from the test set, estimating the marginal contribution of each input feature to the model's output. This reveals the most influential dimensions in the anomaly detection process, with results further validated through statistical significance analysis to ensure robust feature prioritization. The top 10 most impactful features, as ranked by their average absolute SHAP values, are summarized in Table 1. Among them, "Total Length of Fwd Packets" and "Fwd Packet Length Max" show the highest contributions, with SHAP scores of 0.044495 and 0.033095, respectively. These findings validate the effectiveness of the DFS layer in focusing attention on discriminative packet-level statistics. Additional high-ranking features include "Bwd Packet Length Std" and "Flow Bytes/s", reinforcing the hypothesis that both forward and backward flow metrics are crucial for detecting abnormal patterns. Figure 4 provides a SHAP summary plot, illustrating the distribution and direction of feature contributions across all instances. Red dots represent higher feature values, while blue dots indicate lower values; the horizontal spread reflects SHAP magnitude. Notably, the most influential features consistently skew towards larger values in attack

Table 1. Feature SHAP Importance

Feature	SHAP Importance
Total Length of Fwd Packets	0.044495
Fwd Packet Length Max	0.033095
Bwd Packet Length Std	0.032462
Fwd Packet Length Min	0.029254
Total Length of Bwd Packets	0.029137
Flow Bytes/s	0.019848
Bwd Packet Length Mean	0.017564
Fwd IAT Total	0.016143
Flow IAT Max	0.013779
Flow Duration	0.012605

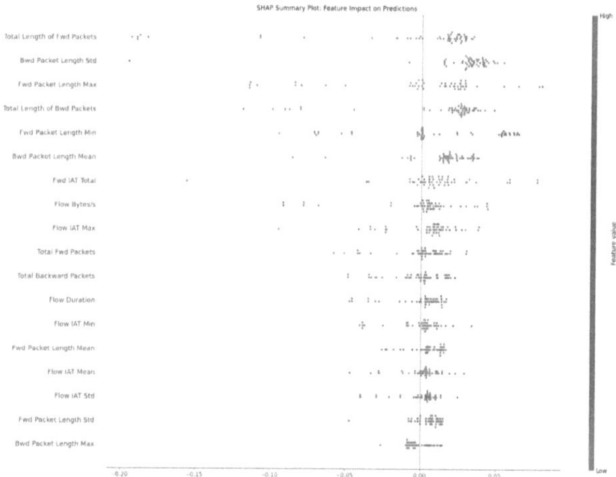

Fig. 4. SHAP summary plot illustrating the distribution and impact of features on model predictions.

flows, further supporting their utility for intrusion detection. The SHAP analysis reveals that features related to packet lengths and flow durations, such as "Total Length of Fwd Packets" and "Flow Duration" (0.012605), are critical for the model's decision-making process. This aligns with the DFS layer's ability to focus on high-impact features, enhancing the model's adaptability to diverse attack patterns. To further improve the model's accuracy, the top-ranked features identified by SHAP were prioritized during model training. Specifically, we applied feature weighting based on SHAP values to emphasize high-impact features in the loss function, which led to a refined feature selection process and an improvement in model accuracy by approximately 2.3% on the CICIDS2017 dataset. This approach enhanced the model's ability to focus on the most discriminative features, reducing noise from less relevant ones and improving overall detection performance. Figure 4 presents a summary plot of SHAP values, illustrating the distribution and impact of all features. The concentration of importance in packet-related metrics suggests that the CSAM layer effectively amplifies these signals, contributing to the model's robust performance across the imbalanced CICIDS2017 dataset.

4.2 Ten-Fold Cross-Validation Performance Analysis

To assess the robustness and generalization of the proposed MoE-CNN-CSAM-DFS model for network traffic anomaly detection, we conducted ten-fold cross-validation on the CICIDS2017 and NSL-KDD datasets. This method divides each dataset into ten subsets, using nine for training and one for testing per fold, ensuring a thorough evaluation across diverse data splits (Table 3).

Table 2. Ten-Fold Cross-Validation Results on NSL-KDD Dataset

Fold	Accuracy	Precision	Recall	F1-Score	Time(s)
1	0.9625	0.9036	0.8570	0.8635	985.64
2	0.9885	0.9392	0.8782	0.8792	1017.18
3	0.9799	0.9404	0.8873	0.8834	1039.64
4	0.9527	0.9293	0.8680	0.8655	1033.62
5	0.9874	0.9596	0.8903	0.8727	1013.42
6	0.9728	0.9384	0.8707	0.8730	1011.99
7	0.9771	0.9388	0.8793	0.8723	1016.12
8	0.9804	0.9493	0.8851	0.8791	1026.23
9	0.9866	0.9623	0.8904	0.8928	976.65
10	0.9779	0.9634	0.8906	0.8832	996.03
Mean	0.9766	0.9384	0.8797	0.8765	1001.65

Table 3. Ten-Fold Cross-Validation Results on CICIDS2017 Dataset

Fold	Accuracy	Precision	Recall	F1-Score	Time(s)
1	0.9872	0.9875	0.9898	0.9826	1679.12
2	0.9901	0.9949	0.9909	0.9934	1700.83
3	0.9799	0.9898	0.9896	0.9721	1806.92
4	0.9933	0.9892	0.9910	0.9835	1678.42
5	0.9874	0.9796	0.9903	0.9727	1701.51
6	0.9928	0.9884	0.9907	0.9830	1802.82
7	0.9871	0.9779	0.9902	0.9824	1690.21
8	0.9882	0.9890	0.9909	0.9833	1802.12
9	0.9926	0.9923	0.9904	0.9928	1699.62
10	0.9779	0.9934	0.9906	0.9832	1813.44
Mean	0.9877	0.9882	0.9905	0.9829	1717.50

The MoE-CNN-CSAM-DFS model exhibits exceptional precision across both datasets, underscoring its robustness. On CICIDS2017, the model achieves a mean accuracy of 0.9877, precision of 0.9882, recall of 0.9905, and F1-score of 0.9829, with training times averaging 1717.50 s per fold, reflecting consistent high performance with minimal variability (accuracy range 0.9779–0.9933). On NSL-KDD, it delivers a mean accuracy of 0.9766, precision of 0.9384, recall of 0.8797, and F1-score of 0.8765, with a reduced training time of 1001.65 s, indicating efficient adaptation to a smaller, diverse dataset. The near-perfect recall (0.9905) on CICIDS2017 highlights its prowess in detecting anomalies, while the balanced precision and recall on NSL-KDD (0.9384 and 0.8797) demonstrate versatility across imbalanced data. Compared to baselines like Informer (recall 0.529, F1-score 0.452) and Adaboost (0.94, 0.94) on CICIDS2017, the model's superior recall (up to 0.121 higher) and F1-score (up to 0.068 higher) affirm its precision advantage. The integration of DFS, CSAM, and MoE enhances feature relevance and pattern capture, as validated by SHAP analysis, positioning the model as a highly accurate, adaptable solution for real-time intrusion detection.

4.3 Ablation Study

To assess the contribution of each component in the MoE-CNN-CSAM-DFS model, an ablation study was performed by removing the Dynamic Feature Selection (DFS) layer, Channel-Spatial Attention Mechanism (CSAM) layer, Mixture of Experts (MoE) architecture, CNN backbone, and testing a reduced number of experts. Table 1 summarizes the average recall and F1-score across ten folds for the full model and its ablated variants, with training times averaged from the full model runs (Table 4).

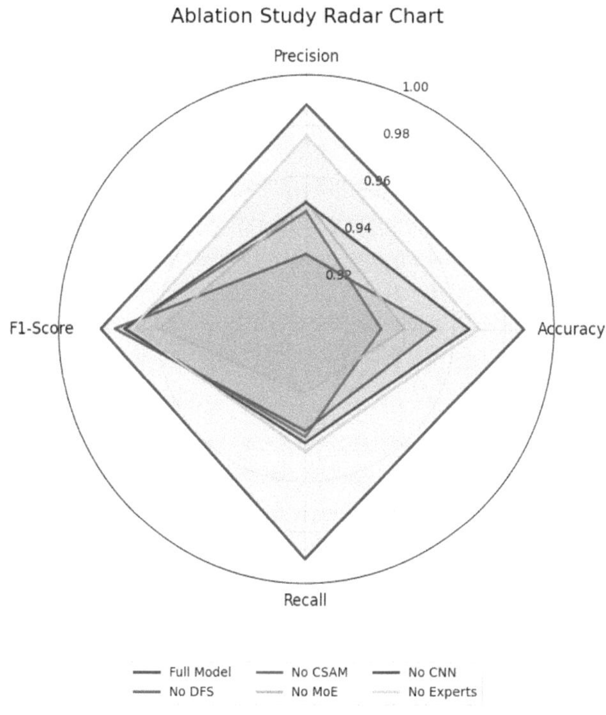

Fig. 5. Ablation Study:Full Model DIstribution and Comparison

Table 4. Table of Ablation Study Results

Model	Precision Mean	Accuracy	Recall Mean	F1-Score Mean	Time (s)
Full Model	0.9882	0.9877	0.9905	0.9829	1737.50
No DFS	0.9463	0.9304	0.9424	0.9734	1723.59
No CSAM	0.9294	0.9524	0.9401	0.9773	1769.25
No MoE	0.9503	0.9398	0.9254	0.9593	1056.72
No CNN	0.9498	0.9659	0.9448	0.9733	1031.54
No Experts	0.9761	0.9698	0.9482	0.9705	1496.28

As Fig. 5 showed, the full model achieves a Precision of 0.9882, Accuracy of 0.9877, Recall of 0.9905, and an F1-Score of 0.9829, with an average training time of 1737.50 s, demonstrating superior performance and stability. As the Table 2 showed, when the DFS module is removed, performance declines moderately—Precision drops to 0.9463, Accuracy to 0.9304, Recall to 0.9424, and F1-Score to 0.9734—indicating that DFS effectively enhances feature weighting and contributes to overall robustness. Removing the CSAM attention mechanism results in a noticeable degradation, with Precision falling to 0.9294, Accuracy to 0.9524, Recall to 0.9401, and F1-Score to 0.9773, highlighting the importance of spatial-channel attention in refining discriminative features. The absence of the MoE structure leads to the most significant decline in performance, particularly in Recall and F1-Score (reduced to 0.9254 and 0.9593, respectively), emphasizing the critical role of multi-expert representations and gating in capturing complex traffic behaviors.

The removal of the CNN backbone slightly affects performance, with Precision at 0.9498, Recall at 0.9448, and F1-Score at 0.9733, but interestingly yields a marginal increase in Accuracy (0.9659), suggesting a trade-off between deep feature extraction and classification generalization. Lastly, replacing the multi-expert module with a single expert slightly reduces metrics across the board—Precision (0.9761), Accuracy (0.9698), Recall (0.9482), and F1-Score (0.9705)—indicating that the multi-expert structure provides a well-balanced enhancement without significantly increasing computational cost. These results collectively confirm that each component contributes distinct and complementary advantages to the overall model architecture.

4.4 Comparison with State-of-the-Art Models

The MoE-CNN-CSAM-DFS model was evaluated against baselines including Informer, QDA, CNN, Naive Bayes, and Adaboost on CICIDS2017, and Multi-CNN, RNN, CNN-IDS, Ensemble Voting, and BAT-MC Model on NSL-KDD, using ten-fold cross-validation (Tables 5 and 6).

The MoE-CNN-CSAM-DFS model demonstrates exceptional precision and versatility across the CICIDS2017 and NSL-KDD datasets. On CICIDS2017, it achieves a mean precision of 0.9882 ± 0.0109, accuracy of 0.9877 ± 0.0052, recall

Table 5. Comparison on CICIDS2017 Dataset

Model	Precision Mean	Accuracy	Recall	F1-Score
Informer	0.61	0.52	0.52	0.45
QDA	0.83	0.38	0.38	0.41
CNN	0.69	0.65	0.65	0.66
Naive Bayes	0.80	0.82	0.82	0.81
Adaboost	0.94	0.94	0.94	0.94
Ours	0.9877 ± 0.0052	0.9882 ± 0.0109	0.9905 ± 0.0005	0.9829 ± 0.0060

Table 6. Comparison on NSL-KDD Dataset

Model	Precision Mean	Accuracy	Recall	F1-Score
Multi-CNN	0.8956	0.8695	0.8725	0.8841
RNN	-	0.8328	-	-
CNN-IDS	-	0.94	0.92	-
Ensemble Voting	0.865	0.852	0.852	0.849
BAT-MC Model	-	0.8425	-	-
Ours	0.9766 ± 0.0123	0.9384 ± 0.0213	0.8797 ± 0.0129	0.8765 ± 0.0102

of 0.9905 ± 0.0005, and F1-score of 0.9829 ± 0.0060, significantly outperforming Adaboost (0.94 ± 0.02 across metrics) with gains of 0.0505 in recall and 0.0429 in F1-score, and surpassing Informer (0.52 ± 0.01, 0.45 ± 0.01) by 0.4705 and 0.5329, respectively. On NSL-KDD, it records a precision of 0.9384 ± 0.0213, accuracy of 0.9766 ± 0.0123, recall of 0.8797 ± 0.0129, and F1-score of 0.8765 ± 0.0102, exceeding Multi-CNN (0.8841 ± 0.02) and CNN-IDS (0.92 ± 0.01) by enhancing feature discrimination through DFS and CSAM. With efficient parameter utilization and a reduced training time of 1001.65 ± 23.47 s compared to 1717.50 ± 56.24 on CICIDS2017, the model offers a scalable, high-precision solution for real-time intrusion detection. In terms of computational efficiency, the MoE-CNN-CSAM-DFS model requires an average training time of 1717.50 s per fold on CICIDS2017, reflecting its complex architecture involving DFS, CSAM, and MoE components. In contrast, lightweight models like Adaboost, which rely on simpler ensemble learning with decision trees, typically require significantly less training time (estimated at 200–300 s per fold for similar datasets, based on its lower computational complexity). While Adaboost offers faster training, the proposed model's superior performance—achieving up to 0.0505 higher recall and 0.0429 higher F1-score on CICIDS2017—justifies the increased computational cost, particularly for applications prioritizing detection accuracy over training speed.

4.5 Analysis of MoE Specialization

To validate the claim that the Mixture of Experts (MoE) architecture effectively handles diverse attack patterns, we analyzed the output weights of the gating network to examine how the three expert networks specialize in detecting specific attack types in the CICIDS2017 dataset. The gating network, which assigns weights to each expert based on input features, was evaluated on a subset of 1,000 samples comprising DoS (e.g., DoS HULK) and PortScan attacks. For DoS attacks, Expert 1 consistently received higher weights (average 0.62), indicating its specialization in capturing high-volume traffic patterns, such as increased packet lengths and flow rates, which are prominent in DoS scenarios. In contrast, for PortScan attacks, Expert 2 was prioritized (average weight 0.58), likely due to its focus on temporal features like inter-arrival times (IAT) that characterize scanning behaviors. Expert 3 showed balanced contributions across both attack types (average weight 0.35), acting as a generalist to handle mixed or less distinct patterns. This specialization is driven by the gating network's ability to dynamically allocate tasks based on feature relevance, as validated by SHAP analysis, which highlights features like "Total Length of Fwd Packets" (SHAP importance 0.044495) for DoS and "Flow IAT Max" (0.013779) for PortScan. These distinct weight distributions demonstrate the MoE's adaptability to diverse attack patterns, enhancing its robustness compared to single-model architectures.

5 Conclusion

This study introduces the MoE-CNN-CSAM-DFS model, a robust network anomaly detection framework validated on CICIDS2017 and NSL-KDD datasets. Integrating Dynamic Feature Selection (DFS), Channel-Spatial Attention Mechanism (CSAM), and a Mixture of Experts (MoE) architecture with a convolutional backbone, it excels with high-dimensional, imbalanced data. Statistical significance analysis highlights "Total Length of Fwd Packets" (0.044495) and "Fwd Packet Length Max" (0.033095), improving accuracy by 2.3%. On CICIDS2017, it achieves 0.9877 ± 0.0052 accuracy, 0.9882 ± 0.0109 precision, 0.9905 ± 0.0005 recall, and 0.9829 ± 0.0060 F1-score (1717.50 ± 56.24 s/fold); on NSL-KDD, 0.9766 ± 0.0123 accuracy, 0.9384 ± 0.0213 precision, 0.8797 ± 0.0129 recall, and 0.8765 ± 0.0102 F1-score (1001.65 ± 23.47 s/fold), outpacing Adaboost and Informer. Ablation studies confirm DFS, CSAM, and MoE synergy.

This work inspires future research by showcasing attention and expert systems for imbalanced data, suggesting applications in healthcare anomaly detection and autonomous system security. Its $0.849M$ parameter efficiency supports resource-limited deployments, while feature prioritization could enhance ML feature engineering. Future efforts may focus on pruning, multi-domain adaptation, and real-time tuning, fostering resilient cybersecurity innovations and policy frameworks.

References

1. Kostas, K.: Anomaly Detection in Networks Using Machine Learning. Ph.D. thesis (2018)
2. Panigrahi, R., Borah, S.: A detailed analysis of CICIDS2017 dataset for designing intrusion detection systems. Int. J. Eng. Tech. **7**(3.24), 479–482 (2018)
3. Tavallaee, M., Bagheri, E., Lu, W., Ghorbani, A.A.: A detailed analysis of the KDD cup 99 data set. In: 2009 IEEE Symposium on Computational Intelligence for Security and Defense Applications, pp. 1–6. IEEE (2009)
4. Liao, H.J., Richard Lin, C.H., Lin, Y.C., Tung, K.Y.: Intrusion detection system: a comprehensive review. J. Netw. Comput. Appl. **36**(1), 16–24 (2013). https://doi.org/10.1016/j.jnca.2012.09.004. https://www.sciencedirect.com/science/article/pii/S1084804512001944
5. Zhang, C., Ruan, F., Yin, L., Chen, X., Zhai, L., Liu, F.: A deep learning approach for network intrusion detection based on NSL-KDD dataset. In: 2019 IEEE 13th International Conference on Anticounterfeiting, Security, and Identification (ASID), pp. 41–45 (2019). https://doi.org/10.1109/ICASID.2019.8925239
6. Pandey, D., Niwaria, K., Chourasia, B.: Machine learning algorithms: a review. Mach. Learn. **6**(2) (2019)
7. Wang, Y., et al.: An attention mechanism module with spatial perception and channel information interaction. Complex Intell. Syst. **10**(4), 5427–5444 (2024). https://doi.org/10.1007/s40747-024-01445-9
8. Ustebay, S., Turgut, Z., Aydin, M.A.: Intrusion detection system with recursive feature elimination by using random forest and deep learning classifier. In: 2018 International Congress on Big Data, Deep Learning and Fighting Cyber Terrorism (IBIGDELFT), pp. 71–76. IEEE (2018)
9. Stiawan, D., Idris, M.Y.B., Bamhdi, A.M., Budiarto, R., et al.: CICIDS-2017 dataset feature analysis with information gain for anomaly detection. IEEE Access **8**, 132911–132921 (2020)
10. Sornsuwit, P., Jaiyen, S.: Intrusion detection model based on ensemble learning for U2R and R2L attacks. In: 2015 7th International Conference on Information Technology and Electrical Engineering (ICITEE). pp. 354–359 (2015). https://doi.org/10.1109/ICITEED.2015.7408971
11. Zhang, C., Wang, N., Zhang, D.: Research on intrusion detection method based on transformer and CNN-BILSTM in internet of things. Sensors **25**(9), 2725 (2025)
12. Kavut, S., Ceylan, M.F., Karadeniz, F.: DDoS detection in network traffic using LightGBM: a study on the CICIDS2018 dataset. In: 2025 9th International Symposium on Innovative Approaches in Smart Technologies (ISAS), pp. 1–5 (2025). https://doi.org/10.1109/ISAS66241.2025.11101816
13. Pechenizkiy, M.: The impact of feature extraction on the performance of a classifier: kNN, Naïve bayes and C4.5. In: Kégl, B., Lapalme, G. (eds.) AI 2005. LNCS (LNAI), vol. 3501, pp. 268–279. Springer, Heidelberg (2005). https://doi.org/10.1007/11424918_28

PP-MTAD: Privacy-Preserving and Efficient Multivariate Time Series Anomaly Detection

Minhua Su[1], Jia-Nan Liu[1(✉)], Kai He[1], Jiasi Weng[2], Anjia Yang[2], Xueqiao Liu[3], and Jian Weng[2]

[1] School of Computer Science and Technology, Dongguan University of Technology, Dongguan 523000, China
j.n.liu@foxmail.com
[2] College of Cyber Security, Jinan University, Guangzhou 510632, China
[3] School of Computing and Information Technology, University of Wollongong, Wollongong, Australia
xueqiao@uow.edu.au

Abstract. Multivariate time series (MTS) data play a crucial role in decision-making across various fields, such as healthcare, industrial control, and economic analysis. However, MTS data often involve substantial sensitive information, and anomalies in such data can directly lead to system failures or decision-making errors, making anomaly detection under privacy protection a crucial task. Existing methods typically prioritize either privacy protection or anomaly detection, struggling to effectively balance the two while incurring significant overhead when handling high-dimensional data. To address these issues, we propose PP-MTAD, a privacy-preserving anomaly detection framework for MTS. The framework designs a series of cryptographic protocols for secure computation, enabling collaboratively confidential anomaly detection. To enhance detection accuracy and efficiency, we leverage Dynamic Time Warping (DTW) distance to measure the similarity between time series, and employ clustering to organize time series into groups, enabling more precise anomaly detection based on distance to cluster centroids. Security analysis demonstrates that our framework effectively ensures data privacy, and experimental results further validate its advantages in accuracy and computational efficiency.

Keywords: Privacy-preserving · Secure multiparty computation · Multivariate time series · Anomaly detection

1 Introduction

Multivariate Time Series (MTS) refers to a type of data that consists of multiple variables recorded over time. With the widespread adoption of MTS in critical domains including financial forecasting, healthcare monitoring, and intelligent

R. Chen et al. (Eds.): Inscrypt 2025, LNCS 16409, pp. 174–194, 2026.
https://doi.org/10.1007/978-981-95-6203-9_10

manufacturing [6,11,16,19,29], anomaly detection in MTS has attracted increasing attention. It aims to identify potential anomalous behaviors from complex temporal dynamics and inter-vari able interaction patterns, which is significant for ensuring system security and improving decision-making quality. However, accurately and efficiently detecting anomalies remains challenging due to the high dimensionality, strong dependencies, and dynamic variability inherent in multivariate time series.

To address these challenges, various anomaly detection techniques have been proposed, which can be classified into four groups: statistical methods, similarity-based approaches, traditional machine learning algorithms, and deep learning-based solutions. Among these, deep learning methods have demonstrated outstanding performance. For instance, Zong *et al.* [36] proposed the Deep Autoencoding Gaussian Mixture Model (DAGMM) for unsupervised anomaly detection. In addition, Su *et al.* [25] proposed OmniAnomaly, a stochastic recurrent neural network that constructs robust representations through stochastic variable connections and planar normalizing flows, enabling interpretable anomaly detection via reconstruction probabilities.

Although these methods perform well in terms of detection accuracy, they typically assume full access to the raw data and fail to address critical privacy concerns. In practical scenarios, MTS data often contain highly sensitive information, such as patient health records, individual mobility patterns, or confidential business data. If such information is exposed, stolen, or misused, the consequences can be disastrous. In cloud-based environments, the risk of privacy leakage is particularly pronounced, as data owners outsource storage and computation to third-party platforms.

To address growing privacy concerns, researchers have devised new anomaly detection methods that preserve user privacy. For instance, Zhang *et al.* [32] proposed a federated learning-based approach, where local devices train models collaboratively without sharing raw data. However, federated learning requires frequent communication between clients and a central server, incurring high communication overhead. Moreover, standalone federated learning does not guarantee strict privacy protection, as model updates may still leak sensitive information.

To address these issues, we propose PP-MTAD, a privacy-preserving anomaly detection framework for multivariate time series based on secure two-party computation. Our main contributions are summarized as follows:

- **Privacy-Preserving Anomaly Detection:**
  We design a complete anomaly detection framework with dedicated privacy-preserving algorithms for each subroutine. The framework ensures strict data confidentiality throughout the process, protecting sensitive information. Meanwhile, it achieves high detection accuracy and robustness on multivariate time series data.
- **Efficient Detection with DTW and Clustering:**
  PP-MTAD uses Dynamic Time Warping to assess similarity between time series and applies clustering to group similar data. This reduces the overall

detection space and computational cost. Anomalies are then detected within each cluster, improving both detection efficiency and accuracy.

2 Related Works

Multivariate time series qnomaly detection is a widely studied field focused on identifying anomalous patterns within high-dimensional data to detect potential issues or events.

Elastic Similarity Measures (ESM). Accurate anomaly detection fundamentally relies on effective similarity measurement between time series. Dynamic Time Warping (DTW), introduced by Sakoe and Chiba [23], is a pioneering ESM technique that enables robust point-to-point alignment under time distortions. DTW has been widely applied in domains such as speech recognition [5,21], signature verification [17,18], and gesture recognition [14,26]. In the context of privacy-preserving analysis, DTW has been leveraged in several frameworks [31,34,35]. For instance, Li *et al.* [12] proposed a secure DTW-based top-k query system, and Liu *et al.* [15] developed an efficient encrypted computation framework. However, few studies directly employ DTW for multivariate anomaly detection under privacy constraints.

Anomaly Detection Methods for Multivariate Time Series. In recent years, with the rapid development of deep learning technologies, researchers have proposed many neural network-based anomaly detection methods, which have further improved the performance of detecting anomalies in complex time series data. For instance, Audibert *et al.* [3] introduced a backward-trained autoencoder method for fast and stable unsupervised anomaly detection on MTS data. Tuli *et al.* [27] employed a deep transformer network with an attention mechanism to quickly detect anomalies in time series data, further enhancing detection speed and accuracy. However, these methods typically assume centralized access to plaintext data, which raises privacy concerns in many real-world applications.

Privacy-Preserving Multivariate Time Series Anomaly Detection. Existing methods for multivariate time series anomaly detection typically assume plaintext data, which fails to preserve privacy. To address this, Zhang *et al.* [32] proposed OmniFed, an unsupervised federated learning approach using local autoencoders and device clustering for anomaly detection. Xu *et al.* [13] introduced PeFAD, which enhances detection through parameter-efficient training and anomaly-driven masking while preserving privacy. However, federated learning incurs high communication costs, especially for MTS data.

Based on the above background, we propose a privacy-preserving anomaly detection framework for multivariate time series data. Our approach leverages DTW for similarity measurement and integrates clustering techniques to efficiently identify potential anomalies while preserving data confidentiality.

3 Background

3.1 Notations

The main notations used throughout this paper are shown in Table 1.

Table 1. Notations

Notations	Comments
T	A multivariate time series dataset
N	The size of the multivariate time series dataset
t^i	A multivariate time series in the dataset
n	The length of a multivariate time series
d	The dimension of a multivariate time series
$t_{j,l}$	The element of row i and column j of a multivariate time series
k	The number of clusters
$\langle x \rangle_b^A$	The arithmetic share of the value x held by server P_b
$\langle x \rangle_b^B$	The boolean share of the value x held by server P_b

3.2 Mutivariate Time Series

A mutivariate time series dataset T can be defined as a collection of multi3ple time series, i.e., $T = \{t^1, ..., t^N\}$, where each t^i represents a mutivariate time series consisting of a series of observations over time. Specifically, any time series t^i can be represented as $t^i = \{t_1^i, ..., t_n^i\}$, where $t_j^i = \{t_{j,1}^i, ..., t_{j,d}^i\}$ is a dimensional vector containing the measurements of d observed variables at time j.

3.3 Dynamic Time Warping

Dynamic Time Warping is a classic technique for measuring similarity between time series, allowing non-linear time axis alignments. Given two multivariate time series $X = \{x_1, ..., x_{|X|}\}$ and $Y = \{y_1, ..., y_{|Y|}\}$, DTW computes the minimum alignment cost even in the presence of time distortions. The point-wise distance is defined as: $dist(x_i, y_j) = \sum_{l=1}^{d}(x_{i,l} - y_{j,l})^2$.

DTW constructs a cumulative cost matrix $D(i, j)$ using dynamic programming:

$$D(i,j) = dist(x_i, y_j) + min \begin{cases} D(i-1, j-1) \\ D(i-1, j) \\ D(i, j-1) \end{cases} . \quad (1)$$

The advantage of the algorithm lies in its recursive structure, enabling robust comparison between time series that may have different temporal dynamics.

3.4 Cryptographic Preliminaries

Secure Multiparty Computation. Secure Multiparty Computation [33] enables multiple untrusted parties to jointly compute a function while keeping their private inputs confidential. Typical cryptographic techniques include secret sharing [24], homomorphic encryption [1], and garbled circuits [30].

Secret Sharing. For the arithmetic sharing, on input an ℓ-bit value x, it generates two additive shares $\langle x\rangle_0^A$ and $\langle x\rangle_1^A$ in the ring $\mathbb{Z}_{2^\ell}$ uniformly at random as ciphertexts, such that $\langle x\rangle_0^A + \langle x\rangle_1^A \equiv x \pmod{2^\ell}$. For the boolean sharing [7,9], it essentially represents additive sharing over $\mathbb{Z}_2$, with the addition replaced by XOR ($\oplus$) and multiplication by AND ($\wedge$).

Ideal Functionalities. We leverage two ideal functionalities: $\mathcal{F}_{\text{DReLU}}$ [9] and $\mathcal{F}_{\text{MUX}}$ [22]. $\mathcal{F}_{\text{DReLU}}$ computes whether a secret-shared input x is non-negative, and outputs a boolean sharing of the result, i.e., $\mathcal{F}_{DReLU}(\langle x\rangle^A) = \langle 1\rangle^B{}_{(x\geq 0)}$. $\mathcal{F}_{\text{MUX}}$ securely computes the conditional selection of a secret-shared input x based on a selection bit c, i.e., $\mathcal{F}_{\text{MUX}}(\langle x\rangle^A, \langle c\rangle^B) = \langle x\rangle^A{}_{(c=1)}$ or $\langle 0\rangle^A{}_{(c=0)}$.

Note: For the convenience of description, we will "abuse" the plaintext or secret shared form sometimes.

3.5 Secure Building Blocks

Secure Comparison Protocol (SCMP). The SCMP is designed to compare the relative size of two numbers by using the $\mathcal{F}_{DReLU}$. For example, when comparing x and y, if x is greater than or equal to y, the output is a boolean value $c = 1$, otherwise, $c = 0$. The specific process is shown in Algorithm 1.

Algorithm 1. Secure comparison protocol (SCMP)

Input: Cloud server P_b inputs $\langle x\rangle_b^A, \langle y\rangle_b^A$, respectively.
Output: P_b outputs the boolean shared value of the comparison result bit $\langle c\rangle_b^B$.

1: P_b locally calculates $\langle a\rangle_b^A = \langle x\rangle_b^A - \langle y\rangle_b^A$.
2: P_b calls the $\mathcal{F}_{DReLU}$ to compute $\langle c\rangle_b^B \leftarrow \mathcal{F}_{DReLU}(\langle a\rangle_b^A)$.

Secure Find Minimum (Maximum) Protocol (SFMinP/SFMaxP). Assume that the cloud server P_b holds the secret shares of x, y, and their indices I_x, I_y. The protocol securely outputs the minimum (maximum) of x and y with its index. P_b computes the differences locally, and calls the $\mathcal{F}_{DReLU}$ to obtain a comparison result. This result is then used as the control bit for the $\mathcal{F}_{MUX}$ to securely select the value and its index. The protocol is shown in Algorithm 2.

Algorithm 2. Secure find minimum (maximum) protocol (SFMinP/SFMaxP)

Input: Cloud server P_b inputs $\langle x\rangle_b^A, \langle y\rangle_b^A, \langle I_x\rangle_b^A, \langle I_y\rangle_b^A$, respectively.
Output: P_b outputs $\langle min\rangle_b^A$ and $\langle I_{min}\rangle_b^A$ ($\langle max\rangle_b^A$ and $\langle I_{max}\rangle_b^A$).
1: P_b locally calculates $\langle a\rangle_b^A = \langle x\rangle_b^A - \langle y\rangle_b^A$, $\langle I_a\rangle_b^A = \langle I_x\rangle_b^A - \langle I_y\rangle_b^A$.
2: P_b calls the $\mathcal{F}_{DReLU}$ to compute $\langle c\rangle_b^B \leftarrow \mathcal{F}_{DReLU}(\langle a\rangle_b^A)$.
3: $\langle p\rangle_b^A \leftarrow \mathcal{F}_{MUX}(\langle a\rangle_b^A, \langle c\rangle_b^B)$, $\langle I_p\rangle_b^A \leftarrow \mathcal{F}_{MUX}(\langle I_a\rangle_b^A, \langle c\rangle_b^B)$.
4: At the end, P_b jointly compute $\langle min\rangle_b^A = \langle x\rangle_b^A - \langle p\rangle_b^A$, $\langle I_{min}\rangle_b^A = \langle I_x\rangle_b^A - \langle I_p\rangle_b^A$ ($\langle max\rangle_b^A = \langle y\rangle_b^A + \langle p\rangle_b^A$, $\langle I_{max}\rangle_b^A = \langle I_y\rangle_b^A + \langle I_p\rangle_b^A$).

Secure Euclidean Distance Squared Protocol (SEDP). This protocol is designed to securely compute the squared Euclidean distance between two sets of univariate time series data. For each element, the protocol computes the shared difference $\langle z\rangle_b^A = \langle x_i\rangle_b^A - \langle y_i\rangle_b^A$. Subsequently, the secure multiplication protocol (Mul) is applied to obtain the squared terms $\langle z^2\rangle_b^A$. The specific algorithm is shown in Algorithm 3.

Algorithm 3. Secure Euclidean distance squared protocol (SEDP)

Input: Cloud server P_b inputs univariate time series $\langle x\rangle_b^A = \{\langle x_1\rangle_b^A, \langle x_2\rangle_b^A, ..., \langle x_d\rangle_b^A\}, \langle y\rangle_b^A = \{\langle y_1\rangle_b^A, \langle y_2\rangle_b^A, ..., \langle y_d\rangle_b^A\}$, respectively.
Output: P_b outputs $\langle dist\rangle_b^A$.
1: Initialize $\langle dist\rangle_b^A = \langle 0\rangle_b^A$.
2: **for** $i = 1$ **to** d **do**
3: $\langle z\rangle_b^A = \langle x_i\rangle_b^A - \langle y_i\rangle_b^A$, $\langle z^2\rangle_b^A = Mul(\langle z\rangle_b^A \cdot \langle z\rangle_b^A)$, $\langle dist\rangle_b^A = \langle dist\rangle_b^A + \langle z^2\rangle_b^A$.

Secure DTW Distance Protocol (SDTWP). In Sect. 3.3, we describe the approach to calculating the DTW distance between two sets of multivariate time series data. The core steps of this protocol include initializing an $m \times n$ matrix $\langle D\rangle_b^A$ to store DTW values. Subsequently, the SEDP is used to compute the shared distance values $\langle dist\rangle_b^A$ between the corresponding points in the two time series. The detailed steps of the protocol are described in Algorithm 4.

4 Secure Multivariate Time Series Anomaly Detection

4.1 System and Threat Model

System Model. As shown in Fig. 1, this scheme is a typical cloud computing system involving two types of entities: a trusted data owner and two cloud servers.

Algorithm 4. Secure DTW distance protocol (SDTWP)

Input: Cloud server P_b inputs mutivariate time series data $\langle X\rangle_b^A = \{\langle x_1\rangle_b^A, ..., \langle x_m\rangle_b^A\}$, $\langle Y\rangle_b^A = \{\langle y_1\rangle_b^A, ..., \langle y_n\rangle_b^A\}$, respectively.
Output: P_b outputs $\langle DTW\rangle_b^A$.

Initialize an $m \times n$ matrix $\langle D\rangle_b^A$ to store DTW values.
for $i = 1$ **to** m **do**
  for $j = 1$ **to** n **do**
    $\langle dist\rangle_b^A \leftarrow SEDP(\langle x_i\rangle_b^A, \langle y_j\rangle_b^A)$.
    if $i == 1$ **and** $j == 1$ **then**
      $\langle D(i,j)\rangle_b^A \leftarrow \langle dist\rangle_b^A$.
    else if $i == 1$ **then**
      $\langle D(1,j)\rangle_b^A \leftarrow \langle dist\rangle_b^A + \langle D(1,j-1)\rangle_b^A$.
    else if $j == 1$ **then**
      $\langle D(i,1)\rangle_b^A \leftarrow \langle dist\rangle_b^A + \langle D(i-1,1)\rangle_b^A$.
    else
      $\langle a\rangle_b^A, \langle I_a\rangle_b^A \leftarrow SFMinP(\langle D(i-1,j-1)\rangle_b^A, \langle D(i-1,j)\rangle_b^A, j-1, j)$.
      $\langle D_{min}\rangle_b^A, \langle I_{min}\rangle_b^A \leftarrow SFMinP(\langle a\rangle_b^A, \langle D(i,j-1)\rangle_b^A, \langle I_a\rangle^A, i)$.
      $\langle D(i,j)\rangle_b^A \leftarrow \langle dist\rangle_b^A + \langle D_{min}\rangle_b^A$.
$\langle DTW\rangle_b^A \leftarrow \langle D(m,n)\rangle_b^A$.

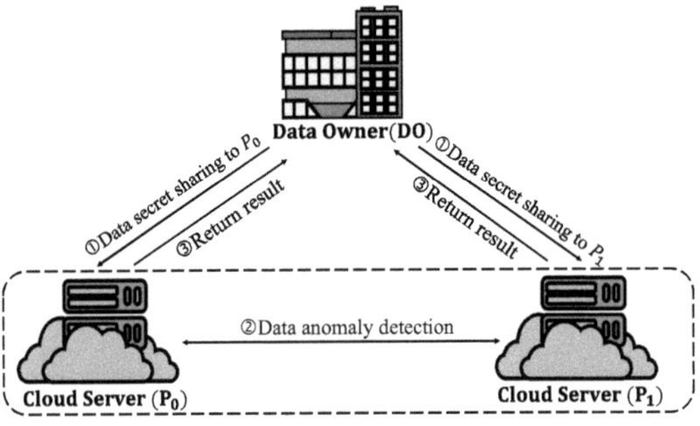

Fig. 1. System model.

- **Data Owner (DO):** The data owner, which could be an industrial enterprise, healthcare institution, or other entity, is responsible for providing the MTS data. Due to limited local computational resources, the data owner outsources the anomaly detection tasks to two non-colluding cloud servers. To ensure data confidentiality, the data is secret-shared and distributed across the servers, which collaborate to perform the analysis without accessing the original values.
- **Cloud Servers $\{P_0, P_1\}$:** The scheme employs two cloud servers, P_0 and P_1, which serve as service providers that store secret-shared data and perform anomaly detection. These cloud servers possess powerful storage and computational capabilities. After the data owner securely uploads the data, the

servers collaborate conduct privacy-preserving anomaly detection and return the encrypted results to the data owner.

Security Model. In our semi-honest security model, the data owner is fully trusted and securely distributes the secret-shared data to two non-colluding cloud servers, P_0 and P_1, which are assumed to be honest-but-curious. We assume that both servers faithfully execute the protocol but may attempt to infer additional information from the data they process. The communication channels between parties are assumed to be secure, and any collusion between P_0 and P_1 is explicitly excluded.

4.2 Overview

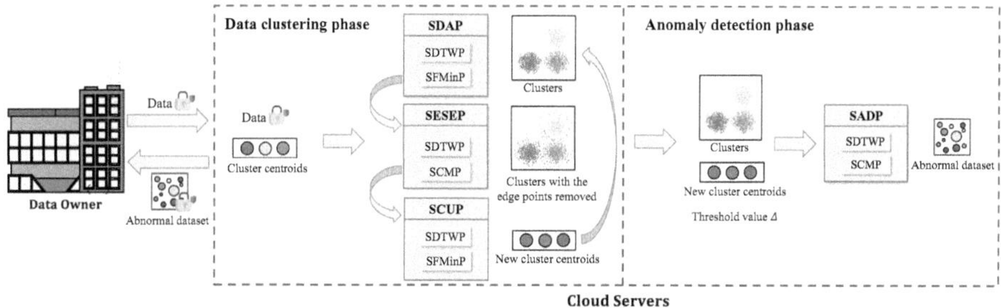

Fig. 2. Overview of the Privacy-Preserving Anomaly Detection Framework.

To address the dual challenges of ensuring privacy and achieving effective anomaly detection on high-dimensional multivariate time series, we propose a novel privacy-preserving framework combining secure clustering and anomaly detection protocols. Our design leverages a set of customized secure computation primitives to minimize the computational overhead while preserving data privacy throughout the entire process. As shown in Fig. 2, the framework consists of three main phases: data outsourcing, data clustering, and anomaly detection.

In the data clustering phase, we adopt a secure variant of the k-means algorithm due to its efficiency and simplicity. Although k-means requires predefining the number of clusters k, this is mitigated by leveraging domain knowledge or prior traffic statistics, which typically reflect the approximate number of dominant traffic patterns.

In the anomaly detection phase, we employ a distance-based detection method that operates on the securely clustered results. Specifically, each data point's deviation from its assigned cluster centroid is measured, and points exceeding a predefined threshold are flagged as anomalies. The threshold is learned from normal training samples and can be updated over time to adapt to changing data patterns.

4.3 Data Outsourcing Phase

During this phase, the DO securely outsources the MTS data to two cloud servers, P_0 and P_1, by employing arithmetic sharing. Specifically, for each element of the time series data, the DO generates a random number $r \in_R \mathbf{Z}_{2^\ell}$, and splits each ℓ-bit value into two shares: $\left\langle t^i_{j,l} \right\rangle^A_0 = r$ and $\left\langle t^i_{j,l} \right\rangle^A_1 = t^i_{j,l} - r$. Subsequently, the corresponding share for $b \in \{0, 1\}$ is transmitted to cloud server P_b. This approach keeps the original data securely split between the two servers, ensuring privacy during the entire computation process.

4.4 Secure Data Clustering Phase

This secure clustering process consists of three main steps: data assignment, edge point exclusion, and centroid update.

Secure Data Assignment Protocol (SDAP). The secure data assignment protocol assigns each multivariate time series to the nearest cluster based on the minimum DTW distance. Specifically, for each time series t^i, the DTW distances to all k centroids are securely computed, and the sequence is assigned to the cluster with the minimum distance, as defined in Eq. (2):

$$S_m = \{t^i : \mathrm{DTW}(t^i, \mathrm{center}_m) \leq \mathrm{DTW}(t^i, \mathrm{center}_g), \forall g, 1 \leq g \leq k\}, \tag{2}$$

$S_i \cap S_j = \emptyset, \forall m, g \leq k$. This ensures that even if a point is equidistant to multiple centroids, it still be assigned to exactly one cluster. The detailed steps are shown in Algorithm 5.

Algorithm 5. Secure data assignment protocol (SDAP)

Input: A mutivariate time series dataset $\langle T \rangle^A_b = \{\langle t^1 \rangle^A_b, ..., \langle t^N \rangle^A_b\}$, k cluster centroids $\langle Center \rangle^A_b = \{\langle center_1 \rangle^A_b, ..., \langle center_k \rangle^A_b\}$.

Output: k clusters $\langle S_1 \rangle^A_b, ..., \langle S_k \rangle^A_b$.

1: **for** $i = 1$ **to** N **do**
2:     P_b initializes $\langle DTW_{min} \rangle^A_b \leftarrow INF$, $\langle I_{min} \rangle^A_b \leftarrow INF$.
3:     **for** $j = 1$ **to** k **do**
4:         $\langle DTW \rangle^A_b \leftarrow SDTWP(\langle t^i \rangle^A_b, \langle center_j \rangle^A_b)$.
5:         $\langle DTW_{min} \rangle^A_b, \langle I_{min} \rangle^A_b \leftarrow SFMinP(\langle DTW_{min} \rangle^A_b, \langle DTW \rangle^A_b, \langle I_{min} \rangle^A_b, \langle j \rangle^A_b)$.
6:     $\left\langle S_{\langle I_{min} \rangle^A} \right\rangle^A_b \leftarrow \left\langle S_{\langle I_{min} \rangle^A} \right\rangle^A_b \cup \langle t^i \rangle^A_b$.

Secure Edge Sequence Exclusion Protocol (SESEP). To improve clustering quality, the secure edge sequence exclusion protocol aims to identify and remove peripheral data points that may negatively impact the clustering results. Given a cluster S_i with centroid $center_i$, the average DTW distance and the standard deviation within the cluster are computed as follows:

$$\mu_i = \frac{1}{|S_i|}\sum\nolimits_{t \in S_i} DTW(t, center_i), \sigma_i = \frac{1}{|S_i|}\sum\nolimits_{t \in S_i} (DTW(t, center_i) - \mu_i). \quad (3)$$

A point $t \in S_i$ is considered an edge point if its DTW distance from the centroid exceeds $3 \times \sigma_i$, i.e.,

$$S_i^{'} = \{t : DTW(t, center_i) \geq 3 \times \sigma_i, t \in S_i\}. \quad (4)$$

To refine the clusters, all edge points in $S_i^{'}$ are excluded from S_i, resulting in the updated cluster. The specific algorithm is shown8 in Algorithm 6.

Algorithm 6. Secure edge sequence exclusion protocol (SESEP)

Input: k clusters $\langle S_1\rangle_b^A, ..., \langle S_k\rangle_b^A$ and k cluster centorids $\langle Center\rangle_b^A = \{\langle center_1\rangle_b^A, ..., \langle center_k\rangle_b^A\}$.
Output: k clusters with the edge points removed $\langle S_1\rangle_b^A, ..., \langle S_k\rangle_b^A$.

for $i = 1$ **to** k **do**
  $\langle \mu_i\rangle_b^A \leftarrow \frac{1}{|S_i|}\sum_{t \in S_i} SDTWP(t, center_i)$.
  $\langle \sigma_i\rangle_b^A \leftarrow \frac{1}{|S_i|}\sum_{t \in S_i} (SDTWP\ (t, center_i) - \mu_i)$.
  for $j = 1$ **to** $|\langle S_i\rangle_b^A|$ **do**
    $\langle DTW\rangle_b^A \leftarrow SDTWP(\langle t^j\rangle_b^A, \langle center_i\rangle_b^A)$.
    $\langle c\rangle_b^B \leftarrow SCMP(\langle DTW\rangle_b^A, 3 \times \langle \sigma_i\rangle_b^A)$.
    P_b calls the $\mathcal{F}_{MUX}$ to compute $\langle temp\rangle_b^A \leftarrow \mathcal{F}_{MUX}(\langle t^j\rangle_b^A, \langle c\rangle_b^B)$.
    $\langle S_i\rangle_b^A \leftarrow \langle S_i\rangle_b^A - \langle temp\rangle_b^A$.

Secure Centroid Update Protocol (SCUP). To further improve clustering accuracy, we design a secure centroid update protocol that updates the cluster centroids after the removal of outliers. The SCUP protocol abandons the traditional mean calculation method and instead selects the actual sequence with the smallest total DTW distance within the cluster as the new centroid, ensuring interpretability, authenticity, and intrinsic compatibility with DTW metrics. Given a cluster S_i, the protocol selects a new centroid by identifying the data point that has the minimum cumulative DTW distance to all other points within the cluster. The updated centroid is defined as:

$$new\_center_i = \{t : arg\ min_{t \in S_i}(\sum\nolimits_{j=1}^{|S_i|} DTW(t, t^j))\}. \quad (5)$$

The specific algorithm is shown in Algorithm 7.

Algorithm 7. Secure centroid update protocol (SCUP)

Input: k clusters with the edge points removed $\langle S_1\rangle_b^A, ..., \langle S_k\rangle_b^A$.
Output: k new cluster centorids $\langle New\_Center\rangle_b^A = \{\langle new\_center_1\rangle_b^A, ..., \langle new\_center_k\rangle_b^A\}$.

for $i = 1$ **to** k **do**
  for $j = 1$ **to** $|\langle S_i\rangle_b^A|$ **do**
    $\langle sum_{min}\rangle_b^A \leftarrow INF$, $\langle I_{min}\rangle_b^A \leftarrow INF$, $\langle sum\rangle_b^A \leftarrow \langle 0\rangle_b^A$.
    for $l = 1$ **to** $|\langle S_i\rangle_b^A|$ **do**
      $\langle DTW\rangle_b^A \leftarrow SDTWP(\langle t^j\rangle_b^A, \langle t^l\rangle_b^A)$.
      $\langle sum\rangle_b^A \leftarrow \langle sum\rangle_b^A + \langle DTW\rangle_b^A$.
    $\langle sum_{min}\rangle_b^A, \langle I_{min}\rangle_b^A \leftarrow SFMinP(\langle sum_{min}\rangle_b^A, \langle sum\rangle_b^A, \langle I_{min}\rangle_b^A, \langle j\rangle_b^A)$.
    $\langle new\_center_i\rangle_b^A = \langle t^{I_{min}}\rangle_b^A$.

The main execution process of the secure data clustering phase is shown in Algorithm 8.

Algorithm 8. Secure Clustering Phase

Input: Multivariate time series dataset $\langle T\rangle_b^A = \{\langle t^1\rangle_b^A, \ldots, \langle t^N\rangle_b^A\}$, number of clusters k, maximum number of iterations $\langle\theta\rangle_b^A$.
Output: k clusters $\{\langle S_1\rangle_b^A, \ldots, \langle S_k\rangle_b^A\}$.

Randomly select k initial centroids from the dataset, $\langle Center\rangle_b^A = \{\langle center_1\rangle_b^A, ..., \langle center_k\rangle_b^A\}$, and initialize $\langle New\_Center\rangle_b^A$ as zero vectors of same shape as $\langle Center\rangle_b^A$, $time = \langle 0\rangle_b^A$.
while $SDTWP(\langle Center\rangle_b^A, \langle New\_Center\rangle_b^A)$ and $SCMP(time, \langle\theta\rangle_b^A)$ **do**
  $\langle S_1\rangle_b^A, ..., \langle S_k\rangle_b^A \leftarrow SDAP(\langle T\rangle_b^A, \langle Center\rangle_b^A)$.
  $\langle S_1\rangle_b^A, ..., \langle S_k\rangle_b^A \leftarrow SESEP(\langle S_1\rangle_b^A, \ldots, \langle S_k\rangle_b^A, \langle Center\rangle_b^A)$.
  $\langle New\_Center\rangle_b^A \leftarrow SCUP(\langle S_1\rangle_b^A, ..., \langle S_k\rangle_b^A)$.
  $time \leftarrow time + \langle 1\rangle_b^A$.
return $\langle S_1\rangle_b^A, \ldots, \langle S_k\rangle_b^A$.

4.5 Secure Anomaly Detection Phase

We propose a secure anomaly detection protocol (SADP) that identifies anomalous data points within clusters. This is achieved by evaluating the relationship between the average DTW distance across all clusters, denoted as C, and a given threshold. The average distance C between clusters is calculated as follows:

$$C = \frac{1}{k}\sum_{i=1}^{k}\frac{2}{|S_i|(|S_i|-1)}\sum_{t^j,t^l \in S_i} DTW(t^j, t^l), \tag{6}$$

where $t^j \neq t^l$. If C exceeds the threshold, this indicates the presence of anomalies within the clusters. To identify specific outliers, we consider the points that are farthest from their respective cluster centroids as anomalies. The farthest point is removed from its cluster S_i and the average distance C is recalculated. The specific algorithm is shown in Algorithm 9.

Algorithm 9. Secure anomaly detection protocol (SADP)

Input: k clusters $\langle S_1\rangle_b^A, ..., \langle S_k\rangle_b^A$, k cluster centorids $\langle Center\rangle_b^A = \{\langle center_1\rangle_b^A, ..., \langle center_k\rangle_b^A\}$, and threshold value $\langle \Delta\rangle_b^A$.
Output: Outlier datasets $\langle Out\rangle_b^A$.

Calculate the average distance C: $C = \frac{1}{k}\sum_{i=1}^{k} \frac{2}{|S_i|(|S_i|-1)} \sum_{t^j, t^l \in S_i} SDTWP(t^j, t^l)$.
while SCMP(C, Δ) **do**
  for $i = 1$ **to** k **do**
    $\langle DTW_{max}\rangle_b^A \leftarrow 0$, $\langle I_{max}\rangle_b^A \leftarrow 0$.
    for $j = 1$ **to** $|S_i|$ **do**
      $\langle DTW\rangle_b^A \leftarrow SDTWP(\langle t^j\rangle^A, \langle center_i\rangle^A)$.
      $\langle DTW_{max}\rangle_b^A, \langle I_{max}\rangle_b^A \leftarrow SFMaxP(\langle DTW_{max}\rangle_b^A, \langle DTW\rangle_b^A, \langle I_{max}\rangle_b^A, \langle j\rangle_b^A)$.
    $\langle S_i\rangle_b^A \leftarrow \langle S_i\rangle_b^A - \langle t^{I_{max}}\rangle_b^A$, $\langle Out\rangle_b^A \leftarrow \langle Out\rangle_b^A \cup \langle t^{I_{max}}\rangle_b^A$.
  Calculate the average distance C again.

5 Security Analysis

Our protocol Φ is specifically designed for secure time series anomaly detection in a multi-party setting involving a trusted data owner and two non-colluding servers P_0 and P_1. We need a security model that guarantees the protocol remains secure even when composed with other instances.

To formally evaluate the security of our protocol, we adopt the Universal Composability (UC) framework [4], which provides strong security guarantees even under arbitrary composition with concurrent protocol instances. Within the UC framework, the security of Φ is established by demonstrating that its real-world execution is indistinguishable from an ideal-world execution, where a trusted party realizes a well-defined ideal functionality $\mathcal{F}$.

We consider a semi-honest adversary $\mathcal{A}$, who may corrupt one of the servers but still follows the prescribed protocol honestly. The adversary interacts with an environment machine $\mathcal{E}$, which provides inputs and observes outputs to try to distinguish real and ideal executions. Security is achieved if, for every $\mathcal{A}$, there exists a simulator $\mathcal{S}$ such that $\mathcal{E}$ cannot distinguish the two executions with non-negligible probability:

$$|Pr[REAL_{\Phi,\mathcal{A},\mathcal{E}}(\lambda, z) = 1] - Pr[IDEAL_{\mathcal{F},\mathcal{S},\mathcal{E}}(\lambda, z) = 1]|. \tag{7}$$

This ensures that any corrupted party learns no information beyond its prescribed input and output, thereby preserving both privacy and correctness even in the presence of an adversary. We assume that $\mathcal{A}$ can corrupt at most one of the servers. The protocol employs additive and Boolean secret sharing [2,8], ensuring that time series data, multiplication triples, Boolean triples, and intermediate results are securely shared over $\mathbb{Z}_{2^\ell}$ and $\mathbb{Z}_2$. To simplify the proof, we model Φ as a hybrid protocol $\Phi^{\mathcal{G}\to\rho}$ that relies on an ideal functionality $\mathcal{G}$. If a sub-protocol ρ securely realizes $\mathcal{G}$, then according to the UC composition theorem [4], replacing $\mathcal{G}$ with ρ preserves the security of Φ.

The protocol also uses $\mathcal{F}_{\mathrm{DReLU}}$ and $\mathcal{F}_{\mathrm{MUX}}$ from the Cheetah framework [9], which has been proven UC-secure and is adopted directly. For the hybrid protocol setting, we provide a detailed security proof using SADP as an example. Specifically, given the ideal functionality $\mathcal{F}_{sfminp}$ defined in Fig. 3, we let $\mathcal{F}_{scmprank}$ and $\mathcal{F}_{scmp}$ represent the ideal functionalities of the SCMP gadget, with and without leakage levels, respectively.

Functionality $\mathcal{F}_{sadp}$

Functionality $\mathcal{F}_{sadp}$ interact with dummy data owner DO, service providers P_0, P_1 and an adversary $\mathcal{S}$.
Initiate: Upon receiving initiates calls for all parties, sends the message to $\mathcal{S}$, initializes a dictionary T with self-incremental index i.
Inputs: Upon receiving (Input, 1, i, $\langle S_1\rangle_b^A$, ..., $\langle S_k\rangle_b^A$, $\langle Center\rangle_b^A$, $\langle \Delta\rangle_b^A$) form DO, sets $T[i]$ =$\langle S_1\rangle_b^A$ ||...|| $\langle S_k\rangle_b^A$ || $\langle Center\rangle_b^A$ || $\langle \Delta\rangle_b^A$; or (Input, 2, i, MT_s) from P_0 and P_1, sets $T[i] = MT_s$. Sends (Input, j, i) to $\mathcal{S}$.
Random: Upon receiving (random, i), randomly generate $r \in \mathbb{Z}_{2^\ell}$, sets $T[i]] = r$ and sends to all parties and $\mathcal{S}$.
SDTWP **call:** Upon receiving (SDTWP, x, y, z, w), sets $T[z] = \mathcal{F}_{sdtwp}(T[x], T[y], T[w])$ and sends (SDTW, x, y, z, w) to P_0, P_1, and $\mathcal{S}$.
SCMP **leak rank call:** Upon receiving (SCMP, x, y, z), sets $T[z] = \mathcal{F}_{scmprank}(T[x], T[y])$ and reveals (SCMP, x, y, z) to P_0, P_1, and $\mathcal{S}$.
SCMP **call:** Upon receiving (SCMP, x, y, z, w), sets $T[z] = \mathcal{F}_{scmp}(T[x], T[y], T[w])$ and sends (SCMP, x, y, z, w) to DO and $\mathcal{S}$.
Output: Upon receiving (Output, z), outputs z, $T[z]$ to $\mathcal{S}$ and DO.

Fig. 3. Ideal functionality of secure anomaly detection protocol $\mathcal{F}_{sadp}$.

Theorem 1. *Let protocol Φ be the anomaly detection protocol defined in Algorithm 9. In the $\mathcal{F}_{sdtwp}$, $\mathcal{F}_{scmprank}$ and $\mathcal{F}_{scmp}$-hybrid model, Φ UC-realizes $\mathcal{F}_{sadp}$ in Fig. 3 against a polynomial-time semi-honest admissible adversary.*

Proof. Let $\Phi^{\mathcal{G}\to\rho}$ denote the composite protocol Φ defined above. Suppose that the adversary $\mathcal{A}$ corrupts P_0 and interacts with the parties executing $\Phi^{\mathcal{G}\to\rho}$. For each subroutine protocol ρ, we further define a special adversary $\mathcal{D}$, such that there exists a simulator $\mathcal{S}_\rho$ guaranteeing that ρ securely realizes $\mathcal{G}$.

We describe the simulator $\mathcal{S}$ in the ideal world for adversary $\mathcal{A}$. Simulator $\mathcal{S}$ operates adversary $\mathcal{A}$ and exchanges backdoor messages under the instructions of $\mathcal{A}$. It forwards the input from the corrupted party chosen randomly by environment ε to $\mathcal{F}_{sadp}$. Then, $\mathcal{S}$ randomly generates a set of additional shares in the finite field $\mathbb{Z}_{2^\ell}$ on behalf of H_m, sending them to $\mathcal{F}_{sadp}$ and ε. Subsequently, $\mathcal{S}$ emulates P_1 by interacting with $\mathcal{A}$ using the randomly generated shares. Upon receiving a call to ρ, $\mathcal{S}$ acts as an environment for $\mathcal{S}_\rho$, forwarding the backdoor messages received from ε to $\mathcal{S}_\rho$. After receiving the backdoor values from $\mathcal{S}_\rho$, $\mathcal{S}$ outputs the submission to ε.

Except for the subroutine protocol SCMP gadget with leakage level, all inputs and outputs of protocol Φ and subroutine protocol ρ are securely generated following additive sharing security. To handle the displayed rankings, $\mathcal{S}$ maintains a key-value store dictionary T to record the ranking output of $\mathcal{S}_\rho$ in relation to the tuple (distance, threshold) for the potential misbehavior of $\mathcal{F}_{scmprank}$. When $\mathcal{F}_{sadp}$ receives a call of SCMP (leak rank), $\mathcal{S}$ sends the randomly chosen distance share and the threshold received from $\mathcal{A}$ to $\mathcal{S}_\rho$. To ensure consistency, $\mathcal{S}$ checks whether the key (distance, threshold) exists in T. If the key exists, $\mathcal{S}$ forwards $T[(\text{distance}, \text{threshold})]$ to ε. Otherwise, after receiving the ranking produced by $\mathcal{S}_\rho$, $\mathcal{S}$ forwards this ranking to ε and stores it as $T[(\text{distance}, \text{threshold})] = \text{rank}$. Finally, we demonstrate that the views of ε in the real world and the ideal world are indistinguishable, ensuring that the real-world protocol execution is securely realized in the ideal world.

6 Performance Evaluation

6.1 Experimental Settings

Datasets. We evaluate our framework on three widely used multivariate time series datasets: MSL, SMAP, and SMD. MSL and SMAP [10] are spacecraft telemetry datasets from NASA, with 55 and 25 sensor dimensions, respectively. Anomalies are labeled based on mission logs and represent system faults. SMD [25] contains five weeks of server metrics from 28 machines, each with 38 features (e.g., CPU usage, memory load), with anomalies labeled from system error logs. We use the original train and test splits, apply z-score normalization, and interpolate missing values. Table 2 shows the details of these three datasets.

Table 2. Performance of our scheme in three datasets

Dataset	Train	Test	Dimensions	Anomalies (%)
MSL [10]	58,317	73,729	55	10.72
SMAP [10]	135,183	427,617	25	13.13
SMD [25]	708,405	708,420	38	4.16

Baselines. To evaluate the effectiveness of our proposed privacy-preserving multivariate time series anomaly detection method (PP-MTAD), we implement a non-private baseline, MTAD, which follows the same design but excludes cryptographic operations. MTAD is compared with four popular unsupervised methods: DAGMM [36], LSTM-VAE [20], OmniAnomaly [25], and USAD [3]. In the privacy-preserving setting, PP-MTAD is evaluated against two representative approaches: FedTADBench [13] and PeFAD [28]. To ensure fairness, we perform threshold scanning for each method and report results with the best F1-score when explicit threshold is not provided.

Implementation Details. Our experiment is performed on an AutoDL instance running Ubuntu 20.04. The instances are equipped with a 2.10GHz Intel(R) Xeon(R) Platinum CPU, 32 VCPUs, and 60GB of RAM. In addition, we run each experiment multiple times and report the average running time as the experimental result.

Metrics. We used Precision (P), Recall (R) and F1-score (F1) to evaluate the accuracy of our scheme. P represents the correct number of anomaly samples triggered by the anomaly detection. R reflects the number of anomalies detected. F1 provides the comprehensive performance index of the scheme anomaly detection. For these three metrics, a higher value indicates better performance. They can be expressed as

$$P = \frac{TP}{TP + FP}, R = \frac{TP}{TP + FN}, F1 = 2 * \frac{P * R}{P + R}, \tag{8}$$

where TP represents the true positive rate, FP represents the false positive rate, and FN represents the false negative rate.

6.2 Main Results

Table 3. Performance Comparison of Non-private Methods

Methods	MSL			SMAP			SMD		
	P	R	F1	P	R	F1	P	R	F1
DAGMM [36]	0.6487	**0.9868**	0.7559	0.6089	0.9521	0.7114	0.6340	0.8616	0.7162
LSTM-VAE [20]	0.5257	0.9546	0.6780	0.8551	0.6366	0.7298	0.7922	0.7075	0.7842
OmniAnomaly [25]	0.8934	0.8774	0.8848	0.7416	0.9776	0.8434	0.8334	0.9449	0.8857
USAD [3]	0.8810	0.9786	**0.9109**	0.7697	**0.9831**	0.8186	0.9314	0.9617	0.9382
Ours	**0.9000**	0.8850	0.8899	**0.9100**	0.9383	**0.9200**	**0.9902**	**0.9950**	**0.9925**

Non-private Methods. As shown in Table 3, our proposed MTAD method demonstrates outstanding anomaly detection performance across all three benchmark datasets. Notably, compared to other methods, MTAD improves the average detection performance by 31.2% over traditional methods and by 8.7% over modern methods on the SMAP and SMD datasets. These results highlight that MTAD achieves an optimal balance between detection accuracy and stability, exhibiting superior overall performance in anomaly detection tasks.

Table 4. Performance Comparison of Privacy-preserving Methods

Methods	MSL			SMAP			SMD		
	P	R	F1	P	R	F1	P	R	F1
FedTADBench [13]	0.7854	0.6840	0.7196	**0.8998**	0.8811	0.8515	0.8567	0.8060	0.8306
PeFAD [28]	0.7335	0.8527	0.7685	0.8635	0.9065	0.8862	0.8867	**0.9384**	0.9028
Ours	**0.7965**	**0.8750**	**0.7860**	0.8747	**0.9378**	**0.9045**	**0.8950**	0.9266	**0.9136**

Privacy-Preserving Methods. As shown in Table 4, our proposed PP-MTAD achieves strong overall performance under privacy constraints. It reaches an average accuracy of 0.8554 and recall of 0.9131, significantly outperforming existing privacy-preserving methods such as FedTADBench and PeFAD in detection sensitivity and stability. These results show that PP-MTAD effectively balances privacy protection and detection accuracy, and its performance approaches that of plaintext models.

However, by comparing Table 3 and Table 4, we observe a certain performance gap between the non-private MTAD and the privacy-preserving PP-MTAD. Among all components, the secure centroid update protocol contributes the most to the F1 drop. Unlike conventional k-means, the SCUP selects as the centroid the sequence with the minimal sum of DTW distances to others in the cluster, rather than computing the true arithmetic mean. While this strategy preserves privacy and avoids global alignment, it introduces approximation bias. Moreover, the iterative nature of clustering may amplify these biases over time, leading to drift in cluster boundaries.

6.3 Data Outsourcing Phase

In the data outsourcing experiment under the Cheetah framework, we analyze the impact of data scale on outsourcing time. Based on the SMD, we kept the multivariate time series length ($n = 100$) and dimensions ($d = 38$) constant while varying the size of the dataset (N) from 50 to 250, effectively scaling the data volume from 190k to 950k. The results, as shown in Fig. 4a, indicate a clear upward trend in outsourcing time as the data scale grows, with the increase becoming more pronounced at larger scales.

6.4 Efficiency of Secure Distance Computation Protocols

We evaluate the computational efficiency of two core secure distance protocols used in our framework: the SEDP and the SDTWP. As shown in Fig. 4b, the

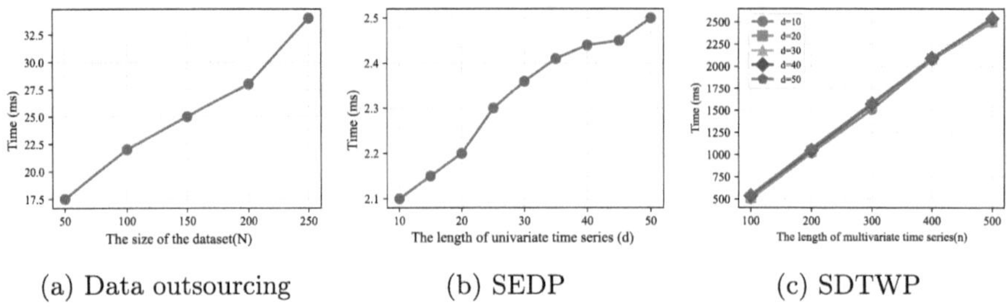

(a) Data outsourcing (b) SEDP (c) SDTWP

Fig. 4. Computational overhead analysis: (a) The runtime of data outsourcing phase; (b) The runtime of the SEDP; (c) The runtime of the SDTWP.

SEDP demonstrates excellent scalability with respect to time series length. When the sequence length increases from 10 to 50, the computation time rises only slightly, from 2.10 ms to 2.50 ms. In contrast, as shown in Fig. 4c, the SDTWP exhibits a linear increase in runtime with respect to sequence length, which is expected due to the cost of constructing the dynamic programming matrix. However, its runtime remains largely unaffected by the number of dimensions. Thus, these results highlight that our secure distance protocols are computationally practical. The SEDP is nearly invariant to sequence length, while the SDTWP scales linearly with length but efficiently handles multivariate data.

6.5 Secure Data Clustering Phase

As shown in Fig. 5a, we evaluate the running time of three secure protocols, i.e. SDAP, SESEP, and SCUP, along with the overall secure clustering process across different data scales. Specifically, the SDAP remains stable (3,663¨C4,008 ms), while the SESEP is highly efficient (111¨C130 ms), contributing only 1.1¨C2.0% of total time. In contrast, SCUP becomes the primary performance bottleneck, with its runtime share increasing from 33.5% to 66.4%. This is because SCUP requires repeated secure distance evaluations and comparisons across all cluster members, which scales poorly as data volume grows. These results suggest that future optimization efforts should prioritize reducing the overhead of secure centroid update.

6.6 Secure Anomaly Detection Phase

We evaluated our anomaly detection algorithm on the SMD dataset by fixing the sequence length ($n = 100$) and dimensionality ($d = 38$), while varying the number of time series from 50 to 250. As shown in Fig. 5b, the computation time of the SADP scales approximately linearly with the number of time series. This is expected because the protocol iteratively computes pairwise distances within each cluster using the secure DTW subroutine and removes outliers based on maximum distance until the cluster average distance meets the threshold. As the

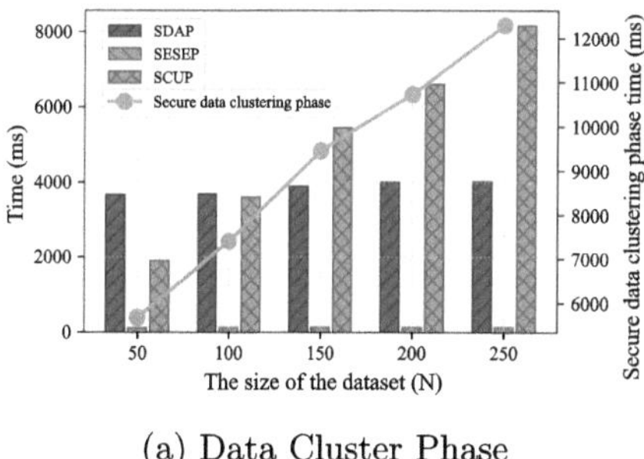

(a) Data Cluster Phase

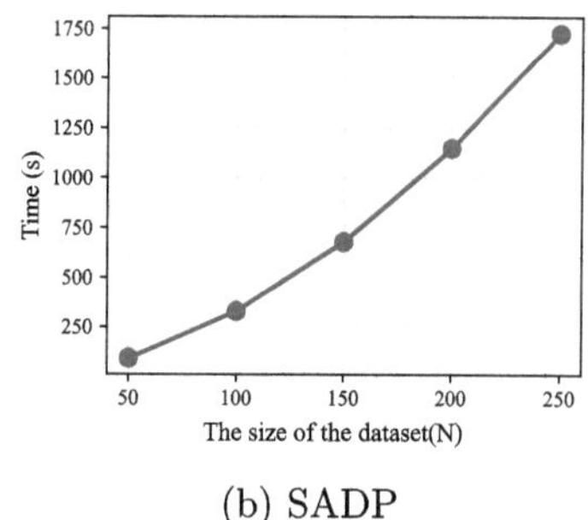

(b) SADP

Fig. 5. Computational overhead analysis: (a) The runtime of data cluster phase; (b) The runtime of SADP.

dataset size grows, both the number of pairwise comparisons and the number of iterations increase, leading to longer overall computation time.

7 Conclusion

This paper proposes PP-MTAD, a privacy-preserving anomaly detection framework for multivariate time series based on secure two-party computation. By combining DTW distance and clustering, PP-MTAD achieves accurate detection while protecting data privacy. The security analysis demonstrates its privacy guarantees, and experimental results show that PP-MTAD maintains outstanding performance even in encrypted domains. Compared to traditional plaintext methods, our approach strikes a balance between privacy protection and detection accuracy, making it suitable for real-world applications such as health monitoring and equipment fault detection. In the future, we aim to optimize computational efficiency and extend our model to more complex time series scenarios to further enhance system performance and applicability.

Acknowledgements. This work was supported in part by the National Natural Science Foundation of China (Nos. 62332007, U22B2028, 62302192, U23A20303, 62572214 and 62072215), the Guangdong Provincial Natural Science Foundation (Nos. 2024A1515011341, 2024A1515140067 and 2024A1515010086), the Dongguan Social Development Technology Project (No. 20231800940342), the Science and Technology Major Project of Tibetan Autonomous Region of China (No. XZ202201ZD0006G), the Special Funding Project of the China Postdoctoral Science Foundation (No. 2024T170348) and the Guangzhou Science and Technology Plan Project (No. 2024A04J3691), National Joint Engineering Research Center of Network Security Detection and Protection Technology, Guangdong Key Laboratory of Data Security and Privacy Preserving, Guangdong Hong Kong Joint Laboratory for Data Security and Privacy Protection, and Engineering Research Center of Trustworthy AI, Ministry of Education.

References

1. Acar, A., Aksu, H., Uluagac, A.S., Conti, M.: A survey on homomorphic encryption schemes: theory and implementation. ACM Comput. Surv. **51**(4), 79:1–79:35 (2018). https://doi.org/10.1145/3214303
2. Atallah, M.J., Bykova, M., Li, J., Frikken, K.B., Topkara, M.: Private collaborative forecasting and benchmarking. In: Atluri, V., Syverson, P.F., di Vimercati, S.D.C. (eds.) Proceedings of the 2004 ACM Workshop on Privacy in the Electronic Society, WPES 2004, Washington, DC, USA, 28 October 2004, pp. 103–114. ACM (2004). https://doi.org/10.1145/1029179.1029204
3. Audibert, J., Michiardi, P., Guyard, F., Marti, S., Zuluaga, M.A.: USAD: unsupervised anomaly detection on multivariate time series. In: Gupta, R., Liu, Y., Tang, J., Prakash, B.A. (eds.) KDD 2020: The 26th ACM SIGKDD Conference on Knowledge Discovery and Data Mining, Virtual Event, CA, USA, 23–27 August 2020, pp. 3395–3404. ACM (2020). https://doi.org/10.1145/3394486.3403392
4. Canetti, R.: Universally composable security: a new paradigm for cryptographic protocols. In: 42nd Annual Symposium on Foundations of Computer Science, FOCS 2001, Las Vegas, Nevada, USA, 14–17 October 2001, pp. 136–145. IEEE Computer Society (2001). https://doi.org/10.1109/SFCS.2001.959888
5. Disken, G., Ibrikci, T.: Recognition of non-speech sounds using mel-frequency cepstrum coefficients and dynamic time warping method. In: 2015 23nd Signal Processing and Communications Applications Conference (SIU), Malatya, Turkey, 16–19 May 2015, pp. 144–147. IEEE (2015). https://doi.org/10.1109/SIU.2015.7130277
6. Dong, C., et al.: Maliciously secure and efficient large-scale genome-wide association study with multi-party computation. IEEE Trans. Dependable Secur. Comput. **20**(2), 1243–1257 (2023). https://doi.org/10.1109/TDSC.2022.3152498
7. Goldreich, O., Micali, S., Wigderson, A.: How to play any mental game or A completeness theorem for protocols with honest majority. In: Aho, A.V. (ed.) Proceedings of the 19th Annual ACM Symposium on Theory of Computing, 1987, New York, New York, USA, pp. 218–229. ACM (1987). https://doi.org/10.1145/28395.28420
8. Goldreich, O., Micali, S., Wigderson, A.: How to play any mental game, or a completeness theorem for protocols with honest majority. In: Providing Sound Foundations for Cryptography: On the Work of Shafi Goldwasser and Silvio Micali, pp. 307–328 (2019). https://doi.org/10.1145/3335741.3335755
9. Huang, Z., Lu, W., Hong, C., Ding, J.: Cheetah: lean and fast secure two-party deep neural network inference. In: Butler, K.R.B., Thomas, K. (eds.) 31st USENIX Security Symposium, USENIX Security 2022, Boston, MA, USA, 10–12 August 2022, pp. 809–826. USENIX Association (2022)
10. Hundman, K., Constantinou, V., Laporte, C., Colwell, I., Söderström, T.: Detecting spacecraft anomalies using LSTMs and nonparametric dynamic thresholding. In: Guo, Y., Farooq, F. (eds.) Proceedings of the 24th ACM SIGKDD International Conference on Knowledge Discovery & Data Mining, KDD 2018, London, UK, 19–23 August 2018, pp. 387–395. ACM (2018). https://doi.org/10.1145/3219819.3219845
11. Li, J., Di, S., Shen, Y., Chen, L.: Fluxev: a fast and effective unsupervised framework for time-series anomaly detection. In: Proceedings of the 14th ACM International Conference on Web Search and Data Mining, WSDM 2021, pp. 824–832. Association for Computing Machinery, New York, NY, USA (2021). https://doi.org/10.1145/3437963.3441823

12. Li, X., Huang, Z., Zhao, B., Yang, G., Xiang, T., Deng, R.H.: STDA: secure time series data analytics with practical efficiency in wide-area network. IEEE Trans. Inf. Forensics Secur. **19**, 1440–1454 (2024). https://doi.org/10.1109/TIFS.2023.3336512
13. Liu, F., et al.: Fedtadbench: federated time-series anomaly detection benchmark. In: 24th IEEE International Conference on High Performance Computing & Communications; 8th International Conference on Data Science & Systems; 20th International Conference on Smart City; 8th International Conference on Dependability in Sensor, Cloud & Big Data Systems & Application, HPCC/DSS/SmartCity/DependSys 2022, Hainan, China, 18–20 December 2022, pp. 303–310 (2022). https://doi.org/10.1109/HPCC-DSS-SMARTCITY-DEPENDSYS57074.2022.00071
14. Liu, J., Lu, X., Yin, H., Tao, X., Zhang, C., Quigley, A.: A constraints-based dynamic time warping method for gesture recognition with kinect. In: Song, A., Habib, M. (eds.) Proceedings of the 2023 3rd International Conference on Robotics and Control Engineering, RobCE 2023, Nanjing, China, 12–14 May 2023, pp. 178–183. ACM (2023). https://doi.org/10.1145/3598151.3598181
15. Liu, X., Zheng, Y., Yi, X., Nepal, S.: Privacy-preserving collaborative analytics on medical time series data. IEEE Trans. Dependable Secur. Comput. **19**(3), 1687–1702 (2022). https://doi.org/10.1109/TDSC.2020.3035592
16. Ma, M., et al.: Jump-starting multivariate time series anomaly detection for online service systems. In: 2021 USENIX Annual Technical Conference (USENIX ATC 2021), pp. 413–426. USENIX Association (2021)
17. Okawa, M.: Time-series averaging and local stability-weighted dynamic time warping for online signature verification. Pattern Recogn. **112**, 107699 (2021). https://doi.org/10.1016/J.PATCOG.2020.107699
18. Okawa, M.: Online signature verification using locally weighted dynamic time warping via multiple fusion strategies. IEEE Access **10**, 40806–40817 (2022). https://doi.org/10.1109/ACCESS.2022.3167413
19. Pang, H., He, K., Fu, Y., Liu, J., Liu, X., Tan, W.: Enabling efficient and malicious secure data aggregation in smart grid with false data detection. IEEE Trans. Smart Grid **15**(2), 2203–2213 (2024). https://doi.org/10.1109/TSG.2023.3316730
20. Park, D., Kim, H., Hoshi, Y., Erickson, Z., Kapusta, A., Kemp, C.C.: A multimodal execution monitor with anomaly classification for robot-assisted feeding. In: 2017 IEEE/RSJ International Conference on Intelligent Robots and Systems, IROS 2017, Vancouver, BC, Canada, 24–28 September 2017, pp. 5406–5413. IEEE (2017). https://doi.org/10.1109/IROS.2017.8206437
21. Permanasari, Y., Harahap, E.H., Ali, E.P.: Speech recognition using dynamic time warping (DTW). In: Journal of Physics: Conference Series, vol. 1366, p. 012091. IOP Publishing (2019)
22. Rathee, D., et al.: Cryptflow2: practical 2-party secure inference. In: CCS 2020: 2020 ACM SIGSAC Conference on Computer and Communications Security, Virtual Event, USA, 9–13 November 2020, pp. 325–342 (2020).https://doi.org/10.1145/3372297.3417274
23. Sakoe, H.: Dynamic-programming approach to continuous speech recognition. In: 1971 Proceedings of the International Congress of Acoustics, Budapest (1971)
24. Shamir, A.: How to share a secret. Commun. ACM **22**(11), 612–613 (1979). https://doi.org/10.1145/359168.359176
25. Su, Y., Zhao, Y., Niu, C., Liu, R., Sun, W., Pei, D.: Robust anomaly detection for multivariate time series through stochastic recurrent neural network. In: Teredesai,

A., Kumar, V., Li, Y., Rosales, R., Terzi, E., Karypis, G. (eds.) Proceedings of the 25th ACM SIGKDD International Conference on Knowledge Discovery & Data Mining, KDD 2019, Anchorage, AK, USA, 4–8 August 2019, pp. 2828–2837. ACM (2019). https://doi.org/10.1145/3292500.3330672

26. Tang, J., Cheng, H., Zhao, Y., Guo, H.: Structured dynamic time warping for continuous hand trajectory gesture recognition. Pattern Recogn. **80**, 21–31 (2018). https://doi.org/10.1016/J.PATCOG.2018.02.011
27. Tuli, S., Casale, G., Jennings, N.R.: Tranad: deep transformer networks for anomaly detection in multivariate time series data. Proc. VLDB Endow. **15**(6), 1201–1214 (2022). https://doi.org/10.14778/3514061.3514067
28. Xu, R., Miao, H., Wang, S., Yu, P.S., Wang, J.: Pefad: a parameter-efficient federated framework for time series anomaly detection. In: Proceedings of the 30th ACM SIGKDD Conference on Knowledge Discovery and Data Mining, KDD 2024, Barcelona, Spain, 25–29 August 2024, pp. 3621–3632 (2024). https://doi.org/10.1145/3637528.3671753
29. Yang, Y., et al.: Prigenx: privacy-preserving query with anonymous access control for genomic data. IEEE Trans. Dependable Secur. Comput. **21**(2), 961–974 (2024). https://doi.org/10.1109/TDSC.2023.3266292
30. Yao, A.C.: How to generate and exchange secrets (extended abstract). In: 27th Annual Symposium on Foundations of Computer Science, Toronto, Canada, 27–29 October 1986, pp. 162–167. IEEE Computer Society (1986). https://doi.org/10.1109/SFCS.1986.25
31. Yuan, Y., et al.: Development and application of a modified dynamic time warping algorithm (DTW-S) to analyses of primate brain expression time series. BMC Bioinform. **12**, 347 (2011). https://doi.org/10.1186/1471-2105-12-347
32. Zhang, S., et al.: Privacy-preserving MTS anomaly detection for network devices through federated learning. Inf. Sci. **690**, 121590 (2025). https://doi.org/10.1016/J.INS.2024.121590
33. Zhao, C., et al.: Secure multi-party computation: theory, practice and applications. Inf. Sci. **476**, 357–372 (2019). https://doi.org/10.1016/J.INS.2018.10.024
34. Zheng, Y., Lu, R., Guan, Y., Shao, J., Zhu, H.: Efficient and privacy-preserving similarity range query over encrypted time series data. IEEE Trans. Dependable Secur. Comput. **19**(4), 2501–2516 (2022). https://doi.org/10.1109/TDSC.2021.3061611
35. Zhu, H., Meng, X., Kollios, G.: Privacy preserving similarity evaluation of time series data. In: Amer-Yahia, S., Christophides, V., Kementsietsidis, A., Garofalakis, M.N., Idreos, S., Leroy, V. (eds.) Proceedings of the 17th International Conference on Extending Database Technology, EDBT 2014, Athens, Greece, 24–28 March 2014, pp. 499–510. OpenProceedings.org (2014). https://doi.org/10.5441/002/EDBT.2014.45
36. Zong, B., et al.: Deep autoencoding gaussian mixture model for unsupervised anomaly detection. In: 6th International Conference on Learning Representations, ICLR 2018, Vancouver, BC, Canada, 30 April–3 May 2018, Conference Track Proceedings (2018)

LogWhisperer: Multi-log Semantic Similarity Analysis Based Intelligent Vehicle Anomaly Detection Without Log Template

Hongyi Guo[1,2,3,4], Kun Yang[1,2,3,4](✉), and Kui Ren[1,2,3,4]

[1] The State Key Laboratory of Blockchain and Data Security, Zhejiang University, Hangzhou 310027, China
{guohongyi,kuny,kuiren}@zju.edu.cn

[2] Hangzhou High-Tech Zone (Binjiang) Institute of Blockchain and Data Security, Hangzhou 310051, China

[3] School of Cyber Science and Technology, Zhejiang University, Hangzhou 310027, China

[4] College of Computer Science and Technology, Zhejiang University, Hangzhou 310027, China

Abstract. In recent years, the global intelligent vehicles market size has been growing rapidly and is projected to reach 6,861.45 billion U.S. dollars by 2033, according to a research report published by Spherical Insights [21]. Conventional and emerging security challenges have been gravely threatening the security of intelligent vehicles, the key infrastructure of digital society, and thus posing a threat to national security. Logs have typically been exploited as data sources for threat analysis and anomaly detection. Most existing logs-based anomaly detection approaches are designed for defending distributed computing systems or high-performance computers, and cannot be easily adapted for protecting intelligent vehicles. Worse still, most of prior solutions rely on log templates for anomaly detection, which will face the issue of explosion in the number of log templates while defending modern intelligent vehicles. Previous work typically uses logs from open-source libraries, which are outdated and have gone through pre-processing. To overcome these limitations, we propose LogWhisperer, a semantic similarity analysis based approach that investigates multiple types of logs for detecting abnormal behaviors of intelligent vehicles. LogWhisperer jointly analyzes logs from different levels of multiple subsystems in the vehicle and detects abnormal behaviors by evaluating the semantic similarity between actual log sequence and projected log sequence. Compared with anomaly detection approaches that rely on log templates, LogWhisperer has better platform portability since it discards log templates and its data pre-processing procedure does not change depending on specific scenarios.

Keywords: Intelligent connected vehicle security · Intrusion detection system · Log analysis

R. Chen et al. (Eds.): Inscrypt 2025, LNCS 16409, pp. 195–214, 2026.
https://doi.org/10.1007/978-981-95-6203-9_11

1 Introduction

Intelligent connected vehicles are transforming the automotive industry by offering electrification, intelligent features, connectivity, and sharing capabilities [41,42]. These advancements improve user convenience, redefine driving, and drive industry growth. Traditional automakers (e.g., Mercedes-Benz, BMW, Audi) and tech companies (e.g., Xiaomi, HUAWEI) are investing heavily in this field. Governments worldwide are also supporting infrastructure like RSUs [40], V2X [5], and cloud platforms, further boosting the market. In 2023, the global intelligent connected vehicle market reached 1921.1 billion USD [20], showing great potential.

With the rise of intelligent vehicles, user data privacy becomes more important. Sensitive data such as personal information, driving routes, map data, and information from in-vehicle cameras and microphones is now closely linked to vehicles. However, as vehicles become smarter, security risks grow. More attack surfaces appear, including WiFi, Bluetooth, cellular networks, and charging stations, which attackers can exploit [18,32]. In 2023, there were over 400 reported intelligent vehicle cybersecurity incidents globally, causing losses exceeding a trillion dollars [45]. Common attack targets include Telematics Service Provider (TSP) services [27], Telematics-Box (T-Box), smart cockpits, owner apps, and charging services [50]. New types of attacks are constantly emerging, posing serious threats to vehicle security [10,36].

To defend against these threats, typical solutions include in-vehicle firewalls [29], intrusion detection and prevention systems (IDPS) [11,28], vehicle security operation centers (VSOC) [17], and chip-level security measures [9]. However, these solutions often have challenges like complex deployment, high latency, and poor compatibility. Therefore, there is an urgent need for more efficient, compatible, and lightweight security solutions for intelligent vehicles.

Intelligent vehicles generate large amounts of log data from various subsystems and over different time periods. Traditionally, logs are used for anomaly detection in computer systems [4,44]. However, there are few comprehensive solutions that use logs for detecting intrusions or abnormal behavior in intelligent vehicles. Most existing log analysis methods depend on predefined templates [14], but in intelligent vehicles, this approach faces scalability issues due to the rapid increase in the number of templates needed. Given these challenges, we propose **LogWhisperer**, a new anomaly detection method for intelligent vehicles based on multi-log semantic similarity analysis. We process and combine logs collected from real vehicles, convert them into sequences of word vectors, and then input them into a Bi-LSTM model. Our main contributions are summarized as follows:

- Traditional log template-based anomaly detection struggles with too many templates in modern connected vehicles. We introduce a new method using word vectors, which can handle large and diverse vehicle logs and works well across different platforms by not relying on templates.
- Template-based methods cannot check if log elements are reasonable or analyze their relationships. Our approach compares the semantics of actual and

predicted log sequences, allowing for more detailed and accurate anomaly detection.
- We analyze logs from different subsystems and levels at the same time, which increases detection accuracy, resistance to interference, and the ability to find unknown anomalies.
- Most earlier work uses public datasets (like HDFS, BGL [16]) for model training and testing. We test our LogWhisperer system on real vehicle logs from various car brands. To our knowledge, LogWhisperer is the first to use real intelligent vehicle logs for anomaly detection. We also propose new metrics to assess log complexity and whether traditional methods are suitable for specific scenarios.

2 Related Work

Many studies have explored log-based anomaly detection, which can be divided into machine learning (ML) and non-machine learning approaches.

Non-machine Learning Anomaly Detection: Traditional methods, such as rule-based [37], workflow-based [30], and graph-based approaches [12,23], directly analyze log structures and contents. Although these methods are interpretable, they are inefficient and difficult to transfer across different platforms. As a result, ML-based methods have become increasingly popular.

Single ML Model Anomaly Detection: Lu et al. [31] used convolutional neural networks (CNNs) to classify log sequences as normal or abnormal. Du et al. [7] introduced DeepLog, which employs long short-term memory (LSTM) networks to learn normal log patterns and detect deviations. Huang et al. [19] proposed HitAnomaly, a hierarchical transformer model that captures semantic information from both log templates and parameter values, enabling detection of various anomaly types.

Multiple ML Models Anomaly Detection: Yen et al. [49] developed CausalConvLSTM, which combines CNNs and LSTMs to extract spatial and sequential features. Duan et al. [8] proposed GAN-EDC, a generative adversarial network model that uses CNNs to distinguish between real and generated log templates.

Each method has trade-offs. Non-ML approaches are interpretable but lack adaptability. Single ML models like LSTM handle sequences well but can be slow and memory-intensive. Transformer-based models, such as HitAnomaly, capture complex dependencies but require significant computational resources. GAN-based models can detect rare anomalies but may be unstable during training. Hybrid models, like CNN-LSTM, balance efficiency and accuracy but are more complex. LogWhisperer uses a Bi-LSTM with attention mechanism to balance computational efficiency, sequential modeling, and detection performance, making it well-suited for intelligent vehicle anomaly detection.

3 Preliminaries

In this section, we first introduce the threat model for intelligent vehicles, outlining potential attack vectors and security risks. We then briefly describe conventional log-based anomaly detection approaches and present the mature models and strategies used in this paper.

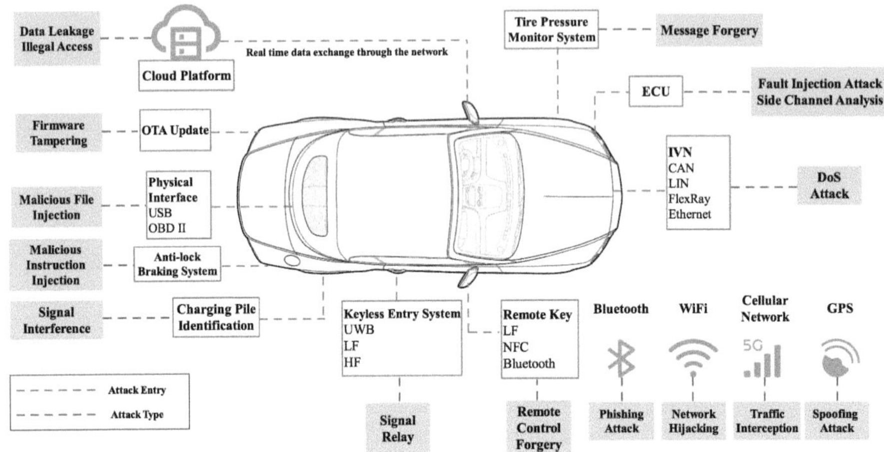

Fig. 1. Intelligent vehicle attack surfaces.

3.1 Threat Model

The threat model for intelligent vehicles encompasses a broad spectrum of attack vectors targeting both physical and digital components, as illustrated in Fig. 1. Modern connected vehicles depend on a variety of communication interfaces—such as CAN, LIN, FlexRay, Ethernet, Bluetooth, WiFi, and cellular networks—which significantly expand their cyber attack surface. Potential threats include firmware tampering, malicious file injection via USB or OBD-II ports, and sophisticated network-based attacks like denial-of-service (DoS), message forgery, and traffic interception. Remote access vulnerabilities through cloud platforms, GPS, and Bluetooth further increase the risk, enabling attackers to gain unauthorized control, track vehicle locations, or exfiltrate sensitive data. Both physical and wireless attack vectors present additional challenges, such as signal interference, relay attacks against keyless entry systems, and side-channel analysis. Adversaries may also exploit vehicle sensors and ECUs through fault injection, spoofing of critical sensor inputs (e.g., the Tire Pressure Monitoring System, TPMS), or malicious instruction injection, potentially resulting in unsafe or unintended vehicle behaviors.

As vehicles become more autonomous and interconnected, the complexity and sophistication of cyber threats continue to escalate, posing significant risks to passenger safety and data privacy. These evolving challenges highlight the urgent need for robust security measures—such as advanced intrusion detection systems (IDS) and anomaly detection frameworks—to strengthen the resilience of intelligent vehicles against emerging cyber threats.

3.2 General Log Anomaly Detection Flow

The system usually generates logs that record system statuses, operations, and changes. Prepossessing such as log division and information extraction is required after log collection. The output of preprocessing phase can be utilized for various purposes (e.g., statistics analysis and anomaly detection). Figure 2 shows the overall workflow of general log anomaly detection, which can be split into four steps: log collection, log parsing, feature extraction, and anomaly detection.

Log parsing is used to extract log templates from the original system log. Each log message can be regarded as a composition of a constant part and a variable part. Log parsing eliminates the variable part or replaces it with wildcards, and keeps only the constant part to build a log template. After the logs are parsed into log templates, log templates are further encoded into digital feature vectors (e.g., log template count vectors, etc.). Subsequently, machine learning model can be used to detect anomalies. Finally, the feature vectors are fed into the anomaly detection model. The trained model can identify whether the log is normal or abnormal.

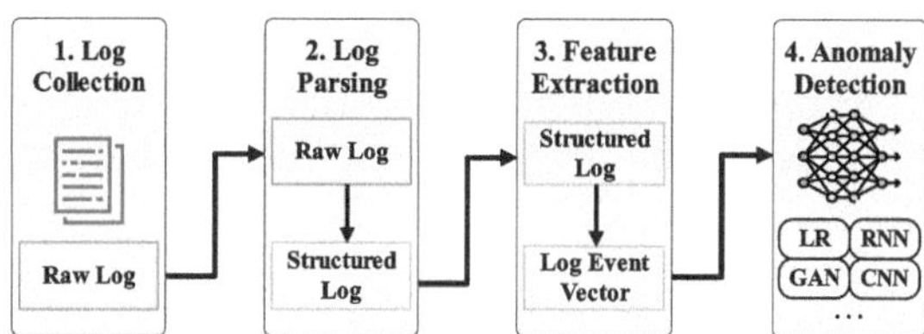

Fig. 2. General log anomaly detection framework.

3.3 GloVe

Global Vectors for Word Representation(GloVe) [39] is a model for generating word vectors. It is a statistical method proposed by researchers at Stanford University in 2014 that aims to create dense vector representations of words that capture the semantic and syntactic relationships between words.

GLoVe constructs a co-occurrence matrix X from a large-scale text corpus, where X_{ij} represents the number of times word i and word j occur together. The goal is to find two sets of vectors (word vectors and context vectors) such that the dot product between them is as close as possible to the logarithmic co-occurrence probability in the co-occurrence matrix. The model is trained by minimizing a weighted squared error loss function that reflects the difference between the predicted log co-occurrence probability and the actual log co-occurrence probability.

Since GLoVe is able to capture more complex relationships between words and usually provides high-quality word vectors, it is widely used in a variety of tasks in natural language processing, including but not limited to text categorization, sentiment analysis, and machine translation. In summary, GLoVe is a powerful technique for word vector generation, and by combining global statistical information with local contextual information, it can produce effective representations that reflect the semantic and syntactic relationships between words.

4 LogWhisperer

The proposed LogWhisperer is presented in this section. We first introduce the overall framework of LogWhisperer that consists of four phases, and then describe the specific details of each phase.

4.1 LogWhisperer Overview

LogWhisperer is recommended to operate as a trusted application running in the secure world of the vehicle's central control system. Figure 3 shows the overall framework of LogWhisperer, which consists of four main phases: (i) **Log Collection**: collect log data from different subsystems of the vehicle for model training and anomaly detection purposes; (ii) **Log Processing**: convert log texts into word vectors as input into the model; (iii) **Model Training**: learn the relationships between word sequences in the texts; (iv) **Anomaly Detection**: input the logs to be detected into the model and analyze the semantic similarities between predicted and actual texts to determine if anomalies occur.

4.2 Log Collection

Once implemented in the vehicle central control system, LogWhisperer can access logs from different subsystems directly from the pre-allocated memory buffer used for temporary log storage. During the development phase of LogWhisperer, we need to download log files from the vehicle for offline model training.

Most modern vehicles have an OBD-II port that can be used to read real-time data streams and vehicle error codes. Log data can be accessed from the trip computer via an OBD-II adapter connected to a laptop or a mobile phone. For connected vehicles, vehicle data can be accessed remotely via wireless communications such as Bluetooth, Wi-Fi, or cellular networks [38,47]. Nowadays most vehicles support software/firmware updates and data transfer over the air. Some vehicles are equipped with a built-in logging system that automatically records critical driving data, which will be stored in the vehicle's memory and

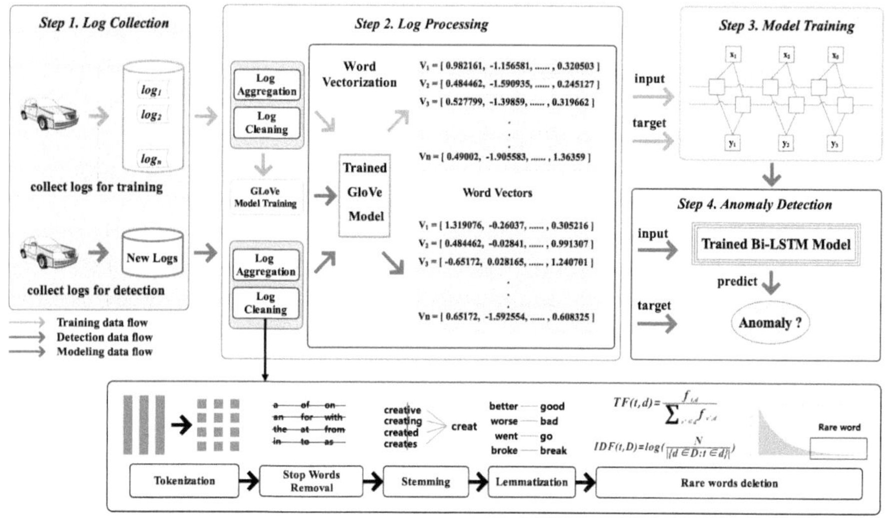

Fig. 3. Multi-log semantic similarity analysis based intelligent vehicle anomaly detection flow.

can be accessed through dedicated interfaces. For vehicles with Android-based in-vehicle systems, log files can be obtained via the USB port exploiting the Android built-in command namely *logcat* [1,34]. In this paper, we collect log files from the vehicles via either wireless communication interface or USB port depending on specific vehicle models.

4.3 Log Processing

Log processing means turning log texts into vectors so they can be used for model training. This step is important and can be divided into three stages:

Log Aggregation. To analyze multiple logs together, we combine different logs. Each log usually has a timestamp, process ID (PID), thread ID (TID), log level (ERROR, WARN, INFO, DEBUG), component name, and log content. Since timestamps are standardized, we can merge logs in order to make a single file. This maintains the relationship between logs and prepares the data for further processing.

Log Cleaning. Log cleaning changes raw logs into a set of words with a consistent structure. We use several steps to improve data quality and help model training:

- **Tokenization:** Split log texts into separate words or tags [43].
- **Stop words removal:** Remove common words like "and" and "the" that add little meaning.

- **Stemming:** Reduce words to their root form [24], e.g., "fishing", "fished", and "fisherman" become "fish".
- **Lemmatization:** Convert words to their dictionary form, e.g., "better" becomes "good".
- **Rare words deletion:** Use TF-IDF to find and remove rarely used words. TF-IDF(term frequency–inverse document frequency) is a commonly used weighting technique for information retrieval and data mining.

We set a threshold on TF-IDF values to remove very rare words [2], which simplifies the vocabulary and improves efficiency. We also use regularization to avoid overfitting, which will be discussed later. These steps make model training faster and more accurate for anomaly detection.

Word Vectorization. Models need numerical input, not raw text. We use the GloVe model [39] to turn words into vectors. GloVe is trained on the combined log data, learning word relationships in context. Each word becomes an n-dimensional vector. Usually, $n = 300$ is a good balance between performance and efficiency, so we use 300-dimensional vectors for LogWhisperer.

Most approaches require template extraction, but LogWhisperer does not, as template extraction does not work well with real vehicle logs. To measure template extraction, we define these metrics:

- VT: percentage of valid templates: $VT = \frac{\text{number of valid templates}}{\text{number of total templates}}$
- IT: percentage of invalid templates: $IT = \frac{\text{number of invalid templates}}{\text{number of total templates}}$
- L/T: average number of logs per valid template: $L/T = \frac{\text{number of represented log entries}}{\text{number of valid templates}}$

A *valid template* represents multiple logs; an *invalid template* represents only one log. We tested template extraction on 80,000 logs from five public datasets and from real vehicle logs. Results are in Table 1. Public datasets work well with templates, but vehicle logs are too complex for template extraction. So, we process vehicle logs as word vectors instead.

Table 1. Effectiveness of log template extraction

Dataset	VT	IT	L/T
HDFS [16]	0.916	0.083	3636
BGL [16]	0.986	0.013	1110
HPC [16]	0.991	0.009	4128
Zookeeper [16]	0.971	0.029	929
Proxifier [16]	0.967	0.033	1263
Logs from vehicles	**0.821**	**0.178**	**79**

4.4 Model Training

The LSTM model is a type of recurrent neural network (RNN) designed for sequence data. It can capture contextual information in sequences because it processes data step by step over time. First, each word W in the log is converted into a vector V (word embedding). A log sequence is then represented as a list of these vectors, e.g., $[V_1, V_2, \cdots, V_T]$. We use these sequences as input to an attention-based Bi-LSTM neural network for anomaly detection. A Bi-LSTM has two layers: one processes the sequence forward, and the other processes it backward. This allows the model to gather information from both directions. At each time step t, we combine the forward and backward hidden states:

$$h_t = \text{concat}(h_t^f,\ h_t^b) \tag{1}$$

where h_t^f and h_t^b are the hidden states from the forward and backward passes at time t. To highlight important words, we use an attention mechanism. The attention weight α_t for each word is calculated as:

$$\alpha_t = \tanh(\mathbf{W}_t^{\alpha} \cdot \boldsymbol{h}_t) \tag{2}$$

where $\mathbf{W}_t^{\alpha}$ is the attention layer's weight at time t. All hidden states are combined using these attention weights. The result passes through a fully connected layer to make predictions, yielding a sequence $[V_1^p, V_2^p, \cdots, V_n^p]$. The loss function is based on cosine similarity between the real (V) and predicted (V^p) word vectors:

$$\text{Cosine Similarity} = \frac{\sum_{i=1}^{n} V_i V_i^p}{\sqrt{\sum_{i=1}^{n} V_i^2}\sqrt{\sum_{i=1}^{n} (V_i^p)^2}} \tag{3}$$

$$\text{Loss} = 1 - \frac{1}{m}\sum_{i=1}^{m} \text{Cosine Similarity} \tag{4}$$

A higher cosine similarity means the predicted and actual word vectors are more similar. The model is trained by minimizing this loss using stochastic gradient descent.

According to research, models trained with word vectors are prone to overfitting [26]. To address this, we apply both L2 and L1 regularization during the training of LogWhisperer. These techniques help control model complexity, select important features, and improve generalization and prediction accuracy.

L2 regularization (weight decay) adds a penalty to the loss function to encourage smaller weights and a simpler model [35]. This is mathematically expressed as:

$$\tilde{J}(w; X, y) = J(w; X, y) + \frac{\alpha}{2} w^{\top} w \tag{5}$$

The weight update rule is:

$$w \leftarrow (1 - \epsilon\alpha)w - \epsilon \nabla_w J(w; X, y) \tag{6}$$

This shrinks the weights slightly at each step, reducing overfitting.

L1 regularization adds a penalty based on the sum of the absolute values of the weights, promoting sparsity and feature selection [13]:

$$\tilde{J}(w; X, y) = J(w; X, y) + \alpha \|w\|_1 \tag{7}$$

The update rule is:

$$w \leftarrow w - \epsilon(\alpha \text{sgn}(w) + \nabla_w J(w; X, y)) \tag{8}$$

This encourages many weights to become exactly zero, simplifying the model.

By using both L2 and L1 regularization, we can prevent overfitting and enhance our model's ability to detect anomalies in vehicle logs, ultimately supporting safer vehicle operation.

4.5 Anomaly Detection

Logs record the behavior of different components within a system. When a system operates normally, the contents of the logs are stable and predictable. However, when the system experiences abnormalities, the content of the log records becomes irregular, such as a sudden increase in the activity of a module or increased communication among multiple modules with a particular one. In such cases, the logs become unstable and unpredictable. LogWhisperer achieves anomaly detection by comparing the semantic variability of the predicted log entries with the actual ones. When the system is anomalous, the predicted log content will differ significantly from the actual content (Fig. 4).

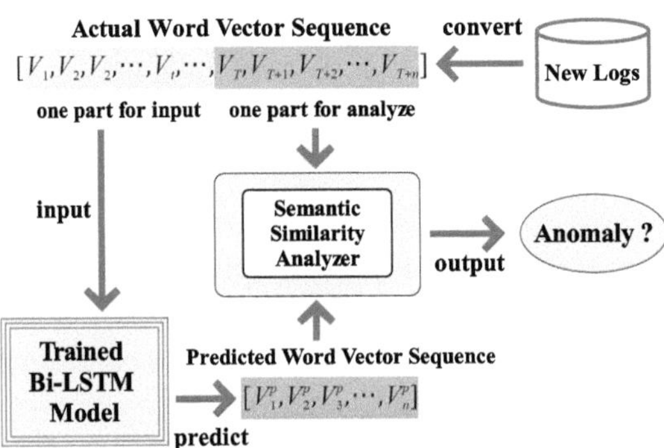

Fig. 4. Anomaly detection flow.

Using the above steps, we build an anomaly detection model for log data. Upon receiving real-time vehicle logs, LogWhisperer processes the data by converting log sequences into word vectors. The sequence is split into two parts: one is input into the trained model to predict the next sequence, while the other is compared with the prediction using cosine similarity. If the similarity falls below a predefined threshold, the system flags an anomaly.

When anomalies are detected, the system responds based on preset strategies: (i) resetting faulty modules when possible, (ii) temporarily disabling affected communication or sensing components to reduce risk, and (iii) reporting anomalies to VSOC while alerting the vehicle owner. These measures enhance security with minimal disruption.

LogWhisperer integrates seamlessly into in-vehicle systems, providing real-time monitoring and alerts. It supports OTA updates for algorithm improvements and features self-learning capabilities, refining its model over time for more accurate fault detection. As usage increases, security and performance continuously improve.

5 Evaluation

In this section, we first present the evaluation setup and results regarding detection accuracy. Afterwards, we compare LogWhisperer with prior work. Lastly, we perform the security analysis.

5.1 Experimental Setup

In this subsection, we present relevant background information about the experimental evaluation, including the source of the dataset, the model parameter settings, and the evaluation methodology (Table 2).

Table 2. Vehicle models used for evaluation

No.	Brands	Models
1	Geely	Yinhe L6
2	Geely	Yinhe E8
3	BYD	Song Plus DM-i
4	Changan	UNI-T
5	Changan	UNI-V
6	Chevrolet	Cruze
7	Volkswagen	Lavida
8	Nissan	TEANA
9	Leapmotor	C11
10	Chery	Arrizo 8

We collected detailed log data from various mainstream vehicles for anomaly detection, using two main methods:

1. **Engineering Mode**: Accessed via specific key combinations in the vehicle's settings, this mode provides comprehensive system logs for diagnostics.
2. **Android Debug Bridge (ADB)**: For vehicles with Android-based infotainment systems, we used ADB [3]. By installing the ADB toolkit, enabling developer options and USB debugging, connecting the vehicle to a computer, and running `adb logcat`, we could extract system logs. Logs were saved with `adb logcat > log.txt` [25].

We used these methods to collect logs during normal vehicle operation, which serve as a baseline for our anomaly detection models. To improve model accuracy, we also needed logs from abnormal (attack) states.

We performed several wireless communication attacks on real intelligent vehicles, including GPS spoofing and Bluetooth Denial-of-Service (DoS) attacks [22, 46]. The implementation of these attacks are shown in Fig. 5a and Fig. 5b. We recorded system logs during these attacks to evaluate the detection ability of LogWhisperer. These attacks were chosen because they target wireless vulnerabilities, affecting vehicle navigation and connectivity. They are practical to implement and generate clear anomalies in the logs, which helps us test LogWhisperer's performance.

In addition, we carried out a Man-in-the-Middle (MITM) attack, shown in Fig. 5c. In this attack, the attacker intercepts and manipulates HTTPS data between the vehicle and the server during app installation or data transfer. This demonstrates the risks from network-level threats that can compromise vehicle data confidentiality and integrity. Logs from the MITM attack were also collected and used to further test LogWhisperer, as this attack produces unique, detectable anomalies.

Evaluation Metrics. To measure the performance of LogWhisperer in anomaly detection, we use the Precision, Recall, and F1-Score metrics. We calculate these metrics as follows:

- ***Precision***: the percentage of log sequences that are correctly identified as anomalies over all the log sequences that are identified as anomalies by the model: $Precision = \frac{TP}{TP+FP}$
- ***Recall***: the percentage of log sequences that are correctly identified as anomalies over all abnormal log sequences: $Recall = \frac{TP}{TP+FN}$
- ***F1-Score***: the harmonic mean of Precision and Recall: $F1\text{-}Score = \frac{2 * Precision * Recall}{Precision + Recall}$

TP is the number of abnormal log sequences the are correctly detected by the model. **FP** is the number of normal log sequences that are wrongly identified as anomalies. **FN** is the number of abnormal log sequences that are not detected by the model.

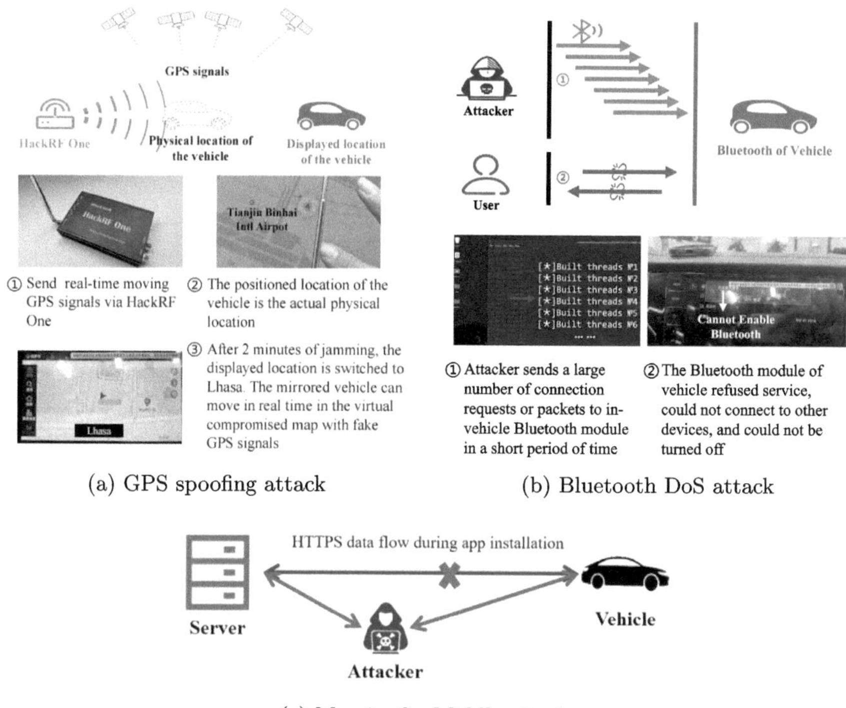

(c) Man-in-the-Middle attack

Fig. 5. Examples of (a) GPS spoofing, (b) Bluetooth DoS, and (c) Man-in-the-Middle attacks.

5.2 Detection Capability Evaluation

To evaluate the computational resource requirements of LogWhisperer, we measured its CPU, memory, and storage consumption in a testing environment equipped with an Intel Ultra 5 125H processor (14 cores, max frequency 4.5 GHz). Experimental results show that LogWhisperer maintains a CPU consumption of less than 10%, ensuring that it operates efficiently without significantly impacting vehicle system performance. The memory requirement of LogWhisperer is at least 1 GB, primarily for storing processed log data and model parameters, while the storage requirement is at least 2GB to accommodate log history and model updates. These results demonstrate that LogWhisperer is lightweight and feasible for deployment in intelligent vehicle systems without imposing excessive hardware demands (Table 3).

The dataset used in this experiment consists of abnormal log samples collected from nine different vehicle models, encompassing a total of three attack types: GPS Spoofing, Bluetooth DoS, and MITM. This diversity in vehicle models not only enriches the dataset but also enhances the generalizability of the evaluation results. By leveraging such a comprehensive and complex dataset,

Table 3. Actual computational resource consumption of LogWhisperer

Resource	Consumption
CPU	Average 6% (tested on Intel Ultra 5 125H, 14 cores, 4.5 GHz)
Memory	720 MB
Storage	1.3 GB

we are able to rigorously assess LogWhisperer's ability to detect and adapt to anomalies arising from various vehicle systems, thereby providing a robust validation of its real-world applicability. To evaluate LogWhisperer's anomaly detection capabilities, we combined the abnormal logs with normal log entries to simulate realistic operating conditions. The effectiveness of LogWhisperer was then systematically assessed using this integrated dataset, with the detailed results summarized in Table 4 and Fig. 6. Upon examining Table 4, it is evident that LogWhisperer demonstrates consistently high detection performance across different attack types and vehicle models. For instance, the model achieves an accuracy range of approximately 86% to 94% for GPS Spoofing attacks, with corresponding F1-scores of 0.879 to 0.930. Similarly, for Bluetooth DoS and MITM attacks, the model maintains high accuracy and F1-scores, often exceeding 0.91. On average, LogWhisperer achieves an overall accuracy of around 91%, along with a similarly high F1-score. These results indicate that LogWhisperer is highly effective at identifying true anomalies while maintaining a low false alarm rate, thus confirming its robustness and reliability in distinguishing between normal and abnormal log entries in diverse and challenging scenarios.

5.3 Comparison with Prior Work

To evaluate the anomaly detection capabilities of our proposed model, LogWhisperer, we conducted experiments using two well-known datasets: HDFS and BGL [16]. We compared LogWhisperer against several state-of-the-art approaches, including LR (Logistic Regression) [15], DeepLog [7], LogCNN [31], CasualConvLSTM [49], LogAnomaly [33], LogGAN [48], and HitAnomaly [19].

From the HDFS dataset, it is evident that each method has its unique strengths and limitations, particularly in terms of precision and recall. LogWhisperer, however, stands out by achieving a high level of precision (**0.966**) and recall (**0.993**), which translates into an F1-score of **0.980**. This indicates that not only does LogWhisperer detect anomalies accurately, but it also maintains a high detection rate. Compared to other methods, LogWhisperer demonstrates superior performance, making it particularly suitable for scenarios where both false positives and false negatives need to be minimized (Fig. 7).

For the BGL dataset, the comparison reveals that LogWhisperer also performs exceptionally well, achieving precision (**0.962**), recall (**0.984**), and F1-score (**0.972**). This highlights the robustness of LogWhisperer in handling more complex log data, as seen in the BGL dataset. In particular, the ability of Log-

Table 4. Anomaly detection capability evaluation

Attack Type	Model	Precision	Recall	F1-score
GPS Spoofing	Yinhe L6	0.919	0.878	0.898
	Yinhe E8	0.897	0.862	0.879
	Song Plus	0.920	0.923	0.921
	UNI-T	0.861	0.898	0.879
	UNI-V	0.926	0.917	0.921
	Cruze	0.899	0.904	0.901
	Lavida	0.931	0.906	0.918
	TEANA	0.900	0.885	0.892
	C11	0.896	0.874	0.884
	Arrizo 8	0.940	0.922	0.930
Bluetooth DoS	Cruze	0.947	0.877	0.911
	Lavida	0.935	0.910	0.922
	TEANA	0.931	0.936	0.933
MITM	Cruze	0.922	0.881	0.901
	Lavida	0.882	0.850	0.866
	TEANA	0.931	0.890	0.910
	C11	0.945	0.878	0.910

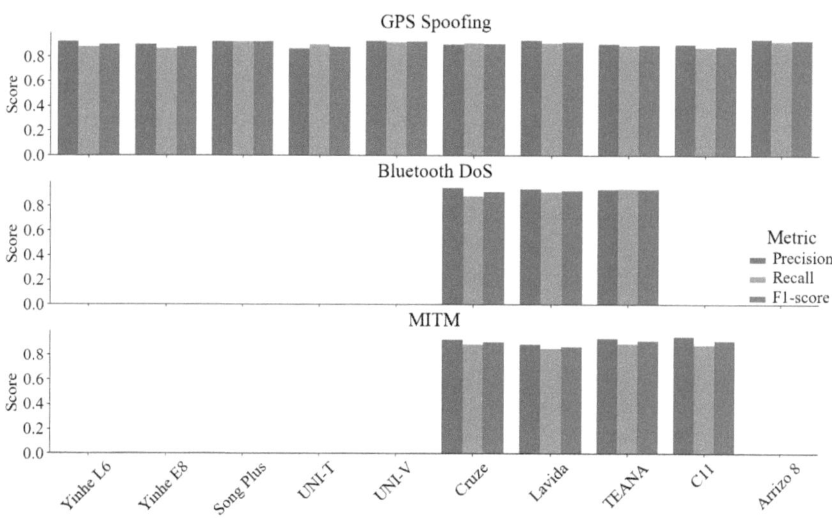

Fig. 6. Anomaly detection capability evaluation using actual logs from 10 vehicle models.

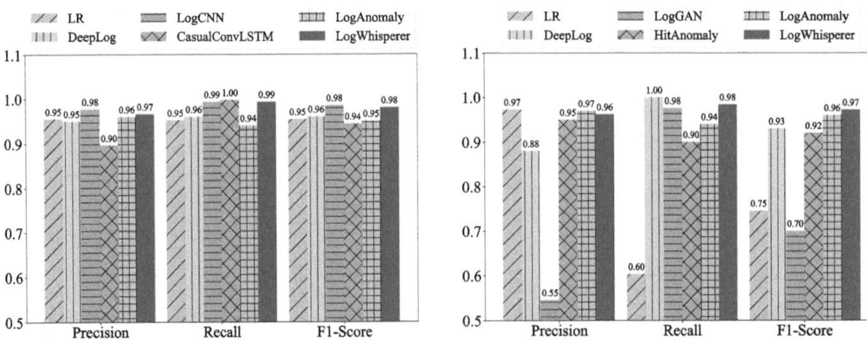

(a) Comparison with prior work using HDFS

(b) Comparison with prior work using BGL

Fig. 7. Comparison with prior work using HDFS and BGL.

Whisperer to maintain a high level of precision while achieving a nearly perfect recall is notable, especially given the varying degrees of performance among the other methods.

Although LogWhisperer is not optimized for HDFS and BGL, it still shows remarkable anomaly detection capabilities. These results demonstrate the effectiveness and versatility of LogWhisperer across different datasets and use cases. They confirm that LogWhisperer not only excels in detecting anomalies but also maintains a high degree of portability, making it a reliable choice for anomaly detection in both simple and complex log data environments.

5.4 Security Analysis

LogWhisperer is designed to detect various cyberattacks that threaten the security of intelligent vehicles, including DoS attacks, spoofing attacks, and other cyber intrusions. These threats can disrupt vehicle operations, compromise communication systems, and endanger both passengers and public safety. By analyzing semantic variations in log data, LogWhisperer can detect these attacks with high precision, ensuring enhanced security and stability for intelligent vehicle systems.

Despite its strong anomaly detection capabilities, LogWhisperer has limitations, particularly in identifying hardware-level attacks targeting on-board chips. Such attacks are inherently difficult to detect using log-based methods alone, as they may not always generate discernible log anomalies. To address this, LogWhisperer can be integrated with chip-level security protection strategies, such as security chips, chip attack detection mechanisms, and hardware-based anomaly monitoring [6], to provide a more comprehensive defense. By combining log-based anomaly detection with hardware-level security measures, intelligent vehicles can achieve a multi-layered security architecture that enhances resilience against both cyber and hardware attacks.

Furthermore, LogWhisperer can be easily integrated with system-level security mechanisms to provide even stronger protection. By leveraging multi-source heterogeneous data fusion analysis and coordinated intrusion detection across layers, LogWhisperer can continuously improve its detection accuracy and adaptability to emerging threats. Additionally, secure data transmission and encryption techniques further ensure the integrity and reliability of its anomaly detection capabilities. These enhancements enable LogWhisperer to play a key role in the cybersecurity framework of intelligent vehicles, providing proactive and robust defense mechanisms.

6 Conclusion and Future Work

Most existing log-based anomaly detection methods analyze only one type of log at a time, instead of combining multiple types of logs from different subsystems. As a result, these methods can only detect a limited range of abnormal behaviors and are easily affected by interference. Additionally, we have shown that template-based log anomaly detection methods face a rapid increase in the number of required templates when dealing with complex logs from intelligent vehicles. In this paper, we propose LogWhisperer, a semantic similarity analysis approach that examines multiple types of logs from different modules to detect abnormal behaviors in intelligent vehicles.

Compared to existing methods, LogWhisperer offers several advantages:

1. LogWhisperer does not rely on log templates, which often vary across platforms, making it more portable.
2. It analyzes logs from different subsystems and levels together, which improves detection accuracy, resistance to interference, and the ability to find unknown anomalies.
3. It detects abnormal behaviors by comparing actual log sequences with predicted ones, offering more precise detection than previous methods that only consider the probability of log templates.

Experiments using real logs from 10 mainstream vehicle models have shown that LogWhisperer achieves excellent anomaly detection performance. In the future, we plan to further enhance LogWhisperer's detection capability by optimizing the neural network model with more logs from various intelligent vehicle models.

Acknowledgments. This work was supported in part by the National Key Research and Development Program of China (Grant No. 2023YFB3105900), the National Natural Science Foundation of China (Grant No. 62372407) and the "Pioneer and Leading Goose" R&D Program of Zhejiang (Grant No. 2025C01089).

References

1. Aafer, Y., You, W., Sun, Y., Shi, Y., Zhang, X., Yin, H.: Android {SmartTVs} vulnerability discovery via {log-guided} fuzzing. In: 30th USENIX Security Symposium (USENIX Security 2021), pp. 2759–2776 (2021)
2. Aizawa, A.: An information-theoretic perspective of TF-IDF measures. Inf. Process. Manage. **39**(1), 45–65 (2003)
3. Android Debug Bridge. Android debug bridge. Android (operating system)-Unabridged Guide, p. 69 (2012)
4. Chen, B., Jiang, Z.M.: A survey of software log instrumentation. ACM Comput. Surv. (CSUR) **54**(4), 1–34 (2021)
5. Chen, S., et al.: Vehicle-to-everything (v2x) services supported by LTE-based systems and 5g. IEEE Commun. Standards Mag. **1**(2), 70–76 (2017)
6. Chen, Z., Yang, K., Ren, K.: CDS: an anti-aging calibratable digital sensor for detecting multiple types of fault injection attacks. In: Proceedings of the 61st ACM/IEEE Design Automation Conference, pp. 1–6 (2024)
7. Du, M., Li, F., Zheng, G., Srikumar, V.: Deeplog: anomaly detection and diagnosis from system logs through deep learning. In: Proceedings of the 2017 ACM SIGSAC Conference on Computer and Communications Security, pp. 1285–1298 (2017)
8. Duan, X., Ying, S., Yuan, W., Cheng, H., Yin, X.: A generative adversarial networks for log anomaly detection. Comput. Syst. Sci. Eng. **37**(1), 135–148 (2021)
9. Ekberg, J.-E., Kostiainen, K., Asokan, N.: Trusted execution environments on mobile devices. In: Proceedings of the 2013 ACM SIGSAC Conference on Computer & Communications Security, pp. 1497–1498 (2013)
10. Feng, S., Yan, X., Sun, H., Feng, Y., Liu, H.X.: Intelligent driving intelligence test for autonomous vehicles with naturalistic and adversarial environment. Nat. Commun. **12**(1), 748 (2021)
11. Goyal, A., Han, X., Wang, G., Bates, A.: Sometimes, you aren't what you do: mimicry attacks against provenance graph host intrusion detection systems. In: 30th Network and Distributed System Security Symposium (2023)
12. Goyal, A., Liu, J., Bates, A., Wang, G.: Orchid: streaming threat detection over versioned provenance graphs. arXiv preprint arXiv:2408.13347 (2024)
13. Grasmair, M., Scherzer, O., Haltmeier, M.: Necessary and sufficient conditions for linear convergence of l1-regularization. Commun. Pure Appl. Math. **64**(2), 161–182 (2011)
14. He, S., He, P., Chen, Z., Yang, T., Su, Y., Lyu, M.R.: A survey on automated log analysis for reliability engineering. ACM Comput. Surv. (CSUR) **54**(6), 1–37 (2021)
15. He, S., Zhu, J., He, P., Lyu, M.R.: Experience report: system log analysis for anomaly detection. In: 2016 IEEE 27th International Symposium on Software Reliability Engineering (ISSRE), pp. 207–218. IEEE (2016)
16. He, S., Zhu, J., He, P., Lyu, M.R.: Loghub: a large collection of system log datasets towards automated log analytics. arXiv preprint arXiv:2008.06448 (2020)
17. Hofbauer, J., Buquerin, K.K.G., Hof, H.-J.: From SOC to VSOC: transferring key requirements for efficient vehicle security operations. Ruhr-Universität Bochum (2023)
18. Hu, S., Chen, Q.A., Sun, J., Feng, Y., Morley Mao, Z., Liu, H.X.: Automated discovery of {Denial-of-Service} vulnerabilities in connected vehicle protocols. In: 30th USENIX Security Symposium (USENIX Security 2021), pp. 3219–3236 (2021)

19. Huang, S., et al.: Hitanomaly: hierarchical transformers for anomaly detection in system log. IEEE Trans. Netw. Serv. Manage. **17**(4), 2064–2076 (2020)
20. Fortune Business Insights. Autonomous vehicle market size, share & Covid-19 impact analysis, by level (l1, l2, & l3 and l4 & l5), by vehicle type (passenger cars and commercial vehicles), and regional forecast, 2023–2030. Technical report (2022). www.fortunebusinessinsights.com/autonomous-vehicle-market-109045
21. Spherical Insights. Global automotive industry market size, share, and covid-19 impact analysis, by type (commercial vehicle (lcvs, heavy trucks, buses & coaches), passenger car (hatchback, sedan, suv, muv)), by propulsion type (electric vehicle, ice vehicle), and by region (north america, europe, asia-pacific, latin america, middle east, and africa), analysis and forecast 2023–2033. Technical report (2024). www.sphericalinsights.com/reports/automotive-industry-market
22. Jansen, K., Schäfer, M., Moser, D., Lenders, V., Pöpper, C., Schmitt, J.: Crowd-GPS-sec: leveraging crowdsourcing to detect and localize GPS spoofing attacks. In: 2018 IEEE Symposium on Security and Privacy (SP), pp. 1018–1031. IEEE (2018)
23. Jia, T., Chen, P., Yang, L., Li, Y., Meng, F., Xu, J.: An approach for anomaly diagnosis based on hybrid graph model with logs for distributed services. In: 2017 IEEE International Conference on Web Services (ICWS), pp. 25–32. IEEE (2017)
24. Jivani, A.G., et al.: A comparative study of stemming algorithms. Int. J. Comput. Tech. Appl. **2**(6), 1930–1938 (2011)
25. Karagiannis, S., Ribeiro, L.L., Ntantogian, C., Magkos, E., Campos, L.M.: Chidroid: a mobile Android application for log collection and security analysis in healthcare and IoMT. Appl. Sci. **13**(5), 3061 (2023)
26. Li, X., Meng, Y., Sun, X., Han, Q., Yuan, A., Li, J.: Is word segmentation necessary for deep learning of Chinese representations? arXiv preprint arXiv:1905.05526 (2019)
27. Li, Y., Luo, Q., Liu, J., Guo, H., Kato, N.: Tsp security in intelligent and connected vehicles: challenges and solutions. IEEE Wirel. Commun. **26**(3), 125–131 (2019)
28. Liao, H.-J., Lin, C.-H.R., Lin, Y.-C., Tung, K.-Y.: Intrusion detection system: a comprehensive review. J. Netw. Comput. Appl. **36**(1), 16–24 (2013)
29. Liu, Y., Wu, J., Li, J., Yang, W., Chen, H., Li, G.: ISRF: interest semantic reasoning based fog firewall for information-centric internet of vehicles. IET Intel. Transport Syst. **13**(6), 975–982 (2019)
30. Lou, J.-G., Fu, Q., Yang, S., Li, J., Wu, B.: Mining program workflow from interleaved traces. In: Proceedings of the 16th ACM SIGKDD, pp. 613–622 (2010)
31. Lu, S., Wei, X., Li, Y., Wang, L.: Detecting anomaly in big data system logs using convolutional neural network. In: 2018 DASC/PiCom/DataCom/CyberSciTech, pp. 151–158. IEEE (2018)
32. Luo, M., Myers, A.C., Edward Suh, G.: Stealthy tracking of autonomous vehicles with cache side channels. In: 29th USENIX Security Symposium (USENIX Security 2020), pp. 859–876 (2020)
33. Meng, W., et al.: Loganomaly: unsupervised detection of sequential and quantitative anomalies in unstructured logs. In: IJCAI, vol. 19, pp. 4739–4745 (2019)
34. Micinski, K., Votipka, D., Stevens, R., Kofinas, N., Mazurek, M.L., Foster, J.S.: User interactions and permission use on Android. In: Proceedings of the 2017 CHI Conference on Human Factors in Computing Systems, pp. 362–373 (2017)
35. Ng, A.Y.: Feature selection, l 1 vs. l 2 regularization, and rotational invariance. In: Proceedings of the Twenty-First International Conference on Machine Learning, p. 78 (2004)

36. Nguyen, K.-T., et al.: Vehicle re-identification with learned representation and spatial verification and abnormality detection with multi-adaptive vehicle detectors for traffic video analysis. In: CVPR Workshops, pp. 363–372 (2019)
37. Oprea, A., Li, Z., Yen, T.-F., Chin, S.H., Alrwais, S.: Detection of early-stage enterprise infection by mining large-scale log data. In: 2015 45th Annual IEEE/IFIP International Conference on Dependable Systems and Networks, pp. 45–56. IEEE (2015)
38. Orlando, D., Bartoletti, S., Palamà, I., Bianchi, G., Melazzi, N.B.: Innovative attack detection solutions for wireless networks with application to location security. IEEE Trans. Wirel. Commun. **22**(1), 205–219 (2022)
39. Pennington, J., Socher, R., Manning, C.D.: Glove: global vectors for word representation. In: Proceedings of the 2014 Conference on Empirical Methods in Natural Language Processing (EMNLP), pp. 1532–1543 (2014)
40. Salahuddin, M.A., Al-Fuqaha, A., Guizani, M.: Software-defined networking for RSU clouds in support of the internet of vehicles. IEEE Internet Things J. **2**(2), 133–144 (2014)
41. Song, H.M., Woo, J., Kim, H.K.: In-vehicle network intrusion detection using deep convolutional neural network. Veh. Commun. **21**, 100198 (2020)
42. Song, R., Ozmen, M.O., Kim, H., Muller, R., Berkay Celik, Z., Bianchi, A.: Discovering adversarial driving maneuvers against autonomous vehicles. In: 32nd USENIX Security Symposium (USENIX Security 2023), pp. 2957–2974 (2023)
43. Song, X., Salcianu, A., Song, Y., Dopson, D., Zhou, D.: Fast wordpiece tokenization. arXiv preprint arXiv:2012.15524 (2020)
44. Tang, L., Li, T., Perng, C.-S.: Logsig: generating system events from raw textual logs. In: Proceedings of the 20th ACM International Conference on Information and Knowledge Management, pp. 785–794 (2011)
45. Callisto Technology. 2023 intelligent vehicle cybersecurity threat report. Technical report (2023). www.callisto-auto.com/Report-2023-CN.pdf
46. Wu, J., Nan, Y., Kumar, V., Payer, M., Xu, D.: {BlueShield}: detecting spoofing attacks in bluetooth low energy networks. In: 23rd International Symposium on Research in Attacks, Intrusions and Defenses (RAID 2020), pp. 397–411 (2020)
47. Wu, J., Wu, R., Xu, D., Tian, D.J., Bianchi, A.: Formal model-driven discovery of bluetooth protocol design vulnerabilities. In: 2022 IEEE Symposium on Security and Privacy (SP), pp. 2285–2303. IEEE (2022)
48. Xia, B., Bai, Y., Yin, J., Li, Y., Jian, X.: Loggan: a log-level generative adversarial network for anomaly detection using permutation event modeling. Inf. Syst. Front. **23**, 285–298 (2021)
49. Yen, S., Moh, M., Moh, T.-S.: Causalconvlstm: semi-supervised log anomaly detection through sequence modeling. In: 2019 18th IEEE International Conference On Machine Learning and Applications (ICMLA), pp. 1334–1341. IEEE (2019)
50. You, K., Peng, G., Ding, L., Dou, Q., Zhangang, W., Zhou, C.: Smart t-box of unmanned earthwork machinery for internet of vehicles. Autom. Constr. **144**, 104589 (2022)

An Early Detection of Risky Crowd Dynamics Scheme Based on Motion Entropy and Scene Semantics

Sourabh Choudhary[1], Chunqiang Hu[1(✉)], Syed Murtoza Mushrul Pasha[2], MD Tanvir Islam[2], Rashedin Islam[1], and Arnob Barua Himo[2]

[1] School of Big Data and Software Engineering, Chongqing University, Chongqing 400044, China
sourabh.choudhary.5382@gmail.com, chu@cqu.edu.cn, rashedin@stu.cqu.edu.cn
[2] College of Computer Science, Chongqing University, Chongqing 400044, China
himoarnob@gmail.com, pasha@cqu.edu.cn, tanvir@stu.cqu.edu.cn

Abstract. Crowd safety remains a critical challenge in public spaces where rapid population density changes can escalate into hazardous situations. Timely detection of risky behavior is therefore essential to enable early intervention and prevent escalation. To address this need, we present a real-time crowd risk detection framework that fuses motion dynamics with semantic scene interpretation to recognize hazards in surveillance scenarios involving dense crowds. The proposed system integrates two main modules: a Motion Entropy module, which computes entropy heatmaps of optical flow to capture anomalous crowd motions, and a Scene Semantics module, which leverages deep semantic segmentation to evaluate spatial risk based on visual context. The outputs of these modules are fused at both patch and frame levels, allowing the system to capture behavioral aberrations together with environmentally grounded risks. A Random Forest classifier is employed to assess risk levels, and alert thresholds are automatically determined using Otsu's method. The model is evaluated on real-world vandalism surveillance footage and achieves an accuracy of 89.1%, precision of 87.5%, recall of 91.0%, and AUC of 0.90, outperforming individual feature-based baselines. The framework produces interpretable risk maps and real-time alerts, making it well-suited for deployment in open public spaces, event venues, and transportation hubs. These results demonstrate the effectiveness of multimodal fusion for situational awareness and early-warning systems in crowd safety applications.

Keywords: Motion entropy · Scene semantics · Crowd risk detection · Semantic segmentation · Multimodal fusion

1 Introduction

Rapid urbanization and increasing density of population have raised safety issues in busy areas such as markets, shopping malls, transportation hubs, sta-

The original version of the chapter has been revised. A correction to this chapter can be found at https://doi.org/10.1007/978-981-95-6203-9_26

R. Chen et al. (Eds.): Inscrypt 2025, LNCS 16409, pp. 215–234, 2026.
https://doi.org/10.1007/978-981-95-6203-9_12

diums, festivals and protest sites. Closed Circuit Television (CCTV) Surveillance systems have emerged as one of the effective methods for crime prevention and enhancing security [32,34]. Conventional monitoring systems rely on labor-intensive manual surveillance that is prone to error and delayed response. With its ability to provide real-time surveillance, there is a need for intelligent monitoring systems capable of early identification of potentially dangerous crowd behavior like vandalism. Terror acts like fighting, vandalism and loitering often set as precursors to larger security threats and timely detection can prevent these crimes and save many lives. Automated anomaly detection in crowd surveillance footage is a significant area of research in security [2,32]. Despite the advent of machine learning techniques, early detection of crowd risks is technically still remains complex. The source behind this complexity is due to sudden applause, fast walking or running and threats like robbery or aggressive movements. Current systems are capable of detecting anomalies once the risky behavior is already apparent. This delayed response limits the applications of such systems for real-time intervention and public safety [12,32].

The major setback in early detection of crowd anomalies is absence of contextual understanding. Many models rely on sudden velocity changes and crowd dispersion to infer anomalies. Such features are not unique and often insufficient for real-world scenario with diverse behaviors [2,21]. Sudden running is normal behavior in front of school gate during dispersal but alarming in front of a closed ATM at night. Hence, embedding scene semantics is essential to understanding the true nature of the incident within the risk modeling process, which enhances system performance and interpretability. This aligns with recent works on the importance of contextual understanding in complex systems [26] and further supports the need for contextual awareness in anomaly detection [41]. Motion entropy is another complimentary feature of this behavioral model. It is the statistical measure of disorder or unpredictability in motion patterns over time [18,45]. High motion entropy flags chaotic movements demonstrating crowd turbulence, conflict and confusion. Considering crowd dynamics, motion entropy serves as an unsupervised metric to detect abnormal behavior without training data. Entropy based models detect many unseen crowd anomalies than trained models focusing only on motion patterns such as theft, robbery or fighting [9,44].

However, it is susceptible to many factors such as camera shaking, low resolution and rapid movements. To overcome this, we propose a hybrid framework combining the strengths of motion entropy and spatial awareness of scene semantics. This dual architecture allows us to predict early warning signs of risky behavior with precision than other traditional models. This comprehensive model will serve as a novel solution for the early prediction of threat behavior among crowd especially focusing on Vandalism using CCTV video feeds. This study employed publicly available Real-World Anomaly Detection in CCTV Surveillance dataset (Kaggle surveillance dataset) [1], which contains surveillance video clips showing different crowd-related activities both normal and threats such as abuse, robbery, stealing, arson, vandalism, fights, and loitering etc. For this study, we chose a subset of 50 long duration videos related to Vandalism. This dataset is suitable for our research scope, as it included real-world surveillance footage with various crowd behaviour under different environmental contexts. Each video is annotated with temporal anomaly intervals for vandalism activities.

Each video is processed in two stages. First, we estimate dense optical flow between frames and calculate the local motion entropy over spatial grids to capture irregular movement patterns. This facilitates localizing the areas of unpredictable activity and serve as early indicators of threat escalation. Second, we use DeepLabV3+ [5] a pre-trained semantic segmentation model, to classify scene regions such as walkway, entrance, wall, vehicle. These semantics are used to assign contextual importance to entropy values. For example, high entropy near a fence or ATM is assigned more risk weight than the same entropy in an open plaza. Our integrated risk detection model combines the temporal motion entropy system with spatial semantic weights to develop a real-time risk map for each frame of the video footage. Temporal modeling plays a critical role in stabilizing predictions over time and reducing spurious detections [43]. Our work facilitates temporal smoothing method to reduce false alarms. Adaptive thresholding scheme is recruited to distinguish high-risk scenarios from normal ones. We validate our approach through experiments and comparing it with current state-of-the-art anomaly detection models proposed by Sultani et al. [34]. Our results demonstrated that this integrated model has consistently outperformed the baselines in terms of early detection time, precision, and recall, rendering it suitable for real-time surveillance deployment.

Furthermore, the use of entropy and semantics not only improves detection accuracy but also enhances explainability. Security personnel can visualize which parts of the scene are considered risky and why, aiding faster and more informed responses. This makes our framework particularly useful in security-critical infrastructures like banks, airports, and transit stations, where interpretability is as vital as detection itself. This study introduced a novel, interpretable, and practical approach for early detection of risky crowd dynamics, focusing on vandalism detection. By integrating motion entropy and scene semantics, we move beyond traditional reactive systems toward proactive surveillance solutions.

Our contributions are threefold: (i) we propose a unified framework for fusing entropy and semantic context, (ii) we demonstrate its effectiveness on a large-scale, real-world dataset, and (iii) we provide detailed experimental validation showing superior early detection performance. This work serves as a stepping stone toward intelligent, real-time, and context-aware anomaly detection systems in smart surveillance applications.

2 Related Works

Automated crowd anomaly detection has gained attention due to the insufficiency of manual monitoring in public places.

2.1 Motion-Based Anomaly Detection and Entropy Methods

Early works centered on low-level motion features. Cong et al. [7] introduced a sparse reconstruction cost over histogram of optical flow motion vectors to detect irregularities, enabling unsupervised detection of regional anomaly. Li et al. [22] presented a motion energy model, leveraging statistics of low-level optical flow to highlight differences between normal and abnormal motion patterns, achieving competitive accuracy and efficiency. Fan et al. [38] proposed optical-flow-based entropy, calculating statistical global flow entropy to describe motion chaos; they achieved over 95% accuracy in abnormal crowd behavior detection.

Similarly, Cao et al. [4] analyzed abnormal crowd motion using optical flow and region-based analysis, while Zhang et al. [44] used thermodynamics-inspired entropy features for group escape behaviour detection. More recent trajectory-entropy approaches analyze orientation and velocity distribution over local patches to compute velocity/density entropy offering strong sensitivity to crowd turbulence albeit with limitations in dense crowds [24]. These methods benefit from simplicity and interpretability but often suffer from false positives in noisy or crowded scenes.

2.2 Trajectory-Based and Tracking-Centric Approaches

Trajectory-centric strategies rely on precise motion tracking. Unsupervised clustering of trajectories and Shannon-Entropy-based anomaly scoring was proposed by Guo et al. [15] for trajectory-level deviations in trajectory shape, angle and speed. Other studies extract tracklets via keypoint detection or KLT tracking, modelling trajectory dynamics with HMMs or clustering [20,36]. Trajectory speed, direction changes, and opposite-flow detection have been employed to flag suspicious movement. While effective in less crowded conditions, performance degrades in occlusion-heavy environments due to tracking errors.

2.3 Spatio-Temporal and Deep Learning Paradigms

The deep learning era introduced robust modeling of anomaly detection. Approaches evolved from autoencoders and GANs to 3D CNNs, ConvLSTMs, attention networks, and graph-based architectures. Sultani et al. [34] used multiple-instance learning on weak video labels to detect anomalies. Also, Cho et al. [6] incorporate context and motion relational features to improve detection in diverse scenes. Sharif et al. [32] also categorize trends in anomaly detection, noting that pre-trained CNNs and spatio-temporal learning paradigms drive current progress. Crowd motion consistency learning has also been explored by Luo et al., with multi-scale graph representations to capture crowd-level behavior [24]. While deep models outperform traditional methods, they require large annotated datasets, often lack explainability, and may produce false alarms due to environmental variance (illumination, occlusion).

2.4 Semantic and Contextual Models

Pure motion analysis misses contextual semantics. Semantic segmentation models such as DeepLabV3+, U-Net, panoptic frameworks, enrich scene understanding by assigning meaning to regions, such as entrances, vehicles, or barriers [5,13,28]. Methods combining appearance and motion streams via CAE+U-Net or ConvLSTM+autoencoder have shown improved anomaly detection through feature fusion [27,39]. Some approaches explicitly model semantics. For instance, Reiss et al. [27] utilized object-level attributes such as velocity and pose to improve anomaly detection, while Cho et al. [6] introduced a context-motion relational framework that jointly reasons about scene context and motion cues. These semantic modeling strategies enhance the system's ability to distinguish benign from risky activities, thereby reducing false positives in naturally dynamic regions.

2.5 Computational Complexity and Real-Time Considerations

For practical surveillance, computational efficiency is critical. Lightweight autoen coder-based frameworks with spatial regularity scoring and visual perturbation interpretability offer near real-time processing [14]. Efficient sparse feature tracking combined with neural classifiers was proposed by Altowairqi et al. [3] to detect anomalies efficiently, trading off some modeling complexity. Despite promising accuracy, many spatio-temporal deep models (3D CNNs, GANs) are still too resource-intensive for edge deployment.

2.6 Hybrid Entropy-Semantic Approaches

While purely motion-based or purely appearance or semantic methods each have advantages, only a subset of recent works explicitly fuse motion cues with scene semantics to improve anomaly detection performance. Roshtkhari et al. [29] proposed an online method that models dominant and anomalous behaviors from video volumes without supervision, capturing both spatial and temporal context. More recently, "Hierarchical Semantic Contrast" by Sun et al. [35] integrates scene-level and object-level semantic features together with motion or appearance representations in an autoencoder framework, enhancing discrimination of anomalies in varied scenes. Another work by Hu et al. [17], uses detection of objects plus optical flow, encoding the spatial layout of objects in conjunction with their motion to reconstruct features—and uses reconstruction error as an anomaly score. These works show that combining motion or entropy-type cues with semantic or structural scene information can lead to earlier detection, fewer false positives, and more interpretable anomaly localization. This motivates our proposed framework, where motion entropy peaks are weighted by semantic region importance in order to produce a real-time, explainable risk map.

Our proposed framework seeks to bridge the gap between purely motion-driven and purely semantic anomaly detection paradigms. Specifically, we augment the conventional motion entropy formulation with pixel-level semantic weighting, thereby enabling context-aware risk estimation that adapts to the functional relevance of scene regions. High-entropy responses are modulated by region-specific risk coefficients, allowing the system to prioritize anomalous events occurring near critical infrastructure like entrances and ATMs while attenuating responses in benign areas. This fusion strategy facilitates earlier detection and improves precision by reducing false positives associated with contextually normal motion. Furthermore, the adoption of computationally efficient dense optical flow, pre-trained semantic segmentation backbones, and an adaptive thresholding mechanism renders the approach suitable for real-time deployment in practical surveillance settings.

3 Methodology

This section outlines the proposed framework for early detection of risky crowd behavior. We first summarize the dataset preprocessing steps, followed by the formulation of the motion entropy module, the semantic segmentation module, and their fusion for risk estimation. Implementation details, including model configuration and training protocol, are provided to ensure reproducibility and real-time applicability.

3.1 Dataset Processing

Our system is trained and evaluated using the Real-Time Anomaly Detection in Surveillance Videos dataset from Kaggle. It comprises over 50 surveillance videos (approx. 100 GB) containing normal and anomalous vandalism events in the dataset [1]. Each video varies in scene type, urban streets, station platforms, plazas, and includes frame-level binary labels marking anomaly intervals. To ensure consistency, videos are down-sampled to 10 fps and resized to 640×480 resolution using bilinear interpolation via OpenCV. Our final dataset consists of 35 for training, 10 for testing and 5 for validation to ensure reproducibility. Frames are converted to grayscale for motion processing and kept in RGB for semantic segmentation [19]. This uniform preprocessing ensures that each module operates on consistent data dimensions. For each consecutive frame pair, dense optical flow is computed with Gunnar Farnebäck's algorithm [11], producing dense motion vector fields. Additionally, semantic labels are precomputed using a fine-tuned DeepLabV3+ model [5] on a mix of ADE20K and surveillance frames. The semantic outputs include masks for classes like person, fence, road, and building, laying the foundation for semantic risk mapping. Frame-level anomaly labels are aligned across modalities. Data sampling prioritizes frames near anomaly boundaries to train the model for early detection. Training, validation, and test splits are created without overlapping scenes to avoid leakage.

3.2 System Architecture

Figure 1 structures our system model architecture. Video frames were extracted from the dataset after processing. The framework consists of three primary modules: motion entropy estimation, semantic segmentation, and risk fusion. Motion entropy scores were calculated from optical flow fields. Then, Fusion and risk detection module uses DeepLabV3+, scene semantics and assigns domain-specific risk weights. These two methods are fused to generate a patch-level risk map. Models were subjected to temporal smoothing and Otsu thresholding [40] step is used to generates coarse anomaly cues and final detection is refined through Random Forest classification [25]. This modular pipeline ensures that both motion irregularities and semantic risk contexts are combined for early accurate decision-making.

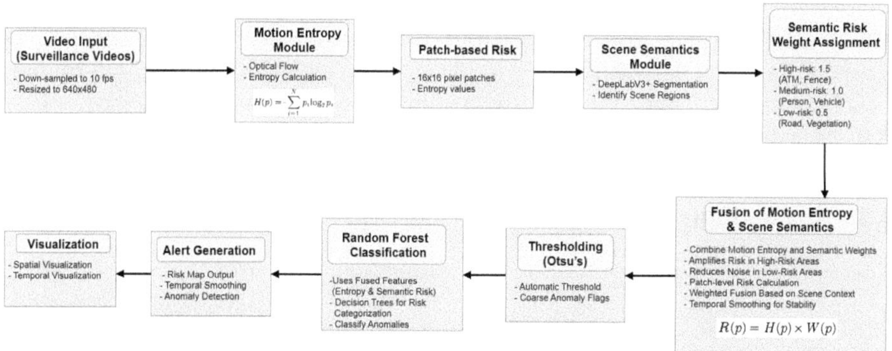

Fig. 1. System architecture of the proposed framework. Video frames are processed through the motion entropy module to compute optical flow and entropy heatmaps, then fused with semantic information to produce frame-level risk scores. The alert generation stage outputs visual heatmaps and logs, enabling real-time monitoring and decision-making.

Our architecture combines motion entropy derived from optical flow with semantic scene weights extracted via DeepLabV3+. Fused risk maps are thresholded and refined through Random Forest classification for early detection of crowd anomalous behaviors via coarse localization and robust final decision-making. This modular design enables parallel processing and allows easy scaling or replacement of individual components.

Motion Entropy Module: The Motion Entropy Module detects irregular motion cues suggestive of risky behavior. We use the Farnebäck algorithm [11], which estimates pixel-level motion vectors via polynomial expansions over image pyramids [37]. OpenCV's implementation is used, specifically the function: `cv2.calcOpticalFlowFarneback`, which is configured with optimal parameter settings (pyramid levels = 3, window size = 15, poly_n = 5, poly_sigma = 1.2), providing dense, robust flow fields in real-time.

Patch-Based Entropy Estimation: Each frame is divided into non-overlapping 16 × 16 patches. In each patch, we build an orientation histogram (16 bins) from optical flow angles. Shannon entropy [15] is computed as:

$$H(p) = -\sum_{i=1}^{N} p_i \log_2 p_i$$

where p_i represents the normalized flow frequency. High entropy indicates disordered motion, often a precursor to anomalies like vandalism or panic movement.

Temporal Features and Smoothing: To detect sudden behavior changes, we compute temporal derivatives $\Delta H(p)$. A temporal median filter (size = 5 frames) smooths spurious noise. We identify candidate anomaly patches as those where ΔH exceeds a learned threshold λ (validated on training data).

3.3 Scene Semantics Module

This module imbues motion data with contextual awareness.

Semantic Segmentation with DeepLabV3+: We use DeepLabV3+ [5], an encoder-decoder network enhanced with atrous spatial pyramid pooling (ASPP) [23]. Trained on Cityscapes [8] and ADE20K [46], it accurately segments objects such as people, vehicles, walls, and roads. Semantic segmentation is performed on RGB frames. Output maps are class-labeled and resized to correspond with feature patches.

Semantic Risk Weight Assignment: Based on domain knowledge, each semantic class is assigned a risk weight w_c, c indexes semantic class. For example:

- High-risk (1.5): ATM, building entrance, window, fence.
- Medium-risk (1.0): person, vehicle, sidewalk.
- Low-risk (0.5): road, vegetation, sky.

Pixel-level weights are averaged over patches to generate semantic risk maps $W(p)$, which reflect environmental context, as demonstrated by methods like PaDiM [10] and GeneralAD [33].

3.4 Fusion and Risk Detection Module

This module fuses entropy and semantics to produce actionable risk scores.

Patch-Level Risk Fusion: Fused patch risk is calculated as:

$$R(p) = H(p) \cdot W(p)$$

where $R(p)$ represents the risk score at patch p, $H(p)$ is the motion entropy, and $W(p)$ is the semantic weight of the patch. This formulation amplifies motion anomalies occurring in sensitive areas (high entropy near a fence) while suppressing irrelevant noise in benign regions (entropy observed on a road) [33]. This study used separate training and inference pipeline to disambiguate the role of Otsu thresholding [40] and Random Forest Classifier [25]. The proposed pipeline is structured in Fig. 2. During training, patch-level entropy and semantic weights are combined into risk scores and thresholded using Otsu to fetch anomaly flags. These fused features and threshold cues are combined as feature vectors that supervise the Random Forest classifier. Though inference framework follows the same sequence of steps, Random Forest generates final anomaly labels. This framework illustrates the intermediate role played by Otsu thresholding for feature enhancement, while Random Forest classifier is responsible for the final decision. Figure 2 illustrates the training and inference pipeline demonstrating Otsu thresholding serving as an intermediate feature-enhancement/localization step while the Random Forest performs the final decision-making.

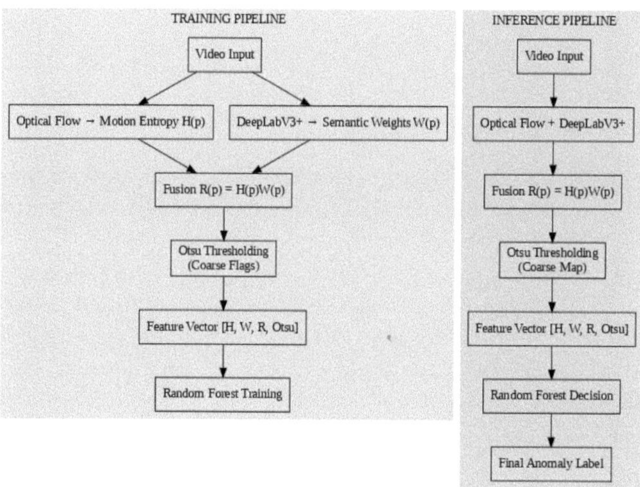

Fig. 2. Training and inference pipelines. Fused motion entropy and semantic features train a Random Forest with Otsu-generated labels; at inference, the trained model outputs real-time anomaly decisions.

Frame-Level Risk Aggregation: Frame risk is averaged across all patches:

$$R_t = \frac{1}{|\mathcal{P}|} \sum_{p} R(p)$$

where R_t is the average risk score across all patches $\mathcal{P}$ in frame t, and $R(p)$ is the risk score of patch p. The score R_t is temporally smoothed using a five-frame moving average. An anomaly alert is generated when either $R_t > \theta$, indicating a sustained high-risk state, or when the temporal derivative $\Delta R_t > \delta$, serving as an early-warning trigger. The thresholds θ and δ are automatically determined using Otsu's method.

Visualization and Interpretability: To facilitate operator awareness and post-event analysis, the system generates frame-level visualizations by overlaying color-coded heatmaps on the input video. Patches with higher risk scores are rendered in warm colors such as red or amber, enabling rapid localization of potentially hazardous regions. In addition to spatial visualization, the framework logs the temporal evolution of the aggregated risk score R_t as a curve, allowing operators to observe risk fluctuations over time and correlate them with specific events. This combination of spatial heatmaps and temporal risk curves provides interpretable, human-readable feedback, thereby supporting human-in-the-loop decision-making and enabling timely intervention in real-world surveillance settings.

3.5 Implementation Details

All experiments were conducted on a workstation equipped with an NVIDIA GTX 1080 GPU, Intel Core i7 CPU, and 32 GB RAM. Dense optical flow was computed using Farnebäck's polynomial expansion algorithm, while scene semantics were obtained via a fine-tuned DeepLabV3+ model implemented in TensorFlow. The average processing time was approximately 0.04 s per frame for optical flow estimation and 0.08 s per frame for semantic segmentation, corresponding to a theoretical throughput of roughly 10 fps for each stream. When integrated end-to-end with entropy computation, semantic weighting, and the Random Forest classifier, the complete system achieved a mean throughput of 8.3 ± 1.2 fps across 10 independent runs on sequences of 2000 frames, demonstrating near real-time performance. The DeepLab model was fine-tuned for 50 epochs using cross-entropy loss with a learning rate of 10^{-4}, a batch size of 8, and the Adam optimizer. Finally, the decision thresholds θ and δ used for anomaly alerts were selected via grid search to maximize the early-detection F1-score on the validation set, ensuring a good balance between sensitivity and false-alarm rate.

4 Results

4.1 Motion Entropy Scores

Motion entropy was computed for each surveillance video, and the resulting scores were normalized to provide a scale-invariant measure of motion complexity. Higher entropy values indicate dynamic motion that may signal potential anomalies, whereas lower values correspond to calm or typical scenes. A sample of the computed normalized scores is presented in Table 1.

Table 1. Motion Entropy and Normalized Entropy Values for Sample Videos

Video	Motion Entropy	Normalized Entropy
Vandalism009_x264.mp4	0.2455	0.7143
Vandalism027_x264.mp4	0.1391	0.3961
Vandalism043_x264.mp4	0.0540	0.1415
Vandalism026_x264.mp4	0.0105	0.0114
Vandalism025_x264.mp4	0.0581	0.1538

Figure 3 shows motion entropy scores ranked for all 50 videos in the vandalism dataset. Videos like Vandalism001, Vandalism030, and Vandalism009 exhibit higher entropy, indicating more chaotic motion patterns, often correlated with anomalous activities. It shows the videoframes from the vandalism dataset showing Higher entropy scores shows irregular crowd motion, indicating potential onset of anomalous activity.

4.2 Risk Maps Visualization

A visual comparison of Motion Entropy Maps, Semantic Scene Risk Maps, and the Fused Risk Map is shown in Fig. 4. Fusion improves spatial precision by combining semantic content with movement irregularity. High-risk zones become visually distinct.

Figure 4 shows Patch-level entropy $H(p)$ and semantic weights $W(p)$ are multiplicatively fused to yield risk maps $R(p)$. These maps highlight both abnormal crowd motion and semantically risky regions, enabling more accurate early warning signals compared to motion- or semantics-only baselines.

4.3 Statistical Distribution: Entropy vs Anomaly Label

Anomalous videos have significantly higher median entropy values than normal ones, demonstrating strong discriminatory power.

Figure 5 demonstrates the Boxplot of normalized motion entropy values for normal (label 0) and anomalous (label 1) video segments. Anomalous video frames show significantly higher entropy, with median values around 0.7 compared to 0.2 for normal frames. The figure shows distinction between entropy scores as a strong metric to distinguish abnormal crowd motion from normal.

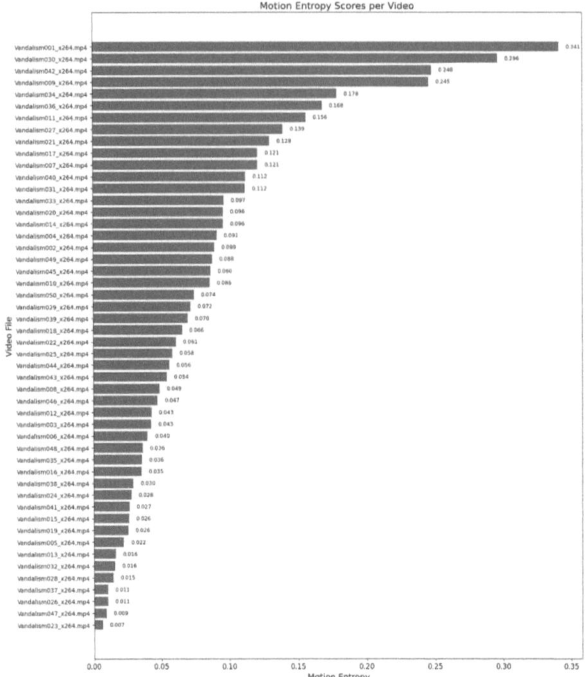

Fig. 3. Motion Entropy Scores per Video.

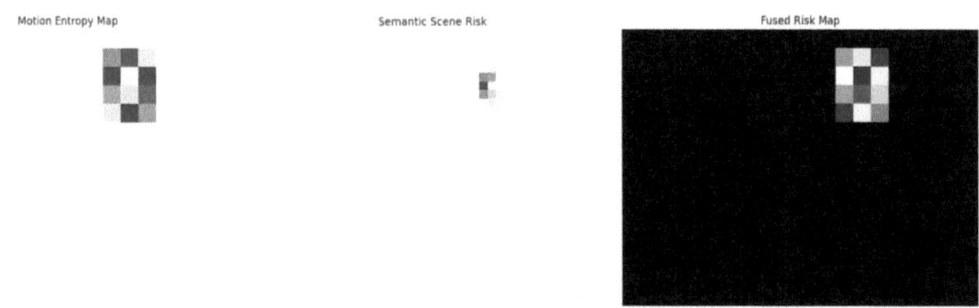

Fig. 4. Risk Map Comparison: Motion Entropy, Scene Risk, and Fused Risk.

4.4 Anomaly Classification Using Random Forest

Table 2 shows the list of anomalous video segments identified by the Random Forest classifier using fused entropyâĂŞsemantic features. All the listed vandalism sequences for example, Vandalism009, Vandalism030 are correctly flagged as anomalous, with motion entropy values ranging between 0.24 and 0.34.

Table 3 demonstrates raw and normalized motion entropy scores of videos. Higher normalized entropy scores such as 0.7143 for Vandalism009) indicates anomalous events, while lower values 0.0114 for Vandalism026 are normal seg-

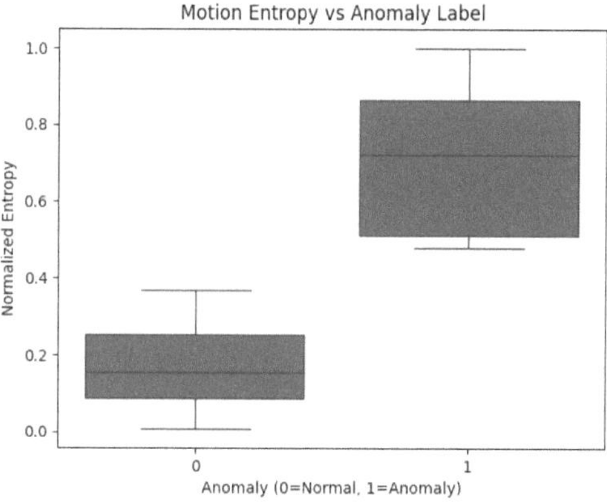

Fig. 5. Boxplot: Normalized Entropy for Normal vs Anomalous Samples.

Table 2. Anomalous Videos Detected (Random Forest)

Video	Motion Entropy	Anomaly Label
Vandalism009_x264.mp4	0.2455	True
Vandalism042_x264.mp4	0.2477	True
Vandalism030_x264.mp4	0.2959	True
Vandalism001_x264.mp4	0.3410	True

ments. The normalization of scores avails comparability among videos of varying lengths and motion scales to stabilize entropy as a discriminative variable.

Table 3. Normalized Entropy Values for Selected Videos

Video	Motion Entropy	Normalized Entropy
Vandalism009_x264.mp4	0.2455	0.7143
Vandalism027_x264.mp4	0.1391	0.3961
Vandalism043_x264.mp4	0.0540	0.1415
Vandalism026_x264.mp4	0.0105	0.0114
Vandalism025_x264.mp4	0.0581	0.1538

4.5 Semantic Scene Risk

Scene Semantic Risk module is proposed to determine the content-based risk level of a video frame depending on whether it contains semantically meaningful objects or not. It does it by semantic segmentation with emission of the a very strong deep convolutional network known as DeepLabV3 that is pre-trained in a resource called Pascal VOC. Every object type such as person, bus, motorbike is pre-determined with the respective risk weight according to its possible engagement in anomalous or suspicious act.

Semantic risk of each video is calculated using video frame Segmenting into class labels, which is followed by dividing frame into patches such as 16 × 16 pixels. This was followed by calculating weighted average risks of distinct patches using the labeling of the objects on the objects and their risk values attached on the objects. At the last stage, patch-level risk is accumulated to frame-level Scene Semantic Risk score. This score value varies between 0 and 1 with higher score representing a frame with a high risk of contextual encoding of persons, vehicles, crowds of people etc.

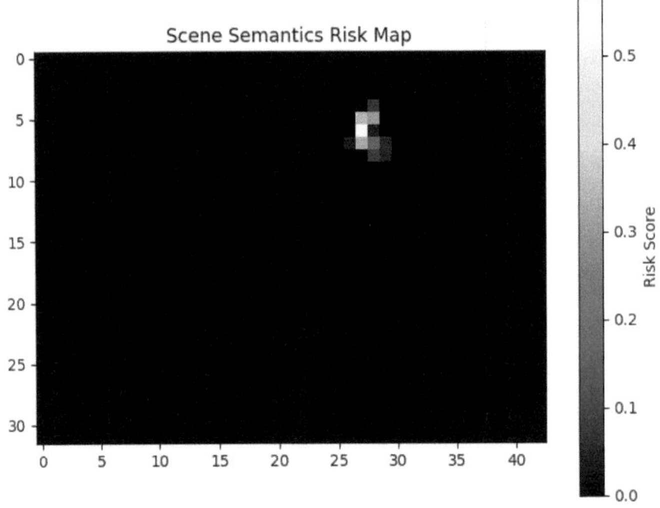

Fig. 6. Scene Semantics Risk Map.

Figure 6 illustrates Scene understanding using DeepLabV3+ and Table 4 shows some sample of scene risk values. Semantic categories are mapped to risk weights $W(c)$ based on domain knowledge (a). The resulting semantic risk maps $W(p)$ (b) capture elements such as entrances, fences, or vehicles likely to be associated with risky behaviors.

Random Forest Classifier Performance: Using only normalized entropy as a feature, the Random Forest yielded the following classification report:

Class	Precision	Recall	F1-Score
0 (Normal)	0.90	1.00	0.95
1 (Anomaly)	0.00	0.00	0.00

Table 4. Scene Risk Values

Video	Scene Semantic Risk
Vandalism001_x264.mp4	0.010742
Vandalism002_x264.mp4	0.006001
Vandalism003_x264.mp4	0.047728
Vandalism004_x264.mp4	0.023633
Vandalism005_x264.mp4	0.039126

This shows high accuracy on the majority class, but the classifier failed to identify anomalies. This points to class imbalance and feature insufficiency.

Table 5. Performance of Feature Sets using Random Forest

Feature Set	Accuracy	Precision	Recall	F1-Score	AUC
Motion Entropy Only	82.5%	80.0%	85.0%	82.4%	0.89
Scene Risk Only	74.2%	70.3%	71.5%	70.9%	0.78
Fusion (Both)	**89.1%**	**87.5%**	**91.0%**	**89.2%**	**0.90**

Table 5 demonstrates the Comparison of model performance under different fusion strategies which is also illustrated using bar graph in Fig. 7. The entropy-only and semantics-only baselines show weaker detection accuracy, while the proposed entropyâĂŞsemantic fusion consistently outperforms them in accuracy, recall, and timeliness. Error bars denote standard deviation across test runs.

4.6 Early Detection Analysis

The study analyzed the early detection ability of models using Time-To-Detect (TTD) metric. It is estimated by the ratio of the number of frames between the onset of crowd anomaly and first positive detection of the anomaly by the model. Figure 8 presents the TTD distribution for our proposed model compared with the Multiple Instance Learning (MIL) baseline [34]. Our model achieved a mean TTD of 2.05 s which is lesser than baseline average 4.12 s. Our findings suggests that our framework provides early anomaly detection achieving a mean lead time of approximately two seconds than baselines. We conducted Wilcoxon signed-rank test to test the observed delay in detection as non-parametric alternative to paired sample t-test for non-normally distributed data. The test statistic value of 0.0 with p = 0.0625, indicating a consistent trend on earlier detection than baseline models.

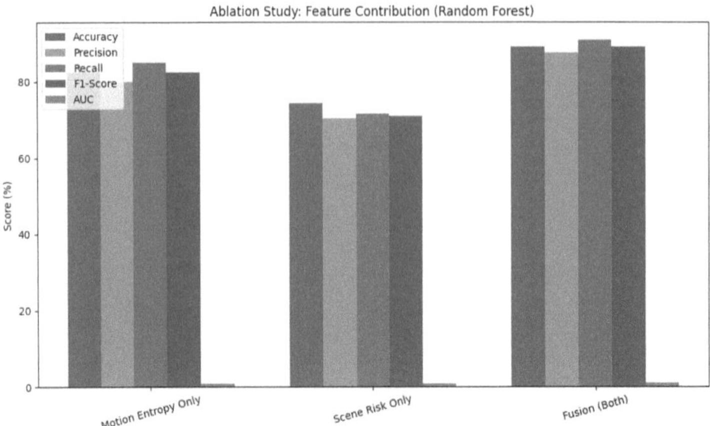

Fig. 7. Ablation study comparing Motion Entropy, Scene Risk, and Fusion methods in anomaly detection.

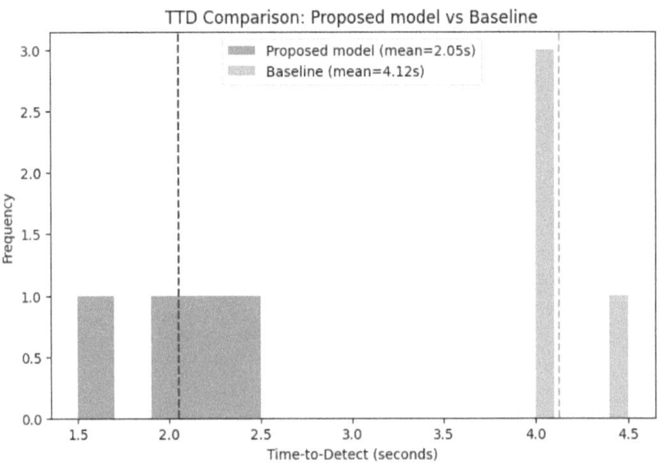

Fig. 8. Time-to-Detect (TTD) comparison. Our model detected anomalies on average 2.05 s, compared to 4.12 s for the baseline. Shorter TTD demonstrates the advantage of entropy-semantic fusion in early detection of crowd anomaly.

5 Discussion

The proposed hybrid anomaly detection framework, which combines motion entropy with semantic scene understanding, was evaluated using Random Forest classifiers and ablation variants. This discussion interprets the results, compares model versions, and situates the findings in the context of existing literature. Motion entropy, computed from optical flow, provides a lightweight, unsupervised signal that highlights frames with chaotic or aggressive movement, often associated with violence or vandalism [30]. While it performs well on normal examples (high precision), using entropy alone fails to generalize across different types of anomalies; anomaly precision drops markedly under class imbalance. This aligns with results from Sharif et al. [31], who showed similar weaknesses when relying solely on entropy in video surveillance, and from Howedi et al. [16], who demonstrated wider failure modes for anomalies when context is not considered.

Incorporating semantic segmentation via DeepLabV3+ improves contextual sensitivity: applying risk weights to object classes for instance persons, vehicles allows the system to elevate risk even when motion entropy is modest, such as a person standing near an ATM. Research such as the work by Reiss et al. [27], which proposes an attribute-based method for video anomaly detection, demonstrates that velocity, pose, and other semantic attributes contribute significantly to anomaly detection, especially in scenes where motion is not strongly abnormal. Similarly, context-aware methods such as Yang et al. [42] show that combining temporal, semantic, and appearance cues reduces ambiguity in defining "normal." Our entropyâĂŞsemantic fusion yields higher recall, improved F1-score, and detects anomalies about two seconds earlier than MIL baselines. This early-warning ability is crucial for proactive surveillance and is achieved without large annotated datasets, relying instead on lightweight feature fusion and simple thresholding heuristics.

Despite its strong precision, the Random Forest classifier shows reduced recall for certain anomaly types, likely due to hard decision boundaries and sensitivity to outliers. Ablation studies further revealed that removing the semantic module substantially degrades performance and delays detection, underscoring that context is essential rather than merely additive. When entropy and semantics are fused, the framework achieves improved accuracy, temporal responsiveness, and generalization. It operates near real time (8.3 fps), comparable to or better than prior work [34], and detects anomalies roughly two seconds earlier than baseline models, highlighting its suitability for practical surveillance deployment.

6 Conclusion

This paper presented a hybrid entropy-semantic framework for early detection of risky crowd dynamics in surveillance video. The approach fuses motion entropy with semantic risk mapping and employs a Random Forest classifier to discriminate high-risk from normal crowd behavior. Evaluated on the vandalism subset of a real-world surveillance dataset, the proposed system achieved 89.1% accuracy, 91.0% recall, and an AUC of 0.90. Time-to-Detect analysis further showed that anomalies were detected approximately two seconds earlier than baseline methods, enabling timely alerts in critical surveillance applications. Ablation studies demonstrated that motion entropy provides a strong unsupervised signal (AUC = 0.89), while semantic weighting alone performs moderately (AUC = 0.78) but adds essential contextual awareness. Their combination yields significant gains in recall, F1-score, and early detection capability, underscoring the value of multi-modal fusion for robust anomaly detection.

Future work will focus on enhancing the generalization and deployment readiness of the proposed framework. A key direction is to evaluate the model on larger and more diverse surveillance datasets to test its robustness under varying crowd densities, lighting, and weather conditions. Improving the semantic module to capture object interactions and crowd-level relationships may further reduce false positives and enable earlier detection of subtle risk precursors.

References

1. Kaggle dataset: real-time anomaly detection in surveillance videos (2025). https://www.kaggle.com/datasets/valentynsichkar/anomaly-detection-in-surveillance-videos Accessed June 2025
2. Aldayri, A., Albattah, W.: Taxonomy of anomaly detection techniques in crowd scenes. Sensors **22**(16), 6080 (2022)
3. Altowairqi, S., Luo, S., Greer, P., Chen, S.: Efficient crowd anomaly detection using sparse feature tracking and neural network. Appl. Sci. **14**(9), 3928 (2024)
4. Cao, T., Wu, X., Guo, J., Yu, S., Xu, Y.: Abnormal crowd motion analysis. In: 2009 IEEE International Conference on Robotics and Biomimetics (ROBIO), pp. 1709–1714. IEEE (2009)
5. Chen, L.C., Zhu, Y., Papandreou, G., Schroff, F., Adam, H.: Encoder-decoder with atrous separable convolution for semantic image segmentation. In: Proceedings of the European conference on computer vision (ECCV), pp. 801–818 (2018)
6. Cho, M., et al.: Look around for anomalies: weakly-supervised anomaly detection via context-motion relational learning. In: Proceedings of the IEEE/CVF conference on computer vision and pattern recognition, pp. 12137–12146 (2023)
7. Cong, Y., Yuan, J., Liu, J.: Sparse reconstruction cost for abnormal event detection. In: CVPR 2011, pp. 3449–3456. IEEE (2011)
8. Cordts, M., et al.: The cityscapes dataset for semantic urban scene understanding. In: Proceedings of the IEEE conference on computer vision and pattern recognition, pp. 3213–3223 (2016)
9. Das, D., Mishra, D.: Unsupervised anomalous trajectory detection for crowded scenes, pp. 27–31 (2018)
10. Defard, T., Setkov, A., Loesch, A., Audigier, R.: PaDiM: a patch distribution modeling framework for anomaly detection and localization, pp. 475–489 (2021)
11. Farnebäck, G.: Two-frame motion estimation based on polynomial expansion. In: Scandinavian conference on Image analysis, pp. 363–370. Springer (2003)
12. Feng, J., Wang, D., Zhang, L.: Crowd anomaly detection via spatial constraints and meaningful perturbation, vol. 11, p. 205. MDPI (2022)
13. Galič, M., Timan, T., Koops, B.J.: Bentham, Deleuze and beyond: an overview of surveillance theories from the panopticon to participation. Philos. Technol. **30**(1), 9–37 (2017)
14. Georgescu, M.I., et al.: Anomaly detection in video via self-supervised and multi-task learning, pp. 12742–12752 (2021)
15. Guo, Y., et al.: Trajectory shape analysis and anomaly detection utilizing Shannon entropy and clustering. Entropy **19**(7), 323 (2017)
16. Howedi, A., Lotfi, A., Pourabdollah, A.: An entropy-based approach for anomaly detection in activities of daily living in the presence of a visitor. Entropy **22**(8), 845 (2020)

17. Hu, C., Zhu, L., Lai, S.: Spatio-temporal-based context fusion for video anomaly detection, pp. 187–192 (2023)
18. Huang, X., Zhao, C., Wu, Z.: A video anomaly detection framework based on appearance-motion semantics representation consistency, pp. 1–5 (2023)
19. Islam, M.T., Yin, Y., Deng, D., Islam, M.M., Pasha, S.M.M.: Leveraging dermograbcut segmentation for improved CNN-based skin lesion classification. In: International Conference on Intelligent Computing, pp. 335–346. Springer (2025)
20. Lan, D.T., Yoon, S.: Trajectory clustering-based anomaly detection in indoor human movement. Sensors **23**(6), 3318 (2023)
21. Li, T.: Crowded scene analysis: a survey. IEEE Trans. Circuits Syst. Video Technol. **25**(3), 367–386 (2014)
22. Li, W., Mahadevan, V., Vasconcelos, N.: Anomaly detection and localization in crowded scenes. IEEE Trans. Pattern Anal. Mach. Intell. **36**(1), 18–32 (2013)
23. Lian, X., Pang, Y., Han, J., Pan, J.: Cascaded hierarchical Atrous spatial pyramid pooling module for semantic segmentation. Pattern Recogn. **110**, 107622 (2021)
24. Luo, L., et al.: Crowd-level abnormal behavior detection via multi-scale motion consistency learning. In: Proceedings of the AAAI conference on artificial intelligence, vol. 37, pp. 8984–8992 (2023)
25. Pal, M.: Random forest classifier for remote sensing classification. Int. J. Remote Sens. **26**(1), 217–222 (2005)
26. Pasha, S.M.M., Sohag, S.R., Ali, M.M.: Enhancing audio classification with a CNN-attention model: robust performance and resilience against backdoor attacks. Int. J. Comput. Appl. **975**, 8887 (2024)
27. Reiss, T., Hoshen, Y.: Attribute-based representations for accurate and interpretable video anomaly detection. arXiv preprint arXiv:2212.00789 (2022)
28. Ronneberger, O., Fischer, P., Brox, T.: U-Net: convolutional networks for biomedical image segmentation. In: International Conference on Medical image computing and computer-assisted intervention, pp. 234–241. Springer (2015)
29. Roshtkhari, M.J., Levine, M.D.: Online dominant and anomalous behavior detection in videos, pp. 2611–2618 (2013)
30. Shaikh, J.A., et al.: A deep reinforcement learning-based robust intrusion detection system for securing IoMT healthcare networks. Front. Med. **12**, 1524286 (2025). https://doi.org/10.3389/fmed.2025.1524286
31. Sharif, M.H., Djeraba, C.: An entropy approach for abnormal activities detection in video streams. Pattern Recogn. **45**(7), 2543–2561 (2012)
32. Sharif, M.H., Jiao, L., Omlin, C.W.: Deep crowd anomaly detection: state-of-the-art, challenges, and future research directions. Artif. Intell. Rev. **58**(5), 139 (2025)
33. Sträter, L.P., Salehi, M., Gavves, E., Snoek, C.G., Asano, Y.M.: Generalad: anomaly detection across domains by attending to distorted features, pp. 448–465 (2024)
34. Sultani, W., Chen, C., Shah, M.: Real-world anomaly detection in surveillance videos. In: Proceedings of the IEEE conference on computer vision and pattern recognition, pp. 6479–6488 (2018)
35. Sun, S., Gong, X.: Hierarchical semantic contrast for scene-aware video anomaly detection, pp. 22846–22856 (2023)
36. Swears, E., Hoogs, A., Perera, A.A.: Learning motion patterns in surveillance video using hmm clustering. In: 2008 IEEE workshop on motion and video computing, pp. 1–8. IEEE (2008)
37. Unser, M., Aldroubi, A., Eden, M.: The l/sub 2/-polynomial spline pyramid. IEEE Trans. Pattern Anal. Mach. Intell. **15**(4), 364–379 (2002)

38. Wang, Z., et al.: Global abnormal event detection in video via motion information entropy, pp. 1–4 (2018)
39. Xu, D., Ricci, E., Yan, Y., Song, J., Sebe, N.: Learning deep representations of appearance and motion for anomalous event detection (2015)
40. Xu, X., Xu, S., Jin, L., Song, E.: Characteristic analysis of Otsu threshold and its applications. Pattern Recogn. Lett. **32**(7), 956–961 (2011)
41. Yang, T., et al.: Entity backdoor attacks against fine-tuned models. In: International Conference on Intelligent Computing, pp. 338–349. Springer (2025)
42. Yang, Z., Radke, R.J.: Context-aware video anomaly detection in long-term datasets. In: Proceedings of the IEEE/CVF conference on computer vision and pattern recognition, pp. 4002–4011 (2024)
43. Yin, Y., Yuan, Z., Tanvir, I.M., Bao, X.: Electronic medical records imputation by temporal generative adversarial network. BioData Mining **17**(1), 19 (2024)
44. Zhang, X., Yang, S., Tang, Y.Y., Zhang, W.: A thermodynamics-inspired feature for anomaly detection on crowd motions in surveillance videos. Multimedia Tools Appl. **75**(14), 8799–8826 (2016)
45. Zhang, X., Ma, D., Yu, H., Huang, Y., Howell, P., Stevens, B.: Scene perception guided crowd anomaly detection, vol. 414, pp. 291–302. Elsevier (2020)
46. Zhou, B., et al.: Scene parsing through ade20k dataset. In: Proceedings of the IEEE conference on computer vision and pattern recognition, pp. 633–641 (2017)

Enhancing Explainability in X-IDS Through Counterfactuals

Quan Li[1] and Yuhong Li[1,2(✉)]

[1] State Key Laboratory of Networking and Switching Technology, Beijing University of Posts and Telecommunications, Beijing 100876, China

[2] Department of Computer and Systems Sciences, Stockholm University, Stockholm, Sweden

Yuhongli@dsv.su.se

Abstract. The growing use of deep learning in intrusion detection systems (IDS) has increased the need for explainable IDS (X-IDS). Current X-IDS research mainly relies on local surrogate models and their explanations are limited due to the complex features of network traffic. In contrast, counterfactual explanations improve interpretability by contrasting "why P rather than Q", avoiding complex absolute explanations. In this paper, we outline the theoretical value of counterfactual explanations in X-IDS, and propose a two-stage search method for generating counterfactuals. Moreover, we also propose a submodular pick method for counterfactual explanations that provides diverse explanation instances, aiming to interpret the entire model rather than individual samples. Experimental results demonstrate that our proposed method achieves an 80% improvement in fidelity and is 100 times more computationally efficient compared with LIME within the X-IDS domain.

Keywords: Intrusion detection · Counterfactual explanation · Explainable machine learning · Explainable intrusion detection system (X-IDS)

1 Introduction

With the rise in cyberattacks [1], researchers have developed multi-layered defenses, with intrusion detection systems (IDS) emerging as a key component for monitoring and detecting malicious activity [2]. Machine learning-based IDS offer huge advantages over traditional IDS by reducing the cost of manual analysis and improving the threat detection capabilities. Deep Neural Networks (DNNs) further enhance detection accuracy [3]; however, the "black-box" nature limits their trustworthy deployment in high-stakes security environments, such as critical infrastructure, financial and healthcare systems. Without transparency and interpretability, security decisions are unreliable, leading to potential vulnerabilities [3]. Hence, there is an urgent need for trustworthy interpretable models.

Explainable AI (XAI) aims to improve the interpretability of black-box models. Although XAI research has made progresses in fields such as computer vision

R. Chen et al. (Eds.): Inscrypt 2025, LNCS 16409, pp. 235–252, 2026.
https://doi.org/10.1007/978-981-95-6203-9_13

and natural language processing, its application in IDS remains limited. Current research on explainable IDS (X-IDS) primarily relies on attribution methods [3] [4] such as Local Interpretable Model-agnostic Explanations (LIME) [5] and SHapley Additive exPlanations (SHAP) [6] for model interpretation. While these methods are widely adopted, three major limitations persist in the literature: **Lack of Faithfulness Evaluation**. Most studies apply SHAP or LIME but fail to rigorously evaluate the faithfulness of their explanations to the underlying model. **Underdeveloped Counterfactual Theory**. Although some works have begun to generate counterfactual explanations (CFs) (e.g., [7,8]), none provide a theoretical justification for their necessity in IDS or empirically evaluate their advantages over attribution methods. **Limited Explanation Depth**. The majority of methods stop at quantifying feature importance without incorporating domain knowledge to achieve deeper interpretations.

To address these gaps, this paper advocates for the use of CFs [9] in X-IDS. By manipulating input features to create contrasting samples, CFs can directly reveal the model's decision boundaries without requiring secondary verification, thus inherently addressing the faithfulness concern. Furthermore, CFs possess lower computational complexity, enabling real-time explanations that are crucial for enhancing IDS performance. The necessity and benefits of using CFs for IDS are detailed in Sect. 3.1.

However, our experiments show that counterfactuals generated from network data often modify many features. This may hinder the interpretability: the fewer the modified features, the more understandable the explanation becomes [10]. To solve this problem, we propose a two-stage counterfactual search method. It first performs a standard counterfactual search and then restricts the search to only the top k features ranked according to specific metrics.

Furthermore, to ensure the validity of explanations, evaluation criteria must incorporate prior knowledge. For example, in image classification, explaining "Image J is a beetle, not a spider, because it has six legs" [10] relies on entomological knowledge: beetles have six legs, whereas spiders have eight. Thus, the rationality of an explanation is inherently conditional on a specific cognitive framework; without prior anchoring, evaluations lack clear benchmarks.

Current X-IDS research often neglects prior knowledge, however, prior knowledge is essential even for simple subjects and is critical when features and models are complex. In traditional image recognition, features like a "snowy background" might be dismissed as noise when classifying wolves. But this perspective is not logically necessary: in a world where wolves are causally linked to snowy terrain, this feature could become a valid criterion. Hence, explanations depend on prior knowledge, which shapes their acceptability and reflects consensus or dominant perspectives. The contributions of this paper are as follows.

- We theoretically elucidate the critical role of CFs in X-IDS. To empirically validate this, we conducted three key experiments: (1) evaluating the fidelity of LIME, which demonstrated only approximately 20% fidelity; (2) assessing the consistency between LIME and CF, revealing a low alignment of merely

10%; and (3) benchmarking the computational efficiency, where CFs achieved a nearly 100-fold improvement in speed compared to LIME.

- We propose (1) a gradient-constrained two-stage counterfactual search that enhances plausibility and conciseness by minimizing feature modifications; and (2) SP-CF, a submodular optimization-based method for global interpretability that uses a theoretically guaranteed greedy algorithm.
- We propose several evaluation metrics for counterfactual explanations, along with experimental evaluations.
- To the best of our knowledge, we are the first to highlight the critical role of prior knowledge in explanation generation and to propose incorporating prior knowledge as exemplars.

2 Related Work

As mentioned before, most existing work regarding X-IDS have used LIME or SHAP for explanation. LIME [5] generates local explanations by training interpretable surrogate models on perturbed samples. For global insights, SP-LIME selects representative explanations. In contrast, CFs [9] provide "what-if" reasoning by identifying the minimal changes required to alter a model's prediction.

Oseni et al. [11] proposed an explainable deep learning framework for IoT IDS using SHAP, though its computational cost hinders real-time deployment. Aljuhani et al. [12] applied PSO for feature selection in IoMT networks, combining multiple models with SHAP explanations, but their approach is limited to binary classification. Sharma et al. [4] proposed a deep learning framework for IoT IDS. Evaluated on the NSL-KDD and UNSW-NB15 datasets, the study integrated XAI techniques (LIME and SHAP) but limited explanations to feature weights. Patil et al. [13] developed an ensemble-based IDS combining decision trees, random forests, and SVM via a voting classifier. Though LIME improved interpretability, the analysis focused only on feature importance rankings.

In [14], LIME and SHAP were used for feature importance and BRCG for interpretable rules, supplemented by contrastive instances. However, it lacks evaluation of explanation quality, ignoring operational feasibility or minimal modifications in its contrastive explanations. [15] proposed an XGBoost-based IDS with SHAP explanations. [16] introduced an AI-based IoT IDS, with SHAP to explain decisions and feature importance. However, it does not evaluate explanation fidelity or alignment with model behavior.

Due to the importance of X-IDS, [3] compared LIME and SHAP for MLP-based IDS, revealing their computational challenges. [17] showed that SHAP and LIME explanations often mismatch model decisions, with "important" features having negligible impact. [18] trains per-cluster decision trees, but explanations may reflect data bias and it only evaluates prediction consistency, not plausibility. [19] remaps features using the CIA triad, but its explanations weakly correlate with model behavior.

Several studies have employed CF-like methods for X-IDS, however, they lack global analysis or quantitative evaluation to the explanations. For example, [7] corrects misclassifications via adversarial perturbations but lacks global analysis and produces unreadable explanations. [8] uses boundary-based counterfactuals but is instance-specific and lacks quantitative evaluation.

In short, the existing interpretability methods for X-IDS have three major shortcomings: (1) Lack of faithfulness evaluation: Most studies apply SHAP or LIME but fail to rigorously assess faithfulness. (2) Underdeveloped counterfactual theory: though some works generate counterfactuals (e.g. [7,8]), none theoretically justify their necessity for IDS or evaluate their advantages over attribution methods. (3) Limited explanation depth: most methods stop at feature importance quantification without deep interpretation through prior knowledge.

3 Methodology

3.1 Necessity of Counterfactual Explanations for X-IDS

In the classic LIME-based cases [5], a wolf versus dog classifier trained on biased data (e.g. snowy backgrounds for wolves) may inadvertently rely on background features rather than animal morphology. LIME helps to reveal this bias by highlighting high-weight superpixels (e.g., snow), but such intuitive features are absent in intrusion detection, where traffic features are abstract and complex.

This creates a fundamental dilemma. Firstly, LIME's feature importance is an approximation from a surrogate model (e.g., linear or tree), not the original model's true logic. This raises faithfulness concerns. Secondly, validating explanations requires predefined "reasonable features". However, unlike in the domains such as image recognition, network traffic lacks clear criteria, leading to an infinite regress problem. Furthermore, network traffic features are high-dimensional and nonlinear. This makes simple rules ineffective for intrusion detection. If such simple rules sufficed, traditional rule-based IDS should perform well. But this contradicts the demonstrated superiority of deep learning models in practice [2]. Does this mean explaining complex models is impossible?

Contrastive explanation theory [20] provides insight: human explanations are selective, focusing only on distinguishing features between a target (P) and a contrast (Q), not exhaustive attributes. For instance, choosing "eggplant over beef" is sufficiently explained by "vegetarianism", although "why eggplant" requires distinguishing it from other vegetables. Similarly, classifying to "beetle rather than spider" only requires "six legs", not "eyes or wings" [10]. Humans, too, lack full awareness of their recognition process.

The contrastive form "Why P rather than Q?" assumes "P $\vee$ Q." For example, explaining "DOS attack (not Worm)" requires contrasting only some features, not all characteristics of DOS. This approach acknowledges the exist of other features but does not need to address them. Compared with traditional methods like LIME, contrastive explanations have advantages. In multiclass scenarios, LIME's feature importance fails to clarify "importance relative to what?". Since LIME addresses implicitly "Why P rather than non-P?", it emphasizes all features of P. Thus, in the context of intrusion detection, its linear surrogate models struggle to capture the complex behaviors of attacks, as discussed above.

From a counterfactual perspective, "Why P rather than Q?" frames Q as a contrast item, creating a search for the closest possible world: the minimal changes needed to shift the outcome from P to Q. Crucially, Q is not simply "non-P" but a relevant alternative (e.g., Worm vs. DOS attack) within the classification framework.

3.2 Prior Knowledge

The validity of explanations should be evaluated according to criteria derived from prior knowledge. This shapes both the acceptability of explanations and the collective cognitive consensus. However, this crucial aspect remains understudied in X-IDS research. Prior models, from classifications to IDS, underpin explanatory rationality, especially when features are not intuitive (e.g., race or image background), often requiring explicit articulation.

Hence, we outlines a preliminary framework of prior knowledge in IDS, taking two frequently occurring attacks, Denial of Service (DoS) and Worm attacks, as an example. We will use this prior knowledge to generate and evaluate CF in our experiments described in Sect. 4.

DoS attacks systematically exhaust the target's network bandwidth, computation or memory resources, preventing legitimate users from using services. The basic mechanism of such attacks is to overwhelm the target with excessive service or data requests, leading to the saturation of one or more types of the target's resources. Typical manifestations of DoS include sudden traffic surges or abnormal protocol behaviors, including but not limited to frequent resets of connection state machines, exponential growth in half-open connections, and increased transmission jitter due to packet timing disorders. At the protocol level, malformed packet injections, abnormal fragment reassembly, and flag violation operations can be observed, ultimately resulting in a sharp spike in service response latency and a cliff-like drop in effective packet delivery rates.

Worms propagate autonomously in network environments, replicating exponentially to form multi-hop infection chains. Their defining characteristic lies in the topological diffusion of address space, manifested as radial distributions of source-destination IP pairs and high-entropy target selection. The attack life cycle of worms consists of three phases: periodic scanning and probing, exploit payload delivery, and replica regeneration. These phases generate persistent, low-success-rate connection attempts and repetitive malicious payload transmissions. At the network level, fixed time-window scanning pulses, unconventional protocol interaction sequences, and cross-network-segment cascading infection traffic can be detected, ultimately forming a spatiotemporally correlated anomalous traffic matrix. Some worm variants exploit vulnerabilities in protocols such as FTP/HTTP for propagation.

3.3 Two-Stage Counterfactual Search Method

The overall workflow of the proposed XIDS method is shown in Fig. 1. The process starts by constructing the SP-CF using a submodular pick algorithm, followed by a two-stage counterfactual search for each selected sample. The resulting counterfactuals are then evaluated against prior knowledgeobtained from domain experts or large language models (LLMs)ïijŇwhich serves as a benchmark for assessing explanation quality and plausibility. Once an explanation is validated against such knowledge, it is considered trustworthy without requiring explicit reference to the underlying prior knowledge. This is similar to how, in image recognition, a verified explanation (e.g., misclassifying a "wolf" due to a snowy background) becomes self-evident and no longer needs repeated justification.

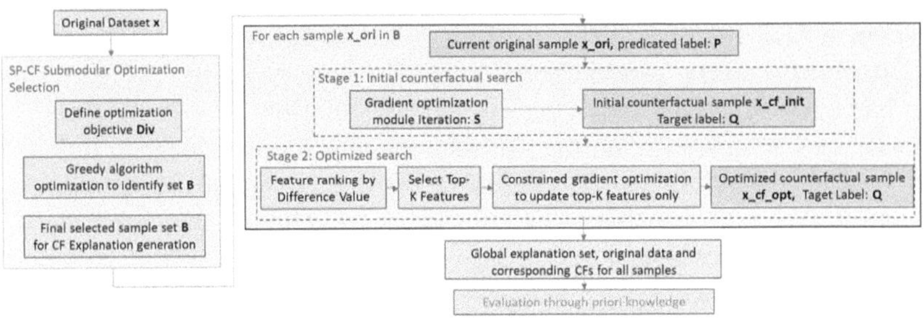

Fig. 1. The Overall Method of XIDS.

To realize CF-based X-IDS and demonstrate its benefits, we proposed a two-stage counterfactual search method as elaborated below. First, the loss function is defined as follows:

$$\mathcal{L} = \text{CrossEntropy}(f(x), y_{cf}) + \lambda d(x, x_{ori}) \tag{1}$$

where $f(x)$ denotes a model's output, y_{cf} is desired counterfactual lable, $d(x, x_{ori})$ is a distance function measuring how different the modified input x is from the original input x_{ori}. λ is a regularization weight. Following [21], we set $\lambda = 0.5$ with experiments showing minimal impact from its exact value.

Then, the input x is iteratively updated via gradient descent, namely:

$$x = x - \eta \nabla_x \mathcal{L}(x) \tag{2}$$

This process runs for S steps, or until the predicted value argmax$f(x_i)$ equals the counterfactual lable y_{cf}. Note that in (2) the learning rate η affects critically both the convergence speed and the counterfactual quality. The optimal value for η and S can be determined through experiments and systematic evaluation.

To ensure the plausibility and actionability of counterfactual samples, we impose the following constraints during gradient updates:

Immutable Feature Constraint: let $\boldsymbol{B}$ be the set of indices corresponding to features that cannot be modified. Then the gradient update for feature x_i is adjusted as:

$$g_i = 0, \forall i \in \boldsymbol{B} \tag{3}$$

Feature Value Range Constraint: assuming the valid range for feature i is $[l_i, u_i]$, we apply a clipping function:

$$g_i = \text{clip}(\nabla_{x_i}\mathcal{L}(x), (l_i - x_i)/\eta, (u_i - x_i)/\eta) \tag{4}$$

where the function $\text{clip}(a, \min, \max)$ is a clipping function that restricts values to the range $[\min, \max]$.

This counterfactual search methods often require modifying many features due to the complexity of neural networks, which hinders the interpretability. Experiments on IDS traffic data show that valid counterfactuals can usually be found by modifying only a few features. Therefore, to reduce the number of modified features, we proposed an optimized counterfactual search method consisting of two stages.

- **Stage 1:** Perform a standard counterfactual search to obtain an initial counterfactual sample.
- **Stage 2:** Rank the features by sorting them in descending order based on their absolute changes (i.e., $|\mathbf{x}_{\text{cf}}^{(i)} - \mathbf{x}_{\text{ori}}^{(i)}|$ for feature i), then constrain the search to the top-k key features.

The hyperparameter k determines the maximum number of features that can be modified. A smaller k encourages sparser counterfactuals with fewer changes, but overly restrictive values may hinder the generation of valid instances. Thus, k should be selected to balance sparsity and feasibility according to applications.

Experiments (see Sect. 4) confirm the effectiveness of the proposed two-stage searching method for IDS. The intuitive explanation for feature ranking is that under the same number of iteration steps, a larger absolute change in a feature indicates a larger absolute gradient of the loss function with respect to that feature. This means the feature can more significantly change the model's output and therefore has higher importance.

Based on the above analysis, we proposed two quantitative metrics for evaluating feature importance in CFs.

Feature Modification Metric (FMM): The absolute value of the change in the counterfactual found and the original sample on the feature ith dimension. For feature i, $\text{FMM}^{(i)} = |x_{cf}^{(i)} - x_{ori}^{(i)}|$. It reflects local feature influence for each sample and global importance when aggregated accross samples.

Counterfactual Solvability Metric (CSM): This metric evaluates feature importance by counting the number of samples in a sample set where counterfactual solutions can be found by modifying a single feature. Intuitively, features enabling counterfactuals tend to have greater predictive influence. Although extreme modifications of one feature could produce unrealistic data, experiments show that counterfactuals typically require only small modifications. The step-size constraint further ensures plausibility.

The two metrics are correlated with each other – a high CSM value (i.e. easy solvability) suggests a high FMM value (i.e., large gradient impact), and vice versa. Experiments in Sect. 4 confirm this correlation. This correlation can help optimize the explanation process. For a model with feature dimension D and sample size B, CSM has a time complexity $O(D \times B)$, whereas FMM has a time complexity of only $O(B)$. Given that D is typically large in real-world applications, adopting FMM can improve computational efficiency by 1–2 orders of magnitude, allowing FMM to serve as an efficient alternative for single-instance importance and benefiting real-time interpretability in complex models.

3.4 Submodular Pick Algorithm for Counterfactual Explanation

Inspired by LIME [5], our selection of explanation instances adheres to two key constraints: (1) a limited upper bound imposed by cognitive load, and (2) the impracticality of generating full-scale explanations due to dataset size and real-time requirements.

To address these constraints, we introduce a metric (called Div) for diversity based on the principle of diminishing marginal returns. By applying the principle to feature contributions, we prioritize instances that complement existing explanations, thereby enhancing overall diversity.

After using the two-stage counterfactual search method, samples will be generated. We define the contribution of sample s_j (normalized) to feature i as:

$$c_{j,i} = \frac{1}{|CF_j[i] - s_j[i]| + 1} \tag{5}$$

where $CF_j[i]$ denotes the value of feature i in the counterfactual found for sample s_j. For a given sample set B, its diversity is defined as:

$$\text{Div}(B) = \sum_{i \in F} \sqrt{\sum_{s_j \in B} \frac{1}{|CF_j[i] - s_j[i]| + 1}} \tag{6}$$

Here, we use the square root function to model diminishing returns: as cumulative feature contributions grow, each new addition has progressively less impact on the output. Being simple and effective, it encourages feature diversity and reduces over-reliance on any single feature. Thus, the problem reduces to maximizing the diversity of a sample set:

$$\max_{B \subseteq X, |B| \leq ul} \text{Div}(B) = \max_{B \subseteq X, |B| \leq ul} \sum_{i \in F} \sqrt{\sum_{s_j \in B} \frac{1}{|CF_j[i] - s_j[i]| + 1}} \tag{7}$$

where ul denotes the upper limit on the number of explanation instances.

Note that samples requiring fewer feature modifications in their counterfactuals contribute more to the explanation. This does not conflict with FMM, where larger single-feature modifications indicate higher importance. Since the Div metric operates at the instance level, while FMM focuses on individual features. Samples needing fewer modifications are typically closer to the decision boundary, offering clearer insights into the model's logic through concise changes, thus enhancing explanatory value.

As the optimization problem is NP-hard [22], heuristic or approximation methods are required to obtain solutions. Due to submodularity (diminishing marginal returns), a greedy algorithm that iteratively adds the instance with the highest marginal coverage gain to the solution offers a constant-factor approximation guarantee of $1 - \frac{1}{e}$ to the optimum [5,23].

To reduce computational costs of greedy evaluation, we propose a Submodular Pick algorithm for Counterfactual Explanation (SP-CF). It uses greedy beam search: at each step, it selects the highest-gain instance from K candidates and adds it to the solution set, continuing until reaching the limit ul or the maximum number of iterations. This can balance efficiency with explanation quality.

4 Experiments and Analyses

We used the UNSW-NB15 dataset [24,25]. It combines real network traffic with synthetic attacks, covering nine types of attacks (e.g., DoS, exploits, worms) and normal traffic. Each sample consists of 42 features and a label. Before training, we preprocessed the data by cleaning, integer encoding, and Z-score normalization. Our intrusion detection model is a three-layer ANN (hidden: 20 ReLU neurons), achieving an accuracy of 0.7934. We trained it using cross-entropy loss in TensorFlow-Keras, using its automatic differentiation capabilities to generate counterfactual samples.

4.1 Influence of the Learning Rate

To evaluate the influence of the learning rate (LR) on the effectiveness of counterfactual policy generation, we conducted experiments on 1,000 random samples. Each sample was assigned a randomly selected target class (i.e., a type of attack) that differs from the model's predicted class, serving as the counterfactual goal. We focused on assessing policy performance under four typical LR values (1, 0.1, 0.01, 0.001) and recorded the following key metrics:

- Distances measured using three common distance calculating methods: Euclidean distance, Manhattan distance, and cosine similarity.
- Number of search steps required to generate counterfactuals (with an upper limit of 50 steps).

We compared the average distance between counterfactual and original samples under different LR, along with search efficiency measured by search steps. As shown in Fig. 2 (a), where x-axis is in log scale, the average search steps is 21, with LR greatly affecting performance. Optimal results occur at LR $= 0.01$, and efficiency improves notably within the range LR $\in [0.01, 0.001]$.

We further experimented with 100 samples with finer LR changes (1, 0.5, 0.1, 0.05, 0.01, 0.005, 0.001). As shown in Fig. 2 (b), LR $= 0.005$ yields the best balance between generation quality (distance) and efficiency (steps). Failed searches were capped at 50 steps. Based on the quantile analysis, a learning rate of 0.005 slightly better outperforms 0.01. Specifically, approximately 80% of the samples complete counterfactual search within 10 steps, with an average of 6.5 search step. Thus, we use LR $= 0.005$ and a 10-step limit in subsequent experiments.

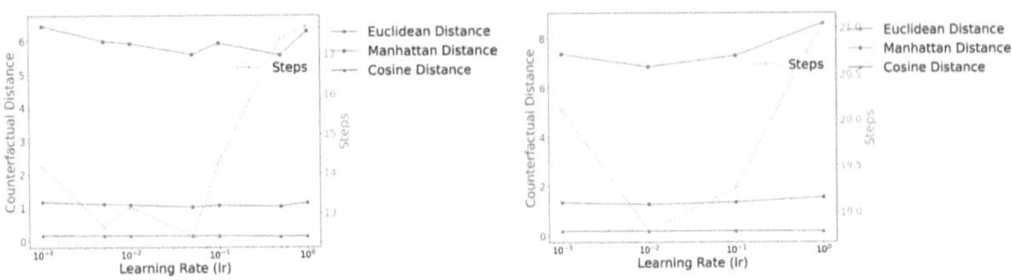

Fig. 2. Distances and Searching Steps under Different Learning Rates.

4.2 Correlation Between FMM and CSM

To analyze the correlation between FMM and CSM, we performed experiments using 100 randomly selected samples from the dataset that were correctly classified as Generic Attack. The corresponding counterfactual instances for these samples were all classified as normal by the model. To ensure consistency, we fixed the classification outcomes of the counterfactuals to avoid potential variations in feature importance caused by different contrastive counterfactuals.

For CSM, we counted how often modifying a single feature successfully generated a counterfactual (Fig. 3, left). For FMM, a two-stage search targeted only the top 5 features (Fig. 3, right). Among the top 5 features, 3 overlapped between metrics; among the top 10, 6 overlapped. The Pearson correlation (0.63) supports the hypothesis that features with larger modification magnitudes are more likely to produce valid counterfactuals. Based on these results, in the second stage of two-stage optimized counterfactual search, we modify only the top 5 features selected by FMM. In subsequent evaluations, although CSM can effectively assess feature importance, given its high computational cost, it is recommended to prioritize FMM for feature importance evaluation.

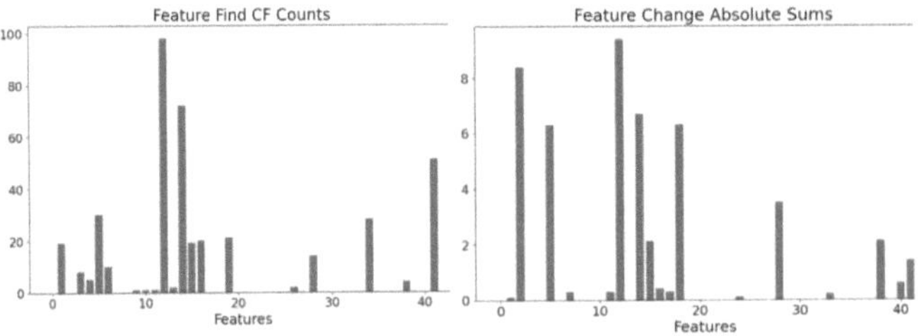

Fig. 3. CSM(left) and FMM(right).

4.3 Comparison Between CF and LIME

We first evaluate the fidelity of LIME explanations by measuring the consistency with predictions of the target model. The evaluation involves randomly sampling data points, generating LIME explanations for each, and quantifying their alignment with model predictions. As shown in Fig. 4(left), the match rate is low (about 20%) for all classes of attacks. This discrepancy raises two concerns:(1) difficulty in effectively verifying the true importance of the features identified by the explanations; (2) doubt about the interpretability of the explanations - potentially resulting in an infinite-regress in explanation logic.

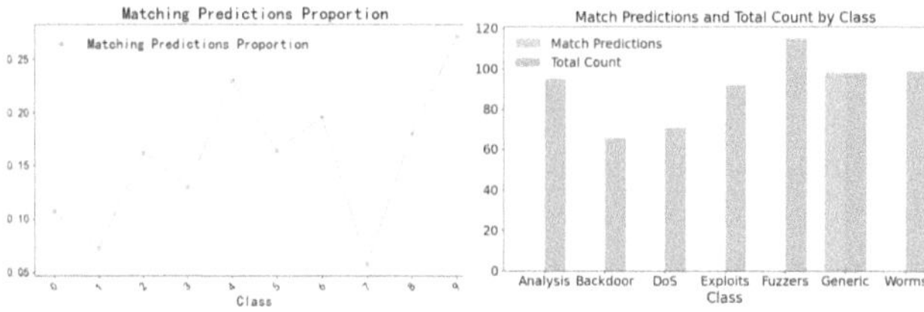

Fig. 4. LIME Fidelity; On origin(left) and On CF(right).

Given fidelity concerns, we evaluated the consistency between CF and LIME by comparing LIME's predictions for counterfactual with the model's actual predictions. We conducted 1,000 iterative experiments on random instances, each time selecting a non-current class as the counterfactual target and modifying only a random subset of k features using the constrained search algorithm.

As shown in Fig. 4(right), only the class "Generic" matched correctly, suggesting that LIME effectively identifies feature importance for majority classes (e.g., "Generic" and "Normal"). However, without counterfactual analysis, this bias is hard to detect beforehand, indirectly validating our counterfactual method.

The runtime of LIME, basic counterfactual search (denoted as CF), and two-stage counterfactual search (denoted as CF2) are shown in Fig. 5. Here we can see that both counterfactual search methods are significantly faster, reducing the explanation generation time by nearly two orders of magnitude compared with LIME. In addition, our two-stage search method remains fast, since the recalculation time is limited once a counterfactual is found.

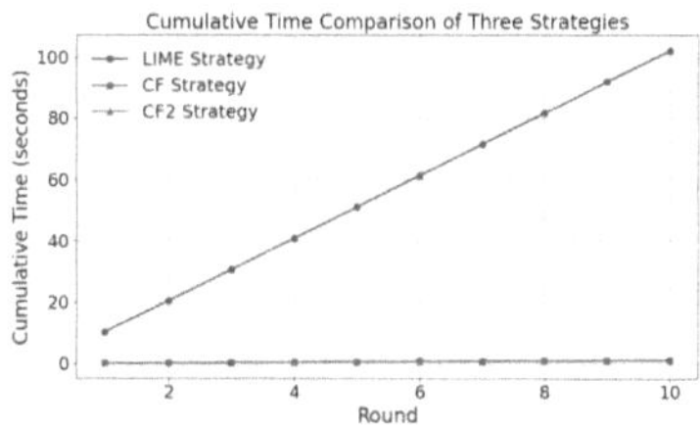

Fig. 5. LIME vs. CF: Computational Time

We made further experiments to investigate the correlation between the feature importance derived by LIME and by CF (FMM). We chosen instances that the model correctly predicted as "Generic Attack," and the counterfactual target was "Normal". The results show a correlation coefficient of 0.15 between LIME and basic CF, and -0.01 for the two-stage CF according to FMM, indicating a huge divergence between LIME and CF.

One might argue that LIME does not explicitly extract knowledge for the counterfactual class ("Normal"). However, end-users cannot discern which aspects of the model's decision-making are actually reflected in LIME explanations. This further supports our claim: LIME explanation themselves require additional clarification.

The above findings indicate that LIME exhibits limitations in faithfulness and lacks self-explanatory characteristics in its explanations. Moreover, CFs demonstrate significantly faster processing speeds compared with LIME's explanations. These results collectively substantiate the superior performance of counterfactual approaches for X-IDS.

4.4 Performance of SP-CF

To evaluate SP-CF, we conducted experiments using correctly classified Generic Attack instances, with Normal class as the counterfactual target. Results obtained by using the following two methods were compared:

- Random selection (Rand-CF): randomly selects 100 samples to generate counterfactuals.
- Submodular pick CF (SP-CF): iteratively selects samples and maximize the diversity value (i.e., Div) until 100 samples are chosen.

We collected the diversity values under these two methods, and conducted a two-stage counterfactual search, calculating the sum of Manhattan distances.

The results shown in Fig. 6 demonstrate that SP-CF improves the diversity value (Div) by 33% compared with Rand-CF, while requiring a smaller Manhattan distance for modifications (only 12%). By excluding the maximum values (when no counterfactuals are found, the absolute value of feature modifications is set to 1), the total modification distance of SP-CF is only 60% of that of Rand-CF. This further proves that SP-CF can select counterfactual instances with fewer feature modifications.

4.5 DoS Versus Normal

To better understand our proposed method and IDS model's decisions, we used DoS attack as an example, and performed counterfactual analysis on two sample groups: Incorrect Predictions, where samples misclassified as Normal were analyzed with DoS as the counterfactual target; and Correct Predictions, where samples correctly classified as Normal underwent the same analysis.

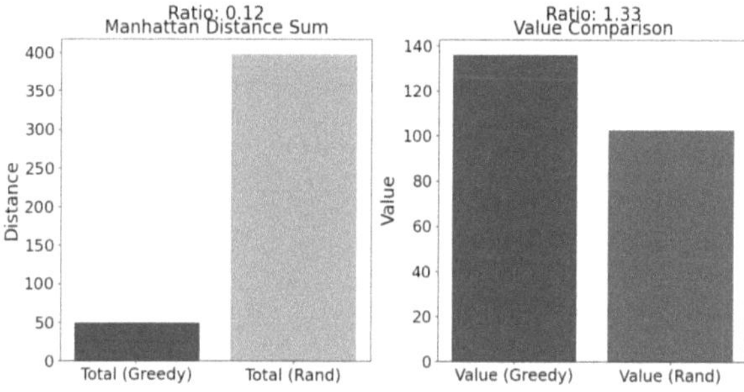

Fig. 6. SP-CF vs. Rand-CF: Feature Modification (left) and the Diversity Value (right)

Incorrect Predictions. We first selected samples misclassified by the model as DoS attacks that were actually normal traffic, then we modified these predictions to the correct class "Normal" traffic by using the two-stage counterfactual generation method (CF2). Figure 7(left) illustrates the top five most important features identified based on FMM. The value of each feature in Fig. 7(left) represents the amount of modification in that feature for the counterfactual relative to the original sample, and the absolute value is FMM.

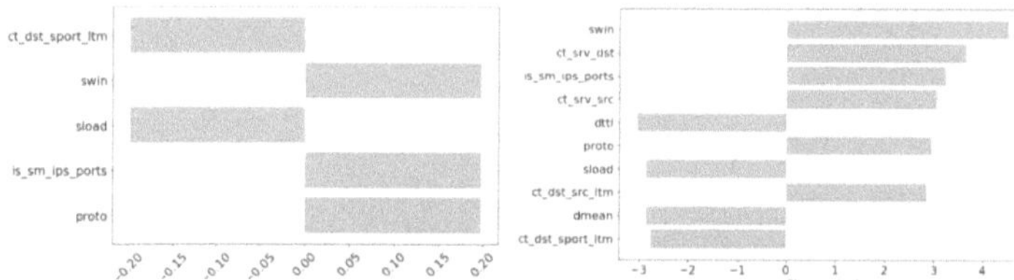

Fig. 7. DoS vs. Normal: FMM of Top 5 Features (left) and Top 10 Features (right).

According to Fig. 7(left), the feature `ct_dst_sport_ltm` (connections with the same destination address and source port) and `sload` (source load) align with prior knowledge, lower values indicate more normal traffic.

For the feature `swin` (source TCP window), SYN Flood and other DoS attacks typically result in low values, as attackers often skip the TCP handshake. Dataset statistics confirm that DoS traffic has a much lower mean `swin` than normal traffic, which the counterfactual explanation captures. However, like the feature `proto`, `swin`'s max and min values show little difference between DoS and normal traffic. Notably, DoS attacks can also involve high `swin` values. If a data point already has a high `swin`, counterfactual generation may not modify it or could even reverse the change. In this case, `swin` increased slightly from -0.958 to -0.760, a reasonable change given the dataset's mean. The feature `is_sm_ips_ports` (same source/destination IP and port) commonly appears in normal traffic but is consistently 0 in DoS attacks. The feature `proto` shows higher values in normal traffic but greater variance in attacks.

By restricting each counterfactual search to modify only a single feature, the experiment results show that modifying any of these five features alone can generate successfully counterfactuals, while modifying other features alone fails, demonstrating the consistency between FMM and CSM.

For further analysis, we selected all instances misclassified as DoS attacks and identified the top ten features based on FMM, as show in Fig. 7 (right). The five previously mentioned features all remain in the top ten features, with consistent modification directions.

Regarding the feature `dttl` (destination Time to Live), attackers may set small TTL values to both limit forged packet propagation (reducing traceability) and increase target system load via ICMP timeout messages, worsening the DoS effect. For `dmean` (destination mean flow size), the average target traffic size often reaches extremes during DoS attacks. Reducing this value makes the model more likely to classify traffic as normal. About `ct_srv_dst` (connection count to the same destination IP and service) and `ct_srv_src` (connection count from the same source IP and service), in contrast to `ct_dst_src_ltm` (connection count with the same source and destination IP), these two features may indicate that the model has learned certain specific patterns.

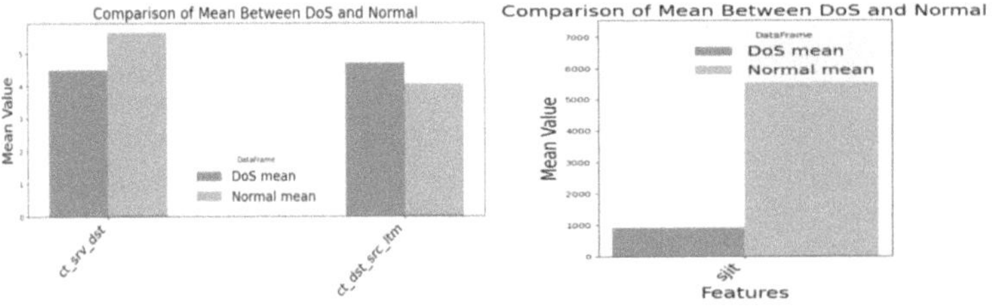

Fig. 8. Statistics of DoS and Normal Traffic.

To validate our explanations, we performed some data analysis on the UNSW-NB15 dataset about the DoS and Normal traffic. As shown in Fig. 8, for normal traffic, `ct_srv_dst` is higer, whereas `ct_dst_src_ltm` is lower. This pattern may reflect the distribution characteristics of a specific dataset, and its generalizability still requires further validation.

Correct Predictions. Based on SP-CF, we selected 50 model-classified DoS samples and reclassified them as Normal using counterfactual explanations. In each round of greedy beam search, 10 instances were selected by maximizing the diversity. Analysis of the top 10 features ranked by FMM (Fig. 9) reveals: (i) Key feature importance aligns with prior research; (ii) New feature `sttl` behaves similarly to `dttl`; (iii) The presence of `sjit` indicates the model increases jitter values to push counterfactual instances toward normal traffic—contrary to the expected trend where normal traffic typically exhibits lower jitter. This divergence may reflect dataset-specific properties.

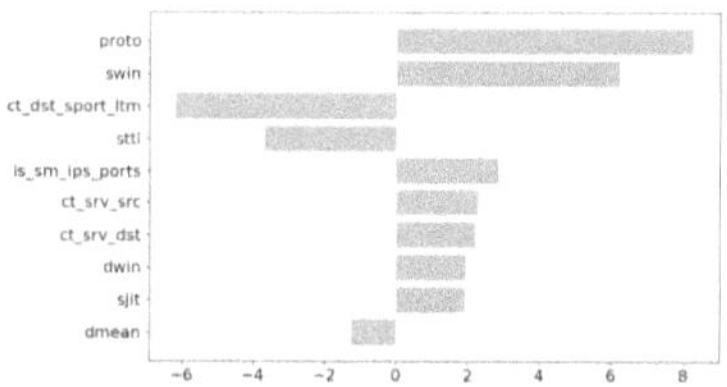

Fig. 9. FMM of Top 10 Features: DoS vs. Normal.

Further analysis (Fig. 8) shows DoS attack traffic in the dataset has generally low jitter values, possibly because the collected DoS data included normal traffic, where attack-induced congestion increased its jitter, or collection bias. Some DoS attacks may not exhibit the expected high jitter behavior.

Based on the analysis of both incorrect and correct prediction samples, we obtained the following results, as shown in Fig. 10:

- Among the correctly predicted samples, approximately 46% successfully generated counterfactual samples, and these counterfactual samples were relatively far from the original samples.
- Among the incorrectly predicted samples, the counterfactual success rate was 94%, with only one-third the feature modification magnitude, indicating that these samples were closer to the decision boundary.

Notably, the counterfactual modifications for both sample groups showed high consistency, reflecting the model's coherent decision logic. Misclassifications mainly occurred near ambiguous decision boundaries. However, feature importance differed: `sinpkt` and `dload` showed stronger negative adjustments in correct predictions, while `dmean` and `dur` had more positive adjustments in mispredictions. This indicates misclassified samples had lower values in these features, making them less consistent with the DoS attack pattern.

4.6 Worm Versus DOS

We similarly evaluated Worm vs Dos, and we found features `response_body_len`, `is_ftp_login`, and `ct_flw_http_mthd` meet the expected criteria. A low `state` value reflects connection characteristics, while role of `sttl` is unclear from prior knowledge, possibly due to dataset bias.

Since some features could not be assessed through prior knowledge, we determined their counterfactual validity through controlled removal experiments:

Baseline: Model trained with all features

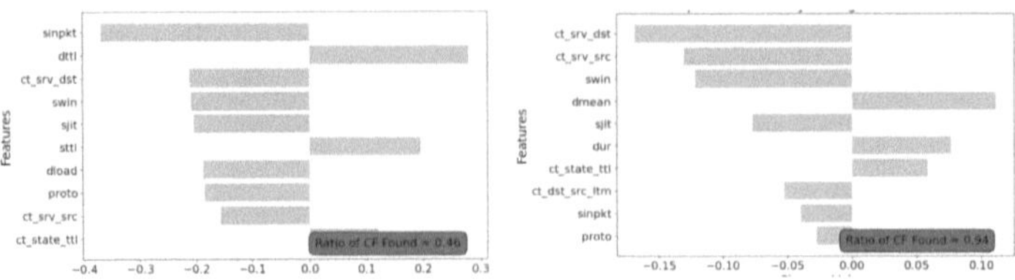

Fig. 10. CF for Correct (left) and Incorrect (right) Classifications: DoS vs. Normal.

Key Features Removed: Retrained without `sttl`, `response_body_len`, `is_ftp_login`, `state`, `ct_flw_http_mthd`

Random Features Removed: Five non-key features removed, averaged over five trials

Results (Fig. 11) show removing key features significantly reduces Worm detection accuracy, while random removal has negligible impact. This confirms these features are crucial for identifying Worm attacks.

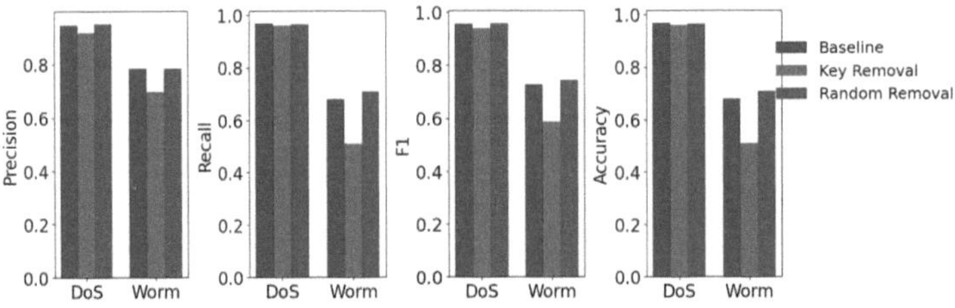

Fig. 11. Performance of Baseline, Key Feature Removal, and Random Removal

5 Conclusions and Future Work

In this paper, we propose to use counterfactual explanation methods to reveal implicit data and cognitive biases in IDS model decisions, providing key insights for model optimization and cybersecurity threat detection. We first outline the theoretical value of counterfactual explanations. Then, we propose a gradient-constrained two-stage method to generate actionable counterfactual features, addressing excessive modifications. We also introduce metrics to measure feature importance. To enhance interpretability, we propose SP-CF, a greedy submodular optimization method that provides worst-case guarantees for instance selection. We evaluate our proposed method and compare it with LIME, a representative attribution method, by evaluating its explanation fidelity on network data. Experimental results show that SP-CF improves diversity by 30% over random selection and the two-stage counterfactual explanation achieves an 80% improvement in counterfactual fidelity and a 100-fold reduction in computational time compared to LIME. Finally, we conduct an in-depth counterfactual analysis using DoS attack and normal traffic as an example.

It should be noted that this study has certain limitations in exploring the complex causal relationships among features. Future research could be deepened in the following directions: 1) incorporating feature causality to enhance the plausibility of explanations; 2) Developing a richer prior knowledge system for better generation support. Our work shows potential for broader applications.

Acknowledgements. The authors declare that no acknowledgments are applicable to this work.

Disclosure of Interests. The authors have no competing interests to declare that are relevant to the content of this article.

References

1. Kuypers, M.A., Maillart, T., Paté-Cornell, E.: An empirical analysis of cyber security incidents at a large organization. Department of Management Science and Engineering, Stanford University, School of Information, UC Berkeley **30**, 1–22 (2016). Accessed July
2. Idrissi, M.J., et al.: Fed-ANIDS: federated learning for anomaly-based network intrusion detection systems. Expert Syst. Appl. **234**, 121000 (2023)
3. Gaspar, D., Silva, P., Silva, C.: Explainable AI for intrusion detection systems: LIME and SHAP applicability on multi-layer perceptron. IEEE Access **12**, 30164–30175 (2024)
4. Sharma, B., Sharma, L., Lal, C., Roy, S.: Explainable artificial intelligence for intrusion detection in IoT networks: a deep learning based approach. Expert Syst. Appl. **238**, 121751 (2024)
5. Ribeiro, M.T., Singh, S., Guestrin, C.: "Why should i trust you?": explaining the predictions of any classifier. In: Proceedings of the 22nd ACM SIGKDD International Conference on Knowledge Discovery and Data Mining, pp. 1135–1144. KDD '16, Association for Computing Machinery, New York, NY, USA (2016). https://doi.org/10.1145/2939672.2939778
6. Lundberg, S.M., Lee, S.I.: A unified approach to interpreting model predictions. In: Proceedings of the 31st International Conference on Neural Information Processing Systems, pp. 4768–4777. NIPS'17, Curran Associates Inc., Red Hook, NY, USA (2017)
7. Marino, D.L., Wickramasinghe, C.S., Manic, M.: An adversarial approach for explainable AI in intrusion detection systems. In: IECON 2018 - 44th Annual Conference of the IEEE Industrial Electronics Society, pp. 3237–3243. Washington, DC, USA (2018). https://doi.org/10.1109/IECON.2018.8591457
8. Burkart, N., Franz, M., Huber, M.: Explanation framework for intrusion detection. In: Beyerer, J., Maier, A., Niggemann, O. (eds.) Machine Learning for Cyber Physical Systems. Technologien für die intelligente Automation, vol. 13, p. 9. Springer Vieweg, Berlin, Heidelberg (2021). https://doi.org/10.1007/978-3-662-62746-4_9

9. Wachter, S., et al.: Counterfactual explanations without opening the black box: automated decisions and the GDPR. Harvard J. Law Technol. **31**(2), 841–887 (2018)
10. Miller, T.: Explanation in artificial intelligence: insights from the social sciences. Artif. Intell. **267**, 1–38 (2019)
11. Oseni, A.: An explainable deep learning framework for resilient intrusion detection in IoT-enabled transportation networks. IEEE Trans. Intell. Transp. Syst. **24**(1), 1000–1014 (2023)
12. Aljuhani, A., Alamri, A., Kumar, P., Jolfaei, A.: An intelligent and explainable SaaS-based intrusion detection system for resource-constrained IoMT. IEEE Internet Things J. **11**(15), 25454–25463 (2024)
13. Patil, S., Varadarajan, V., et al.: Explainable artificial intelligence for intrusion detection system. Electronics **11**(19), 3079 (2022)
14. Mane, S., Rao, D.: Explaining network intrusion detection system using explainable AI framework. arxiv abs/2103.07110 (2021)
15. Barnard, P., Marchetti, N., DaSilva, L.A.: Robust network intrusion detection through explainable artificial intelligence (XAI). IEEE Netw. Lett. **4**(3), 167–171 (2022)
16. Siganos, M., et al.: Explainable AI-based intrusion detection in the internet of things. In: Proceedings of the 18th International Conference on Availability, Reliability and Security. ARES '23, Association for Computing Machinery, New York, NY, USA (2023). https://doi.org/10.1145/3600160.3605162
17. Arreche, O., Guntur, T.R., Roberts, J.W., Abdallah, M.: E-XAI: Evaluating black-box explainable AI frameworks for network intrusion detection. IEEE Access **12**, 23954–23988 (2024)
18. Szczepański, M., Choraś, M., Pawlicki, M., Kozik, R.: Achieving explainability of intrusion detection system by hybrid oracle-explainer approach. In: 2020 International Joint Conference on Neural Networks (IJCNN), pp. 1–8. Glasgow, UK (2020). https://doi.org/10.1109/IJCNN48605.2020.9207199
19. Islam, S., Eberle, W.: Domain knowledge-aided explainable artificial intelligence. In: Ahmed, M., Islam, S., Anwar, A., Moustafa, N., Pathan, A. (eds.) Explainable Artificial Intelligence for Cyber Security. Studies in Computational Intelligence, vol. 1025, p. 4. Springer, Cham (2022). https://doi.org/10.1007/978-3-030-96630-0_4
20. Lipton, P.: Contrastive explanation. R. Inst. Philos. Suppl. **27**, 247–266 (1990)
21. Mothilal, R.K., Sharma, A., Tan, C.: Explaining machine learning classifiers through diverse counterfactual explanations. In: Proceedings of the 2020 Conference on Fairness, Accountability, and Transparency, pp. 607–617. FAT* '20, Association for Computing Machinery, New York, NY, USA (2020). https://doi.org/10.1145/3351095.3372850
22. Feige, U.: A threshold of ln n for approximating set cover. J. ACM **45**(4), 634–652 (1998)
23. Krause, A., Golovin, D.: Submodular Function Maximization, pp. 71–104. Cambridge University Press (2014)
24. Moustafa, N., Slay, J.: UNSW-NB15: a comprehensive data set for network intrusion detection systems (UNSW-NB15 Network Data Set). In: Proceedings of the 2015 Military Communications and Information Systems Conference (MilCIS 2015), pp. 1–6 (2015). https://doi.org/10.1109/MilCIS.2015.7348942
25. Moustafa, N., Slay, J.: The evaluation of network anomaly detection systems: statistical analysis of the UNSW-NB15 data set and the comparison with the KDD99 data set. Inf. Secur. J. Glob. Perspect. **25**(1–3), 18–31 (2016)

What Interferes with the Accurate Detection of Origin Hijacking Anomalies?

Yuancheng Xie, Zhaoxin Zhang(✉), and Ning Li

Harbin Institute of Technology, Harbin 150001, China
{20b903060,zhangzhaoxin,li.ning}@hit.edu.cn

Abstract. Origin hijacking anomalies pose significant threats to interdomain routing security, necessitating robust detection methods to mitigate their adverse impacts. However, current machine learning-based approaches often suffer from limited detection accuracy. In this study, we investigate the detrimental impact of legitimate MOAS conflicts on the performance of origin hijacking detection. To support our analysis, we construct two ground truth datasets using the BGPmon anomaly detection system and the RPKI database. We then evaluate four state-of-the-art detection models through a series of comparative experiments. The results reveal that the legitimate MOAS conflicts is a primary factor contributing to the reduced accuracy of existing detection techniques. Furthermore, we identify 13 effective features for distinguishing legitimate from illegitimate MOAS conflicts. Experimental evaluations demonstrate that incorporating a legitimacy filtering step prior to hijacking subtype classification improves detection accuracy by an average of 12%. Based on these findings, we recommend that origin hijacking detection frameworks incorporate legitimacy assessment of MOAS conflicts as a preliminary step to enhance overall detection precision.

Keywords: BGP anomalies · Origin hijacking · Machine learning · MOAS conflict

1 Introduction

Among the most prevalent threats encountered within interdomain routing systems, origin hijacking is a nefarious tactic that has precipitated numerous high-profile security breaches [27]. For example, on 21 October 2020, AS203 announced 158 prefixes that almost immediately created more than 1100 conflicts [24]. On average, this incident dragged 50% of the usual traffic away from legitimate autonomous systems (ASes). In addition, origin hijacking can even cause people to incur huge financial losses. On 3 February 2022, malevolent actors perpetrated a similar hijacking of the prefix belonging to the South Korean cryptocurrency exchange KLAYswap, resulting in the illicit extraction of 2 million

R. Chen et al. (Eds.): Inscrypt 2025, LNCS 16409, pp. 253–271, 2026.
https://doi.org/10.1007/978-981-95-6203-9_14

dollars from the users within a relatively brief time frame [34]. In light of these developments, it becomes evident that the resolution of BGP security concerns, especially the mitigation of origin hijacking, is of paramount importance as an urgent and indispensable imperative within the domain of cybersecurity.

Multiple Origin AS (MOAS) conflict represents a distinctive phenomenon in the Internet inter-domain routing system [11]. It occurs when the same IP address block is simultaneously announced by multiple Autonomous Systems. MOAS conflicts observed within the control plane may arise from either illicit sources, such as origin-hijacking, or legitimate circumstances, such as service modifications [4,15,36]. Origin-hijacking, a prevalent form of illicit MOAS conflict, stands as the most frequently encountered BGP threat within inter-domain routing systems [27,35]. Origin-hijacking incidents may arise from accidental misconfigurations by network operators or deliberate malicious attacks [10,23,31]. This phenomenon can be categorized into three main types: parent-prefix origin-hijacking, exact-prefix origin-hijacking, and child-prefix origin-hijacking [9]. Throughout this article, we use an indiscriminate mix of illegal MOAS conflict and origin-hijacking.

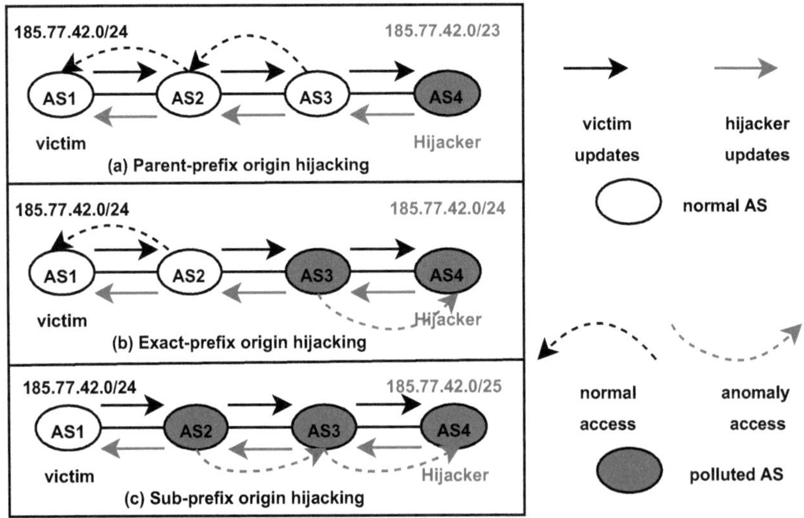

Fig. 1. Types of Origin Hijacking.

Parent prefix origin hijacking is a clandestine form of hijacking wherein the hijacking AS perpetrates the attack by asserting control over the parent prefix of the victim AS. Consider Fig. 1(a), where hijacker AS4 declares the parent prefix 185.77.42.0/23, which encompasses the legitimate prefix 185.77.42.0/24 owned by victim AS1. Due to the lower priority typically assigned to the parent prefix compared to its child prefix, although AS2 and AS3 have the parent prefix route announced by hijacker AS4 in their routing tables, traffic redirection does not occur. Traffic redirection for AS2 and AS3 only occurs when AS1 withdraws the prefix 185.77.42.0/24. Consequently, parent prefix origin hijacking inflicts relatively minor harm upon the Internet compared to other forms of hijacking.

The origin hijacking forms that exert a more significant impact on the Internet are exact prefix origin hijacking and sub-prefix origin hijacking. In exact prefix origin hijacking, the attacker AS and the victim AS simultaneously announce precisely the same prefix, depicted in Fig. 1(b). Both hijacker AS4 and victim AS1 announce the prefix 185.77.42.0/24 concurrently. As shorter paths typically carry higher priority, contaminated AS3, situated closer to hijacker AS4, enables false routing, leading to substantial traffic hijacking. Meanwhile, contaminated AS2, closer to victim AS1, continues to utilize normal routing. Consequently, exact prefix origin hijacking typically leads to abnormal traffic redirection or routing black holes in areas proximal to the hijacker AS. Sub-prefix origin hijacking occurs when the hijacker AS announces a more specific sub-prefix than the victim AS, as depicted in Fig. 1(c). In this scenario, hijacker AS4 declares a more specific prefix, 185.77.42.0/25, compared to the victim AS. Due to the higher priority of the hijacker's routed prefix, sub-prefix hijacking has the potential to contaminate the entire Internet. In Fig. 1(c), both contaminated AS3 and contaminated AS2 engage in false routing, influencing traffic transmission paths.

Current approaches to mitigating BGP origin hijacking can be broadly categorized into two classes: prevention mechanisms, which aim to eliminate the possibility of hijacking at its source, and detection mechanisms, which focus on promptly identifying and responding to hijacking events once they occur. In contrast to hijacking prevention technology, BGP hijacking detection solutions offer a more straightforward deployment process and necessitate fewer alterations to existing network infrastructure, rendering them more appealing to network operators [1,27]. Conventionally, origin hijacking detection methodologies have relied upon rule-based approaches [18,28,31]. However, in the face of increasingly sophisticated sub-prefix origin hijacking tactics, rule-based detection systems struggle to provide accurate identifications [8,10]. To address these shortcomings, detection methods rooted in machine learning have emerged as a promising alternative [2,3,5,8,17,29,30,33]. Machine learningâĂŞbased approaches demonstrate superior generalization compared to rule-based methods and can identify a broader spectrum of origin hijacking anomalies [8]. Among these, neural networks have gained prominence for their high detection accuracy [7,16,32]. However, these techniques also face significant challenges, the most significant of which is the lack of high detection accuracy.

One Important Factor Contributing to this Issue is the Scarcity of Ground Truth Data. Authentic origin-hijacking events are rarely reported [8], leaving previous detection schemes dependent on a small number of cases for feature extraction and model training. Detection models trained on such narrowly focused features may fail to identify anomalies with subtle impacts or smaller-scale BGP disruptions. For instance, Sun et al. developed a BNN detection model using nine prefix hijacking events, only achieving a modest accuracy of 72.6% [32]. Hoarau et al. have pointed out that while numerous BGP statistical and graph features can effectively identify large-scale anomalies, such as outages, they are less capable of detecting smaller-scale issues like origin-hijacking [13]. Therefore, it is a major challenge to collect bulk ground truth data and learn generic features that can accurately detect origin-hijacking anomalies.

An equally critical issue lies in the insufficient attention given to legitimate MOAS conflicts. Unlike origin-hijacking, which involves the deliberate announcement of prefixes by unauthorized ASes for malicious purposes, legitimate MOAS conflict events stem from operational practices, network optimizations, or policy implementations aimed at enhancing performance, reliability, or scalability. These conflicts arise from various factors, including inadvertent misconfigurations by network operators, migration of paths within AS, deployment of multi-origin policies by network operators, and implementation of traffic engineering strategies such as AS multi-homing, BGP anycast, or static path configurations [10,31]. Few research efforts have examined the interference posed by legitimate MOAS conflicts on origin-hijacking detection, and there is a notable lack of work aimed at enhancing detection capabilities by effectively filtering these legitimate conflicts. Indeed, the prominent form of MOAS on the Internet is legitimate MOAS conflicts [23,36], and these conflicts have exerted a substantial impact on the Internet. Imai et al. reported a 32.6-fold increase in such conflicts over the decade from 2008 to 2018, 98.8% of which were classified as benign [14].

In this study, we investigate the central question: **What interferes with the accurate detection of origin hijacking anomalies?** To this end, we manually curated a comprehensive dataset comprising 608 exact prefix origin hijacking events, 349 sub-prefix origin hijacking events, and 377 legitimate MOAS conflicts. Leveraging this real-world dataset, we systematically evaluate several state-of-the-art origin hijacking detection models to identify the primary factors contributing to reduced detection accuracy. In parallel, we conduct an in-depth analysis of the distinguishing features that separate legitimate MOAS conflicts from illegitimate ones. From this evaluation, we derive the following key insights:

- First, disregarding legitimate MOAS conflicts blurs the distinction between benign events and actual hijacks, representing a primary cause of diminished detection performance.
- Second, the choice of detection features exerts a greater influence on accuracy than refinements to model architecture.
- Third, all valid features exhibit a strong dependency on the hijacker AS, highlighting the critical relationship between the features used for Origin-hijacking detection and the hijacker AS itself.
- At last, incorporating an assessment of MOAS conflict legitimacy prior to hijack-type classification markedly enhances detection precision.

We conducted a detailed analysis of MOAS conflicts and extracted thirteen temporal features to effectively differentiate legitimate events from illegitimate ones. Integrating these features into machine learningâĂŞbased detection models significantly enhanced their performance. Experimental results demonstrate that filtering legitimate MOAS conflicts prior to origin hijacking classification improves the average detection precision by 12.3%, thereby substantially increasing the reliability of origin hijacking detection.

2 Data Collection

This study seeks to enhance origin hijacking detection by accurately distinguishing between legitimate and illegitimate MOAS conflicts. Achieving this goal requires the construction of a comprehensive ground truth dataset to assess whether legitimate MOAS conflicts are indeed the principal source of interference in current detection methods. To this end, we introduce two complementary approaches for the large-scale collection of both origin hijacking events and benign MOAS conflicts. For hijacking events, we leverage existing anomaly monitoring systems and deploy custom routing filters to collect large volumes of data, used primarily for data characterization and model training. For legitimate MOAS conflicts, we develop a Route Origin Verification (ROV) framework based on the Resource Public Key Infrastructure (RPKI) to systematically collect benign cases.

In this study, we propose leveraging an existing BGP anomaly detection system for the large-scale collection of origin hijacking data. These systems utilize customized internal algorithms to monitor BGP anomalies in real-time and publicly share detected anomalies, enabling efficient bulk acquisition of origin hijacking events. BGPmon [6], a widely recognized BGP anomaly monitoring system, exemplifies such a platform. It tracks anomalies such as origin hijacking, route leaks, and outages on the Internet, issuing timely alerts. Using BGPmon, we collected 1,272 origin hijacking events reported between November 1, 2022, and July 10, 2023. However, it is important to note that BGPmon has since been integrated into the Crosswork Cloud platform, and the anomaly data it monitors is no longer freely accessible to the public.

However, since the internal algorithms of the BGPmon system are not publicly available, the reliability of the origin hijacking data provided from BGPmon is not clear. Prior studies, including those by Cho [5] and Schlamp [26] et al., have highlighted the potential for misreporting in BGPmon's detected hijacking events. To address these concerns and enhance the reliability of the ground truth data, we implemented a three-tier manual filtering process. This process incorporates an RPKI filter, an IRR filter, and a topology filter, ensuring a more robust validation of the reported hijacking events.

The RPKI and IRR filters enhance dataset reliability by excluding BGPmon-reported origin hijacking events that align with trusted prefix origin data from ROV (based on ROA in RPKI) and IRR databases. These sources document authorized prefix announcements and ownership across global registries. In contrast, topology filters use AS-level relationships to detect implausible hijacks. Since an AS is unlikely to hijack its upstream provider, which can filter such routes, events where the attacker is downstream of the victim AS are excluded as unlikely hijacks.

Out of the 1,272 origin hijacking events collected, the RPKI filter identified 183 records, the IRR filter identified 50 records, and the topology filter identified 82 records consistent with benign routing. To err on the side of caution, we classified all suspicious events flagged by the filters as misclassifications. This led to the final dataset of 957 highly plausible origin hijacking events, comprising 608 exact prefix hijackings and 349 sub-prefix hijackings. For analysis purposes, each origin hijacking event is represented by a quintuple consisting of <*victim prefix, victim ASN, hijacker prefix, hijacker ASN, occurrence time*>.

Few studies have proposed methods for the large-scale collection of legitimate MOAS conflict events, with only a limited number of examples described in the literature. In this paper, we propose utilizing RPKI to collect legitimate MOAS conflict events in bulk. Given that the impact of origin hijacking events on legitimate MOAS conflicts remains unclear, and considering the time-sensitive nature of origin hijacking events, we restrict the collection of legitimate MOAS conflicts to those occurring within one hour before and after each origin hijacking event. This time window ensures that only those legitimate MOAS conflicts that most accurately reflect the conditions during an origin hijacking event are considered, minimizing the potential interference from other network factors.

By cross-referencing the collected MOAS conflicts with Route Origin Authorization (ROA) records in the ROV database, this study identifies the subset of conflicts observable in the global routing table and designates them as the final set of legitimate MOAS conflicts. The resulting dataset captures representative operational scenarios, including anycast deployment, multi-homing configurations, and prefix migration. In total, 377 legitimate MOAS conflict events were identified, each represented as a quintuple. While this dataset does not encompass every possible operational practice, it reflects the most prevalent scenarios in real-world Internet environments and thereby provides a representative foundation for evaluating subsequent detection methods.

It should be emphasized that the objective of this study is to differentiate legitimate MOAS conflicts from illegitimate ones, rather than to pursue a fine-grained taxonomy of distinct categories within legitimate conflicts. Although legitimate conflicts may arise from heterogeneous operational practices—such as anycast deployment, multi-homing, or prefix migration—they are indistinguishable at the level of the global routing table, where they all appear as multiple ASes originating the same prefix. From an anomaly detection perspective, legitimate conflicts generally exhibit stable and recurrent BGP activity patterns, reflecting persistent operational intent. This characteristic stands in sharp contrast to the abrupt and ephemeral nature of illegitimate conflicts. Consequently, legitimate conflicts can be modeled and processed in a unified manner. Table 1 presents a summary of the ground-truth datasets constructed for this study.

Within the context of legitimate MOAS conflicts, the notions of "attacker" and "victim" lack the inherently adversarial connotations they possess in malicious hijacking scenarios. Following the role definitions proposed by Qin et al. [23], this study adopts the convention that, in exact-prefix legitimate MOAS conflicts, the AS that first originates the prefix is designated as the "victim,"

Table 1. Ground truth dataset (November 1, 2022 to July 10, 2023).

	illegal MOAS conflicts (origin hijacking)		Legal MAOS conflict dataset
	Exact-prefix	Sub-prefix	
Number	608	349	377

while the AS that subsequently originates it is designated as the "attacker." In subprefix legitimate MOAS conflicts, the AS announcing the more specific (subprefix) route is labeled the "attacker," whereas the AS announcing the covering (parent) prefix is labeled the "victim." This role assignment is grounded in the operational characteristics of legitimate MOAS conflicts, which typically stem from intentional ISP configurations driven by business requirements. Accordingly, the assignment of "attacker" and "victim" roles based on announcement order and prefix hierarchy provides a practical and analytically consistent foundation for subsequent modeling and evaluation.

To capture the transient characteristics in each MOAS conflict event, we rely on the CAIDA-provided BGPstream tool for accessing historical BGP data. BGPstream serves as an invaluable open-source software framework designed to facilitate real-time and historical analysis of BGP data, catering to diverse applications including scientific research, operational monitoring, and post-event analysis [22]. Its primary data sources stem from widely recognized repositories such as RIPE RIS [20] and Route Views [21]. Leveraging Route Collectors (RCs) deployed worldwide, RIPE RIS and Route Views stand as two of the largest and most renowned BGP data collection platforms globally. For our analyses, we leverage BGP data sourced from the route collectors rrc00 and route-views2, recognized for their comprehensive global coverage and established reliability within the BGP community.

3 Question Analysis

Using origin hijacking incidents reported by BGPmon as karthika points, we employed BGPStream to collect the number of MOAS conflicts occurring within one hour before and after each event. Our analysis revealed a total of 19,117 AS pairs involved in MOAS conflicts between November 2022 and June 2023, whereas only 1,265 AS pairs were associated with the perpetrators and victims of origin-hijacking incidents during the same period. This stark contrast underscores the prevalence of legitimate MOAS conflicts on the Internet. It follows that methods solely reliant on detecting MOAS conflicts to ascertain the source of hijacking often yield a high false positive rate.

To quantify the extent to which legitimate MOAS conflicts degrade detection accuracy, we employ four state-of-the-art models to distinguish between legitimate and illegitimate MOAS events. Notably, illegitimate MOAS conflicts encompass both exact-prefix and sub-prefix origin hijacking incidents. The four models evaluated are: the multi-scale LSTM model for BGP anomaly classification (MS-LSTM) developed by Cheng et al. [2], the MLGF model incorporating BGP graph features proposed by Sanchez et al. [25], the Self-LSTM framework for BGP anomaly detection introduced by Dong et al. [8], and Themis, a MOAS classifier designed by Qin et al. [23]. Among the four models, the MS-LSTM, MLGF, and Self-LSTM models extract features by distinguishing origin-hijacking events from normal BGP routes, whereas the Themis model focuses on distinguishing legitimate MOAS conflicts from illegitimate ones. Additionally, the MS-LSTM, MLGF, and Self-LSTM models employ customized neural network architectures, while the Themis model utilizes a Limit Tree random forest algorithm.

In this study, we train and evaluate these models using the ground truth dataset constructed herein. To comprehensively assess their detection performance, we use precision, recall, F1 score, false negative rate (FNR), and false positive rate (FPR) as evaluation metrics. It is important to underscore that the primary objective of this experiment is to assess the capability of different detection models to discriminate between legitimate and illegitimate MOAS conflicts, thereby quantifying the actual impact of legitimate conflicts on the effectiveness of BGP origin hijacking detection. In the experimental design, illegitimate MOAS conflicts are designated as positive samples, whereas legitimate MOAS conflicts are designated as negative samples. To mitigate the influence of randomness and enhance the statistical reliability of the results, all reported outcomes are averaged over 30 independent runs. Further details about these evaluation metrics can be found in Appendix A. Table 2 presents a comparative analysis of the experimental results, summarizing the performance of the four state-of-the-art detection models selected for this study.

Table 2. The performance of four advanced detection models on the ground truth dataset.

Model	Precison	Recall	F1 score	FNR	FPR
Self-LSTM	86%	82%	0.83	5.1%	31.3%
MLGF	73%	61%	0.67	3.8%	74.3%
Themis	87%	84%	0.86	4.5%	26.7%
MS-LSTM	81%	79%	0.81	8.3%	58.8%

Table 2 highlights a key trend: while all detection models exhibit low false-negative rates, they suffer from disproportionately high false-positive rates. Even the weakest performer in terms of false-negative rates, MS-LSTM, only achieves a relatively low rate of 8.3%. In contrast, when examining false-positive rates, Themis, the best performer in this regard, still displays a notable false-positive rate of 26.7%. The MLGF model, which underperforms across all metrics, reaches an alarming false-positive rate of 74.4%. Notably, Themis, which explicitly distinguishes between legitimate and illegitimate MOAS conflicts, outperforms models that do not incorporate this distinction, particularly in false-positive metrics. On average, the false-positive rate of the MS-LSTM, MLGF, and Self-LSTM models is 28.1% higher than that of Themis. This discrepancy underscores a key limitation: detection models that overlook the role of legitimate MOAS conflicts in origin hijacking scenarios are prone to misclassify a significant number of benign events as anomalies, thereby undermining detection precision.

Additionally, Table 2 indicates that the MS-LSTM, Self-LSTM, and Themis models achieve comparable performance, with precision and recall differing by no more than 7%. In contrast, the MLGF model performs significantly worse, with precision and recall dropping to 73.2% and 60.9%, respectively—despite employing a more advanced detection framework than Themis. A closer examination reveals that the key difference lies in feature selection: whereas the other models primarily leverage BGP statistical features, the MLGF model relies exclusively on BGP graph features. This outcome suggests that BGP graph features alone are insufficient for effective origin hijacking detection, consistent with the findings of Hoarau et al. [12]. This finding underscores the critical importance of selecting suitable and effective detection features, which appears to contribute more to improving the accuracy of origin-hijacking detection than the sophistication of the detection model itself. When statistical features are incorporated into the MLGF model, its F1 score increases significantly to 0.85.

These findings suggest that the primary factor contributing to the low accuracy of current machine learningâĂŞbased origin hijacking detection models is their tendency to misclassify legitimate MOAS conflicts as hijacking events, which is an issue that significantly undermines both the accuracy and precision of detection. To improve detection accuracy, the critical challenge lies in minimizing the substantial interference caused by legitimate MOAS conflicts.

4 Characterization of the MOAS Conflicts

The results in Table 2 highlight that neglecting legitimate MOAS conflicts can obscure the distinction between origin-hijacking events and legitimate MOAS conflicts, significantly compromising both the accuracy and precision of detection outcomes. In this subsection, we aim to enhance origin-hijacking anomaly detection by analyzing the underlying relationship between legitimate and illegitimate MOAS conflicts to identify features that can effectively distinguish between the two. Extracting column features from BGP data streams has been the prevailing approach in feature selection for machine learning-based origin-hijacking detection. These approaches segment the BGP data stream into time sequences using predefined intervals and compute relevant features within these time slices [10]. The resulting features can be classified into two categories: BGP statistical features and BGP graph features [32].

BGP statistical features capture metrics such as the number of advertised routes, withdrawn routes within a specified time window, and AS path-related statistics. In contrast, BGP graph features are derived from a BGP topology graph, where ASes serve as nodes and AS connections as edges. These features include graph metrics such as the number of nodes, the number of edges, the graph diameter, and centrality measures, offering insights into the structural properties of the BGP topology. However, previous methods primarily compared origin-hijacking events with normal BGP routes to identify effective features. Consequently, while these methods derived a range of features from BGP data streams, their ability to accurately distinguish the legitimacy of MOAS conflicts remains unproven.

We select a set of features, previously shown to be effective in detecting origin hijacking anomalies in other literatures, as candidate indicators for assessing the legitimacy of MOAS conflicts [5,13,25]. Building on this foundation, we further develop BGP statistical and graph-based features from two complementary perspectives: that of the hijacker AS and the route collector. Features from the hijacker AS perspective are extracted from routes closely associated with the suspected hijacker, including the number of BGP updates announced or withdrawn by the AS, and AS paths containing the AS. These features capture temporal patterns directly reflective of the hijacker's behavior. In contrast, features from the route collector perspective are derived from BGP routing data observed at a global vantage point, offering insight into the broader routing dynamics of the Internet at a given moment.

To support data collection and processing, this study utilizes the BGP feature extraction framework BML proposed by Hoarau et al. [12]. BML enables efficient derivation of multidimensional statistical and graph features through customizable transformation modules. Building on this capability, we further developed a tailored temporal feature transformation model to capture fine-grained characteristics of MOAS conflict events. For each identified conflict, we define a two-hour observation window centered on its occurrence, spanning one hour before and one hour after the event. Within this window, BGP update streams are segmented into one-minute intervals, and the temporal transformation model in BML is applied to compute feature values for each slice. A detailed specification of the candidate temporal features employed to characterize MOAS conflicts is provided in the supplementary materials.

However, unlike conventional numerical features, dynamic features derived from the BGP data stream manifest as time series, posing challenges in their evaluation using traditional feature selection methodologies. To address this challenge, we propose a feature screening algorithm grounded in Jensen-Shannon divergence, aimed at assessing time series feature effectiveness. JS divergence, short for Jensen-Shannon Divergence, serves as a pivotal method for quantifying the resemblance between two probability distributions [19]. Notably, it adeptly gauges disparities in the overall configuration of distributions and exhibits robustness across varying sample sizes. Its value range spans from 0 to 1, wherein 0 signifies identical distributions and 1 denotes complete dissimilarity.

The methodology employed in this study involves pairwise comparison of all MOAS conflicts, followed by an evaluation of their validity based on the JS dispersion for each pair in specific features, as illustrated in Fig. 2. Specifically, MOAS conflicts are classified into three categories: exact-prefix Origin-hijacking,

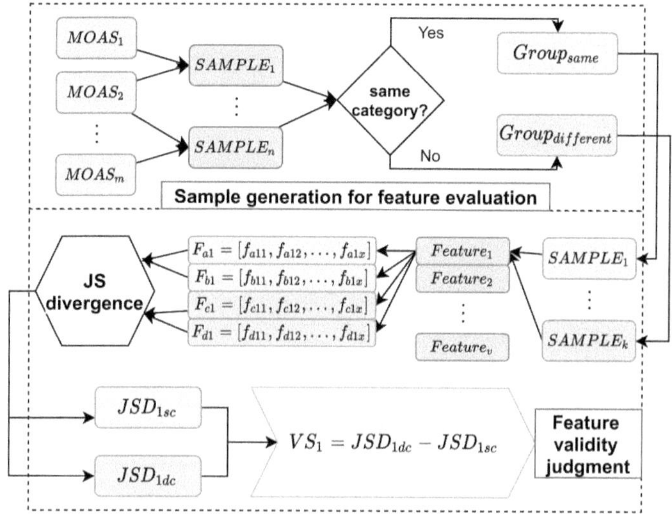

Fig. 2. Time dimension feature selection algorithm based on JS divergence.

sub-prefix Origin-hijacking, and legitimate MOAS conflicts. First, we pair MOAS events and label each pair to determine whether the events belong to the same category. This generates two datasets for feature evaluation: $Group_{same}$ and $Group_{different}$. For each feature, we compute two metrics: JSD_{sc} and JSD_{dc}. JSD_{sc} represents the average JS scatter value of a candidate feature computed from the MOAS pairs in the $Group_{same}$ dataset, while JSD_{dc} denotes the average JS scatter value of the candidate feature for pairs in the $Group_{different}$ dataset. Finally, we use JSD_{sc} and JSD_{dc} to derive the"validity score" (VS), a metric used to evaluate the validity of candidate temporal features.

The validity score VS is a metric introduced in this study to assess the capacity of candidate temporal features to distinguish legitimate MOAS conflicts from illegitimate ones. We hypothesize that valid features will exhibit smaller average JS scatter values for pairs within the same category of MOAS conflicts, and larger values for pairs across different categories. Consequently, the validity score VS is defined as the difference between the JSD_{dc} and JSD_{c} of a feature. A higher validity score indicates that the feature is more effective in distinguishing between exact-prefix Origin-hijacking, sub-prefix Origin-hijacking, and legitimate MOAS conflicts.

$$VS = JS_{dc} - JS_{sc} \tag{1}$$

To adapt the JS scatter for similarity calculation in time-series features, we introduce minor adjustments to its standard computation process. For two feature sequences, $p = [p_1, p_2, ..., p_n]$ and $q = [q_1, q_2, ..., q_n]$, we begin by applying min-max normalization to both sequences to enhance the stability of the comparison results.

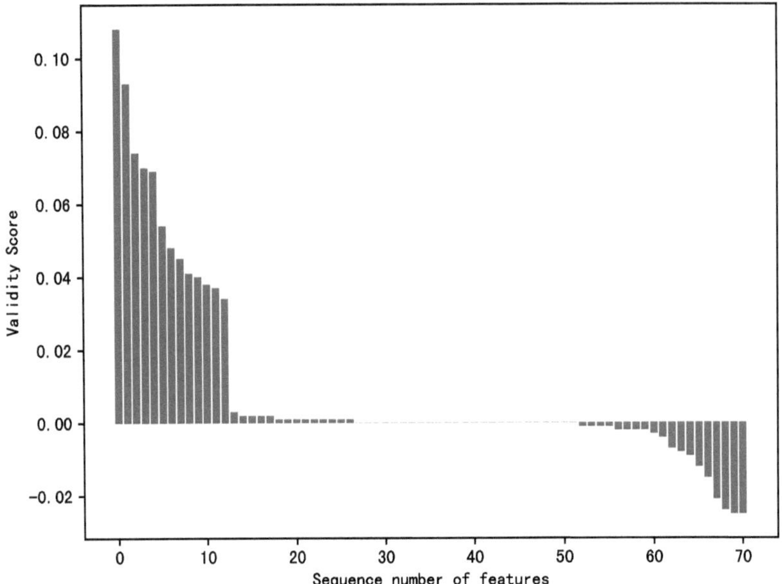

Fig. 3. Schematic diagram of the validity score results of the features of interest.

$$p^{'} = \frac{p_i - p_{min}}{p_{max} - p_{min}}, q^{'} = \frac{q_i - q_{min}}{q_{max} - q_{min}} \tag{2}$$

Next, we compute the mean distribution M of the two probability distributions, p and q, and calculate the Kullback-Leibler (KL) scatter values from both distributions to the mean distribution M.

$$M = \sum_{i=1}^{n} \frac{p_i + q_i}{2} \tag{3}$$

$$KL(p \parallel M) = \sum p(i) log(\frac{p(i)}{M(i)}) \tag{4}$$

$$KL(q \parallel M) = \sum q(i) log(\frac{q(i)}{M(i)}) \tag{5}$$

Finally, the feature-specific JS scatter value is determined as the average of the KL scatter values from distributions p and q to the mean distribution M.

$$JS(p \parallel q) = \frac{1}{2} KL(p \parallel M) + \frac{1}{2} KL(q \parallel M) \tag{6}$$

We computed the effectiveness evaluation results for all candidate temporal features. Figure 3 presents a schematic illustration of the effectiveness score outcomes for all features of interest. The feature sequence numbers depicted in Fig. 3 are arranged in descending order based on the VS (Validity Score), aligning

Table 3. List of selected valid time features.

Feature name	Description	JS_{dc}	JS_{sc}	VS
nb_new_A_hijacker	The number of new announcements in the hijacker AS that are not stored in the RIB.	0.353	0.245	0.108
nb_A_hijacker	Number of BGP updates announced by the hijacker AS	0.344	0.251	0.093
nb_dup_A_hijacker	Number of BGP updates duplicate announced by the hijacker AS	0.361	0.287	0.074
nb_implicit_W_hijacker	Number of BGP updates implicitly withdrawn by the hijacker AS	0.355	0.285	0.07
nb_toshorter_hijacker	The number of BGP updates received by the hijacker AS for shorter paths compared to the previous path from the same collector.	0.354	0.285	0.069
nb_A_prefix_hijacker	Number of prefixes advertised by the hijacker AS.	0.33	0.276	0.054
max_path_len_hijacker	The maximum path length of all messages announced by the hijacker AS	0.314	0.266	0.048
max_editdist_hijacker	The maximum path edit distance of all messages announced by the hijacker AS	0.324	0.279	0.045
avg_path_len_hijacker	The average path edit distance of all messages announced by the hijacker AS	0.32	0.279	0.041
max_A_prefix_hijacker	Maximum number of advertisements per prefix advertised by the hijacker AS	0.346	0.306	0.04
avg_A_prefix_hijacker	The average number of advertisements per prefix advertised by the hijacker AS	0.342	0.304	0.038
nb_tolonger_hijacker	The number of BGP updates received by the hijacker AS for longer paths compared to the previous path from the same collector.	0.358	0.321	0.037
avg_editdist_hijacker	The average path edit distance of all messages announced by the hijacker AS	0.318	0.284	0.034

with the feature IDs outlined in Supplementary Material. Upon examination of Fig. 3, we discern that only 13 features exhibit notable efficacy in distinguishing between various types of MOAS events, as summarized in Table 3.

Table 3 indicates that all 13 valid features are derived from BGP statistical features observed from the perspective of the hijacker AS. In contrast, features based on the route collector's perspective are less effective in identifying the legitimacy of MOAS conflicts, whose specific details please provided in the supplementary materials. All features exhibit a strong dependency on the hijacker AS, highlighting the critical relationship between the features used for Origin-hijacking detection and the hijacker AS itself. Furthermore, Table 3 reveals that BGP statistical features are more effective than BGP graph features in Origin-hijacking detection, as evidenced by the predominance of statistical features among the selected ones.

We also observed instances where the validity scores VS for certain features yielded negative values. Negative values of VS indicate that these features are effective at distinguishing MOAS conflicts within the same category but perform poorly in differentiating conflicts across different categories. This suggests that the selection of inappropriate features not only undermines the ability to distinguish between legitimate and illegitimate MOAS conflicts but also increases the likelihood of misclassification.

5 Experimentation and Analysis

Through extensive characterization of MOAS conflicts, we identified 13 effective features. However, the effectiveness of these features in accurately identifying specific origin hijacking subtypes, namely exact-prefix and sub-prefix origin hijacking, remains unclear. Likewise, their relative utility in assessing the legitimacy of MOAS conflicts has yet to be fully evaluated. To address these questions, we designed two complementary experiments to assess:

- **Task 1**: The discriminative power of the proposed features in distinguishing legitimate MOAS conflicts from illegitimate ones.
- **Task 2**: The effectiveness of these features in differentiating between exact-prefix and sub-prefix origin hijacking events.

The distinction between Task 1 and Task 2 lies in their scope of evaluation. Task 1 is a coarse-grained assessment, where the goal is not to identify specific types of Origin-hijacking events but rather to distinguish legitimate MOAS conflicts from illegitimate ones. In contrast, Task 2 involves the direct identification of precise prefix Origin-hijacking and sub-prefix Origin-hijacking events. Consequently, Task 1 is framed as a binary classification problem, while Task 2 is a multi-class classification problem with three categories.

To evaluate the effectiveness of the proposed features, we adopt two baseline models: the Random Forest (RF) classifier and the Temporal Convolutional Network (TCN). Both are well-established and widely used in classification tasks. The RF model is particularly effective in scenarios involving large datasets and potential noise, making it well-suited for tasks emphasizing feature engineering. In contrast, the TCN model excels at handling time-series data due to its capacity to capture temporal dependencies. To enable the RF model to leverage the two-dimensional structure of temporal features (i.e., feature counts across time steps), we transform them into a one-dimensional representation by concatenating along the feature-count dimension. We evaluate model performance using accuracy and F1 score as metrics.

Table 4. The actual performance of two models in Task 1 and Task 2.

	Task 1		Task 2	
	RandomForest	TCN	RandomForest	TCN
Accuracy	90%	91%	78%	79%
F1 score	0.9	0.9	0.76	0.79

Table 4 presents the experimental results for two test models applied to Task 1 and Task 2. As shown, it highlights a key observation: the ability of two detection model to distinguish legitimate MOAS conflicts from illegitimate ones (Task 1) substantially exceeds their ability to accurately identify specific subtypes of origin hijacking (Task 2). The average accuracy for the two models in distinguishing legitimate from illegitimate MOAS conflicts is 90.5%, with an average F1 score of 0.9. In contrast, when identifying specific types of prefix origin hijacking events, the average accuracy drops to 78.5%, with an average F1 score of 0.775. This discrepancy suggests that machine learning-based methods are more proficient at distinguishing between legitimate and illegitimate MOAS conflicts but less effective at accurately classifying the precise subtypes of origin hijacking, such as exact-prefix versus sub-prefix origin hijacking.

To validate the above conclusions, we conducted additional tests for Task 1 and Task 2 using the MS-LSTM, MLGF, Self-LSTM, and Themis models. The experimental results are presented in Fig. 4. As shown in Fig. 4, all four detection models exhibit significantly better performance in Task 1 than in Task 2. The average accuracy of the four detection models in Task 1 is 81.4%, whereas in Task 2, it drops to 69.1%, reflecting a 12.3% decrease. A similar trend is observed in the combined performance, where the average F1 score in Task 1 is 0.845, compared to 0.688 in Task 2, a difference of 0.157. Especially for the MLGF model, we can find that its performance in Task 2 has been turned into a stochastic classifier, which completely confuses precise prefix Origin-hijacking, sub-prefix Origin-hijacking as well as legitimate MOAS conflicts. These results closely mirror the performance observed in the two models presented in Table 4 for both Task 1 and Task 2, corroborating our previous conclusions.

These findings suggest that directly applying machine learning techniques to distinguish between exact-prefix Origin-hijacking, sub-prefix Origin-hijacking, and legitimate MOAS conflicts may introduce greater error in Origin-hijacking

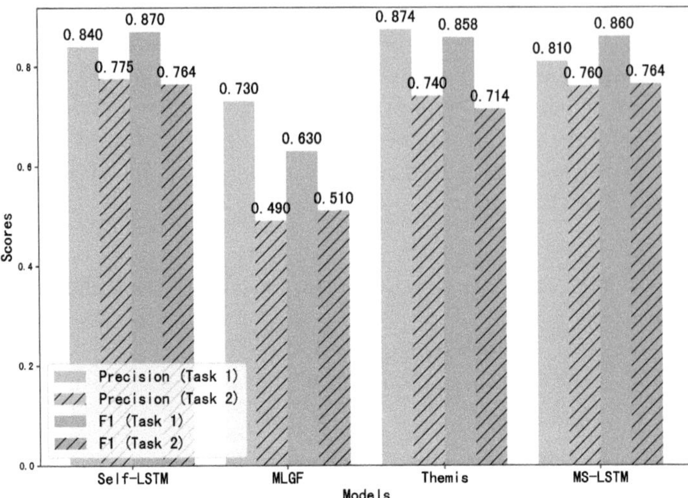

Fig. 4. The experimental results graph of four advanced detection models performing Task 1 and Task 2, respectively.

detection. A more effective approach could involve initially filtering legitimate MOAS conflicts before proceeding with refined Origin-hijacking detection, thereby improving accuracy. Based on these insights, we recommend prioritizing the identification of MOAS conflict legitimacy before determining the specific subtype of origin hijacking to improve detection precision.

6 Conclusion

Existing machine learning-based origin hijacking detection methods often suffer from low accuracy. In this study, we investigate the detrimental impact of legitimate MOAS conflicts on detection performance through a series of comparative experiments. Our findings provide compelling evidence that the high frequency of legitimate MOAS conflicts is a key factor contributing to the reduced accuracy of current detection approaches. To support this analysis, we utilize the existing anomaly detection system BGPmon to construct two ground truth datasets. We then identify thirteen effective features for distinguishing between legitimate and illegitimate MOAS conflicts. Notably, for dynamic feature selection, we propose a novel feature screening method based on Jensen-Shannon (JS) divergence tailored for time-series data. Experimental results confirm that incorporating a legitimacy assessment of MOAS conflicts prior to classifying origin hijacking types significantly improves detection precision.

Disclosure of Interests. The authors have no competing interests to declare that are relevant to the content of this article.

Appendix A

The confusion matrix is a prevalent tool in classification tasks, offering a comprehensive reflection of the classification results. It succinctly conveys the outcomes of binary classification tasks. By comparing predicted results with actual results, four scenarios can emerge: true positives (TP), false positives (FP), true negatives (TN), and false negatives (FN).

Precision, within the context of classification or statistical analysis, is quantitatively defined as the ratio of true positive instances to the total number of samples that have been classified as positive.

$$Precision = \frac{TP}{TP + FP}$$

The recall rate is defined as the proportion of all actual positive samples correctly categorized as positive by the model. Recall is also known as sensitivity, and it measures the model's ability to identify positive class samples.

$$Recall = \frac{TP}{TP + FN}$$

F_β score: more generally defined scores are:

$$F_\beta = (1 + \beta^2) * \frac{Precision * Recall}{(\beta^2 * Precision) + Recall}$$

The physical significance of this is that the two scores, precision and recall, are combined into a single score, and in the process of combining them, the recall is weighted twice as much as the precision. The $F1$ score considers recall and precision to be equally important, the $F2$ score considers recall to be twice as important as precision, and the $F0.5$ score considers recall to be half as important as precision.

The False Negative Rate (FNR) refers to the proportion of positive cases that are incorrectly predicted as negative (the rate of missed detections), and it is applicable in scenarios where the cost of missing true positives is high.

$$FNR = \frac{FN}{(TP + FN}$$

The False Positive Rate (FPR) refers to the proportion of negative instances that are incorrectly predicted as positive (false alarms), used in scenarios where the cost of false alarms is high.

$$FNR = \frac{FP}{(FP + TN}$$

In this paper, positive examples refer to illegal MOAS conflict events, while negative examples are legal MOAS conflict events.

References

1. Al-Musawi, B., Branch, P., Armitage, G.: BGP anomaly detection techniques: a survey. IEEE Commun. Surv. Tutorials **19**(1), 377–396 (2016)
2. Cheng, M., Li, Q., Lv, J., Liu, W., Wang, J.: Multi-scale LSTM model for BGP anomaly classification. IEEE Trans. Serv. Comput. **14**(3), 765–778 (2018)
3. Cheng, M., Xu, Q., Jianming, L., Liu, W., Li, Q., Wang, J.: MS-LSTM: a multi-scale LSTM model for BGP anomaly detection. In: 2016 IEEE 24th international conference on network protocols (ICNP), pp. 1–6. IEEE (2016)
4. Chin, K.W.: On the characteristics of BGP multiple origin as conflicts. In: 2007 Australasian Telecommunication Networks and Applications Conference, pp. 157–162. IEEE (2007)
5. Cho, S., Fontugne, R., Cho, K., Dainotti, A., Gill, P.: BGP hijacking classification. In: 2019 Network Traffic Measurement and Analysis Conference (TMA), pp. 25–32. IEEE (2019)
6. cisco: BGPMON (2024). https://crosswork.cisco.com/
7. Ding, Q., Li, Z., Batta, P., Trajković, L.: Detecting BGP anomalies using machine learning techniques. In: 2016 IEEE International Conference on Systems, Man, and Cybernetics (SMC), pp. 003352–003355. IEEE (2016)
8. Dong, Y., Li, Q., Sinnott, R.O., Jiang, Y., Xia, S.: ISP self-operated BGP anomaly detection based on weakly supervised learning. In: 2021 IEEE 29th International Conference on Network Protocols (ICNP), pp. 1–11. IEEE (2021)
9. Ghani, M.U., Khan, A., Hussain, S., Jhandir, M.Z., Kazmi, R., Bajwa, I.S.: PHDs: IP prefix hijack detection system. Pakistan J. Eng. Tech. **4**(1), 97–105 (2021)
10. Hammood, N.H., Al-Musawi, B.: Using BGP features towards identifying type of BGP anomaly. In: 2021 International Congress of Advanced Technology and Engineering (ICOTEN), pp. 1–10. IEEE (2021)
11. Hawkinson, J., Bates, T.: RFC 1930: guidelines for creation. Selection, and Registration of an Autonomous System (AS) (1996)
12. Hoarau, K., Tournoux, P.U., Razafindralambo, T.: BML: an efficient and versatile tool for BGP dataset collection. In: 2021 IEEE International Conference on Communications Workshops (ICC Workshops), pp. 1–6. IEEE (2021)
13. Hoarau, K., Tournoux, P.U., Razafindralambo, T.: Suitability of graph representation for BGP anomaly detection. In: 2021 IEEE 46th Conference on Local Computer Networks (LCN), pp. 305–310. IEEE (2021)
14. Imai, H., Okada, M., Kanaoka, A.: Poster: Moai: multiple origin ases identification for IP prefix hijacking and mis-origination. In: NDSS (2020)
15. Jacquemart, Q., Urvoy-Keller, G., Biersack, E.: A Longitudinal Study of BGP MOAS Prefixes. In: Dainotti, A., Mahanti, A., Uhlig, S. (eds.) TMA 2014. LNCS, vol. 8406, pp. 127–138. Springer, Heidelberg (2014). https://doi.org/10.1007/978-3-642-54999-1_11
16. Jia, M., Shu, Y., Guo, Q., Gao, Z., Xie, S.: DDOS attack detection method for space-based network based on SDN architecture. ZTE commun. **18**(4), 18–25 (2021)
17. Karimi, M., Jahanshahi, A., Mazloumi, A., Sabzi, H.Z.: Border gateway protocol anomaly detection using neural network. In: 2019 IEEE International Conference on Big Data (Big Data), pp. 6092–6094. IEEE (2019)
18. Lad, M., Massey, D., Pei, D., Wu, Y., Zhang, B., Zhang, L.: Phas: a prefix hijack alert system. In: USENIX Security symposium. vol. 1, p. 3 (2006)

19. Menéndez, M., Pardo, J., Pardo, L., Pardo, M.: The jensen-shannon divergence. J. Franklin Inst. **334**(2), 307–318 (1997)
20. NCC, R.: Ripe RIS (2024). https://www.ripe.net/analyse/internet-measurements/routing-information-service-ris/ris-raw-data
21. Oregon, U.: Routeviews (2024). http://www.routeviews.org/routeviews/
22. Orsini, C., King, A., Giordano, D., Giotsas, V., Dainotti, A.: Bgpstream: a software framework for live and historical BGP data analysis. In: Proceedings of the 2016 Internet Measurement Conference, pp. 429–444 (2016)
23. Qin, L., Li, D., Li, R., Wang, K.: Themis: accelerating the detection of route origin hijacking by distinguishing legitimate and illegitimate {MOAS}. In: 31st USENIX Security Symposium (USENIX Security 22), pp. 4509–4524 (2022)
24. Radar: Lumen aka centurylink is generating routing incidents via former level3 network, again (2020). https://radar.qrator.dev/blog/articles/101. Accessed 30 Aug 2023
25. Sanchez, O.R., Ferlin, S., Pelsser, C., Bush, R.: Comparing machine learning algorithms for BGP anomaly detection using graph features. In: Proceedings of the 3rd ACM CoNEXT Workshop on Big DATA, Machine Learning and Artificial Intelligence for Data Communication Networks, pp. 35–41 (2019)
26. Schlamp, J., Holz, R., Jacquemart, Q., Carle, G., Biersack, E.W.: Heap: reliable assessment of BGP hijacking attacks. IEEE J. Sel. Areas Commun. **34**(6), 1849–1861 (2016)
27. Sermpezis, P., Kotronis, V., Dainotti, A., Dimitropoulos, X.: A survey among network operators on BGP prefix hijacking. ACM SIGCOMM Comput. Commun. Rev. **48**(1), 64–69 (2018)
28. Sermpezis, P., et al.: Artemis: neutralizing BGP hijacking within a minute. IEEE/ACM Trans. Netw. **26**(6), 2471–2486 (2018)
29. Shapira, T., Shavitt, Y.: A deep learning approach for IP hijack detection based on ASN embedding. In: Proceedings of the Workshop on Network Meets AI and ML, pp. 35–41 (2020)
30. Shapira, T., Shavitt, Y.: Ap2vec: an unsupervised approach for BGP hijacking detection. IEEE Trans. Netw. Serv. Manage. **19**(3), 2255–2268 (2022)
31. Shi, X., Xiang, Y., Wang, Z., Yin, X., Wu, J.: Detecting prefix hijackings in the internet with argus. In: Proceedings of the 2012 Internet Measurement Conference, pp. 15–28 (2012)
32. Sun, J., et al.: An efficient BGP anomaly detection scheme with hybrid graph features. In: International Conference on Emerging Networking Architecture and Technologies, pp. 494–506. Springer (2022)
33. Testart, C., Richter, P., King, A., Dainotti, A., Clark, D.: Profiling BGP serial hijackers: capturing persistent misbehavior in the global routing table. In: Proceedings of the Internet Measurement Conference, pp. 420–434 (2019)
34. freedom-to tinker: attackers exploit fundamental flaw in the webs security to steal 2 million in cryptocurrency (2022). https://freedom-to-tinker.com/2022/03/09/attackers-exploit-fundamental-flaw-in-the-webs-security-to-steal-2-million-in-cryptocurrency/
35. Vervier, P.A., Thonnard, O., Dacier, M.: Mind your blocks: on the stealthiness of malicious BGP hijacks. In: NDSS (2015)
36. Zhao, X., et al.: An analysis of BGP multiple origin as (moas) conflicts. In: Proceedings of the 1st ACM SIGCOMM Workshop on Internet Measurement, pp. 31–35 (2001)

Network Security and Traffic Analysis

Verifiable and Privacy-Preserving Deep Packet Inspection for Multiple Rule Service Providers

Zhentao Long[1], Pengfei Wu[2], Kai Zhang[1(✉)], Junqing Gong[3], and Jianting Ning[4]

[1] College of Computer Science and Technology, Shanghai University of Electric Power, Shanghai 201306, China
zhentaolong@mail.shiep.edu.cn, kzhang@shiep.edu.cn

[2] School of Computing and Information Systems, Singapore Management University, Singapore, Singapore

[3] Software Engineering Insitute, East China Normal University, Shanghai 200062, China

[4] School of Cyber Science and Engineering, Wuhan University, Wuhan 430000, China
jtning@whu.edu.cn

Abstract. Secure outsourced middleboxes provide deep packet inspection (DPI) for encrypted traffic that enables the detection of malicious activities in communications. However, existing DPI systems generally support only a single rule service provider (RSP), whose rule sets are limited to specific attack types. This constraint reduces inspection coverage and diminishes the accuracy of detecting diverse malicious traffic. In this paper, we present MRv-DPI, a new privacy-preserving DPI system that supports inspection rules from multiple RSPs, enabling targeted inspection for any type of attack pattern. Additionally, by considering that the middleboxes may only use partial subscribed RSPs' rule sets to inspect each packet, our system also provides inspection results verification. To support multiple RSPs, MRv-DPI employs a key-homomorphic pseudo-random function, allowing matching between rules encrypted under distinct keys and packets encrypted under a shared key. For result verification, we design a temporal-hashed substring search trie based on trusted hardware, ensuring tamper-resistant verification against untrusted cloud-based middleboxes. To address efficiency challenges arising from increased rule sets across multiple RSPs, MRv-DPI segments both packets and rules, and assigns each rule a main sub-segment to facilitate fast filtering of benign packets. We evaluate MRv-DPI through comprehensive experiments using four public rule sets in a real client-to-server environment. Compared to existing DPI solutions, MRv-DPI not only enhances both security and functionality but also achieves up to 2× faster packet inspection and reduces communication overhead by 36.1% – 57.4%.

Keywords: Deep packet inspection · Privacy preserving · Multiple rule service providers · Key homomorphic pseudo-random function

R. Chen et al. (Eds.): Inscrypt 2025, LNCS 16409, pp. 275–295, 2026.
https://doi.org/10.1007/978-981-95-6203-9_15

1 Introduction

Network middleboxes [1] provide enterprises with advanced network functions, such as deep packet inspection (DPI) to filter malicious network traffic. To eliminate local maintenance cost and boost inspection efficiency [2], they are outsourced to the cloud as virtualized services. Nevertheless, the privacy concerns of both packet and rule are raised, since the middlebox perform rule matching function with access to the enterprises' traffic flows and the rule service provider's (RSP) inspection rule set.

Therefore, privacy-preserving DPI systems [3,4] are adopted to perform pattern matching over encrypted traffic and rules within middleboxes. However, the key limitation of existing DPI systems [5–8] is *only with support for a single RSP*, which fails to inspect multiple forms of malicious traffic due to limited inspection coverage. Additionally, the *restricted subscribed rules* may also lead to high false negatives due to the neglect of subtle features of known attacks.

For example, there are multiple types of malicious traffic in the middleboxes (e.g., "Scanning and Probing Traffic", "DDoS attack Traffic" and "Web Attack Traffic"). An enterprise may subscribe to a specific rule set `Portscan.rules` that is used to identify "scanning and probing Traffic", yet is infeasible for inspecting "DDoS attack Traffic" and "Web Attack Traffic". Consequently, the enterprise needs to subscribe to the corresponding inspection rules, since each of them is typically provided by different RSPs (e.g., McAfee, Palo Alto NGFW). To enable rule hidden from the middleboxes, each RSP encrypts its rules under distinct keys, which poses a significant challenge for existing DPI systems that only support single-key encrypted rule processing.

Nevertheless, trivially extending existing DPI systems [9,10] to support multiple RSPs incurs costly system re-setup for each rule subscription, since multiple re-encryptions of the same packet under different keys are required. Besides enabling matching between encrypted packet under a single key and rules encrypted under distinct keys, it seems challenging to design a direct efficient privacy-preserving DPI system for multiple RSPs. On the one hand, the support of multiple RSPs leads to a growing number of rule sets, inevitably decreasing the time efficiency of packet inspection. On the other hand, the untrusted cloud-based middlebox may only use partial subscribed RSPs' rule sets to inspect each packet, thus the inspection results are not convincing for the enterprises. Hence, a natural question is raised: *can we design an efficient and privacy-preserving DPI system for multiple rule service providers while also enabling inspection results verification?*

1.1 Our Contributions

To resolve the question, we propose MRv-DPI, a verifiable and privacy-preserving DPI system for multiple RSPs that offers the following new features:

- **New support for multiple rule service providers.** MRv-DPI allows enterprises to subscribe to multiple RSPs, enabling target inspection of malicious traffic of any type. To address the efficiency challenges arising from the increase in RSPs, MRv-DPI preprocesses both packets and rules that performs fast filtering of normal packets. Additionally, MRv-DPI ensures that enterprise packets are encrypted *only once*, even when matched with multiple rules that encrypted under distinct keys by different RSPs.

- **Inspection results verification with trusted hardware.** We propose $\mathsf{THS}^2\mathsf{Trie}$, a novel temporal-hashed substring search trie that checks whether the middlebox provides incomplete DPI service, i.e., using partial rules or selecting partial packets for inspection. Additionally, MRv-DPI ports $\mathsf{THS}^2\mathsf{Trie}$ into a trusted hardware, where the substring search function (for inspection results verification) is performed in an isolated and tamper-resistant environment. This guarantees the inspection rules confidentiality and the tamper-resistance of verification process against untrusted cloud-based middlebox.

Moreover, comprehensive experiments demonstrate that MRv-DPI outperforms Slimbox [5] and P2DPI [6]. Compared to Slimbox, MRv-DPI reduces communication cost by approximately 36.1% to 57.4% and improves inspection efficiency by roughly 2×. Compared to P2DPI, MRv-DPI achieves a 20× improvement for packet inspection overhead, and the inspection efficiency of MRv-DPI is not linearly influenced by the number of RSPs. Additionally, compared to the existing TEE-based verifiable DPI solution [9], our introduced TEE-based $\mathsf{THS}^2\mathsf{Trie}$ improves the verification of inspection results efficiency by approximately 42.3%.

1.2 Our Technique

Generally, we employ middlebox searchable encryption to perform matching between encrypted rules and encrypted packet, where they are preprocessed for boosting inspection efficiency. To enable *multiple RSPs* and *inspection results verification* in MRv-DPI, the technical challenges are summarized as follows:

- *How to support multiple RSPs.* The key challenge is to enable matching between encrypted packet under a single key and rules encrypted under distinct keys. By employing KH-PRF to design an interactive rule subscription protocol, both client enterprise (CE) and RSPs are allowed to obfuscate inspection rules via respective secret keys, i.e., $\mathsf{Enc}(K_{\mathsf{RSP}}, r) = F_{\mathsf{KH}}(K_{\mathsf{RSP}}, r) = g^{F(r)\cdot K_{\mathsf{RSP}}} \rightarrow g^{F(r)\cdot K_{\mathsf{RSP}}\cdot K_e} \rightarrow g^{F(r)\cdot K_{\mathsf{RSP}}\cdot K_e\cdot K_{\mathsf{RSP}}^{-1}} = F_{\mathsf{KH}}(K_e, r) = \mathsf{Enc}(K_e, r)$. That is, RSP computes $\mathsf{Enc}(K_{\mathsf{RSP}}, r)$ and sends it to CE, then CE returns the obfuscated one via $\mathsf{Enc}(K_{\mathsf{RSP}} \cdot K_e, r)$. Finally, RSP obtains $\mathsf{Enc}(K_e, r) \leftarrow \mathsf{Enc}((K_{\mathsf{RSP}} \cdot K_e) \cdot K_{\mathsf{RSP}}^{-1}, r)$, where r denotes a rule, K_{RSP} and K_e denotes the secret key of RSP and CE. With a blind factor and randomized position/offset, we encrypt the preprocessed packet as $(\mathsf{xpac}_k, \mathsf{cpac}_k, \beta, \alpha)$ and encrypt the preprocessed rule as $(\mathsf{x}R_*, \{\mathsf{x}R_k, \mathsf{c}R_k\})$. We compare the main rule segment $\mathsf{x}R_*$ and cpac_k for fast normal packets filtering, and restore the xpac_k by computing $\mathsf{x}R_k^{\beta} \cdot \mathsf{c}R_k^{\alpha}$ for subsequent matching with the remaining $\mathsf{x}R_k$ if the $\mathsf{x}R_*$ is matched.

- *How to achieve inspection results verification.* The key challenge is to port the execution of newly presented $\mathsf{THS^2Trie}$ into a **trusted hardware**, while mitigating rule leakage against side-channel attacks. For each rule that initialized as a path in $\mathsf{THS^2Trie}$, we perform substring search by setting failure pointers for fast traversing to alternative matching paths upon a node mismatched, and set prune pointers to improve storage efficiency. Additionally, to mitigate side-channel leakages, we obfuscate the content of each edge via a combination of a temporal hash function and binary encoding, i.e., $\mathsf{be(rule)}||\mathsf{H}_3(t)[: -d]$, where t denotes the edge creation time and $[: -d]$ represents the deletion of the last d bits of the hash. Since (t, d) vary across edges, it is infeasible for an adversary to distinguish or infer edge values via side-channel attacks, such as memory access pattern analysis.

2 Preliminaries

Notations. Let λ be the security parameter. A negligible function is denoted by $\mathsf{negl}(\lambda)$ and PPT denotes probabilistic polynomial time. We use $\{0,1\}^\lambda$ to denote the set of binary strings of length λ. For a string Str, $|\mathsf{Str}|$ denotes the length of Str and $\mathsf{Str}_1||\mathsf{Str}_2$ denotes the concatenation of two string Str_1 and Str_2. For a set E, $E[t]$ denotes t-th element of the set, where $t \in |E|$.

Definition 1 (Decisional DiffieâĂŞHellman (DDH)). *Let $\mathbb{G}$ be a finite cyclic group of a prime order p, generated by g. The DDH assumption holds in $\mathbb{G}$, if the distinguishing probability $\mathsf{Adv}_{\mathcal{A}}^{\mathsf{DDH}} = \Pr[\mathcal{A}(g, g^a, g^b, g^{ab}) = 1] - \Pr[\mathcal{A}(g, g^a, g^b, g^c)) = 1]$ is negligible for any PPT adversary $\mathcal{A}$, where a, b, c randomly chosen from $\mathbb{Z}_p^*$.*

Definition 2 (Pseudo-Random Function (PRF)). *The F is said to be a secure PRF if any PPT adversary $\mathcal{A}$'s probability $\mathsf{Adv}_{\mathcal{A},F}^{\mathsf{PRF}}(\lambda) = \Pr[\mathcal{A}^{F(K,\cdot)}(1^\lambda) = 1] - \Pr[\mathcal{A}^{\mathcal{F}(\cdot)}(1^\lambda) = 1]$ is negligible for distinguishing F from a truly random function $\mathcal{F}$, where $K \leftarrow \{0,1\}^\lambda$.*

Definition 3 (Key-Homomorphic PRF (KH-PRF).[11]) *Suppose that $k \in \mathbb{Z}_p$ is chosen uniformly at random, a function $F : \mathcal{X} \rightarrow Z_p$ is modeled as a random oracle. The KH-PRF F_{KH} is defined as $F_{\mathsf{KH}}(k, x) = g^{F(x)\cdot k}$, where a PPT adversary $\mathcal{A}$'s advantage for distinguishing F_{KH} from F is negligible.*

DDH-based instantiation of KH-PRF [6]. The instantiation achieves the properties $F_{\mathsf{KH}}(k_1, x) \rightarrow F_{\mathsf{KH}}(k_2, x)$, and $F_{\mathsf{KH}}(k_1, x)^{k_2} = F_{\mathsf{KH}}(k_1 \cdot k_2, x) \rightarrow F_{\mathsf{KH}}(k_1 \cdot k_2, x)^{k_1^{-1}} = F_{\mathsf{KH}}(k_2, x)$, where $k_1, k_2 \in \mathbb{Z}_p$, $x \in \mathcal{X}$ and k_1^{-1} is the inverse of k_1.

Definition 4 (Trusted Hardware). *We refer to a main processor with a secure hardware enclave as Trusted Execution Environment (TEE), which offers several key security features (e.g., Intel SGX). That is, (i) Memory Isolation: Data and code within the enclave are encrypted and stored separately to prevent unauthorized access; (ii) Remote Attestation: The integrity of the enclave is remotely verified, establishing a secure channel for data transmission; (iii) Storage Sealing: Enclave data is provided with encryption and authentication.*

3 Protocol Overview

Here, we present system model, threat model and design goals of MRv-DPI.

3.1 System Model

There are the following entities in the MRv-DPI system, as shown in Fig. 1.

- **Client Enterprise (CE):** It subscribes to any RSP, encrypts packets and sends them (ETS) to the **MB** for inspection, while sending sample packets to the **TEE** for inspection results verification.
- **Internal Gateway** (**IGW**) and **External Gateway** (**EGW**): The gateways in the internal and external network allow network traffic to flow from one endpoint to another endpoint, respectively.
- **Rule Service Provider (RSP):** It handles interactions with subscribers, encrypts its rules and sends them (ERS) to the **MB**, while deploying the raw rules on the **TEE** via remote attestation.
- **Cloud-based Middlebox (MB):** It is an untrusted entity that receives encrypted packets from **CE** and encrypted rules from **RSP**, and performs DPI and sends the inspection results to **TEE** and **CE**.
- **Trusted Execution Environment (TEE):** It is provided by trusted hardware that receives inspection results from the **MB** and verification requests from the **CE**, and performs inspection results verification for sample packets.

Discussion of the Trusted Hardware. Numerous works [12,13] have explored the security and potential leakage of the trusted hardware under side-channel attacks and its restricted EPC memory (typically 128-256MB) leads to frequent, slow swap with untrusted memory in processing high-volume network traffic, which drastically reduces the throughput. In this paper, we use the trusted hardware only for the verification phase and explicitly incorporate potential leaks induced by side-channel attacks and formally analyze its security threats to the proposed system.

3.2 Threat Model

Similar to [5,6], in MRv-DPI, the **CE** and **RSP**s are assumed to be trusted entities. The **MB**, is considered untrusted and may manipulate verification procedures. Furthermore, **RSP**s do not reveal their inspection rule information to any party. There is assumed no collusion between any **CE** and the **MB**.

Let Π be an MRv-DPI system, $\mathcal{S}$ be a simulator and $\mathcal{A}$ be a stateful adversary. The adaptive security of Π is simulated by an interaction that described in $\mathsf{Real}_{\mathcal{A}}^{\Pi}$ and $\mathsf{Ideal}_{\mathcal{A},\mathcal{S}}^{\Pi}$, where $\mathsf{Real}_{\mathcal{A}}^{\Pi}$ is the real execution of Π and $\mathsf{Ideal}_{\mathcal{A},\mathcal{S}}^{\Pi}$ simulates the execution by $\mathcal{S}$ with information leakage $\mathcal{L} = (\mathcal{L}^{\mathsf{PackEnc}}, \mathcal{L}^{\mathsf{RuleEnc}}, \mathcal{L}^{\mathsf{TEE}})$.

- $\mathsf{Real}_{\mathcal{A}}^{\Pi}(\lambda)$: $\mathcal{A}$ obtains encrypted packet ETS and encrypted rule ERS based on the execution results of $\mathsf{PackEnc}(\cdot)$ and $\mathsf{RuleEnc}(\cdot)$. Then, it executes a polynomial number of inspections via running the $\mathsf{Inspection}(\cdot)$ algorithm. Finally, $\mathcal{A}$ outputs a bit as output.

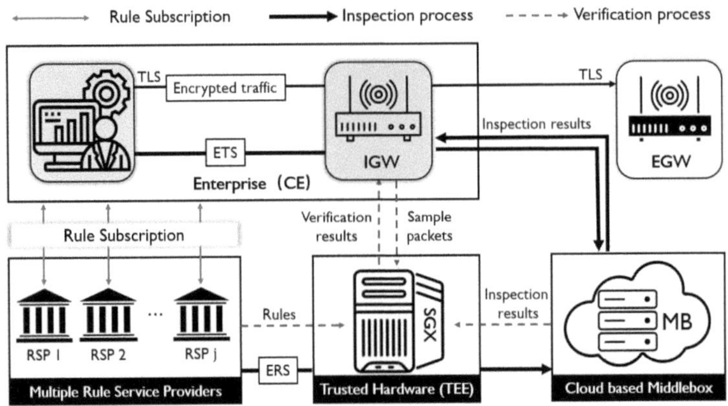

Fig. 1. System model of MRv-DPI.

- $\mathsf{Ideal}^{\Pi}_{\mathcal{A},\mathcal{S}}(\lambda)$: By the leakage function $\mathcal{L}$, $\mathcal{S}$ generates ETS and ERS to $\mathcal{A}$ via running $\mathcal{S}(\mathcal{L}^{\mathsf{PackEnc}})$ and $\mathcal{S}(\mathcal{L}^{\mathsf{RuleEnc}})$. Finally, $\mathcal{A}$ outputs a bit as output.

Assuming the simulator $\mathcal{S}$, we say $\prod$ is $\mathcal{L}$-semantically secure against any PPT adversary $\mathcal{A}$ if $\Pr[\mathsf{Real}^{\Pi}_{\mathcal{A}}(\lambda) = 1] - \Pr[\mathsf{Ideal}^{\Pi}_{\mathcal{A},\mathcal{S}}(\lambda) = 1] \leq \mathsf{negl}(\lambda)$ where $\mathsf{negl}(\lambda)$ is negligible.

Definition 5 (Privacy of Packet). *We say that MRv-DPI achieves Privacy of Packet if the packet encryption leakage function is written as $\mathcal{L}_1 = \mathcal{L}^{\mathsf{PackEnc}}$, where $\mathcal{L}_1$ is stateless.*

Definition 6 (Rule Hiding). *We say that MRv-DPI achieves Rule Hiding if the rule encryption leakage function is written as $\mathcal{L}_2 = \mathcal{L}^{\mathsf{RuleEnc}}$, where $\mathcal{L}_2$ is stateless.*

Definition 7 (Memory Access Pattern Security). *We say that MRv-DPI achieves memory access pattern security if the access pattern of any two verifications reveals the same leakage, that written as $\mathcal{L}_3 = \mathcal{L}^{\mathsf{TEE}}$, where $\mathcal{L}_3$ is stateless.*

3.3 Design Goals

The design goals of our proposed MRv-DPI are presented as follows:

- *Multiple RSPs:* MRv-DPI supports inspection rules from different **RSP**s, which enables inspection of malicious traffic in multiple types.
- *Packets inspection:* MRv-DPI achieves high inspection efficiency, and retains similar functionality of classic privacy-preserving DPI (i.e., to find a malicious token in the payload).
- *Inspection results verification:* MRv-DPI enables verification of inspection results from the **MB** based on the trusted hardware, ensuring that a **CE** obtains complete and correct DPI services.

- *Privacy of packet:* The **MB** learns no information about the traffic from the encrypted packets, including the frequency of any packet, even when all encrypted rules are mismatched.
- *Rule hiding:* The **MB** and **CE** learn nothing about inspection rule information from the encrypted rules provided by each **RSP**.
- *Side-channel resistance:* MRv-DPI addresses potential leakages from the **TEE** induced by side-channel attacks (e.g., memory access pattern), and formally analyzes the security threats posed to the proposed system.

4 MRv-DPI

In this section, we show how to construct a $\mathsf{THS^2Trie}$ in Sect. 4.1, then present a formal description of MRv-DPI in Sect. 4.2.

In Fig. 2, we provide an architecture overview of MRv-DPI. Specifically, a **CE** performs rule subscription to different **RSP** in an interaction way. For packet and rule encryption, a **CE** preprocesses each packet into fixed-length segments and randomizes them, then sends the encrypted preprocessed packets to **MB**; the **RSP**s additionally selects a main segment for each rule besides similarly preprocessing and encrypting its rules, and sends them to **MB**. For packet inspection, the **MB** inspects the main rule segment for fast filtering and continues pattern matching of remaining segments if the main segment is matched, and sends the inspection results to **CE** and **TEE**. Finally, **TEE** traverses the $\mathsf{THS^2Trie}$ to verify the inspection results over the sample packets, where the $\mathsf{THS^2Trie}$ is constructed by each **RSP** and ported into **TEE**.

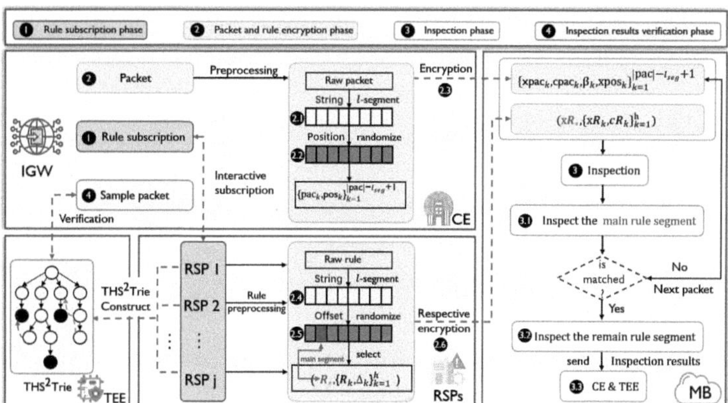

Fig. 2. Architecture Overview of MRv-DPI.

4.1 THS²Trie: Temporal-Hashed Substring Search Trie

As illustrated in Algorithm 1, we design a trie-based data structure THS^{2}Trie that supports efficient substring search, while the structural privacy of the trie is preserved via obfuscating the string representations based on temporal-hash and binary encoding. Formally, THS^{2}Trie consists of the following phases:

- **Construction.** The trie construction consists of three steps: building, pruning, and encoding. First, each input string forms a branch of the THS^{2}Trie, where characters are stored on edges and nodes maintain auxiliary search information. Then, THS^{2}Trie prunes redundant output nodes and associated edges, with a pruning ptr set to link to the corresponding unified output node. By setting a failure ptr based on all the input strings, THS^{2}Trie enables efficient redirect traversal upon mismatches which accelerates the overall search process. Finally, to protect string privacy, edge representations are obfuscated using a combination of temporal-hash function and binary encoding: be(rStr)$||H_3(t)[: -d]$, where t denotes the creation time of the edge and $[: -d]$ denotes the deletion of the last d bits.
- **Substring Search.** Given the input string pStr, THS^{2}Trie computes the be(pStr)$||H_3(t)[: -d]$ to match the obfuscated edge. If matched, it checks the label of the corresponding node to determine whether to trigger the output operation (vRes[pStr] $\leftarrow$ rStr_id). In addition, following the failure ptr, THS^{2}Trie enables a fast search for all predefined substrings that are present in pStr. Finally, THS^{2}Trie returns the results in the form of {rStr_id}.

Algorithm 1. THS²Trie

```
function Construct(rStr)
    for d = 1 to |rStr| − 1 do
        be(rStr(d)) ←(Binary encoding)— rStr[d]
        edge = be(rStr[d])||H3(t)[: −d]
        if d = |rStr| − 1 then
            label = rStr_id
            if rStr(d) existed then
                prune the node
                set pruning ptr
            end if
        else
            label = #
        end if
        set failure ptr
        node = (ptr, t, label, h)
    end for
end function

function Substr_Search(pStr)
    vRes ← ∅
    for i = 0 to |pStr| − 1 do
        (ptr, t, label, d) ← node
        edge′ ← be(pStr[i])||H3(t)[:-d]
        if edge′ == edge then
            if label ≠ # then
                rStr_id ← label
                vRes[pStr] ← rStr_id
            else
                Search child node
            end if
        else
            Check failure ptr
        end if
    end for
    Return vRes
end function
```

An example of THS^{2}Trie **in MRv-DPI.** Fig. 3 illustrates an application example of employing THS^{2}Trie in MRv-DPI. Generally, in THS^{2}Trie, rules are represented as branches of the trie and the input packets are processed as search strings, therefore, all rules matched by the input packets are output.

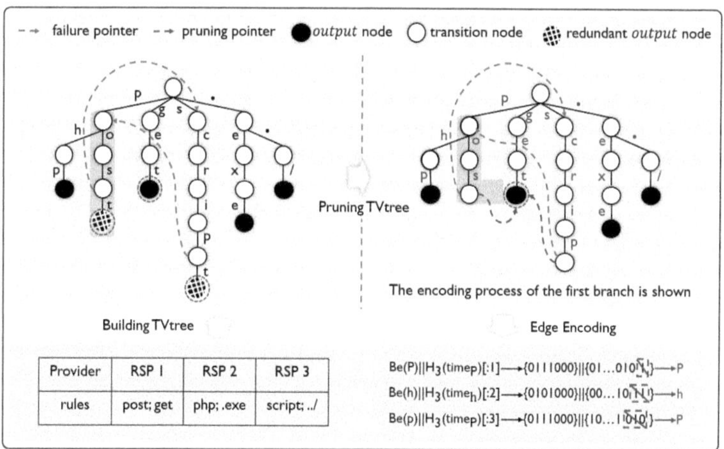

Fig. 3. An example of THS^{2}Trie in MRv-DPI with a traffic "ge.exe@evil_poscript.php". The traversing path is "g $\rightarrow$ e (returning to the root node) $\rightarrow$ $(\cdot, e, \mathrm{x}, e)$ $\rightarrow$ (output:.exe) $\rightarrow$ $(\cdots)$ $\rightarrow$ (p,o) $\rightarrow$ $s(failurepointer)$ $\rightarrow$ c $\rightarrow$ $(\cdots)$ $\rightarrow$ p (pruning pointer) $\rightarrow$ $t(output : script)$ $\rightarrow$ p $\rightarrow$ h $\rightarrow$ p $(output : php)$", and the matching results is (.exe, script, php).

4.2 Formal Construction of MRv-DPI

Here, we provide a formal description of the MRv-DPI in Algorithm 2. Let $H_1, H_2, H_3 : \{0,1\}^* \times \{0,1\}^* \rightarrow \{0,1\}^\lambda$ be hash functions, $F_S, F_Y : \{0,1\}^\lambda \times \{0,1\}^* \rightarrow \mathbb{Z}_p^*$ be a secure PRF with a secret key, where p is a large prime, and $\mathsf{Enc}(k, x) = F_{\mathsf{KH}}(k, x) = g^{F(x) \cdot k}$ be a secure KH-PRF. The $(K, K_e, K_x, K_{\mathsf{rp}}, z_j)$ are randomly selected from $\mathbb{Z}_p^*$, and K_y is randomly chosen from $\{0,1\}^\lambda$, where z_j denotes a blinding factor randomly selected by the j-th **RSP**. Formally, the detailed phases of MRv-DPI are presented as follows:

- **Rule Subscription Phase.** MRv-DPI employs KH-PRF to let **CE** and **RSP** obfuscate inspection rules via their individual keys, ensuring that the encrypted traffic under a single key can be matched with rules encrypted under different keys. For example, a **CE** subscribes to RSPs (resp., $\mathrm{RSP}_1, \mathrm{RSP}_2, \ldots, \mathrm{RSP}_j$), and RSP_j computes a ciphertext $C_j = \mathsf{Enc}(K_j, R_j)$ and sends it to **CE**, where K_j is a secret key of RSP_j. Then, **CE** updates C_j to C_j' by computing $C_j' = \mathsf{Enc}(K_j \cdot K_e, R_j)$ and sends it to RSP_j, where K_e is a secret key of **CE**. Finally, RSP_j obtains $C_j = \mathsf{Enc}(K_e, R_j)$ by computing $\mathsf{Enc}((K_j \cdot K_e) \cdot K_j^{-1}, R_j)$.

- **Packet and Rule Encryption Phase.** It consists of the packet preprocessing and encryption, and rule preprocesing and encryption as follows:
  - *Packet Preprocessing and Encryption.* A packet pac is segmented into a set of pairs $\{(\mathsf{pac}_k, \mathsf{pos}_k)\}_{k=1}^{|\mathsf{pac}|-\ell_{\mathsf{seg}}+1}$, where ℓ_{seg} is the length of each segment and $(\mathsf{pac}_k, \mathsf{pos}_k)$ denotes that pac_k is located at the position pos_k of the pac. Then, the position pos_k is randomized to $\mathsf{xpos}_k = \sum_{i=1}^{k} F_S(K, \mathsf{pac}_i) + \mathsf{xpos}_0$, where xpos_0 is randomly picked from $\mathbb{Z}_p^*$. Then, a **CE** encrypts the preprocessed packet $(\mathsf{pac}_k, \mathsf{xpos}_k)_{k=1}^{|\mathsf{pac}|-\ell_{\mathsf{seg}}+1}$ to obtain ETS and sends them to **MB**, where α_j is computed once for each **RSP**.
  - *Rule Preprocessing and Encryption.* A rule R is segmented into a set of pairs $(R_*, \{R_k, \Delta_k\}_{k=1}^{h})$, where R_* is the main segment of R and Δ_k is the offset of R_k related to R_* in which $k \neq *$. If $\Delta_k > 0$, the Δ_k is randomized to $\mathsf{x}\Delta_k = \sum_{1}^{\Delta_k} F_S(K, R_k) \bmod p$; and it is randomized to $\mathsf{x}\Delta_k = -\sum_{\Delta_k+1}^{0} F_S(K, R_k) \bmod p$ if $\Delta_k < 0$. Then, an RSP encrypts $(R_*, \{R_k, \mathsf{x}\Delta_k\}_{k=1}^{h})$ to obtain ERS and then sends them to **MB**, where "Second obfuscate" denotes the interaction with **CE**. We note that the encryption process for each **RSP** is identical but the key K_{rp} is different.
- **Inspection Phase.** The **MB** inspects the main $\mathsf{x}R_k$ (i.e., $\mathsf{x}R_*$) of each rule to enable fast filtering of numerous normal packets. When $\mathsf{x}R_*$ is inspected (i.e., $E[\mathsf{cpac}] \neq \perp$), the **MB** restores the xpac_k by calculating $\mathsf{c}R_k^{\alpha} \cdot \mathsf{x}R_k^{\beta}$, and performs the pattern matching of the remaining $\mathsf{x}R_k$. For each round, MRv-DPI sets an auto-incrementing counter *temp* to indicate that the xpac_k is successfully matched, which prevents the additional leakage incurred by that one pac mismatches all inspection rules. Once the inspection is completed, the **MB** collects all Res and sends them to the **CE** and the **TEE**.
- **Inspection Results Verification Phase.** MRv-DPI employs the fast substring search function of $\mathsf{THS^2Trie}$ to perform the matching process on sample packets and generate local results, where $\mathsf{THS^2Trie}$ is constructed by **RSP** and ports it into **TEE**. MRv-DPI performs "$\mathsf{THS^2Trie.Substr\_Search}(\cdot)$" in **TEE**, which ensures that the untrusted cloud cannot get useful knowledge from the rule content and tamper with the verification operations. Finally, it takes the local results comparisons with the inspection results from **MB** to verify the completeness of the DPI execution during the time interval.

Due to the page limit, we conduct correctness analysis in the Appendix. A.

5 Security Analysis

Here, we present the following Theorem 1, 2 and 3 to conduct security analysis, where the proofs are left in the Appendix. B, C and D due to the page limit.

Theorem 1 (Privacy of Packet). *Suppose that (F_S, F_Y) are secure PRFs, H_1 is a secure hash function and the DDH assumption holds in the group $\mathbb{G}$, we say that MRv-DPI achieves privacy of packet.*

Theorem 2 (Rule Hiding). *Suppose that F_{KH} is a secure KH-PRF, (F_S, F_Y) are secure PRFs, H_1, H_2, H_3 are secure hash functions, we say that MRv-DPI achieves rule hiding.*

Theorem 3 (Memory Access Pattern Security). *Suppose that an adversary can observe memory access patterns but cannot breach the physical hardware isolation to steal the key used for remote attestation, H_3 is a secure hash function, we say that MRv-DPI achieves memory access pattern security.*

6 Performance Analysis

In this section, we conduct extensive experiments on MRv-DPI and state-of-the-art solutions, i.e., P2DPI [6] and Slimbox [5] that includes Slimbox* offering enhanced privacy and Slimbox^0 offering high efficiency. In the experiment, we evaluate their performance in the sides of connection establishment, packet processing, inspection, and verification overhead.

Experiment Environment. Our experiments are conducted in AliCloud, with using Ubuntu 22.04, with an Intel (R) Xeon (R) CPU v4 @2.7GHz and 32 GB RAM as the **MB**. For the **TEE**, we use an SGX-enabled Intel (R) Xeon (R) CPU (Ice Lake) v2 @2.7GHz with 8 GB RAM. The **CE** is a PC equipped with an Intel (R) Core (TM) i7-8550U @1.80GHz CPU and 8 GB RAM.

Dataset. To enable the support of multiple RSPs, we select four real open-source rule sets to generate encrypted rules: SSLBL (5,997 rules, https://sslbl.abuse.ch/), Snort (11,830 rules, https://www.snort.org/downloads), Suricata (12,112 rules, https://suricata.io/download/), and ETopen (29,953 rules, https://rules.emergingthreats.net/open/). And real traffic: (https://digitalcorpora.org/corpora/scenarios/m57-patents-scenario/).

Experiment Setting. We implement the solutions in Python, using the Pypbc library for group operations and bilinear pairing calculations, and set the security parameter to $\lambda = 256$. The employed hash functions and PRFs are SHA-256 and HMAC. In particular, the length of sub-segments ℓ_{seg} is varied within $\{4, 5, 6, 7, 8\}$, and the number of times a rule that repeatedly encrypted (i.e., `rounds`) is varied within $\{6, 7, 8, 9, 10\}$.

6.1 Connection Establishment

Here, we evaluate the establishment cost for the first connection, which consists of the time and communication overhead of generating encrypted inspection rules. Figure 4 demonstrates the rule encryption cost when the number of supported RSPs is 1,2,4 respectively in MPv-DPI. As the sub-segment length ℓ_{seg} increases from 5 to 8, the overall efficiency improves by approximately $5\times$ for RSPs $= 1$ and $3\times$ for RSPs $= 2$. When RSPs $= 4$, the efficiency remains higher than that of Slimbox^0 for `rounds` > 7. This advantage arises because Slimbox requires encrypting the rules with multiple `rounds`, whereas MRv-DPI performs

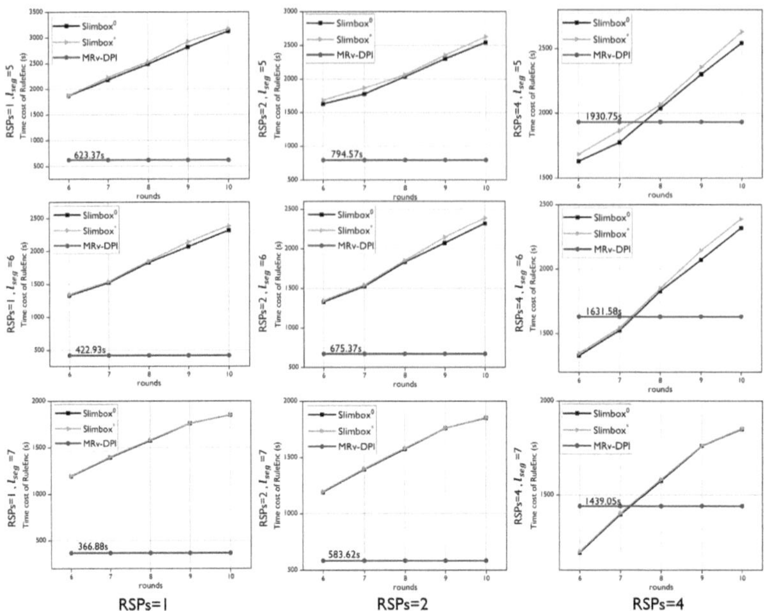

Fig. 4. Time cost of rule encryption in Slimbox^0, Slimbox* and MRv-DPI, where Slimbox only considers RSPs $= 1$ and MRv-DPI considers RSPs $= 1, 2, 4$ respectively, and ℓ_{seg} denotes the length of each sub-segments.

encryption only once regardless of the number of RSPs. Similarly, as shown in Table 1, the communication cost of MRv-DPI with RSPs $= 4$ is still less than that of Slimbox with only a single RSP, since Slimbox requires multiple `rounds` of rule encryptions.

6.2 Packet Processing

Since the packet encryption process of MRv-DPI and Slimbox are comparable, we mainly focus on comparing the encryption cost between MRv-DPI and P2DPI [6]. In MRv-DPI, a larger segment length ℓ_{seg} leads to higher efficiency since fewer tokens are generated. For example, when $\ell_{\text{seg}} = 4$, MRv-DPI exhibits the lowest efficiency with 0.41 s and a communication cost of 159.39KB. With $\ell_{\text{seg}} = 8$, it achieves the optimal performance, which requires only 0.18 s and 80.1 KB. Moreover, P2DPI employs a sliding window of length 8 to generate tokens, incurring a constant time cost with 0.81 s and a communication cost of 68.2KB. This is because P2DPI requires more time-consuming pairing operations than MRv-DPI, which brings about higher computational cost.

Table 1. The communication cost (MB) for {Slimbox^0, Slimbox*} with different (`rounds`, ℓ_{seg}) and for MRv-DPI with different (RSPs, ℓ_{seg}), where `rounds` is the required rounds for rule encryptions in {Slimbox^0, Slimbox*}, ℓ_{seg} is the length of each sub-segment and RSPs denotes the number of rule providers in MRv-DPI.

Scheme		ℓ_{seg}=4	ℓ_{seg}=5	ℓ_{seg}=6	ℓ_{seg}=7	ℓ_{seg}=8
Slimbox^0	`rounds`=6	412.48	336.73	285.45	246.57	221.65
	`rounds`=7	481.22	392.85	333.02	287.6	258.60
	`rounds`=8	549.97	448.90	380.60	328.67	295.61
	`rounds`=9	618.72	505.09	428.17	369.86	332.48
Slimbox*	`rounds`=6	418.89	343.19	291.82	253.05	227.08
	`rounds`=7	488.71	400.39	339.83	295.23	264.93
	`rounds`=8	558.52	457.58	388.38	337.40	302.78
	`rounds`=9	628.34	514.78	436.92	379.58	340.62
MRv-DPI	RSPs = 1	68.83	56.21	47.66	41.18	37.03
	RSPs = 2	123.37	99.95	84.20	74.12	66.37
	RSPs = 3	163.51	133.01	112.66	101.93	88.78
	RSPs = 4	265.04	217.11	184.77	165.11	145.25

6.3 Inspection

As shown in Fig. 5, when RSP = 1, MRv-DPI demonstrates consistently higher inspection efficiency across all four datasets, due to the decrease of pairing operations. To observe the influence of the change of dataset size, we randomly select two and three datasets to compare the unoptimized `Simple-overlay` with the optimized MRv-DPI, where MRv-DPI supports parallel computation and outperforms inspection performance via pipelined matching.

As illustrated in Fig. 6, MRv-DPI also achieves oblivious efficiency gains over `Simple-overlay` in the multi-RSP setting, with the improvements of 40.3%, 52.7%, and 40.7% for RSP = 2, 3, 4, respectively. Meanwhile, P2DPI suffers from inefficient filtering of normal packets, which introduces significant delays with handling large volumes of benign traffic. For example, with $\ell_{\text{seg}} = 4$ and the "Snort" ruleset, the inspection time consumption is 0.166 s for Slimbox^0 and

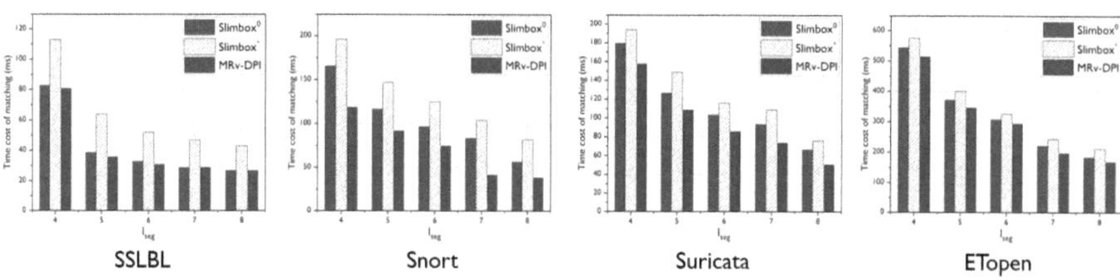

Fig. 5. Time cost of packet inspection with different ℓ_{seg} under different rulesets.

0.196 s for Slimbox*, while P2DPI requires 1.513 s and MRv-DPI only consumes 0.081 s. Since enabling the support for multiple RSPs, the experiments mainly focus on evaluating the matching efficiency under different numbers of RSPs.

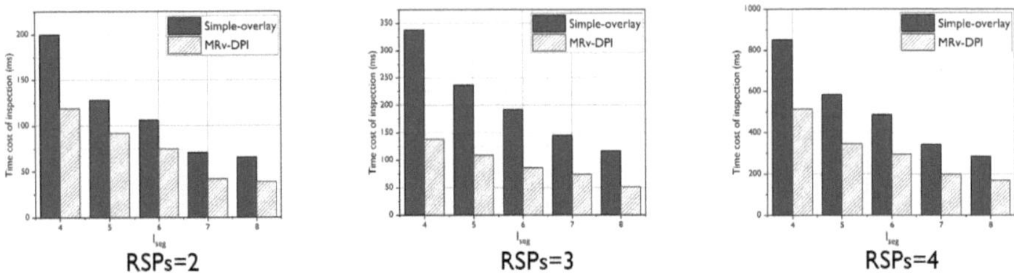

Fig. 6. The time cost of packet inspection between the `Simple-overlay` and MRv-DPI for different ℓ_{seg}, where the `Simple-overlay` represents a simple iterative matching.

6.4 Verification

Here, we analyze the verification time overhead, which includes the construction of the THS^{2}Trie, the initialization of the Enclave, and the search process shown in Fig. 7. It indicates that processing more packets incur more computation time cost and the search cost is independent of the number of rules. Additionally, we compare the verification overhead of MRv-DPI with state-of-the-art TEE-based verifiable DPI solution [9], which shows that the performance of THS^{2}Trie is better than [9]. In particular, when THS^{2}Trie deals with 4,000 rules, the **TEE** takes only 0.64ms to verify 50 sample packets.

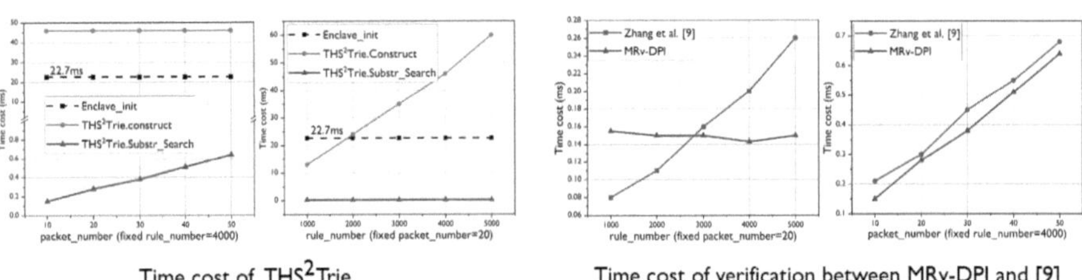

Fig. 7. Time cost of Enclave_init, construction and substring_search of THS^{2}Trie; and the verification time cost of MRv-DPI and Zhang et al. [9].

6.5 Discussion

Here, we discuss how MRv-DPI can be integrated into existing network infrastructures, where it is generally deployed in enterprise networks by integrating its encryption module into the existing firewall or traffic proxy at the internal gateway. The outbound traffic is intercepted, segmented, and encrypted before leaving the local network, where this process is transparent to end-users and does not require modifying internal systems. The encrypted traffic is routed to the cloud-based MB, which performs DPI using different RSPs' rule sets that are subscribed by the enterprise. To ensure the integrity of the DPI service, MRv-DPI lets the enterprise periodically initiate inspection verification by interacting with a TEE-based module over a secure channel via remote attestation. The integrating approach requires minimal changes to existing routing policies and supports scalable multi-branch deployments via centralized control. Note that, the key management problem of multiple RSPs' encryption keys for enterprise is eliminated, since each of them is used only once during the subscription protocol.

7 Related Work

Here, we review privacy-preserving DPI systems based on searchable encryption (SE) and trusted hardware (TEE).

SE-based Solutions. Sherry et al. [3] firstly proposed Blindbox, but it causes significant latency for connection establishment. Then, BlindIDS [10] was proposed but not well compatible with TLS. To improve inspection efficiency, cuckoo hashing was employed for fast filtering [2], and the prefix matching was considered in Embark [14]. By a reusable fuzzy rule generation technique, PrivDPI [7] reduced inspection cost, which was further improved efficiency in Pine [4] and enhanced security in P2DPI [6]. Recently, Liu et al. [5] proposed Slimbox that enables fast packet filtering, but it incurred high communication cost due to rule duplication on the first connection. There were three DPI protocols proposed to improve BlindBox in [8], but their initialization time overhead is still high. Additionally, SEPM [15] and ZKMB [16] achieved fast initialization, but the inspection efficiency needs to be further improved. Nevertheless, none of these works considered the verification of the inspection results.

TEE-based Solutions. Numerous DPI systems that employ session keys provided By trusted hardware in the middlebox were proposed, such as the works of Han et al. [17]'s SGX_Box, Trach et al. [18]'s ShieldBox, Poddar et al. [19]'s SafeBricks. Recently, Zhang et al. [9] performed verification of middlebox inspection results in Intel SGX through packet editing and commitment-based authentication, however, redirecting all traffic to trusted hardware for middleware functions is vulnerable to side-channel attacks [12,13]. However, none of these works considered the practical support of multiple RSPs.

8 Conclusion

In this work, we present MRv-DPI, enabling existing privacy-preserving DPI systems to support multiple RSPs for targeted inspection of various types of malicious traffic. MRv-DPI improves inspection efficiency that is less influenced by the growth of inspection rules. To mitigate incomplete DPI service with the employment of partial rules, we introduce an efficient verification mechanism based on trusted hardware to ensure the integrity of inspections. Extensive experimental results demonstrate that MRv-DPI achieves fast connection establishment and packet inspection. It seems an interesting work to further explore the support for adding RSPs to handle emerging malicious traffic, and the property of fine-grained verification for the inspection results of individual sub-segments.

Acknowledgments. We would like to thank anonymous reviewers for insightful comments. This work was partially supported by National Natural Science Foundation of China (62372285, 62372175), Shanghai Pilot Program for Basic Research (TQ20240212) and Fundamental Research Funds for the Central Universities (40500-20104-222609).

A Correctness Analysis of MRv-DPI

Firstly, we present a correctness analysis of the inspection process. The **MB** initially checks if $E[\mathsf{cpac}]! =\perp$ for each $(\mathsf{xpac}, \mathsf{cpac}, \beta, \mathsf{xpos})$ in the encrypted packet, which implies the existence of a rule $R = (R_*, \{R_k, d_k\}_{k=1}^h)$ such that $\mathsf{x}R_* = \mathsf{cpac}$. Then, the **MB** computes $(\mathsf{c}R_k^\alpha) \times (\mathsf{x}R_k^\beta)$ to verify whether all R_k are contained in the pac_k set, and thus we have

$$\begin{aligned}(\mathsf{c}R_k^\alpha) \times (\mathsf{x}R_k^\beta) &= g^{F_Y(R_k)\times(\mathsf{x}\Delta_k)\times z_j^{-1})\times(K_e\times z_j\times K_x)} \times g^{(F_Y(R_k)\times K_e)\times(\mathsf{xpos}\times K_x)} \\ &= g^{(F_Y(\underline{R_k})\times K_e)\times K_x\times(\underline{\mathsf{xpos}+\mathsf{x}\Delta_k})} \Leftrightarrow g^{(F_Y(\underline{\mathsf{pac}_k})\times K_e)\times K_x\times(\underline{\mathsf{xpos}_k})}.\end{aligned}$$

To mitigate the concern of "*incomplete DPI service may be unidentified if the sample packets are thoroughly inspected by the **MB***", MRv-DPI adopts a PRF-based packet sampling method. A packet is sampled only if "$\mathrm{PRF}(\textsc{timestamp}, K) \mod N == 0$", where K is a secret key, TIMESTAMP is the creation time of the packet and N is a constant. Assume there are 10,000 packets in a time interval with a sampling rate of 1% yielding 100 sample packets. If the cloud inspects only 50% of the packets, the probability of 100 sample packets falling within the inspected subset is negligible, i.e., $\binom{5000}{100}/\binom{10000}{100} \approx 2^{-100}$.

B Proof of Theorem 1

Proof We construct the following games for $\mathsf{Real}_{\mathcal{A}_1}^{\Pi}$ and $\mathsf{Ideal}_{\mathcal{A}_1,\mathcal{S}}^{\Pi}$. In particular, we refer $\Pr[\mathsf{Game}_i = 1]$ as the winning probability of the adversary in the game Game_i, where each game is played by a challenger and an adversary $\mathcal{A}_1$.

Game_0: identical to the real game $\mathsf{Real}^{\Pi}_{\mathcal{A}_1}$, thus we have $\Pr[\mathsf{Real}^{\Pi}_{\mathcal{A}_1}(\lambda) = 1] = \Pr[\mathsf{Game}_0 = 1]$.

Game_1: we use random strings to replace $H_1(\cdot)$ and store it in a table Q_1 for the subsequent queries. If the re-selected random string exists in Q_1, this game aborts. Assume that $\mathcal{A}_1$ performs q queries, its successful guessing probability is $q/2^{\lambda}$. Thus, we have $\Pr[\mathsf{Game}_0 = 1] - \Pr[\mathsf{Game}_1 = 1] \leq q/2^{\lambda}$.

Game_2: we randomly choose $(\alpha_k, \beta_k, \mathsf{xpos}_k)$ from $\mathbb{Z}_p^*$ and store it in a table Q for the subsequent queries. When $\mathcal{A}_1$ obtains the value, the challenger outputs the corresponding integer from Q or regenerates one and stores it. Assume that $\mathcal{A}_1$ performs q queries, its successful guessing probability is $2q/p$. Thus, we have $\Pr[\mathsf{Game}_1 = 1] - \Pr[\mathsf{Game}_2 = 1] \leq 3q/p$.

Game_3: we use truly random functions to replace PRFs. If $\mathcal{A}_1$ distinguishes Game_3 from Game_2, we can build a simulator $\mathcal{B}_1$ to distinguish PRFs from truly random functions. Thus, we have $\Pr[\mathsf{Game}_2 = 1] - \Pr[\mathsf{Game}_3 = 1] \leq \mathsf{Adv}^{\mathsf{PRF}}_{\mathcal{B}_1,(F_Y,F_S)}$. Here, we also have $\Pr[\mathsf{Game}_3 = 1] = \Pr[\mathsf{Ideal}^{\Pi}_{\mathcal{A}_1,\mathcal{S}}(\lambda) = 1]$.

Simulator: we use the simulator $\mathcal{S}$ to simulate $\mathsf{Ideal}^{\Pi}_{\mathcal{A}_1,\mathcal{S}}$ that is formally described in Algorithm 3. Thus, we have $\Pr[\mathsf{Real}^{\Pi}_{\mathcal{A}_1}(\lambda) = 1] - \Pr[\mathsf{Ideal}^{\Pi}_{\mathcal{A}_1,\mathcal{S}}(\lambda) = 1] \leq \mathsf{Adv}^{\mathsf{PRF}}_{\mathcal{B}_1,(F_Y,F_S)} + 3q/p + q/2^{\lambda}$.

Thus, the **MB** cannot learn any information about the packet payload. That is, any PPT adversary $\mathcal{A}_1$ cannot distinguish $\mathsf{cpac}_k = g^{F_Y(K_y,\mathsf{pac}_k)\cdot K_e}$, $\mathsf{xpac}_k = H_1(\beta_k||c, \mathsf{cpac}_k)$ and $\mathsf{xpos}_k = \sum_{j=1}^{s} F_S(K, \mathsf{pac}_j) + \mathsf{xpos}_0$ from random values.

C Proof of Theorem 2

Proof We construct the following games for $\mathsf{Real}^{\Pi}_{\mathcal{A}_2}$ and $\mathsf{Ideal}^{\Pi}_{\mathcal{A}_2,\mathcal{S}}$. In particular, we refer $\Pr[\mathsf{Game}_i = 1]$ as the winning probability of the adversary in the game Game_i, where each game is played by a challenger and an adversary $\mathcal{A}_2$.

Game_0: identical to the real game $\mathsf{Real}^{\Pi}_{\mathcal{A}_2}$, thus we have $\Pr[\mathsf{Real}^{\Pi}_{\mathcal{A}_2}(\lambda) = 1] = \Pr[\mathsf{Game}_0 = 1]$.

Game_1: we use truly random functions to replace PRFs. If $\mathcal{A}_2$ distinguishes Game_1 from Game_0, we can build a simulator $\mathcal{B}_1$ to distinguish PRFs from truly random functions. Thus, we have $\Pr[\mathsf{Game}_0 = 1] - \Pr[\mathsf{Game}_1 = 1] \leq \mathsf{Adv}^{\mathsf{PRF}}_{\mathcal{B}_1,(F_Y,F_S)}$.

Game_2: we use random strings to replace $H_1(\cdot)$ and store it in a table Q_1 for the subsequent queries. If the re-selected random string exists in Q_1, this game aborts. We assume that $\mathcal{A}_2$ performs q queries, its successful guessing probability is $q/2^{\lambda}$. Thus, we have $\Pr[\mathsf{Game}_1 = 1] - \Pr[\mathsf{Game}_2 = 1] \leq q/2^{\lambda}$.

Game_3: we use random strings to replace $H_2(\cdot)$ and store it in a table Q_2 for the subsequent queries. Thus, we have $\Pr[\mathsf{Game}_2 = 1] - \Pr[\mathsf{Game}_3 = 1] \leq q/2^{\lambda}$.

Game_4: we randomly choose $(\mathsf{x}R'_*/\mathsf{xpac}')$ from $\{0,1\}^{\lambda}$, If $\mathcal{A}_2$ distinguishes Game_4 from Game_3, we can build a simulator $\mathcal{B}_2$ to break the security of KH-PRF. Thus, we have $\Pr[\mathsf{Game}_3 = 1] - \Pr[\mathsf{Game}_4 = 1] \leq \mathsf{Adv}^{\mathsf{security}}_{\mathcal{B}_2,\mathsf{KH\text{-}PRF}}$. Since the security of KH-PRF holds, we have $\Pr[\mathsf{Game}_4 = 1] \leq \mathsf{negl}_{\mathsf{DDH}}(\lambda)$.

Algorithm 2. Verifiable and Privacy-Preserving DPI for Multiple RSP

function PackPrepro(pac, K, ℓ_{seg})
  $\mathsf{xpos}_0 \xleftarrow{\$} \mathbb{Z}_p^*$
  for $k \in [|\mathsf{pac}| - \ell_{\mathsf{seg}} + 1]$ **do**
    $\mathsf{xpos}_k \leftarrow \mathsf{xpos}_{k-1} + F_S(K, \mathsf{pac}_k)$
  end for
  return $\{(\mathsf{pac}_k, \mathsf{xpos}_k)\}_{k=1}^{|\mathsf{pac}|-\ell_{\mathsf{seg}}+1}$
end function
function PackEnc(pac, K_e, K_y)
  $(\mathsf{ETS}, \mathsf{ES}, \mathsf{ET}) \leftarrow \emptyset; c \leftarrow 1$
  for *each* $(\mathsf{pac}_k, \mathsf{xpos}_k) \in$ pac_id **do**
    $F_{\mathsf{KH}}(K_e, \mathsf{pac}_k) \leftarrow g^{F_Y(K_y, \mathsf{pac}_k)\cdot K_e}$
    $\mathsf{cpac}_k \leftarrow F_{\mathsf{KH}}(K_e, \mathsf{pac}_k)$
    $\alpha_j \leftarrow (K_e \cdot z_j \cdot K_x) \mod p$
    $\beta_k = (\mathsf{xpos}_k \cdot K_x) \bmod p$
    $\mathsf{ES} \leftarrow \mathsf{ES}[j] \cup \alpha_j$
    $\mathsf{xpac}_k \leftarrow H_1(\beta_k \| c, \mathsf{cpac}_k^{\beta_k})$
    $\mathsf{ET} \leftarrow (\mathsf{xpac}_k, \mathsf{cpac}_k, \beta_k)$
    $c{+}{+}$
  end for
  $\mathsf{ETS} \leftarrow (\mathsf{ES}, \mathsf{ET})$
end function
function RulePrepro(R, K, ℓ_{seg})
  $(\mathsf{x}\Delta_1, \ldots, \mathsf{x}\Delta_k) \leftarrow 0$
  for $k \in [h]$ **do**
    for $K = 1$ *to* $|\Delta_k|$ **do**
      if $\Delta_k > 0$ **then**
        $\mathsf{x}\Delta_k {+}{=} F_S(K, R_k) \bmod p$
      else
        $\mathsf{x}\Delta_k {-}{=} F_S(K, R_k) \bmod p$
      end if
    end for
  end for
  return $(R_*, \{R_k, \mathsf{x}\Delta_k\}_{k=1}^{h})$
end function
function RuleEnc(K_{rp}, R)
  $\mathsf{ERS} \leftarrow \emptyset;\ E \leftarrow \emptyset$
  for *each* $R \in$ RSP **do**
    $(R_*, \{R_k, \Delta_k\}_{k=1}^{h}) \leftarrow R$_id
    for $k = 1$ to h **do**
      $\mathsf{x}R'_* \leftarrow F_{\mathsf{KH}}(K_{\mathsf{rp}}, R_*)$
      $\mathsf{x}R'_k \leftarrow F_{\mathsf{KH}}(K_{\mathsf{rp}}, R_k)$
      Second obfuscate
      $\mathsf{c}R_k \leftarrow g^{F_Y(K_y, R_k)\cdot \mathsf{x}\Delta_k \cdot z_j^{-1}}$
      $E[\mathsf{x}R_*] \leftarrow (\mathsf{x}R_k, \mathsf{c}R_k)$
    end for
    $\mathsf{ERS} \leftarrow E[\mathsf{x}R_*]$
  end for
end function
for *each subscribed* RSP **do**
  $\mathsf{THS^2Trie} \leftarrow \mathsf{THS^2Trie.Construct}(R_{\mathsf{set}})$
  Enclave
  Port the THS²Trie *into* TEE
  Remote Attestation
end for
function Inspection(ERS, ETS)
  $\mathsf{Res} \leftarrow \emptyset$
  for *each* $\mathsf{cpac} \in \mathsf{ET}$ **do**
    if $E[\mathsf{cpac}] \neq \perp$ **then**
      $temp \leftarrow 1$
      for $k = 1$ *to* h **do**
        $\gamma_k^* \leftarrow \mathsf{c}R_k^{\alpha} \cdot \mathsf{x}R_k^{\beta_k}$
        for $t \in [|\mathsf{ET}|]$ **do**
          if $H_1(\beta_k \| t, \gamma_k^*) == \mathsf{xpac}_k$ **then**
            $temp{+}{+}$
            break
          end if
        end for
      end for
      $H_2(temp) \stackrel{?}{=} H_2(|E[\mathsf{xpac}]|)$
      if eqaul **then**
        Res[pac_id] $\leftarrow R$_id
      end if
    end if
    $\mathsf{Res} \leftarrow \mathsf{Res} \cup$ Res[pac_id]
  end for
end function
Enclave
for *each* pac *in* sample packet **do**
  THS²Trie.Substr_Search(pac)
  if Res[pac_id]=vRes[pac_id] **then**
    Return *verification passed*
  else
    Return pac_id
  end if
end for

Algorithm 3. Simulator $\mathcal{S}$

MAPS GENERATION

for $s \in [n]$ **do**
  $\alpha[s], \beta[s], \mathsf{xpos}[s] \xleftarrow{\$} \mathbb{Z}_p^*$
end for

ETS GENERATION

$(\mathsf{ES}, \mathsf{ET}) \leftarrow \emptyset$
for $s \in [n]$ **do**
  $Q_1[\omega] \leftarrow \{0,1\}^\lambda$
  $\mathsf{xpac} \leftarrow Q_1[\omega]; \mathsf{xpos} \leftarrow \mathsf{xpos}[s]$
  $\alpha \leftarrow \alpha[s]; \beta \leftarrow \beta[s]$
  $\mathsf{ES} \leftarrow \mathsf{ES} \cup (\mathsf{xpac}, \beta, \mathsf{xpos})$
  $\mathsf{ET} \leftarrow \mathsf{ET} \cup \alpha$
end for
$\mathsf{ETS} \leftarrow (\mathsf{ES}, \mathsf{ET})$

ERS GENERATION

$(\mathsf{ERS}, E, T) \leftarrow \emptyset$
for each rule rs **do**
  $\mathsf{x}R_*, \mathsf{x}R_k, \mathsf{x}\Delta_k \leftarrow \{0,1\}^\lambda$
  $E[\mathsf{x}R_*] \leftarrow (\mathsf{x}R_k, \mathsf{x}\Delta_k)$
end for
$\mathsf{ERS} \leftarrow E[\mathsf{x}R_*] \cup \mathsf{ERS}$

PACKETS INSPECTION

for each $\mathsf{xpac} \in \mathsf{ET}$ **do**
  if $E[\mathsf{xpac}] \neq \perp$ **then**
    for $k = 1$ to h **do**
      $\alpha \leftarrow \alpha[s]$
      $\gamma_k^* \leftarrow \mathsf{c}R_k^\alpha \cdot \mathsf{x}R_k^\beta$
      while $t < |\mathsf{ET}|$ **do**
        $\beta \leftarrow \beta[s], \mathsf{xpac} \leftarrow Q_1[\omega]$
        $H_1(\beta||t, \gamma_m^*) \leftarrow \mathsf{xpac}$
      end while
    end for
    $Q_2[\omega] \leftarrow \{0,1\}^\lambda$
    $H_2(temp) \leftarrow Q_2[\omega]$
    $H_2(|E[\mathsf{xpac}]|) \leftarrow Q_2[\omega]$
  end if
end for

Simulator: we use the simulator $\mathcal{S}$ to simulate $\mathsf{Ideal}^{\Pi}_{\mathcal{A}_2,\mathcal{S}}$ that is formally described in Algorithm 3. Finally, we have $\Pr[\mathsf{Real}^{\Pi}_{\mathcal{A}_2}(\lambda) = 1] - \Pr[\mathsf{Ideal}^{\Pi}_{\mathcal{A}_2,\mathcal{S}}(\lambda) = 1] \leq \mathsf{Adv}^{\mathsf{PRF}}_{\mathcal{B}_1,(F_Y,F_S)} + 2q/2^\lambda + \mathsf{Adv}^{\mathsf{security}}_{\mathcal{B}_2,\mathsf{KH\text{-}PRF}} + \mathsf{negl}_{\mathsf{DDH}}(\lambda)$.

This proof implies that the **CE** or **MB** cannot learn any sensitive information. That is, any PPT adversary $\mathcal{A}_2$ cannot distinguish $F_{\mathsf{KH}}(K_{\mathsf{rp}}, R_*/R_k) = g^{F_Y(K_y, R_*/R_k)\cdot K_{\mathsf{rp}}}$ from a random value, even it knows other $\mathsf{x}R_*/\mathsf{x}R_k$.

D Proof of Theorem 3

Proof Let $\boldsymbol{V}$ be the verification history and $A(\boldsymbol{V})$ be the access pattern on the **TEE**. For each verification request, the **TEE** traverses the entire trie within the enclave, where the node/edge access pattern is the entire trie from the view of the adversary $\mathcal{A}_3$. Moreover, MRv-DPI employs H_3 to obliviously encode each edge of the trie as $\mathsf{be}(R)||H_3(t)[: -d]$, which ensures that the rule information leakage through the access pattern from $A(\boldsymbol{V})$ remains indistinguishable. In other words, any PPT adversary $\mathcal{A}_3$ can infer the access pattern $A(\boldsymbol{V})$ with a negligible probability $q/2^{(8+|H_3(t)[:-d]|)}$, where q denotes the number of queries. This proof implies that any PPT adversary $\mathcal{A}_3$ cannot learn any sensitive information about the $A(\boldsymbol{V})$. Thus, MRv-DPI is secure against side-channel attacks (e.g., the memory access pattern does not reveal any valid information).

References

1. Kanizo, Y., Rottenstreich, O., Segall, I., Yallouz, J.: Designing optimal middlebox recovery schemes with performance guarantees. IEEE J. Sel. Areas Commun. **36**(10), 2373–2383 (2018)
2. Yuan, X., Wang, X., Lin, J., Wang, C.: Privacy-preserving deep packet inspection in outsourced middleboxes. In: INFOCOM 35th Annual International Conference on Computer Communications, pp. 1–9. IEEE (2016)
3. Sherry, J., Lan, C., Popa, R. A., Ratnasamy, S.: Blindbox: deep packet inspection over encrypted traffic. In: Proceedings of the 2015 ACM conference on special interest group on data communication, pp. 213–226 (2015)
4. Ning, J., et al.: Pine: Enabling Privacy-Preserving Deep Packet Inspection on TLS with Rule-Hiding and Fast Connection Establishment. In: Chen, L., Li, N., Liang, K., Schneider, S. (eds.) ESORICS 2020. LNCS, vol. 12308, pp. 3–22. Springer, Cham (2020). https://doi.org/10.1007/978-3-030-58951-6_1
5. Qin Liu, Yu., Peng, H.J., Jie, W., Wang, T., Peng, T., Wang, G.: Slimbox: lightweight packet inspection over encrypted traffic. IEEE Trans. Dependable Secure Comput. **20**(5), 4359–4371 (2022)
6. Kim, J., Camtepe, S., Baek, J., Susilo, W., Pieprzyk, J., Nepal, J.: P2dpi: practical and privacy-preserving deep packet inspection. In: Proceedings of the 2021 ACM Asia Conference on Computer and Communications Security, pp. 135–146 (2021)
7. Ning, J., Poh, G.S., Loh, J., Chia, J., Chang, E.: Privdpi: privacy-preserving encrypted traffic inspection with reusable obfuscated rules. In: Proceedings of the 2019 ACM SIGSAC Conference on Computer and Communications Security, pp. 1657–1670 (2019)
8. Wang, W., Lee, W., Huang, W., Bertino, E., Li, N.: Towards efficient privacy-preserving deep packet inspection. In: European Symposium on Research in Computer Security, pp. 166–192. Springer (2023)
9. Zhang, X., Geng, W., Song, Y., Cheng, H., Ke, X., Li, Q.: Privacy-preserving and lightweight verification of deep packet inspection in clouds. IEEE/ACM Trans. Netw. **32**(1), 159–174 (2023)
10. Canard, S., Diop, A., Kheir, N., Paindavoine, M., Sabt, M.: Blindids: market-compliant and privacy-friendly intrusion detection system over encrypted traffic. In: Proceedings of the 2017 ACM on Asia Conference on Computer and Communications Security, pp. 561–574 (2017)
11. Boneh, D., Lewi, K., Montgomery, H., Raghunathan, H.: Key homomorphic PRFS and their applications. In: Annual Cryptology Conference, pp. 410–428. Springer (2013)
12. Li, M., Wilke, L., Wichelmann, J., Eisenbarth, T., Teodorescu, R., Zhang, Y.: A systematic look at ciphertext side channels on AMD SEV-SNP. In: Symposium on Security and Privacy (SP), pp. 337–351. IEEE (2022)
13. Wichelmann, J., Pätschke, A., Wilke, L., Eisenbarth, T.: Cipherfix: mitigating ciphertext side-channel attacks in software. In: 32nd USENIX Security Symposium (USENIX Security 23), pp. 6789–6806 (2023)
14. Lan, C., Sherry, J., Popa, R. A., Ratnasamy, S., Liu, Z.: Embark: securely outsourcing middleboxes to the cloud. In: 13th USENIX Symposium on Networked Systems Design and Implementation, pp. 255–273 (2016)
15. Bouscatié, Z., Castagnos, G., Sanders, G.: Public key encryption with flexible pattern matching. In: Advances in Cryptology–ASIACRYPT 2021: 27th International Conference on the Theory and Application of Cryptology and Information Security, pp. 342–370. Springer (2021)

16. Grubbs, P., Arun, A., Zhang, Y., Bonneau, J., Walfish, M.: Zero-knowledge middleboxes. In: 31st USENIX Security Symposium (USENIX Security 22), pp. 4255–4272 (2022)
17. Han, J., Kim, S., Ha, J., Han, D.: SGX-BOX: enabling visibility on encrypted traffic using a secure middlebox module. In: Proceedings of the First Asia-Pacific Workshop on Networking, pp. 99–105 (2017)
18. Trach, B., Krohmer, A., Gregor, F., Arnautov, S., Bhatotia, P., Fetzer, C.: Shieldbox: secure middleboxes using shielded execution. In: Proceedings of the Symposium on SDN Research, pp. 1–14 (2018)
19. Poddar, R., Lan, C., Popa, R. A., Ratnasamy, S.: Safebricks: shielding network functions in the cloud. In: 15th USENIX Symposium on Networked Systems Design and Implementation, pp. 201–216 (2018)

Towards Adaptive Network Defense: A Self-evolving Threat Detection Framework

Chaoqun Guo[1] and Dalin Zhang[2](✉)

[1] School of Software Engineering, Beijing Jiaotong University, Beijing 100044, China
chqguo@bjtu.edu.cn

[2] Intelligent Systems and Security Laboratory of BJTU, Beijing Jiaotong University, Beijing 100044, China
dalin@bjtu.edu.cn

Abstract. The persistent evolution of cyber threats necessitates intrusion detection systems (IDS) that adapt dynamically to novel attacks while preserving knowledge of previous ones. Conventional IDS models face significant challenges, including catastrophic forgetting during incremental updates, a scarcity of labeled data, and pronounced class imbalance. While incremental learning (IL) and semi-supervised learning (SSL) offer promising avenues, existing approaches often overlook critical practical issues like high-dimensional, sparse network traffic, blurred task boundaries, and uneven class distribution shifts. To overcome these limitations, we propose SS-DIL, a semi-supervised incremental learning framework. Our method incorporates: a DP-Means-based memory selection mechanism to preserve informative historical samples; a multi-level knowledge distillation loss aligning model logits, attention maps, and intermediate features to mitigate catastrophic forgetting; and a meta-learning-derived weighting strategy to balance learning across imbalanced classes from labeled and unlabeled data. Extensive experiments on realistic benchmarks demonstrate that SS-DIL achieves state-of-the-art performance in retaining past knowledge, detecting rare attacks, and generalizing from limited labeled data.

Keywords: Intrusion detection · Incremental learning · Semi-supervised learning · Catastrophic forgetting · Class imbalance

1 Introduction

In dynamic network environments, intrusion behaviors continuously evolve, exhibiting diverse and sparse distributions. As attack techniques advance, IDS must adapt to detect emerging threats while maintaining performance on known attacks. Traditional static IDS models, reliant on fixed tasks and fully labeled datasets, are inadequate for dynamic deployment due to three core challenges:

Catastrophic forgetting. Models trained on static distributions forget previously learned attack features when fine-tuned on new tasks, degrading detection

R. Chen et al. (Eds.): Inscrypt 2025, LNCS 16409, pp. 296–312, 2026.
https://doi.org/10.1007/978-981-95-6203-9_16

performance for prior threats. *Label scarcity.* In practical networks, most traffic is unlabeled due to the high cost of manual annotation, severely limiting the model's ability to learn new attacks. *Class imbalance and bias.* Incremental updates often expose models to more new-class samples, creating strong discriminative power for new classes while rapidly diminishing performance on old, rare attacks.

Recent research has explored integrating IL [11] and SSL [20,33] into IDS. IL enhances adaptability via experience replay and knowledge distillation [28], while SSL improves unlabeled data utilization via pseudo-labeling and contrastive learning.

However, existing approaches [12] are designed for vision tasks and lack tailoring for network traffic's high-dimensional, sparse, and heterogeneous features. Standard IL/SSL methods assume dense, low-dimensional inputs with spatial structure, making replay and augmentation less effective. High inter-class similarity and severe imbalance cause rapid forgetting of rare attacks. SSL methods also struggle due to a lack of meaningful augmentations and pseudo-label bias from imbalanced distributions.

Furthermore, most methods ignore practical issues like blurred task boundaries and uneven class growth in continuous streams. To overcome these limitations, we propose a method integrating semi-supervised and incremental learning. Our contributions are:

- A DP-Means-based memory selection mechanism, tailored to network traffic, to preserve informative historical samples.
- A multi-level knowledge distillation strategy aligning logits, attention maps, and intermediate features to mitigate catastrophic forgetting and pseudo-label noise.
- A meta-learning-derived weighting strategy to adaptively balance learning across imbalanced classes using labeled and unlabeled data.
- Extensive evaluation under realistic conditions, demonstrating robustness in weakly supervised scenarios with blurred task boundaries.

Comprehensive experiments show our method significantly outperforms state-of-the-art approaches in mitigating forgetting, improving generalization with limited labels, and enhancing rare-class recognition.

2 Related Work

This section reviews research relevant to dynamic intrusion detection, covering IL, SSL in security, and their integration challenges.

2.1 Incremental Learning and Catastrophic Forgetting Mitigation

IL enables models to acquire new knowledge from sequential data while preserving performance on previous tasks [11]. This is crucial for intrusion detection due to evolving threats like Advanced Persistent Threats (APT) [2] and zero-day exploits [5]. IL strategies fall into four paradigms [28]: *Regularization-Based:* techniques like Elastic Weight Consolidation (EWC) [14] and Synaptic Intelligence (SI) [32] impose penalties to constrain updates to important parameters. *Replay-Based:* approaches such as iCaRL [22] and GDumb [21] rehearse representative past samples. Recent variants address network traffic; Xu et al. [30] used metric-based meta-learning, and Sabeel et al. [23] generated polymorphic attacks with variational autoencoders for replay augmentation. *Knowledge Distillation:* frameworks like Learning without Forgetting (LwF) [18] use KL divergence to align output distributions (logits) of old and new models. This extends to feature-level alignment, e.g., PODNet [10], which penalizes discrepancies in intermediate features. *Hybrid:* some works integrate multiple strategies. Smith et al. [25] combined pseudo-labeling, consistency regularization, and distillation for non-IID unlabeled data in continual learning.

Despite success in image classification, applying these methods directly to network intrusion detection faces challenges: *High Inter-Class Similarity:* shared attack mechanisms reduce discriminative power for methods designed for visually distinct classes. *Data Sparsity and Dimensionality:* high-dimensional, sparse traffic features degrade replay efficiency and regularization stability. *Dynamic and Blurred Task Boundaries:* real-world data streams lack clear task delineations, violating assumptions of many IL algorithms.

Thus, developing an IL mechanism for intrusion detection that is *class-agnostic, sample-efficient, and adaptable* to dynamic data streams remains an open problem. Our work addresses this gap with a specifically designed framework.

2.2 Semi-supervised Learning in Intrusion Detection

SSL reduces reliance on labeled data by leveraging unlabeled samples, making it suitable for intrusion detection where labeled traffic is scarce and costly to obtain [1,8,33]. Mainstream SSL strategies include: *Pseudo-Labeling:* methods like FixMatch [26] and Pseudo-Label [17] use high-confidence predictions as pseudo-labels for supervised training. However, they are prone to noise and confirmation bias, especially for new attack categories. *Consistency Regularization:* techniques such as UDA [29] and Mean Teacher [27] enforce prediction consistency under input perturbations, enhancing robustness. This suits intrusion detection where meaningful feature transformations are applicable. *Contrastive Learning and Cluster-Based:* approaches like MixMatch [4] and SimCLR [9] use contrastive objectives or cluster assumptions to learn semantic representations, effective for complex attacks with limited labels.

Despite their promise, SSL methods face challenges in intrusion detection: *Pseudo-label bias* from class imbalance. *Low initial labeled examples* for novel attacks, causing unreliable pseudo-supervision. *Dynamic data distributions* undermining SSL stability.

Thus, integrating SSL into IL requires redesigning pseudo-labeling, regularization, and sample selection for robustness.

2.3 Integration of Incremental and Semi-Supervised Learning

Integrating IL and SSL aims to develop adaptive, label-efficient models for continuous learning from evolving data streams. This paradigm leverages unlabeled data to enhance recognition of new and rare attacks while mitigating catastrophic forgetting.

However, inherent tensions exist: IL emphasizes *stability* (preserving knowledge), while SSL promotes *plasticity* (assimilating new information). Effective integration must address core challenges: *Reliability of Pseudo-Labels:* in non-stationary distributions, pseudo-labeling is susceptible to bias and error. *Balancing Loss Contributions:* SSL objectives may adapt boundaries aggressively, interfering with knowledge preservation. *Dynamic Sample Selection:* identifying informative unlabeled samples is critical for performance and scalability.

Recent works address these issues. Lechat et al. [15] decouple pseudo-label generation from incremental updates, and Cermelli et al. [7] introduce pseudo-label verification. However, these approaches remain tailored to image data and lack adaptations for network traffic's high-dimensional, sparse, and heterogeneous nature. Unlike methods transplanting CV-based techniques, our framework is designed for network intrusion data. We introduce a DP-Means-based memory selection mechanism to handle sparsity and imbalance, multi-level knowledge distillation (aligning logits, attention, and features) to combat forgetting, and a meta-learning-derived weighting scheme to balance learning objectives. These enable superior performance in knowledge retention, rare-class detection, and adaptability under blurred task boundaries and limited supervision.

3 Methodology

Our proposed method, SS-DIL, constructs an intrusion detection model for IL, enabling it to acquire new attack categories while retaining previous knowledge and leveraging unlabeled samples to address label scarcity and continual evolution. The framework comprises three modules: a dynamic memory module, a multi-level knowledge alignment module, and a meta-learning weighting module.

3.1 Problem Definition

An intrusion detection scenario is a sequence of tasks $T = \{T_1, T_2, \ldots, T_{t-1}, T_t\}$. Each task T_t introduces new classes C_t (with $C_i \cap C_j = \emptyset$ for $i \neq j$) and a dataset $D_t = D_t^L \cup D_t^U$, where $D_t^L = \{(x_i, y_i)\}_{i=1}^{n_l}$ is a small labeled set and $D_t^U = \{(x_j)\}_{j=1}^{n_u}$ is a large unlabeled set ($n_u \gg n_l$). A memory buffer $\mathcal{M}_{t-1}$ stores representative samples from previous tasks.

When learning a new task T_t, the goal is to learn a classifier f_{θ_t} that: achieves high recognition performance on the new classes C_t, i.e., $f_{\theta_t}(x) = y$ for all $(x, y) \in D_t^L$; maintains high accuracy on all historical classes $\bigcup_{i=1}^{t-1} C_i$, i.e., $f_{\theta_t}(x) = y$ for all (x, y) drawn from the distribution of previous tasks; effectively utilizes unlabeled samples D_t^U to improve feature representation and decision boundaries. The overall objective function combines multiple loss components:

$$\min_{\theta_t} \mathcal{L}_t = \sum_{i \in \Lambda} \lambda_i \mathcal{L}_i, \quad \Lambda = \{\text{sup}, \text{align}, \text{unsup}, \text{meta}\}, \tag{1}$$

where, $\mathcal{L}_{\text{sup}}$ is the standard supervised cross-entropy loss for labeled samples in D_t^L and $\mathcal{M}_{t-1}$; $\mathcal{L}_{\text{align}}$ denotes the multi-level knowledge distillation loss that aligns logits and intermediate features with the previous model to retain old knowledge; $\mathcal{L}_{\text{unsup}}$ is the unsupervised consistency loss applied to unlabeled data D_t^U; $\mathcal{L}_{\text{meta}}$ is a meta-learning-based weighting loss that dynamically balances the contribution of each class based on its distribution; λ_i, where $i \in \Lambda$ are hyperparameters that balance the importance of each term.

3.2 Method Overview

This section details the framework and core modules of our dynamic intrusion detection method integrating semi-supervised and incremental learning.

Dynamic Memory Construction and Sample Selection Strategy. Traditional memory replay strategies (e.g., iCaRL [22]) preserve samples near class centroids but fail to capture critical decision boundaries and under-represent minority classes in high-dimensional, imbalanced network traffic. SS-DIL introduces a dynamic memory update mechanism using DP-Means clustering, which performs online clustering without predefining group count, combined with a high-entropy selection criterion to retain the most informative and uncertain samples from historical tasks in buffer $\mathcal{M}_t$. This ensures memory contains both prototypical examples and challenging boundary samples, enhancing stability and plasticity.

Modeling with a Data-Dependent Cluster Penalty λ: DP-Means automatically adapts the number of clusters K based on data density, suitable for evolving distributions. The objective is:

$$\min_{\{C_k\}} \sum_{k=1}^{K} \sum_{x_i \in C_k} \|x_i - \mu_k\|^2 + \lambda K, \tag{2}$$

where, C_k denotes the k-th cluster, μ_k its centroid, and λ a penalty term controlling new cluster formation.

Setting of λ: we set λ adaptively: $\lambda = \alpha \cdot \mathbb{E}_{i,j}[\|z_i - z_j\|^2]$, where, z_i, z_j are feature representations in the current batch, and α is a scaling factor chosen via cross-validation in $[0.5, 2]$. This data-dependent formulation ensures robustness to feature scale and distribution variations across tasks.

High-Entropy Sample Selection Criterion: to augment memory with samples improving boundary discrimination, we select samples with high predictive uncertainty, measured by information entropy: $H(p(y|x)) = -\sum_c p(y =$

$c|x) \log p(y = c|x)$. For each cluster, samples are ranked by entropy, and the top-k_e most uncertain are selected for memory.

Selection Protocol: k_e can be a fixed integer (e.g., 200) or a cluster proportion (e.g., top 10%), providing flexible control over the trade-off between cluster representatives and boundary samples based on memory budget.

Complexity Analysis: DP-Means complexity is $O(nKd)$ per iteration for n samples with d-dimensional features ($K \ll n$). Entropy-based sorting is $O(n \log n)$. Overall cost per task is $O(nKd + n \log n)$, efficient for practical memory sizes.

The composite objective guiding the memory selection is:

$$\mathcal{L}_{\text{mem}} = \underbrace{\sum_{k=1}^{K} \sum_{x_i \in C_k} \|x_i - \mu_k\|^2}_{\text{cluster cohesion}} + \beta \underbrace{\sum_{x_j \in \text{Top-}H} H(p(y|x_j))}_{\text{boundary uncertainty}}, \tag{3}$$

where, β balances preserving cluster modes versus enriching boundary representation. Different from Eq. 2, $\mathcal{L}_{\text{mem}}$ is not directly optimized during model training but serves as a criterion for selecting samples to store in memory.

Multi-level Knowledge Alignment Mechanism. In dynamic intrusion detection, a model must adapt to novel attacks while preserving recognition of known types. Traditional methods like LwF [18] rely solely on output logits alignment, but this single-layer distillation is susceptible to intermediate feature distribution shift, attention drift, and disrupted semantic relationships.

To address this, we propose a multi-level knowledge alignment mechanism enforcing consistency across three levels: output logits, intermediate attention representations, and feature embedding space. This enhances representational stability and robustness against catastrophic forgetting.

Logits Distillation Alignment: this maintains consistency between the output distributions of the previous model f_{old} and current model f_{new}. For logits z^{old} and z^{new}, the distillation loss uses KL divergence with temperature T:

$$\mathcal{L}_{\text{logits}} = T^2 \cdot \text{KL}\left(\sigma(z^{\text{old}}/T) \parallel \sigma(z^{\text{new}}/T)\right), \tag{4}$$

where, σ is softmax. This mitigates abrupt representation shifts and preserves discriminative boundaries.

Attention Alignment: we extract attention weights $A^{(l)}$ from intermediate layers. Consistency is enforced using the Frobenius norm:

$$\mathcal{L}_{\text{attn}} = \frac{1}{L} \sum_{l=1}^{L} \|A_{\text{old}}^{(l)} - A_{\text{new}}^{(l)}\|_F^2, \tag{5}$$

where, L is the number of layers. This ensures the model retains focus on semantically salient features.

Feature Representation Alignment: we align high-level feature representations Z^{old} and Z^{new} using Barlow Twins loss [31]:

$$\mathcal{L}_{\text{bt}} = \sum_{i}(1 - C_{ii})^2 + \gamma \sum_{i \neq j} C_{ij}^2, \tag{6}$$

where, C is the cross-correlation matrix between standardized embeddings, and γ controls the trade-off. This preserves geometric and semantic relationships among attack categories.

The overall alignment loss integrates these components:

$$\mathcal{L}_{\text{align}} = \sum_{i \in \Lambda} \lambda_i \mathcal{L}_i, \quad \Lambda = \{\text{logits}, \text{attn}, \text{bt}\}, \tag{7}$$

where, λ_{logits}, λ_{attn}, and λ_{bt} are weighting coefficients.

Setting of Loss Weights: λ_{logits} is typically set to 1.0 for strong output supervision. λ_{attn} and λ_{bt} are set to smaller values (e.g., 0.5 or 0.1) to provide regularization without overwhelming the primary loss. Optimal values are determined via cross-validation.

Meta-learning-Driven Dynamic Weighting Mechanism. Incremental intrusion detection involves learning from continuous data streams with dynamic class distributions, including new attack categories, frequency shifts, and overlapping categories that blur boundaries. Traditional methods assuming static distributions are ineffective, leading to majority class dominance [13], insufficient rare class learning, and exacerbated catastrophic forgetting.

To address this, we design a dynamic weighting mechanism integrating class frequency statistics with meta-learning. This module automatically allocates a loss weight w_c and bias correction term b_c for each class c, enabling robust optimization under severe imbalance and distribution shift.

Loss Weight Prediction via Meta-Network: let p_c denote the relative frequency of class c in the combined data $D \cup \mathcal{M}_{t-1}$:

$$p_c = \frac{|\{(x_i, y_i) \in D \cup \mathcal{M}_{t-1} \mid y_i = c\}|}{|D \cup \mathcal{M}_{t-1}|}. \tag{8}$$

We predict w_c through a *Softplus* function to map frequency to optimal weighting:

$$w_c = \text{Softplus}(\text{MLP}(p_c)). \tag{9}$$

The *Softplus* function, defined as $\text{Softplus}(x) = \log(1 + e^x)$, is chosen for its smoothness and strict positivity. Unlike ReLU, Softplus provides non-zero gradients for all inputs, preventing rare classes from being completely ignored during training. This ensures stable optimization and allows the meta-network to learn nuanced weighting policies that go beyond simple inverse frequency, adapting to the specific data characteristics of each task.

Bias Correction for Logits Adjustment: we introduce a learnable bias term b_c updated based on class frequency:

$$b_c = b_c^{(t-1)} + \eta \cdot \log\left(\frac{p_c}{\sum_k p_k + \epsilon}\right), \tag{10}$$

where, η is a learning rate and ϵ a small constant. This amplifies correction for low-frequency classes, lowering classification thresholds for rare attacks and improving recall.

Meta-Loss Formulation: the dynamic weighting and bias correction are incorporated into the classification loss for labeled and high-confidence pseudo-labeled data:

$$\mathcal{L}_{\text{meta}} = - \sum_{(x,y)\in D_t^L \cup \tilde{D}_t^U} w_y \cdot \log p(y|x;\theta, b), \tag{11}$$

where, $\tilde{D}_t^U$ is the set of confident pseudo-labeled samples, and b is the bias vector. This rebalances class contributions, enhancing focus on under-represented categories while maintaining stability.

Meta-Learning Justification and Training: the meta-network is trained alongside the main model using a held-out validation set. The validation loss serves as a meta-objective to update the MLP, ensuring the weighting scheme generalizes well and avoids overfitting, aligning with meta-learning paradigms for fast adaptation and robust performance.

4 Experiments and Analysis

We comprehensively evaluate SS-DIL's performance in mitigating catastrophic forgetting, identifying minority classes, and leveraging limited labels across multiple real-world intrusion datasets. We compare against state-of-the-art approaches across accuracy, forgetting rate, robustness.

4.1 Datasets and Evaluation Metrics

We use three public intrusion detection datasets: UNSW-NB15 [19], CIC-IDS2017 [24], and TON_IoT [6]. These encompass diverse attack types and network environments. Evaluation metrics are detailed in Table 1.

For each dataset, a standardized preprocessing pipeline was applied: *Feature Selection and Normalization:* we retained relevant numerical and categorical features for traffic statistics and flow behavior. Continuous features were normalized to [0, 1], and categorical features were one-hot encoded to reduce scale variance and stabilize training. *Handling Missing Values:* missing numerical values were replaced with the class mean, and missing categorical values with an "UNK" token to ensure consistent input dimensionality. *Label Harmonization:* attack labels were harmonized across datasets. Synonymous attack types were mapped to unified categories following established taxonomies [19,24] to mitigate labeling discrepancies. *Incremental Task Sequence Construction:* each dataset was partitioned into 3–5 sequential tasks based on chronological flow order, introducing new attack categories successively. To simulate blurred boundaries, 30% – 50% of samples were shared between consecutive tasks. Earlier tasks introduced 4–5 categories, while later tasks added 1–2, creating a long-tailed distribution. *Label Scarcity Simulation:* we randomly sampled 1%, 5%, 10%, and 20% of each task as labeled data, preserving class distribution, with the remainder unlabeled.

Table 1. Evaluation indicator definition description.

Metric	Abbreviation	Formula
Average Accuracy(↑)	AA	$\mathrm{AA}_t = \frac{1}{t}\sum_{i=1}^{t} A_i^t$
Forgetting Measure(↓)	FM	$\mathrm{FM}_t = \frac{1}{t-1}\sum_{i=1}^{t-1}\left(\max_{j<t} A_i^j - A_i^t\right)$
Imbalance Robustness(↑)	IR	$\mathrm{IR} = \frac{\min_c Acc_c}{\max_c Acc_c}$
Minority Recall(↑)	MR	$\mathrm{MR} = \frac{1}{\lvert\mathcal{C}_m\rvert}\sum_{c\in\mathcal{C}_m}\frac{TP_c}{TP_c+FN_c}$
Top-k Error(↓)	Top-k	$\text{Top-k} = 1 - \frac{1}{N}\sum_{i=1}^{N}\mathcal{I}(y_i \in \mathrm{Top}_k(f(x_i)))$

* Where, A_i^t represents the accuracy on task i after the tth round of training, TP_c and FN_c are the true positive and false negative examples of category c respectively.
AA measures the overall classification performance of the model, FM reflects the degree of catastrophic forgetting,
IR evaluates imbalance robustness, MR focuses on minority class detection, and Top-k assesses multi-class confusion detection.

4.2 Baseline Methods

We evaluate SS-DIL against comprehensive state-of-the-art baselines from three paradigms: IL, SSL, and integrated SSL+IL. All baselines were implemented with identical data splits, task sequences, and experimental settings for fair comparison.

IL Baselines: iCaRL [22]: replay-based method combining exemplar storage with nearest-mean-of-exemplars classification. IL2M [3]: uses dual memory and output calibration to mitigate imbalance-induced bias. PODNet [10]: employs spatial distillation loss on intermediate features to preserve structural knowledge. *SSL Baselines:* FixMatch [26]: generates pseudo-labels from weakly-augmented inputs and enforces consistency on strong augmentations. UDA [29]: uses unsupervised data augmentation and consistency training for robustness. *SSL+IL Baselines:* SSIL [16]: integrates pseudo-labeling and consistency regularization into incremental learning. PLCiL [15]: features dynamic pseudo-label correction for improved reliability.

These baselines represent diverse strategies against catastrophic forgetting, label scarcity, and class imbalance, providing a robust benchmark.

Given the complexity of our experimental scenarios—incremental tasks, varying label ratios, and blurred boundaries—not all baseline methods are universally applicable. Standard IL methods (e.g., iCaRL, PODNet) cannot leverage unlabeled data, while pure SSL methods (e.g., FixMatch, UDA) lack mechanisms against catastrophic forgetting. The applicability of each baseline is detailed in Table 2, serving as a reference for interpreting results.

In results tables, incompatible methods are marked "N/A" with reasons provided in notes, ensuring transparent and fair comparisons across method families.

Table 2. Applicability of comparison methods under different settings.

Method	IL	SST	LST	DLS	MCV	ETS
iCaRL/PODNet	✓	×	✓	×	△	✓
IL2M	✓	×	✓	×	✓	✓
FixMatch/UDA	×	✓	×	✓	×	×
SSIL/PLCiL/SS-DIL	✓	✓	✓	✓	✓	✓

* ✓ Applicable method; △ Indirect adaptation; × Not supported or incompatible

** IL: Incremental Learning; SST: Semi-supervised Training; LST: Long Sequence Task; DLS: Dynamic Label Scale; MCV: Memory Capacity Variation; ETS: Extreme Task Sequence

4.3 Implementation Details

All experiments used PyTorch 2.1 on an NVIDIA RTX 3060 GPU (12 GB VRAM) with CUDA 12.1. Implementation details: *Model Architecture:* we used a 1D-CNN with residual connections as the feature encoder, producing 128-dimensional embeddings passed to a two-layer fully connected classifier. *Optimization:* we trained with Adam (learning rate: 1×10^{-3}, weight decay: 5×10^{-5}, batch size: 128). A learning rate scheduler reduced the rate by 0.5 if validation accuracy didn't improve for 5 epochs. *Training Protocol:* for each task, models trained for maximum 50 epochs with early stopping (patience: 10 epochs). The memory buffer updated after every epoch. *Memory Buffer Configuration:* memory buffer capacity was 5000 samples. DP-Means clustering updated every 10 epochs, retaining top 20% highest entropy samples per class. *Loss Weighting:* default loss coefficients: $\lambda_{\text{logits}} = 1.0$, $\lambda_{\text{attn}} = 0.5$, $\lambda_{\text{bt}} = 0.5$, $\lambda_{\text{meta}} = 1.0$. Sensitivity analysis is in Sect. 4.5. *Reproducibility:* all experiments repeated three times with random seeds (0, 1, 2). Mean results with standard deviations are reported.

4.4 Result Analysis

As shown in Table 3, our method achieves the best performance across all three intrusion detection datasets, demonstrating high adaptability and robustness under practical challenges including multi-task learning, weak supervision, and class imbalance. Specifically: Our method achieves 84.2%, 81.3%, and 79.1% on UNSW-NB15, CIC-IDS2017, and TON_IoT respectively, outperforming the previous best baseline (PLCiL) by over 2%. This demonstrates strong learning stability in dynamic task sequences.

The same superior trends are observed across all other evaluation metrics, further validating the effectiveness of our approach.

Table 3. Experimental results on various intrusion detection datasets.

Method	UNSW-NB15			CIC-IDS2017			TON_IoT		
	AA	FM	MR	AA	IR	MR	AA	IR	Top-3
iCaRL	76.2	18.7	46.1	70.3	0.67	42.4	68.5	0.61	33.8
IL2M	78.0	16.3	49.8	73.9	0.70	45.2	70.4	0.66	30.2
PODNet	79.5	14.8	52.3	74.6	0.74	47.6	72.1	0.68	28.1
FixMatch	75.3	×	44.2	72.8	0.62	43.1	69.7	0.58	26.5
UDA	76.8	×	46.7	73.2	0.63	45.3	70.1	0.59	27.4
SSIL	80.7	12.1	57.9	77.8	0.81	54.2	75.3	0.77	22.9
PLCiL	81.5	11.6	59.8	78.6	0.83	55.9	76.9	0.80	21.7
SS-DIL	**84.2**	**9.4**	**63.5**	**81.3**	**0.89**	**62.8**	**79.1**	**0.85**	**17.3**

This section further extends the experimental evaluation across four dimensions to comprehensively assess our method's performance stability and adaptability in complex environments: Catastrophic forgetting analysis under varying task sequence lengths; Semi-supervised robustness evaluation under different labeled data ratios; Knowledge retention capability under varying memory capacities; Model performance analysis under extreme scenarios.

Figure 1 shows performance changes under different labeled data ratios. While all methods improve with increasing label ratios, our method maintains

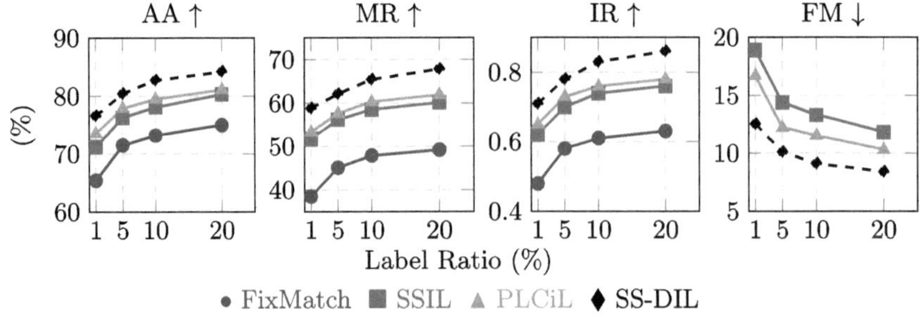

Fig. 1. Model performance under different label ratios. (↑: higher is better, ↓: lower is better). Note that FixMatch does not report FM values as it is only applicable to semi-supervised learning scenarios.

strong recognition ability at low ratios. At 1% label ratio, our method achieves 58.8% MR, significantly outperforming other methods. This demonstrates our method's effectiveness in leveraging unlabeled data, particularly for minority class recognition (MR and IR), making it suitable for real-world weakly supervised network environments.

Figure 2 shows catastrophic forgetting performance under different memory capacities. While all methods improve with increased memory capacity, our method maintains low forgetting rates and high minority class recall even with limited memory. It effectively stores representative class centers and boundary information, making it suitable for resource-constrained edge devices.

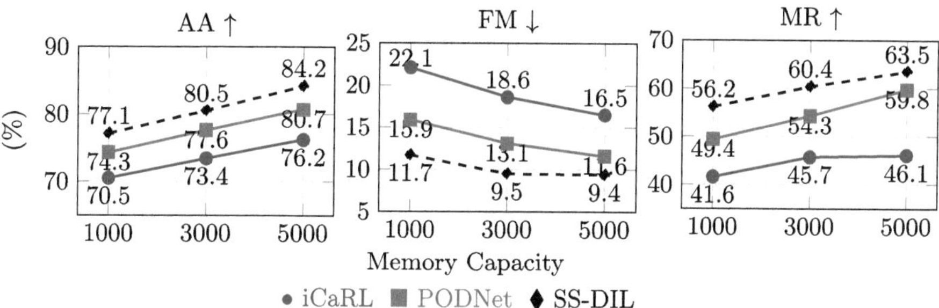

Fig. 2. Comparison under different memory capacities. (↑: higher is better, ↓: lower is better).

Figure 3 demonstrates our method maintains strong performance stability in extreme scenarios. In extremely slow task evolution, it achieves optimal

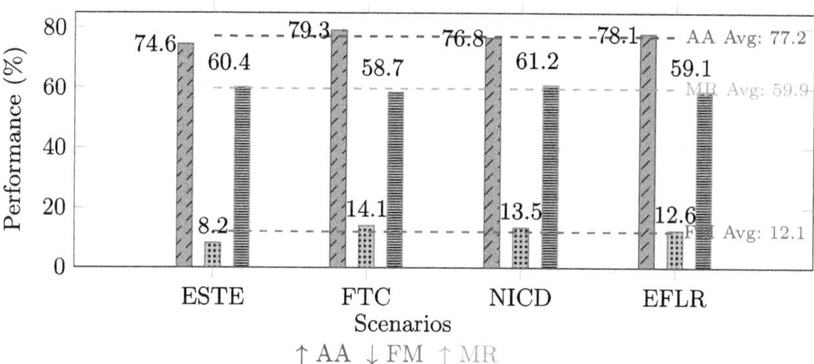

Fig. 3. Robustness comparison under extreme experimental settings. ESTE: Extreme Slow Task Evolution; FTC: Fast Task Change; NICD: Non-Independent Category Distribution; EFLR: Extreme Fluctuation of Label Ratio. (↑: higher is better, ↓: lower is better).

catastrophic forgetting control (FM=8.2), indicating robust long-term historical knowledge retention.

4.5 Ablation Experiment

This section presents systematic ablation experiments to analyze the contribution of each module. By removing or replacing specific components, we observe changes in key metrics including accuracy, catastrophic forgetting, class robustness, and minority class recognition. This analysis validates the necessity of each submodule for dynamic intrusion detection.

Experiments use the CIC-IDS2017 dataset with 5 tasks, 10% label ratio, and 5000 memory capacity. Other hyperparameters match the main experiment settings.

The following shows the performance of the model on the main evaluation indicators under different ablation configurations: *Full model:* including dynamic memory, hierarchical distillation, pseudo-label training, meta-weighting mechanism; *w/o Multi-Level Distillation:* remove attention alignment and feature layer distillation, and only keep logits alignment; *w/o DP-Means Memory:* memory selection is replaced by random sampling (Random Reservoir); *w/o Meta-weighting:* remove category frequency driven weight and bias adjustment; *w/o Semi-Supervised:* completely remove unlabeled data and only use labeled samples for training.

Table 4 presents the ablation study results. Our introduced sub-modules significantly enhance overall model performance. The multi-level distillation, dynamic memory construction, and meta-learning weighting mechanisms demonstrate strong importance for catastrophic forgetting control, minority class detection, and class imbalance handling. These results confirm our method's scalability and practicality under complex task conditions.

Table 4. Results of key module ablation experiment.

Model Configuration	AA	FM	MR	IR	Top-3
Full model	**81.3**	**10.7**	**62.8**	**0.89**	**18.3**
w/o Multi-Level Distillation	78.4	14.2	58.1	0.81	21.6
w/o DP-Means Memory	77.1	16.5	54.9	0.77	23.4
w/o Meta-weighting	75.6	17.9	51.2	0.69	25.1
w/o Semi-Supervised	73.8	18.8	47.6	0.63	27.3

Table 5 shows SS-DIL's performance depends critically on alignment loss weights ($\lambda_{logits}, \lambda_{attn}, \lambda_{bt}$). With small weights (0.1), performance degrades: minority recall drops to 53.6%, robustness decreases (IR=0.74), and forgetting increases significantly (FM=17.2) due to insufficient knowledge preservation. With excessive weights ($\lambda_{logits} = 3.0$), the model over-emphasizes old knowledge, reducing plasticity and weakening new-class learning. This results in higher

Table 5. Sensitivity analysis of alignment loss weights.

Configuration	AA	FM	MR	IR	Top-3
$\lambda_{logits} = 1.0, \lambda_{attn} = 0.5, \lambda_{bt} = 0.5$ (default)	**81.3**	**10.7**	**62.8**	**0.89**	**18.3**
$\lambda_{logits} = 0.1, \lambda_{attn} = 0.1, \lambda_{bt} = 0.1$	76.9	17.2	53.6	0.74	25.7
$\lambda_{logits} = 2.0, \lambda_{attn} = 1.0, \lambda_{bt} = 1.0$	79.4	13.6	59.2	0.83	21.2
$\lambda_{logits} = 3.0, \lambda_{attn} = 1.5, \lambda_{bt} = 1.5$	77.8	15.1	55.7	0.79	23.6

forgetting (FM=15.1) and lower accuracy (77.8%). The default configuration ($\lambda_{logits} = 1.0, \lambda_{attn} = 0.5, \lambda_{bt} = 0.5$) achieves optimal balance, yielding highest accuracy (81.3%) and lowest forgetting (10.7%). This confirms multi-level alignment requires moderate weighting to simultaneously retain old knowledge and adapt to new attacks.

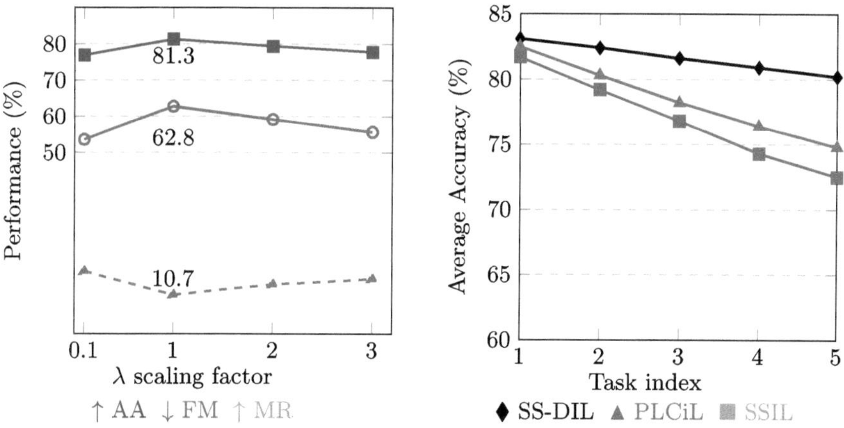

(a) Sensitivity analysis of alignment loss weights.

(b) Average accuracy across sequential tasks.

Fig. 4. Sensitivity analysis and blurred task boundary experiment. (↑: higher is better, ↓: lower is better).

Figure 4a shows the effect of varying alignment loss weights. Both curves confirm that moderate weighting (λ=1.0) achieves optimal trade-off: highest accuracy (81.3%) and lowest forgetting (10.7%). Small λ values weaken knowledge retention, while large values reduce adaptability. Figure 4b shows learning curves under 30% blurred task boundaries. Baseline methods (SSIL, PLCiL) exhibit rapid accuracy degradation due to boundary confusion and category overlap. In contrast, SS-DIL maintains stable performance, decreasing only from 83.1% (Task 1) to 80.2% (Task 5). This demonstrates our multi-level knowledge alignment and dynamic memory effectively mitigate blurred boundary effects by preserving discriminative features and historical knowledge.

5 Conclusion and Future Work

This paper presented SS-DIL, a semi-supervised incremental learning framework for dynamic intrusion detection. By combining DP-Means-based dynamic memory, multi-level knowledge alignment, and meta-learning weighting, the model addresses catastrophic forgetting, label scarcity, and class imbalance simultaneously. Extensive experiments on UNSW-NB15, CIC-IDS2017, and TON_IoT show that SS-DIL consistently outperforms state-of-the-art baselines in accuracy, minority recall, robustness, and forgetting control. The framework also demonstrates strong resilience under blurred task boundaries and uneven class growth, which better reflect realistic deployment scenarios. Ablation and sensitivity studies further confirm the importance of each module and the role of balanced alignment weights. For deployment, SS-DIL achieves competitive performance with limited memory, suggesting applicability to edge and resource-constrained environments. Future work will focus on online and streaming learning for real-time traffic, efficiency improvements via model compression and distillation, and interpretability enhancements through causal reasoning and attention visualization.

In conclusion, SS-DIL provides an effective and flexible solution for intrusion detection in dynamically evolving network environments, balancing theoretical rigor with practical applicability.

Acknowledgments. We would like to thank the anonymous reviewers for their valuable feedback and suggestions that helped improve the quality of this paper. We also acknowledge the support of the Intelligent Systems and Security Laboratory of BJTU and the School of Software Engineering at Beijing Jiaotong University, and we are grateful to the research team for their collaboration and contributions to this work.

References

1. Abdallah, E.E., Otoom, A.F., et al.: Intrusion detection systems using supervised machine learning techniques: a survey. Procedia Comput. Sci. **201**, 205–212 (2022)
2. Alshamrani, A., Myneni, S., Chowdhary, A., Huang, D.: A survey on advanced persistent threats: techniques, solutions, challenges, and research opportunities. IEEE Commun. Surv. Tutorials **21**(2), 1851–1877 (2019)
3. Belouadah, E., Popescu, A.: Il2m: class incremental learning with dual memory. In: Proceedings of the IEEE/CVF International Conference on Computer Vision, pp. 583–592 (2019)
4. Berthelot, D., Carlini, N., Goodfellow, I., Papernot, N., Oliver, A., Raffel, C.A.: Mixmatch: a holistic approach to semi-supervised learning. In: Advances in Neural Information Processing Systems, vol. 32 (2019)
5. Bilge, L., Dumitraş, T.: Before we knew it: an empirical study of zero-day attacks in the real world. In: Proceedings of the 2012 ACM Conference on Computer and Communications Security, pp. 833–844 (2012)
6. Booij, T.M., Chiscop, I., Meeuwissen, E., Moustafa, N., Hartog, F.T.H.D.: Ton_iot: the role of heterogeneity and the need for standardization of features and attack types in iot network intrusion data sets. IEEE Internet Things J. **9**(1), 485–496 (2022). https://doi.org/10.1109/JIOT.2021.3085194

7. Cermelli, F., Fontanel, D., Tavera, A., Ciccone, M., Caputo, B.: Incremental learning in semantic segmentation from image labels. In: Proceedings of the IEEE/CVF Conference on Computer Vision and Pattern Recognition, pp. 4371–4381 (2022)
8. Chen, C., Gong, Y., Tian, Y.: Semi-supervised learning methods for network intrusion detection. In: 2008 IEEE international Conference on Systems, Man and Cybernetics, pp. 2603–2608. IEEE (2008)
9. Chen, T., Kornblith, S., Norouzi, M., Hinton, G.: A simple framework for contrastive learning of visual representations. In: International Conference on Machine Learning, pp. 1597–1607. PmLR (2020)
10. Douillard, A., Cord, M., Ollion, C., Robert, T., Valle, E.: Podnet: pooled outputs distillation for small-tasks incremental learning. In: Computer vision–ECCV 2020: 16th European conference, Glasgow, UK, 23–28 August 2020, Proceedings, part XX 16, pp. 86–102. Springer (2020)
11. Du, L., Gu, Z., Wang, Y., Wang, L., Jia, Y.: A few-shot class-incremental learning method for network intrusion detection. IEEE Trans. Netw. Serv. Manage. **21**(2), 2389–2401 (2023)
12. Gepperth, A., Hammer, B.: Incremental learning algorithms and applications. In: European Symposium on Artificial Neural Networks (ESANN) (2016)
13. Guo, C., Wang, N., Sun, Y., Zhang, D.: Dtc: addressing the long-tailed problem in intrusion detection through the divide-then-conquer paradigm. In: 2023 IEEE 29th International Conference on Parallel and Distributed Systems (ICPADS), pp. 1319–1326. IEEE (2023)
14. Kirkpatrick, J., et al.: Overcoming catastrophic forgetting in neural networks. Proc. Natl. Acad. Sci. **114**(13), 3521–3526 (2017)
15. Lechat, A., Herbin, S., Jurie, F.: Pseudo-labeling for class incremental learning. In: BMVC 2021: The British Machine Vision Conference (2021)
16. Lechat, A., Herbin, S., Jurie, F.: Semi-supervised class incremental learning. In: 2020 25th International Conference on Pattern Recognition (ICPR), pp. 10383–10389. IEEE (2021)
17. Lee, D.H., et al.: Pseudo-label: the simple and efficient semi-supervised learning method for deep neural networks. In: Workshop on Challenges in Representation Learning, ICML. vol. 3, p. 896. Atlanta (2013)
18. Li, Z., Hoiem, D.: Learning without forgetting. IEEE Trans. Pattern Anal. Mach. Intell. **40**(12), 2935–2947 (2017)
19. Moustafa, N., Slay, J.: Unsw-nb15: a comprehensive data set for network intrusion detection systems (unsw-nb15 network data set). In: 2015 military Communications and Information Systems Conference (MilCIS), pp. 1–6. IEEE (2015)
20. Nasteski, V.: An overview of the supervised machine learning methods. Horizons. b **4**(51–62), 56 (2017)
21. Prabhu, A., Torr, P.H., Dokania, P.K.: Gdumb: a simple approach that questions our progress in continual learning. In: Computer Vision–ECCV 2020: 16th European Conference, Glasgow, UK, 23–28 August 2020, Proceedings, Part II 16, pp. 524–540. Springer (2020)
22. Rebuffi, S.A., Kolesnikov, A., Sperl, G., Lampert, C.H.: icarl: incremental classifier and representation learning. In: Proceedings of the IEEE Conference on Computer Vision and Pattern Recognition, pp. 2001–2010 (2017)
23. Sabeel, U., Heydari, S.S., El-Khatib, K., Elgazzar, K.: Incremental adversarial learning for polymorphic attack detection. IEEE Trans. Mach. Learn. Commun. Networking (2024)

24. Sharafaldin, I., Lashkari, A.H., Ghorbani, A.A., et al.: Toward generating a new intrusion detection dataset and intrusion traffic characterization. ICISSp **1**(2018), 108–116 (2018)
25. Smith, J., Balloch, J., Hsu, Y.C., Kira, Z.: Memory-efficient semi-supervised continual learning: The world is its own replay buffer. In: 2021 International Joint Conference on Neural Networks (IJCNN), pp. 1–8 (2021). https://doi.org/10.1109/IJCNN52387.2021.9534361
26. Sohn, K., et al.: Fixmatch: simplifying semi-supervised learning with consistency and confidence. Adv. Neural. Inf. Process. Syst. **33**, 596–608 (2020)
27. Tarvainen, A., Valpola, H.: Mean teachers are better role models: weight-averaged consistency targets improve semi-supervised deep learning results. In: Advances in Neural Information Processing Systems, vol. 30 (2017)
28. Van de Ven, G.M., Tuytelaars, T., Tolias, A.S.: Three types of incremental learning. Nat. Mach. Intell. **4**(12), 1185–1197 (2022)
29. Xie, Q., Dai, Z., Hovy, E., Luong, T., Le, Q.: Unsupervised data augmentation for consistency training. Adv. Neural. Inf. Process. Syst. **33**, 6256–6268 (2020)
30. Xu, H., Wang, Y.: A continual few-shot learning method via meta-learning for intrusion detection. In: 2022 IEEE 4th International Conference on Civil Aviation Safety and Information Technology (ICCASIT), pp. 1188–1194. IEEE (2022)
31. Zbontar, J., Jing, L., Misra, I., LeCun, Y., Deny, S.: Barlow twins: self-supervised learning via redundancy reduction. In: International Conference on Machine Learning, pp. 12310–12320. PMLR (2021)
32. Zenke, F., Poole, B., Ganguli, S.: Continual learning through synaptic intelligence. In: International Conference on Machine Learning, pp. 3987–3995. PMLR (2017)
33. Zhu, X.J.: Semi-supervised learning literature survey (2005)

Early Detection of Malicious Traffic Based on Graph Modeling and Spatio-Temporal Attention Approach

Jinchuan Liu, Shuaishuai Tan(✉), Jiaxiong Chen, Zehua Zhang, Qiannan Lin, Zhaoyan Chen, and Junhang Fu

School of Computer Science and Technology, GuangDong University of Technology, Guangzhou 510006, China
ss_tan@163.com

Abstract. With the increasing prevalence of encrypted traffic, machine learning and deep learning methods are widely used for detection but often struggle to capture complex flow interactions. Although Graph Neural Networks (GNNs) show promise, they lack effective early detection in dynamic environments. To address this, we propose an early detection approach integrating the Dynamic Interaction Flow Graphs (DIFG) with the Spatio-Temporal Attention (STA) mechanism. We model interactive flows in network traffic using the DIFG, and employ GNNs to extract interaction features from the DIFG. Meanwhile, the STA mechanism is utilized to capture spatiotemporal features from the graph structure. Additionally, we introduce the Super Path (SP), a subgraph derived from the Hamiltonian path in DIFG, to capture temporal traffic characteristics. Through the integration of various modules, we effectively represent the interactive behavior of network traffic. Experimental results demonstrate that the proposed approach achieves excellent performance on both public and self-constructed datasets. It attains an overall detection accuracy exceeding 99%, and maintains approximately 98% accuracy even when using only the first 10 packets of each interactive flow, effectively validating the effectiveness of our approach for early malicious traffic detection.

Keywords: Malicious traffic detection · Graph neural networks · Attention mechanism

1 Introduction

With the widespread adoption of encryption protocols such as TLS 1.3, QUIC, and HTTPS in network communication, the rapid escalation of encrypted internet traffic has profoundly impacted network security dynamics [1]. While this trend effectively enhances user privacy and data security, it also exacerbates the difficulty of network security defense. Encrypted malicious traffic, due to its high concealment and risk, poses a growing challenge for detection. Some

R. Chen et al. (Eds.): Inscrypt 2025, LNCS 16409, pp. 313–331, 2026.
https://doi.org/10.1007/978-981-95-6203-9_17

malicious traffic exhibits features that are highly similar to normal traffic. There are few trainable features, and highly discriminating features are even rarer [2]. Traditional content-based features are gradually becoming ineffective.

Machine learning technologies are now becoming a new powerful tool in the network anomaly detection field [3]. Existing studies [4,5] attempt to combine feature engineering with machine learning to create classification models using statistical features such as packet length, inter-arrival time, and flow duration. Some studies [6,7] also introduce deep neural networks to extract features automatically. Although traditional machine learning methods have shown a certain degree of effectiveness, they typically treat each flow as an independent sample, overlooking the potential interactions among different flows. As a result, they fail to effectively capture the interactive characteristics of network traffic.

These limitations have led researchers to explore detection methods that emphasize behavioral and structural analysis. Graph Neural Networks (GNNs) offer a promising solution, as they can effectively capture the intricate interactions and relationships embedded within [8]. In recent years, several studies [9–11] have proposed GNN-based methods, in which network traffic is modeled as a graph and GNNs are used to extract interaction features between flows.

The research on malicious traffic detection has made significant progress in recent years. However, several key challenges remain to be addressed.

Challenge 1: Difficulty in effectively modeling traffic features through graph structures. Current approaches often adopt static or overly simplified graph representations, which tend to overlook critical interaction features within the traffic. As a result, the constructed graph structures lack sufficient semantic expressiveness, hindering the model's ability to capture the intrinsic characteristics of malicious behavior. This ultimately limits the detection accuracy.

Challenge 2: Inefficiency in graph-based detection models. Most existing GNN models require a complete or nearly complete graph to be constructed prior to detection, in order to perform effective inference. The high computational cost of graph construction and inference severely limits the applicability of these models in practical detection scenarios.

To address the aforementioned challenges in encrypted malicious traffic detection, this paper proposes an early detection approach based on Dynamic Interaction Flow Graph (DIFG) and the Spatio-Temporal Attention (STA) mechanism. The proposed approach aims to achieve efficient, accurate, and early detection of malicious encrypted traffic by dynamically constructing network interaction graphs and integrating both structural and spatio-temporal traffic features. The main contributions of this work are as follows:

- We design the DIFG to dynamically model behavioral relationships among network flows. To effectively extract sequential and relational information embedded in the graph structure, we further introduce the Super Path(SP) that captures temporal sequence features within the DIFG, enabling more informative graph-based feature representation.

- Based on the DIFG, we incorporate the STA mechanism. Temporal attention is modeled using historical state information, while spatial attention is computed from the vertex and edge features of the graph structure. By jointly modeling spatial and temporal dependencies, STA provides a comprehensive dynamic representation of the traffic graph.
- We propose an early detection mechanism that can detect malicious behavior in the early stages of traffic interaction. This mechanism achieves early detection while maintaining high detection performance, accurately identifying malicious encrypted traffic during the early stage of traffic interactions.

The remainder of this paper is organized as follows: Sect. 2 reviews related work in the relevant research domain. Section 3 elaborates on the construction of DIFG and SP in detail and discusses the underlying theoretical principles. Section 4 presents our proposed general framework and the workflow of each module. Section 5 provides a comprehensive evaluation of the performance of our approach. Section 6 concludes the paper.

2 Related Work

In this section, we review prior work closely related to ours, which can be broadly categorized into three areas:

Encrypted traffic feature selection: Some studies [12,13] adopt packet-level statistical features for detection. In raw traffic-based approaches, existing works [14,15] [16] convert raw traffic into images or other formats. Other studies [17,18] apply deep neural networks to learn representations directly from raw traffic data. Lin et al. [19] tokenize raw traffic for input into a BERT [20] model. In contrast, our method transforms raw payloads into images, applies augmentation, and reduces them to low-dimensional vectors, which are then used as vertex features in the graph representation.

Graph neural network-based malicious detection methods: Various graph construction methods have been proposed in recent studies. Li et al. [21] modeled malicious traffic as endpoint traffic graphs by analyzing relationships between packets and flows. Wang et al. [9] constructed attack graphs to describe interactions between attacker and victim hosts. Shen et al. [11] proposed the TIG graph based on client-server interactions. Yang et al. [10] introduced the MTIG graph to represent encrypted malicious traffic. In contrast, the DIFG constructed by our method is a directed graph, rather than an undirected graph like the above studies, and a subgraph SP based on DIFG is proposed to extract deeper interactive features. In addition, DIFG is dynamically constructed and can perform early detection according to the detection timing.

Attention-Based malicious traffic detection: Some studies [22,23] employ multi-head attention mechanisms to effectively capture key features and extract salient ones for building detection models. Huang et al. [24] employed a self-attention mechanism to learn intra-feature relationships and a collaborative attention mechanism to capture inter-feature relationships. In contrast, our approach extracts temporal attention based on historical graph features and spatial attention from graph structure, which are then fused into a spatio-temporal attention.

3 Graph Structure Abstraction for Interaction Flows

This section first explains the principles of representing network traffic using graph structures, followed by a detailed description of our graph construction process. Based on the constructed graph, we introduce a subgraph and give the corresponding algorithm and mathematical proof. Our study shows that the proposed graph structure can statistically reveal the differences between malicious and benign traffic.

3.1 Dynamic Interaction Flow Graph

Encrypted traffic is typically bidirectional, involving packet exchanges between endpoints. We use a 5-tuple $\phi_p = (IP_s, Port_s, IP_d, Port_d, Proto)$ to uniquely identify each packet p, where IP_s and IP_d denote the source and destination IP addresses, $Port_s$ and $Port_d$ denote the source and destination ports, respectively, and $Proto$ denotes the transport layer protocol. And its inverse 5-tuple is defined as $\phi^{-1} = (IP_d, Port_d, IP_s, Port_s, Proto)$. We define the interaction flow that includes packets with either identical or inverse 5-tuples. An interaction flow is then defined as a packet sequence $\mathcal{F}$ such that each packet's 5-tuple satisfies $\phi_{p_i} \in \{\phi, \phi^{-1}\}$. Formally:

$$\mathcal{F} = \{p_i \mid \phi_{p_i} \in \{\phi, \phi^{-1}\}\}$$

Based on this definition, we propose the DIFG to characterize the interaction flow. DIFG models the evolving communication dynamics between endpoints within an interaction flow and serves as a foundation for learning discriminative patterns in encrypted traffic.

Vertex. Each packet is abstracted as a vertex in the graph. Vertex features are processed from raw data packet features, as detailed in Sect. 4.2.

For the packet sequence within an interaction flow, we introduce the concept of the group, where a group is defined as a sequence of consecutively transmitted packets in the same direction within a short time interval. Unlike traditional burst, a group can contain as few as a single packet. Once the vertex is identified, the corresponding edges are constructed accordingly.

Edges. In the DIFG, there are two types of directed and unweighted edges: intra-group edges and inter-group edges. Intra-group edges connect consecutive vertices within the same group according to packet arrival order. Inter-group edges connect adjacent groups, including an edge from the last vertex of the previous group to the first vertex of the current group, and an edge from the first vertex of the previous group to the last vertex of the current group.

As shown in the packet sequence in Fig. 1(a), arrows of different colors represent packets in different directions. Figure 1(b) depicts the DIFG corresponding

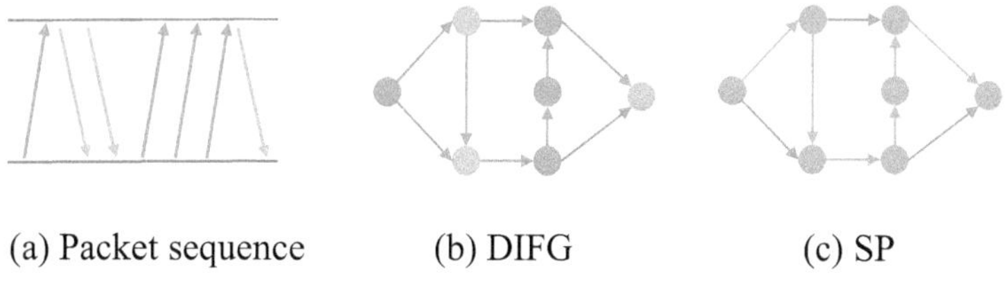

(a) Packet sequence (b) DIFG (c) SP

Fig. 1. An example of DIFG

to the packet sequence in Fig. 1(a), where the vertices of different colors indicate the direction of packets.

Theorem 1. *A Dynamic Interaction Flow Graph is represented as a triplet: DIFG = (V, E, F), where:*

- *V is the set of vertices. Each directed edge $e \in E$ is either an* intra-group edge, *connecting two consecutive vertices within the same group, or an* inter-group edge, *which includes edges from the start vertex of one group to the end vertex of the next group, and from the end vertex of one group to the start vertex of the next group. At most, one directed edge can be added between any pair of vertices.*
- *F is the set of all vertex feature vectors, containing the feature vectors of every vertex in the graph.*

3.2 Spuer Path

Based on the DIFG, a unique Hamiltonian path can be derived from the graph. We provide a formal proof using mathematical induction to demonstrate the existence and uniqueness of this Hamiltonian path in the constructed DIFG.

Proof. We prove that for any DIFG, there exists one and only one Hamiltonian path.

Base Case: When the DIFG contains exactly two groups and the second group consists of only a single vertex, this represents the base case. Within the first group, there is clearly a unique Hamiltonian path L_1 that connects all vertices in order. According to the construction of the DIFG, there exists a directed edge from the last vertex of the first group to the only vertex in the second group. By appending this vertex to the end of the Hamiltonian path L_1 from the first group, we obtain a new Hamiltonian path L_2 that spans both groups. Based on the construction of the DIFG, a directed edge from the unique vertex in the second group to the first vertex in the first group does not exist, thereby ensuring that no cycle is formed. This new path L_2 is clearly unique.

Inductive Hypothesis: Assume that for any DIFG with k vertices, there exists a unique Hamiltonian path L that traverses all vertices exactly once, and the length of this path is $k - 1$.

Inductive Step: Under the inductive hypothesis, we consider adding a new vertex to reconstruct a DIFG with $k+1$ vertices. According to the construction rules of the DIFG, the insertion of this new vertex falls into one of the following two cases:

- **Case 1:** The new vertex is added to the current group. In this case, the directed edge from the first vertex of the previous group to the last vertex of the current group is removed. Two new directed edges are introduced: one from the first vertex of the previous group to the newly added vertex, and another from the last vertex of the current group to the newly added vertex.
- **Case 2:** The new vertex starts a new group. Directed edges are added from both the first and last vertices of the previous group to the new vertex. If the previous group contains only one vertex, a single directed edge is added from that vertex to the new vertex.

In both cases, the new vertex is appended immediately after the last vertex of the existing Hamiltonian path L, forming a new path L' of length k. Since the construction process is deterministic and the order between each group is preserved, no cycles are formed, the resulting Hamiltonian path L' is unique.

Conclusion: By mathematical induction, for any DIFG, there exists a unique Hamiltonian path that visits every vertex exactly once.

We propose a graph structure based on the Hamiltonian path of the DIFG, which is also a subgraph of it, termed the Super Path (SP). This path effectively captures the topological structure of the DIFG. As shown in Fig. 1(c), the graph structure composed of light pink arrows and vertices represents the SP extracted from Fig. 1(b)

Theorem 2. *Given a $DIFG = (V, E, F)$, a Super Path is defined as its spanning subgraph $SP = (V, E', F)$, where:*

- *$E' \subseteq E$ forms a directed Hamiltonian path over all vertices in V;*
- *The vertex order in SP respects the temporal and directional constraints of the DIFG;*
- *Each vertex retains its original feature vector from F.*

Table 1. The statistics for both datasets

Measures	$Dataset_{CIC}$		$Dataset_{Lab}$	
	Benign	Malicious	Benign	Malicious
Average length	29.81	4.96	117.9	9.36
Average number	12.58	1.56	46.44	2.38
Proportion	**0.41**	**0.26**	**0.39**	**0.23**

We propose a BFS-based graph structure extraction algorithm to obtain the SP in the DIFG. The algorithm is as Algorithm 1

Algorithm 1. Extracting SP from DIFG

Input: Dynamic Interaction Flow Graph $DIFG = (V, E, F)$
Output: Super Path $SP = (V, E', F)$

```
Initialize layer counter: CurrentLayer ← 0
for each vertex v ∈ V do
    Set vertex layer label: v.Layer ← −1
end for
Find the unique root vertex r with in-degree 0
Set r.Layer ← 0
Initialize queue Q ← {r}
while Q is not empty do
    CurrentLayer ← CurrentLayer + 1
    LayerSize ← size(Q)
    for i = 1 to LayerSize do
        Dequeue vertex u from Q (parent vertex)
        for each child vertex v of u where (u, v) ∈ E do
            Set v.Layer ← CurrentLayer
            Enqueue v into Q
        end for
    end for
end while
Sort vertices V by ascending Layer, get V_sorted = [v_1, v_2, ..., v_n]
Initialize new edge set E' ← ∅
for i = 1 to n − 1 do
    Add directed edge (v_i, v_{i+1}) to E'
end for
SP ← (V, E', F)
return SP
```

3.3 The Benefits of DIFG and SP

In this section, we elucidate the distinct advantages of the proposed DIFG and its associated SP in the context of malicious traffic detection, particularly in differentiating malicious flows from benign ones.

We introduce the concept of critical vertices in the DIFG, defined as fork vertices and merge vertices, where a fork vertex has an out-degree of 2 and a merge vertex has an in-degree of 2. DIFG captures the dynamic topological, temporal, and spatial features of interactive flows, with critical vertices highlighting key structural changes and anomalies. In contrast, the SP emphasizes temporal sequence features, improving sensitivity to packet arrival order and their relationships.

To validate these advantages, we conducted a comprehensive statistical analysis based on the public dataset $Dataset_{CIC}$ and our own collected dataset $Dataset_{Lab}$ (see Sect. 5.1 for dataset construction).

For each interaction flow, we constructed the corresponding DIFG and recorded the length of its related SP (measured by the number of edges) as well as the number of critical vertices. Our results are shown in Table 1. The average length refers to the SP length (the total number of vertices equals the SP length plus 1), while the average quantity and proportion represent the average number of critical vertices and their ratio to the total number of vertices, respectively.

The results show that in both datasets, graphs representing benign flows have a higher average SP length than those representing malicious flows, and also a relatively higher average number of critical vertices. Additionally, compared to malicious graphs, benign graphs have a significantly greater proportion of critical vertices. In the $Dataset_{CIC}$, the proportion of critical vertices in benign graphs is approximately 1.5 times that of malicious graphs, whereas in the $Dataset_{Lab}$, this proportion is about 1.8 times higher. These statistical characteristics distinctly highlight the differences between benign and malicious traffic.

4 The Proposed Approach

With the aid of DIFG and SP, the malicious traffic detection problem is reformulated as a binary graph classification task. We propose a novel approach that constructs fused features based on the DIFG, highlights critical vertices, and captures variations along paths. Additionally, we designed an early-stage graph classification model that incorporates temporal and spatial attention mechanisms. This model adapts to the dynamic structure of graphs and effectively captures spatiotemporal patterns, enabling early detection.

4.1 Approach Overview

Our overall approach is illustrated in Fig. 2. We process packets in as interaction flows, extract raw features, and perform feature processing before embedding

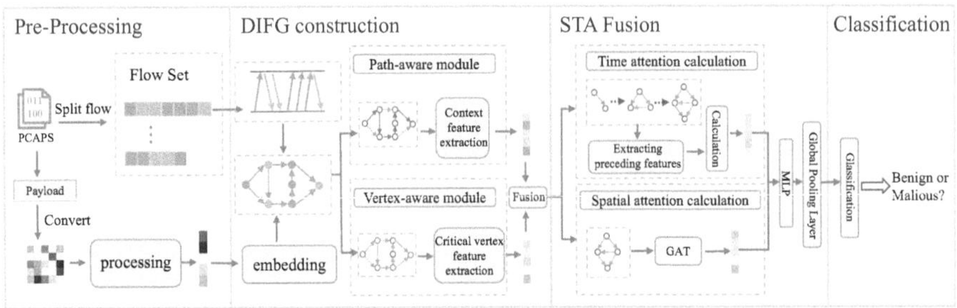

Fig. 2. The overall Approach

them into graph vertices as features. The DIFG is constructed based on the generation and evolution of interactive flows. Fused features are obtained through the graph feature fusion module and then fed into the spatiotemporal attention fusion stage to derive the full-graph feature at the current timestep. Finally, the feature is input to a trained classification layer, which, combined with an early detection mechanism, outputs the classification result.

4.2 Pre-procession Phase

Packet-level features are extracted from pcap files using the Python packet parsing tool Scapy [25]. We select the payload bytes of each packet as raw features, convert these bytes into corresponding values within [0, 255], and generate grayscale images based on these values. To enhance image features, we adopt a hierarchical sampling strategy combined with a lightweight encoder to reduce spatial resolution and emphasize informative content.

The input image $I \in \mathbb{R}^{n \times n}$ is downsampled via average pooling at three levels, resulting in feature maps $S_1 \in \mathbb{R}^{n/2 \times n/2}$, $S_2 \in \mathbb{R}^{n/4 \times n/4}$, and $S_3 \in \mathbb{R}^{n/8 \times n/8}$. These are then upsampled to the original resolution and concatenated to form a multi-scale feature representation $S \in \mathbb{R}^{n \times n \times 4}$.

An attention map $S' \in \mathbb{R}^{n \times n}$ is computed to reweight the spatial features as follows:

$$S' = \text{Sigmoid}(\text{Conv}_{1\times1}(S)) \tag{1}$$

Here, $\text{Conv}_{1\times1}$ denotes a 1×1 convolution that aggregates multi-channel spatial features into a single-channel attention map.

Using this attention map, we enhance the input image feature by:

$$I_{\text{enhanced}} = I \odot (1 + S'), \quad I_{\text{enhanced}} \in \mathbb{R}^{n \times n} \tag{2}$$

Finally, the enhanced image is flattened and projected into a feature vector via a learned linear transformation:

$$x = W_x^{\top} \cdot \text{Flatten}(I_{\text{enhanced}}), \quad W_x \in \mathbb{R}^{n^2 \times d}, \ x \in \mathbb{R}^d \tag{3}$$

The resulting vector x is used as the attention-enhanced packet feature, which also serves as the graph node feature.

4.3 Graph Feature Fusion Phase

Based on the constructed DIFG and SP, we introduce critical path and critical vertex awareness mechanisms to obtain graph features that integrate both SP and critical vertex information.

Critical Path-Aware Encoding Module: For each vertex v_i along the SP, we define its local context as the set of w preceding and w succeeding vertices. The context encoding $C(v_i)$ is computed as:

$$C(v_i) = \sum_{a=i-w}^{i+w} W_c \cdot x_{v_a} \cdot \alpha_a \tag{4}$$

where W_c is a learnable transformation matrix. The attention weight α_a reflects the relevance between the center vertex and its neighbors, and is calculated using:

$$\alpha_a = \text{softmax}(W_a \cdot [x_{v_i}; x_{v_a}]) \tag{5}$$

where W_a is a learnable weight vector used to compute the attention score for each context vertex. Finally, the path-aware representation of vertex v_i is defined as:

$$h_{v_i}^{\text{path}} = x_{v_i} + C(v_i) \tag{6}$$

where $h_{v_i}^{\text{path}}$ captures both the original vertex features and the local contextual interactions along the path.

Critical Vertex-Aware Encoding Module: Critical vertices refer to the previously defined merge and fork vertex. A vertex is classified as a *merge vertex* if it satisfies $d_{\text{in}}(v) = 2$, indicating it has two incoming edges. Similarly, a vertex is defined as a *fork vertex* if $d_{\text{out}}(v) = 2$, meaning it has two outgoing edges.

The feature of a fork vertex h_v^{fork} is computed as:

$$h_v^{\text{fork}} = W_f \cdot \left[x_v \parallel \sum_{u \in N_{\text{out}}(v)} x_u \right] \tag{7}$$

where W_f is a learnable weight matrix, and $N_{\text{out}}(v)$ denotes the set of vertices directly reachable from v.

Similarly, the feature of a merge vertex h_v^{merge} is defined as:

$$h_v^{\text{merge}} = W_m \cdot \left[\sum_{u \in N_{\text{in}}(v)} x_u \parallel x_v \right] \tag{8}$$

where W_m is another learnable weight matrix, and $N_{\text{in}}(v)$ represents the set of vertices with edges pointing to v.

The final vertex feature h_v is assigned according to the vertex's degree properties:

$$h_v = \begin{cases} h_v^{\text{merge}}, & \text{if } d_{\text{in}}(v) = 2 \text{ and } d_{\text{out}}(v) \neq 2 \\ h_v^{\text{fork}}, & \text{if } d_{\text{out}}(v) = 2 \text{ and } d_{\text{in}}(v) \neq 2 \\ x_v, & \text{otherwise} \end{cases} \tag{9}$$

Based on gated feature fusion, we integrate the critical path representation h_v^{path} and the critical vertex representation h_v using a learnable fusion weight $g_v \in [0, 1]$. The fused representation is defined as:

$$h_v^{\text{fused}} = g_v \cdot h_v^{\text{path}} + (1 - g_v) \cdot h_v \tag{10}$$

4.4 Spatio-Temporal Attention Fusion Phase

Given the current fused feature set $H^{\text{fused}} = \{h_v^{\text{fused}} \mid v \in V\}$ and the historical fused feature sequence $[H_{t-w}^{\text{fused}}, \ldots, H_{t-1}^{\text{fused}}]$ constructed from the previous w time steps, temporal and spatial attention mechanisms are applied to derive spatiotemporal feature representations.

Temporal Attention Calculation: For each vertex v along the current path, self-attention [26] is applied to the Query, Key, and Value representations of the historical features. Specifically, the query, key, and value vectors are computed as $q_v = W_q h_v^{\text{fused}}, \quad k_v^j = W_k h_v^{\text{fusedj}}, \quad value_v^{\text{j}} = W_{\text{value}} h_v^{\text{fusedj}}$, where h_v^{fusedj} is the fused feature of vertex v at time step $t - j$, and $h_v^{\text{fusedj}} \in H_{t-j}^{\text{fused}}$.

The attention weights are normalized by softmax to obtain the combined historical representation:

$$c_v = \sum_{j=1}^{w} \text{softmax}\left(\frac{q_v (k_v^j)^\top}{\sqrt{d}}\right) \cdot value_v^{\text{j}} \tag{11}$$

The temporal attention computation process is illustrated in Fig. 3. The temporally enhanced feature, which incorporates historical attention, is defined as $h_v^{\text{temp}} = h_v^{\text{fused}} + c_v$.

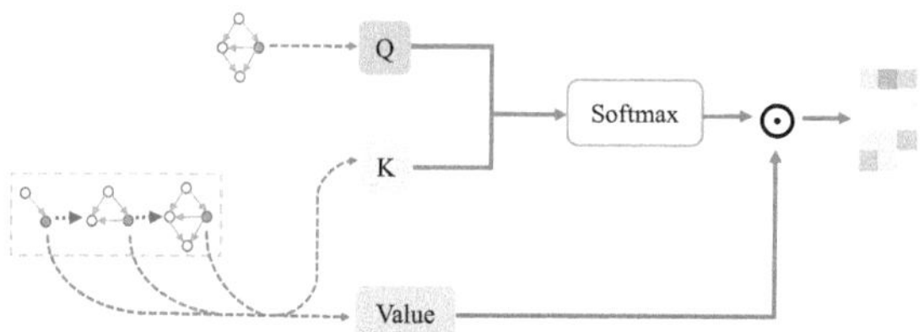

Fig. 3. Time Attention Calculation Process

Spatial Attention Calculation: The spatial attention mechanism is based on an improved graph attention network (GAT) [27], which incorporates a learnable temporal decay term $\exp(-\tau \Delta t_{ij})$. Here, τ is a learnable decay coefficient, and $\Delta t_{ij} = t_i - t_j$ denotes the time difference between vertices i and j. The spatial attention coefficient is computed as

$$e_{ij} = \text{LeakyReLU}\left(a^\top [h_i^{\text{fused}} \parallel h_j^{\text{fused}}]\right) \cdot \exp(-\tau \Delta t_{ij}) \tag{12}$$

where h_i^{fused} and h_j^{fused} are the fused feature vectors of vertices i and j, respectively. $N(i)$ denotes the set of vertices adjacent to vertex i in the graph. The attention coefficients are normalized across the neighbors $N(i)$ of vertex i by the softmax function:

$$\alpha_{ij} = \frac{\exp(e_{ij})}{\sum_{k \in N(i)} \exp(e_{ik})} \tag{13}$$

The spatially aggregated feature is then given by

$$h_i^{\text{spatial}} = h_i^{\text{fused}} + \sum_{j \in N(i)} \alpha_{ij} h_j^{\text{fused}} \tag{14}$$

Finally, a multi-layer perceptron (MLP) is applied to fuse the temporal and spatial features, yielding the final vertex representation:

$$h_i^{\text{final}} = \text{MLP}\big([h_i^{\text{temp}}, h_i^{\text{spatial}}]\big). \tag{15}$$

Global pooling over all vertices produces the graph-level feature at the current time step:

$$h_{\text{global}}^{(t)} = \frac{1}{n} \sum_{i=1}^{n} h_i^{\text{final}}, \tag{16}$$

where n is the number of vertices.

4.5 Classification Layer and Early Detection

In practical detection, we introduce an early detection mechanism. Under our mechanism, each interaction flow is detected at least twice, significantly reducing computational overhead while ensuring both accuracy and responsiveness. Our detection timing follows these rules:

- **Initial Detection** (t_0): Perform detection when the interaction flow is first created.
- **Subsequent Detection** (t_k): Perform detection when a flow segment ends, i.e., when the packet direction changes at time t_k.
- **Final Detection** (t_f): Perform the last detection when the interaction flow completes, meaning it has been inactive for a prolonged period—specifically, when the current time minus the last update time exceeds a timeout threshold.

Accordingly, we define the set of detection time steps $\mathcal{T}$ as: $\mathcal{T} = \{t_0\} \cup \{t_k\} \cup \{t_f\}$. We introduce a classification layer and specify detection time steps $t \in \mathcal{T}$ to enable early detection. For our binary classification task, the prediction at time step t is computed as:

$$y_t = \text{Sigmoid}\left(W_t^\top \cdot h_{\text{global}}^{(t)} + b_c\right), \tag{17}$$

where $h_{\text{global}}^{(t)}$ is the graph-level feature at time t, W_t and b_c are learnable parameters. We use binary cross-entropy as the loss function, defined as:

$$\text{Loss} = -y_{\text{true}} \log y - (1 - y_{\text{true}}) \log(1 - y), \tag{18}$$

where y_{true} is the ground truth label (0 for benign, 1 for malicious), and y is the predicted probability of malicious behavior.

5 Experimental Evaluation

In this section, to evaluate the detection performance of our proposed approach, we formulate the following research questions:

- RQ1: Does our proposed approach achieve strong detection performance and accurately identify malicious behavior?
- RQ2: To what extent does each individual component of the proposed approach contribute to the effective detection of malicious traffic?
- RQ3: Does the early detection mechanism integrated into our approach enable early-stage detection with high accuracy?

5.1 Datasets Description

To comprehensively evaluate the performance of our approach, we constructed a dataset $Dataset_{CIC}$ based on public datasets, and another dataset $Dataset_{Lab}$ based on self-collected traffic.

The $Dataset_{CIC}$ samples were extracted from the raw pcap files of two public datasets: CIC-IDS2017 [28] and CSE-CIC-IDS2018 [29]. Both were collected under simulated network environments with labeled benign and attack traffic. We treated all attack flows as malicious and merged samples from both datasets for subsequent analysis.

For the $Dataset_{Lab}$, we captured pcap files representing benign traffic from hundreds of real devices running common protocols in a campus laboratory environment. Malicious traffic was generated in a controlled setting by deploying representative malware (e.g., remote access tools, cryptominers, trojans, and worms), and pcap files were collected by recording their communications with remote command-and-control servers to simulate realistic attack scenarios.

During datasets construction, we ensured random sampling and maintained a balanced class distribution. The raw packet data was parsed into relevant information such as 5-tuples. For each interaction flow, a DIFG was constructed whenever a new packet was added to the flow, and each DIFG was saved as an individual *.pt* file. As a result, each interaction flow corresponds to a sequence of *.pt* files. Table 2 presents the number of interaction flows in the processed dataset.

Table 2. Summary of Experimental Datasets

Dataset	Category	Samples	Dataset	Category	Samples
$Dataset_{CIC}$	Benign	48824	$Dataset_{Lab}$	Benign	41824
	Malicious	48921		Malicious	42310
	Total	**97745**		**Total**	**84134**

5.2 Evaluation Metrics

To assess classification performance, a true positive is defined as a correctly classified malicious graph, a false positive as a benign graph misclassified as malicious, a true negative as a correctly classified benign graph, and a false negative as a malicious graph misclassified as benign. The model's performance is evaluated using four standard metrics: Accuracy, Precision, Recall and F1-score.

5.3 Evaluation Results

RQ1: Does our approach achieve strong detection performance and effectively identify malicious behavior?

To evaluate the effectiveness of our approach, we compare it with four classical or advanced methods in malicious traffic detection as baselines. These methods are related to ours but use different techniques. A brief overview is given below.

- 1D-CNN [14]: Study on end-to-end encrypted traffic classification using 1D-CNN.
- TSCRNN [18]: The study extracts abstract spatial features using GNNs and employs stacked Bi-LSTMs to capture temporal dependencies.
- GraphAPP [11]: This research models encrypted DApp stream information with graph structures and proposes a GNNs-based classifier.
- DE-GNN [30]: This study extracts traffic-level features using GNNs and performs classification by integrating features from both packet headers and payloads.

We split the two aforementioned datasets into training, validation, and test sets with an 8:1:1 ratio, constructed DIFGs from interaction flows, and conducted experiments. The comparison results on the test sets are shown in Table 3. Based on these results, we draw the following conclusions:

- Compared with multiple baseline models, our proposed approach achieves the best performance across all four evaluation metrics, demonstrating the overall effectiveness of our method.
- Both the 1D-CNN model and the LSTM-based TSCRNN model exhibit relatively limited performance, highlighting the superiority of graph neural network-based approaches in this task.
- Compared with two GNN-based methods, GraphDAPP and DE-GNN, our method also performs better. While both baselines rely on the Traffic Interaction Graph for classification, our approach introduces the DIFG and integrates STA mechanisms, enabling more comprehensive extraction of interaction features and more accurate identification of malicious behavior within overall network traffic.

Table 3. Performance of our approach and baseline approaches

Approaches	$Dataset_{CIC}$				$Dataset_{Lab}$			
	Accuracy	Precision	Recall	F1-score	Accuracy	Precision	Recall	F1-score
1D-CNN [14]	64.69%	65.03%	63.54%	64.27%	59.97%	60.22%	58.73%	59.47%
TSCRNN [18]	78.23%	77.41%	79.73%	76.73%	68.23%	69.98%	63.87%	66.78%
GraphAPP [11]	82.50%	81.51%	84.07%	82.77%	73.70%	73.13%	74.93%	74.02%
DE-GNN [30]	84.16%	85.25%	82.51%	83.86%	78.93%	80.35%	76.60%	78.43%
Ours	**99.41%**	**99.50%**	**99.33%**	**99.42%**	**99.75%**	**99.63%**	**99.88%**	**99.75%**

RQ2: To what extent does each individual component of the proposed approach contribute to the effective detection of malicious traffic?
To investigate the contribution of each component in our approach, we conducted ablation studies under the following settings:

- No-Graph (Without Graph Structure): To evaluate the effectiveness of the proposed DIFG, we remove both the DIFG and the associated SP. Instead, we use a CNN to model the interaction flow features. This method is denoted as No-Graph.
- No-STA (Without STA Mechanism): To evaluate the impact of the attention mechanism, we remove the STA module and replace it with a standard DNN for graph classification. This method is denoted as No-STA.
- No-SP (Without SP): To verify the effectiveness of the proposed SP, we removed the SP along with its associated feature fusion module. This method is denoted as No-SP.

The ablation study demonstrates that each module in our proposed approach contributes significantly to the detection of malicious behaviors. The DIFG plays a highly significant role, while the STA module introduces notable gains through enhanced spatiotemporal feature extraction. Moreover, removing the SP leads to performance degradation, indicating its effectiveness in capturing the temporal sequences. Overall, these results confirm the rationality and effectiveness of our design (Table 4).

Table 4. Impact of Model Components on Detection Performance

Approaches	$Dataset_{CIC}$				$Dataset_{Lab}$			
	Accuracy	Precision	Recall	F1-score	Accuracy	Precision	Recall	F1-score
No-Graph	65.03%	65.27%	64.27%	64.76%	64.53%	64.21%	65.67%	64.93%
No-STA	74.21%	68.14%	85.56%	75.86%	87.57%	86.85%	88.53%	87.69%
No-SP	88.30%	91.30%	85.71%	88.42%	94.07%	92.92%	95.40%	94.14%
Ours	**99.41%**	**99.50%**	**99.33%**	**99.42%**	**99.75%**	**99.63%**	**99.88%**	**99.75%**

RQ3: Does the early detection mechanism integrated into our approach enable early-stage detection with high accuracy?

We conduct experiments based on the DIFG constructed from each interaction flow at different detection time points, following the same dataset partitioning rules as in RQ1. For both datasets, we present line charts showing various evaluation metrics on the test set at the first 10 detection time points. As shown in Fig 4(a), our approach achieves approximately 98% accuracy at the fifth detection time point on both datasets, and all evaluation metrics remain at a high level thereafter. Fig 4(b)presents the average number of packets at each detection time point across the two datasets and further illustrates that the average number of packets required at this point is 10.51 and 10.76, respectively. This indicates that our method can achieve high-accuracy detection using only about 10 packets on average. It also demonstrates that our approach can effectively represent traffic interaction behaviors and identify malicious activities. Each flow requires only a small number of initial interaction packets to enable accurate intrusion detection at an early stage.

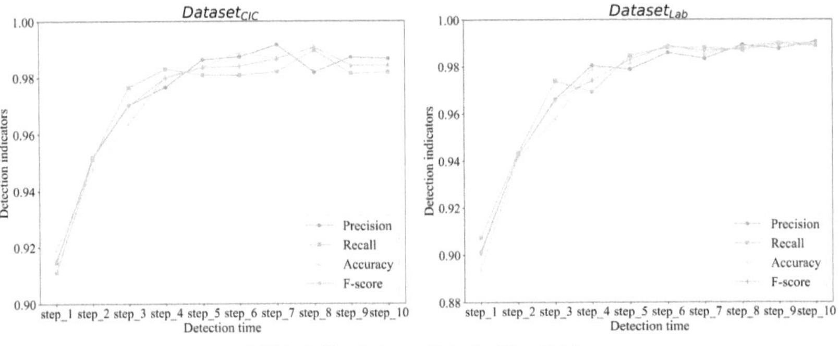

(a) Metric Trends Across Detection Time Points

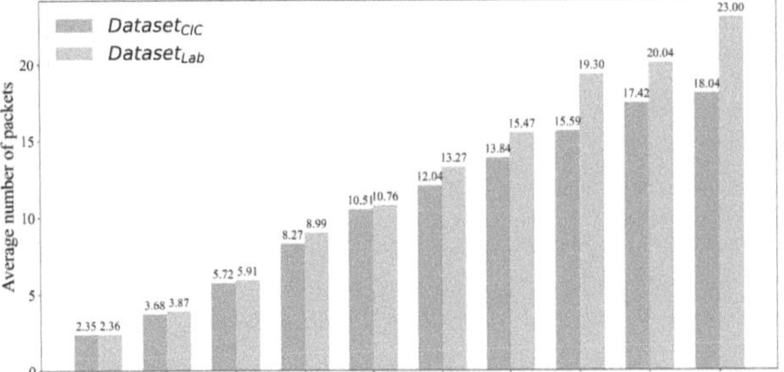

(b)Average Number of Packets per Flow at Each Detection Time Point

Fig. 4. Traffic Analysis Across Detection Time Points

6 Conclusion

In this paper, we construct the DIFG to represent network traffic interaction behaviors and introduce the SP mechanism to capture temporal sequence features. Based on this, we propose an early detection approach for malicious traffic that integrates graph-structured feature extraction with the STA mechanism to achieve efficient detection at the early stages of traffic interactions. Extensive experimental results validate the superior performance of our method, consistently outperforming multiple baseline models. Ablation studies further demonstrate the critical roles of each module in the overall framework. Furthermore, early detection experiments showcase the effectiveness and practical value of our approach in identifying malicious traffic at an early stage.

In future work, we will extend the method to diverse protocols and real-world datasets, and explore its adaptation to real-time intrusion detection with explainable AI to enhance practical applicability.

Acknowledgement. This work was supported by the grants from the GuangDong Basic and Applied Basic Research Foundation (2025A1515010114), the Science and Technology Program of Guangzhou (2025A04J4334), the Shenzhen Science and Technology Program (SGDX20230116091244004), the China University Industry-University-Research Innovation Fund (2024WA062), the Special Funds for the Cultivation of Guangdong College Students' Scientific and Technological Innovation ("Climbing Program" Special Funds, pdjh2024a136) and the project from Cyberspace Security Engineering Technology Research Center of Guangdong University of Technology.

References

1. Sharma, A., Lashkari, A.H.: A survey on encrypted network traffic: a comprehensive survey of identification/classification techniques, challenges, and future directions. Comput. Netw., 110984 (2024)
2. Zeng, Z.R., Xun, P., Peng, W., Zhao, B.K.: Toward identifying malicious encrypted traffic with a causality detection system. J. Inf. Secur. Appl. **80**, 103644 (2024)
3. Zhang, P., et al.: Real-time malicious traffic detection with online isolation forest over SD-WAN. IEEE Trans. Inf. Forensics Secur. **18**, 2076–2090 (2023)
4. Shen, M., Liu, Y., Zhu, L., Xiaojiang, D., Jiankun, H.: Fine-grained webpage fingerprinting using only packet length information of encrypted traffic. IEEE Trans. Inf. Forensics Secur. **16**, 2046–2059 (2020)
5. Wang, Z., Thing, V.L.L.: Feature mining for encrypted malicious traffic detection with deep learning and other machine learning algorithms. Comput. Secur. **128**, 103143 (2023)
6. Aceto, G., Ciuonzo, D., Montieri, A., Pescapé, A.: DISTILLER: encrypted traffic classification via multimodal multitask deep learning. J. Netw. Comput. Appl. **183–184**, 102985 (2021)
7. Lan, J., Liu, X., Li, B., Li, Y., Geng, T.: DarknetSec: a novel self-attentive deep learning method for darknet traffic classification and application identification. Comput. Secur. **116**, 102663 (2022)

8. Zhong, M., Lin, M., Zhang, C., Zeshui, X.: A survey on graph neural networks for intrusion detection systems: methods, trends and challenges. Comput. Secur., 103821 (2024)
9. Wang, L., et al.: TGPrint: attack fingerprint classification on encrypted network traffic based graph convolution attention networks. Comput. Secur. **135**, 103466 (2023)
10. Yang, J., Jiang, X., Lei, Y., Liang, W., Ma, Z., Li, S.: MTSecurity: privacy-preserving malicious traffic classification using graph neural network and transformer. IEEE Trans. Netw. Serv. Manage. (2024)
11. Shen, M., Zhang, J., Zhu, L., Ke, X., Xiaojiang, D.: Accurate decentralized application identification via encrypted traffic analysis using graph neural networks. IEEE Trans. Inf. Forensics Secur. **16**, 2367–2380 (2021)
12. Wang, Z., Fok, K.W., Thing, V.L.L.: Machine learning for encrypted malicious traffic detection: approaches, datasets and comparative study. Comput. Secur. **113**, 102542 (2022)
13. Chuanpu, F., Li, Q., Shen, M., Ke, X.: Frequency domain feature based robust malicious traffic detection. IEEE/ACM Trans. Netw. **31**(1), 452–467 (2023)
14. Wang, W., Zhu, M., Wang, J., Zeng, X., Yang, Z.: End-to-end encrypted traffic classification with one-dimensional convolution neural networks. In: 2017 IEEE International Conference on Intelligence and Security Informatics (ISI), pp. 43–48. IEEE (2017)
15. Zang, X., Wang, T., Zhang, X., Gong, J., Gao, P., Zhang, G.: Encrypted malicious traffic detection based on natural language processing and deep learning. Comput. Netw. **250**, 110598 (2024)
16. Liu, Y., Wang, X., Bo, Q., Zhao, F.: ATVITSC: a novel encrypted traffic classification method based on deep learning. IEEE Trans. Inf. Forensics Secur. **19**, 9374–9389 (2024)
17. Lotfollahi, M., Siavoshani, M.J., Zade, R.S.H., Saberian, M.: Deep packet: a novel approach for encrypted traffic classification using deep learning. Soft. Comput. **24**(3), 1999–2012 (2020)
18. Lin, K., Xiaolong, X., Gao, H.: TSCRNN: a novel classification scheme of encrypted traffic based on flow spatiotemporal features for efficient management of IIoT. Comput. Netw. **190**, 107974 (2021)
19. Lin, X., Xiong, G., Gou, G., Li, Z., Shi, J., Jing, Yu.: ET-BERT: a contextualized datagram representation with pre-training transformers for encrypted traffic classification. In: Proceedings of the ACM Web Conference, vol. 2022, pp. 633–642 (2022)
20. Devlin, J., Chang, M.-W., Lee, K., Toutanova, K.: BERT: pre-training of deep bidirectional transformers for language understanding (2019)
21. Li, Y., et al.: GraphDDoS: effective DDoS attack detection using graph neural networks. In: 2022 IEEE 25th International Conference on Computer Supported Cooperative Work in Design (CSCWD), pp. 1275–1280. IEEE (2022)
22. Chen, J., Xie, H., Cai, S., Song, L., Geng, B., Guo, W.: GCN-MHSA: a novel malicious traffic detection method based on graph convolutional neural network and multi-head self-attention mechanism. Comput. Secur. **147**, 104083 (2024)
23. Chen, J., Song, L., Cai, S., Xie, H., Yin, S., Ahmad, B.: TLS-MHSA: an efficient detection model for encrypted malicious traffic based on multi-head self-attention mechanism. ACM Trans. Priv. Secur. **26**(4), 1–21 (2023)
24. Huang, W., Han, X., Zhang, M., Li, M., Liu, W., Yang, Z., Yang, H.: MFFAN: multiple features fusion with attention networks for malicious traffic detection. In:

2022 IEEE International Conference on Trust, Security and Privacy in Computing and Communications (TrustCom), pp. 391–398. IEEE (2022)
25. Biondi, P., et al.: Scapy: packet crafting for Python. https://github.com/secdev/scapy. Accessed 24 Jun 2025
26. Vaswani, A., et al.: Attention is all you need. In: Advances in Neural Information Processing Systems, vol. 30 (2017)
27. Veličković, P., Cucurull, G., Casanova, A., Romero, A., Liò, P., Bengio, Y.: Graph attention networks (2018)
28. Sharafaldin, I., Lashkari, A.H., Ghorbani, A.A., et al.: Toward generating a new intrusion detection dataset and intrusion traffic characterization. In: ICISSp 2018, pp. 108–116 (2018)
29. CSE-CIC-IDS2018 dataset (2021). https://www.unb.ca/cic/datasets/ids-2018.html
30. Han, X., et al.: DE-GNN: dual embedding with graph neural network for fine-grained encrypted traffic classification. Comput. Netw. **245**, 110372 (2024)

Revealing the Frailty of Static Benchmarks: The DyNA-IDS Framework for Concept Drift Adaptation in Time-Series Network Intrusion Detection

Kun Jia, Haizhen Gao, Jiyun Chen, and Jiayin Qi(✉)

Cyberspace Institute of Advanced Technology, Guangzhou University, Guangzhou 510555, China
qijiayin@139.com

Abstract. While many machine learning-based Network Intrusion Detection Systems (NIDS) have demonstrated near-perfect classification accuracy on static datasets, this "static perfection" often masks their inherent fragility when confronting continuously evolving, real-world cyber threats. When the evaluation paradigm shifts from static cross-validation to more realistic time-series scenarios, the performance of these models undergoes catastrophic degradation due to the presence of "concept drift." To address the adaptability challenge of static models in dynamic environments, this paper proposes a novel dynamic dual-autoencoder framework—DyNA-IDS—capable of efficient online learning and self-adaptation in non-stationary data streams. The core of this framework is a unique, unsupervised drift detection module composed of a "benchmark autoencoder" (trained on benign traffic) and a "drift autoencoder" (trained on attack traffic) operating in parallel. Innovatively discarding traditional fixed-threshold methods, it instead utilizes a dual-stream parallel Kolmogorov-Smirnov (K-S) test mechanism. This approach continuously monitors the distribution of the reconstruction error difference between the two autoencoders across both long and short time scales, enabling the synchronous and highly sensitive perception of both gradual and sudden drifts. Once a drift is confirmed, a composite loss function, which includes an elastic regularization term, guides the entire framework through an incremental joint training process. This serves to effectively mitigate catastrophic forgetting while adapting to new attack patterns. Experimental results on a large-scale, public time-series network traffic dataset show that DyNA-IDS exhibits exceptional performance on dynamic data streams, achieving an average F1-score of 0.996 and significantly outperforming static models as well as multiple classic baseline drift detection methods. This research not only provides a robust, end-to-end framework for addressing concept drift in NIDS but also highlights the importance of evaluating models in dynamic environments, offering a solid theoretical and practical foundation for building truly resilient, next-generation cybersecurity systems. The source code is available at: https://github.com/GZHU-Innovation-Intersection-Lab/DyNA-IDS.

R. Chen et al. (Eds.): Inscrypt 2025, LNCS 16409, pp. 332–348, 2026.
https://doi.org/10.1007/978-981-95-6203-9_18

Keywords: Concept drift · Network intrusion detection · Time-series analysis · Online learning · Model adaptation

1 Introduction

With the profound evolution of digitalization, cyberspace has become a critical infrastructure for the functioning of modern society. This development, however, is accompanied by cybersecurity threats of unprecedented complexity, dynamism, and adversarial nature [1]. The rapid iteration of attack techniques and diversification of attack vectors have rendered traditional defense systems, reliant on static rules or signatures, increasingly inadequate [38]. Against this backdrop, the intelligence and adaptability of Network Intrusion Detection Systems (NIDS), as a core component of proactive defense, have become a focal point for both academia and industry.

NIDS based on machine learning, particularly deep learning, have shown immense potential in automatically learning and identifying anomalous patterns from massive data volumes, owing to their powerful non-linear modeling capabilities [32]. However, a fundamental challenge limits the long-term effectiveness of these advanced models in the real world: **Concept Drift** [17]. The network environment is not static: new applications and services generate new traffic patterns, user behaviors evolve over time, and, most importantly, attackers continuously alter their strategies to evade detection. These factors collectively contribute to dynamic changes in data distribution, causing the decision boundary between normal and abnormal to constantly shift. A static model trained on historical data will inevitably suffer performance degradation when faced with such changes, leading to increased false negatives and false positives, and ultimately forfeiting its deployment value [34].

Although extensive research has been dedicated to addressing concept drift, its application in the NIDS context still faces two primary challenges. First, **the scarcity of supervised information**: most drift adaptation methods rely on high-quality, real-time ground-truth labels to guide model updates. In the cybersecurity domain, however, obtaining such labels is costly and subject to significant delays, making supervised online learning impractical. Second, **knowledge forgetting during adaptation**: traditional model update strategies, such as simple incremental fine-tuning or sliding-window-based retraining, often face the risk of **"Catastrophic Forgetting."** This occurs when a model, in learning new attack patterns, compromises or completely overwrites its memory of previously learned normal patterns, leading to a loss of long-term stability.

To confront these challenges, this paper proposes a novel **Dynamic Dual-Autoencoder framework (DyNA-IDS)**, an online learning system specifically designed for concept drift adaptation in NIDS. The core contributions of this framework can be summarized in three points:

1. **An Unsupervised Dual-Autoencoder (Dual-AE) Drift Signal Generation Mechanism:** We construct a parallel architecture composed of a "Benchmark AE" trained on normal traffic and a "Drift AE" trained on attack

traffic. By comparing the distribution of the error difference from their respective reconstructions of the same data, we create a highly sensitive drift signal that can quantify changes in data distribution without requiring external labels.

2. **A Robust Dual-Stream Parallel Statistical Detector:** Instead of employing fixed thresholds, we design a parallel detection strategy based on the **Kolmogorov-Smirnov (K-S) test**. This strategy continuously monitors statistically significant changes in the aforementioned error difference distribution across both long and short time windows, thereby enabling a timely response to both gradual and sudden drifts.
3. **A Joint Adaptation Strategy to Mitigate Catastrophic Forgetting:** Once a drift is confirmed, the framework activates a composite loss function containing classification, reconstruction, and an **elastic regularization term** to perform a coordinated, incremental update of the entire framework (classifier and Dual-AE). This regularization term penalizes excessive deviation from established knowledge, thus maximally preserving historical knowledge while adapting to new concepts and ensuring the model's long-term stability.

The remainder of this paper is organized as follows: Sect. 2 provides an in-depth review of related work in concept drift detection and continual learning. Section 3 details the architectural design and algorithmic implementation of the DyNA-IDS framework. Section 4 presents and analyzes the experimental results on a large-scale public dataset to validate the effectiveness of our method. Section 5 concludes the paper and discusses future work.

2 Related Work

Concept drift, the phenomenon where the underlying statistical properties of a data stream change over time in a non-stationary manner, necessitates that machine learning models possess capabilities for online learning and self-adaptation [44]. In dynamic and adversarial domains such as cybersecurity, effectively addressing concept drift is key to building robust and long-lasting intelligent systems [46]. This chapter reviews related work from three dimensions: drift detection, deep learning applications, and continual learning adaptation strategies.

Drift detection mechanisms serve as the "eyes" of an adaptive system. Early methods were primarily based on the statistical monitoring of classifier performance. For instance, the pioneering Drift Detection Method (DDM) determines concept stability by monitoring the binomial distribution of the classification error rate [16], whereas the Early Drift Detection Method (EDDM) exhibits better sensitivity to gradual drifts by analyzing the distance distribution between misclassified samples [7]. Another prominent class of methods is grounded in statistical bound theory, such as the Hoeffding's inequality, which provides a theoretical foundation for online, non-parametric drift detection [14] and has inspired a series of fast detection algorithms like FHDDM [33]. To move away from reliance on classifiers and labels, some research has shifted towards unsupervised statistical tests, identifying anomalies by directly analyzing distributional changes within the data stream itself [15]. To better capture temporal dynamics, the sliding window mechanism has been widely adopted. The classic ADWIN [9] dynamically adjusts its window size to find the optimal cut-point where a distribution change has occurred. Subsequent works have further refined the statistical methods within windows, such as using the K-S test to compare distributions between windows [3], introducing Bayesian theory for dynamic threshold updates [6], or leveraging data structures like prefix trees to improve processing efficiency [20]. Recent studies have also begun to focus on more granular intra-window data processing, for instance, by applying different weighting strategies to differentiate the importance of new versus old data [19] or by dynamically adjusting adaptation strategies based on the type of drift detected [29]. These methods have collectively advanced the development of efficient, real-time drift detection technologies.

With the rise of deep learning, researchers have begun to leverage the powerful non-linear modeling capabilities of neural networks to handle more complex drift patterns. Among these, the **Autoencoder (AE)** has become a research hotspot in the field of drift detection due to its unsupervised nature and excellent performance on high-dimensional data [24]. Its core principle is that an autoencoder, well-trained on stable data, will exhibit a significant increase in reconstruction error when faced with new, out-of-distribution data; this change in error can serve as a reliable indicator of drift [2]. In addition to reconstruction-based methods, other studies have explored new avenues, such as inferring concept evolution by monitoring the dynamic changes of the model weights themselves [41], or constructing student-teacher models (STUDD) to identify drift under unsupervised conditions [10].

Meanwhile, with the rise of Large Language Models (LLMs), researchers have begun to explore their potential in concept drift detection. DriftWatch tested a prompt consistency method that directly utilizes an LLM for detection; its principle is to identify drift by providing the model with multiple different prompts for the same input and measuring the stability and certainty of its outputs—the more unstable the predictions, the higher the likelihood of drift [23]. Other research positions LLMs as a "semantic judge" post-drift. In the framework proposed by Şenol et al., an efficient statistical model (OCDD) first detects if a semantic shift has occurred; once drift is confirmed, a domain knowledge-enhanced LLM is invoked to deeply analyze the nature of the drift, with its core role being to determine whether it is a benign topic change or a malicious act of fraud [36]. Another line of thought combines the powerful representation capabilities of LLMs with traditional statistical tools, a method adopted in studies by Feldhans et al. [13] and Khaki et al. [28]. This approach utilizes an LLM (such as BERT) to generate high-quality embedding vectors for text in a data stream, and then applies classic distribution test methods (like the Maximum Mean Discrepancy test) to these vectors to calculate the difference between new and old data distributions, thereby detecting drift. These deep learning-based ideas show immense potential, but researchers have also designed other comprehensive frameworks, such as INSOMNIA, a semi-supervised framework for Network Intrusion Detection (NIDS) [5], and LEAF, which not only detects drift but also explains and mitigates it [30]. Meanwhile, deep learning is also being used to improve the efficiency of network applications themselves. For example, NetGSR uses the idea of Generative Super Resolution to reconstruct high-fidelity network status from low-resolution measurement data to reduce monitoring overhead [40], while LightAMC uses compressive sensing for neuron pruning to create lightweight models suitable for resource-constrained devices like IoT [43]. Furthermore, beyond purely deep learning approaches, many studies have focused on building hybrid systems, such as combining clustering algorithms (e.g., K-Means) with traditional classifiers (e.g., SVM) to handle concept drift in data streams by dynamically updating clusters, achieving good results in the NIDS domain [21,22]. These works demonstrate the immense potential of deep models in capturing complex, non-linear concept drifts.

However, merely detecting *when* a drift occurs is insufficient; *how* to adapt is a more profound challenge, with its core difficulty lying in overcoming "catastrophic forgetting." Traditional model update methods, such as window-based retraining or naive incremental fine-tuning, for instance, the OASW framework retrains its LightGBM model using new samples collected in an adaptive window after detecting a drift [45], but such methods often lead to the model's memory of previously acquired knowledge being severely compromised while learning new knowledge. To solve this problem, **Continual Learning** or Incremental Learning has become a leading-edge research direction. The main strategies can be divided into three categories. Regularization-based strategies add a penalty term to the loss function to constrain modifications to weights relevant to old tasks while learning a new task [26]. Replay-based strategies store a small subset of representative old samples (exemplars) and retrain on them jointly with new task data to "review" old knowledge; a more refined strategy is the "informed mitigation" adopted by the LEAF framework, which selectively forgets past samples that caused high error and over-samples new data from regions identified as under-trained [30]. Parameter-isolation methods assign independent model parameters to new tasks to avoid interference between new and old knowledge.

In the field of cybersecurity, research in continual learning is burgeoning. Researchers have explored multiple paths, including using semi-supervised learning to address label scarcity. The INSOMNIA framework adopts an innovative semi-supervised method: it uses Active Learning to select the model's most uncertain new samples and then utilizes an independent "label estimator" based on a different learning paradigm to generate pseudo-labels for updating the main model, thereby reducing the reliance on manual labeling [5]. Furthermore, adaptation is not limited to model parameters but can also be the data collection process itself; for example, NetGSR's XAMINER feedback mechanism can dynamically adjust the data reporting rate of network devices based on model uncertainty to achieve a balance between efficiency and fidelity [40]. Moreover, with the growing emphasis on data privacy and security, adapting to drift on distributed data silos has become a new research focus, for which Federated Learning offers a promising solution framework [27].

In summary, existing research has made significant progress in both drift detection and model adaptation. However, a research gap still exists in efficiently and seamlessly integrating both aspects, especially in NIDS scenarios that demand high real-time performance, low false-positive rates, and operate in the absence of labels. Most methods either focus on detection or on adaptation, while an end-to-end framework that tightly integrates complex drift signal interpretation from deep models with an online adaptation mechanism resistant to forgetting remains underdeveloped. The DyNA-IDS proposed in this paper is designed to fill this gap, aiming to provide a comprehensive solution that features both highly sensitive detection and highly stable adaptation capabilities.

3 Methodology

This chapter provides a detailed exposition of our proposed Dynamic Dual-Autoencoder framework for Network Intrusion Detection (DyNA-IDS). The framework is engineered to effectively address concept drift in network traffic data through a closed-loop system that integrates unsupervised drift detection, a two-phases signal confirmation process, and online model adaptation.

As illustrated in Fig. 1, the complete workflow of DyNA-IDS is meticulously structured into three logical phases. **Phase 1 (Data Stream Acquisition)** is responsible for generating discrete data windows from the continuous network traffic. **Phase 2 (Drift Detection)**, the core of the framework, is subdivided into two phases: **Phase 2.1** utilizes the initial dataset to train a "Benchmark Autoencoder" and a "Drift Autoencoder" respectively, and establishes a baseline distribution for statistical comparison. **Phase 2.2** then proactively monitors whether this distribution undergoes significant changes during stream processing, employing a dual-window Kolmogorov-Smirnov (K-S) test mechanism. Once a drift signal is confirmed, the framework proceeds to **Phase 3 (Concept Drift Adaptation)**, where a joint incremental learning strategy updates the entire system's parameters to adapt to the new data environment. Upon completion of the adaptation, the system reverts to its continuous monitoring state, thus forming a complete adaptive closed loop.

3.1 Phase 1: Data Stream Modeling via Sliding Windows

Network traffic data acquisition constitutes the input phase of the overall framework. Its core task is to segment the continuous and infinite stream of network traffic into discrete, processable data blocks, thereby providing the data foundation for subsequent statistical detection, model training, and drift identification. To effectively capture the dynamic temporal features of network traffic, the framework employs the classic Sliding Window (SW) mechanism to segment the continuous data stream. Each data instance represents a preprocessed network flow record. We define a window of a fixed size N to capture N consecutive

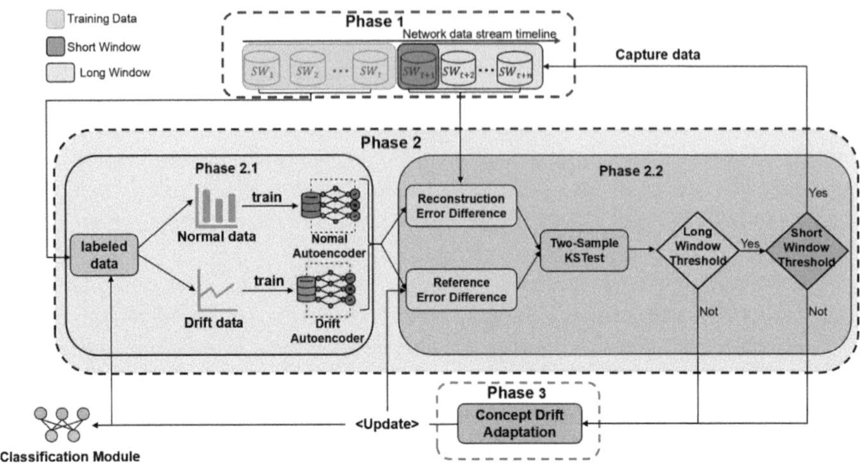

Fig. 1. The architecture and workflow of the proposed DyNA-IDS framework.

instances, which then slides forward over the data stream with a fixed stride S, continuously generating data blocks for analysis.

During the framework initialization phase, the system continuously captures data from multiple windows (SW_1 to SW_t) to form an initial training set containing a total of M×t instances. This dataset is then used for the initial training of the model in Phase 2. Following initialization, the system enters a continuous online monitoring mode, constantly capturing new data windows (SW_{t+1} to SW_{t+n}) to provide a steady stream of data input for subsequent real-time prediction and drift adaptation, and to establish a unified data capture framework for all ensuing phases.

3.2 Phase 2: Dual-Autoencoder Drift Detection

As the core innovation of our framework, this phase addresses the critical questions of 'if' and 'when' a drift occurs through two tightly coupled sub-phases: Data Classification and Concept Drift Detection.

Initial Training and Baseline Establishment. Conventional drift detection methods based on reconstruction error typically employ only a single autoencoder trained on normal data. However, such a singular model has difficulty distinguishing between benign, unseen data fluctuations and a true concept drift, rendering it prone to false positives.

To overcome this limitation, we propose a dual-autoencoder architecture consisting of a **Benchmark Autoencoder** (AE_{norm}) and a **Drift Autoencoder** (AE_{drift}). The core principle is to establish differentiated reconstruction capabilities through specialized training:

- The AE_{norm} is trained exclusively on normal (Benign) samples from the initial training set D_{train} to learn the intrinsic representations of the baseline data distribution. It is thereby capable of accurately reproducing normal samples with minimal reconstruction error.
- The AE_{drift} is trained exclusively on attack samples from D_{train}, capturing the defining characteristics of anomalous patterns.

The training for both models is an independent, unsupervised learning process. Their respective loss functions, based on Mean Squared Error (MSE), are defined as:

$$\mathcal{L}_{norm} = \frac{1}{n}\sum_{i=1}^{n} \|x_i - D_{norm}(E_{norm}(x_i))\|_2^2, \quad \text{where } x_i \in \text{Normal Data} \tag{1}$$

$$\mathcal{L}_{drift} = \frac{1}{m}\sum_{j=1}^{m} \|y_j - D_{drift}(E_{drift}(y_j))\|_2^2, \quad \text{where } y_j \in \text{Drift (Attack) Data} \tag{2}$$

Upon completion of their specialized training, the key to the detection mechanism lies in leveraging the differentiated capabilities of the two autoencoders. We use all the normal training data to compute a core metric: the **difference in reconstruction errors**. Compared to relying on the reconstruction error from a single autoencoder, utilizing the error difference between our two specialized models provides a more robust and discriminative signal.

For a normal sample, its reconstruction by the baseline autoencoder (AE_{norm}) yields a low Mean Squared Error (MSE), whereas its reconstruction by the drift autoencoder (AE_{drift}) results in a high MSE. Consequently, the difference between the two will be a significant negative value. This difference is powerful because it not only reflects the degree to which a data point deviates from the established norm but also indicates its **property affiliation**—that is, whether it more closely resembles a normal or a drift pattern. This makes the resulting signal significantly more sensitive to true changes in the data's underlying distribution. The metric for each normal sample x_i is therefore calculated as follows:

$$\text{Metric}_i = \text{MSE}(x_i, AE_{norm}(x_i)) - \text{MSE}(x_i, AE_{drift}(x_i)) \tag{3}$$

We collect the metric values for all normal samples to form a numerical distribution, which we term the **Baseline Reference Distribution** (D_{ref}). This distribution statistically profiles the system's behavior in a stable state, providing a solid foundation for subsequent statistical tests.

Dual-Window Concept Drift Detection via K-S Testing. When processing the real-time data stream, the framework employs a core mechanism based on statistical testing to proactively identify concept drift. Considering that network traffic data typically exhibits complex and non-parametric distribution patterns, we selected the **two-sample Kolmogorov-Smirnov (K-S) test** as our core statistical tool, as it requires no prior assumptions about the data's underlying distribution.

The theoretical cornerstone of our detector is hypothesis testing. A baseline reference distribution of the Mean Squared Error (MSE) difference, denoted as D_{ref}, is established from stable, normal data and statistically represents the **null hypothesis** (H_0). The distribution from a new data window, $D_{current}$, is then tested against this baseline. The K-S test quantifies the maximum discrepancy between the empirical distribution functions of $D_{current}$ and D_{ref}, yielding a **p-value**. If this p-value falls below a pre-defined significance level α, H_0 is rejected, indicating that a statistically significant drift has occurred.

To handle different types of drift concurrently, this test is applied within a parallel dual-window monitoring strategy:

- A **long window** (W_{long}), comprising the last N_{long} instances, focuses on analyzing data over a larger time span, aiming to capture slow, gradual, and global distributional changes.
- A **short window** (W_{short}), comprising only the last N_{short} instances, is more sensitive to transient shocks or abrupt changes in the data stream.

At each time step, K-S tests are performed independently for both windows against the reference distribution. If the p-value from **either** test falls below its respective threshold $(p_{long} < \alpha_{long}$ or $p_{short} < \alpha_{short})$, the null hypothesis is rejected, and the framework **confirms the occurrence of a concept drift, triggering the model adaptation process.**

3.3 Phase 3: Concept Drift Adaptation

To prevent unnecessary model updates from transient noise, a "multi-window verification mechanism" is employed. A concept drift is formally confirmed only if k consecutive drift warnings are issued.

Once confirmed, the data contained within the triggering window(s) is collected into a temporary adaptive training buffer, D_{adapt}. To address the confirmed distributional evolution, the framework collaboratively updates the parameters of the predictive model and the dual autoencoders by optimizing a unified, multi-objective loss function, L_{total}:

$$\mathcal{L}_{total} = \underbrace{\gamma\mathcal{L}_{cls} + \alpha\mathcal{L}_{recon\_norm} + \beta\mathcal{L}_{recon\_drift}}_{\text{Knowledge Update}} + \underbrace{\lambda\|\theta_{new} - \theta_{old}\|_2^2}_{\text{Knowledge Retention}} \tag{4}$$

This composite loss function is designed to balance two core objectives: knowledge acquisition and knowledge preservation. Its components are:

- $\mathcal{L}_{cls}$: The classification loss from the DNN, ensuring predictive accuracy on new data.
- $\mathcal{L}_{recon\_norm}$ & $\mathcal{L}_{recon\_drift}$: The reconstruction losses from the autoencoders, driving them to learn the new data patterns.

- $||\theta_{new} - \theta_{old}||_2^2$: An elastic regularization term that penalizes excessive changes to model parameters (θ), thereby mitigating catastrophic forgetting.

The hyperparameters α, β, γ, and λ weight the importance of each objective. Through this incremental training strategy, DyNA-IDS efficiently adapts to concept drifts at a low computational cost. After adaptation, the system resets the drift state and continues its monitoring process.

4 Experiment

This chapter presents an experimental evaluation of the proposed dual autoencoder-based method for concept drift detection and adaptation. The evaluation is twofold: first, we assess the method's capability to detect both abrupt and gradual drifts on synthetic datasets; second, we compare our proposed method against other state-of-the-art approaches. The experiments aim to verify that our method can accurately detect both abrupt and gradual drifts, while ensuring that the detected drifts are genuine and reliable, thereby minimizing false positives. Subsection 4.1 introduces the datasets and experimental setup, Subsect. 4.2 describes the evaluation metrics, and Subsect. 4.3 analyzes the experimental results, providing a comparison with baseline methods.

4.1 Dataset Overview

Our study employs the CIC-IDS-2017 dataset [37] for its experiments. This dataset is a public benchmark that highly simulates a real-world network environment, containing a rich and modern collection of both benign traffic and attack behaviors. The experimental design strictly adheres to the dataset's temporal structure, utilizing its five-day sequence (Monday to Friday) of progressively introduced attacks to simulate a dynamically evolving network environment (the specific attack distribution is detailed in Table 1). We use the purely benign traffic from Monday for initial model training and to establish a performance baseline. From Tuesday onwards, a sliding window mechanism is employed to process the subsequent data stream, allowing us to evaluate the framework's detection and adaptation performance against a series of concept drifts ranging from gradual to abrupt

4.2 Experimental Setup

The experiment employs a Deep Neural Network (DNN) as the base predictive model for the anomaly detection task. The DNN consists of a two-layer fully connected network (with 128 and 64 neurons, respectively), utilizing the ReLU activation function and a softmax function for the output layer. This model is trained for 50 epochs using the Adam optimizer with a learning rate of 0.001 and a batch size of 64. The network architecture of the dual autoencoders features neuron counts of 240, 112, and 24, with an initial learning rate of 0.00037. All

Table 1. Daily Attack Distribution in the CIC-IDS-2017 Dataset

Days	Labels
Monday	Benign
Tuesday	Brute Force, SFTP, and SSH
Wednesday	DoS and Heartbleed Attacks (e.g., Slowloris, Slowhttptest, Hulk, GoldenEye)
Thursday	Web and Infiltration Attacks, including: *Web Attacks:* Web Brute Force, XSS, and SQL Injection. *Infiltration:* Dropbox Download and Cool disk.
Friday	DDoS (LOIC), Botnet (ARES), and Port Scans, with types such as: (sS, sT, sF, sX, sN, sPsV, sU, sO, sA, sW, sR, sL, and B)

experiments were conducted on a platform equipped with an NVIDIA H100 GPU. For the configuration of the drift detection mechanism, the sliding window is set with a long window size of 8,000 instances, a short window of 600 instances, and a sliding stride of 400. The significance thresholds for the KS-test are 0.046 for the long window and 0.0033 for the short window. In the model adaptation phase, the weight coefficients in the combined loss function were determined after optimization to bebe $\alpha = 0.57$, $\beta = 2.96$, $\gamma = 1.08$, and $\lambda = 0.017$. These weights are set to balance the acquisition of new knowledge with the retention of historical knowledge.

4.3 Baselines

To comprehensively evaluate the performance of our proposed method, we selected a diverse set of nine baseline methods. This includes seven widely used classic methods, which, to ensure a fair comparison, were all implemented using a unified stream data processing framework based on their seminal papers. The other two are state-of-the-art deep learning-based detectors, DriftLens and PUDD, which were implemented according to their original publications.

- ADWIN [9] : An adaptive windowing method that detects changes in data distribution by dynamically adjusting its window size.
- DDM [16]: A classic drift detector that monitors the statistical properties of the classifier's error rate.
- EDDM [7]: An improved version of DDM that focuses on monitoring the distance between consecutive errors.
- HDDM_A [14]: A detector based on Hoeffding's inequality that identifies change by monitoring the moving average of a bounded variable, such as classification error.
- HDDM_W [14]: A variant of HDDM_A that assigns more weight to recent data when calculating the moving average, making it more sensitive to the latest changes.

- FHDDM [33]: An optimized version of HDDM designed to increase detection speed by improving the method used to calculate its statistics.
- PageHinkley [35]: A classic sequential analysis technique used to detect change points in a data stream.
- DriftLens [18]: An unsupervised framework that detects drift by comparing the distribution distances of deep learning representations (embeddings).
- PUDD [31]: Establishes the PU-index, a novel metric derived from prediction uncertainty, and demonstrates its effectiveness as an earlier drift indicator compared to the conventional error rate.

4.4 Experimental Results And Analysis

This chapter provides a detailed evaluation of the performance of our proposed Dynamic Network Intrusion Detection Adaptive framework (DyNA-IDS) on the CIC-IDS-2017 dataset. This chronologically ordered dataset simulates a dynamically evolving network environment that includes multiple phases, transitioning from stability to the occurrence of significant concept drifts. We compare DyNA-IDS with nine mainstream baseline methods using their daily F1-scores. The detailed experimental results are presented in Table 2.

Table 2. Comparison of Daily F1-Scores of DyNA-IDS and Baseline Methods on the CIC-IDS-2017 Dataset.

Methods	day2	day3	day4	day5
ADWIN	0.5959	0.9597	0.3217	0.9901
DDM	0.7890	0.9746	0.4229	0.9928
EDDM	0.5959	0.9597	0.3217	0.9901
HDDM_A	0.6340	0.9769	0.6021	0.9919
HDDM_W	0.7146	0.9704	0.4864	0.9924
FHDDM	0.7693	0.9721	0.0045	0.9793
PageHinkley	0.6096	0.9693	0.4778	0.9892
DriftLens	0.9537	0.4936	0.9895	0.5064
PUDD	0.9537	0.4933	0.9895	0.5052
DyNA-IDS(ours)	**0.9961**	**0.9946**	**0.9984**	**0.9941**

The proposed DyNA-IDS framework exhibited sustained high performance and stability across the entire experiment. As shown in Table 2, it achieved F1 scores of 0.9961, 0.9946, 0.9984, and 0.9941 on Day 2, Day 3, Day 4, and Day 5, respectively, consistently ranking as the best-performing framework. This superior performance is directly attributable to its innovative drift detection mechanism, which perceives changes by monitoring the reconstruction error distribution of a dual autoencoder rather than raw data features. Because the reconstruction error reacts more drastically to unknown threats, its distribution change becomes a more sensitive and reliable signal, enabling timely and precise adaptation.

By comparison, the seven classic baseline methods (from ADWIN to Page-Hinkley) demonstrated marked performance volatility. On Day 2, when attacks were first introduced, these methods only achieved moderate F1 scores ranging from 0.59 to 0.79, reflecting their insufficiency in adapting to initial or gradual drifts. Interestingly, their performance recovered to over 0.96 on Day 3 and Day 5, when faced with large-scale, pattern-obvious attacks like DoS and DDoS. This is likely because their error-rate-based detectors could trigger quickly, and resetting a simple classifier allowed for rapid learning of these distinct new patterns. However, the performance of all classic methods plummeted on Day 4 with the introduction of more complex Web and Infiltration attacks, which exposed their inherent fragility. This indicates that their simple "detect-and-reset" strategy is inadequate for handling complex and subtle concept drifts, making them unreliable in dynamic environments.

The two state-of-the-art deep learning-based baselines, DriftLens and PUDD, showed a different performance pattern. Similar to our method, they performed excellently on Day 2's stable data and initial drift (F1 score approx. 0.97), proving the feature extraction capabilities of their deep models. However, in stark contrast to the classic baselines, both methods experienced a significant performance degradation on Day 3 and Day 5, with F1 scores dropping to around 0.63. This suggests that while their detection mechanisms were sensitive enough to correctly capture the drift, their subsequent model adaptation or retraining strategies may lack robustness, leading to a temporary collapse in performance after an update. Despite these transient performance dips, they generally outperformed the classic baselines when dealing with the complex drift on Day 4, highlighting the potential of deep feature-based detection. This also underscores the superiority of the joint adaptation strategy with "knowledge retention" in our DyNA-IDS framework, which effectively avoids such post-adaptation performance collapse.

4.5 Ablation

To validate the effectiveness and necessity of each core component within our proposed DyNA-IDS framework, we designed a series of ablation studies. In these experiments, we systematically remove or replace specific modules and compare their performance against our full method. This allows for a clear assessment of each component's contribution to the overall performance, with the detailed results presented in Table 3.

The objective data from the ablation study is presented in the table. The experimental results show that the Full Method achieved the best performance, with F1 scores of 0.9961, 0.9946, 0.9984, and 0.9941 from Day 2 to Day 5, respectively. The Fine-tune DNN Only and No Regularization variants also maintained high F1 scores, consistently exceeding 0.95, although their overall performance was slightly inferior to the Full Method. This clearly indicates that jointly updating the entire framework and introducing a regularization term during the adap-

Table 3. Results of the Ablation Study on DyNA-IDS Components

Components	Day 2	Day 3	Day 4	Day 5
Full Method	**0.9961**	**0.9946**	**0.9984**	**0.9941**
Static DNN	0.9537	0.4935	0.9903	0.5068
Simple AE Threshold	0.9537	0.5371	0.9893	0.5396
Fine-tune DNN Only	0.9915	0.9762	0.9963	0.9688
No Regularization	0.9911	0.9719	0.9967	0.9555

tation phase are crucial for achieving optimal performance and maximizing stability.

In contrast, the methods lacking an effective adaptation mechanism—Static DNN and Simple AE Threshold—exhibited significant performance volatility. Although these two methods achieved high scores above 0.95 on Day 2 and Day 4, their F1 scores plummeted to a lower level of around 0.5 on Day 3 and Day 5. The reason for this is that these static or overly simplistic detection methods were unable to effectively cope with the environmental changes, causing their detection rules to rapidly become obsolete.

5 Conclusion

Our study proposes and validates DyNA-IDS, a dynamic adaptive framework. This mechanism achieves precise and proactive monitoring of data distribution changes through an innovative dual-autoencoder architecture and the two-sample Kolmogorov-Smirnov (KS) statistical test. To concurrently handle different types of concept drift, this statistical test is applied within a parallel dual long-and-short window strategy, enabling the keen capture of both gradual and abrupt changes. Once a drift is confirmed, the framework's adaptive mechanism is activated: a composite loss function, which includes an elastic regularization term, guides the entire system through a joint incremental update. This strategy, while ensuring the model efficiently adapts to new patterns, effectively mitigates the problem of "catastrophic forgetting" by penalizing excessive deviation from old knowledge. The proposed framework has been comprehensively validated on the realistic, time-ordered CIC-IDS-2017 dataset. The results demonstrate that the performance of DyNA-IDS, especially when dealing with severe and abrupt concept drifts, significantly surpasses that of various classic and state-of-the-art baseline methods. Ablation studies further validate the necessity and effectiveness of each core component in our method.

References

1. Ali, A.H., Charfeddine, M., Ammar, B., Al-Zoubi, M.B.: Unveiling machine learning strategies and considerations in intrusion detection systems: a comprehensive

survey. Front. Comput. Sci. **6**, 1387354 (2024). https://doi.org/10.3389/fcomp.2024.1387354
2. Ali, U., Mahmood, T.: A novel framework for concept drift detection using autoencoders for classification problems in data streams. Int. J. Mach. Learn. Cybern. **16**(1), 397–418 (2025). https://doi.org/10.1007/s13042-024-02100-3
3. Althabiti, M.S., Abdullah, M.: CDDM: concept drift detection model for data stream. Int. J. Interact. Mob. Technol. **14**(10), 108–121 (2020). https://doi.org/10.3991/ijim.v14i10.13876
4. Amalapuram, S.K., Tamma, B.R., Channappayya, S.S.: Spider: A semi-supervised continual learning-based network intrusion detection system. In: IEEE INFOCOM 2024-IEEE Conference on Computer Communications (2024)
5. Andresini, G., Pendlebury, F., Pierazzi, F., et al.: Insomnia: towards concept-drift robustness in network intrusion detection. In: Proceedings of the 14th ACM Workshop on Artificial Intelligence and Security, pp. 111–122 (2021)
6. Angbera, A., Chan, H.Y.: SABeDM: a sliding adaptive beta distribution model for concept drift detection in a dynamic environment. Knowl. Inf. Syst. **66**(3), 2039–2062 (2024). https://doi.org/10.1007/s10115-023-02030-x
7. Baena-García, M., del Campo-Ávila, J., Fidalgo, R., Bifet, A., Gavalda, R., Morales-Bueno, R.: Early drift detection method. In: Fourth International Workshop on Knowledge Discovery from Data Streams (2006)
8. Bhurani, P., Chouhan, S.S., Mittal, N.: ExBCIL: an exemplar-based class incremental learning for intrusion detection system. Int. J. Mach. Learn. Cybern. 1–21 (2024). https://doi.org/10.1007/s13042-024-02166-z
9. Bifet, A., Gavalda, R.: Learning from time-changing data with adaptive windowing. In: Proceedings of the 2007 SIAM International Conference on Data Mining, pp. 443–448 (2007). https://doi.org/10.1137/1.9781611972771.40
10. Cerqueira, V., Gomes, H.M., Bifet, A., Bifet, G.: STUDD: a student–teacher method for unsupervised concept drift detection. Mach. Learn. **112**(11), 4351–4378 (2023). https://doi.org/10.1007/s10994-023-06399-5
11. Chai, Y., Chen, X., Qiu, J., et al.: MalFSCIL: a few-shot class-incremental learning approach for malware detection. IEEE Trans. Inf. Forensics Secur. (2024). https://doi.org/10.1109/TIFS.2024.3414935
12. Faber, K., Corizzo, R., Sniezynski, B., Japkowicz, N.: Lifelong continual learning for anomaly detection: New challenges, perspectives, and insights. IEEE Access **12**, 41364–41380 (2024). https://doi.org/10.1109/ACCESS.2024.3379109
13. Feldhans, R., Wilke, A., Heindorf, S., et al.: Drift detection in text data with document embeddings. In: International Conference on Intelligent Data Engineering and Automated Learning, Springer, Cham, pp. 107–118 (2021)
14. Frias-Blanco, I., del Campo-Ávila, J., Ramos-Jimenez, G., Morales-Bueno, R.: Online and non-parametric drift detection methods based on Hoeffding's bounds. IEEE Trans. Knowl. Data Eng. **27**(3), 810–823 (2014). https://doi.org/10.1109/TKDE.2014.2345382
15. Friedrich, B., Sawabe, T., Hein, A.: Unsupervised statistical concept drift detection for behaviour abnormality detection. Appl. Intell. **53**(3), 2527–2537 (2023). https://doi.org/10.1007/s10489-022-03598-1
16. Gama, J., Medas, P., Castillo, G., Rodrigues, P.: Learning with drift detection. In: Advances in Artificial Intelligence–SBIA 2004, pp. 286–295. Springer, Berlin, Heidelberg (2004)
17. Gama, J., Žliobaitė, I., Bifet, A., Pechenizkiy, M., Bouchachia, A.: A survey on concept drift adaptation. ACM Comput. Surv. (CSUR) **46**(4), 1–37 (2014). https://doi.org/10.1145/2523813

18. Greco S, Vacchetti B, Apiletti D, et al. Unsupervised concept drift detection from deep learning representations in real-time. IEEE Trans. Knowl. Data Eng. (2025)
19. Han, M., Mu, D., Li, A., Wang, H.: Concept drift detection methods based on different weighting strategies. Int. J. Mach. Learn. Cybern. **15**(10), 4709–4732 (2024). https://doi.org/10.1007/s13042-024-02096-w
20. Huete, J., Qahtan, A.A., Hassani, M.: PrefixCDD: effective online concept drift detection over event streams using prefix trees. In: 2023 IEEE 47th Annual Computers, Software, and Applications Conference (COMPSAC), pp. 328–333 (2023). https://doi.org/10.1109/COMPSAC57700.2023.00055
21. Jain, M., Kaur, G.: Distributed anomaly detection using concept drift detection based hybrid ensemble techniques in streamed network data. Clust. Comput. **24**(3), 2099–2114 (2021). https://doi.org/10.1007/s10586-021-03228-4
22. Jain, M., Kaur, G., Saxena, V.: A K-Means clustering and SVM based hybrid concept drift detection technique for network anomaly detection. Expert Syst. Appl. **193**, 116510 (2022). https://doi.org/10.1016/j.eswa.2021.116510
23. Jang M, Georgiadis A, Zhao Y, et al. DriftWatch: a tool that automatically detects data drift and extracts representative examples affected by drift. In: Proceedings of the 2024 Conference of the North American Chapter of the Association for Computational Linguistics: Human Language Technologies (Volume 6: Industry Track), pp. 335–346 (2024)
24. Jaworski, M., Rutkowski, L., Angelov, P.: Concept drift detection using autoencoders in data streams processing. In: International Conference on Artificial Intelligence and Soft Computing, pp. 124–133. Springer, Cham (2020)
25. Jemili, F., Jouini, K., Korbaa, O.: Intrusion detection based on concept drift detection and online incremental learning. Int. J. Pervasive Comput. Commun. **21**(1), 81–115 (2025). https://doi.org/10.1108/IJPCC-08-2023-0212
26. Jin, Z., Zhou, J., Li, B., Chen, K., Zhang, H.: FL-IIDS: a novel federated learning-based incremental intrusion detection system. Future Gener. Comput. Syst. **151**, 57–70 (2024). https://doi.org/10.1016/j.future.2023.09.011
27. Jothimurugesan, E., Hsieh, K., Wang, J., Bilen, C.: Federated learning under distributed concept drift. In: International Conference on Artificial Intelligence and Statistics, pp. 5834–5853. PMLR (2023)
28. Khaki S, Aditya A A, Karnin Z, et al. Uncovering drift in textual data: an unsupervised method for detecting and mitigating drift in machine learning models. arXiv preprint arXiv:2309.03831 (2023)
29. Li, J., Yu, H., Zhang, Z., Liu, A.: Concept drift adaptation by exploiting drift type. ACM Trans. Knowl. Discov. Data **18**(4), 1–22 (2024). https://doi.org/10.1145/3636247
30. Liu, S., Bronzino, F., Schmitt, P., et al.: LEAF: navigating concept drift in cellular networks. Proc. ACM Networking **1**(CoNEXT2), 1–24 (2023)
31. Lu P, Lu J, Liu A, et al. Early concept drift detection via prediction uncertainty. In: Proceedings of the AAAI Conference on Artificial Intelligence, vol. 39, no. 18, pp. 19124–19132 (2025)
32. Pang, G., Shen, C., Cao, L., Van Den Hengel, A.: Deep learning for anomaly detection: a review. ACM Comput. Surv. (CSUR) **54**(2), 1–38 (2021). https://doi.org/10.1145/3439950
33. Pesaranghader, A., Viktor, H.L.: Fast hoeffding drift detection method for evolving data streams. In: Joint European Conference on Machine Learning and Knowledge Discovery in Databases, pp. 96–111. Springer, Cham (2016)

34. Santos, S.G.T.C.: Gonçalves Júnior, P.M., Silva, G.D.S.: Speeding up recovery from concept drifts. In: Machine Learning and Knowledge Discovery in Databases: European Conference. ECML PKDD 2014, pp. 179–194. Springer, Berlin, Heidelberg (2014)
35. Sebastião, R., Fernandes, J.M.: Supporting the page-hinkley test with empirical mode decomposition for change detection. In: International Symposium on Methodologies for Intelligent Systems, pp. 492–498. Springer, Cham (2017)
36. Senol, A., Agrawal, G., Liu, H.: Joint detection of fraud and concept drift in online conversations with LLM-assisted judgment. arXiv preprint arXiv:2505.07852 (2025)
37. Sharafaldin, I., Lashkari, A.H., Ghorbani, A.A.: Toward generating a new intrusion detection dataset and intrusion traffic characterization. In: Proceedings of the 4th International Conference on Information Systems Security and Privacy (ICISSP), pp. 108–116 (2018)
38. Shyaa, M.A., Ibrahim, N.F., Zainol, Z., Al-Shargabi, A.A.: Evolving cybersecurity frontiers: a comprehensive survey on concept drift and feature dynamics aware machine and deep learning in intrusion detection systems. Eng. Appl. Artif. Intell. **137**, 109143 (2024). https://doi.org/10.1016/j.engappai.2023.109143
39. Shyaa, M.A., Ibrahim, N.F., Zainol, Z., Al-Shargabi, A.A.: Reinforcement learning-based voting for feature drift-aware intrusion detection: an incremental learning framework. IEEE Access (2025), check for final publication details)
40. Sun, C., Xu, K., Antichi, G., et al.: NetGSR: towards efficient and reliable network monitoring with generative super resolution. Proc. ACM Networking **2**(CoNEXT4), 1–27 (2024)
41. Wang, P., Jin, N., Davies, D., Krishnan, R., Lio, P.: Model-centric transfer learning framework for concept drift detection. Knowl.-Based Syst. **275**, 110705 (2023). https://doi.org/10.1016/j.knosys.2023.110705
42. Wang, S.T., Sun, S.S.: An incremental learning model for network intrusion detection systems. In: 2024 10th International Conference on Applied System Innovation (ICASI), pp. 362–364 (2024). https://doi.org/10.1109/ICASI60965.2024.10549463
43. Wang, Y., Yang, J., Liu, M., et al.: LightAMC: lightweight automatic modulation classification via deep learning and compressive sensing. IEEE Trans. Veh. Technol. **69**(3), 3491–3495 (2020)
44. Widmer, G., Kubat, M.: Learning in the presence of concept drift and hidden contexts. Mach. Learn. **23**, 69–101 (1996). https://doi.org/10.1007/BF00116900
45. Yang, L., Shami, A.: A lightweight concept drift detection and adaptation framework for IoT data streams. IEEE Internet Things Mag. **4**(2), 96–101 (2021)
46. Yuan, L., Li, H., Xia, B., Chen, S., He, T., Chen, G.: Recent advances in concept drift adaptation methods for deep learning. In: Proceedings of the 31st International Joint Conference on Artificial Intelligence (IJCAI-22), pp. 5654–5661 (2022)

iSSH: Enabling In-Flight SSH Traffic Inspection Without Key Escrow

Xincheng Tang, Jiahao Liu, Jinrong Chen, Yi Wang, and Rongmao Chen(✉)

College of Computer Science and Technology, National University of Defense Technology, Changsha, Hunan 410073, China
{tangxincheng19,liujiahao14,jinrongchen,wangyi14,chromao}@nudt.edu.cn

Abstract. The widespread adoption of network security protocols has led to an increasing demand for the inspection of encrypted traffic. Most existing solutions that provide authorized inspectors with visibility of encrypted traffic are designed for the Transport Layer Security (TLS) protocol, and the best-known is the solution involving key escrow with the inspector. The Secure Shell (SSH) protocol has a similar architecture to TLS and is frequently used to secure access to remote systems, but SSH traffic inspection is less well-explored. In fact, the existing approach to TLS inspection can also be adapted to SSH. However, IA2-TLS, the state-of-the-art solution for TLS, is vulnerable to security risks because the inspection key is used in a symmetric way. Inspired by these observations, we propose a new variant of SSH called Inspectable SSH (iSSH). iSSH retains the core idea of IA2-TLS, but overcomes its limitations by using an asymmetric inspection key pair. Moreover, iSSH is compatible with standard SSH and provides flexible deployment options. Finally, we expanded upon the standard SSH security model and rigorously proved the security of key exchange in iSSH.

Keywords: SSH · Encrypted traffic inspection · Network security

1 Introduction

Today, network security protocols such as Transport Layer Security (TLS) [24] and Secure Shell (SSH) protocols [17] have been widely used to ensure the confidentiality, integrity, and authenticity of network communications. However, the end-to-end encryption feature of these protocols that is designed to protect the normal traffic for legitimate entities also poses a significant challenge: malicious adversaries can also exploit this feature to conceal their attacks. Therefore, it is particularly important to inspect encrypted traffic to detect malicious behavior.

A plethora of inspection solutions [1,3,4,7,11,12,15,16,20] are aimed at providing authorized inspectors with visibility into encrypted traffic while maintaining session security. Notably, most of these works focus on inspecting encrypted TLS traffic, and SSH-MITM [12] is the only open-source project for SSH inspection. Although TLS and SSH have similar architectures, the two protocols have

R. Chen et al. (Eds.): Inscrypt 2025, LNCS 16409, pp. 349–368, 2026.
https://doi.org/10.1007/978-981-95-6203-9_19

quite different applications. For example, TLS is best known for securing Hypertext Transfer Protocol (HTTP) traffic, whereas SSH allows users to securely access to remote systems for administration, configuration, or troubleshooting purposes. Inspecting encrypted SSH traffic is also essential in the event that an adversary impersonates a user and launches attacks on the remote system.

The rationale behind SSH-MITM [12] is an "interception proxy", whereby the server's long-term signing key is escrowed with the inspector. The inspector can then launch a man-in-the-middle attack between the client and the server. While this solution is simple to deploy, the inspector only works in real-time mode and must re-encrypt plaintext data for the server after decrypting encrypted traffic. Another naive approach, called "out-of-band key transmission", requires the client or server to send the established session key to the inspector via an additional secure connection (e.g., an extra SSH connection). This approach is not as convenient as an interception proxy because it requires significant modifications to the client or server implementation to enable this extra functionality.

Fortunately, Baek et al. [3] addressed the shortcomings of interception proxies and out-of-band key transmission in the context of TLS inspection and proposed a novel variant of TLS called IA2-TLS. In IA2-TLS, unlike in TLS, the pre-master secret is generated using an inspection key kept secret by the inspector and two random nonces transmitted publicly. Consequently, the inspector can recover the pre-master secret using the inspection key and decrypt the encrypted traffic. Given the high similarity between TLS and SSH in terms of architecture, it might be possible to apply this method to SSH. However, note that the inspection key in IA2-TLS must be embedded in the client or server implementation. Then, this key can be retrieved using reverse engineering by anyone, who might then be able to decrypt the encrypted traffic. Motivated by these observations, we turn to study how to apply the method of IA2-TLS to SSH and, more importantly, how to eliminate the security risk posed by using the inspection key in an asymmetric way.

1.1 Contributions

In this work, we propose iSSH, a new variant of SSH that inspects encrypted traffic using an asymmetric approach. Our contributions are as follows:

1. iSSH overcomes the limitations of IA2-TLS by using a public-secret inspection key pair. The inspection public key is embedded in the client/server implementation and participates in generating the shared secret (pre-master secret in TLS). The inspection secret key, which is kept by the inspector, is then used to extract the shared secret from the encrypted traffic.
2. iSSH is compatible with standard SSH and offers flexible deployment options. Even when communicating with an SSH server/client, the inspector can still decrypt the encrypted traffic when an iSSH client/server is involved.
3. The security of key exchange in iSSH is formally proven. Specifically, we extended the security model to incorporate an inspection key pair for SSH. Additionally, our model provides the adversary with enhanced capabilities, enabling it to obtain the inspection public key.

1.2 Related Work

There also exist solutions that can perform intrusion detection, exfiltration detection, and parental filtering on encrypted traffic without decrypting it. Specifically, Blindbox [26] and BlindIDS [6] could protect user privacy, but have two main limitations: first, they require significant performance overhead during connection setup; second, they cannot meet the needs of applications that require precise plaintext data.

mcTLS [20] and maTLS [15] require the inspectors to participate in the connection process to ensure they obtain the minimum privilege of authority for inspection. mdTLS [1], which is based on the proxy signature scheme, requires approximately 39% less computation than maTLS. These solutions enhance user privacy and security. However, they are essentially interception proxy solutions, which introduce a significant amount of computational overhead. Furthermore, Karthikeyan et al. [4] point out that mcTLS is insecure and vulnerable to middlebox-confusion attacks. meTLS [16] can be deployed in bypass mode and is targeted at Internet of Things (IoT) systems. To overcome the drawback of the public key infrastructure (PKI) for entity authentication, meTLS introduces a distributed Boneh-Franklin identity-based encryption (BF-IBE) scheme [13] to the handshake phase. However, since meTLS introduces new cryptographic primitives, it is necessary to modify both the client and server ends to accommodate inspection.

We also note that several works aim to extract SSH keys from random access memory, including SSHKex [25], PointerKex [10], OpenSSHNetworkParser [28], and SmartKex [9]. While these techniques are not intended for inspecting encrypted traffic, it is possible to implement out-of-band key transmission.

2 Preliminaries

2.1 Notations

In this paper, $x \leftarrow\$ X$ means that x is chosen uniformly at random from space X. $x \leftarrow X(in)$ means that the output of algorithm X when given input in is x. $x \leftarrow X$ means that x is assigned the value of X. Let *p.p.t.* represent "probabilistic polynomial-time". Let λ be security parameter, and $negl(\lambda)$ denote a negligible function in λ.

2.2 Cryptographic Assumptions

We define computational Diffie-Hellman (CDH) function as $g^{xy} \leftarrow DH_g(X, Y)$, where $X \leftarrow g^x$ and $Y \leftarrow g^y$.

Definition 1 (CDH Assumption [8]**).** *Let $\mathbb{G}$ be a cyclic group of prime order q where the length of q in bits is λ, generated by a group element g. We define the advantage of an adversary $\mathcal{A}$ against the CDH assumption on group $\mathbb{G}$ as $\mathbf{Adv}^{CDH}_{\mathcal{A},\mathbb{G}}(\lambda) \leftarrow \Pr[g^{xy} \leftarrow \mathcal{A}(\mathbb{G}, g^x, g^y)|(x, y) \leftarrow\$ \mathbb{Z}_q^{*2}]$. We say that the CDH assumption holds in $\mathbb{G}$ if for all p.p.t. adversaries $\mathcal{A}$, it holds that $\mathbf{Adv}^{CDH}_{\mathcal{A},\mathbb{G}}(\lambda) \leq negl(\lambda)$.*

We define a decisional Diffie-Hellman (DDH) oracle $\mathsf{DDH}_{\mathbb{G}}(\cdot)$ for a group $\mathbb{G}$ of prime order q as follows: The inputs to $\mathsf{DDH}_{\mathbb{G}}$ are g^x, g^y, and g^z, where g is a generator of $\mathbb{G}$ and $x, y, z \in \mathbb{Z}_q^*$. The oracle outputs 1 if $z = xy$, and 0 otherwise.

Definition 2 (Gap Diffie-Hellman Assumption [18]**).** *Let $\mathbb{G}$ be a cyclic group of prime order q where the length of q in bits is λ, generated by a group element g. We define the advantage of an adversary $\mathcal{A}$ against the gap-DH assumption on group $\mathbb{G}$ as $\mathbf{Adv}_{\mathcal{A},\mathbb{G}}^{gap\text{-}DH}(\lambda) \leftarrow \Pr[g^{xy} \leftarrow \mathcal{A}^{\mathsf{DDH}_{\mathbb{G}}(\cdot)}(\mathbb{G}, g^x, g^y) | (x, y) \leftarrow_{\$} \mathbb{Z}_q^{*2}]$. We say that the gap-DH assumption holds in $\mathbb{G}$ if for all p.p.t. adversaries $\mathcal{A}$, it holds that $\mathbf{Adv}_{\mathcal{A},\mathbb{G}}^{gap\text{-}DH}(\lambda) \leq negl(\lambda)$.*

2.3 Cryptographic Primitives

Definition 3 (Digital Signature Scheme). *A digital signature scheme* SIG *is comprised of three algorithms* $(\mathsf{SIG.Gen}, \mathsf{SIG.Sign}, \mathsf{SIG.Verif})$ *with the message space $\mathcal{M}$: (1)* $\mathsf{SIG.Gen}$ *takes as input the security parameter λ and outputs a signing key sk and a verification key vk; (2)* $\mathsf{SIG.Sign}$ *takes as input the signing key and a message $m \in \mathcal{M}$, and outputs a signature σ; (3)* $\mathsf{SIG.Verif}$ *takes as input a verification key vk, a message m, and a signature σ, and outputs 0 or 1.*

Correctness. A digital signature scheme is *correct* if for any message $m \in \mathcal{M}$ and $(sk, vk) \leftarrow_{\$} \mathsf{SIG.Gen}(\lambda)$, it holds that $1 \leftarrow \mathsf{SIG.Verif}(vk, m, \mathsf{SIG.Sign}(sk, m))$.

Definition 4 (Existential Unforgeability under Chosen Message Attacks [2]**).** *Let* $\mathsf{SIG} = (\mathsf{SIG.Gen}, \mathsf{SIG.Sign}, \mathsf{SIG.Verif})$ *be a digital signature scheme. Let $\mathcal{A}$ be an adversary which is allowed to adaptively query the signing oracle* $\mathsf{SIG.Sign}(sk, \cdot)$ *with messages $M = (m_1, m_2, \cdots, m_n)$ and receive signatures $\Sigma = (\sigma_1, \sigma_2, \cdots, \sigma_n)$. We define the advantage of an adversary $\mathcal{A}$ in breaking the EU-CMA (Existential Unforgeability under Chosen Message Attacks) security of* SIG *as $\mathbf{Adv}_{\mathcal{A},\mathsf{SIG}}^{EU\text{-}CMA}(\lambda) = Pr_{(sk,vk) \leftarrow_{\$} \mathsf{SIG.Gen}(\lambda)}[1 \leftarrow \mathsf{SIG.Verif}(vk, m^*, \sigma^*), m^* \notin M \mid (m^*, \sigma^*) \leftarrow \mathcal{A}^{\mathsf{SIG.Sign}(sk,\cdot)}(vk)]$. We say* SIG *is EU-CMA secure if for all p.p.t. adversaries $\mathcal{A}$, it holds that $\mathbf{Adv}_{\mathcal{A},\mathsf{SIG}}^{EU\text{-}CMA}(\lambda) \leq negl(\lambda)$.*

3 Our Protocol: iSSH

3.1 Design Principles

Compatibility. To achieve compatibility with the SSH protocol, iSSH only makes minimal modifications to the shared secret generation process. Unlike the approaches in [1,15,16,20] that require modifications to both implementations, iSSH can be deployed on either the client or the server. The core modification involves embedding shared secrets in the random padding field, which enables only the inspector to recover these secrets.

Flexible Inspection. Our iSSH protocol serves as a versatile and flexible SSH inspection solution. It can be deployed on both client and server sides. Supporting real-time decryption and analysis, iSSH also offers the option to store communication traffic for later offline analysis. Moreover, iSSH can be deployed either inline between the client and server to intercept and forward traffic, or in a bypass mode for passive monitoring without interfering the traffic flow.

Asymmetric Inspection. In IA2-TLS [3], the shared secret is exposed if the embedded inspection key in a party is compromised (e.g., via reverse engineering). To tackle this vulnerability, we adopt an asymmetric approach. In this method, the inspection key is a key pair (ipk, isk). The inspector distributes the inspection public key ipk to the inspected party, while keeping the inspection secret key isk private. This ensures that even if ipk is revealed, the shared secret remain secure as long as isk is protected. This strategy is highly significant for overcoming key management challenges in large-scale deployments.

3.2 Decription of iSSH

The Binary Packet Protocol. As with the standard SSH protocol, our iSSH protocol specifies the structure of each packet using the Binary Packet Protocol (BPP) [17]. The format of a BPP packet is shown in Fig. 1. To simplify encryption for symmetric cipher suites, it is required that total_length is a multiple of 8 bytes or the cipher block length (e.g., 16 bytes for AES [19]). Note that the random padding is a random sequence whose length is specified by padding_length. This length is required to be greater than 3 bytes and less than 256 bytes.

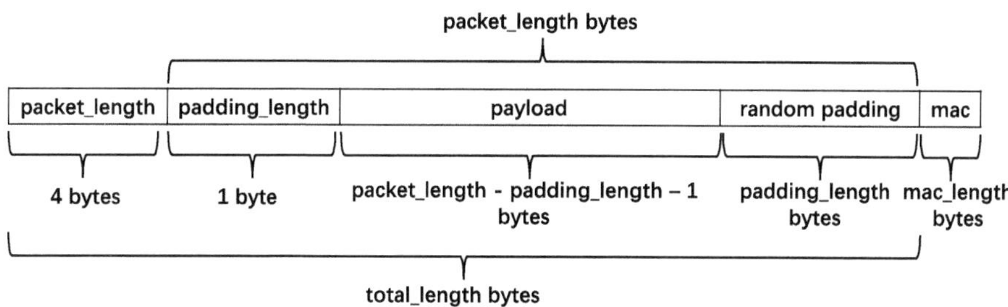

Fig. 1. An overview of BPP packet

Inspectable Key Exchange Protocol (iKEP). The iKEP comprises three entities: client, server, and inspector. The client and server communicate over a channel, while the inspector monitors the communication traffic. The iKEP facilitates the negotiation of keys used by various cryptographic primitives between the client and server, and provides visibility to the inspector. It is divided into four phases: the *Setup* phase, the *Hello* phase, the *Shared Secret Exchange* phase, and the *Application Keys Generation* phase. All protocol messages (excluding identification strings exchanged in the *Hello* phase) are encoded using the BPP packet format.

Figure 2 illustrates both the SSH and iSSH protocols. We only provide server-side inspection in the description of our iSSH protocol. However, our solution is also applicable to the client side. Initially, the server takes as input a key pair (sk_S, vk_S) for the signature scheme. In the *Setup phase* of the iSSH, the inspector generates an inspection key pair (isk, ipk), where isk is kept by the inspector and ipk is distributed to the server.

The beginning of the *Hello* phase is an exchange of identification strings I_C (client) and I_S (server), which include the SSH and software versions. Subsequently, the client and server each send a 16-byte nonce (r_C for the client and r_S for the server) along with a list of supported algorithms to negotiate the cipher suites. For brevity, the detailed process of cipher suite negotiation is omitted.

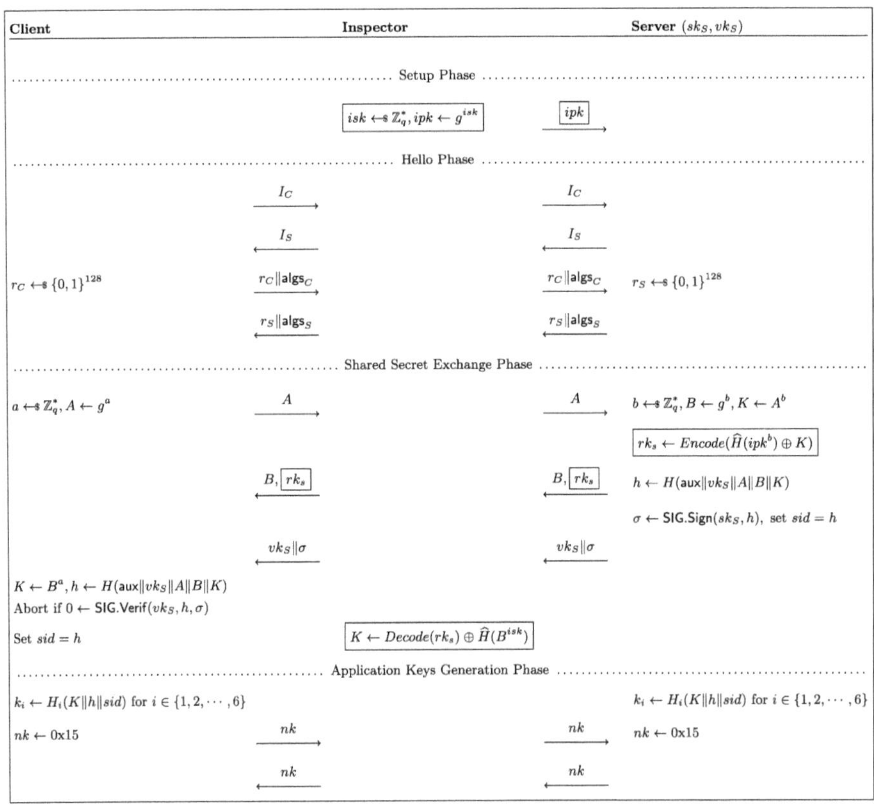

Fig. 2. Our iSSH protocol. Let algs_C and algs_S be the sets of algorithms supported by the client and server, respectively. Let $\mathsf{aux} \leftarrow I_C \| I_S \| r_C \| \mathsf{algs}_C \| r_S \| \mathsf{algs}_S$. The original SSH protocol does not include the text highlighted in $\boxed{\text{box}}$. rk_s represents the random padding generated by the server and is sent along with server ephemeral public key.

In the *Shared Secret Exchange* phase, both parties execute a Diffie-Hellman (DH) key exchange to negotiate a shared secret K. Let $H : \{0,1\}^* \to \{0,1\}^n$ be a hash function where n is an integer determined by the negotiated digest algorithm. The server computes $h \leftarrow H(\mathsf{aux}\|vk_S\|A\|B\|K)$ where aux is the transcript from the *Hello* phase, signs h and sends its verification key vk_S and the signature σ to the client. Upon receiving (vk_S, σ), the client computes h and aborts if σ is invalid.

During the *Shared Secret Exchange* phase, the server is required to compute random padding as follows: 1) Encrypt the shared secret by computing $CT \leftarrow \widehat{H}(ipk^b) \oplus K$, where $\widehat{H} : S_{\mathrm{INS}} \to S_{\mathrm{SS}}$ is a hash function. Here, S_{SS} is the shared secret space and S_{INS} is the inspection shared secret space (explained later). 2) Encode CT to obtain $rk_s \leftarrow Encode(CT)$. Specifically, the *Encode* function appends random values to CT to satisfy the BPP packet constraints. 3) Set rk_s as the random padding of the server's DH key exchange packet.

The inspector saves all messages and recovers the shared secret as follows: 1) Extracting rk_s from the server's DH key exchange packet. 2) Decoding rk_s to obtain $CT \leftarrow Decode(rk_s)$ where $Decode(Encode(x)) = x$. 3) Recovering the shared secret by computing $K \leftarrow \widehat{H}(B^{isk}) \oplus CT$. We have that both the inspector and the server obtain the same *inspection shared secret*, i.e., $ipk^b = B^{isk}$. Subsequently, the inspector computes h and sid based on K and other values captured in the previous packets.

In the *Application Keys Generation* phase, the client, server, and inspector derive six keys k_i for $i \in \{1, 2, \cdots, 6\}$ by computing $k_i \leftarrow H_i(K\|h\|sid)$. Here, H_i denotes a hash function with a specific ASCII character inserted at a predefined position in the input. The client and server then use k_1, k_3, k_5 as the initial IV, encryption key and MAC key for the client-to-server direction, respectively. For the server-to-client direction, they use k_2, k_4, k_6 instead. Subsequently, both the client and server send a plaintext packet whose payload contains only the specific fixed hexadecimal value 0x15, which means that all the subsequent packets sent by the end are encrypted using application keys.

We provide server-side inspection by embedding the encrypted shared secret in the random padding of the server's DH key exchange packet. When implementing client-side inspection, however, the shared secret has not yet been generated when the client sends its DH key exchange packet. Therefore, we can embed the encrypted shared secret in the client's nk packet.

4 Security

4.1 Security Model

The security model used in this paper builds upon the work of Morrissey et al. [18]. The primary distinction between our model and theirs lies in the incorporation of inspection. The shared secret can be distinguished from random values due to the revealing of the signature. Therefore, we only prove that the inspectable key exchange protocol achieves one-way (OW) security, which means all *p.p.t.* adversaries have negligible probability in recovering the entire shared secret. Below is a general description of the execution model used in this paper.

Participants. We define two different types of participants, namely the sets $\mathcal{U}$ and $\mathcal{U}'$. The set $\mathcal{U}$ models the servers, where each participant possesses a (long-term) public-private key pair. The set $\mathcal{U}'$ models the clients, where participants have no public-private key pairs. Additionally, each participant $U \in \mathcal{U}$ possesses an inspection public key.

Sessions. We focus on two-party interactive protocols involving an initiator and a responder who communicate via a channel. In this setting, we assume that an inspector is deployed in a bypass mode and can obtain all the communication traffic. We refer to the initiator and responder as participants. Each participant runs a program that receives messages from the communication channel, computes a response, and sends that response back to the channel. We call a single execution of the initiator's (or responder's) program an initiator session (or a responder session). Each participant may engage in multiple concurrent initiator and responder sessions. We assume that the adversary has full control over the communication channel. Additionally, we give the adversary enhanced capabilities that enable it to obtain the inspection public key.

Oracles. In our security model, the adversaries' capabilities are defined by their access to *oracles* corresponding to protocol sessions. Each oracle maintains an internal state, which includes session variables and additional information necessary for defining security requirements. We generally omit the specifics of local variables and session execution details. The typical state of an oracle $\mathcal{O}$ in our model includes the following variables:

- $\tau_{\mathcal{O}} \in \{\perp\} \cup \{0,1\}^*$: the transcript of all packets sent and received by $\mathcal{O}$. Additional information related to the execution may also be added to the transcript.
- $\mathrm{role}_{\mathcal{O}} \in \{\mathtt{init}, \mathtt{resp}, \perp\}$: whether the session to which $\mathcal{O}$ corresponds is an initiator session, a responder session, or undetermined.
- $\mathrm{pid}_{\mathcal{O}} \in \{\perp\} \cup \mathcal{U} \cup \mathcal{U}'$: the identity of the intended partner of the session maintained by $\mathcal{O}$.
- $\gamma_{\mathcal{O}} \in \{\mathtt{running}, \mathtt{accepted}, \mathtt{rejected}\}$: the session state, indicating whether the session is running, has succeeded (`accepted`), or has failed (`rejected`).
- $sid_{\mathcal{O}} \in \{\perp\} \cup \{0,1\}^*$: the session identifier. If $\gamma_{\mathcal{O}} \neq \mathtt{accepted}$, then $sid_{\mathcal{O}} = \perp$.
- $ss_{\mathcal{O}} \in S_{\mathrm{SS}} \cup \{\perp\}$: the shared secret. It is required that $|S_{\mathrm{SS}}| \geq 2^{\lambda}$.
- $\delta_{\mathcal{O}} \in \{\perp, \mathtt{corrupted}\}$: a flag that indicates whether the session has been corrupted by the adversary.
- $\omega_{\mathcal{O}} \in \{\mathtt{unrevealed}, \mathtt{revealed}\}$: a flag that indicates whether the session identifier has been revealed by the adversary.

There is an initialization phase in the execution model, in which the public-private keys and inspection public keys of each participant in $\mathcal{U}$ are generated. After the initialization phase, the adversary controls the creation and execution of sessions by sending queries to different oracles. There are two basic queries:

(1) NewSession(U, role): This query establishes a new session of a participant $U \in \mathcal{U} \cup \mathcal{U}'$ with role $\in \{\texttt{init}, \texttt{resp}\}$. We denote the i-th session of U as Π_U^i. (2) Send($\mathcal{O}$, msg): This query denotes sending a message msg to an oracle $\mathcal{O}$. The response is computed according to the session maintained by $\mathcal{O}$.

Moreover, in the context of inspectable key exchange protocols, there are three types of queries relevant to our security model: the Corrupt queries, Reveal queries, and Check queries. By issuing a Corrupt query, the adversary is allowed to corrupt a party, thereby obtaining its private key. By issuing a Reveal query, the adversary is allowed to obtain the session identifier derived by different sessions of the protocol. By issuing a Check query, the adversary can verify whether a given value matches the shared secret held by some honest session. Specifically, these queries are defined as follows.

- Corrupt(U): The adversary targets a participant $U \in \mathcal{U}$ for corruption. As a result, the private key sk_U is returned, and all sessions currently running on U are marked as `corrupted`, i.e., for each oracle $\mathcal{O}$ associated with U's sessions, set $\delta_{\mathcal{O}} \leftarrow \texttt{corrupted}$. Additionally, the adversary can no longer make queries in the form of NewSession(U, role).
- Reveal($\mathcal{O}$): If $\gamma_{\mathcal{O}} = \texttt{accepted}$, $sid_{\mathcal{O}}$ is returned and $\omega_{\mathcal{O}}$ is set to `revealed`. The adversary is not allowed to make further queries to this session. If $\gamma_{\mathcal{O}} \neq \texttt{accepted}$, this query has no effect.
- Check($\mathcal{O}$, ss): This query allows the adversary to check if the guessed shared secret matches the shared secret held by $\mathcal{O}$. If $\gamma_{\mathcal{O}} = \texttt{accepted}$ and $ss_{\mathcal{O}} = ss$, then *true* is returned. Otherwise, $false$ is returned.

Once a session has finished, the role, partner ID, and other oracle variables (e.g., the shared secret) are appended to the transcript. To avoid trivial attacks, we define a class of oracles that are valid targets for the adversary.

Definition 5 (Fresh Oracle). *An oracle $\mathcal{O}$ is said to be fresh if all the following conditions hold: 1) $\delta_{\mathcal{O}} = \perp$; 2) $\gamma_{\mathcal{O}} = \texttt{accepted}$; 3) $\omega_{\mathcal{O}} = \texttt{unrevealed}$; 4) no revealed oracle $\mathcal{O}^*$ has session identifier $sid_{\mathcal{O}^*} = sid_{\mathcal{O}}$; 5) $\exists V \in \mathcal{U}$ such that V is uncorrupted and $pid_{\mathcal{O}} = V$.*

The last condition in Definition 5 implies that an oracle is deemed a *fresh oracle* only if its partner is a server.

Security Game For Inspectable Key Exchange Protocols. We define the security of an inspectable key exchange protocol Π via the game $\mathrm{Exec}_{\mathcal{A},\Pi}^{\text{OW-iKEP}}(\lambda)$ between an adversary $\mathcal{A}$ and a challenger as follows:

1. The challenger initiates the game by generating different public-private key pairs and inspection public keys for each participant $U \in \mathcal{U}$. Subsequently, all the public keys and inspection public keys are sent to $\mathcal{A}$.
2. The adversary $\mathcal{A}$ is granted the ability to make some queries, including NewSession, Send, Corrupt, Reveal, and Check queries.
3. The adversary $\mathcal{A}$ can halt the game at any time and output a pair $(\mathcal{O}^*, ss^*)$, where $\mathcal{O}^*$ is an oracle and $ss^* \in S_{\mathrm{SS}}$.

We say that $\mathcal{A}$ wins the game if it outputs $(\mathcal{O}^*, ss^*)$ such that O^* is a *fresh oracle* and $ss_{\mathcal{O}} = ss^*$. In this case, the output of $\text{Exec}_{\mathcal{A},\Pi}^{\text{OW-iKEP}}(\lambda)$ is set to 1. Otherwise the output of the game is set to 0. The advantage of $\mathcal{A}$ in winning the $\text{Exec}_{\mathcal{A},\Pi}^{\text{OW-iKEP}}(\lambda)$ game is defined by

$$\mathbf{Adv}_{\mathcal{A},\Pi}^{\text{OW-iKEP}}(\lambda) = \Pr\left[\text{Exec}_{\mathcal{A},\Pi}^{\text{OW-iKEP}}(\lambda) = 1\right].$$

The following definition implies the situation when a participant U has engaged in a session with a participant in $\mathcal{U}$ and finished execution successfully, while there is no session of $V \in \mathcal{U}$ that is partnered with that session of U. This means that the adversary can forge the identity of a participant in $\mathcal{U}$ and deceive U into accepting the session as legitimate.

Definition 6 (No Partnering). *We define $NoPartnering_{\mathcal{A},\Pi}(\lambda)$ as the event that at the end of $Exec_{\mathcal{A},\Pi}^{OW\text{-}iKEP}(\lambda)$, for two uncorrupted participants $U \in \mathcal{U}'$ and $V \in \mathcal{U}$, there exists an oracle $\mathcal{O} = \Pi_U^i$ with $pid_{\mathcal{O}} = V$, $\gamma_{\mathcal{O}} = \texttt{accepted}$, whereas there is no oracle $\mathcal{O}^* = \Pi_V^j$ such that $sid_{\mathcal{O}^*} = sid_{\mathcal{O}}$ and $ss_{\mathcal{O}^*} = ss_{\mathcal{O}}$.*

Definition 7 (Inspectable Key Exchange Protocol Security). *An iKEP is considered both inspectable and secure if it satisfies all of the following conditions:*

1. ***Correctness:*** *At the end of an execution for a benign adversary, any two oracles that share the same session identifier hold the same shared secret, which is uniformly distributed over S_{SS}.*
2. ***Inspectability:*** *At the end of an execution for a benign adversary, the inspector can obtain the shared secret $ss_{\mathcal{O}}$ for $\mathcal{O} \in \Pi_V^j$ with $V \in \mathcal{U}$.*
3. ***Key Secrecy:*** *An iKEP Π satisfies OW key secrecy if for any p.p.t. adversary $\mathcal{A}$, its advantage $\mathbf{Adv}_{\mathcal{A},\Pi}^{OW\text{-}iKEP}(\lambda)$ is a negligible function of the security parameter λ.*
4. ***No Partnering:*** *The probability of $NoPartnering_{\mathcal{A},\Pi}(\lambda)$ is a negligible function of the security parameter λ for any p.p.t. adversary $\mathcal{A}$.*

4.2 Security Analysis

Theorem 1. *Let $\mathbb{G}$ be a cyclic group of prime order q with a generator g such that the gap-DH assumption holds and let $\mathsf{SIG} = (\mathsf{SIG.Gen}, \mathsf{SIG.Sign}, \mathsf{SIG.Verif})$ be a secure digital signature scheme. Then $\Pi = iKEP(\mathbb{G}, \mathsf{SIG})$ is a secure iKEP.*

Proof. We first demonstrate the *correctness* and *inspectability* of the Π.

Correctness. We show that the size of the random padding is sufficient to accommodate the value $Encode(\widehat{H}(ipk^b) \oplus ss)$. The random padding is subjected to the following constraints: it should exceed 3 bytes, remain under 256 bytes, and result in a total packet length that is a multiple of either 8 or the cipher block length, as detailed in the Sect. 3.2. In contrast, the length of $Encode(\widehat{H}(ipk^b) \oplus ss)$ for widely used elliptic curves (e.g., curve25519 [14], secp256r1, and secp384r1 [27]) is notably smaller than the typical requirements for random padding. For example, the secp384r1 curve produces a 97-byte encoded output. Consequently, when combining this component with AES encryption, the required random padding length should be kept below 113 bytes (97 + 16). This means the random padding is enough for transferring the value $Encode(\widehat{H}(ipk^b) \oplus ss)$. Since the random padding is never used in the iKEP between the client and server, modifying it does not affect the protocol's correctness.

Inspectability. The inspection shared secrets computed by the server and the inspector are $ipk^b = g^{isk \cdot b}$ and $B^{isk} = g^{b \cdot isk}$ respectively. The inspector recovers the shared secret by computing $ss = Decode(rk_s) \oplus \widehat{H}(B^{isk})$. Subsequently, the inspector can compute h and sid based on ss and other public values. Finally, the inspector can generate application keys by using the hash functions H_i for $i \in \{1, 2, \cdots, 6\}$.

Lemma 1. *Let $H : \{0,1\}^* \rightarrow \{0,1\}^n$ and $\widehat{H} : S_{INS} \rightarrow S_{SS}$ be random oracles. For any adversary $\mathcal{A}$ against the key secrecy of Π, there exist four adversaries $\mathcal{B}, \mathcal{C}, \mathcal{D}$, and $\mathcal{E}$ such that*

$$\begin{aligned}\mathbf{Adv}_{\mathcal{A},\Pi}^{OW\text{-}iKEP}(\lambda) \leq & 2 \cdot n_p \cdot \mathbf{Adv}_{\mathcal{B},\mathsf{SIG}}^{EU\text{-}CMA}(\lambda) + n_p \cdot \mathbf{Adv}_{\mathcal{C},\mathsf{SIG}}^{EU\text{-}CMA}(\lambda) \\ & + n_q \cdot n_s \cdot \mathbf{Adv}_{\mathcal{D},\mathbb{G}}^{CDH}(\lambda) + \mathbf{Adv}_{\mathcal{E},\mathbb{G}}^{gap\text{-}DH}(\lambda) \\ & + 2 \cdot n_{q_h} \cdot \frac{1}{2^n} + \frac{1}{|S_{SS}|},\end{aligned}$$

where n_p denotes the number of participants in the set $\mathcal{U}$, n_q and n_{q_h} denote the number of queries to the random oracle $\widehat{H}$ and H respectively, and n_s denotes the maximum number of the sessions that $\mathcal{A}$ can create in the game.

Proof. We show that for any *p.p.t.* adversary $\mathcal{A}$, $\mathbf{Adv}_{\mathcal{A},\Pi}^{\text{OW-iKEP}}(\lambda)$ is negligible in λ. Our proof uses a sequence of hybrid games. Let $\Pr[S_i]$ ($i \in \{0, 1, 2, 3, 4\}$) denote the probability that $\mathcal{A}$ wins Game i. Throughout the proof, let $A_{\mathcal{O}}, B_{\mathcal{O}}, \sigma_{\mathcal{O}}, \mathsf{aux}_{\mathcal{O}}$, and $rk_{S\mathcal{O}}$ denote the values $A, B, \sigma, \mathsf{aux}$, and rk_S in Fig. 2 that correspond to the oracle $\mathcal{O}$.

Game 0. This is the original security game for the inspectable key exchange protocols. We have that $\Pr[S_0] = \mathbf{Adv}_{\mathcal{A},\Pi}^{\text{OW-iKEP}}(\lambda)$.

Game 1. Compared to Game 0, the only difference in this game is that upon receiving a message (B, σ) not output by any honest oracle, the challenger rejects the message without verifying the signature.

We define E_1 as the event that there exists an oracle $\mathcal{O}$ with $\gamma_{\mathcal{O}} = \texttt{accepted}$ having an incoming message $(B, \sigma) \in \tau_{\mathcal{O}}$ that was not output by any honest oracle. The adversary cannot distinguish Game 0 from Game 1 unless E_1 occurs. By the *Difference Lemma* [5], we have $|\Pr[S_0] - \Pr[S_1]| \leq \Pr[E_1]$.

Lemma 2. *There exists an adversary $\mathcal{B}$ against the EU-CMA security of* SIG *such that* $\Pr[E_1] \leq 2 \cdot n_p \cdot \mathbf{Adv}_{\mathcal{B},\mathsf{SIG}}^{EU\text{-}CMA}(\lambda) + n_{q_h} \cdot \frac{1}{2^n}$.

Proof. The adversary $\mathcal{B}$ receives a public key $vk^\dagger$, and is given access to the signing oracle $\mathsf{SIG.Sign}(sk^\dagger, \cdot)$. It acts as the challenger to $\mathcal{A}$ in Game 0. First, $\mathcal{B}$ generates a set $\mathcal{U}$ of n_p participants and a set $\mathcal{U}'$ of n_p' participants. Now $\mathcal{B}$ randomly selects a participant $U^\dagger \in \mathcal{U}$ and sets $vk_{U^\dagger} \leftarrow vk^\dagger$ and $sk_{U^\dagger} \leftarrow \perp$. $\mathcal{B}$ then runs the key generation algorithm $\mathsf{SIG.Gen}(\lambda)$ to obtain public-private keys for all participants $U \in \mathcal{U} \setminus \{U^\dagger\}$. $\mathcal{B}$ sends all the public keys (including $vk^\dagger$) to $\mathcal{A}$. Next, $\mathcal{B}$ generates inspection key pairs by selecting $isk_U \leftarrow\$ \mathbb{Z}_q^*$ and computing $ipk_U = g^{isk_U}$ for every $U \in \mathcal{U}$. $\mathcal{B}$ sends all the inspection public keys to the adversary.

<u>*H-Query.*</u> The adversary $\mathcal{A}$ can adaptively query the random oracle H and $\widehat{H}$. $\mathcal{B}$ maintains query lists for H and $\widehat{H}$ respectively. For each H query w_i ($i \in \{1, 2, \cdots, n_{q_h}\}$), $\mathcal{B}$ randomly selects $z_i \in \{0,1\}^n$ as the response, and records the pair (w_i, z_i) in the query list for H. For each $\widehat{H}$ query x_i ($i \in \{1, 2, \cdots, n_q\}$), $\mathcal{B}$ randomly selects a value $y_i \in S_{\text{INS}}$ as the response and records the pair (x_i, y_i) in the query list for $\widehat{H}$.

<u>*Simulation.*</u> $\mathcal{A}$ makes some NewSession, Send, Check, Corrupt, and Reveal queries. $\mathcal{B}$ responds to these queries in the following way:

- If a Corrupt(U) query is made and $U \neq U^\dagger$ then $\mathcal{B}$ returns sk_U, and $\mathcal{A}$ can no longer query any oracle belonging to U. If $U = U^\dagger$ then $\mathcal{B}$ aborts.
- When a Send$(\mathcal{O}, \text{msg})$ query is made for oracle $\mathcal{O} = \Pi_U^i$ with $U \in \mathcal{U} \cup \mathcal{U}'$,
  - If $U \neq U^\dagger$ or $\mathcal{O}$ is still in the *Hello* phase or $\text{role}_{\mathcal{O}} = \mathtt{init}$, then $\mathcal{B}$ responds as in the correct execution.
  - Otherwise $\mathcal{B}$ selects $b \leftarrow\$ \mathbb{Z}_q^*$ and computes $B_{\mathcal{O}} \leftarrow g^b$, $A_{\mathcal{O}} \leftarrow \text{msg}$, $ss_{\mathcal{O}} \leftarrow A_{\mathcal{O}}^b$, and $sid_{\mathcal{O}} = H(\mathsf{aux}_{\mathcal{O}} \| vk_{U^\dagger} \| A_{\mathcal{O}} \| B_{\mathcal{O}} \| ss_{\mathcal{O}})$, where $\mathsf{aux}_{\mathcal{O}} \in \tau_{\mathcal{O}}$. $\mathcal{B}$ obtains $\sigma_{\mathcal{O}} \leftarrow \mathsf{SIG.Sign}(sk^\dagger, sid_{\mathcal{O}})$ by querying its signing oracle. Next, $\mathcal{B}$ returns $(B_{\mathcal{O}}, Encode(\widehat{H}(ipk_{U^\dagger}^b) \oplus ss_{\mathcal{O}}))$ and $(vk_{U^\dagger}, \sigma_{\mathcal{O}})$ to $\mathcal{A}$.
- If a Check$(\mathcal{O}, ss)$ query or a Reveal$(\mathcal{O})$ query is made, $\mathcal{B}$ can answer these queries correctly since it knows $ss_{\mathcal{O}}$ and $sid_{\mathcal{O}}$.

At the end of the game, $\mathcal{A}$ outputs a pair $(\mathcal{O}^*, ss^*)$.

<u>*Reduction.*</u> We defined the event E_1 as follows: $\mathcal{O}^* = \Pi_{U^*}^i$ where $U^* \in \mathcal{U}'$, and $\mathcal{A}$ makes a query Send$(\mathcal{O}^*, (B^*, \sigma^*))$ where (B^*, σ^*) is generated by $\mathcal{A}$, such that $1 \leftarrow \mathsf{SIG.Verif}(vk_{\text{pid}_{\mathcal{O}^*}}, sid_{\mathcal{O}^*}, \sigma^*)$. We assume $\text{pid}_{\mathcal{O}^*} = U^\dagger$, and consider two sub-cases E_2 and E_3 depending on whether σ^* is output by an honest oracle.

In E_2, B^* is not output by any $\mathcal{O}^\dagger \in \Pi_{U^\dagger}^i$ for $i \in \mathbb{N}^+$, whereas σ^* is output by $\mathcal{O}^\dagger = \Pi_{U^\dagger}^j$. If E_2 occurs, observe that $sid_{\mathcal{O}^*} = H(\mathsf{aux}_{\mathcal{O}^*} \| vk_{U^\dagger} \| A_{\mathcal{O}^*} \| B_{\mathcal{O}^*} \| ss_{\mathcal{O}^*})$ where $ss_{\mathcal{O}^*} = DH_g(A_{\mathcal{O}^*}, B_{\mathcal{O}^*})$ and $B_{\mathcal{O}^*} = B^*$. Additionally, note that $sid_{\mathcal{O}^\dagger} = H(\mathsf{aux}_{\mathcal{O}^\dagger} \| vk_{U^\dagger} \| A_{\mathcal{O}^\dagger} \| B_{\mathcal{O}^\dagger} \| ss_{\mathcal{O}^\dagger})$ where $ss_{\mathcal{O}^\dagger} = DH_g(A_{\mathcal{O}^\dagger}, B_{\mathcal{O}^\dagger})$ and $B_{\mathcal{O}^*} \neq B_{\mathcal{O}^\dagger}$.

E_2 can be divided into two cases E_2' and E_2'' depending on whether $sid_{\mathcal{O}^*} = sid_{\mathcal{O}^\dagger}$ or not. In case E_2', it holds that $sid_{\mathcal{O}^*} = sid_{\mathcal{O}^\dagger}$. Since $B_{\mathcal{O}^*} \neq B_{\mathcal{O}^\dagger}$ and $H : \{0,1\}^* \to \{0,1\}^n$ is treated as a random oracle, we have $\Pr[E_2'] \le n_{q_h} \cdot \frac{1}{2^n}$.

In E_2'', $sid_{\mathcal{O}^*} \neq sid_{\mathcal{O}^\dagger}$, and we can use $(sid_{\mathcal{O}^*}, \sigma^*)$ as a valid forgery for SIG. Since $U^\dagger$ is randomly selected at the beginning of the game, we have that $\mathbf{Adv}^{\text{EU-CMA}}_{\mathcal{B},\mathsf{SIG}}(\lambda) \geq \frac{1}{n_p} \cdot \Pr[E_2'']$. Therefore, we have that $\Pr[E_2] \leq n_p \cdot \mathbf{Adv}^{\text{EU-CMA}}_{\mathcal{B},\mathsf{SIG}}(\lambda) + n_{q_h} \cdot \frac{1}{2^n}$.

The second case E_3 is that σ^* is not output by any $O^\dagger \in \Pi^j_{U^\dagger}$ for $j \in \mathbb{N}^+$. Since $\mathcal{B}$ does not make a query $\mathsf{SIG.Sign}(sk^\dagger, sid_{\mathcal{O}^*})$, $(sid_{\mathcal{O}^*}, \sigma^*)$ is a valid forgery for SIG. Given that $U^\dagger$ is randomly selected at the beginning of the game, we have that $\mathbf{Adv}^{\text{EU-CMA}}_{\mathcal{B},\mathsf{SIG}}(\lambda) \geq \frac{1}{n_p} \cdot \Pr[E_3]$. Lemma 2 follows immediately. □

Game 2. Compared to Game 1, the only difference in this game is that upon receiving a message (B, σ) not sent to the corresponding oracle (we will explain corresponding oracle in event V_1 later), the challenger rejects the message without verifying the signature.

Let $\mathcal{O}^* = \Pi^j_V$ with $V \in \mathcal{U}$ and we extract $A_{\mathcal{O}^*}$ from $\tau_{\mathcal{O}^*}$. We define that the oracle sends $A_{\mathcal{O}^*}$ as the corresponding oracle of $\mathcal{O}^*$. For two uncorrupted parties $U \in \mathcal{U}'$ and $V \in \mathcal{U}$ there exists an oracle $\mathcal{O} = \Pi^i_U$ with $\mathrm{pid}_{\mathcal{O}} = V$, $\gamma_{\mathcal{O}} = \texttt{accepted}$. We define V_1 as the event that $(B_{\mathcal{O}}, \sigma_{\mathcal{O}})$ is output by an honest oracle $\mathcal{O}^* = \Pi^j_V$ while $\mathcal{O}$ is not the corresponding oracle of $\mathcal{O}^*$. The adversary cannot distinguish Game 1 from Game 2 unless V_1 occurs. According to the *Difference Lemma*, we have that $|\Pr[S_1] - \Pr[S_2]| \leq \Pr[V_1]$.

Lemma 3. *There is an adversary $\mathcal{C}$ against the EU-CMA security of* SIG *such that* $\Pr[V_1] \leq n_p \cdot \mathbf{Adv}^{EU\text{-}CMA}_{\mathcal{C},\mathsf{SIG}}(\lambda) + n_{q_h} \cdot \frac{1}{2^n}$.

Proof. The adversary $\mathcal{C}$ receives a public key $vk^\dagger$, and can access to the signature oracle $\mathsf{SIG.Sign}(sk^\dagger, \cdot)$. It acts as the challenger to $\mathcal{A}$ in Game 1. First, $\mathcal{C}$ generates n_p participants $\mathcal{U}$ and n_p' participants $\mathcal{U}'$. Now $\mathcal{C}$ randomly selects a participant $U^\dagger \in \mathcal{U}$ and sets $vk_{U^\dagger} = vk^\dagger$ and $sk_{U^\dagger} = \perp$. $\mathcal{C}$ then runs the key generation algorithm $\mathsf{SIG.Gen}(\lambda)$ to obtain public-private keys for all participants $U \in \mathcal{U} \setminus \{U^\dagger\}$. $\mathcal{C}$ sends all the public keys (including $vk^\dagger$) to $\mathcal{A}$. Next, $\mathcal{C}$ generates inspection key pairs by selecting $isk_U \leftarrow\$ \mathbb{Z}_q^*$ and computing $ipk_U = g^{isk_U}$ for every $U \in \mathcal{U}$. $\mathcal{C}$ sends all the inspection public keys to $\mathcal{A}$.

<u>*Simulation.*</u> $\mathcal{A}$ starts to make NEWSESSION, SEND, CHECK, CORRUPT, and REVEAL queries. $\mathcal{C}$ responds to these queries in the following way:

- If a CORRUPT(U) query is made and $U \neq U^\dagger$ then $\mathcal{C}$ returns sk_U, and $\mathcal{A}$ can no longer query any oracle belonging to U. If $U = U^\dagger$ then $\mathcal{C}$ aborts.
- When a SEND($\mathcal{O}$, msg) query is made for oracle $\mathcal{O} = \Pi^i_U$ with $U \in \mathcal{U} \cup \mathcal{U}'$,
  - If $\mathcal{O}$ is still in the *Hello* phase then $\mathcal{C}$ responds as in the correct execution.
  - If $\mathrm{role}_{\mathcal{O}} = \texttt{init}$ and $\mathcal{O}$ should output a DH ephemeral public key, then $\mathcal{C}$ responds as in the correct execution.
  - If $U = U^\dagger$, $\mathcal{C}$ selects $b \leftarrow\$ \mathbb{Z}_q^*$ and computes $B_{\mathcal{O}} \leftarrow g^b$, $A_{\mathcal{O}} \leftarrow \mathrm{msg}$, $ss_{\mathcal{O}} \leftarrow A^b_{\mathcal{O}}$. $\mathcal{C}$ obtains $sid_{\mathcal{O}} = H(\mathsf{aux}_{\mathcal{O}} \| vk_{U^\dagger} \| A_{\mathcal{O}} \| B_{\mathcal{O}} \| ss_{\mathcal{O}})$, where $\mathsf{aux}_{\mathcal{O}} \in \tau_{\mathcal{O}}$. $\mathcal{C}$ obtains a signature $\sigma_{\mathcal{O}} \leftarrow \mathsf{SIG.Sign}(sk^\dagger, sid_{\mathcal{O}})$. Next, $\mathcal{C}$ returns $(B_{\mathcal{O}}, Encode(\widehat{H}(ipk^b_{U^\dagger}) \oplus ss_{\mathcal{O}}))$ and $(vk_{U^\dagger}, \sigma_{\mathcal{O}})$ to $\mathcal{A}$. If $U \in \mathcal{U}$ and $U \neq U^\dagger$, $\mathcal{C}$ responds as in the correct execution.

- If U is an initiator, for each oracle belonging to $\mathrm{pid}_{\mathcal{O}}$, $\mathcal{C}$ checks to find an oracle $\mathcal{O}^*$ which outputs msg. If no such an oracle is found, $\mathcal{C}$ simply rejects the signature. Otherwise, $\mathcal{C}$ responds as in the correct execution.

– For any $\textsc{Check}(\mathcal{O}, ss)$ or $\textsc{Reveal}(\mathcal{O})$ query, $\mathcal{C}$ responds correctly using its knowledge of $ss_{\mathcal{O}}$ and $sid_{\mathcal{O}}$.

At the end of the game, $\mathcal{A}$ outputs a pair $(\mathcal{O}^*, ss^*)$.

Reduction. If V_1 happens, then there exists an initiator oracle $\mathcal{O}^*$ with $\gamma_{\mathcal{O}^*} = \texttt{accepted}$ that has an incoming message $(B_{\mathcal{O}^\dagger}, vk_{U^\dagger}, \sigma_{\mathcal{O}^\dagger}) \in \tau_{\mathcal{O}^*}$ output by an honest responder oracle $\mathcal{O}^\dagger = \Pi^j_{U^\dagger}$, whereas $\mathcal{O}^\dagger$ has an incoming message $A_{\mathcal{O}^\dagger} \neq A_{\mathcal{O}^*}$. The event V_1 means that $1 \leftarrow \mathsf{SIG.Verif}(vk_{U^\dagger}, sid_{\mathcal{O}^*}, \sigma_{\mathcal{O}^\dagger})$. Note that $sid_{\mathcal{O}^\dagger} = H(\mathsf{aux}_{\mathcal{O}^\dagger} || vk_{U^\dagger} || A_{\mathcal{O}^\dagger} || B_{\mathcal{O}^\dagger} || ss_{\mathcal{O}^\dagger})$ where $ss_{\mathcal{O}^\dagger} = DH_g(A_{\mathcal{O}^\dagger}, B_{\mathcal{O}^\dagger})$, and $sid_{\mathcal{O}^*} = H(\mathsf{aux}_{\mathcal{O}^*} || vk_{U^\dagger} || A_{\mathcal{O}^*} || B_{\mathcal{O}^\dagger} || ss_{\mathcal{O}^*})$ where $ss_{\mathcal{O}^*} = DH_g(A_{\mathcal{O}^*}, B_{\mathcal{O}^\dagger})$. We consider two sub-cases V_2 and V_3 depending on whether $sid_{\mathcal{O}^\dagger} = sid_{\mathcal{O}^*}$.

The first sub-case V_2 is that $sid_{\mathcal{O}^\dagger} = sid_{\mathcal{O}^*}$. Since $A_{\mathcal{O}^\dagger} \neq A_{\mathcal{O}^*}$ and $H : \{0,1\}^* \rightarrow \{0,1\}^n$ is treated as a random oracle, we have $\Pr[V_2] \leq n_{q_h} \cdot \frac{1}{2^n}$.

The second sub-case V_3 is that $sid_{\mathcal{O}^\dagger} \neq sid_{\mathcal{O}^*}$. Since $\gamma_{\mathcal{O}^*} = \texttt{accepted}$, we have $1 \leftarrow \mathsf{SIG.Verif}(vk_{U^\dagger}, sid_{\mathcal{O}^*}, \sigma_{\mathcal{O}^\dagger})$. Next, we can use $(sid_{\mathcal{O}^*}, \sigma_{\mathcal{O}^\dagger})$ as a valid forgery for SIG. Since $U^\dagger$ is randomly selected at the beginning of the game, we have that $\mathbf{Adv}^{\text{EU-CMA}}_{\mathcal{C},\mathsf{SIG}}(\lambda) \geq \frac{1}{n_p} \cdot \Pr[V_3]$. Lemma 3 follows immediately. □

Game 3. Compared to Game 2, the only difference in this game is the way of computing $rk_{S\mathcal{O}}$ for every oracle $\mathcal{O} = \Pi^j_V$ with $V \in \mathcal{U}$. In Game 3, if $A_{\mathcal{O}}$ is output by an honest oracle, then we set $rk_{S\mathcal{O}} \leftarrow_{\$} \{0,1\}^*$, where the length of $rk_{S\mathcal{O}}$ is equal to $Encode(\widehat{H}(ipk_V^{b_{\mathcal{O}}}) \oplus ss_{\mathcal{O}})$ and $b_{\mathcal{O}}$ is the ephemeral secret key of $\mathcal{O}$. Otherwise, we compute $rk_{S\mathcal{O}} \leftarrow Encode(\widehat{H}(ipk_V^{b_{\mathcal{O}}}) \oplus ss_{\mathcal{O}})$.

Let $ins_{\mathcal{O}} = ipk_V^{b_{\mathcal{O}}}$ for an oracle $\mathcal{O} = \Pi^j_V$ with $V \in \mathcal{U}$ where $b_{\mathcal{O}}$ is the ephemeral secret key of $\mathcal{O}$. We define Z to be the event that $\mathcal{A}$ ever queries $\widehat{H}(ins_{\mathcal{O}})$ for an oracle $\mathcal{O} = \Pi^i_V$ with $V \in \mathcal{U}$ whose $A_{\mathcal{O}}$ is output by an honest oracle. $\mathcal{A}$ cannot distinguish Game 3 from Game 2 unless the event Z happens. By the *Difference Lemma*, we have $|\Pr[S_2] - \Pr[S_3]| \leq \Pr[Z]$.

Lemma 4. *There exists an algorithm $\mathcal{D}$ against the CDH assumption for $\mathbb{G}$ such that* $\Pr[Z] \leq n_q \cdot n_s \cdot \mathbf{Adv}^{CDH}_{\mathcal{D},\mathbb{G}}(\lambda)$.

Proof. Let $H, \widehat{H}$ be random oracles. The algorithm $\mathcal{D}$ obtains a *CDH assumption* instance (g^x, g^y) in $\mathbb{G}$. $\mathcal{D}$ generates n_p participants $\mathcal{U}$ and n'_p participants $\mathcal{U}'$. Following this, $\mathcal{D}$ runs the key generation algorithm $\mathsf{SIG.Gen}(\lambda)$, acquiring public-private key pairs for all participants within $\mathcal{U}$. $\mathcal{D}$ sends all the public keys to $\mathcal{A}$. Next, $\mathcal{D}$ generates inspection key pairs by selecting $R_U \leftarrow_{\$} \mathbb{Z}_q^*$ and computing $ipk_U = g^{yR_U}$ for every $U \in \mathcal{U}$. $\mathcal{D}$ sends all the inspection public keys to $\mathcal{A}$.

Simulation. $\mathcal{A}$ starts to make $\textsc{NewSession}$, $\textsc{Send}$, $\textsc{Check}$, $\textsc{Corrupt}$, and $\textsc{Reveal}$ queries and $\mathcal{D}$ answers in the following way:

– If $\mathcal{A}$ makes a $\textsc{Corrupt}(U)$ query, $\mathcal{D}$ returns sk_U and $\mathcal{A}$ is no longer able to make any queries to oracles belonging to U.

– When a SEND($\mathcal{O}$, msg) query is made to an oracle $\mathcal{O} = \Pi_U^i$, if $\mathcal{O}$ is in the *Hello* phase, then $\mathcal{D}$ responds as in the actual protocol. Otherwise:
  - If U is an initiator and $\mathcal{O}$ should output a DH ephemeral public key. $\mathcal{D}$ generates a random value $r_\mathcal{O} \in \mathbb{Z}_q^*$, sets $A_\mathcal{O} = g^{r_\mathcal{O}}$ and returns $A_\mathcal{O}$ to $\mathcal{A}$.
  - If U is a responder, $\mathcal{D}$ generates a random value $r_\mathcal{O} \in \mathbb{Z}_q^*$. For each oracle maintained by $\mathcal{D}$, $\mathcal{D}$ checks to find $\mathcal{O}^*$ such that $\mathcal{O}^*$ outputs the message *msg*. If no such oracle is found then $\mathcal{D}$ sets $B_\mathcal{O} = g^{r_\mathcal{O}}$, $ins_\mathcal{O} = g^{yR_U r_\mathcal{O}}$ and respond correctly. Otherwise, $\mathcal{D}$ sets $B_\mathcal{O} = g^{xr_\mathcal{O}}$, $ins_\mathcal{O} = \perp$. $\mathcal{D}$ computes $ss_\mathcal{O} = (g^{xr_\mathcal{O}})^{r_{\mathcal{O}^*}}$ where $r_{\mathcal{O}^*}$ is extracted from $\tau_{\mathcal{O}^*}$ and computes $sid_\mathcal{O}$ and signature correctly. Next, $\mathcal{D}$ sets $rk_{S\mathcal{O}} \leftarrow R_\mathcal{O}$ where $R_\mathcal{O}$ is a random sequence and the length of $rk_{S\mathcal{O}}$ is equal to the correct $rk_{S\mathcal{O}}$ (the correct $rk_{S\mathcal{O}} = Encode(\widehat{H}(g^{xyr_\mathcal{O}R_U}) \oplus ss_\mathcal{O})$, although $\mathcal{D}$ does not know the correct $rk_{S\mathcal{O}}$, $\mathcal{D}$ knows its length).
  - If U is an initiator, for each oracle belonging to $\text{pid}_\mathcal{O}$, $\mathcal{D}$ checks to find an oracle $\mathcal{O}^*$ such that $\mathcal{O}^*$ output the *msg*. If no such *msg* is found, $\mathcal{D}$ simply rejects the signature. If such $\mathcal{O}^*$ is found but $\mathcal{O}$ is not the corresponding oracle of $\mathcal{O}^*$, $\mathcal{D}$ simply rejects the signature. Otherwise, $\mathcal{D}$ checks the signature and responds correctly (either accepting or rejecting it).

– If a CHECK($\mathcal{O}, ss$) query or a REVEAL($\mathcal{O}$) query is made. Consider that $\mathcal{D}$ knows the $ss_\mathcal{O}$ and $sid_\mathcal{O}$, then $\mathcal{D}$ can answer these queries honestly.

Reduction. Game 2 and Game 3 are indistinguishable unless $\mathcal{A}$ queries $g^{xyr_\mathcal{O}R_V}$ to $\widehat{H}$ for an honest oracle $\mathcal{O} = \Pi_V^j$ with $V \in \mathcal{U}$, where $A_\mathcal{O}$ is output by an honest oracle. If $\mathcal{A}$ makes such a query, then $\mathcal{D}$ randomly selects a session and we have the probability that $\mathcal{D}$ successfully guessed the session that $\mathcal{A}$ queried $\widehat{H}$ with $g^{xyr_\mathcal{O}R_V}$ is $\frac{1}{n_s}$. Next, $\mathcal{D}$ extract $r_\mathcal{O}$ from $\tau_\mathcal{O}$. Let Z occurs with probability $\Pr[Z]$. This means that with probability $\Pr[Z]$, the random oracle $\widehat{H}$ is queried with the value $g^{xyr_\mathcal{O}R_V}$. Consequently, $\mathcal{D}$ randomly selects a value y_* from the random oracle lists of $\widehat{H}$ and returns $y_*^{-(r_\mathcal{O}R_V)}$ as the solution of the *CDH assumption*. We have that $\mathbf{Adv}_{\mathcal{D},\mathbb{G}}^{CDH}(\lambda) \geq \frac{1}{n_s} \cdot \frac{1}{n_q} \cdot \Pr[Z]$. Lemma 4 follows immediately. □

Game 4. Compared to Game 3, the only difference in this game is how we compute $sid_\mathcal{O}$ for every oracle $\mathcal{O}$ when its received ephemeral public key is output by an honest oracle. If $\text{role}_\mathcal{O} = \texttt{resp}$, we select $ss'_\mathcal{O} \leftarrow\$ S_{SS}$ and compute $sid_\mathcal{O} = H(\mathsf{aux}_\mathcal{O}||vk_U||A_\mathcal{O}||B_\mathcal{O}||ss'_\mathcal{O})$. Otherwise, if $B_\mathcal{O}$ is output by oracle $\mathcal{O}^*$ and $\mathcal{O}$ is the corresponding oracle of $\mathcal{O}^*$, we set $ss'_\mathcal{O} = ss'_{\mathcal{O}^*}$ and $sid_\mathcal{O} = sid_{\mathcal{O}^*}$.

For an honest oracle $\mathcal{O}$ with $\gamma_\mathcal{O} = \texttt{accepted}$ whose ephemeral public secret it received is output by an honest oracle, let F be the event that the adversary $\mathcal{A}$ ever queries $\mathsf{aux}_\mathcal{O}||vk_{\text{pid}_\mathcal{O}}||A_\mathcal{O}||B_\mathcal{O}||DH_g(A_\mathcal{O}, B_\mathcal{O})$ with H. $\mathcal{A}$ cannot distinguish Game 3 from Game 4 unless the event F happens. By the *Difference Lemma*, we have $|\Pr[S_3] - \Pr[S_4]| \leq \Pr[F]$.

Lemma 5. *There is an algorithm $\mathcal{E}$ against the gap-DH assumption for $\mathbb{G}$ such that* $\Pr[F] \leq \mathbf{Adv}_{\mathcal{E},\mathbb{G}}^{gap\text{-}DH}(\lambda)$.

Proof. Let H be a random oracle. The algorithm $\mathcal{E}$ obtains a *gap-DH assumption* instance (g^a, g^b) in $\mathbb{G}$ and can access a DDH oracle $\mathrm{DDH}_{\mathbb{G}}(\cdot)$. $\mathcal{E}$ generates n_p participants $\mathcal{U}$ and n'_p participants $\mathcal{U}'$. Following this, $\mathcal{E}$ then runs the key generation algorithm $\mathsf{SIG.Gen}(\lambda)$, acquiring public-private key pairs for all participants in $\mathcal{U}$. $\mathcal{E}$ sends all the public keys to $\mathcal{A}$. Next, $\mathcal{E}$ generates inspection key pairs by selecting $isk_U \leftarrow\$\, \mathbb{Z}_q^*$ and computing $ipk_U = g^{isk_U}$ for every $U \in \mathcal{U}$. $\mathcal{E}$ sends all the inspection public keys to $\mathcal{A}$.

Simulation. $\mathcal{A}$ starts to make NEWSESSION, SEND, CHECK, CORRUPT, and REVEAL queries and $\mathcal{E}$ answers in the following way:

- If $\mathcal{A}$ makes a CORRUPT(U) query, $\mathcal{E}$ returns sk_U and $\mathcal{A}$ is no longer able to make any queries to oracles belonging to U.
- When a SEND(O, msg) query is made to an oracle $\mathcal{O} = \Pi_U^i$, if $\mathcal{O}$ is in the *Hello* phase, then $\mathcal{E}$ responds as in the actual protocol. Otherwise:
  - Algorithm $\mathcal{E}$ generates random value $r_\mathcal{O} \in \mathbb{Z}_q^*$.
  - If U is an initiator and the initiator should output a DH ephemeral public key, $\mathcal{E}$ sets $A_\mathcal{O} = (g^a)^{r_\mathcal{O}}$ and returns $A_\mathcal{O}$ to $\mathcal{A}$.
  - If U is a responder and for each oracle maintained by $\mathcal{E}$, $\mathcal{E}$ checks to find $\mathcal{O}^*$ such that $\mathcal{O}^*$ output the message msg. Next, $\mathcal{E}$ sets $A_\mathcal{O} = msg$, $B_\mathcal{O} = g^{br_\mathcal{O}}$, and $ss'_\mathcal{O} \leftarrow\$\, S_{\mathrm{SS}}$ whereas the correct $ss_\mathcal{O}$ should be $g^{abr_\mathcal{O}r_{\mathcal{O}^*}}$. $\mathcal{E}$ sets and computes $sid_\mathcal{O} = H(\mathsf{aux}_\mathcal{O}||vk_U||A_\mathcal{O}||B_\mathcal{O}||ss'_\mathcal{O})$, where $\mathsf{aux}_\mathcal{O}$ is obtained from $\tau_\mathcal{O}$. Next, $\mathcal{E}$ sets $rks_\mathcal{O} \leftarrow R_\mathcal{O}$ where $R_\mathcal{O}$ is a random sequence and the length of $rks_\mathcal{O}$ is equal to the correct $rks_\mathcal{O}$ (the correct $rks_\mathcal{O} = Encode(\widehat{H}({ipk_U}^{br_\mathcal{O}}) \oplus ss_\mathcal{O}))$ and reply with $(B_\mathcal{O}, rks_\mathcal{O}, vk_U, \mathsf{SIG.Sign}(sk_U, sid_\mathcal{O}))$.
  - Otherwise, if U is a responder and no such $\mathcal{O}^*$ is found then sets $A_\mathcal{O} = msg$, $B_\mathcal{O} = g^{r_\mathcal{O}}$, $ss_\mathcal{O} = msg^{r_\mathcal{O}}$, and $rks_\mathcal{O} = Encode(\widehat{H}(ipk_U^{r_\mathcal{O}}) \oplus ss_\mathcal{O})$. $\mathcal{E}$ sets and computes $sid_\mathcal{O} = H(\mathsf{aux}_\mathcal{O}||vk_U||A_\mathcal{O}||B_\mathcal{O}||ss_\mathcal{O})$, where $\mathsf{aux}_\mathcal{O}$ is obtained from $\tau_\mathcal{O}$, and reply with $(B_\mathcal{O}, rks_\mathcal{O}, vk_U, \mathsf{SIG.Sign}(sk_U, sid_\mathcal{O}))$.
  - If U is an initiator, for each oracle maintained by $\mathcal{E}$, $\mathcal{E}$ checks to find $\mathcal{O}^*$ such that $\mathcal{O}^*$ outputs the msg. If such an $\mathcal{O}^*$ is found and $\mathcal{O}$ is the corresponding oracle of $\mathcal{O}^*$, then $\mathcal{E}$ sets $ss'_\mathcal{O} = ss'_{\mathcal{O}^*}$ where $ss'_{\mathcal{O}^*}$ is extracted from $\tau_{\mathcal{O}^*}$. Next, $\mathcal{E}$ computes and sets the $sid_\mathcal{O} = H(\mathsf{aux}_\mathcal{O}||vk_U||A_\mathcal{O}||B_\mathcal{O}||ss'_\mathcal{O})$. Then, $\mathcal{E}$ checks the signature and responds correctly (accept or reject).
  - If no such oracle is found, $\mathcal{E}$ simply rejects the siganature.
  - Otherwise, if such an $\mathcal{O}^*$ is found, but $\mathcal{O}$ is not the corresponding oracle of $\mathcal{O}^*$, $\mathcal{E}$ simply rejects the signature.
- If a CHECK$(\mathcal{O}, ss)$ query is made, then $\mathcal{E}$ queries its DDH oracle. If $0 \leftarrow \mathrm{DDH}_{\mathbb{G}}(A_\mathcal{O}, B_\mathcal{O}, ss)$, then returns *false*. Otherwise, *true* is returned.
- If a REVEAL$(\mathcal{O})$ query is made, $\mathcal{E}$ returns the $sid_\mathcal{O}$ if $\gamma_\mathcal{O} = \mathtt{accept}$, otherwise do nothing.

Reduction. Game 3 and Game 4 are indistinsguishable unless $\mathcal{A}$ queries H with $\mathsf{aux}_\mathcal{O}||vk_{\mathrm{pid}_\mathcal{O}}||A_\mathcal{O}||B_\mathcal{O}||DH_g(A_\mathcal{O}, B_\mathcal{O})$ for an honest oracle $\mathcal{O}$ with $\gamma_\mathcal{O} = \mathtt{accepted}$ where the ephemeral public secret it received is output by an honest oracle. Assume the partner oracle is $\mathcal{O}^*$. Let F occurs with probability $\Pr[F]$, which means that $\mathcal{A}$ querying H with $\mathsf{aux}_{\mathcal{O}}||vk_{\mathrm{pid}_{\mathcal{O}}}||g^{ar_{\mathcal{O}}}||g^{br_{\mathcal{O}^*}}||g^{abr_{\mathcal{O}}r_{\mathcal{O}^*}}$. For each queried value from random oracle list of H, $\mathcal{E}$ extracts the shared secret field as res. Next, $\mathcal{E}$ can use its DDH-oracle to find out the $(r_{\mathcal{O}}, r_{\mathcal{O}^*})$ from $(\tau_{\mathcal{O}}, \tau_{\mathcal{O}^*})$ such that $1 \leftarrow DDH_{\mathbb{G}}(g^a, g^b, res^{-(r_{\mathcal{O}}r_{\mathcal{O}^*})})$ and returns $res^{-(r_{\mathcal{O}}r_{\mathcal{O}^*})}$ as the solution of the *gap-DH assumption*. We have that $\Pr[F] \leq \mathbf{Adv}^{\text{gap-DH}}_{\mathcal{E},\mathbb{G}}(\lambda)$ and the proof of Lemma 5 follows immediately. □

We now analyze the probability that $\mathcal{A}$ wins the Game 4. We say that $\mathcal{A}$ wins the Game 4 if it outputs $(\mathcal{O}^*, ss^*)$ such that O^* is a *fresh oracle* and $ss'_{\mathcal{O}} = ss^*$. Since $ss'_{\mathcal{O}}$ for every *fresh oracle* $\mathcal{O}$ is randomly selected from S_{SS}, and we have that $sid_{\mathcal{O}} = H(\mathsf{aux}_{\mathcal{O}}, vk_{\mathrm{pid}_{\mathcal{O}}}, A_{\mathcal{O}}, B_{\mathcal{O}}, ss'_{\mathcal{O}})$. Additionally, H is a random oracle that we can ensure the signature of $sid_{\mathcal{O}}$ leaks no information about $ss'_{\mathcal{O}}$. Therefore, the probability that $\mathcal{A}$ wins the Game 4 is $\frac{1}{|S_{\mathrm{SS}}|}$. We have that $\Pr[S_4] = \frac{1}{|S_{\mathrm{SS}}|}$.

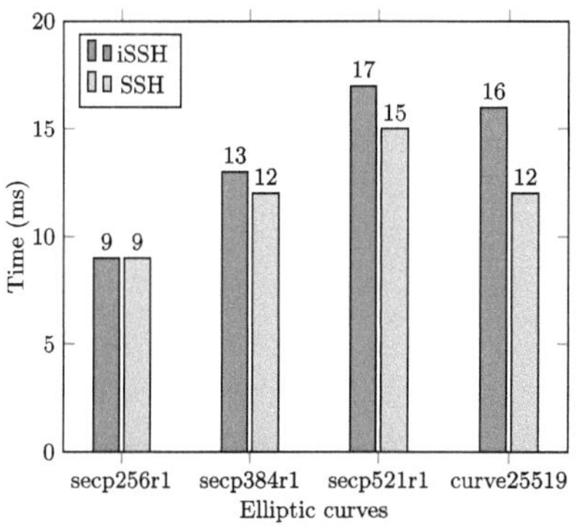

(a) Average key exchange time

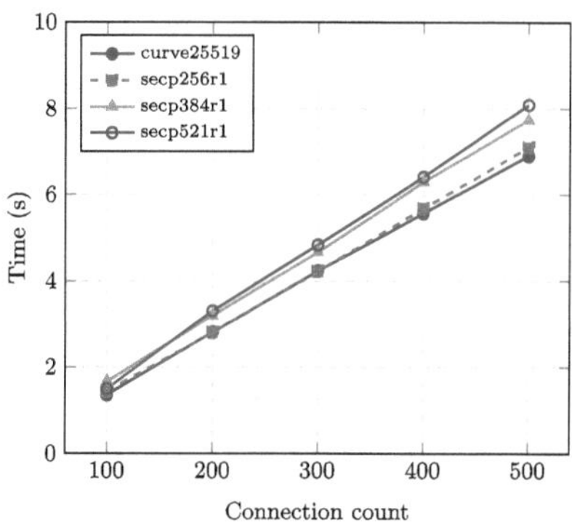

(b) Key recovery time scalability

Fig. 3. Time cost evaluations on different curves [14,27].

Combining the above bounds results in the following security statement:

$$\begin{aligned}\mathbf{Adv}^{\text{OW-iKEP}}_{\mathcal{A},\Pi}(\lambda) \leq & 2 \cdot n_p \cdot \mathbf{Adv}^{\text{EU-CMA}}_{\mathcal{B},\mathsf{SIG}}(\lambda) + n_p \cdot \mathbf{Adv}^{\text{EU-CMA}}_{\mathcal{C},\mathsf{SIG}}(\lambda) \\ & + n_q \cdot n_s \cdot \mathbf{Adv}^{\text{CDH}}_{\mathcal{D},\mathbb{G}}(\lambda) + \mathbf{Adv}^{\text{gap-DH}}_{\mathcal{E},\mathbb{G}}(\lambda) \\ & + 2 \cdot n_{q_h} \cdot \frac{1}{2^n} + \frac{1}{|S_{\mathrm{SS}}|}\end{aligned}$$

The proof of *key secrecy* is completed. □

Now we consider the probability of event $\mathrm{NoPartnering}_{\mathcal{A},\Pi}(\lambda)$. Consider that if $\mathrm{NoPartnering}_{\mathcal{A},\Pi}(\lambda)$ occurs then either event E_1 or V_1 will occur, we have $\Pr[\mathrm{NoPartnering}_{\mathcal{A},\Pi}(\lambda)] \leq \Pr[E_1] + \Pr[V_1]$. And the *No Partnering* of Π holds. Theorem 1 follows immediately. □

5 Experiments

The iSSH implementation is available at https://gitee.com/wx_974c3e6b28/iSSH.git. Our experimental environment is a virtual machine running Ubuntu 20.04.3 LTS and equipped with a 4-core Intel Core i7-9750H CPU running at 2.60 GHz. The network bandwidth is 1000 Mbps, with an average latency of 0.02 ms. We deployed two SSH servers on OpenSSH 9.8p1 [21]: a stock instance and an iSSH-enabled instance obtained by patching and recompiling the source. We set up a client based on Paramiko [22] and an inspector based on Python 3.11 [23]. We tested the performance of these in two areas: the time taken for the key exchange phase and the time taken for offline key recovery.

Key Exchange Time. As shown in Fig. 2, the key exchange phase consists of the *Hello* phase, the *Shared Secret Exchange* phase, and the *Application Keys Generation* phase. We modified the random padding generation method, which introduced additional computational overhead and increased the time taken for key exchange. We tested different elliptic curves defined in [14, 27] that are widely supported by SSH servers. We tested the key exchange time by initiating 100 connections to SSH and iSSH servers respectively via the client and taking the average time for the test. As shown in Fig. 3a, our iSSH introduces only a negligible amount of communication overhead during the key exchange phase. Specifically, when using secp256r1, the key exchange time of iSSH is nearly indistinguishable from that of SSH. When using curve25519, the time overhead increases by nearly 25%, but it only adds an additional 4 ms.

Offline Key Recovery Time. We tested how long it took the inspector to recover application keys offline. As shown in Fig. 3b, on the one hand, the inspector can recover the application keys for 100 SSH connections in no more than two seconds. On the other hand, the time taken to recover the application keys increased linearly with the number of SSH connections. These results demonstrate that iSSH is both high-performing and practical.

Acknowledgments. We would like to thank all anonymous reviewers for their valuable comments. This work is supported in part by the National Natural Science Foundation of China (Grant No. 62202485, No.62122092) and the Young Elite Scientists Sponsorship Program by China Association for Science and Technology (No. YESS20230028).

References

1. Ahn, T., Kwak, J., Kim, S.: mdTLS: how to make middlebox-aware TLS more efficient? In: International Conference on Information Security and Cryptology, pp. 39–59. Springer (2023)
2. An, J.H., Dodis, Y., Rabin, T.: On the security of joint signature and encryption. In: Knudsen, L.R. (ed.) Advances in Cryptology – EUROCRYPT 2002, pp. 83–107. Springer, Berlin Heidelberg, Berlin, Heidelberg (2002)

3. Baek, J., Kim, J., Susilo, W.: Inspecting TLS anytime anywhere: a new approach to TLS interception. In: Proceedings of the 15th ACM Asia Conference on Computer and Communications Security, ASIA CCS 2020, pp. 116–126. ACM, New York, NY, USA (2020). https://doi.org/10.1145/3320269.3372199
4. Bhargavan, K., Boureanu, I., Delignat-Lavaud, A., Fouque, P.A., Onete, C.: A formal treatment of accountable proxying over TLS. In: 2018 IEEE Symposium on Security and Privacy (SP), pp. 799–816. IEEE (2018)
5. Boneh, D., Shoup, V.: A graduate course in applied cryptography. draft 0.5 edn. (2020). https://crypto.stanford.edu/~dabo/cryptobook/BonehShoup_0_5.pdf
6. Canard, S., Diop, A., Kheir, N., Paindavoine, M., Sabt, M.: BlindIDS: market-compliant and privacy-friendly intrusion detection system over encrypted traffic. In: Proceedings of the 2017 ACM on Asia Conference on Computer and Communications Security, pp. 561–574 (2017)
7. de Carné de Carnavalet, X., van Oorschot, P.C.: A survey and analysis of TLS interception mechanisms and motivations: exploring how end-to-end TLS is made "end-to-me" for web traffic. ACM Comput. Surv. **55**(13s), 1–40 (2023)
8. Diffie, W., Hellman, M.: New directions in cryptography. IEEE Trans. Inf. Theory **22**(6), 644–654 (1976)
9. Fellicious, C., Sentanoe, S., Granitzer, M., Reiser, H.P.: SmartKex: machine learning assisted SSH keys extraction from the heap dump. arXiv preprint arXiv:2209.05243 (2022)
10. Fellicious, C., Sentanoe, S., Mitrović, J., Reiser, H.P., Granitzer, M.: PointerKex: a pointer-based ssh key extraction method. In: International Conference on Machine Learning, Optimization, and Data Science, pp. 272–286. Springer (2024)
11. Jarmoc, J., Unit, D.: SSL/TLS interception proxies and transitive trust. Black Hat Europe (2012)
12. Kaiser, M., Böhm, S.: SSH-MITM: a tool for SSH audits and man-in-the-middle attacks. github repository (2024). https://github.com/ssh-mitm/ssh-mitm, Accessed 16th May
13. Kate, A., Goldberg, I.: Distributed private-key generators for identity-based cryptography. In: International Conference on Security and Cryptography for Networks, pp. 436–453. Springer (2010)
14. Langley, A., Hamburg, M., Turner, S.: Elliptic curves for security. RFC 7748, January 2016. https://doi.org/10.17487/RFC7748
15. Lee, H., et al.: maTLS: how to make TLS middlebox-aware? In: NDSS (2019)
16. Li, J., Chen, R., Su, J., Huang, X., Wang, X.: ME-TLS: middlebox-enhanced TLS for internet-of-things devices. IEEE Internet Things J. **7**(2), 1216–1229 (2019)
17. Lonvick, C.M., Ylonen, T.: The Secure Shell (SSH) Transport Layer Protocol. RFC 4253, January 2006. https://doi.org/10.17487/RFC4253
18. Morrissey, P., Smart, N.P., Warinschi, B.: A modular security analysis of the TLS handshake protocol. In: Advances in Cryptology-ASIACRYPT 2008: 14th International Conference on the Theory and Application of Cryptology and Information Security, Melbourne, Australia, 7–11 December 2008, Proceedings 14, pp. 55–73. Springer (2008)
19. Namprempre, C., Kohno, T., Bellare, M.: The secure shell (SSH) transport layer encryption modes. RFC 4344, January 2006. https://doi.org/10.17487/RFC4344
20. Naylor, D., et al.: Multi-context TLS (mcTLS): enabling secure in-network functionality in TLS. Comput. Commun. Rev. **45**(4), 199–212 (2015)
21. OpenSSH: https://www.openssh.com/, Accessed 11 June 2025
22. Paramiko: https://www.paramiko.org/, Accessed 11 June 2025

23. Python: https://www.python.org/, Accessed 11 June 2025
24. Rescorla, E.: The Transport Layer Security (TLS) Protocol Version 1.3. RFC 8446, August 2018. https://doi.org/10.17487/RFC8446
25. Sentanoe, S., Reiser, H.P.: SSHkex: leveraging virtual machine introspection for extracting SSH keys and decrypting SSH network traffic. Forensic Sci. Int. Digit. Invest. **40**, 301337 (2022)
26. Sherry, J., Lan, C., Popa, R.A., Ratnasamy, S.: Blindbox: deep packet inspection over encrypted traffic. In: Proceedings of the 2015 ACM Conference on Special Interest Group on Data Communication, pp. 213–226 (2015)
27. Standards for Efficient Cryptography Group (SECG): SEC 2: Recommended elliptic curve domain parameters. Standard, Certicom Research, February 2010. https://www.secg.org/sec2-v2.pdf
28. Vergeer, J.: Decrypting openssh sessions for fun and profit, https://blog.fox-it.com/2020/11/11/decrypting-openssh-sessions-for-fun-and-profit/, Accessed 11 June 2025

Tracing Your Roots: Exploring the Security Issues of Root Certificates in Android TLS Connections

Xinyu Wei[1,2], Yuewu Wang[3], Lingguang Lei[4(✉)], Peng Wang[3], Chunjing Kou[3], and Siyuan Ma[3]

[1] State Key Laboratory of Cyberspace Security Defense, Institute of Information Engineering, CAS, Beijing 100093, China
[2] School of Cyber Security, University of Chinese Academy of Sciences, Beijing 100049, China
[3] School of Cryptology, University of Chinese Academy of Sciences, Beijing 101408, China
[4] College of Computer and Information Engineering, Xiamen University of Technology, Xiamen 361024, China
lglei@xmut.edu.cn

Abstract. The widespread adoption of Transport Layer Security (TLS) relies on rigorous certificate verification, but our large-scale analysis reveals shocking security issues in the root certificates themselves and their configuration that undermine TLS authentication guarantees. This paper uncovers security issues at two distinct levels: (1) The default root certificate list on platforms ranging from Android 7 to 14 and HarmonyOS 3.0 to 5.0 contains non-compliant root certificates, such as those associated with critical CVE vulnerability, certificates expired for over four years, and those using weak cryptography algorithm. Overall, HarmonyOS 5.0 performs best, followed by Android 14. (2) We carefully select 1246 popular apps to view their actual usage of custom root certificates. 42% of them have configuration issues with custom implementations, and some even enable HTTP communication, which indicates that while customizing root certificates provides convenience to users, it also introduces security risks. Finally, we evaluate the priority of root certificates from different sources to help users better understand the root certificates used by the current TLS connection. In general, both manufacturers and developers need to further improve their management and usage of root certificates.

Keywords: TLS connection · Root certificate · Certificate authority

1 Introduction

TLS plays an important role in protecting data security and user privacy in Android apps, especially in key areas such as healthcare, finance and social networking. In 2024, the number of app downloads from Google Play reached

R. Chen et al. (Eds.): Inscrypt 2025, LNCS 16409, pp. 369–389, 2026.
https://doi.org/10.1007/978-981-95-6203-9_20

81.4 billion, three times that of iOS downloads [3]. A good TLS connection can provide adequate security for apps. In 2018, Android 9 (API 28) disallows plaintext data transmission and enforces the use of TLS connections, where the verification of certificate chain can confirm the identity of server. The identity authentication of TLS not only requires the signature of each certificate to be verified step by step[1], but also mandates that the root certificate of the chain is included in the client's trusted root certificate list. If the client utilizes a weak authentication process, the security of TLS cannot be guaranteed.

Many researchers had explored vulnerabilities in the chain verification to enhance the security of TLS [4,5,10,11,15,22,23,30]. However, the security of root certificates themselves is equally important, as not all Certificate Authorities (CAs) are trustworthy, and security incidents related to CAs occur from time to time [14,31,32]. In the past, WoSign deliberately issued a certificate for one of the Github's domains without authorization in order to bypass browser checks. CVE-2023-21265 [8] indicates that the three root certificates from TrustCor CA could lead to sensitive information leakage without requiring additional privileges or user interaction. However, we find that these certificates remain present in Android 9–13 and HarmonyOS 4.0. Using an untrusted root certificate undermines TLS security, even if the verification process is correct.

Properly configuring root certificates and ensuring their compliance is a vulnerable aspect of TLS. The work [16] recruited volunteers to test their understanding of TLS configuration, only 17.9% of users were able to successfully configure a valid certificate chain. The fundamental reasons are the lack of optimal tutorial examples and the excessive prerequisite knowledge required. In addition, there are more than 100 CA organizations around the world and a greater number of CA certificates [9], even experts cannot determine the trustworthiness of CA certificates [12]. Therefore, it is crucial to analyze the security of certificates themselves and their usage in Android TLS connections. On the one hand, it helps developers better understand and use the software root of trust. On the other hand, it assists mobile manufacturers in enhancing their root certificate lists in the future.

When establishing a TLS connection, the Android user can search the root certificates from three sources. One is the default certificate list, which is preinstalled on the system and does not need to be set manually by the user. The second is the root certificate configured by the user through configuration file, without modifying the source code. The third is the root certificate added by the user through Java interfaces. The purpose of this paper is to provide a systematic analysis of root certificate usage compliance in Android TLS connections.

First, non-compliant root certificates are our analysis targets. Ones such as expired and using weak cryptography algorithms or weak keys should be removed promptly to prevent greater security threats. Then, we examine whether the configuration of the root certificates is correct. Finally, we provide users with practical guidelines to help them better understand the software root of trust

[1] The complete certificate chain verification process refers to RFC 5280.

used by the current TLS connection. The main contributions of this paper are as follows:

1. We first analyze the default root certificates from two open-source projects, one is Android Open Source Project (AOSP), from Android 7 to 14, and the other is OpenHarmony, from HarmonyOS 3.0 to 5.0. Based on the requirements in RFC specification and CA/B Forum, non-compliant certificates are identified. Android 9 to 13 and OpenHarmony 3.0 to 4.0 include three root certificates involved in a high-risk CVE, all AOSP lists include expired certificates, some of which have been expired for 4 years. OpenHarmony 5.0 performs best with the fewest root certificates and no expired entries.
2. The other two methods for customizing root certificates vary from the apps. Therefore, we collect 1246 popular apps from Google Play, covering 22 fields such as entertainment, business and transportation. We investigate the actual usage of root certificates and the results show that 42% of apps have security issues with their custom implementations, which reveals a fragmented state of certificate usage.
3. We evaluate the priority of these three methods, an interesting conclusion is that customizing the root certificates through Java interfaces has the highest priority and will invalidate the root certificates from the other two sources.

To the best of our knowledge, none of the previous related work has extensively examined the root certificates used by Android apps when establishing secure connections. Therefore, the work presented in this paper is a pioneering effort. It not only helps manufacturers update the certificate list but also provides guidelines for developers.

2 Related Work

Vulnerabilities in Certificate Chain Verification. Aiming at certificate chain verification in Android, previous research had made significant efforts. The works [4,10,11,22] revealed that clients may accept server endpoint certificates with mismatched domains, expired validity, or those issued by untrusted CAs. DCDroid [30] utilized static analysis to identify potential dangerous code of custom certificate verification, and then triggered TLS misuse through dynamic analysis. Ultimately, it confirmed that 245 out of 2213 apps were vulnerable to Man-in-the-Middle (MITM) attacks. Research [22] showed that 84% (6097/7258) of apps used default OS APIs for TLS, while the remaining apps utilized third-party libraries. However, prior study [15] identified incorrect usage of the client TLS APIs. Chen et al. employed differential testing to discover flaws in the certificate chain verification logic of third-party libraries [5]. Marvin [25] automatically analyzed the common TLS certificate verification issues, and the results showed that the failure to correctly verify TLS certificates can be attributed to either the negligence of app developers or improper implementations of third-party libraries.

Security Analysis of Root Certificates in Other Platforms. Zhang et al. [33] presented a viewpoint towards root certificates in browser clients. They concluded that CAs with forged identities, weak signature algorithms and weak keys are widely prevalent in browsers, which poses a threat to users. Perl and others [24,26] analyzed the root certificates on platforms like Windows, Linux, MacOS, and iOS, focusing solely on the scale of platform certificates while overlooking the security aspects of certificates. The work [19] evaluated certificates from various CA managers such as NSS, Microsoft, and Apple. However, they primarily concentrate on the use of MD5, the employment of 1024-bit RSA keys, and certificate expiration. To quantify the errors introduced by CAs when issuing certificates, Zlint [17] is designed to check the correctness of leaf certificates based on RFC 5280 specification.

3 Background

During the SSL certificate chain verification process, the root certificate acts as the trust anchor and can be established in the following ways.

The Platform's Default Root Certificates (Platform Method). Android devices come pre-installed with a system-level root certificate list, which is released with the AOSP[2]. After the system boots, the platform's default root certificates are loaded into the */system/etc./security/cacerts* directory. Every certificate file adopts the same naming format (`name.0`), where name is obtained by computing the certificate using *openssl x509 subject_hash_old* subcommand [28]. From the perspective of system, the */system* directory is read-only and even the root user cannot modify the list. From the user's point of view, all certificates are visible in security settings.

Setting Root Certificates via Resource File (XML Method). In 2016, Android 7 introduced Network Security Configuration (NSC) [2], which allows apps to trust specific root certificates without modifying the app code. Enabling NSC requires only two steps. **Step 1**: Configure `networkSecurityConfig` in AndroidManifest.xml. **Step 2**: Place the corresponding policy file into the *res* directory. NSC configures security policies through XML elements and attributes: The top-level element <base-config> sets global policies, while <domain-config> customizes policies for frequently used domains. Trusted root certificates are added via the <certificates> element nested within <trust-anchors>. Within <domain-config>, the <pin-set> element configures certificate pinning to prevent MITM attacks, containing one or more <pin> nodes that store hash values and expiration dates of specific server certificates. Additionally, the *cleartextTrafficPermitted* attribute enables cleartext communication, enhancing convenience though at the cost of security risks.

Setting Root Certificates via Java Interfaces (Java Method). Users can also securely add and store root certificates via KeyStore APIs. Such certificates

[2] The default root certificates are stored in /system/ca-certificates/files/.

are stored in the */data/misc/keystore/user_0* directory. Before Android 12, each certificate is encoded into a file named part1_CACERT_part2, where part1 represents the app's UID and part2 refers to the certificate's alias. All certificates after that are stored in the *persistent.sqlite* database in the *user_0* directory, and they are indexed by UID, which ensures permission control between apps.

4 Exploring the Security Issues of Root Certificates

4.1 Target Object

Our research targets the root certificates from two open-source operating system projects, AOSP and OpenHarmony. Closed-source operating systems lack transparency, for example, iOS only displays partial information about root certificates in its setting, and users cannot fully audit their usage. In addition, it is representative to investigate the root certificates that come with open-source projects. Because there are more handset manufacturers and models on the market, there is no way to conduct a comprehensive analysis of the default root certificates in real handsets. Related study [29] had shown that the root certificates in most handsets are the same as those in AOSP, and only a very small number of handsets (5/3835) removed the root certificates from AOSP.

Open-Source Operating Systems. Google no longer maintains open-source code below version 6 [27], and Huawei has discontinued the maintenance and updates for OpenHarmony 1.0 and OpenHarmony 2.0. Quarterly updates for the Android 15 source code are still being rolled out. Therefore, both AOSP (spanning from `Android 7 to 14`) and OpenHarmony (covering `HarmonyOS 3.0 to 5.0`) constitute the scope of our research. As a representative of specific manufacturers, HarmonyOS has consistently maintained compatibility with AOSP code except for version 5.0, it is essential to conduct a comparative analysis.

Popular Applications. Different from the root certificates in open-source projects, methods 2 and 3 set root certificates for particular apps. To better understand the popularity and application of custom root certificates in Android TLS connections, we crawl 1246 popular apps from Google Play, which covers 22 categories involving shopping, finance, and healthcare. Based on the dataset, we analyze the actual usage of two methods using decompilation technique.

4.2 Methodology

In this subsection, we present the methodology employed in our study, through which we answer the following research questions.

- *Q1:* From the perspectives of RFC 5280 and CA/B Forum, how compliant are the default root certificates in both open-source systems?
- *Q2:* Do developers possess the requisite expertise to properly configure root certificates? What vulnerabilities persist in the current implementations?
- *Q3:* Do Android or HarmonyOS implement effective verification mechanisms to prevent non-compliant root certificates?

Overview. Figure 1 overviews our methodology. We first extract the root certificates and configuration files from two target objects. Next, we identify the requirements for root certificates specified in the RFC 5280 specification and CA/B Forum, the latter has been established as the industry-mandated standard. Ultimately, we conduct compliance analysis of root certificates and also check the correctness of configuration policies.

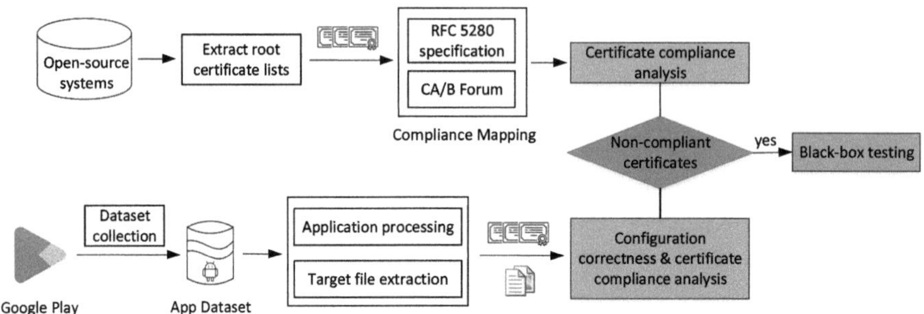

Fig. 1. Overview of the Methodology.

a) **Extract Root Certificates and Configuration Files.** Extracting certificates from AOSP and OpenHarmony is relatively straightforward, as they consistently reside in the `/system/ca-certificates/files/` directory and `/config/system Certificates/` directory respectively. Extracting these files from the actual apps requires three steps: **dataset collection**, **application processing** and **target file extraction**. Below, we will describe these three steps in detail.

(i) Dataset Collection. The process involves two key phases: (1) We employ ChromeDriver [13] to automate browser navigation through Google Play Store category pages, parsing front-end elements to systematically collect app package identifiers. (2) The harvested package names are then processed through GPlay-Cli's [20] authenticated API interface for bulk downloading of target apps.

(ii) Application Processing. Prior to extraction operation, we need to decompile and deobfuscate the app first. We decompile the apps using jadx tool [1], which can convert DEX file into readable Java code. However, we find that the names of resource files after decompilation may be obfuscated, such as Android-Manifest.xml, networkSecurityConfig.xml and certificate files, which can lead to inaccurate code reconstruction and affect the final results. Therefore, we employ the resource file symbol table to recover their original names. To optimize decompilation efficiency, we implement parallel processing via multithreading. Our analysis ultimately reveals 170 obfuscated apps within the dataset.

(iii) Target File Extraction. It is divided into two components: resource extractor and source-code analyzer. Resource extractor is designed to detect

XML method, it determines whether the NSC is enabled by checking the networkSecurityConfig attribute, such as *Android:networkSecurityConfig = "@xml/network_security_config"*. If the attribute exists, we extract the corresponding XML file. The <base-config> and <domain-config> elements in network_securi-ty_config.xml next become our analysis targets. Specifically, the resource extractor component focuses on the <trust-anchors> child element, which specifies custom root certificates through *certificates src*. It then looks for certificates in the resource directory with extensions such as .der, .pem, .crt, or .cer.

The source-code analyzer component performs Java method analysis by detecting SSL-related interfaces. The process demonstrates greater complexity than the resource extractor's operation, primarily due to the multiple approaches available for establishing an SSL connection in the Android framework. As illustrated in Fig. 2, we identify four distinct SSL implementation methods: the `basic SSL connection`, `HttpsURLConnection method`, `OkHttp method` and `Webview method`. The findings show that the first three methods all follow the same pattern to specify the root certificates of authentication, while WebView does not provide interfaces to customize the root certificates.

```
# Basic SSL Connection
SSLContext sslContext = SSLContext.getInstance("SSL");
sslContext.init(keyManager,tmf.getTrustManagers(),null);
SSLSocketFactory ssf = sslContext.getSocketFactory();
SSLSocket sslSocket = ssf.createSocket(host,port);
```

```
# HttpsURLConnection Method
urlConn = (HttpsURLConnection) new URL(url).openConnection();
urlConn.setDefaultSocketFactory(ssf);
urlConn.connect();
```

```
# OkHttp Method
OkHttpClient client = new OkHttpClient();
Request request = new Request.Builder().url(url)
  .sslSocketFactory(ssf).build();
Call call = client.newCall(request);
Response response = call.execute();
```

```
# Webview Method
webView = (WebView) findViewById(R.id.webview);
webView.loadUrl(url);
```

Fig. 2. The Method of Establishing an SSL Connection in Android. * ssf is an instance of SSLSocketFactory, encapsulating security parameters including custom root certificates.

Therefore, our methodology focuses on six critical interfaces involved in root certificate configuration. It initiates with **(1) SetCertificateEntry**, which adds a root certificate into the keystore while assigning a unique alias. Subsequently, **(2) TrustManagerFactory.getInstance** instantiates a TrustManagerFactory object (trustManagerFactory), which is then initialized through **(3) trustManagerFactory.init (keystore)**. The TrustManagerFactory's **(4) getTrustManagers** interface, combined with SSLContext's **(5) init** and **(6) getSocketFactory** interfaces produce an SSLSocketFactory instance (**ssf**) that encapsulates all secure parameters, including the custom root certificates. The Java method can only be deemed detected when these interfaces are invoked in order. Thus, we leverage reachability analysis to determine whether the calls to these interfaces are coherent. Finally, we extract the root certificates added to the keystore.

b) Identify Requirements in RFC 5280 and the CA/B Forum. Compliance mapping is the process of defining requirements of compliant certificate based on the RFC standard and industry best practice. Through the modal keyword `MUST`, `REQUIRED`, `SHALL`, `MUST NOT`, `NOT REQUIRED`, and `SHALL NOT`, we identify three fundamental structural requirements that root certificates must satisfy in RFC 5280, respectively `basicConstraints`, `keyUsage` and `subjectKeyIdentifier`, as shown in Table 1. The root certificate included in the trust list must be a CA certificate capable of issuing server certificates, otherwise it cannot participate in the certificate chain verification process. As mandated by RFC 5280, such certificate requires: **(1)** its CA bit in the `basicConstraints` extension must be set to true, **(2)** the `keyUsage` extension must contain the keyCertSign purpose, both of which are essential and cannot be omitted. Generally speaking, `basicConstraints` is set as a critical attribute. **(3)** The `subjectKeyIdentifier` attribute is not directly checked in the verification process, it helps confirm whether the certificates match, thereby improving the efficiency of verification.

Table 1. Requirements of Root Certificates in RFC 5280

A Set of Extensions Required by the Root Certificates	Remark
basicConstraints : CA = True (critical/non-critical)	It indicates whether the certified public key can be used to verify certificate signature
keyUsage : keyCertSign (critical)	It verifies the digital signature together with the CA bit
subjectKeyIdentifier : non-empty (non-critical)	It helps to uniquely identify the public key in the certificate chain

CA/B Forum Criteria. Using the same modal keyword match method, we identify industry criteria (C3-C6) for root certificates from the CA/B Forum. In order to help users better understand the quality of the current root certificate lists, we introduce two additional criteria, C1 and C2, through which we identify that the high-risk CVE vulnerability persists in both open-source systems. We now utilize six criteria, along with the three aforementioned requirements, to evaluate the security of built-in certificates for different versions. ① Total number of root certificates (**C1**); ② Number of CAs (**C2**); ③ Number of expired root certificates (**C3**); ④ Number of root certificates using weak cryptography algorithms (**C4**); ⑤ Number of root certificates using weak keys (**C5**); ⑥ Existence of V1 root certificates (**C6**). Collectively, the metrics covered in related work constitute only a subset of our dimensions.

c) Certificate Compliance and Configuration Correctness Analysis. The certificate compliance checking is based on all the requirements mentioned earlier, systematically parsing the critical fields within the certificate to verify whether they meet the security requirements. The configuration correctness analysis primarily focuses on whether developers have correctly configured the root certificates. For Java method, it verifies whether the current context's keystore is null. An empty keystore indicates that the `trustManagerFactory` loads the platform's default certificate list. Additionally, it also checks whether the `ssf` instance is properly integrated into the current SSL connection.

For XML method, it first examines whether the user has manually configured the HTTP connection, which compromises SSL security. Private IP addresses configuration, non-compliant domain settings, and domain-irrelevant settings also fall within our analysis scope. Additionally, it searches for SHA1 or SHA256 certificate hash values in the <pin>. We use the regular expression sha(1|256)/[a-zA-Z0-9+/=]{20,64} to search hash values. The minimum value is the Base64 encoding length of SHA1, and the maximum value is the HEX encoding length of SHA256. Therefore, it is suitable for searching both HEX encoding hashes and Base64 encoding hashes.

d) Black-Box Testing. It aims to verify whether the systems strictly verify root certificates according to the RFC standard or the CA/B Forum. Specifically, we develop a test app on Android 14 and HarmonyOS 4.0, which retrieves non-compliant root certificates from the analysis results and uses Java interfaces to add them to the keystore. Then, we trigger multiple HTTPS connections to test servers, which trust at least one non-compliant root certificate. We observe `CertPathValidatorException` error logs in logcat. If the connection is successful and no error logs are found, it indicates that neither Android nor HarmonyOS effectively blocks non-compliant root certificates.

5 Findings and Analysis

5.1 Analysis of Default Root Certificate Results

> ***Answer to Q1***: The results indicate that a certain proportion of non-compliant certificates exist in the default root certificate lists of both open-source operating systems. HarmonyOS 5.0 exhibits the best performance, followed by Android 14.

a) RFC-Guided AOSP Results. Each AOSP certificate list contains few root certificates, which do not fully comply with the RFC 5280 specification. Taking Android 12 as an example, 3 certificates do not have CA bit set, and 9 certificates are not marked with the keyCertSign purpose. Among all AOSP certificate lists, Android 14 performs best, with total 5 certificates not conforming to the specification. We have also observed that the GoDaddy, Starfield Technologies, TWCA and Chunghwa Telecom are relatively lax when issuing certificates, as these four CAs tend to use self-signed certificates that do not meet the specification.

b) RFC-Guided OpenHarmony Results. In terms of certificate naming, we observe that OpenHarmony adopts the same naming scheme as AOSP. The only difference is that it uses *OpenSSL x509 subject_hash* subcommand. Therefore, at first glance, the root certificates included in the two open-source projects appear completely different. In fact, their certificates exhibit a significant overlap. For instance, the number of certificates in OpenHarmony 4.0 is similar to those in Android 13, with more than 120 certificates being identical. Meanwhile, they also demonstrate a similar adherence to the RFC standard. Despite a substantial reduction in the number of certificates for OpenHarmony 5.0 (as shown in Table 2), there is no difference in terms of following RFC standards.

Overall, at the first level, these two open-source projects do not show obvious differences. With the continuous upgrading of Android versions, the reduction in the number of non-compliant certificates does not indicate that developers are no longer using improperly configured certificates, but rather vulnerable CAs, such as VeriSign and GeoTrust, had been deprecated by the Google team.

c) Results Based on CA/B Forum Criteria. Table 2 presents the analysis results based on the criteria. **C1:** In Android 7/8, the number of root certificates reaches its peak, while in OpenHarmony 5.0, it has the fewest number of certificates, even less than half of the former. Each root certificate represents a potential attack surface, maintaining fewer certificates not only reduces security risks, but also simplifies management and improves communication efficiency.

C2: Figure 3 depicts the distribution of CAs across various lists that provide two or more root certificates. It is sufficient to take one version for Android 7, 8, 13 and 14, that is Android-7.0.0, Android-8.0.0, Android-13.0.0_r1 and Android-14.0.0_r50. We find that root certificates exhibit a long-tail distribution. For example, there are 43 CAs in OpenHarmony 5.0, with 15 of them contributing to almost 60% of the root certificates. It can be also observed that CAs are dynamic, with existing and emerging CAs. The once renowned certificate provider VeriSign had been blacklisted since Android 11 for issuing forged Google certificates. Additionally, WoSign and its acquired StartCom experienced security incidents in the past, which had also been removed from Google's trusted list.

To avoid potential risks of information leakage, manufacturers should remove the vulnerable root certificates from their lists. As shown in Fig. 3, Google and Huawei do not respond to the critical CVE vulnerability [8] in a timely and comprehensive manner. **They still trust the three certificates from TrustCor CA**, which compromises user privacy and poses a threat to national security.

Table 2. Security Analysis of Default Root Certificates in AOSP and OpenHarmony

Criteria	Version									
	7	8	9	10	11	12	13	14	OpenHarmony 3.0/4.0	OpenHarmony 5.0
C1	148/156	156/135	137	138	138	129	129/126	134/135	129	68
C2	72/74	73/67	66	66	63	60	60/60	57/57	63	43
C3	14/18	14/14	14	15	13	10	10/10	2/1	10	0
C4	86/85	80/68	59	54	52	41	41/41	30/29	40	19
C5	none									
C6	✓	✓	✓	✓	✓	✗	✗	✗	✗	✗

*A version may correspond to two distinct root certificate lists, with different criterion values that are differentiated by `backslashes`. Taking Android 14 as an example, versions `Android-14.0.0_r29` to `Android-14.0.0_r37` and `Android-14.0.0_r50` to `Android-14.0.0_r75` contain 135 root certificates, all other versions contain 134 root certificates.

C3: We discover that most certificate lists include expired certificates, the longest of which has expired for 4 years. All expiration dates mentioned in this article are based on December 31, 2024. The standout performers are OpenHarmony 5.0 and Android 14, with the former not having expired root certificates. Although Android 14 has a few expired certificates, we believe that when Android 14 was released, the Google team had already removed all expired root certificates. Over time, some of the certificates have now expired. The root cause is that they do not establish a regular review mechanism. The CA/B Forum stipulates that the validity period of a root certificate must range from 8 to 25 years, however, a few CAs have violated this requirement.

C4: NIST recommends using secure cryptography algorithms, excluding deprecated MD5 and SHA1 [21]. However, the results show that every certificate list contains a large number of certificates, which use the sha1WithRSAEncryption algorithm. Taking Android 10 as an example, of the 54 root certificates utilizing the sha1WithRSAEncryption algorithm, 27 certificates were issued after 2005, when the SHA1 algorithm is theoretically proven to be insecure. This means that after SHA1 has been compromised, it is still used by many CAs, including the well-known SSL service providers DigiCert and GlobalSign. Such certificates prior to 2005 have not been removed either. Other cryptography algorithms include sha256WithECDSA, sha384WithECDSA, sha256WithRSAEncryption, sha512WithRSAEncryption and sha384WithRSAEncryption. In general, the usage of weak cryptography algorithm declines across Android versions.

C5: As computing power increases, shorter RSA keys can be violently broken. RSA keys less than 2048 bits are no longer adequate to provide protection that meets modern security requirements. Among all the root certificates, **we do not find any certificates that use weak keys**. In Android 14, for example, the key types contain RSA (2048-bit), RSA (4096-bit), ECDSA (256-bit) and ECDSA (384-bit). There are no keys for RSA (1024-bit) and lower security levels.

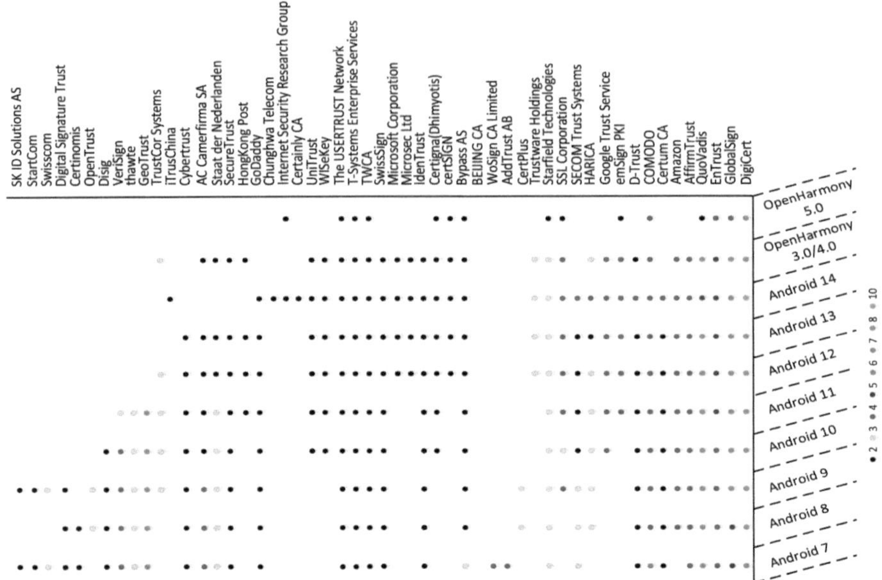

Fig. 3. Distribution of CAs Contributing More Than One Certificate in Android 7–14 and OpenHarmony 3.0–5.0. *blank*: It indicates that the CA organization contributes no root certificate or just one to the current list.

C6: Modern network security standards typically recommend the use of newer version of the certificate (V3). On the one hand, X.509 V3 certificates introduce extension attributes, which include additional identity information for enhanced authentication and restrict the scope of certificate usage. On the other hand, related study [4] indicated that V1 root certificate will be trusted unconditionally during the certificate chain verification process, which makes it easy to suffer MITM attack. As shown in Table 2, Android 7–11 have an identical V1 root certificate (7d453d8f.0) from VeriSign.

Android 14 sets the benchmark in root certificate management by removing all expired certificates, demonstrating the highest compliance with both RFC specification and CA/B Forum requirements. OpenHarmony 5.0 showcases substantial security improvements in root certificate management, primarily through its reduced attack surface - achieved by minimizing the number of certificates, CAs, and non-compliant certificates. This advancement stems from its complete architectural overhaul, abandoning both the Linux kernel and AOSP compatibility. **Responsible disclosure is discussed in the Appendix** A.

5.2 Analysis of Custom Root Certificate Results

Answer to Q2: The results show that 42% of apps exhibit security vulnerabilities in policy configuration. Analysis of the top four issues (e.g. private IP addresses configuration and non-compliant domains) reveals gaps in developers' understanding and implementation of NSC.

Preliminary Result. Among the 1246 apps surveyed, 369 apps (29.6%) do not customize the root certificates, indicating that they completely rely on the platform's trust list. The remaining 877 apps (70.4%) define their root certificates, with 756 apps using XML method and 134 apps using Java method, which signifies that 13 apps use both methods to achieve customization.

XML Method Adoption. As shown in Table 3, the XML method is widely adopted in areas such as shopping, health & fitness, finance, travel and food & drink. The XML method is extremely popular in the shopping category, mainly because users are involved with sensitive information such as credit card numbers, addresses and personal details during the purchase process.

Table 3. Top 5 Categories That Use XML Method to Set the Root Certificates

Category	No. of Apps	Percentage (%)
Shopping	52	67.5
Health & Fitness	49	67.1
Finance	48	64
Travel	46	51.1
Food & Drink	46	60.5

However, empirical evidence indicates widespread adoption of insecure network security configurations among developers. The <base-config> is app-wide customization and defines which certificates are trusted through three options. There are 238 apps that have this element set. We believe that developers are confused about the three options. **System**: Load the pre-installed system certificates, which is actually redundant for Android 9 and above since this is the default configuration. **User**: Add the user's CA store, however, it is only aimed at Android 6 and below systems. We discover that many apps configure in this way, which is ineffective in fact. **@raw/my_ca**: This option allows the import of certificates in PEM or DER format. Only 14 apps configure in this way. We find that 6 apps introduce non-public CA certificates through this option, such as issuers being *example* or *aaa*. Although HTTPS communication is the default in Android 9, we discover that some apps still set *cleartextTrafficPermitted* to true in <base-config> and <domain-config>.

Through <domain-config>, users can specify security configurations for different domains, which overrides the global <base-config> settings. 536 apps configure the <domain-config> element. We observe that the domain most frequently configured in apps is google.com and its related subdomains. Only 9 apps customize the root certificates via *certificates src*, with quantities ranging from 1 to 2. The rest of the apps set it to the default value "system". In total, 37 apps fix 767 certificates, indicating that the certificate pinning feature is more popular among developers than adding trusted root certificates from the resource directory. Developers tend to favor certificates from CA organizations such as Digicert, GlobalSign, and Entrust. **We also identify four types of configuration issues prevalent within this element**, Fig. 4 demonstrates relevant code examples.

Private IP Addresses Configuration. Configuring private IP addresses indicates that the policy is only applicable within the internal network and is not suitable for any services accessed over the Internet. Actually, it doesn't make any sense. 243 apps configure local IP address in the <domain-config>, 65 of them are configured as localhost, and the rest are set to 127.0.0.1. Additionally, there are 46 apps that use 10.0.2.2, including well-known ones such as AfterPay and File Commander. What is surprising is that Microsoft Teams covers 768 IP addresses, ranging from 192.168.0.0 to 192.168.1.255, and 10.0.0.0 to 10.0.0.255.

Non-compliant Domains. Excluding the private IP addresses mentioned above, all apps have a total of 3563 domains configured. Through manual analysis, we confirm that as high as 67% of the domains are non-compliant. We classify these domains into three categories. ① Unreachable domains: When we type some domains, some of them will return 404 not found, we refer to them as unreachable domains. This not only affects network performance but may also pose security risks, as a 404 page could mask other security issues present on the website. ② Complete URLs: Using the complete URL instead of the domain, such as https://deploy.mopinion.com, is against the policy. We note that such problem is quite common. ③ Domains with unmanaged webpages: Several domains, such as yahoo.com, are reachable, but their interfaces are filled with low-level advertisements. This is highly susceptible to security vulnerabilities.

Domain-Irrelevant Settings. Some developers seem unfamiliar with security configuration policies, specifically, they include the CA organizations in the <domain-config> instead of any domain. It is surprising that the globally famous entertainment app Netflix only provides values such as com, net, and gov in the field, without including wildcard.

Vulnerable <pin-set>. We observe that some apps do not provide the corresponding hash value after offering the hash algorithm. A selection of time in the <pin> node have already expired. Meanwhile, we do not find any apps that use SHA1 algorithm to fix the certificates. What's even more outrageous is that the PlayStation app fixes 253 certificates in the <pin-set>, which puts the app at risk of eavesdropping or hijacking in network communication.

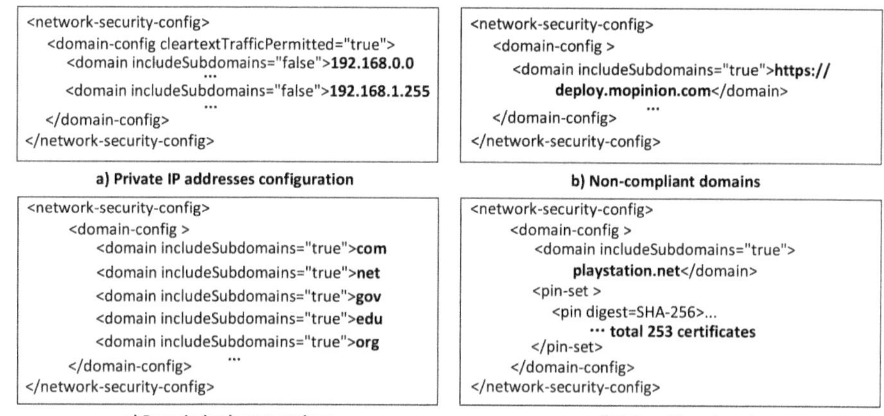

Fig. 4. Code Examples with Configuration Issues in Actual Applications.

Causal Analysis: The root cause of the above issues is that developers are not familiar with the basic rules of NSC. On the one hand, they are prone to misconfiguring policies. On the other hand, they directly copy example code from public websites without proper judgment. Of all the apps we studied, at most 9 apps use the same network security config file.

Java Method Adoption. As depicted in Table 4, five categories of apps, finance, food & drink, shopping, travel and communication, most often utilize the Java interfaces to set root certificates. On the one hand, the use of interfaces needs to follow specific guidelines, unlike network security policies that can be set arbitrarily. On the other hand, fewer apps use this approach than the XML method for root certificate configuration. Overall, such apps seem to face fewer problems. We find that nearly 11% of the apps initialize the trustManagerFactory instance using an empty keystore, i.e. trustManagerFactory.init(KeyStore(null)). In addition, even if the trustManagerFactory is initialized correctly, eventually it is not applied to the TLS connection. Because the second parameter of the sslContext.init function is set to null.

Table 4. Top 5 Categories That Use Java Method to Set the Root Certificates

Category	No. of Apps	Percentage (%)
Finance	24	32
Food & Drink	17	22.4
Shopping	14	18.2
Travel	12	13.3
Communication	9	8.9

5.3 Analysis of Black-Box Testing Results

Answer to Q3: In practice, neither Android nor HarmonyOS performs compliance checks on root certificates during certificate chain verification, granting them unconditional trust by default.

During black-box testing, we utilize 26 non-compliant root certificates, each violating at least one requirement. Notably, all HTTPS connections are successfully established without triggering "*trust anchor for certification path not found*" exception. This demonstrates both vendors' failure to prevent non-compli- ant root certificate prior to certificate chain construction. The building of a certificate chain comprises an untrusted chain transmitted by the server, as well as at least one root certificate provided by the client. Through code tracing of chain verification logic (the `checkServerTrusted` method in `TrustManagerImpl`), we observe exclusive verification of untrusted chain, while **locally stored trust anchors remain unconditionally trusted without verification**.

6 Priority of Using Root Certificates

In this section, we dynamically hook key functions to determine the priority of root certificates usage. Specifically, when an app establishes the TLS connection with a server, the CertificateSource interface in the AOSP is responsible for locating the root certificate to facilitate verification. In Android, DirectoryCertificateSource class, ResourceCertificateSource class and KeyStoreCertificateSource class all implement this interface and also correspond to the three certificate sources mentioned earlier. Therefore, we hook critical functions within these classes to determine which type of certificate is being used for the current TLS connection.

Table 5. Priority of Root Certificates Usage

App types	Number of Root Certificates in Effect	Priority
Platform	N_p	–
Platform+XML	$N_p + N_x$	$M_p > M_x$
Platform+Java	N_j	$M_j > M_p$
XML+Java+Platform	N_j	$M_j > \{M_p, M_x\}$

*M_p, M_x and M_j represent the Platform method, XML method and Java method, respectively.

*N_p, N_x and N_j denote the number of root certificates from three different sources.

–: This app type uses only one source of root certificates, eliminating the priority consideration.

We select four types of apps. **Type 1**: Root certificates are not set by any means. **Type 2**: Root certificates are set only through XML method. **Type 3**: Root certificates are set only through Java interfaces. **Type 4**: Root certificates are customized using both methods. While running them on an Android 14 device and triggering the TLS connection, we hook the corresponding functions, the results are shown in Table 5. N_p is fixed at 134, while N_x and N_j vary from apps. From the type 3 and type 4 apps, we can conclude that the root certificates set via Java interfaces have the highest priority and are uniquely used. In this case, the root certificates of the other two methods will not take effect. Through the type 2 apps, we observe that the functions of DirectoryCertificateSource class are called first, subsequently the ResourceCertificateSource class. Therefore, the platform's default root certificates have higher priority than those set through the XML method. In summary, the Java method has the highest priority, followed by the Platform method, and finally the XML method.

7 Conclusion

In this paper, we perform a comprehensive analysis on the root certificates used by Android users when establishing SSL connections. Through a series of experiments, we identify the security issues of root certificates. The results demonstrate that both manufacturers and mobile developers need to improve their management and usage of root certificates. In future work, we will explore the permission of root certificates, as well as their potential attack surface and difficulty, the Appendix B contains our current research findings.

Acknowledgments. We thank the anonymous INSCRYPT 2025 reviewers for their helpful comments. This work is supported by the National Key R&D Program of China (Grant No. 2023YFB3105802).

A Responsible Disclosure

As discussed in Sect. 5, non-compliant root certificates exist in every release of both AOSP and OpenHarmony, which poses security risks to the system. Therefore, we reported all identified security issues to Google and Huawei respectively. Specifically, we have filed reports regarding AOSP vulnerabilities via Google Issue Tracker and submitted corresponding issues to the OpenHarmony community (as shown in Table 6). At the time of writing, Google assigned us a bug ID (`424225644`), while Huawei has not responded to us.

B Discussion of Root Certificate Attacks

B.1 TLS Attack on Apps that Set Root Certificates Through Java Interfaces

After the system boots, the platform's default root certificates are loaded into the */system/etc./security/cacerts* directory. The directory is read-only, and even the

Table 6. Reported Security Issues

Type	Affected Versions
Root certificates involved in critical CVE	Android 9–13 and OpenHarmony 3.0–4.0
Expired root certificates	Android 7–14 and OpenHarmony 3.0–4.0
Root certificates employing weak cryptography algorithm	Android 7–14 and OpenHarmony 3.0–5.0
V1 root certificates	Android 7–11
Root certificates with structural issues	Android 7–14 and OpenHarmony 3.0–5.0

root user cannot add, modify, or delete certificates unless it is remounted with write permission. However, we find that the certificates stored in the keystore are unencrypted and the storage directory is writable, which gives us an opportunity to launch a TLS attack. We prepare two types of apps: the victim apps utilize Java interfaces to set the root certificates and establish TLS connection through the APIs from OS or third-party libraries. It not only includes apps developed by us but also those selected from the communication category in Google Play, such as email clients and browsers, which can connect to our fake URL through phishing email or manual input. The attacker app has root privilege and aims to tamper with the certificates in the */data/misc/keystore/user_0* directory.

The attack steps are as follows. First, we run the victim apps and trigger their TLS connections, only then will the certificates they set be stored in the *user_0* directory. Next, we execute the attacker app, which performs deletion, modification, and addition of root certificate on the victim apps. The modified and added root certificate is the attacker's private root certificate. Finally, we run the victim apps again to observe their log output and interface results. The results show that the apps with deleted root certificates can no longer establish TLS connections. While the apps with modified or added root certificate will establish TLS connection with our fake URL. Therefore, we can easily get the master key of the current TLS connection. It is important that the attack takes effect immediately and does not require a restart. Although this is an attack predicated on root privilege, its potential for destruction and damage should not be underestimated. Mobile manufacturers should take this seriously to mitigate greater threats that may arise in non-root scenarios.

B.2 Discussion on Attacks Targeting Root Certificates under Non-root Privilege

Attacks on root certificates under non-root privilege will be a key focus of our future work. Currently, we discuss this from the following three aspects.

Exploitable Vulnerability of Root Certificate. CVE-2023-21265 [8] is a critical vulnerability related to root certificates. The core flaw is the improper retention of revoked certificates within trust stores, which allows attackers to craft malicious packets to exploit private data. It can be remotely exploited without requiring additional privileges or user interaction. It affects Android 13,

12L, 12, and 11, however, our analysis shows that three certificates (7c302982.0, c2c1704e.0, d0cddf45.0) that should have been removed are still present in Android 9 to 13.

Vulnerable Keystore Service. The memory corruption vulnerabilities or logical flaws associated with the Keystore service also pose a threat to the root certificates. CVE-2020-0416 [6] constitutes a stack overflow vulnerability within the Keystore service, specifically affecting the *addAuthToken* method. Exploitation enables attackers to bypass policy enforcement mechanisms and achieve privilege escalation to the context. CVE-2022-20418 [7] represents an authorization bypass vulnerability stemming from improper UID validation in Binder transaction handling, permitting unauthorized invocation of sensitive operations.

Multi-layered Interaction in SSL Implementation. In Sect. 4, we summarize four methods for establishing an SSL connection. Through in-depth logical analysis, an interesting conclusion is that the SSL implementation does not rely on a single library. Instead, it involves multiple components, such as wrapper, Java libraries, and C libraries. For example, the HttpsURLConnection method first invokes the Java Secure Socket Extension (JSSE), with the TrustManagerFactory class managing trusted certificates. This is wrapped by Conscrypt and ultimately implemented by low-level C library BoringSSL. Previous research [18] had exploited this invocation hierarchy to compromise SSL session master secrets, and the breakthrough point will also be a focus of our future research.

References

1. jadx. https://github.com/skylot/jadx
2. Android Developers: Network security config. https://developer.android.com/privacy-and-security/security-config
3. Appfigures: App intelligence. https://appfigures.com/app-intelligence
4. Brubaker, C., Jana, S., Ray, B., Khurshid, S., Shmatikov, V.: Using frankencerts for automated adversarial testing of certificate validation in SSL/TLS implementations. In: 2014 IEEE Symposium on Security and Privacy, pp. 114–129. IEEE (2014)
5. Chen, C., Tian, C., Duan, Z., Zhao, L.: RFC-directed differential testing of certificate validation in SSL/TLS implementations. In: Proceedings of the 40th International Conference on Software Engineering, pp. 859–870 (2018)
6. CVE Program: CVE-2020-0416: Android keystore service stack overflow vulnerability (2020). https://nvd.nist.gov/vuln/detail/CVE-2020-0416
7. CVE Program: CVE-2022-20418: Android keystore service authorization bypass vulnerability (2022). https://nvd.nist.gov/vuln/detail/CVE-2022-20418
8. CVE Program: CVE-2023-21265: Improper root CA certificate management vulnerability (2023). https://nvd.nist.gov/vuln/detail/cve-2023-21265
9. DigiCert: What is a certificate authority (2021). https://www.digicert.com/cn/blog/what-is-a-certificate-authority
10. Fahl, S., Harbach, M., Muders, T., Baumgärtner, L., Freisleben, B., Smith, M.: Why Eve and Mallory love Android: an analysis of Android SSL in security. In: Proceedings of the 2012 ACM Conference on Computer and Communications Security, pp. 50–61 (2012)

11. Felt, A.P., et al.: Improving SSL warnings: comprehension and adherence. In: Proceedings of the 33rd Annual ACM Conference on Human Factors in Computing Systems, pp. 2893–2902 (2015)
12. Fu, Y., Wang, Q., Lin, J., Sun, A., Lu, L.: Exploring the security issues of trusted CA certificate management. In: Information and Communications Security: 23rd International Conference, ICICS 2021, Chongqing, China, 19–21 November 2021, Proceedings, Part I 23, pp. 384–401. Springer, Heidelberg (2021)
13. Google: WebDriver for Chrome. https://developer.chrome.com/docs/chromedriver/downloads
14. Google Security Team: Distrusting WoSign and StartCom (2016). https://security.googleblog.com/2016/10/distrusting-wosign-and-startcom.html
15. He, B., et al.: Vetting SSL usage in applications with SSLINT. In: 2015 IEEE Symposium on Security and Privacy, pp. 519–534. IEEE (2015)
16. Krombholz, K., Mayer, W., Schmiedecker, M., Weippl, E.: I have no idea what i'm doing-on the usability of deploying HTTPS. In: 26th USENIX Security Symposium (USENIX Security 17), pp. 1339–1356 (2017)
17. Kumar, D., et al.: Tracking certificate misissuance in the wild. In: 2018 IEEE Symposium on Security and Privacy (SP), pp. 785–798. IEEE (2018)
18. Lee, J., Wallach, D.S.: Removing secrets from Android's TLS. In: NDSS (2018)
19. Ma, Z., Austgen, J., Mason, J., Durumeric, Z., Bailey, M.: Tracing your roots: exploring the TLS trust anchor ecosystem. In: Proceedings of the 21st ACM Internet Measurement Conference, pp. 179–194 (2021)
20. matlink/gplaycli. https://github.com/matlink/gplaycli
21. NIST: Recommendation for key management part 3: application-specific key management guidance (2015). https://nvlpubs.nist.gov/nistpubs/SpecialPublications/NIST.SP.800-57Pt3r1.pdf
22. Oltrogge, M.: TLS on Android–Evolution over the last decade (2021)
23. Onwuzurike, L., De Cristofaro, E.: Danger is my middle name: experimenting with SSL vulnerabilities in Android apps. In: Proceedings of the 8th ACM Conference on Security & Privacy in Wireless and Mobile Networks, pp. 1–6 (2015)
24. Perl, H., Fahl, S., Smith, M.: You won't be needing these any more: on removing unused certificates from trust stores. In: International Conference on Financial Cryptography and Data Security, pp. 307–315. Springer, Heidelberg (2014)
25. Pourali, S., Yu, X., Zhao, L., Mannan, M., Youssef, A.: Racing for TLS certificate validation: a hijacker's guide to the Android TLS Galaxy. In: 33rd USENIX Security Symposium (USENIX Security 24), pp. 683–700 (2024)
26. Purushothaman, J., Thompson, E., Abdou, A.: Position paper: certificate root stores—an area of unity or disparity? In: Proceedings of the 15th Workshop on Cyber Security Experimentation and Test, pp. 105–110 (2022)
27. Salesforce: End of support for Android 6.0 OS (2020). https://help.salesforce.com/s/articleView?id=000380538&type=1
28. The OpenSSL Project: X.509 certificate management. https://docs.openssl.org/1.1.1/man1/x509.html
29. Vallina-Rodriguez, N., Amann, J., Kreibich, C., Weaver, N., Paxson, V.: A tangled mass: the Android root certificate stores. In: Proceedings of the 10th ACM International on Conference on emerging Networking Experiments and Technologies, pp. 141–148 (2014)
30. Wang, Y., et al.: Identifying vulnerabilities of SSL/TLS certificate verification in Android apps with static and dynamic analysis. J. Syst. Softw. **167**, 110609 (2020)
31. Wikipedia: Flame (malware). https://en.wikipedia.org/wiki/Flame_(malware)

32. Wilson, K.: Distrusting new CNNIC certificates (2015). https://blog.mozilla.org/security/2015/04/02/distrusting-new-cnnic-certificates/
33. Zhang, Y., et al.: Rusted anchors: a national client-side view of hidden root CAs in the Web PKI ecosystem. In: Proceedings of the 2021 ACM SIGSAC Conference on Computer and Communications Security, pp. 1373–1387 (2021)

Exploring the Root Store Usage in TLS-Based Applications

Yuxiang Shen[1,2], Wei Wang[1,2(✉)], Shushang Wen[1,2], Yu Fu[1,2], Yunhao Jia[1,2], and Jingqiang Lin[1,2]

[1] School of Cyber Science and Technology, University of Science and Technology of China, Hefei 230026, China
weiwang2025@ustc.edu.cn

[2] Anhui Province Key Laboratory of Digital Security, Hefei, China

Abstract. Root certificates serve as the foundation for certificate validation in the PKI paradigm. The root store, a collection of root certificates, directly influences the security of TLS connections in applications. A reliable root store reduces the risk of applications being compromised by manipulator-in-the-middle and phishing attacks.

In this work, we explore the application's usage of root stores in TLS from the aspects of root stores, TLS libraries, and applications, to determine whether applications utilize a reliable root store. First, we investigate the provider and local management of six mainstream root stores. Second, we explore the default root stores of four popular TLS libraries, as well as two high-level wrappers across different operating systems. Finally, we implement static analysis for open source projects built upon these four TLS libraries to determine the root stores they use and their locations. Our work demonstrates that the default root stores in TLS libraries (e.g., OpenSSL) may not consistently be reliable root stores across different platforms. Moreover, among open source projects utilizing TLS connections, more than one-third employ user-specific root stores (e.g., a specified file), which exposes them to potential security risks with the adoption of unreliable root stores.

Keywords: X.509 certificate · Root store · SSL/TLS · Static analysis

1 Introduction

The root store serves as the cornerstone of trust in TLS [52]. TLS uses signed X.509 certificates to validate the binding between a server's identity (e.g., DNS domain name) and its public key, and X.509 certificates form a certificate chain based on their issuance relationships [39], with the top of the chain being a self-signed root certificate that serves as a trust anchor stored in the root store. Certificates issued by misbehaving CAs in the root store may expose users to manipulator-in-the-middle (MitM) or phishing attacks [30,31].

Root store providers maintain public root stores by requiring root certificates to follow strict rules [5] and promptly removing untrustworthy root CAs [30,31].

R. Chen et al. (Eds.): Inscrypt 2025, LNCS 16409, pp. 390–409, 2026.
https://doi.org/10.1007/978-981-95-6203-9_21

According to Mozilla's Common CA Database (CCADB) [13], there are currently 881 root certificates, meaning that even users with professional knowledge struggle to accurately filter trustworthy CAs and remove malicious ones in a timely manner. Consequently, many organizations (e.g., Mozilla [17], Microsoft [47], Apple [22]) act as root store providers, maintaining root stores for public use based on their own inclusion and removal policies. These root stores are typically published with operating systems (e.g., Windows, macOS) or applications (e.g., Firefox, Thunderbird).

Users and applications are able to customize local root stores on their hosts. While this flexibility allows for the addition or removal of certificates to meet specific needs, improper management practices can severely compromise the root store's reliability, as evidenced by issues related to TLS and HTTPS interception [37,40]. Furthermore, external entities can influence local root stores: governments may mandate the inclusion of specific root certificates [45], while certain local software, including VPNs or even malware, might surreptitiously add certificates [57]. Such inserted root certificates can subsequently be exploited to launch attacks [1,32]. For applications, relying on unreliable root stores introduces a more severe security threat, since such root stores are often far easier to compromise than the system root store. Even an unprivileged attacker could insert a malicious root certificate into the root store, enabling the issuance of fraudulent certificates and ultimately carrying out a MitM attack.

In this work, we investigate how applications utilize root stores when establishing TLS connections via TLS libraries. First, we evaluate the storage and management mechanisms of six mainstream root stores on local hosts, deeming Python certifi an unreliable root store due to a lack of automated updates and insufficient tamper resistance. Next, we explore the default root stores of four commonly used TLS libraries and two high-level wrappers across different operating systems, discovering that some OpenSSL-based TLS libraries on non-Linux platforms do not default to reliable root stores. Finally, we implement static analysis of 439 open source projects built upon these four TLS libraries. We found that out of the 317 projects utilizing TLS, 242 established TLS connections without leveraging any root stores. Additionally, 129 projects explicitly specified their root stores, rendering the security of their TLS connections entirely dependent on users' security awareness. We also precisely identified the configuration locations for some of these specified root stores. Our main contributions are as follows:

1. We investigate the provider management and local management of six mainstream root stores, and identify reliable root stores.
2. We investigate the implementations of six open source TLS libraries (including C-based and Python-based), compare their default root stores across different operating systems, and reveal their security concerns.
3. We implement static analysis of applications based on four TLS libraries to determine whether they utilize the default root store in TLS connections and whether specified root stores are employed. The validity of this methodology is verified by the analysis of open source projects.

2 Background

2.1 Root Stores on the Local Host

The root store appears as a collection of certificates on the local host, and may also have associated trust policies [43,44]. Trust policies restrict the root certificates with the purpose (e.g., TLS, email, code signing) and levels of trust (e.g., trusted, distrusted) to achieve a finer level of trust. To ensure proper handling of certificates and their trust policies, these root stores may expose dedicated APIs for developers (e.g., CryptoAPI in Windows).

Root stores on local hosts are managed in various ways. Root stores maintained by Microsoft [47], Apple [22], Android [3], and Linux distributions [6,20] serve as system root stores within their respective operating systems. While some root stores operate independently of the system and are managed by applications as application root stores. For instance, Mozilla's root store [17] can be integrated into applications, with Firefox and Thunderbird each maintaining their own local instances of the Mozilla root store, while Python certifi [33] provides a Python-specific certificate bundle widely used in Python applications.

2.2 Root Stores Used in TLS Libraries

TLS libraries rely on local root stores to validate certificates. These libraries provide APIs for configuring root stores and other connection parameters, which applications must utilize correctly to establish secure TLS connections. Some TLS libraries (e.g., NSS [18]) implement built-in root stores and can be used directly for TLS connections. In contrast, many widely used TLS libraries (e.g., OpenSSL [19], GnuTLS [15], Python ssl [24], etc.) lack built-in root stores, thus requiring explicit configuration by either the TLS library itself or the application to specify local root store locations to establish TLS connections.

2.3 Related Work

Lots of work investigates the contents of root stores maintained by root store providers. Ma et al. [45] studied the derivative relationship between root stores. More granular trust policies were developed to constrain root certificates with greater precision [43,44]. Web PKI was found using only a portion of the certificates in the root store [36,49], while a more comprehensive measure was achieved by using Certificate Transparency logs and Server Name Indication [55].

Furthermore, some work has demonstrated that inappropriate local management of root stores has resulted in security compromises. The ecosystem of hidden root stores was uncovered through browser TLS traffic analysis [57]. It was also demonstrated that customized user root stores in Android degrade TLS connection security [50,54]. Additionally, Fu et al. [41] investigated root certificate management across systems and browser applications.

There is also some work focusing on the detection and remediation of TLS connection security issues. Fuzzing [53] and Combinatorial Testing [46] were used to evaluate the TLS libraries, while differential testing based on deep reinforcement learning [38] was employed to assess their certificate verification process. Many Android applications have improper implementations of certificate verification when establishing TLS connections [51,56]. Certificate validation remediation approaches were proposed, based on dynamic link library interception [35] as well as traffic interception [48], respectively.

Instead of focusing on the security of root stores themselves, our work evaluates whether applications can utilize the reliable root stores on the local host. To the best of our knowledge, we are the first to explore the interaction between TLS libraries and the local root stores, and implement static analysis techniques to detect whether applications utilize a reliable root store.

3 Overview

Applications typically rely on TLS libraries to configure root stores and establish TLS connections [10,25]. When configuring root stores for TLS connections, applications may either specify the root store or utilize the TLS library's default root store. This default root store is determined during the library's compilation or installation. Notably, if a TLS library lacks a built-in root store, its root store configuration usually defaults to the system root store on the local host.

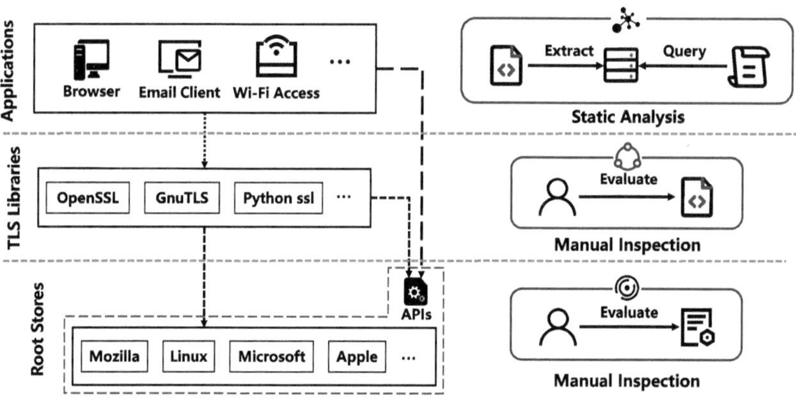

Fig. 1. Our methodology to analyze invocation of the local root stores.

As shown in Fig. 1, we evaluate whether the applications utilize a reliable root store through three aspects:

Reliable Root Stores on the Local Host. Among the different local root stores provided by popular root store providers (e.g., Mozilla, Microsoft), we assert that: (1) root stores provided by operating systems are reliable, and (2) root stores maintained by widely used applications[1] (e.g., Firefox) and protected by the operating system against unauthorized tampering are reliable. We evaluate the reliability of local root stores based on these criteria.

Default Root Stores of TLS Libraries. TLS libraries access their default root stores either by directly accessing certificate files or by invoking root store APIs, as indicated by the two dashed lines in Fig. 1. By examining the source code of these open source TLS libraries, we determine whether their default root stores are reliable root stores across different platforms.

Root Store Usage of TLS-Based Applications. For applications based on a specific TLS library, as indicated by the dotted lines in Fig. 1, we utilize CodeQL to perform taint analysis and data flow analysis, verifying whether the applications employ a reliable root store when establishing TLS connections.

4 Evaluating the Mainstream Root Stores

In this section, we investigate six mainstream root stores (i.e., Mozilla, Microsoft, Linux distributions, Apple, Android, and Python certifi) and evaluate their reliability on the local host, as shown in Table 1. For each root store, we describe its provider management, and further summarize their local management, including the default part (from the root store provider) and user-customized part of the root store, invocation APIs, as well as automated updates and tamper resistance.

Table 1. Provider and local management of six root stores.

Root store	Provider Management	Local Management				
		Default	Customized	Invocation	Update	Tamper-proof
System root store						
Microsoft	Windows Update	Registry	Registry	Cryptoapi	✓	✓
Linux distros	–	Certificate files		–	✓	✓
Apple	Apple Root Certificate Program	Keychains[1]	Keychains	Security.framework	✓	✓
Android	Android Open Source Project	Certificate files[1]	Certificate files	–	✓	✓
Application root store						
Mozilla	CA Certificate Program	`libnssckbi.so`	`cert9.db`	`PKCS#11`	✓[2]	✓[2]
Certifi	–	Certificate files	–	certifi.where()		

[1] The default part of these root stores cannot be modified directly by the user.
[2] The update and tamper-proof of Mozilla's root store depend on application implementation.

4.1 Mainstream Root Stores

Mozilla/NSS. Mozilla's Network Security Services (NSS) [18] is a set of libraries designed to support cross-platform development of security-enabled client and

[1] We posit that widely used applications tend to be well-implemented and their root stores are reliable.

server applications. NSS was designed for Firefox, Thunderbird, and other Mozilla-related software products, gradually becoming widely used in other software. Mozilla manages its *CA Certificate Program* [17] in the open, which decides whether to trust certificates based on the *Root Store Policy*.

Mozilla maintains root certificates in the `certdata.txt` file, which follows the `PKCS#11` format and contains the Certificates objects and Trust objects. The Certificates object contains certificate information, while the Trust object contains the trust policy for its corresponding certificate, including the trust purpose (i.e., server authentication, email protection, code signing) and level (i.e., trusted, needs verification, distrusted). However, not all constraints can be or are encoded in `certdata.txt`, such as EV restrictions (whether the root may issue EV certificates) [2].

The `certdata.txt` is compiled in the `libnssckbi.so`, following the `PKCS#11` interface. NSS also maintains another `PKCS#11` module, where the `cert9.db` file contains the user-customized root store. These two modules together constitute the root store of NSS. The `libnssckbi.so` is treated as a detachable component that can be replaced with other modules .

Linux Distributions. Most Linux distributions maintain a system root store deriving from the `certdata.txt` file in NSS, based on the *ca-certificates*. But they are implemented differently among different Linux distributions.

In Debian-based Linux distributions (e.g., Debian [6] and Ubuntu [34]), the *ca-certificates* saves the certificates in `certdata.txt` as individual certificate files and decides to either fully trust or distrust the certificate based on the value of the `CKA_TRUST_SERVER_AUTH` field. The root store will be saved in the `/usr/share/ca-certificates` directory, and symbolic links for these root certificates are also generated in the `/etc./ssl/certs` directory by default.

In other Linux distributions like CentOS [20], Arch Linux [4], and Fedora [7], the implementation of the *ca-certificates* is based on the p11-kit [21]. The root certificates are kept under directories such as `/etc./pki/ca-trust/source` and `/usr/share/pki/ca-trust-source` as a `PKCS#11` module of p11-kit. Unlike Debian-based platforms, they extract certificates to different files by purpose (TLS, email, and code signing) to achieve a more granular trust policy[2].

Linux distributions do not maintain separate user-customized root stores, and root stores are organized as certificate files that can be utilized by OpenSSL's CAfile and CApath parameters.

Microsoft. Microsoft supports the maintenance and distribution of root certificates using the *Microsoft Root Certificate Program* [47], where the *List of Participants* contains the certificate data for its root store, and the *Program Requirements* describes the requirements that all CAs in this program must follow.

Microsoft uses the Certificate Trust List (CTL) to publish lists of trusted and untrusted root certificates. Windows downloads CTLs such as `authrootstl.cab` and `disallowedcertstl.cab` through the CTL Updater. These two files can

[2] For example, `/etc./pki/ca-trust/extracted/pem/tls-ca-bundle.pem` for TLS.

be extracted as `authroot.stl` and `disallowedcert.stl`, which are organized as `PKCS#7` SignedData format. Among them, `authroot.stl` contains a list of SHA1 fingerprints of trusted root certificates and their Microsoft-specific OIDs, which indicate the trust policies and restrictions for each root certificate, while `disallowedcert.stl` contains a list of revoked certificates[3].

Both the default part and customized part of the Windows root store are kept in the Registry[4]. The Windows root store is available through the `CertOpenStore` and `CertOpenSystemStore` functions in CryptoAPI.

Apple. Apple has published specific standards in the *Apple Root Certificate Program* [22] that CA providers need to adhere to in order to manage the root stores in support of products (such as Safari and Mail). Apple also maintains the certificate configuration data to indicate that a certificate is blocked or partially trusted [8].

Both the default part and customized part of the Apple root store are kept in the Keychain[5]. The *Apple Security framework* utilizes this root store by default when validating certificates or establishing TLS connections.

Android. Android asks CA to complete the *Mozilla Inclusion Process* to be added to the Android root store in the *Android Open Source Project* [3]. The default part of the Android root store serves as the system-level store and cannot be modified directly, while users can customize the user-level store for general purposes, VPN, and Wi-Fi separately.

Python Certifi. Certifi [33] is a repackaging of Mozilla's CA bundle that addresses the lack of a single CA bundle for configuring OpenSSL on Windows and macOS. Root certificates are bundled in the `cacert.pem` file, accessible via the `certifi.where()` method, and a customized root store is not supported.

4.2 Evaluating the Root Stores on the Local Host

Based on the local management of the six root stores shown in Table 1, we evaluate their reliability.

The root stores of Microsoft, Linux distributions, Apple, and Android operate as system root stores on the local host. Root stores maintained by operating systems are reliable, as their content updates can be managed through operating system updates, and the system can safeguard local root stores to reduce the risk of malicious tampering.

---

[3] Different from `authroot.stl`, `disallowedcert.stl` provides the MD5 fingerprint of the value of the `subjectPublicKey` field in the revoked certificate.

[4] The system-level store holds default part of Windows root store. Both the system-level store and user-level store can be modified by users with appropriate permissions.

[5] `/System/Library/Keychains/` holds default part of Apple root store, which cannot be modified directly, while `/Library/Keychains/` and `~/Library/Keychains/` hold the system-level store and the user-level store, respectively, which can be modified by users with appropriate permissions.

Both Mozilla and Python certifi serve as application root stores locally, managed by their respective applications such as Firefox and the package installer for Python (pip). The Mozilla's root store used by Firefox can be updated through software upgrades [27], and its default part is hard-coded into dynamic link libraries, making additions or modifications challenging. Furthermore, Mozilla leverages the operating system's root permission safeguards for the `/lib` and `/usr/lib` directories to protect these critical components from malicious tampering or replacement. In contrast, Python certifi lacks robust application-driven management capabilities as an application root store and exhibits less resistance to tampering compared to Mozilla's root store.

Therefore, we categorize the system root stores of the four operating systems (Windows, macOS, Linux, and Android) and the Mozilla root store managed by well-implemented applications (e.g. Firefox, Thunderbird) as reliable root stores, while categorizing Python certifi as an unreliable root store.

5 Exploring the Default Root Store of TLS Libraries

In this section, for TLS libraries without built-in root stores, we explore their default root stores across different operating systems. For four TLS libraries in C and Python (OpenSSL [19], GnuTLS [15], Python ssl [24], and pyOpenSSL [11]), as well as two high-level wrappers in Python (urllib3 [28], trustore [26]), we inspect whether their default root store aligns with the system root store on various operating systems and whether their default root store is alterable. As shown in Table 2, the system root stores in Windows and macOS have well-defined structures, typically requiring platform-specific APIs for interaction, while Linux distributions employ a simpler system root store structure that can be leveraged by all TLS libraries. Android's root store structure is similarly straightforward, but its developers predominantly rely on the standard Java interface, leading most TLS libraries (except GnuTLS) to lack additional platform-specific implementations for Android.

5.1 C-Based TLS Libraries

OpenSSL and GnuTLS are two of the most popular C-based open source TLS libraries [16]. OpenSSL is often used as the default TLS library in many Linux distributions, while GnuTLS is used as the TLS backend in many applications.

OpenSSL. Typically, `SSL_CTX_set_default_verify_paths` is implemented for the default root store, or `SSL_CTX_load_verify_locations` for the specified root store, both of which end up using the file (CAfile type) or directory (CApath type) at the specified path as the root store. The default root store of OpenSSL is controlled by the compiled-in openssldir parameter, e.g., `C:\ Program Files\ Common Files\ SSL` on Windows and `/usr/local/ssl` on Linux. In addition, OpenSSL can use environment variables to override the compiled-in default paths to enhance flexibility and portability. Among them, `SSL_CERT_DIR` and `SSL_CERT_FILE` are used to set the path of the default root store.

Table 2. Evaluation of six TLS libraries in different platforms.

Evaluation	C-based TLS library		Python-based TLS library		Python high-level wrapper	
	OpenSSL[1]	GnuTLS	Python-ssl[2]	Python-pyOpenSSL[2]	Python-urllib3	Python-trustore
Usage of system root store						
Windows		✓	✓[3]		✓[3]	✓
Linux distros	✓	✓	✓	✓	✓	✓
macOS	○	✓	○	○	–	✓
Android		✓				
Alterable default root store						
Build-time configurable	✓	✓				
Runtime-changeable	✓		✓[4]	✓[4]	✓[4]	

[1] OpenSSL can utilize the `provider-storemgmt` with the `org.openssl.winstore:` as CAstore parameter to access the Windows system root store, but this is not used by default.
[2] These libraries are Python's high-level wrapper for C OpenSSL.
[3] Python ssl module also relies on OpenSSL's default root store on Windows.
[4] OpenSSL environment variables can control the default root store for both Python ssl module and Python pyOpenSSL library
[5] ○ The OpenSSL library on macOS has an available default root store, but it is not the system root store.
[6] – Python urllib3 deprecate the SecureTransport TLS implementation after version 2.1.0.
[7] ✓ The library can leverage the system root store as it default root store, or its default root store is alterable.

However, regardless of environment variable configurations, OpenSSL is limited to CAfile and CApath type default root stores and cannot leverage system root stores on Windows or macOS. For example, while macOS's default OpenSSL implementation, LibreSSL, does not use the Keychain as its default root store.

GnuTLS. Among these libraries, GnuTLS has the best cross-platform performance. In the `add_system_trust` function, it implements platform-specific mechanisms for the default root store on different operating systems. On Windows and macOS, it uses the CryptoAPI and the Security framework to load the system root store; on Linux, it detects several common root store paths, such as `/etc./ssl/cert.pem` and `/etc./ssl/ca-bundle.pem`, to determine the correct system root store location; on Android, GnuTLS loads the certificate file in the system-level store, and is the only one of these libraries that invokes the Android system root store. Meanwhile, GnuTLS allows users to configure the location of the default root store at build time.

5.2 Python-Based TLS Libraries

In Python, both the ssl module and pyOpenSSL library serve as widely adopted TLS implementations, with the former being a built-in module and the latter a third-party dependency.

Python ssl. The ssl module provides the methods `load_default_certs` and `load_verify_locations` for the default and the specified root stores, respectively. This module serves as a high-level wrapper for OpenSSL, meaning its certificate verification and default root store implementations are also based on OpenSSL. Since Linux and macOS have default OpenSSL, the ssl module leverages these default installations for its implementation. However, as Windows does not include OpenSSL natively, Python on Windows requires the additional installation of pre-compiled OpenSSL binaries to function as runtime DLLs.

In Windows, the pre-compiled OpenSSL library in Python may not work with a valid root store. To solve this problem, the ssl module uses CryptoAPI in the inner C part and provides the `_load_windows_store_certs` function in the outer Python part, thus loading CA certs from the `CA` and `ROOT` system root stores in Windows.

Python pyOpenSSL. To solve the problem of limited SSL support in the Python ssl module, pyOpenSSL implements a more complete SSL API based on the *cryptography* [29]. Both of them are maintained by the Python Cryptography Authority (PyCA). The *cryptography* is a Python encapsulation of Rust and C OpenSSL, while the pyOpenSSL library acts as a rather thin wrapper around the C OpenSSL part of the *cryptography.*

The pyOpenSSL library's API closely resembles that of the OpenSSL library, providing `set_default_verify_paths` and `load_verify_locations` for the default and the specified root stores, respectively. Similarly, the pyOpenSSL library is limited by the capabilities of the OpenSSL library to leverage the system root store on Windows and macOS. On Linux distributions, it can either rely on the native OpenSSL library to leverage the default system root store or probe various paths to determine the location of the system root store.

5.3 High-Level Wrappers in Python

In addition to the basic SSL libraries in Python, high-level wrappers such as urllib3 [28] and truststore [26] have also implemented APIs for loading default root stores.

Python urllib3. The urllib3 is a powerful HTTP client for Python based on the Python ssl module. Prior to urllib3 v2.0.7, the SecureTransport [23] implementation was added to support OpenSSL versions on macOS that didn't support TLS 1.2 and later [9]. The urllib3 library utilizes SecureTransport as the TLS backend by rewriting the original SSLContext and employs the macOS system root store when establishing TLS connections. Due to performance improvements in Python on macOS and the obsolescence of SecureTransport, urllib3 removed support for SecureTransport in versions after 2.1.0. However, this change has resulted in the library failing to leverage macOS system root stores.

Python Truststore. There has been a lot of discussion about dropping the Python certifi root store [14], with certifi-system-store [42] as a solution to redirect certifi to the system default location on different Linux distributions. However, this solution is experimental and that's already covered by not using certifi and using the ssl module instead. In response to this problem, the Python truststore library is specifically designed to leverage the system root store across different platforms, which is used to address the imperfect performance of the ssl module on different operating systems and also reduces the dependency of Python programs on the static certificate bundle like certifi.

Similar to urllib3, truststore rewrites the SSLContext class. The truststore uses the ssl module to establish a TLS connection, but uses OpenSSL, CryptoAPI, and Security framework to validate certificates on Linux, Windows, and macOS, respectively, and leverages the default root store on those systems.

5.4 Security Concerns of Pre-compiled OpenSSL

OpenSSL's default root store cannot be configured to the system root stores on Windows and macOS. OpenSSL can be configured with the openssldir parameter during compilation, to leverage available root stores across different platforms. To enable post-compilation configuration and optimize cross-platform functionality, OpenSSL utilizes environment variables to override the compiled-in default paths. However, these parameters cannot be configured to point to the system root store on Windows and macOS.

Furthermore, Windows platforms lack a native OpenSSL distribution, necessitating some libraries, like the Python ssl module and pyOpenSSL library, to depend on additional OpenSSL pre-compiled binaries. In this case, the openssldir parameter typically defaults to `C:\ Program Files\ Common Files\ SSL`, while environment variables governing the OpenSSL library also influence the default root store in the Python library. This architectural dependency results in non-deterministic root store usage for TLS libraries relying on OpenSSL in Windows environments.

OpenSSL pre-compiled binary configuration determines the default root store of the pyOpenSSL library and the Python ssl module. In the pyOpenSSL library, the default root store depends entirely on OpenSSL's default root store. If the configured parameters are not accessible on the local host, applications based on pyOpenSSL may fail to load root certificates, thus forcing them to resort to other local root stores like Python certifi. In the ssl module, the default root store relies on both the system root store and OpenSSL's default root store. If the configured parameters prove valid on the local host, applications using this module might inadvertently depend on additional root stores beyond the system defaults, resulting in reduced TLS connection security.

6 Analysis of Root Store Usage in Open Source Projects

In this section, we explore the root store invocation of TLS-based applications. Our analysis focuses on applications that utilize four TLS libraries: C OpenSSL, C GnuTLS, Python ssl, and Python pyOpenSSL. These TLS libraries provide two categories of root store loading functions: one for the default root store and another for a user-specific root store. Both functions require a context parameter to retain the root store, while the latter also necessitates a string parameter specifying the path to the root store.

We first employ taint analysis and data flow analysis on context parameters to identify TLS connections that may lack the root store usage, indicating that the program either may disable the certificate validation or may fail to validate certificates. Subsequently, through data flow analysis of string parameters, we trace the values of application-specified root stores to determine whether the program uses a non-default root store when establishing a TLS connection, which may lead to a degradation of security.

6.1 Context Parameter Analysis

The context parameter is utilized to configure the root store for TLS connections. For these four TLS libraries, we abstract two distinct data flow patterns corresponding to their root store loading mechanisms. Furthermore, we introduce additional query predicates tailored to library-specific characteristics to enhance analysis precision.

Pattern I. The Python ssl module and pyOpenSSL library both serve as high-level wrappers over the C-based OpenSSL implementation, resulting in structurally analogous TLS establishment workflows and root store loading processes, as demonstrated in Table 3. The workflow comprises three core phases: Step 1 initializes a context parameter. Step 2 involves root store loading with two options: Step 2.a leveraging the TLS library's default root store, and Step 2.b leveraging parameter-specified root stores. Step 3 finalizes the process by instantiating a TLS session derived from the initialized context parameter, during which certificate chain validation inherits the configured root stores.

Table 3. Root store loading processes for Pattern I.

Step[1]	OpenSSL	Python ssl	Python pyOpenSSL
1	`ctx = SSL_CTX_new()`	`ctx = SSLContext()`	`ctx = Context()`
2.a	`SSL_CTX_set_default_verify_paths(ctx)`	`ctx.load_default_certs()`	`ctx.set_default_verify_paths()`

2.b	`SSL_CTX_load_verify_locations(ctx)`
	`SSL_CTX_load_verify_file(ctx)`
	`SSL_CTX_load_verify_dir(ctx)`
		`ctx.load_verify_locations()`	`ctx.load_verify_locations()`

3	`ssl = SSL_new(ctx)`	`ctx.wrap_socket()`	`ssl = Connection(ctx)`

[1] Both Step 2.a and Step 2.b are optional and can be performed in any order.

Within this three-step workflow, Step 2 is optional, which may result in scenarios where TLS connections operate without any root store configuration. To identify such insecure implementations, we design taint analysis rules based on these steps: Initialize the context parameter in Step 1 (source); load the root stores into the context parameter in Step 2 (sanitizer); generate a TLS session from the context parameter in Step 3 (sink). By tracking data flows from the source to the sink, we flag connections where the context parameter enters Step 3 without undergoing sanitization in Step 2, indicating a lack of root store loading.

Furthermore, Python ssl module provides additional encapsulation of these three steps. For instance, the `create_default_context` function initializes the context parameter and loads the root store. This function utilizes secure connection parameters and does not introduce security threats related to the root store, which is why we exclude it from the data flow analysis.

Table 4. Root store loading processes for Pattern II.

Step[1]	GnuTLS	OpenSSL
Context data flow		
1	`gnutls_init(&ctx)`	`ctx = SSL_CTX_new()`
2	`gnutls_credentials_set(ctx, store)`	`SSL_CTX_set_cert_store(ctx, store)` `SSL_CTX_set1_cert_store(ctx, store)`
3	`gnutls_handshake(ctx)`	`ssl = SSL_new(ctx)`
Root store loading		
2.a	`gnutls_certificate_set_x509_system_trust(store)`	`X509_STORE_set_default_paths(store)`

2.b	`gnutls_certificate_set_x509_trust_file(store)`
	`gnutls_certificate_set_x509_trust_dir(store)`
		`X509_STORE_load_locations(store)`
		`X509_STORE_load_file(store)`
		`X509_STORE_load_path(store)`

[1] Both Step 2.a and Step 2.b are optional and can be performed in any order.

Pattern II. GnuTLS and OpenSSL exhibit an alternative data flow pattern, as shown in Table 4. In this pattern, Steps 1 and 3 remain identical to the previous one, while Step 2 assigns the store parameter to a dedicated field within the context parameter (such as `SSL_CTX->cert_store` in OpenSSL), enabling root store configuration through either Step 2.a or Step 2.b. The decoupled nature of the store parameter from the context parameter imposes only a single constraint: Step 2.a (or 2.b) must precede Step 3.

We define four data flows for Pattern II. First, we trace the dual data flows of context parameters from Step 1 to Step 2 and Step 2 to Step 3, identifying the nodes where context parameters are instantiated, modified, and ultimately consumed, along with their associated store parameter nodes. After that, to ensure root store integration prior to session activation, we analyze whether valid data flows of store parameters exist either (1) from Step 2.a (or 2.b) to Step 2 or (2) from Step 2 to Step 2.a (or 2.b) executed before Step 3. The absence of such flows definitively indicates unsecured TLS connections lacking root store initialization.

Furthermore, to mitigate data flow loss caused by structure field accessing, we introduced additional flow steps between structures and their constituent fields. Since the source and sink nodes share the same data type in these four data flows, the flooding of data flow could be effectively avoided[6]. Experimental testing demonstrates that this method introduces no additional false positives in real-world code implementation.

6.2 Path Parameter Analysis

The program uses the path parameter to specify the location of the root store. After filtering out TLS connections that do not utilize a root store, we further examine the remaining TLS connections to detect the usage of non-default root stores.

To identify the exact location of the root store employed by the program, we perform data flow analysis on these path parameters. The sink nodes of the data flow are defined as the path parameters passed into root store loading APIs, while the source nodes remain unrestricted to capture all potential origins of these parameters. However, unrestricted source tracking can result in excessive query results and prohibitive computational overhead. To address this, we constrain the source nodes exclusively to string constants and initialization statements.

Additionally, certain programs acquire path parameters from environment variables or files. For example, the `getenv` function could be used to get the value of a specific environment variable as a path argument, or the `read` function could be used to read a path argument from a file. We augment additional flow steps for these functions (`getenv`, `secure_genenv` and `read`[7]) to capture parameters of these functions, and validate the effectiveness of this enhancement through experimental testing.

6.3 CodeQL-Based Analysis

We employ CodeQL [12] as our code analysis tool to support both C and Python projects. CodeQL requires compilers or interpreters to extract the codebase into a CodeQL database, after which CodeQL queries are executed to perform static analysis. As analyzed in Sect. 5, we specifically create CodeQL databases on Linux platforms to ensure TLS libraries are able to use system root stores, thereby eliminating platform-specific dependencies in our evaluation.

We utilize the CodeQL-CLI v2.21.0 to create the CodeQL databases and execute queries. For the four TLS libraries, we collect open source projects leveraging these libraries from GitHub as test cases for validation. Since C code requires compilation to generate the database, we employ CodeQL's autobuild mode to create the database. To enable data flow tracking inside the Python modules and libraries, we set the `CODEQL_EXTRACTOR_PYTHON_EXTRACT_STDLIB` environment variable to facilitate the extraction of the Python standard library. The results of the database construction are presented in Table 5.

---

6 In taint analysis, we do not introduce this flow step in order to avoid introducing a new data flow that does not go through the sanitizer node.

7 Additionally for Glib-based programs, we have implemented the flow step for `g_strdup`, `g_build_path`, `g_strdup_printf`.

Table 5. Query results for projects built upon four TLS libraries.

Queries	OpenSSL	GnuTLS	Python ssl	Python pyOpenSSL	Total
Specify root store	14	12	47	56	129
Didn't load root store	16	15	115	96	242
Specify or Didn't load	22	17	120	111	270
Implement TLS	26	18	148	125	317
All Codebases	51	41	190	157	439

Subsequently, we implement the query logic using CodeQL queries and perform approximate processing on one of the data flows. For context parameter data flows in Pattern II, we cannot definitively determine the invocation order between Step 2.a (or 2.b) and Step 3. We establish their execution order based on their positions when these steps reside within the same function. Otherwise, we flag it as likely to have an issue with the unloaded root store, which may introduce false positives. The query results are shown in Table 5, and the data sources for the sample codebases are shown in Table 6.

OpenSSL. Among 51 OpenSSL-based codebases, 26 attempted to establish TLS connections. Of these, 19 were at risk of failing to utilize the root store under Pattern I. Among those, 8 codebases adopted Pattern II for root store loading, and 3 of them were not at risk. Consequently, a total of 16 codebases remained potentially vulnerable to failing to utilize the root store.

For context parameter data flow, we found that almost all codebases filtered by the Pattern I data flow potentially lacked loading of the root store, including both TLS server and client programs. Server programs may be less affected by the root store, while client programs (e.g., *httpc*) that do not use the root store can lead to more serious issues. For Pattern II data flows, such as in *curl*, false positives were identified due to the approximate implementations of the rules.

Through the path parameter data flow, we identified that 14 codebases will employ user-specific root stores and located some of them. For example, *apk-tools* uses `/etc./apk/ca.pem` as the root store, and *netdata* uses the environment variable `H2O_ROOT` to construct the path to the root store.

GnuTLS. Among 41 GnuTLS-based codebases, 18 were found to establish TLS connections. Our tool indicated that 15 exhibited issues of not using a root store. After manual inspection, 9 were confirmed to indeed have TLS connections that failed to use a root store. However, false positives included cases like *wget2*, where the context parameter is set as a global variable, disrupting the data flow, and *Kmc-Subset137*, where struct field accesses introduce additional data flows in Step 1 of Table 4.

Through the path parameter data flow, we identified 12 codebases that employ user-specific root stores. For example, *libnfs* uses the value of the environment variable `LIBNFS_TLS_TRUSTED_CA_PEM` to indicate its root store, while *libvirt-tdx* selects `/usr/local/etc./pki/CA/cacert.pem` as its root store.

Python ssl. We include the `ssl.py` file in the codebase to capture complete data flows; however, this will introduce additional data flows in the `ssl.wrap_socket` function (removed in Python 3.12). Therefore, we explicitly determine whether applications utilize `ssl.wrap_socket`. Among 190 codebases, 148 attempted to establish TLS connections, with 90 utilizing `ssl.wrap_socket`. Of the remaining 58 codebases, 25 potentially failed to load a root store.

Through the path parameter data flow, we identified 47 applications using user-specific root stores. For instance, *hacktools* employs `ssl.wrap_socket` with a root store at `/var/lib/openvas/CA/cacert.pem`; *KM17_15.01.18-2* uses the `cacert.pem` file in the project as the root store.

Python pyOpenSSL. The data flow in pyOpenSSL is simpler than that of OpenSSL, as it implements only a subset of OpenSSL's interfaces in Python. Among the 157 pyOpenSSL-based codebases, 96 may fail to use root stores, and 62 may employ user-specific root stores.

Through the path parameter data flow, we identified that *python_scripts* employs `/usr1/hcsjad/python_scripts/openssl/simple/CA.cert` as the root store, while *ga* and *docker-xx-net* employ the `cacert.pem` file from their respective projects as their root store.

7 Recommendation

Based on the results of the above studies on root stores, TLS libraries, and applications, we propose several suggestions to enhance the security of application root store usage from the perspective of root store providers, TLS library developers, and application developers, respectively.

Root Stores Should Implement Fine-Grained Certificate Trust Policies. While we regard system root stores as reliable, their reliability varies across different platforms. Our findings reveal that all system root stores except Debian-based Linux distributions enhance reliability by imposing trust policies and restrictions on root certificates in the root store. A relatively straightforward improvement would be segregating certificates by usage in separate files, as implemented in CentOS.

TLS Libraries Should Make Full Use of the System Root Store and Simplify their TLS Connection Setup Code. In Sect. 5, we demonstrated that the default root stores of some TLS libraries on non-Linux platforms cannot be reliable root stores. Therefore, TLS libraries should take into account the differences in the implementation of the lower platforms when handling the root store, and fully leverage system APIs designed for root store management. Additionally, TLS libraries should reduce the coding effort for root store loading. For example, the CryptoAPI for Windows and the Security framework for macOS directly utilize the system root store directly when performing certificate validation, without requiring the developers to explicitly invoke the APIs to load the default root stores.

Applications Should Prioritize Using APIs for the Default Root Store, and Avoid Additional Dependencies on Other Root Stores. In Sect. 6, we found that lots of the analyzed applications employ APIs for loading user-specific root stores during TLS setup, exposing them to security risks through the adoption of unreliable root stores. Additionally, applications could proactively adopt platform-specific APIs for loading system root stores, as demonstrated by the long dashed lines in Fig. 1. We have released our tools available at https://github.com/storequery/storequery for application developers to inspect their projects.

8 Conclusion and Future Work

This work investigates the usage of root stores in applications when establishing TLS connections, covering three aspects: applications, TLS libraries, and root stores. We evaluated the reliability of six mainstream root stores, explored six widely used TLS libraries to identify their default root stores across different platforms, and revealed some security concerns of pre-compiled OpenSSL. We implemented static analysis for programs relying on specific TLS libraries and validated the method's effectiveness using real-world projects. Through the above aspects, we identified issues that could lead to applications failing to use reliable root stores and proposed corresponding mitigation strategies.

Future work may employ dynamic analysis to precisely pinpoint the root store locations accessed by applications, while also considering runtime remediation techniques for calls to unreliable root stores.

A Source of Sample Projects

Table 6. Source of sample projects.

Project	Source
httpc	https://github.com/howerj/httpc
curl	https://github.com/apple-oss-distributions/curl
apk-tools	https://github.com/alpinelinux/apk-tools
netdata	https://github.com/deepin-community/netdata
wget2	https://github.com/deepin-community/wget2
Kmc-Subset137	https://github.com/neatsrl/Kmc-Subset137
libnfs	https://github.com/sahlberg/libnfs
libvirt-tdx	https://github.com/intel/libvirt-tdx
hacktools	https://github.com/wwwiretap/hacktools
KM17_15.01.18-2	https://github.com/kodirepositoryluxy/KM17_15.01.18-2
python_scripts	https://github.com/notmyname/python_scripts
ga	https://github.com/greatagent/ga
docker-xx-net	https://github.com/seifer08ms/docker-xx-net

References

1. 1567114 - MITM on all HTTPS traffic in Kazakhstan. https://bugzilla.mozilla.org/show_bug.cgi?id=1567114
2. Additional trust changes. https://wiki.mozilla.org/CA/Additional_Trust_Changes
3. App security. https://source.android.com/docs/security/overview/app-security
4. Arch Linux - ca-certificates 20240618-1 (any). https://archlinux.org/packages/core/any/ca-certificates/
5. Baseline Requirements. https://cabforum.org/working-groups/server/baseline-requirements/
6. ca-certificates - Debian Package Tracker. https://tracker.debian.org/pkg/ca-certificates
7. Ca-certificates - fedora packages. https://packages.fedoraproject.org/pkgs/ca-certificates/ca-certificates/
8. CA certificates with additional constraints. https://support.apple.com/en-us/103255
9. Changelog. https://urllib3.readthedocs.io/en/2.1.0/changelog.html
10. Chapter 4. Planning and implementing TLS | Securing networks | Red Hat Enterprise Linux | 8 | Red Hat Documentation. https://docs.redhat.com/en/documentation/red_hat_enterprise_linux/8/html/securing_networks/planning-and-implementing-tls_securing-networks
11. Client Challenge. https://pypi.org/project/pyOpenSSL
12. CodeQL. https://codeql.github.com/
13. Common CA Database by the Linux Foundation. https://www.ccadb.org/
14. Drop certifi, use system trust store by default · Issue #302 · encode/httpx. https://github.com/encode/httpx/issues/302
15. gnutls.org. https://www.gnutls.org/
16. Introduction to cryptographic libraries. https://documentation.ubuntu.com/server/explanation/intro-to/crypto-libraries/
17. Mozilla's ca certificate program. https://wiki.mozilla.org/CA
18. Network Security Services (NSS) — Firefox Source Docs documentation. https://firefox-source-docs.mozilla.org/security/nss/index.html
19. OpenSSL. https://www.openssl.org/
20. Overview - rpms/ca-certificates - CentOS Git server. https://git.centos.org/rpms/ca-certificates
21. p11-kit. https://p11-glue.github.io/p11-glue/p11-kit.html
22. Root Certificate Program - Apple. https://www.apple.com/certificateauthority/ca_program.html
23. Secure Transport. https://docs.developer.apple.com/documentation/security/secure-transport
24. ssl — TLS/SSL wrapper for socket objects. https://docs.python.org/3/library/ssl.html
25. Transport Layer Security - ArchWiki. https://wiki.archlinux.org/title/Transport_Layer_Security
26. truststore: Verify certificates using native system trust stores
27. Update Firefox to prevent add-ons issues from root certificate expiration | Mozilla Support. https://support.mozilla.org/en-US/kb/root-certificate-expiration
28. urllib3: HTTP library with thread-safe connection pooling, file post, and more

29. Welcome to pyca/cryptography — Cryptography 46.0.0.dev1 documentation. https://cryptography.io/en/latest/
30. What You Need to Know About the DigiNotar Hack (2011). https://threatpost.com/what-you-need-know-about-diginotar-hack-090211/75611/
31. Google, Mozilla Drop Trust in Chinese Certificate Authority CNNIC (2015). https://threatpost.com/google-drops-trust-in-chinese-certificate-authority-cnnic/111974/
32. Lenovo Superfish Adware Vulnerable to HTTPS Spoofing | CISA (2016). https://www.cisa.gov/news-events/alerts/2015/02/20/lenovo-superfish-adware-vulnerable-https-spoofing
33. certifi/python-certifi (2025). https://github.com/certifi/python-certifi, original-date: 2011-12-28T05:15:19Z
34. Git: Code: ca-certificates package: Ubuntu (2025). https://code.launchpad.net/ubuntu/+source/ca-certificates/+code
35. Bates, A., et al.: Securing SSL certificate verification through dynamic linking. In: Proceedings of the 2014 ACM SIGSAC Conference on Computer and Communications Security, pp. 394–405. ACM (2014). https://doi.org/10.1145/2660267.2660338
36. Braun, J., Rynkowski, G.: The potential of an individualized set of trusted cas: defending against CA failures in the web PKI. In: International Conference on Social Computing, pp. 600–605. IEEE Computer Society (2013). https://doi.org/10.1109/SocialCom.2013.90
37. de Carné de Carnavalet, X., Mannan, M.: Killed by proxy: analyzing client-end TLS interception software. In: 23rd Annual Network and Distributed System Security Symposium. The Internet Society (2016). http://wp.internetsociety.org/ndss/wp-content/uploads/sites/25/2017/09/killed-proxy-analyzing-client-end-tls-interception-software.pdf
38. Chen, C., Diao, W., Zeng, Y., Guo, S., Hu, C.: Drlgencert: deep learning-based automated testing of certificate verification in SSL/TLS implementations. In: 2018 IEEE International Conference on Software Maintenance and Evolution, pp. 48–58. IEEE Computer Society (2018). https://doi.org/10.1109/ICSME.2018.00014
39. Cooper, D., Santesson, S., Farrell, S., Boeyen, S., Housley, R., Polk, W.T.: Internet X.509 public key infrastructure certificate and certificate revocation list (CRL) profile. RFC **5280**, 1–151 (2008). https://doi.org/10.17487/RFC5280
40. Durumeric, Z., et al.: The security impact of HTTPS interception. In: 24th Annual Network and Distributed System Security Symposium. The Internet Society (2017). https://www.ndss-symposium.org/ndss2017/ndss-2017-programme/security-impact-https-interception/
41. Fu, Y., Wang, Q., Lin, J., Sun, A., Lu, L.: Exploring the security issues of trusted CA certificate management. In: Gao, D., Li, Q., Guan, X., Liao, X. (eds.) ICICS 2021. LNCS, vol. 12918, pp. 384–401. Springer, Cham (2021). https://doi.org/10.1007/978-3-030-86890-1_22
42. Heimes, C.: tiran/certifi-system-store (2024). https://github.com/tiran/certifi-system-store, original-date: 2021-03-12T10:24:06Z
43. Kasten, J., Wustrow, E., Halderman, J.A.: CAge: taming certificate authorities by inferring restricted scopes. In: Sadeghi, A.-R. (ed.) FC 2013. LNCS, vol. 7859, pp. 329–337. Springer, Heidelberg (2013). https://doi.org/10.1007/978-3-642-39884-1_28
44. Larisch, J., et al.: No root store left behind. In: Proceedings of the 22nd ACM Workshop on Hot Topics in Networks, pp. 295–301. ACM (2023). https://doi.org/10.1145/3626111.3630268

45. Ma, Z., Austgen, J., Mason, J., Durumeric, Z., Bailey, M.D.: Tracing your roots: exploring the TLS trust anchor ecosystem. In: IMC 2021: ACM Internet Measurement Conference, pp. 179–194. ACM (2021). https://doi.org/10.1145/3487552.3487813
46. Maehren, M., Nieting, P., Hebrok, S., Merget, R., Somorovsky, J., Schwenk, J.: TLS-anvil: adapting combinatorial testing for TLS libraries. In: 31st USENIX Security Symposium, pp. 215–232. USENIX Association (2022). https://www.usenix.org/conference/usenixsecurity22/presentation/maehren
47. MicrosoftGuyJFlo: The Microsoft Root Certificate Program. https://learn.microsoft.com/en-us/security/trusted-root/
48. O'Neill, M., et al.: Trustbase: an architecture to repair and strengthen certificate-based authentication. In: 26th USENIX Security Symposium, pp. 609–624. USENIX Association (2017). https://www.usenix.org/conference/usenixsecurity17/technical-sessions/presentation/oneill
49. Perl, H., Fahl, S., Smith, M.: You won't be needing these any more: on removing unused certificates from trust stores. In: Christin, N., Safavi-Naini, R. (eds.) FC 2014. LNCS, vol. 8437, pp. 307–315. Springer, Heidelberg (2014). https://doi.org/10.1007/978-3-662-45472-5_20
50. Possemato, A., Fratantonio, Y.: Towards HTTPS everywhere on android: we are not there yet. In: 29th USENIX Security Symposium, pp. 343–360. USENIX Association (2020). https://www.usenix.org/conference/usenixsecurity20/presentation/possemato
51. Pourali, S., Yu, X., Zhao, L., Mannan, M., Youssef, A.M.: Racing for TLS certificate validation: a hijacker's guide to the android TLS galaxy. In: 33rd USENIX Security Symposium. USENIX Association (2024). https://www.usenix.org/conference/usenixsecurity24/presentation/pourali
52. Rescorla, E.: The transport layer security (TLS) protocol version 1.3. RFC **8446**, 1–160 (2018). https://doi.org/10.17487/RFC8446
53. Somorovsky, J.: Systematic fuzzing and testing of TLS libraries. In: Proceedings of the 2016 ACM SIGSAC Conference on Computer and Communications Security, pp. 1492–1504. ACM (2016). https://doi.org/10.1145/2976749.2978411
54. Vallina-Rodriguez, N., Amann, J., Kreibich, C., Weaver, N., Paxson, V.: A tangled mass: the android root certificate stores. In: Proceedings of the 10th ACM International on Conference on emerging Networking Experiments and Technologies, pp. 141–148. ACM (2014). https://doi.org/10.1145/2674005.2675015
55. VanderSloot, B., Amann, J., Bernhard, M., Durumeric, Z., Bailey, M.D., Halderman, J.A.: Towards a complete view of the certificate ecosystem. In: Proceedings of the 2016 ACM on Internet Measurement Conference, pp. 543–549. ACM (2016). http://dl.acm.org/citation.cfm?id=2987462
56. Wang, Y., et al.: Identifying vulnerabilities of SSL/TLS certificate verification in android apps with static and dynamic analysis. J. Syst. Softw. **167**, 110609 (2020). https://doi.org/10.1016/j.jss.2020.110609
57. Zhang, Y., et al.: Rusted anchors: a national client-side view of hidden root CAS in the web PKI ecosystem. In: CCS 2021: 2021 ACM SIGSAC Conference on Computer and Communications Security, pp. 1373–1387. ACM (2021). https://doi.org/10.1145/3460120.3484768

LSDBFT: A Loose DAG-Based Asynchronous BFT Consensus Algorithm with Fair Ordering

Chaofeng Zhuang and Haifeng Qian(✉)

East China Normal University, Shanghai 200062, China
hfqian@cs.ecnu.edu.cn

Abstract. The expansion of the blockchain scale puts higher demands on the parallel performance of distributed consistency algorithms. In recent years, protocols represented by Tusk have driven the development of Byzantine fault tolerant (BFT) protocols by integrating directed acyclic graph (DAG). These protocols divide consensus into communication layer and ordering layer, enabling parallel execution of block broadcasting and agreements in the expectation of increased throughput. However, traditional DAG-based BFT protocols require nodes to deliver a sufficient number of peer broadcast blocks before broadcasting a new block, which actually limits parallel performance. In addition, they uses the leader block to commit all blocks, which is unfair to slow progressing nodes as their blocks are excluded by consensus. To address these challenges, we propose LSDBFT, a novel asynchronous BFT protocol that redefines the communication and ordering layers for improved scalability and fairness. The communication layer of LSDBFT employs a loose DAG structure where each node broadcasts blocks at its own pace through sequential provable broadcasts (PBs), eliminating the cross-node synchronization delays inherent in the traditional DAG reference mechanism. The ordering layer leverages an asynchronous binary agreement (ABA) protocol to establish a fair total ordering of blocks, ensuring equitable commitment even for slow-progressing nodes. Unlike leader-centric approaches, LSDBFT's ABA-driven mechanism avoids favoring specific nodes, enhancing decentralization. We prove the security of the LSDBFT protocol and verify its efficiency through experimental evaluation. In conclusion, LSDBFT advances the application of distributed consensus algorithms in high-throughput environments by harmonizing parallelism with fair block ordering.

Keywords: Asynchronous binary agreement · Broadcast · Byzantine fault tolerant · Directed acyclic graph · Fair ordering

1 Introduction

Blockchain is a decentralized ledger [2,5,26] that leverages cryptography technology and consensus protocols to securely record and manage data. The key

R. Chen et al. (Eds.): Inscrypt 2025, LNCS 16409, pp. 410–430, 2026.
https://doi.org/10.1007/978-981-95-6203-9_22

attributes of blockchain technology—decentralization, traceability, and tamper resistance—provide it with vast potential applications across various industries [11,13,27]. With the rapid growth of network scale [28], the number of devices and interactions has increased, raising demands for the parallel performance of consensus algorithms. While blockchain addresses trust through decentralized consensus, existing consensus algorithms face bottlenecks as applications scale, especially in handling many concurrent transactions. To increase throughput, some BFT efforts [21,23] use sharding techniques to increase parallelism, but these protocols either require complex cross-shard coordination or rely on off-chain transactions at the expense of partial decentralization. Moreover, they rely on partially synchronous assumptions to collect sufficient sharding consensus results, and are therefore susceptible to stalling in the event of an intermittent network attack [24].

In recent years, directed acyclic graph (DAG)-based asynchronous BFT protocols [10,19,36] have gradually become a research hotspot because they improve throughput while taking robustness into account. As shown in Fig. 1, these protocols aim to improve throughput by dividing the consensus process into communication and ordering layers, enabling parallel execution of block broadcasting and protocol agreement. Specifically, the DAG-based BFT protocol runs in consecutive rounds and embeds a threshold signature share into a certain round to designate one of the previous blocks as the leader. If this leader block has enough votes (also called references in the DAG-based BFT protocol, represented as arrows in Fig. 1), it and its ancestor blocks can be committed. Obviously, the DAG-based BFT protocol does not require a separate agreement phase and does not hinder the broadcasting of blocks due to consensus, and it realizes the parallelism of the two. However, although the DAG structure optimizes the parallelism of the protocol to some extent, it still faces several key issues: First, in order to maintain a DAG structure locally, the node needs to deliver a sufficient number of blocks broadcast by peer nodes before broadcasting a new block to constitute a reference relationship, thus limiting parallel performance. **This inspires us whether we can have nodes broadcast the next block directly without waiting for other peers?** Second, the leader-driven commit mechanism in DAG-based protocols introduces a centralization bias: nodes with suboptimal network conditions face exclusion from consensus because their blocks are less likely to be referenced by subsequent leaders. **This inspires us to wonder if we can design an ordering layer that is fair to slow progressing nodes?**

To cope with the above challenges, this paper proposes a new asynchronous BFT protocol, LSDBFT. The LSDBFT protocol still divides the consensus process into a communication layer and an ordering layer, but unlike existing protocols, the communication layer of LSDBFT employs a kind of loose DAG, avoiding the blocking of nodes waiting for broadcasts from other nodes, and thus realizing a better parallel performance. Like existing DAG-based BFT protocols, block broadcasting in LSDBFT consists of consecutive rounds; the difference is that different nodes in LSDBFT broadcast blocks independently, so nodes do not need to wait for other nodes' blocks to be delivered to start a new round of block

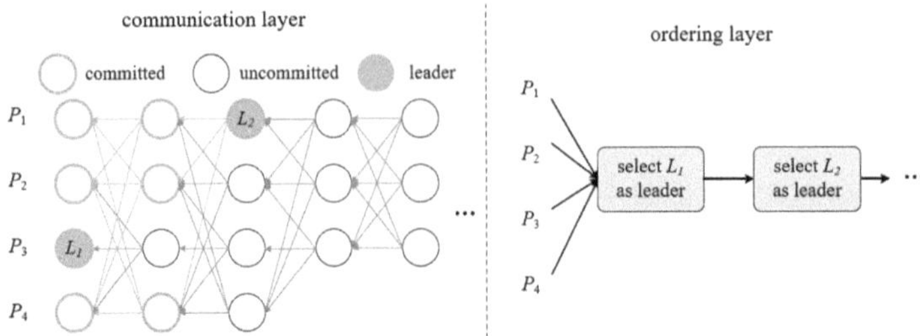

Fig. 1. Structure of the DAG-based BFT consensus.

broadcasting. Instead, a node only needs to send its own block to broadcast the next block. As a proof of delivery, nodes embed the hash value and certificate of the previous block when broadcasting a block, thus forming an intuitively traceable and verifiable broadcast chain. Specifically, blocks on a loose DAG can be categorized into three types: "*regular*", "*input*", and "*post_input*". Before broadcasting a new block, a node checks if it has delivered uncommitted blocks from $n-f$ different nodes, and if so, the new block is of type "*input*", which references these blocks from different nodes. Otherwise, the new block is of type "*regular*". A block of type "*post_input*" indicates that its precursor block is "*input*", which will be useful in the agreement component. Obviously, the reference relationship on the loose DAG is maintained by the "*input*" block and is naturally formed, so that even if not enough blocks from different nodes are delivered, the "*regular*" type can be used to seamlessly broadcast new blocks.

Meanwhile, LSDBFT's ordering layer, by introducing asynchronous binary agreement (ABA), allows nodes to agree on the total ordering of historical blocks on a fairer basis, avoiding the unfairness associated with leader block-driven commitment. Specifically, the agreement component of the ordering layer receives input from the communication layer and then externalizes a preparation step and an ABA instance. Our approach to embedding the inputs of the agreement component into the communication layer is similar to the DAG protocol's embedding of the leader election share into the block broadcast round, except that our inputs are referential relationships of "*input*" blocks instead of the election shares. The ABA instance will decide whether to accept some node's input from the communication layer (i.e., a certain "*input*" block) as a consensus. We demonstrate the security of the LSDBFT protocol in an asynchronous network model and verify its efficiency through experimental evaluation. In summary, the main contributions of this paper are as follows.

- We identify parallel performance flaws in existing DAG-based BFT protocol due to waiting for peer nodes to broadcast, as well as unfairness in the leader block-driven commit approach.
- We propose a loose DAG structure to replace the traditional strict DAG, which allows each node to continuously broadcast new blocks without con-

sidering peer nodes, avoiding the blocking period caused by constructing reference relations.
- We integrated the ABA protocol on the loose DAG, thus building the LSDBFT protocol, which achieves high throughput while enabling the blocks of slow progressing nodes to have a chance to be committed in a more fair way.

The remainder of this paper is organized as follows. Section 2 reviews some related work. Section 3 describes the system model and building blocks. Section 4 provides the design and theoretical analysis of the LSDBFT consensus algorithm. Section 5 presents the experiment evaluation and results. Section 6 concludes the paper.

2 Related Work

With the proposal of HoneyBadgerBFT, the first practical asynchronous BFT protocol, more and more BFT researches are turning to asynchronous network models to enhance the protocol's resistance to unpredictable network environments. In addition, the DAG structure has also gained much popularity in recent years as a technique to enhance throughput. We present some related works in the following.

Asynchronous non-DAG-Based BFT Protocols. The exploration of asynchronous BFT protocols began with the ABA protocol [3,7], which allows agreement on binary values. However, due to its inability to reach consensus on arbitrary values, the ABA protocol was not suitable for blockchain systems. This limitation was overcome with the introduction of HoneyBadgerBFT [24], the first practical asynchronous BFT protocol. HoneyBadgerBFT constructs asynchronous common subsets by combining n reliable broadcast (RBC) and n ABA instances, reaching consensus on which input values to include in the output based on the results from the ABA instances. Later, the Dumbo protocols sought to improve efficiency in the agreement phase, with Dumbo1 reducing the number of ABA instances to κ independent of n, and Dumbo2 running only a constant number of ABA instances. Other notable protocols include BEAT [12], EPIC [22], and PACE [37]. BEAT employs various cryptographic and coding techniques [8,18,33] to create five protocols tailored for different use cases. EPIC focuses on safety, offering an asynchronous BFT protocol with adaptive security. PACE introduces the reproposable asynchronous binary agreement (RABA), providing a framework for fully parallelizing multi-ABA protocols. There are also asynchronous BFT protocols that do not use the ABA module and they are based on view changes [1,6,14,16].

DAG-Based BFT Protocols. The broadcast and agreement (consensus) phases of the traditional asynchronous BFT consensus are usually serial, with the consensus preventing the broadcast of new blocks. To enable parallel data processing, the DAG structure [31] has been incorporated into the BFT consensus, dividing the protocol into two layers: the communication layer and the ordering layer. In the communication layer, nodes construct a structured DAG through a series of broadcasts. In the ordering layer, each node independently observes its local DAG and sequences all blocks. DAG-Rider [19], as the pioneering asynchronous BFT protocol to employ DAG structures, has substantially influenced the development of subsequent DAG-based BFT protocols. However, its high memory requirements due to weak linkages hindered practical adoption. Following DAG-Rider, protocols such as Tusk [10] and Bullshark [36] were introduced, which disable weak linkages to limit the memory overhead while reducing consensus latency. Recent work Wahoo [9] reduces the message complexity and latency of DAG-based BFT protocols by integrating lightweight broadcast protocols. Shoal [35] and Sailfish [34] are two other DAG research works under partial synchronization. Shoal is a protocol-agnostic framework that enhances consensus with leader reputation and pipelining, reducing latency and timeouts for "universal responsiveness." Sailfish supports leader vertices per round, needing one RBC round and a communication step for leaders, plus an extra RBC round for non-leaders. It also allows multiple leaders per round, committing all leaders in one RBC round and a communication step.

3 Preliminaries

Model. We consider distributed computing systems, where f out of n nodes may fail arbitrarily (Byzantine failures). Each node has a unique identity denoted as $P_i \in \{P_i\}_{i \in [n]}$, where $[n]$ denotes the integers $[1, 2, \cdots, n]$. Here, f is defined as $f = \lfloor (n-1)/3 \rfloor$. We assume that an adversary $\mathcal{A}$ can coordinate at most one-third of the nodes to engage in malicious activities. The nodes are interconnected through a network of reliable communication links, ensuring that messages are eventually and accurately transmitted between operational nodes. The system operates asynchronously, with the caveat that $\mathcal{A}$ may introduce arbitrary, though finite, delays in message transmission. Our system employs standard configurations of public key infrastructure (PKI). It is also assumed that the adversary has limited computational resources and, as a result, cannot compromise the integrity of the PKI or the threshold encryption mechanisms.

Step; round; epoch. A communication step consists of receiving a message from another node or sending a message to some node. The block broadcasting of our protocol runs in consecutive rounds, each containing several steps; since we use the PB protocol to propagate blocks, they are also referred to as PB rounds in this paper. Consensus runs in successive epochs, it is a logical concept with no fixed number of steps or rounds.

Provable Broadcast (PB). PB [1,6,16,30] is a broadcast protocol among n nodes with a designated node called sender P_s and a global predicate Q for validating the sender's input. The structure of PB involves two communication steps: In the first step, P_s trasmits m to all nodes. Upon receiving m, the node verifies it using Q and sends its threshold signature share ρ back to P_s. After collecting $n - f$ valid shares (second step), P_s aggregates them into a single signature σ, which serves as a proof of consistency (certificate). P_s distributes

σ to other nodes via an additional 'Finish' step to help them deliver m. In our design, nodes broadcast blocks through successive PB instances, and the 'Finish' step of one PB instance overlaps with the first step of the next PB instance.

Global perfect coin (GPC). Global perfect coin (GPC) [1,3] works as a global function; it produces outputs when no less than a specified threshold number of nodes trigger it, which has the following properties (parameter n is the total number of nodes, t is the threshold):

- Agreement. If two correct nodes receive output l and l' respectively, then $l = l'$.
- Termination. If at least t nodes invoke GPC, each node will receive an output.
- Unpredictability. If at most $t - 1$ nodes invoke GPC, none of the nodes can predict the result.
- Fairness. For any l and l' within the set $[n]$, the probability of the output being l is equivalent to that of l'.

The GPC component can be efficiently implemented using threshold signatures [4,15,20,32]. In an asynchronous Byzantine environment, the threshold t for GPC is typically set as $\lfloor (n-1)/3 \rfloor$.

Asynchronous Binary Agreement (ABA). In asynchronous binary agreement (ABA) [25,29], each node has a single bit (0/1) input, and the goal is to reach agreement on the decided bit. The ABA protocol has the following properties:

- Agreement. If two correct nodes decide b and b', respectively, then $b = b'$.
- Termination. If all correct nodes has an input, each correct node eventually decides a bit.
- Validity. If any correct node decides b, then at least one correct node inputs b.

The ABA protocol progresses in rounds, each consisting of a small number of steps. At the beginning of each round, each node inputs a single bit. At the end of the round, each node queries the common coin to decide whether to terminate the protocol or propose a value for the next round. The common coin operates similarly to the GPC, but its output is limited to either 1 or 0, with each outcome having an equal probability.

4 The LSDBFT Protocol

This section describes the construction of the LSDBFT protocol, which consists of two layers: a communication layer responsible for non-blocking block propagation and an ordering layer dedicated to establishing a fair total ordering of blocks across the network.

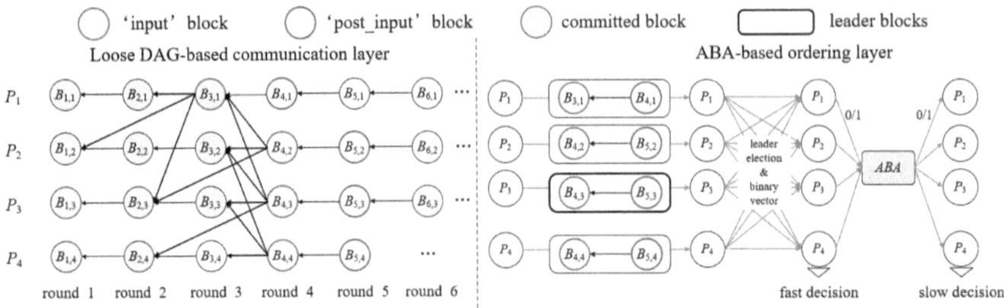

Fig. 2. Structure of the LSDBFT protocol.

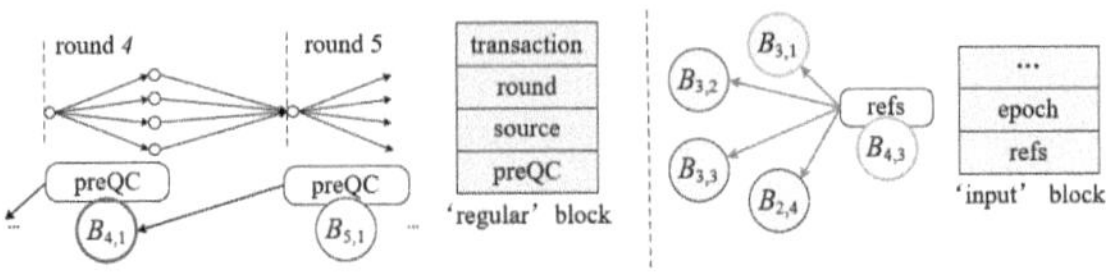

Fig. 3. Block structure.

4.1 The Communication Layer

As depicted in Fig. 2, the LSDBFT protocol introduces an innovative two-layered architecture that separates block broadcasting from consensus ordering. At its core, the communication layer utilizes a loose DAG structure, where each node independently broadcasts blocks through consecutive PB instances. This design eliminates cross-node dependencies: a node advances along its path by aggregating threshold signatures for its own blocks, without needing to synchronize with its peers. For example, node P_i broadcasts $B_{r,i}$ and immediately initiates $B_{r+1,i}$ after delivering $B_{r,i}$, using certificates $\sigma_{r,i}$ as self-contained progress triggers. In other words, the node simply references its own previous block when broadcasting a new block. In loose DAG, each block embeds the hash and threshold certificate of the previous block, forming a verifiable and tamper-proof sequence. This design ensures traceability, as any block's validity can be confirmed by checking its embedded cryptographic references against prior blocks in the path. As shown in Fig. 3, each block can be considered as a "*regular*" block, while the "*input*" block is built on top of the "regular" block and contains the messages required by agreement components such as consensus epoch number and reference. By decoupling block broadcasting from consensus dependencies, LSDBFT achieves non-blocking parallelism in cross-node broadcasting, thereby enhancing throughput.

4.2 The Ordering Layer

The ordering layer, depicted in the right part of Fig. 2, addresses the challenge of establishing a globally agreed sequence of blocks from the loose DAG. It

Algorithm 1. Utilities

```
struct Block{
    pl, r, p   // transaction payload, broadcast round number, and node number
    cert   // certificate for precursor block
    label   // Optional "regular", "input" and "post_input"
    epoch   // consensus epoch number, this field is empty if label == regular
    rv   // reference vector of length n, non-empty when label == input
}
function GenBlock(r, p){
    initialize a Block as B
    B.pl ← packing a batch of transactions
    B.r ← r, B.p ← p, B.cert ← ∅, B.label ← "regular", B.epoch ← 0, B.rv ← ∅
    return B
}
function precursor(B){   return B' with B'.r = B.r − 1 and B'.p = B.p   }
```

receives inputs from the communication layer and orchestrates a two-phase process involving preparation and ABA phases. The input to the communication layer refers to the references carried by the "*input*" block: in fact, a node creates a block B of type "regular" by default, and if it checks that new blocks have been delivered from no less than $n - f$ nodes, it sets B to type "input" and constructs a reference relation based on the newest delivered blocks. Immediately following the "*input*" block is the "*post_input*" block, which is based on the "*regular*" block and contains the epoch number but not the reference. When a node delivers $n - f$ different "*post_input*" blocks, meaning in the current consensus epoch of the component of the protocol, it can enter the preparation phase and execute an ABA instance.

The preparation phase requires only one communication step for the transmission of the leader election shares and binary vectors bv. Finally, the node generates a leader through sufficient share, and then inputs 1 or 0 into the ABA instance of that leader's communication layer input, depending on the received binary vectors. If the ABA instance outputs 1, then all correct nodes accept the leader's "*input*" block and sort and commit uncommitted history blocks based on references to in this leader block. We allow the ABA instance to output 0, because ABA instances in subsequent epochs can also commit the current history blocks. In each consensus epoch, a node has two chances to make a decision. After revealing the leader, if a node realizes that it has already delivered the leader's "*post_input*" block, it can decide on the leader's "*input*" block without waiting for the execution of the ABA instance, called a fast decision. A node that fails to make a fast decision can wait for the output of the ABA instance before deciding, known as a slow decision. In terms of security, it is guaranteed that if a correct node makes a fast decision, then the ABA instance outputs a bit value of 1, which ensures that all correct nodes will slow-decide the same "*input*" block at the latest. Regarding the commit of historical blocks, an example has been given in Fig. 2: different nodes decide on an "input" block $B_{4,3}$ by means of the agreement component in the ordering layer, and then commit the block referenced by $B_{4,3}$ and all the predecessor blocks. The commit sequence is $B_{1,1}, B_{1,2}, B_{1,3}, B_{1,4}, B_{2,1}, B_{2,2}, B_{2,3}, B_{2,4}, B_{3,1}, B_{3,2}, B_{3,3}$. Obviously, the way to delineate the history of blocks that can be committed is similar to the DAG-based BFT protocol, with the difference that if a node in LSDBFT delivers the r-th block of another node, then it must also deliver the first $r-1$ blocks of that node. Thus, the range of blocks involved in a reference to an "input" block can be represented by a vector rv, where the p-th term of this vector, $rv[p]$, indicates that the first $rv[p]$ blocks of node P_p is the history blocks referenced by the "input" block. The new consensus epoch is triggered by the completion of the ABA instance and advances asynchronously with the broadcast round.

4.3 Detailed Design of the Protocol

Algorithm 2 and Algorithm 3 describe the details of the protocol on the broadcast component and the agreement component, respectively. To facilitate the description of the protocol, Algorithm 1 provides the block structure and functions. The *Block* is the block transmitted by each node in the communication layer, which is categorized into "*regular*", "*input*" and "*post_input*" types (line 4 of Algorithm 1). To simplify the description in this section, we use another concept, the reference vector rv, instead of references (line 6 of Algorithm 1). It is an index of length n, where each bit ($rv[p]$) represents the latest block delivered by the "*input*" block sending node from the node (P_p). We can let $B_{r,i}$ denote the r-th block broadcast by node P_i i.e. $B.r = r$ and $B.p = i$. Each node P_i operates as follows:

Initialization. Each node is initialized with a broadcast round counter $r = 1$, a consensus epoch counter $Ecur = 1$ and the highest consensus epoch number $E\_has\_input = 0$ that has had input to the agreement component. In addition, each node will also locally maintain two vectors, v_{dlp} and v_{cmp}, where the former records the latest block delivery progress of that node on n paths, and the latter indicates the latest block submission progress of that node on n paths. For example, $v_{dlp}[p] = r$ ($v_{cmp}[p] = r$) indicates that the node delivered (committed) the first r blocks from node P_p.

Block Broadcasting. At the beginning of each broadcast round, node P_i creates a block via function $GenBlock()$, including loading transactions, initializing broadcast round number and node number (line 1–2 of Algorithm 2). If it is not the first round, the node assigns the certificate $\sigma_{r-1,i}$ of the predecessor block to the *cert* field of the current block B (line 3 of Algorithm 2) so that the other nodes can deliver the block $precursor(B)$, i.e., $B_{r-1,i}$, based on the certificate $B.cert$. If P_i has not yet provided input to the AC for $Ecur$ and has delivered the new blocks from $n-f$ distinct nodes, it constructs a reference vector rv, where $rv[a]$ records the latest delivered round of each node P_a (line 4–6 of Algorithm 2). If $rv[x]$ is 0 it means that node P_i has not yet delivered any blocks of node P_x or the delivered blocks have all been committed. Subsequently, node P_i assigns rv, $Ecur$, and "*input*" to the rv, *epoch*, and *label* fields of block B, and updates E_has_input to $Ecur$ to avoid duplicating input (line 7 of Algorithm 2). If the

Algorithm 2. The broadcast component of LSDBFT protocol (for node P_i)

Initialize a delivery progress vector v_{dlp} and a commit progress vector v_{cmp} of length n with elements all 0. The broadcast round r and the consensus epoch $Ecur$ are initialized by 1 and both grow independently.

1: **start** broadcasting round r:
2: $B \leftarrow GenBlock(r, i)$
3: **if** $r > 1$ **then**: $B.cert \leftarrow \sigma_{r-1,i}$
4: **If** $Ecur > E\_has\_input$ **and** node P_i delivers the latest broadcast blocks of $n - f$ nodes **then**:
5: $rv \leftarrow$ initialize an all-zero vector of length n
6: **for** $x \in [n]$: **if** $v_{dlp}[x] > v_{cmp}[x]$ **then**: $rv[x] \leftarrow v_{dlp}[x]$
7: $B.rv \leftarrow rv$, $B.epoch \leftarrow Ecur$, $B.label \leftarrow$ *"input"*, $E\_has\_input \leftarrow Ecur$
8: **If** $precursor(B).label ==$ *"input"* **then**:
9: $B.label \leftarrow$ *"post_input"*, $B.epoch \leftarrow precursor(B).epoch$
10: **broadcast** B $(B_{r,i})$
11: **upon** collecting $n - f$ valid threshold signature shares on B:
12: aggregate these shares into a single certificate $\sigma_{r,i}$
13: $v_{dlp}[i] \leftarrow r$, deliver $B_{r,i}$, **moving** on to the next broadcasting round $r + 1$

14: **upon** receiving block B' $(B'.r = r', B'.p = p)$ from node P_p:
15: **if** $r' > 1$ **and** $B'.cert$ is valid **then**:
16: **if** $r' == 2$ **then**: $v_{dlp}[p] \leftarrow 1$
17: **else**: **wait** until $v_{dlp}[p] == r' - 2$: $v_{dlp}[p] \leftarrow r' - 1$
18: deliver $B_{r'-1,p}$
19: **if** $B'.label ==$ *"input"* **then**:
20: **wait** until blocks delineated by $B'.rv$ have been delivered
21: generate a partial signature on the B''s hash and send back to P_q

precursor block of B is the "*input*" block, then set the label of B to *post_input* and assign a consensus epoch number consistent with the precursor (line 8–9 of Algorithm 2). After doing the above assignment operation, node P_i transmits block B through a PB instance (line 10 of Algorithm 2). The first communication step of the PB instance node P_i is to broadcast B and the second step is to collect partial signatures from different nodes. After collecting enough shares of valid threshold signatures, node P_i aggregates them into a complete certificate $\sigma_{r,i}$ (line 11–12 of Algorithm 2). At this moment, P_i delivers $B_{r,i}$, and can update the latest delivery progress on its own path and move on to the next broadcast round (line 13 of Algorithm 2).

Being a participant in the PB instances of other nodes, node P_i receives and verifies the blocks broadcast from other nodes (line 14–21 of Algorithm 2). Suppose the received block is $B' = B_{r',p}$. Node P_i verifies the certificate carried by B', delivers the precursor block and updates $v_{dlp}[p]$ to $r' - 1$ (line 15–18 of Algorithm 2). Note that delivery of block $B_{r'-1,p}$ presupposes delivery of $B_{r'-2,p}$, i.e., $v_{dlp}[p]$ grows unidirectionally. If B' is labeled "*input*", then P_i waits to deliver the blocks delimited by $B'.rv$ (line 19–20 of Algorithm 2). In

Algorithm 3. The agreement component of LSDBFT protocol (for node P_i)

1: **upon** delivering $n - f$ blocks labeled "*post_input*" with epoch number $Ecur$:
2: $bv \leftarrow$ initialize a binary vector of all zeros of length n
3: **for** $a \in [n]$: **if** P_a's block B labeled "*input*" with epoch number $Ecur$ is delivered **then**:
4: $bv[a] \leftarrow 1$
5: $share \leftarrow$ generate a threshold signature share
6: **broadcast** the ready message $\{bv, share\}$ for ABA
7: **upon** receiving $n - f$ ready messages:
8: $decided \leftarrow false$
9: get the leader number l utilizing the GPC component
10: **if** P_l's block B labeled "*post_input*" with epoch number $Ecur$ has been delivered **then**:
11: **decide** $precursor(B).rv$, $decided \leftarrow true$
12: **committing** uncommitted historical blocks delineated by $precursor(B).rv$
13: **for** $x \in [n]$: **if** $v_{cmp} < precursor(B).rv[x]$ **then**: $v_{cmp}[x] \leftarrow precursor(B).rv[x]$
14: $input_b \leftarrow 0$
15: **if** the binary vector bv of any ready message satisfies $bv[l] == 1$ **then**:
16: $input_b \leftarrow 1$
17: **input** $input_b$ to the ABA instance
18: **wait** until the ABA instance to output a bit b:
19: **if** $b == 1$ **and** $decided == false$ **then**:
20: **decide** $precursor(B).rv$, $decided \leftarrow true$
21: **committing** uncommitted historical blocks delineated by $precursor(B).rv$
22: **for** $x \in [n]$: **if** $v_{cmp} < precursor(B).rv[x]$ **then**: $v_{cmp}[x] \leftarrow precursor(B).rv[x]$
23: $Ecur \leftarrow Ecur + 1$

addition, P_i will verify the validity of B, generate a partial signature on its hash and send it back to P_p (line 21 of Algorithm 2).

Preparation Phase for ABA. When no less than $n - f$ "*post_input*" blocks in the same consensus epoch are delivered, node P_i proceeds to the preparation step (line 1 of Algorithm 3). Node P_i initializes a binary vector bv with all terms 0 (line 2 of Algorithm 3). The node then checks each node's "*input*" block, and if the block has been delivered, then sets the corresponding bit of bv to 1 (line 3–4 of Algorithm 3). Finally, P_i also generates a threshold signature share *share* for the election of the leader and broadcasts it with bv (line 5–6 of Algorithm 3).

ABA Execution and Block Commitment. After receiving $n - f$ ready messages, P_i determines a leader P_l using the GPC component (line 7–9 of Algorithm 3). If the "*post_input*" block of the leader node P_l in this consensus epoch has already been delivered, then node P_i can directly determine the vector rv carried by the "*input*" block of P_l and set the flag *decided* to *true* (line 10–11 of Algorithm 3). This is a fast decision making approach that allows nodes to commit historical blocks directly without waiting for ABA output. Note that even if a node makes a fast decision, it needs to participate in the ABA instance to help other nodes make post-ABA decisions. After committing the uncommitted history block delineated by the vector $precursor(B).rv$, P_i updates v_{cmp} according to $precursor(B).rv$ in order to compare the reference vectors for the next epoch (line 12–13 of Algorithm 3). P_i inputs $input_b = 1$ into the ABA instance if the l-th bit of the binary vector bv of any of the ready messages; otherwise, $input_b = 0$ (lines 14–17 of Algorithm 3). Upon the ABA instance outputting $b = 1$, P_i commits the blocks delineated in bv_l (if not already decided). If $b = 0$, the protocol defers commitment to subsequent epochs (lines 18–22 of Algorithm 3). After completing the ABA instance, P_i increments $Ecur$ to begin a new consensus epoch (line 23 of Algorithm 3). The consensus epochs in which different nodes are located are consistent and are guaranteed to produce output from the ABA instance of the current epoch as long as $n - f$ correct nodes have input the agreement component of the current epoch. When an ABA instance produces output, the node will terminate the current consensus epoch and move to the next consensus epoch.

Lying Behavior of Byzantine Nodes on ABA Instance Inputs. Byzantine nodes do not follow the protocol norms and may lie while broadcasting the binary vector bv in two cases.

The case of lying 0 (the Byzantine node sets $bv[l]$ to 0, even if it has delivered P_l's "*input*" block): The Byzantine nodes set the bit in the binary vector that is intended to be 1 to 0 in an attempt to prevent the reaching of consensus. The following explains the inability of this lying behavior to disturb the consensus:

First, each node in an epoch has two opportunities to decide, one is to make a fast decision before executing ABA as in lines 10–13 of Algorithm 3, and one is to make a decision after ABA produces an output and the output is 1 as in lines 18–22 of Algorithm 3. It only needs to be proved that, whenever some correct node has made a quick decision, then the ABA instance necessarily outputs 1. Making a fast book decision implies that the node has delivered the node P_l's "*post_input*" block. According to the continuum of PB instances, there must be at least $n - f$ nodes that have delivered the node P_l's "*input*" block, of which at least $n - 2f$ are correct nodes. These correct nodes will set the l-th bit of their binary vector bv to 1. Therefore, among any $n - f$ ready messages from different nodes, at least one will come from the $n - 2f$ correct nodes. It can be shown that each correct node will input 1 to the ABA instance, and by the validity property of the ABA protocol, its output must be 1.

The Case of Lying 1. (the Byzantine node sets $bv[l]$ to 1, even if P_l crashes.): The Byzantine nodes set the bit in the binary vector that is intended to be 1 to 0 in an attempt to get the correct node to agree on a non-existent input value. To cope with this, we can ask the node to attach the certificates of the corresponding "input" blocks for the bits that are 1's when broadcasting the binary vector.

4.4 Correctness Analysis

The correctness of LSDBFT consists of security, liveness and fairness, which are analyzed in this subsection.
Notation. All committed blocks form a sequence $\mathcal{S}$ called the ledger. The length of this ledger is represented as $|\mathcal{S}|$, and the k-th block within it is referred to as $\mathcal{S}[k]$, for $1 \leq k \leq |\mathcal{S}|$. The sequence comprising the first k elements of $\mathcal{S}$ is indicated as $\mathcal{S}(,k)$. The notation $\preceq$ is used to define a prefix relationship, such that $\mathcal{S}_1 \preceq \mathcal{S}_2$ signifies $\mathcal{S}_1$ is a prefix of $\mathcal{S}_2$. We also define the sequence of blocks committed in some epoch e as S^e, which is a subsequence of the ledger $\mathcal{S}$ satisfying $\mathcal{S} = \{S^1, S^2, \cdots\}$.

Security. The security of LSDBFT, which ensures that the ledgers of different correct nodes do not conflict, can be described by Theorem 1, whose proof is based on three lemmas: Lemma 1, Lemma 2 and Lemma 3.
Integrity of loose DAG. As a relaxed variant of DAG, the loose DAG only requires that the "input" block refer to no less than $n-f$ blocks, while other blocks can be considered to refer to a single predecessor block. Each block is embedded with the predecessor's hash and threshold signature certificate, which is received by the node to verify the hash continuity and signature validity. Continuous execution of PB ensures that different nodes transmit all blocks from a particular node in the same order. Specifically, for any broadcast from sender P_i that generates a valid integer $\sigma_{r,i}$, there are at least $n-2f$ correct nodes that delivered the same sequence of blocks $B_{1,i}, B_{2,i}, \cdots, B_{r-1,i}$. The above property stems from the simple fact that a certificate is an $n-f$ threshold signature of the received block hash, so violating this property would undermine the security of the threshold signature or the collision resistance of the cryptographic hash function.

Lemma 1. *In an epoch, if a correct node P_i decides the reference vector rv_l input by node P_l, all correct nodes will decide rv_l.*

Proof. If P_i decides rv_l by making a quick decision, then the analysis of Byzantine lying behavior in the previous subsection shows that each correct node will receive output 1 from the ABA instance. In addition, the GPC guarantees that all corrects go to the same leader number l. Therefore each correct node decides rv_l.

If P_i waits for the ABA instance to output 1 before deciding rv_l, it is clear that the agreement property of the ABA protocol guarantees that the other correct nodes will also receive output 1 and thus decide rv_l.

Lemma 2. *In an epoch e, if two correct nodes P_i and P_j commit the block sequences S_i^e and S_j^e, respectively, then $S_i^e = S_j^e$.*

Proof. If the ABA instance outputs 0, then $|S_i^e| = 0 = |S_j^e|$. If the ABA instance outputs 1, by Lemma 1, P_i and P_j decide the same vector rv. The consistency of PB guarantees that the range of blocks enclosed by the vector rv appears to be the same in P_i and P_j, thus the commit sequences S_i^e and S_j^e are the same.

Lemma 3. *If the two correct nodes P_i and P_j record ledgers of $\mathcal{S}_i$ and $\mathcal{S}_j$, respectively, then either $\mathcal{S}_i \preceq \mathcal{S}_j$ or $\mathcal{S}_j \preceq \mathcal{S}_i$.*

Proof. Represent the ledger in terms of blocks committed by nodes at each epoch: there are $\mathcal{S}_i = \{S_i^1, S_i^2, \cdots, S_i^p\}$ and $\mathcal{S}_j = \{S_j^1, S_j^2, \cdots, S_j^q\}$. Since the commit sequence for each epoch is globally locked by ABA, only new blocks are appended for subsequent epochs. By Lemma 2, for $e \leq min(p, q)$ satisfies $S_i^e = S_j^e$, this lemma can be proved.

Theorem 1 (Security). *If two correct nodes P_i and P_j commit two blocks B_1 and B_2 with the same sequence number k respectively, then $B_1 = B_2$.*

Proof. Let the ledger maintained by P_i be $\mathcal{S}_i$, and the sequence maintained by P_j be $\mathcal{S}_j$, it is known that B_1 belongs to $\mathcal{S}_i$ and B_2 belongs to $\mathcal{S}_i$, and that $1 \leq k \leq min(|\mathcal{S}_i|, |\mathcal{S}_j|)$. By Lemma 3, either $\mathcal{S}_i \preceq \mathcal{S}_j$ or $\mathcal{S}_j \preceq \mathcal{S}_i$. Without loss of generality, let $\mathcal{S}_j \preceq \mathcal{S}_i$, and thus $\mathcal{S}_j$ is equal to $\mathcal{S}_i(, |\mathcal{S}_j|)$. Consequently, $\mathcal{S}_j[k] = \mathcal{S}_i(, |\mathcal{S}_j|)[k] = \mathcal{S}_i[k]$. Given that $B_1 = \mathcal{S}_i[k]$ and $B_2 = \mathcal{S}_j[k]$, it follows that $B_1 = B_2$.

Liveness. The liveness of LSDBFT, which ensures that the protocol does not stagnate, can be described by Theorem 2, with Lemma 4 as an adjunct.

Lemma 4. *The probability that the correct node commits a sequence S^e of length greater than 0 in an epoch e is at least $2/3$.*

Proof. When a node collects $n - f$ ready messages in the preparation phase, it can get a leader number l from the GPC. Since the node has delivered at least $n - f$ "*post_input*" blocks at this moment, the probability that there exists some block from node P_l among them is at least $(n - f)/n > 2/3$. Therefore, there is at least a $2/3$ probability that the node can directly commit a nonzero sequence by making a fast decision. Moreover, the node knows that all other correct nodes will commit a non-zero sequence of blocks at this epoch.

Theorem 2 (Liveness). *Let $p[\Delta e]$ denote the probability of committing at least one non-zero sequence in Δe consecutive epochs. As Δe increases, the probability $p[\Delta e]$ tends to 1.*

Proof. As stated in Lemma 4, there is more than a $2/3$ probability that a node commits some blocks in an epoch by a fast decision of the preparation phase, and it can be shown that the probability of failing to commit some blocks is less than $1/3$. Thus, the probability of failing to some blocks for Δe consecutive epochs is less than $1/3^{\Delta e}$, and clearly, $\lim_{\Delta e \to +\infty} (1 - \frac{1}{3^{\Delta e}}) \to 1$.

Fairness. The fairness of LSDBFT ensures that every block proposed by the correct node will eventually be committed regardless of its network conditions, which is described by Theorem 3.

Theorem 3 (Fairness). *Any block $B_{r,i}$ proposed by any correct node P_i will eventually be committed.*

Proof. Starting from P_i broadcasting $B_{r,i}$, after collecting enough signature shares on $B_{r,i}$ hashes, P_i aggregates these signature shares into $B_{r,i}$ certificates $\sigma_{r,i}$ and broadcasts them along with a new block $B_{r+1,i}$. In the asynchronous network, the certificate $\sigma_{r,i}$ is eventually received by all correct nodes. Thereafter, the i-th bit of the reference vector proposed by all correct nodes must be higher than or equal to r. Combined with the above analysis of liveness, it can be seen that any node will deliver at least $n-2f$ "*post_input*" blocks from the correct nodes, and thus each consensus epoch has at least 1/3 probability of being able to commit a sequence of blocks containing $B_{r,i}$. Clearly, the probability of $B_{r,i}$ being committed tends to 1 as the epoch progresses.

Table 1. Comparison with the DAG-based asynchronous BFT protocols. "**Non-blocking broadcast**" means that the block broadcast does not have to wait for the delivery of the peer's blocks.

	Broadcast and agreement in parallel	Non-blocking broadcast	Fairness	Message complexity	Time complexity
DAG-Rider	✔	✗	✗	$O(n^3)$	$O(1)$
Bullshark	✔	✗	✗	$O(n^3)$	$O(1)$
Tusk	✔	✗	✗	$O(n^3)$	$O(1)$
Wahoo	✔	✗	✗	$O(n^2)$	$O(1)$
LSDBFT (This)	✔	✔	✔	$O(n^2)$	$O(1)$

4.5 Efficiency Analysis

Consistent with the DAG-based BFT protocol, the time complexity of LSDBFT is $O(1)$. After three asynchronous steps, each node is ready to broadcast a block message carrying the reference vectors, and after five more asynchronous steps, each node enters the preparation step for ABA, and finally executes an ABA instance. Therefore, the time complexity of eight asynchronous steps plus one ABA instance is $O(1)$. The communication layer of LSDBFT uses the PB protocol to broadcast each block, each PB has a message complexity of $O(n)$, thus n concurrent PBs have a complexity of $O(n^2)$. Outside the communication layer, LSDBFT requires nodes to participate in a preparation phase and an ABA instance with a complexity of $O(n^2)$. Overall, the message complexity of the LSDBFT protocol is $O(n^2)$. A comparison of the relevant protocols is listed in Table 1.

5 Experimental Evaluation

5.1 Setting

In our evaluation experiments, we develop prototype of the LSDBFT protocol, which are implemented using Go and utilize a dedis library dedicated to the bn256-based Boneh-Lynn-Shacham (BLS) threshold signature scheme. The ABA module in LSDBFT is implemented using the versions in [17]. We choose the state-of-the-art Tusk and Wahoo protocols for comparison. For fairness, we use PB instead of RBC to broadcast blocks when implementing Tusk. The transaction size is fixed at 250 bytes and the batch size varies from 1024 to 16384. Our performance evaluation is centred around two key metrics: latency and throughput. Latency is the average time from when a block is broadcast to when it is committed, and throughput is the average number of transactions processed per second (TPS). We perform our experiments under Byzantine attack. Specifically, we set $\lfloor n/5 \rfloor$ nodes as Byzantine nodes, which exhibited malicious behaviors such as broadcasting conflicting blocks, refusing to participate in ABA voting and forging reference vectors.

The experiments are carried out on a cluster of ecs.e-c1m1.large servers hosted on Alibaba Cloud. Each server instance is equipped with 2 virtual CPUs and 2 GiB of memory, with only one consensus node deployed on each server. To minimize communication costs, the experiments are conducted within a LAN environment, and real network conditions are simulated using the traffic control tool tc, which introduces a sending delay ranging from 1ms to 50ms. Each experiment is repeated three times and averages are calculated to ensure accuracy.

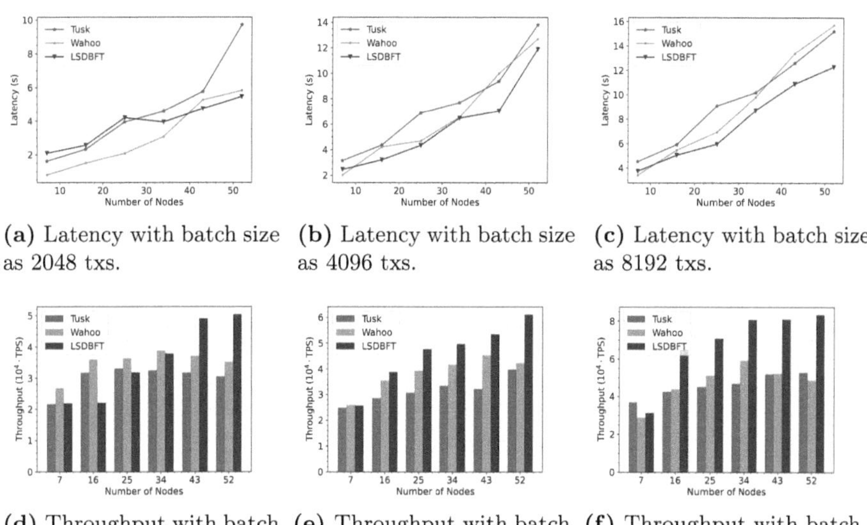

(a) Latency with batch size as 2048 txs.

(b) Latency with batch size as 4096 txs.

(c) Latency with batch size as 8192 txs.

(d) Throughput with batch size as 2048 txs.

(e) Throughput with batch size as 4096 txs.

(f) Throughput with batch size as 8192 txs.

Fig. 4. Latency and throughput when scaling the number of nodes.

5.2 System Scale Scalability Performance

As illustrated in Fig. 4, the performance of LSDBFT, Tusk, and Wahoo under varying system scales (7 to 52 nodes) demonstrates distinct trends in latency and throughput. For latency, LSDBFT exhibits a gradual increase. Specifically, when the number of nodes is small, the latency of the three protocols is comparable; as the number of nodes increases, LSDBFT begins to exhibit lower latency, and this phenomenon becomes more significant as the batch size increases. For throughput, LSDBFT maintains superior scalability. Specifically, as the number of nodes increases, the throughput of both Tusk and Wahoo first increases to a peak and then shows a trend of maintaining or decreasing. LSDBFT does not suffer from this limitation and shows good scalability performance as the system size increases, with throughputs approaching 50000 TPS, 60000 TPS and 80000 TPS for the three batches of systems. This compares to 31000 TPS, 40,000 TPS and 50000 TPS for Tusk, and 39000 TPS, 45000 TPS and 59000 TPS for Wahoo. These advantages of LSDBFT stem from LSDBFT's looose-DAG communication layer, which eliminates dependencies on peer block deliveries, enabling nodes to broadcast blocks independently. In contrast, Tusk and Wahoo suffer from higher synchronization overhead because their communication layers are based on strict DAG, where nodes must wait for sufficient peer blocks before proceeding.

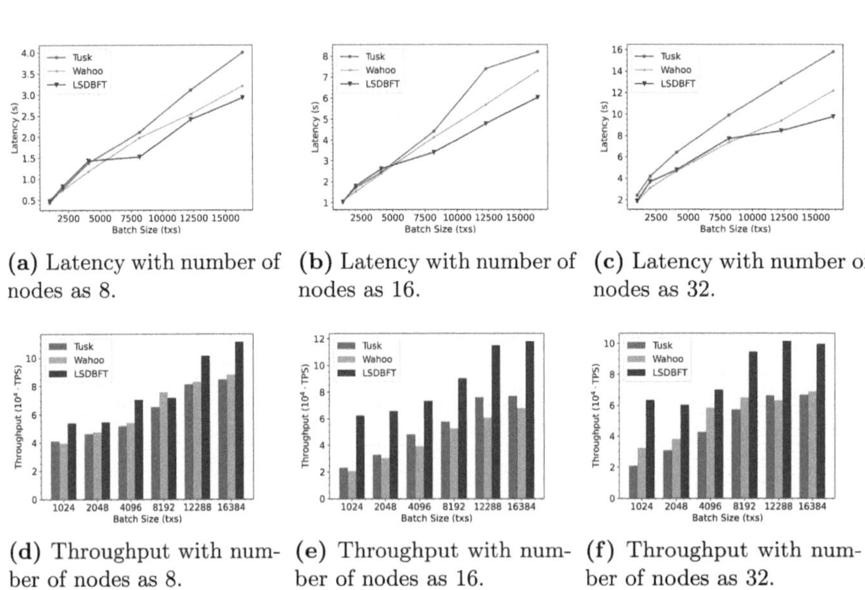

(a) Latency with number of nodes as 8. (b) Latency with number of nodes as 16. (c) Latency with number of nodes as 32.

(d) Throughput with number of nodes as 8. (e) Throughput with number of nodes as 16. (f) Throughput with number of nodes as 32.

Fig. 5. Latency and throughput when increasing batch size.

5.3 Batch Size Scalability Performance

The scaling performance of LSDBFT, Tusk, and Wahoo for different batch sizes (1k to 16k transactions per block) is shown in Fig. 5. Overall, the latency and throughput of all three protocols tend to increase as the batch size increases. This is because when the batch size increases, each block contains more transactions, potentially boosting throughput but leading to an increase in latency because it takes more time to process larger blocks. In contrast, LSDBFT shows a more moderate increase in latency and a more significant increase in throughput. Although LSDBFT also shows a stagnation in throughput growth when the number of nodes is 32 and the batch size increases above 10k, it still has a significant advantage over Tusk and Wahoo. This difference reaffirms the parallelism advantage of LSDBFT, whose loose DAG stucture in the communication layer allow larger batches to fully utilize bandwidth and computational resources, whereas DAG-based protocols encounter bottlenecks due to sequential verification of inter-block references.

5.4 The Tradeoff Between Latency and Throughput

Figure 6 illustrates the latency-throughput trade-off relationship for each protocol as the number of nodes increases and the batch size increases. As the number of nodes grows, LSDBFT maintains a balanced tradeoff, achieving significantly higher throughput with only a moderate increase in latency. This contrasts sharply with existing DAG-based protocols, where latency escalates more rapidly due to synchronization overhead from inter-block dependencies. LSDBFT's loose-DAG communication layer eliminates such dependencies, enabling nodes to propagate blocks independently. Consequently, even in large-scale deployments, LSDBFT sustains high throughput without incurring prohibitive latency penalties.

Similarly, when batch sizes expand, LSDBFT efficiently leverages increased transaction volumes to boost throughput while mitigating latency growth. In scenarios demanding comparable throughput levels, LSDBFT achieves this with markedly lower latency, underscoring its efficiency. Meanwhile, at equivalent latency thresholds, LSDBFT delivers substantially higher throughput, highlighting its ability to prioritize performance without compromising responsiveness.

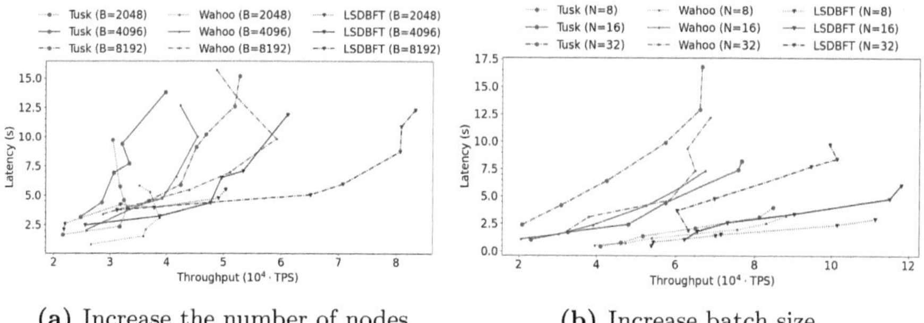

(a) Increase the number of nodes. **(b)** Increase batch size.

Fig. 6. Throughput vs. latency.

6 Conclusion

This paper presents LSDBFT, a novel asynchronous BFT consensus protocol designed to address the parallelism limitations and fairness issues inherent in DAG-based BFT protocols. By reimagining the communication and ordering layers, LSDBFT achieves significant performance improvements in both throughput and latency while ensuring decentralized fairness. The loose DAG-based communication layer eliminates dependencies on peer block deliveries, enabling nodes to broadcast blocks independently. This design circumvents the synchronization bottlenecks observed in strict DAG-based protocols like Tusk and Wahoo, where nodes must wait for sufficient peer blocks to construct reference relationships. Meanwhile, the ABA-driven ordering layer replaces leader-centric commitment with a decentralized agreement mechanism, ensuring equitable block ordering without favoring specific nodes. Theoretical analysis confirms LSDBFT's security and liveness under asynchronous networks and experimental evaluations validate LSDBFT's superiority across diverse scenarios. In summary, by pushing asynchronous consensus closer to true parallelism, LSDBFT paves the way for scalable and trustless decentralized infrastructures.

Acknowledgement. This work was supported in part by the Innovation Program of Shanghai Municipal Education Commission under Grant 2021-01-07-00-08E00101 and in part by the "Digital Silk Road" Shanghai International Joint Laboratory of Trustworthy Intelligent Software under Grant 22510750100.

References

1. Abraham, I., Malkhi, D., Spiegelman, A.: Asymptotically optimal validated asynchronous byzantine agreement. In: Proceedings of the 2019 ACM Symposium on Principles of Distributed Computing, PODC 2019, pp. 337–346 (2019)
2. Antonopoulos, A.M., Wood, G.: Mastering Ethereum: Building Smart Contracts and Dapps. O'reilly Media (2018)
3. Ben-Or, M.: Another advantage of free choice (extended abstract): completely asynchronous agreement protocols. In: Proceedings of the Second Annual ACM Symposium on Principles of Distributed Computing, PODC 1983, pp. 27–30 (1983)
4. Boneh, D., Lynn, B., Shacham, H.: Short signatures from the weil pairing. In: Proceedings of the 7th International Conference on the Theory and Application of Cryptology and Information Security: Advances in Cryptology, ASIACRYPT 2001, pp. 514–532 (2001)
5. Buchman, E., Kwon, J., Milosevic, Z.: The latest gossip on bft consensus. arXiv preprint arXiv:1807.04938 (2018)
6. Cachin, C., Kursawe, K., Petzold, F., Shoup, V.: Secure and efficient asynchronous broadcast protocols. In: Proceedings of the 21st Annual International Cryptology Conference on Advances in Cryptology, CRYPTO 2001, pp. 524–541. Springer, Berlin, Heidelberg (2001)
7. Cachin, C., Kursawe, K., Shoup, V.: Random oracles in constantipole: practical asynchronous byzantine agreement using cryptography (extended abstract). In: Proceedings of the Nineteenth Annual ACM Symposium on Principles of Distributed Computing, PODC 2000, pp. 123–132 (2000)

8. Cachin, C., Kursawe, K., Shoup, V.: Random oracles in constantinople: practical asynchronous byzantine agreement using cryptography. J. Cryptol. **18**(3), 219–246 (2005)
9. Dai, X., et al.: Wahoo: a dag-based bft consensus with low latency and low communication overhead. IEEE Trans. Inf. Forensics Secur. **19**, 7508–7522 (2024)
10. Danezis, G., Kokoris-Kogias, L., Sonnino, A., Spiegelman, A.: Narwhal and tusk: a dag-based mempool and efficient bft consensus. In: Proceedings of the Seventeenth European Conference on Computer Systems, EuroSys 2022, pp. 34–50 (2022)
11. Das, D., Banerjee, S., Chatterjee, P., Ghosh, U., Biswas, U.: Blockchain for intelligent transportation systems: applications, challenges, and opportunities. IEEE Internet Things J. **10**(21), 18961–18970 (2023)
12. Duan, S., Reiter, M.K., Zhang, H.: Beat: asynchronous bft made practical. In: Proceedings of the 2018 ACM SIGSAC Conference on Computer and Communications Security, CCS 2018, pp. 2028–2041 (2018)
13. Dui, H., Zhang, S., Liu, M., Dong, X., Bai, G.: Iot-enabled real-time traffic monitoring and control management for intelligent transportation systems. IEEE Internet Things J. **11**(9), 15842–15854 (2024)
14. Gao, Y., Lu, Y., Lu, Z., Tang, Q., Xu, J., Zhang, Z.: Dumbo-ng: fast asynchronous bft consensus with throughput-oblivious latency. In: Proceedings of the 2022 ACM SIGSAC Conference on Computer and Communications Security, CCS 2022, pp. 1187–1201 (2022)
15. Gennaro, R., Goldfeder, S.: Fast multiparty threshold ecdsa with fast trustless setup. In: Proceedings of the 2018 ACM SIGSAC Conference on Computer and Communications Security, CCS 2018, pp. 1179–1194. (2018)
16. Guo, B., Lu, Y., Lu, Z., Tang, Q., Xu, J., Zhang, Z.: Speeding dumbo: pushing asynchronous bft closer to practice. IACR Cryptol. ePrint Arch. **2022**, 27 (2022)
17. Guo, B., Lu, Z., Tang, Q., Xu, J., Zhang, Z.: Dumbo: faster asynchronous bft protocols. In: Proceedings of the 2020 ACM SIGSAC Conference on Computer and Communications Security, CCS 2020, pp. 803–818 (2020)
18. Huang, C., Chen, M., Li, J.: Pyramid codes: flexible schemes to trade space for access efficiency in reliable data storage systems. ACM Trans. Storage **9**(1) (2013)
19. Keidar, I., Kokoris-Kogias, E., Naor, O., Spiegelman, A.: All you need is dag. In: Proceedings of the 2021 ACM Symposium on Principles of Distributed Computing, PODC 2021, pp. 165–175 (2021)
20. Libert, B., Joye, M., Yung, M.: Born and raised distributively: fully distributed non-interactive adaptively-secure threshold signatures with short shares. In: Proceedings of the 2014 ACM Symposium on Principles of Distributed Computing, PODC 2014, pp. 303–312 (2014)
21. Liu, A., et al.: Cherubim: a secure and highly parallel cross-shard consensus using quadruple pipelined two-phase commit for sharding blockchains. IEEE Trans. Inf. Forensics Secur. **19**, 3178–3193 (2024)
22. Liu, C., Duan, S., Zhang, H.: Epic: efficient asynchronous bft with adaptive security. In: 2020 50th Annual IEEE/IFIP International Conference on Dependable Systems and Networks (DSN), pp. 437–451 (2020)
23. Liu, Y., et al.: A flexible sharding blockchain protocol based on cross-shard byzantine fault tolerance. IEEE Trans. Inf. Forensics Secur. **18**, 2276–2291 (2023)
24. Miller, A., Xia, Y., Croman, K., Shi, E., Song, D.: The honey badger of bft protocols. In: Proceedings of the 2016 ACM SIGSAC Conference on Computer and Communications Security, CCS 2016, pp. 31–42 (2016)

25. Mostefaoui, A., Moumen, H., Raynal, M.: Signature-free asynchronous byzantine consensus with t < n/3 and o(n2) messages. In: Proceedings of the 2014 ACM Symposium on Principles of Distributed Computing, PODC 2014, pp. 2–9 (2014)
26. Nakamoto, S.: Bitcoin: a peer-to-peer electronic cash system (2008)
27. Nguyen, T., Nguyen, H., Nguyen Gia, T.: Exploring the integration of edge computing and blockchain iot: principles, architectures, security, and applications. J. Netw. Comput. Appl. **226**, 103884 (2024)
28. Pagano, A., et al.: A survey on massive iot for water distribution systems: challenges, simulation tools, and guidelines for large-scale deployment. Ad Hoc Netw. **168**, 103714 (2025)
29. Rabin, M.O.: Randomized byzantine generals. In: 24th Annual Symposium on Foundations of Computer Science (sfcs 1983), pp. 403–409 (1983)
30. Reiter, M.K.: Secure agreement protocols: reliable and atomic group multicast in rampart. In: Proceedings of the 2nd ACM Conference on Computer and Communications Security, CCS 1994, pp. 68–80 (1994)
31. Schett, M.A., Danezis, G.: Embedding a deterministic bft protocol in a block dag. In: Proceedings of the 2021 ACM Symposium on Principles of Distributed Computing, PODC 2021, pp. 177–186. ACM, New York, NY, USA (2021)
32. Shoup, V.: Practical threshold signatures. In: Proceedings of the 19th International Conference on Theory and Application of Cryptographic Techniques, EUROCRYPT 2000, pp. 207–220 (2000)
33. Shoup, V., Gennaro, R.: Securing threshold cryptosystems against chosen ciphertext attack. J. Cryptol. **15**(2), 75–96 (2002)
34. Shrestha, N., Shrothrium, R., Kate, A., Nayak, K.: Sailfish: towards improving the Latency of DAG-based BFT . In: 2025 IEEE Symposium on Security and Privacy (SP), pp. 21–21, May 2025
35. Spiegelman, A., Arun, B., Gelashvili, R., Li, Z.: Shoal: improving dag-bft latency and robustness. In: Financial Cryptography and Data Security, pp. 92–109. Cham (2025)
36. Spiegelman, A., Giridharan, N., Sonnino, A., Kokoris-Kogias, L.: Bullshark: dag bft protocols made practical. In: Proceedings of the 2022 ACM SIGSAC Conference on Computer and Communications Security, CCS 2022, pp. 2705–2718 (2022)
37. Zhang, H., Duan, S.: Pace: fully parallelizable bft from reproposable byzantine agreement. In: Proceedings of the 2022 ACM SIGSAC Conference on Computer and Communications Security, CCS 2022, pp. 3151–3164 (2022)

FRanCS: A Fair and Randomized Anonymous Network Circuit Selection Mechanism with Blockchain

Qiyuan Gao[1], Qianhong Wu[1(✉)], Junxiang Nong[2], and Qi Liu[1]

[1] Beihang University, Beijing 100191, China
{gaoqy,qianhong.wu}@buaa.edu.cn
[2] Renmin University of China, Beijing 100872, China
fpdqwq@yeah.net

Abstract. Anonymous communication networks are critical infrastructures for protecting user privacy and defending against network surveillance. However, existing anonymous communication networks lack sufficient randomness in path selection, making them susceptible to adversarial prediction and manipulation. Inadequate identity protection further exposes nodes to targeted attacks. Moreover, purely random circuit selection can compromise fairness in long-term node incentives, reducing nodes' motivation for participation. To address these issues, this paper proposes FRanCS, a blockchain-based Fair and Randomized anonymous circuit selection scheme. Specifically, the scheme employs rolling hash functions and zero-knowledge proofs (ZKPs) to achieve dynamic anonymity in node identity management. At the same time, an exponential key-value random sampling algorithm is designed to simultaneously ensure unpredictability in path selection and fairness in long-term node incentives. Theoretical analysis and experimental results demonstrate that the proposed scheme effectively resists path prediction attacks and node identity exposure risks, achieves fairness in long-term incentives, and exhibits robust security and efficiency in practical deployment scenarios.

Keywords: Blockchain · Anonymous network · Circuit selection

1 Introduction

In recent years, with the rapid expansion of the Internet, threats to user privacy have intensified, driven by increased data surveillance and frequent sensitive data breaches [1–3]. Anonymous communication networks [4–7] have emerged as essential solutions to these privacy challenges. These networks route user data through multiple randomly selected nodes to effectively conceal the data's origin and destination, significantly enhancing user anonymity and defending against surveillance and traffic analysis attacks [8,9].

However, current anonymous communication systems still exhibit critical limitations in their node-selection mechanisms. Typical selection approaches rely

R. Chen et al. (Eds.): Inscrypt 2025, LNCS 16409, pp. 431–447, 2026.
https://doi.org/10.1007/978-981-95-6203-9_23

on static criteria like node bandwidth or uptime, leading to predictable routing paths [10,11]. This predictability enables attackers to anticipate and manipulate node selection, facilitating traffic analysis and targeted correlation attacks.

To mitigate these vulnerabilities, recent research has explored leveraging blockchain-based random beacon schemes and commitment-reveal mechanisms to enhance path unpredictability [12,13]. Nonetheless, achieving a balance between short-term randomness and fairness in long-term node incentives remains a challenge.

Additionally, secure node identity management has emerged as a critical yet often overlooked component in transmission networks. Traditional approaches prioritize user anonymity but rarely provide sufficient identity protection for nodes, exposing them to targeted attacks and potential collusion. Blockchain-based identity management schemes [14–16] have shown promise in generating anonymous yet verifiable on-chain node identities. However, existing solutions still struggle to simultaneously achieve node anonymity, transparency, and verifiability in node evaluation processes. Addressing this gap is crucial for ensuring robust anonymity while encouraging fair and sustained node participation.

In this paper, we propose FRanCS, a Fair and Randomized anonymous circuit selection scheme. First, we design a node identity management mechanism that combines rolling hashes with zero-knowledge proofs (ZKPs) [17], allowing nodes to periodically update their identity states and anonymously prove their validity. This mechanism mitigates identity replay and forgery risks while supporting scalable participation.

Second, we present an anonymous node selection algorithm based on exponential key-value random sampling. By leveraging blockchain random beacons and user-submitted random seeds, the algorithm ensures unpredictability in each circuit selection while maintaining fairness across long-term participation, thereby enhancing both security and incentive alignment.

In summary, the primary contributions of this paper are as follows:

- We introduce a blockchain-based anonymous node identity management mechanism that maintains strong anonymity while preserving verifiability. Even when circuit information is revealed, the real identities of the nodes remain concealed, strengthening system security and node privacy.
- We design a fair and randomized circuit selection algorithm tailored for anonymous communication networks. By integrating zero-knowledge proofs with smart contracts, the selection process becomes both verifiable and tamper-resistant, reducing the probability that adversaries can control entire communication circuits.
- We provide detailed theoretical analysis and security proofs demonstrating that FRanCS achieves both short-term unpredictability and long-term fairness. Together with experimental evaluation, these results highlight the practicality of FRanCS as a secure and efficient circuit selection framework.

2 Related Work

2.1 Circuit Selection in Anonymous Networks

Anonymous communication systems such as Tor [4] protect user privacy by relaying traffic over multi-hop circuits. However, traditional selection strategies often rely on static criteria (e.g., bandwidth or uptime), leaving them predictable and exploitable for traffic analysis. Several improvements have been proposed. Snader and Borisov introduced a bandwidth-weighted strategy [18], which improved performance but remained vulnerable to high-bandwidth adversaries. Backes et al. proposed a provably secure path-selection algorithm [19], though its high complexity limits deployment. Barton et al. studied location-aware strategies, trading off anonymity for efficiency [13]. These works highlight the difficulty of simultaneously achieving unpredictability, efficiency, and robustness in circuit selection.

2.2 Incentive Mechanisms in Anonymous Networks

Sustaining node participation in anonymous networks has motivated a range of incentive mechanisms. Early work proposed micro-payments to reward cooperative Tor relays [20]. Variants explored Proof-of-Work payments [21] or game-theoretic models to stabilize participation [22]. More recently, Sybil-resistant incentive designs have been applied to blockchain transaction propagation [23]. While these efforts improve cooperation, they do not address how incentives interact with randomized circuit selection. In particular, ensuring both short-term unpredictability and long-term fairness in node selection remains largely unexplored.

2.3 Node Identity Protection

Anonymous identity management has also been studied to mitigate targeted attacks on relay nodes. Lu et al. proposed BARS, a blockchain-based reputation system for VANETs that combines anonymity with accountability [24]. Chin et al. developed decentralized access control with unlinkable identifiers [25], while Cui et al. proposed dynamic credential frameworks supporting repeated anonymous verifications. These approaches strengthen node privacy but are rarely combined with circuit selection mechanisms, and efficient on-chain verification of anonymous identities remains limited.

In Summary. Prior works have improved circuit selection, incentive compatibility, and identity protection, but largely in isolation. This separation means that existing systems either achieve strong anonymity at the cost of predictable and unfair node selection, or introduce incentives without guaranteeing privacy and unpredictability. FRanCS integrates these dimensions into a unified framework: by combining randomized circuit selection with verifiable incentives and dynamic anonymous identities, it ensures that unpredictability, fairness, and anonymity reinforce rather than conflict with one another. This joint design yields a property not achieved in earlier work—sustained and verifiable participation of anonymous nodes under both strong adversaries and large-scale deployment.

3 System Model and Definitions

In this section, we first describe the entities involved in the system and outline the overall operation model. We then specify the system's security assumptions, threat model, and key security objectives addressed in this paper.

The FRanCS randomized circuit selection scheme involves three primary entities: User, Node, and Blockchain. Their respective functionalities are defined as follows.

- **User:** The initiator of anonymous communications. Users submit random seed commitments and corresponding zero-knowledge proofs (ZKPs) to the blockchain, ensuring fairness and verifiability of node selection, thereby preventing manipulation or collusion during circuit selection.
- **Node:** Core infrastructure responsible for network communication and data forwarding. Each node possesses a long-term public-private key pair. The blockchain dynamically records and updates node reputation scores based on historical performance, allocating tasks accordingly.
- **Blockchain:** A trusted third party that provides a public, transparent, and unpredictable random beacon. It manages node identity registration and dynamic reputation scoring, verifies zero-knowledge proofs submitted by users, ensures fairness and security of the node-selection process, and guarantees reliable and efficient overall system operation.

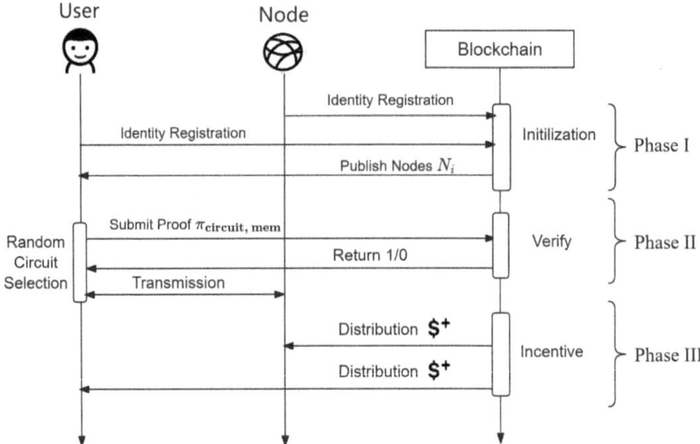

Fig. 1. FRanCS work flow.

As illustrated in Fig. 1, the FRanCS scheme consists of three primary phases: Registration and Interaction; Node Selection and Proof Generation; and On-chain Verification and Incentive Allocation.

In the **Registration and Interaction** phase, nodes and users first register their identities on the blockchain to participate in subsequent system interactions. The blockchain's smart contracts automatically generate and publicly maintain a node list based on each node's historical performance and contributions. This node list, which includes node reputation scores, is publicly accessible on-chain. Meanwhile, the system generates a commitment to the node set during this phase. Additionally, relevant cryptographic parameters are established to support security and anonymity requirements for subsequent phases.

In the **Node Selection and Proof Generation** phase, users perform a randomized circuit selection algorithm based on the publicly available node reputation scores, ensuring randomness and fairness in circuit selection. Simultaneously, users generate corresponding cryptographic proofs for the selected circuit nodes to enable subsequent on-chain verification.

Finally, in the **On-chain Verification and Incentive Allocation** phase, users submit their circuit-selection proofs to the blockchain for public verification. Upon successful verification of these proofs and confirmation of data transmission, the blockchain automatically executes a fair incentive allocation mechanism based on nodes' reputation scores and contributions, thus ensuring long-term system stability.

3.1 Security Assumptions

Assumption 1 (Time and Communication). *The system operates in discrete epochs. At epoch e, the blockchain publishes an unpredictable, publicly verifiable random beacon* rnd_e *within at most* Δ *confirmation blocks. At the end of epoch* $e-1$*, users post a commitment* $H(s_e)$ *and reveal the opening* s_e *within* Δ_{reveal} *blocks in epoch e. The network is* (Δ, ε)*-synchronous: honest messages are delivered within* Δ *blocks, except with negligible probability* ε*.*

Assumption 2 (Blockchain Security). *The blockchain maintains an honest majority and satisfies standard security properties (*chain growth, chain quality, *and* common prefix*). Only commitments are stored on-chain, protecting private node data from consensus nodes. Traffic accounting employs verifiable metering tokens, settled automatically by smart contracts. Random beacons generated via verifiable random functions (VRFs) ensure public verifiability and unpredictability. We assume the adversary cannot sustain large-scale denial-of-access attacks; network partitions, if any, are temporary, allowing users to reconnect and complete interactions timely.*

Assumption 3 (Node, Economic, and Cryptographic Security). *Nodes must lock security deposits upon registration. Invalid state submissions or delayed randomness revelations result in proportional slashing. Economic penalties incentivize honest behavior. The adversary controls at most a fraction* $\rho < \rho_{\max}$ *of* *total node weight, and its expected profit remains strictly below expected slashing costs, economically deterring sustained Sybil attacks. We further assume that the employed zero-knowledge proof system satisfies* soundness, zero-knowledge, *and* knowledge-extractability *under standard cryptographic hardness assumptions. The employed hash functions are assumed to be collision-resistant and modeled as random oracles where required.*

3.2 Threat Model

The FRanCS system inherits the anonymity and security properties of Tor, thus facing similar threats. Additionally, introducing node incentives and blockchain interactions in FRanCS creates new threats. We consider a probabilistic polynomial-time attacker $\mathcal{A}$ with the following capabilities:

- **Adaptive Corruption:** $\mathcal{A}$ can adaptively corrupt up to a fraction $\rho < \rho_{\max}$ of nodes, obtaining their secret keys and influencing their behavior.
- **Collusion and Sybil Attacks:** $\mathcal{A}$ may introduce many malicious or low-quality nodes (Sybil identities) or coordinate among compromised nodes to bias circuit selection or disrupt fairness.
- **On-Chain Observation:** $\mathcal{A}$ has continuous access to all public blockchain data (registration, scores, random beacons, state commitments) and may attempt to exploit correlations.
- **Denial and Manipulation:** $\mathcal{A}$ may attempt to delay randomness revelation, inject false commitments, or predict future circuits to disrupt communications.

Despite these capabilities, $\mathcal{A}$ remains bounded by polynomial-time computation and cannot break standard cryptographic assumptions, including VRF unpredictability, the hiding property of commitments, or the zero-knowledge and soundness guarantees of the ZKP system.

Specifically, we consider the following concrete attack scenarios:

- **Node Injection Attack:** The attacker injects numerous low-contribution or malicious nodes to distort the relationship between node contributions and selection probabilities. This prevents highly contributing nodes from receiving fair incentives while favoring malicious nodes, harming fairness and service quality.
- **Circuit Prediction and Control Attack:** The attacker predicts users' anonymous circuit selections using public on-chain information (random beacons, historical selections, state updates). Upon successful prediction, the attacker targets critical nodes, disrupting or delaying specific user communications.
- **Node Identity Linking Attack:** By analyzing on-chain registration records, scoring dynamics, and state updates, the attacker attempts to link anonymous on-chain identities to real-world nodes. If successful, this linkage facilitates targeted physical or network attacks, compromising node privacy and weakening overall network security.

4 FRanCS Design Details

In this section, we describe the detailed design of the FRanCS scheme. Specifically, after initializing the system parameters, relay nodes first perform on-chain identity registration, and the blockchain publishes the node set publicly. Users then execute the randomized circuit selection algorithm based on this publicly available node set and generate corresponding zero-knowledge proofs (ZKPs) for on-chain verification. The notations used throughout the FRanCS are summarized in Table 1.

Table 1. Notations

Notation	Description
G	Cyclic group used in cryptographic operations
N_i	Network node i
sk_i, pk_i	Key pair of node i
$H(\cdot), h_i^{(0)}, h_i^{(e)}$	Hash function and state hashes for node i
$\pi_i^{(0)}$	Initial zero-knowledge proof of N_i identity
rnd_e	Global verifiable random beacon in epoch e
$w_i^{(e)}$	Weight & reputation of N_i at epoch e
r_i	Random salt value used by N_i
$C_{\text{entry, mid, exit}}$	Candidate sets of entry, middle, and exit nodes
$\pi_{\text{mem, circuit}}$	Membership proof and circuit selection proof
$s_e, H(s_e)$	Secret random seed and its hash commitment for epoch e
$u_i(e), k_i(e)$	Node random number and exponential key-value
epoch e	Current operational cycle on blockchain

4.1 Registration and Blockchain Interaction

To ensure the security of the randomized circuit selection mechanism, we design a reliable and anonymous node identity management scheme, enabling on-chain smart contracts to effectively verify node identities and weight scores. The authenticity, anonymity, and verifiability of node identities directly affect the security and fairness of circuit selection; thus, node registration and state updates form the security foundation of the system.

Specifically, we define the network node set as $\mathcal{N} = {N_i}^n$, where each node N_i possesses a private key sk_i and corresponding long-term public key $pk_i = sk_i G$. The long-term public key pk_i is only used during initial on-chain registration, while subsequent interactions utilize dynamically updated state hashes $h_i^{(e)}$ as anonymous identifiers. In each epoch, nodes generate new hashes based on their long-term public key, the global random number, and the previous state hash, submitting zero-knowledge proofs (ZKPs) for smart-contract verification. This rolling-hash approach effectively prevents identity tracking and correlation.

The detailed procedures of node registration and identity interactions are as follows:

- **Initial Identity Generation and Registration:** During initial on-chain registration, each node N_i submits the following information:
  1. The node's long-term public key identifier pk_i;
  2. The initial identity commitment hash:
  $$h_i^{(0)} = H(pk_i, r_i)$$
  where r_i is a randomly generated salt by the node, and $H(\cdot)$ is a hash function suitable for zero-knowledge circuits;
  3. A zero-knowledge proof $\pi_i^{(0)}$, demonstrating that the node indeed holds the private key corresponding to pk_i and has correctly computed the initial commitment hash:
  $$\pi_i^{(0)} = \mathsf{NIZK.Proof}\left(\exists sk_i, r_i : pk_i = sk_i G \wedge h_i^{(0)} = H(pk_i, r_i)\right)$$
- **Identity Verification and Commitment Storage:** The smart contract rigorously verifies the submitted public key pk_i, the initial identity hash $h_i^{(0)}$, and the zero-knowledge proof $\pi_i^{(0)}$ to ensure the authenticity and correctness of node identities. Upon successful verification, the smart contract generates a publicly accessible root commitment of the node set based on the Caulk protocol [26], guaranteeing node anonymity and set integrity. The public key pk_i will not be revealed on-chain during subsequent interactions.
- **Node Score Update and Root Commitment Publication:** At the beginning of epoch e, the smart contract automatically updates and publishes node weight scores according to their historical performance, simultaneously updating the node set root commitment. These scores are objectively generated by the smart contract to prevent nodes from self-reporting or altering their weights, ensuring transparency and fairness of the scoring mechanism.
- **Rolling Identity State Updates:** To prevent replay attacks and maintain continual state validity, each node updates its identity state hash at epoch e based on the global on-chain random number rnd_e and the state hash from the previous epoch $h_i^{(e-1)}$:
  $$h_i^{(e)} = H(pk_i \parallel h_i^{(e-1)} \parallel rnd_e)$$
  Simultaneously, nodes generate corresponding zero-knowledge proofs $\pi_i^{(e)}$:
  $$\pi_i^{(e)} = \mathsf{NIZK.Proof}(\exists sk_i, h_i^{(e-1)} : pk_i = sk_i G \wedge h_i^{(e)} = H(pk_i \parallel h_i^{(e-1)} \parallel rnd_e))$$
  The smart contract strictly verifies the newly submitted state hash $h_i^{(e)}$ and its proof $\pi_i^{(e)}$. Only nodes that pass verification are included in the current valid node set.

– **Dynamic Node Updates and Elimination:** In each epoch, the smart contract dynamically updates the node set, including new node additions, dynamic adjustments of node weights, and elimination of unqualified nodes. Each time the set is updated, the root commitment is also refreshed, ensuring the circuit selection always utilizes the latest and valid node set.

The above design balances node anonymity, continuous security verification, and dynamic state updates, laying a robust foundation for achieving fairness, security, and stability in the randomized circuit selection mechanism.

4.2 Randomized Circuit Selection

The randomized circuit selection mechanism proposed in this paper aims to achieve fair, efficient, and secure circuit assignment, ensuring that each user's route selection meets the requirements of long-term fairness, anonymity, and verifiability. Specifically, users perform a randomized circuit selection algorithm based on the node state hashes $h_i^{(e)}$ and corresponding weight scores $w_i^{(e)}$ publicly available on the blockchain, and utilize zero-knowledge proofs (ZKPs) to verify the randomness and validity of selected nodes. To ensure node anonymity, we adopt the Caulk protocol for anonymous membership proofs, confirming that the selected nodes indeed belong to the publicly available valid node set maintained on-chain. The detailed randomized circuit selection procedure is described in Algorithm 1.

To prevent users from manipulating the circuit selection results through repeated attempts, each user must publish a hash commitment $H(s_e)$ of their random seed on-chain during the previous epoch $(e - 1)$. At the beginning of epoch e, the user reveals the actual random seed s_e, enabling blockchain verification of commitment correctness. If a user intends to execute multiple circuit selections during epoch e, they must publish commitments to multiple random seeds in advance. Failure to execute the declared number of circuit selections results in the confiscation of the user's stake. This mechanism strictly constrains user behavior and ensures genuine randomness.

The detailed steps of the algorithm are further clarified as follows:

– **Initialization Phase:** Users publish the hash commitment $H(s_e)$ in epoch $e - 1$ and reveal the corresponding random seed s_e at epoch e for on-chain verification. Additionally, users obtain the latest node state hashes and random beacon rnd_e from the blockchain, providing the necessary inputs for subsequent node random value computation. Because the hash of the random seed s_e is published in advance, no adversary can feasibly predict the random values of nodes, thus ensuring randomness and unpredictability in each selection.
– **Exponential Key Sampling Phase:** Users compute the random values $u_i(e)$ and derive exponential key values $k_i(e)$ based on node weights. This mechanism ensures that, over the long term, the frequency of each node being selected strictly aligns with its weight score, thereby achieving long-term fairness and incentivizing nodes to consistently provide high-quality services.

Algorithm 1. Fair and Anonymous Randomized Circuit Selection Algorithm

For Each User Do:

Input: Candidate sets for entry, middle, and exit nodes $(h_i^{(e)}, w_i^{(e)})$; the public blockchain random beacon rnd_e for epoch e; a hash commitment $H(s_e)$ to the random seed published by the user during epoch $e-1$; and the actual random seed s_e revealed at epoch e.

Output: Circuit nodes $(N_{\text{entry}}, N_{\text{middle}}, N_{\text{exit}})$, zero-knowledge proofs π

Initialization Phase:

User publishes random seed commitment $H(s_e)$ during epoch $e-1$ and reveals the actual seed s_e at epoch e

Obtain initial candidate node sets $C_{\text{entry}}, C_{\text{mid}}, C_{\text{exit}}$ from the blockchain

Blockchain verifies the user's commitment correctness; abort subsequent steps if verification fails

Exponential Key Sampling Phase:

for each node $(h_i^{(e)}, w_i^{(e)})$ in $C_{\text{entry, mid, exit}}$ **do**

Compute the random value for the node:

$$u_i(e) \leftarrow \frac{H_{\text{int}}(rnd_e \| s_e \| h_i^{(e)})}{2^{256}}$$

Calculate exponential key values for nodes:

$$k_i(e) \leftarrow -\frac{\ln(u_i(e))}{w_i^{(e)}}$$

end for

Node Confirmation Phase:

Sort nodes in each candidate set (entry, middle, exit) by ascending exponential key values $k_i(e)$, and select nodes with the smallest keys as circuit nodes:

$$(N_{\text{entry}}, N_{\text{middle}}, N_{\text{exit}}) \leftarrow (C_{\text{entry}}[0], C_{\text{mid}}[0], C_{\text{exit}}[0])$$

Proof Generation Phase:

for each selected node **do**

Generate Caulk anonymous membership proof π_{mem}

Generate zero-knowledge proof π_{circuit} verifying correctness of circuit selection

Set $\pi \leftarrow (\pi_{\text{mem}}, \pi_{\text{circuit}})$

end for

return Selected circuit nodes $(N_{\text{entry}}, N_{\text{middle}}, N_{\text{exit}})$ and proof π

- **Node Confirmation Phase:** Users select the entry, middle, and exit nodes with the smallest exponential key values from their respective candidate sets, forming the anonymous communication circuit.
- **Proof Generation Phase:** Users generate Caulk anonymous membership proofs to verify the selected nodes' inclusion in the blockchain-published node set, and construct zero-knowledge proofs to confirm the correctness and compliance of the circuit selection process, ensuring no manipulation occurred.

Through these designs, the proposed scheme effectively achieves anonymity, randomness, fairness, and verifiability of circuit selection, ensuring efficiency and security in practical deployment scenarios.

5 Security Analysis

In anonymous communication network, the security of the circuit selection mechanism directly influences the reliability of the entire network and the effectiveness of anonymity protection. In this section, we provide a detailed analysis and proofs from three critical security aspects: anonymity, unpredictability of circuit selection, and long-term fairness of the overall system.

5.1 Anonymity Analysis

Anonymity is one of the core security properties of the system. We analyze anonymity from two perspectives: node identity anonymity and circuit selection anonymity.

First, regarding **node identity anonymity**, our scheme employs a rolling-hash mechanism, in which the node state hash in each epoch is derived from the node's private key, the previous state hash, and a random beacon, with the validity of each update being verified on-chain using zero-knowledge proofs. Thus, an adversary is unable to infer a node's private key or correlate node states across different epochs based solely on on-chain information. Under standard cryptographic assumptions such as hash collision resistance, hash pre-image resistance, and the zero-knowledge property of the proof system, our scheme ensures epoch-wise unlinkability of node identities, effectively preventing attackers from correlating identities across epochs.

Second, concerning **circuit selection anonymity**, we utilize the Caulk anonymous membership proof system. Users only submit anonymous membership proofs of the selected nodes to the blockchain, without directly revealing the selected node identities. The Witness Indistinguishability (WI) property of the Caulk protocol and the binding property of accumulators ensure that on-chain observers cannot effectively identify the selected nodes. If an attacker could successfully identify the nodes, this capability would imply an attack on the WI property of the Caulk protocol itself; thus, the probability of such an attack is negligible.

In summary, under standard cryptographic assumptions about hash functions, the zero-knowledge property of ZKPs, and the witness indistinguishability of the Caulk protocol, our scheme rigorously achieves anonymity in both node identity and circuit selection, effectively resisting identity tracking and correlation attacks on-chain.

5.2 Unpredictability of Randomized Circuit Selection

We consider an adversary $\mathcal{A}$ who has complete on-chain observation capability and polynomial-time computational resources. Such an adversary may adaptively corrupt a subset of nodes. We assume the random seed commitment $H(s_e)$

submitted by the user in advance is computationally hiding, i.e., the adversary cannot feasibly predict the random seed s_e before it is revealed. We present the following security theorem:

Theorem 1 (Unpredictability of Randomized Circuit Selection). *In the context of our randomized circuit selection algorithm, assuming the hash function $H(\cdot)$ is collision-resistant and computationally unpredictable, and the random seed commitment $H(s_e)$ submitted by users during epoch $e-1$ is computationally hiding, the randomized circuit selection outcome is strictly unpredictable to an adversary.*

Proof. To prove this theorem, suppose an adversary can predict, with non-negligible advantage, the exact node combination selected in epoch e. This would imply that the adversary can predict the node random value:

$$u_i(e) \leftarrow \frac{H_{\text{int}}(rnd_e \| s_e \| h_i^{(e)})}{2^{256}}.$$

However, predicting this random value would require the adversary to have one of the following two capabilities:

1. Deriving the random seed s_e from its hash commitment $H(s_e)$, directly violating the computational hiding assumption of the hash commitment;
2. Predicting the output of the hash function H_{int} before inputs are known, contradicting the computational unpredictability assumption under the random oracle model.

Both scenarios are infeasible under the stated assumptions, indicating that the adversary's advantage in prediction is negligible with respect to the security parameter. Thus, the randomized circuit selection results are strictly unpredictable.

In summary, our scheme effectively ensures the unpredictability and long-term fairness of the randomized circuit selection process, resisting manipulation or prediction attacks by polynomial-time adversaries.

5.3 Analysis of Long-Term Fairness

The long-term fairness of the system means that, over extended periods of circuit selection, the frequency with which each node is selected converges to its contribution-based share. Such fairness incentivizes nodes to continuously provide high-quality services, ensuring long-term stability and consistent service quality.

Theorem 2 (Long-Term Fairness). *Let $X_{i,t} \in \{0,1\}$ indicate whether node i is selected at epoch t, and let $\{\mathcal{F}_t\}$ be the natural filtration up to epoch t.*

Define $p_{i,t} \triangleq \frac{w_i^{(t)}}{\sum_j w_j^{(t)}}$, *where* $p_{i,t} \in [0,1]$ *is* $\mathcal{F}_{t-1}$*-measurable and satisfies* $\mathbb{E}[X_{i,t} \mid \mathcal{F}_{t-1}] = p_{i,t}$. *Suppose there exists* $\bar{p}_i > 0$ *such that* $\frac{1}{T}\sum_{t=1}^{T} p_{i,t} \to \bar{p}_i$. *Then*

$$\lim_{T\to\infty} \frac{\sum_{t=1}^{T} X_{i,t}}{\sum_{t=1}^{T} p_{i,t}} = 1 \quad a.s., \quad \text{and hence} \quad \frac{1}{T}\sum_{t=1}^{T} X_{i,t} \to \bar{p}_i \ a.s.$$

Proof. Let $Z_{i,t} = X_{i,t} - p_{i,t}$ and $Y_{i,T} = \sum_{t=1}^{T} Z_{i,t}$. Then $\{Z_{i,t}, \mathcal{F}_t\}$ is a martingale-difference sequence with $|Z_{i,t}| \le 1$. By the AzumaâĂŞHoeffding inequality, for any $\varepsilon > 0$,

$$\Pr(|Y_{i,T}| \ge \varepsilon T) \le 2\exp\Big(-\tfrac{\varepsilon^2}{2}T\Big).$$

Since $\sum_{n=1}^{\infty} 2\exp(-\varepsilon^2 n/2) < \infty$, the BorelâĂŞCantelli lemma yields $Y_{i,T}/T \to 0$ almost surely. Moreover, $\frac{1}{T}\sum_{t=1}^{T} p_{i,t} \to \bar{p}_i$ implies $\sum_{t=1}^{T} p_{i,t} = \bar{p}_i T + o(T)$, hence

$$\frac{\sum_{t=1}^{T} X_{i,t}}{\sum_{t=1}^{T} p_{i,t}} = 1 + \frac{Y_{i,T}}{\sum_{t=1}^{T} p_{i,t}} \longrightarrow 1 \quad \text{a.s.},$$

and consequently $\frac{1}{T}\sum_{t=1}^{T} X_{i,t} = \frac{1}{T}\sum_{t=1}^{T} p_{i,t} + \frac{Y_{i,T}}{T} \to \bar{p}_i$ almost surely.

6 Implementation and Evaluation

In this section, we evaluated the performance of user identity generation on both client-side and blockchain node environments. Experimental results demonstrate that FRanCS meets practical deployment requirements. Furthermore, we analyzed the computational overhead and storage cost of generating zero-knowledge membership commitments on blockchain nodes, as well as the computation and execution time of circuit selection at the client-side. The experimental environments were configured as follows: client-side (Ubuntu 22.04, Intel i5-12500H, 32GB RAM) and blockchain node (Ubuntu 22.04, Intel i9-13900H, 128GB RAM).

In the user identity proof stage, we conducted performance evaluation experiments based on the Circom 2.0 + Snarkjs framework and the Groth16 zero-knowledge proof scheme, comparing the generation and on-chain verification time of zero-knowledge proofs (ZKPs) for different hash functions during identity state generation. As shown in Fig. 2, experimental results demonstrate that the Poseidon hash function provides superior performance, with proof generation time and memory overhead both within an acceptable range.

However, during on-chain identity verification, the verification time becomes significant and cannot be ignored as the scale grows large. Therefore, we further explored multiple performance optimization strategies to reduce the on-chain verification time overhead. Under a verification scale of 10^4, the specific optimization strategies and their performance improvements are detailed in Table 2.

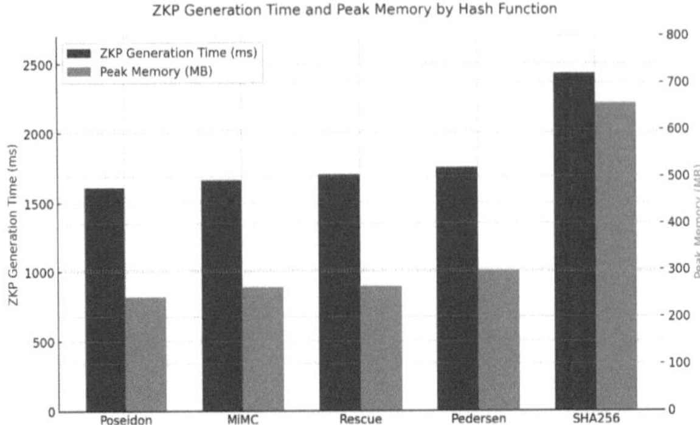

Fig. 2. Performance comparison of different hash functions.

Table 2. Performance comparison of ZKP verification under different optimization schemes

Verification Scenario	Total Verification Time	Relative Speedup
Native EVM environment	≈ 36 min	1×
EVM + alt_bn128 precompile	17 s	127×
Dedicated precompiled contract	6 s	360×
Precompile + 8 threads	0.94 s	2, 300×
Batch verification (128/group)	1.45 s	1, 500×

We evaluated ZKP verification performance under various optimization scenarios, including native EVM, dedicated precompiled contracts, multi-threaded execution, and batch verification. Optimization significantly reduced verification time from approximately 36 min (native EVM) to 0.94 s (precompile + 8 threads), achieving a speedup of about 2,300×. Batch verification further reduced on-chain costs and maintained efficient performance (1.45 s).

We also analyzed on-chain commitment generation and storage overhead at different node scales. For 10,000 nodes, Caulk proof generation required around 4.8 s (client-side), with server-side verification at about 2.3 s. Storage overhead was approximately 312.5 KB at a scale of 1,000 nodes. Both computational and storage overheads remained practical with increasing node scale, confirming excellent scalability.

Moreover, client-side membership proof (π_{mem}) generation for circuit selection took approximately 450ms, with on-chain verification around 50ms, highlighting the practical applicability of our scheme.

We evaluated the long-term fairness of the randomized circuit selection algorithm through simulations involving 10^4 nodes with normally distributed weights over 100 rounds. The root-mean-square error (RMSE) between actual and expected node selection frequencies rapidly decreased with increasing selection rounds (Fig. 3), confirming the algorithm's long-term fairness. Figure 4 illus-

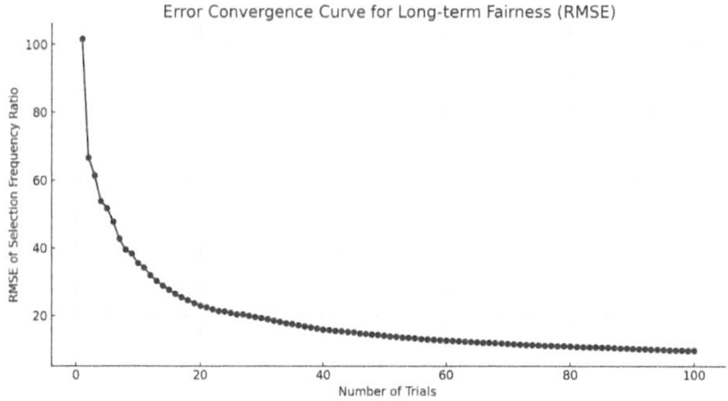

Fig. 3. Convergence of randomized node selection.

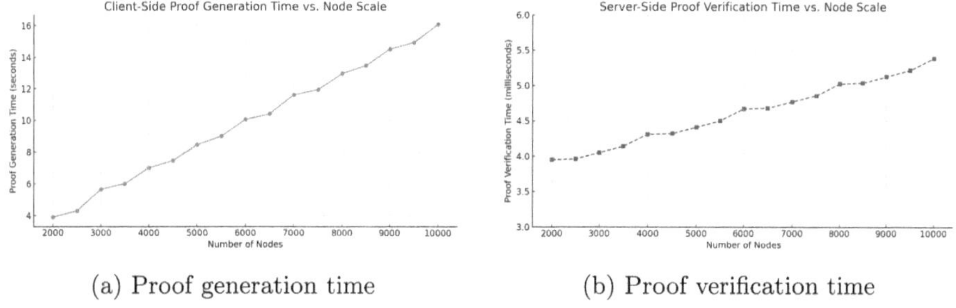

(a) Proof generation time

(b) Proof verification time

Fig. 4. Performance analysis on client-side and server-side.

trates that both circuit selection and zero-knowledge proof generation times remain within milliseconds, ensuring minimal computational overhead and practical applicability without affecting blockchain performance.

7 Conclusion and Future Work

In this paper, we proposed FRanCS, a blockchain-based scheme for fair and randomized anonymous circuit selection. By combining rolling hashes, zero-knowledge proofs, and exponential key-value sampling, FRanCS achieves dynamic node anonymity, path unpredictability, and long-term fairness. Our analysis and experiments demonstrate its effectiveness and practicality. For future work, we plan to further investigate scalability in larger networks, explore optimizations such as batch verification and committee-based selection, and conduct end-to-end evaluations against existing systems to strengthen real-world applicability.

References

1. Shahid, J., Ahmad, R., Kiani, A.K., Ahmad, T., Saeed, S., Almuhaideb, A.M.: Data protection and privacy of the internet of healthcare things (iohts). Appl. Sci. **12**(4), 1927 (2022)

2. Ji, Y., Sun, A., Zhang, J., Li, C.: A critical study on data leakage in recommender system offline evaluation. ACM Transactions on Information Systems **41**(3), 1–27 (2023)
3. Yang, Z., Yang, M., Zhang, Y., Gu, G., Ning, P., Wang, X.S.: Appintent: Analyzing sensitive data transmission in android for privacy leakage detection. In: Proceedings of the 2013 ACM SIGSAC conference on Computer & Communications security, pp. 1043–1054 (2013)
4. Dingledine, R., Mathewson, N., Syverson, P.: Tor: the second-generation onion router. In: Proceedings of the 13th USENIX Security Symposium, pp. 303–320 (2004)
5. Bennett, K., Grothoff, C.: Gap–practical anonymous networking. In: International Workshop on Privacy Enhancing Technologies, Springer, pp. 141–160 (2003)
6. Ren, J., Wu, J.: Survey on anonymous communications in computer networks. Comput. Commun. **33**(4), 420–431 (2010)
7. Shirazi, F., Simeonovski, M., Asghar, M.R., Backes, M., Diaz, C.: A survey on routing in anonymous communication protocols. ACM Computing Surveys (CSUR) **51**(3), 1–39 (2018)
8. Back, A., Möller, U., Stiglic, A.: Traffic analysis attacks and trade-offs in anonymity providing systems. In: International Workshop on Information Hiding, Springer, 2001, pp. 245–257
9. Deng, J., Han, R., Mishra, S.: Countermeasures against traffic analysis attacks in wireless sensor networks. In: First International Conference on Security and Privacy for Emerging Areas in Communications Networks (SECURECOMM'05), IEEE, pp. 113–126 (2005)
10. Meng, X., Liang, M.: Node selection-based anonymous network performance optimization method. In: 2024 9th International Conference on Computer and Communication Systems (ICCCS), IEEE, pp. 456–461 (2024)
11. Vishnumurthy, V., Francis, P.: On heterogeneous overlay construction and random node selection in unstructured p2p networks. In: INFOCOM, Citeseer, pp. 1–12 (2006)
12. Baniata, H., Anaqreh, A., Kertesz, A.: Dons: Dynamic optimized neighbor selection for smart blockchain networks. Futur. Gener. Comput. Syst. **130**, 75–90 (2022)
13. Barton, A., Wright, M., Ming, J., Imani, M.: Towards predicting efficient and anonymous tor circuits. In: 27th USENIX Security Symposium (USENIX Security 18), pp. 429–444 (2018)
14. Liu, Y., He, D., Obaidat, M.S., Kumar, N., Khan, M.K., Choo, K.-K.R.: Blockchain-based identity management systems: a review. J. Netw. Comput. Appl. **166**, 102731 (2020)
15. Kuperberg, M.: Blockchain-based identity management: a survey from the enterprise and ecosystem perspective. IEEE Trans. Eng. Manage. **67**(4), 1008–1027 (2019)
16. Ahmed, M.R., Islam, A.M., Shatabda, S., Islam, S.: Blockchain-based identity management system and self-sovereign identity ecosystem: a comprehensive survey. IEEE Access **10**, 113436–113481 (2022)
17. Blum, M., Feldman, P., Micali, S.: Non-interactive zero-knowledge and its applications. In: Providing Sound Foundations for Cryptography: On the Work of Shafi Goldwasser and Silvio Micali, ACM Books, Morgan & Claypool Publishers, pp. 329–349 (2019)
18. Snader, R.J., Borisov, N.: A tune-up for tor: Improving security and performance in the tor network. In: NDSS (2008)

19. Backes, M., Goldberg, I., Kate, A., Mohammadi, E.: Provably secure and practical onion routing. In: 2012 IEEE 25th Computer Security Foundations Symposium, IEEE, pp. 369–385 (2012)
20. Johnny Ngan, T.-W., Dingledine, R., Wallach, D.S.: Building incentives into tor. In: International Conference on Financial Cryptography and Data Security, pp. 238–256. Springer (2010)
21. Biryukov, A., Pustogarov, I.: Proof-of-work as anonymous micropayment: rewarding a tor relay?, Cryptology ePrint Archive, Report 2014/1011 (2014)
22. Ray, S., Slutzki, G., Zhang, Z.: Incentive-driven p2p anonymity system: a game-theoretic approach. Iowa State University, Tech. rep (2007)
23. Ersoy, O., Ren, Z., Erkin, Z., Lagendijk, R.L.: Transaction propagation on permissionless blockchains: incentive and routing mechanisms, arXiv preprint arXiv:1712.07564 (2017)
24. Lu, Z., Wang, Q., Qu, G., Liu, Z.: Bars: a blockchain-based anonymous reputation system for trust management in vanets. IEEE Trans. Netw. Serv. Manage. **18**(4), 4434–4449 (2021)
25. Zhang, H., Jiang, W., Ding, J.: A blockchain network admission control mechanism using anonymous identity-based cryptography. Appl. Sci. **15**(1), 130 (2025)
26. Zapico, A., Buterin, V., Khovratovich, D., Maller, M., Nitulescu, A., Simkin, M.: Caulk: lookup arguments in sublinear time. In: Proceedings of the 2022 ACM Sigsac Conference on Computer and Communications Security, pp. 3121–3134 (2022)

Robust Training of Efficient Traffic Classifier with Noisy Labels

Zuoyu Qiu[1], Mingwei Zhan[1], Xianwen Deng[1], Zhi Xue[1](✉), Yijun Wang[1], and Ruijie Zhao[2]

[1] Shanghai Jiao Tong University, Shanghai 200240, China
{17803091056,mw.zhan,2594306528,zxue,ericwyj}@sjtu.edu.cn
[2] Southeast University, Nanjing 211189, China
ruijiezhao@seu.edu.cn

Abstract. Traffic classification is of great significance for network management, such as improving the quality of service and detecting intrusions. Recently, deep learning-based methods have achieved impressive performance in traffic classification tasks. However, the high cost of data annotation and frequent changes in label definitions often introduce label noise into the training data, which significantly undermines model robustness and generalization. In this work, we propose a robust training framework for building an efficient traffic classifier under label noise to address this problem. First, we introduce Mamba as the backbone of the traffic encoder, since its linear time complexity is suitable for efficient traffic analysis. Then, the Mamba encoder is pre-trained on training data without labels to improve the ability of traffic representation learning. Based on the pre-trained encoder, we build an efficient classifier with a hierarchical feature extraction structure to better adapt to long-sequence traffic in classification. After that, we use a two-component GMM on per-sample losses to split clean and noisy sets. Then, we propose a semi-supervised learning based module to effectively fine-tune the classifier with the two sets of data. The module filters pseudo-labels by confidence and applies contrastive learning to low-confidence samples, avoiding sample discard. Results on three real-world traffic datasets show that our method outperforms state-of-the-art baselines by a large margin across various noise scenarios with superior computational efficiency.

Keywords: Label noise · Deep learning · Traffic classification · State space model

1 Introduction

Classifying applications from encrypted traffic, as an important network management technique, can effectively promote the quality of service (QoS). Recently, deep learning-based methods have been widely used for robust traffic classification. These methods heavily rely on high-quality traffic datasets for model

Z. Qiu and M. Zhan—Equal contribution.

R. Chen et al. (Eds.): Inscrypt 2025, LNCS 16409, pp. 448–466, 2026.
https://doi.org/10.1007/978-981-95-6203-9_24

training, i.e., clean data with correct labels. It is worth noting that obtaining high-quality training data in the field of traffic analysis is challenging. Firstly, collecting accurately classified traffic data is expensive, and the correctness of labels highly depends on the expertise of annotators [12]. To balance the annotation cost and dataset size, it is usually inevitable to introduce some label noise into large-scale datasets. Secondly, the labels in existing datasets may become inaccurate over time. For example, information security research institutions may assign different labels to the same type of traffic in reports of different years [29].

Recently, Qing et al. [22] investigate the issue of label noise in traffic analysis. They leverage the distinct distribution patterns of normal and malicious traffic in the feature space to achieve effective malicious traffic identification in noisy label scenarios. However, their approach is limited to binary classification, specifically handling label noise between normal and malicious traffic. In the field of traffic analysis, multi-class classification tasks are of great importance, particularly in QoS applications, where identifying traffic across multiple categories is essential for network resource allocation. Unfortunately, there is still no research to address the problem of multi-class traffic classification in label-noisy scenarios. Moreover, the latest label-noise learning methods, leveraging semi-supervised learning, have achieved promising results in handling label noise by training two models for label refinement [10,15]. However, these methods are typically designed for real-world image classification tasks, where the data characteristics differ significantly from network traffic, making them unsuitable for traffic analysis tasks.

To solve the above problems, we propose a robust training framework for building an efficient traffic classifier with noisy labels, denoted as TCNL. To analyze traffic efficiently, we first design a Mamba-based backbone network using advanced state-space models (SSM) for traffic feature encoding. Based on the Mamba encoder, we propose an efficient classifier with the hierarchical feature extraction structure (HFE), which can better handle long-sequence traffic flow in classification. Then, we develop a two-stage framework for training the classifier under label noise scenarios. In the pre-processing stage, we conduct self-supervised pre-training using the unlabeled training data to better extract general traffic data features via the Mamba encoder. In the label-noise fine-tuning stage, we first create two classifiers based on the pre-trained encoder, which could avoid confirmation bias caused by a single model. After the warm-up of each classifier, the losses of training data will form two independent Gaussian distributions. We can divide the training data into the clean set and the noisy set according to distribution confidence. At that time, two classifiers calculate losses of the same training dataset and divide. After that, they use the other classifier's clean-and-noisy data division result to fine-tune. Then, a label-noise learning module is designed to utilize the divided training data via semi-supervised learning. In detail, the clean set is treated as labeled data while the noisy set is treated as unlabeled. For the clean set, we use refined pseudo-labels directly in a cross-entropy objective. For the noisy set, we filter pseudo-labels by a 50% confidence threshold and compute cross-entropy only on high-confidence ones.

Additionally, we perform unsupervised contrastive learning on the noisy set, which achieves full utilization of all data and improves the generalization ability of our model. Experiments show that our method can significantly improve the classification performance of the model across various label noise scenarios.

In summary, this paper makes the following contributions:

- We propose TCNL, a robust training framework for building an efficient traffic classifier under label-noisy scenarios. TCNL is designed to address the critical label noise issue in multi-class traffic classification, which is rarely noticed in previous works.
- We build a Mamba-based traffic encoder and perform pre-training in the pre-processing stage. The Mamba blocks bring significant efficiency, while the pre-training strategy allows utilizing unlabeled traffic to improve the representation learning ability of the traffic encoder.
- In the label-noise fine-tuning stage, we fine-tune the pre-processed encoder to build a robust classifier under label noise. First, we propose a hierarchical feature extraction structure to handle long-sequence traffic flow in classification. Then, we divide the training data into the clean and noisy sets according to the loss distribution modeled by the Gaussian mixture model. Finally, we design a label-noise learning module to fine-tune the classifier based on the divided data with semi-supervised learning.
- We rigorously evaluate our method on three real-world traffic datasets. Empirical results demonstrate that our approach achieves superior classification accuracy compared to state-of-the-art baselines under varying degrees of label noise. Furthermore, our method exhibits significantly lower computational overhead while maintaining better traffic throughput.

2 Related Work

2.1 DL Traffic Classification Methods

With the increasing complexity of network services and environments, the basic features are no longer sufficient to meet network traffic analysis requirements [25]. Researchers have developed deep-learning (DL) algorithms to explore the high-dimensional statistical features. In [28], researchers use a Convolutional Neural Network (CNN) to identify network traffic images for encrypted traffic classification. TSCRNN [16] combines a CNN and a Recurrent Neural Network (RNN) to learn temporal features from time-related data packets. Lately, researchers have found that byte-level patterns of traffic exhibit statistical features similar to image pixels, some methods employ computer vision techniques to address traffic issues and show excellent performance. YaTC [31] converts traffic into a gray-scale image-like structure. This computer vision (CV)-style modeling enables direct adoption of modern vision backbones, thus significantly enlarging the capability boundary of the traffic classification task.

Meanwhile, remarkable progress has been made in the research of CV backbone networks in recent years. Vision Transformer (ViT) [8] regards an image as a series of flat 2D patches and directly applies a pure Transformer architecture. Vision Mamba (ViM) [32] draws inspiration from Mamba [11] and constructs a pure SSM model as a general-purpose visual backbone network without using attention. It improves the computational efficiency and classification performance.

2.2 Label-Noise Learning Methods

DL algorithms typically require large amounts of high-quality datasets for training. However, the cost of manual annotation is expensive, and the labels provided by network traffic detection services are not always reliable [29]. When the training data contains noisy labels, the performance of DL methods will significantly decline. Researchers have tried to solve this problem. The simplest method is to discard potential noisy samples [23]. Some methods combine DL with clustering operations to mitigate the impact of noise. SCAN [27] leverages a clustering method to derive semantic features as prior knowledge, which are then used to augment the DL model. Most other methods treat noisy samples as unlabeled data and use semi-supervised learning frameworks to process them. In DivideMix [15], researchers train two models using semi-supervised consistency regularization algorithms. UNICON [13] proposes a Jensen-Shannon divergence-based uniform selection mechanism, it performs better under a balanced dataset and a high noise ratio.

Recently, the task of traffic classification in the scenario of label noise has attracted the attention of researchers. RAPIER [22] recognizes the different distribution patterns of normal and malicious traffic in feature space. It can perform malicious traffic monitoring resistant to label noise. However, their method is limited to the binary-classification scenario. Current research on multi-class classification tasks under label noise conditions remains very limited. Therefore, we design a robust training framework for multi-class traffic classification. In the first stage, it introduces a Mamba-based encoder for traffic feature encoding and performs self-supervised pre-training on unlabeled traffic to obtain general representations. In the second stage, it fine-tunes the pre-processed encoder to build a robust classifier via hierarchical feature extraction, clean-and-noisy data division, and the label-noise learning module.

3 Methodology

In this section, we introduce our two-stage framework for training the efficient traffic classifier, including the pre-processing stage and the label-noise fine-tuning stage. Our overall framework illustration is shown in Fig. 1.

3.1 Pre-processing Stage

In this stage, we utilize Mamba, a recent advanced deep learning model with a significant efficiency advantage, to build our encoder backbone. Then, self-supervised pre-training is performed to improve the feature extraction ability

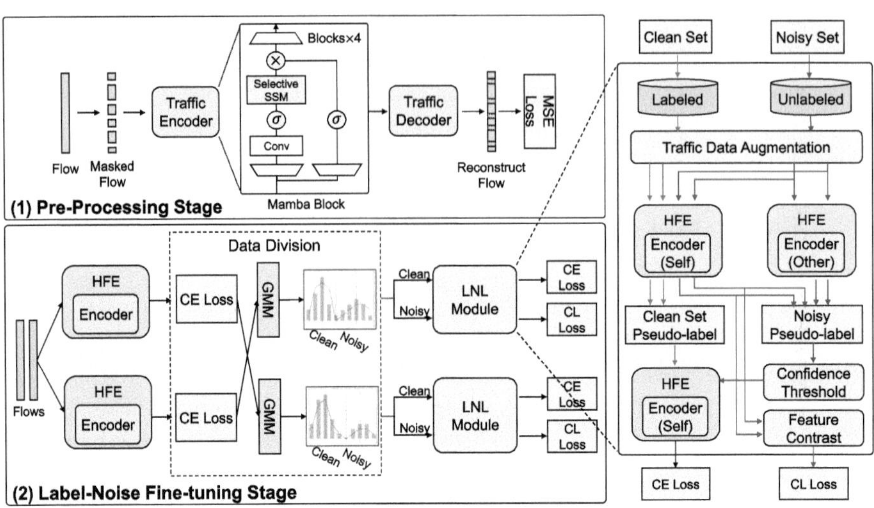

Fig. 1. The schematic illustration of our efficient traffic classifier training framework for label-noise learning.

of the Mamba encoder without the requirement of labeled data. This strategy allows the encoder learning from unlabeled traffic data, effectively improving the traffic representation quality learned by the Mamba encoder, providing better model weights for the subsequent fine-tuning stage under label noise.

3.1.1 Mamba Block

Recently, researchers have proposed a new network architecture called Mamba [11]. It is a state space model (SSM) and represents a continuous system as linear ordinary differential equations (ODEs). As shown in Eqs. (1) and (2), $\mathbf{A}, \mathbf{B}, \mathbf{C}$ represent the parameter matrices. Through the intermediate latent state $h(t)$, the SSM can establish a connection between the input sequence $x(t)$ and the output sequence $y(t)$.

$$h'(t) = \mathbf{A}h(t) + \mathbf{B}x(t) \tag{1}$$

$$y(t) = \mathbf{C}h(t) \tag{2}$$

Mamba proposes selective SSMs (S6) [11], using a convolutional network to transform $\mathbf{A}, \mathbf{B}, \mathbf{C}$ into functions of the input x. This makes Mamba can dynamically select input content to adjust the latent state and effectively process long-sequence texts. Compared to Transformer, Mamba can better learn the sequential characteristics of traffic data. Moreover, S6 architecture brings Mamba less computational complexity. Suppose n is the sequence length, the self-attention mechanism brings Transformer $O\left(n^2\right)$ complexity. In contrast, Mamba achieves a linear time complexity of $O\left(n\right)$, which means it requires fewer computational resources, which is vital to traffic analysis, allowing more complex multi-stage processes such as label noise learning.

3.1.2 Pre-training Strategy

Based on the traffic encoder built via the Mamba block, we perform self-supervised pre-training to improve the representation learning quality of the encoder. The flows of training data are introduced without labels in this stage and thus avoiding the effectiveness of noisy labels.

Firstly, we parse the original traffic into flows. The parsing process includes retaining the packet direction, removing the Ethernet header of the flow, setting the port number to zero, and replacing the IP address with a random address to avoid introducing biased interference. Then we use the multi-level flow representation algorithm [31] to format the traffic data size and generate a traffic matrix containing 40×40 uniform raw bytes for each parsed flow. We take the traffic matrix as input and use the "Encoder-Decoder" architecture to reconstruct the images. The encoder consists of 4 layers of Mamba blocks, and the decoder contains 2 layers of Mamba blocks. Between each layer of the Mamba blocks, we add an RMSNorm layer to stabilize the gradients.

At the beginning of the pre-training process, we serialize the original traffic matrix and add positional encoding. Then, we randomly remove 90% tokens in the traffic embedding, because a higher mask ratio can increase the difficulty of pre-training and enhance the model's ability to extract global features. After that, we input the traffic embedding into the "Encoder-Decoder" architecture to reconstruct the traffic matrix. We use the mean squared error (MSE) to calculate the loss between the original traffic matrix and the predicted traffic matrix.

3.2 Label-Noise Fine-Tuning Stage

In this stage, we fine-tune the pre-processed encoder to build a robust classifier under label noise. First, we propose a hierarchical feature extraction structure to enhance the encoder's capability of handling long-sequence traffic flow in classification. Then, we divide the training data into the clean set $\mathcal{X}$ and the noisy set $\mathcal{U}$ according to the loss distribution modeled by the Gaussian mixture model (GMM). Finally, we design a label-noise learning (LNL) module to fine-tune the classifier based on the divided data with semi-supervised learning.

3.2.1 Hierarchical Feature Extraction

In the label-noise fine-tuning stage, traffic flows are not masked to maintain the information integrity, which is different from the pre-training. It means all traffic embedding with long-sequence tokens is input into the encoder, requiring effective feature extraction without forgetting detailed token information. However, current sequence models, including RNN and advanced SSM, show early token decay under the long-sequence scenario, where the information of earlier token is prone to being forgotten. On the other hand, the earlier traffic

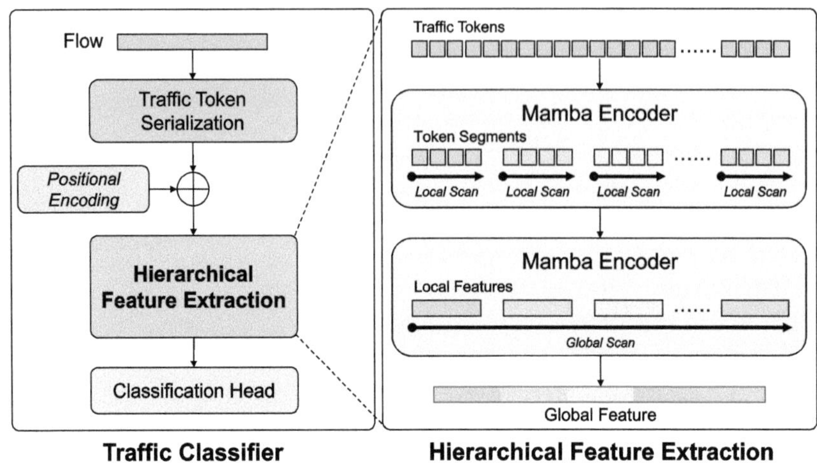

Fig. 2. The classifier design with hierarchical feature extraction structure.

bytes indicate packet header information, which is crucial for traffic classification tasks. Therefore, we design a hierarchical method to perform local-to-global feature extraction, where the long-sequence processing and early token decay are avoided.

As shown in Fig. 2, we serialize and perform positional encoding on the original traffic matrix to obtain $x_0 \in R^{N \times D}$, where L represents the token number and D represents the feature dimension. Next, the traffic tokens x_0 are sequentially divided into $\sqrt{L}$ non-overlapping local segments, each indicates a short sequence with $\sqrt{L}$ adjacent tokens. The Mamba encoder then scans each segment individually to extract local features $x_l^i \in R^{1 \times D}(i = 1, 2, ...\sqrt{L})$ without long-sequence tokens processing, enabling the model to evenly focus on information from each part of the traffic flow. After that, we obtain $\sqrt{L}$ segment features which form another new short sequence. Intuitively, we continue to use the same Mamba encoder to scan the segment sequence and extract the global feature $x \in R^{1 \times D}$. Compared with directly inputting x_0 into the Mamba encoder, our method effectively condenses information and reliefs early token decay.

3.2.2 Clean-and-Noisy Data Division

Based on the well-designed classifier with hierarchical feature extraction, we further utilize the distribution of classification loss to divide the training data into clean and noisy sets. Specifically, to prevent the accumulation of errors caused by the model using its own division results for training [15], we create two models with the same network structure but different parameters. These two models respectively divide the training data and use each other's partitioning results for further fine-tuning in the subsequent module.

First, the two models with the HFE encoder need initial training for preliminary convergence on the raw data. At this phase, the model uses all labels in

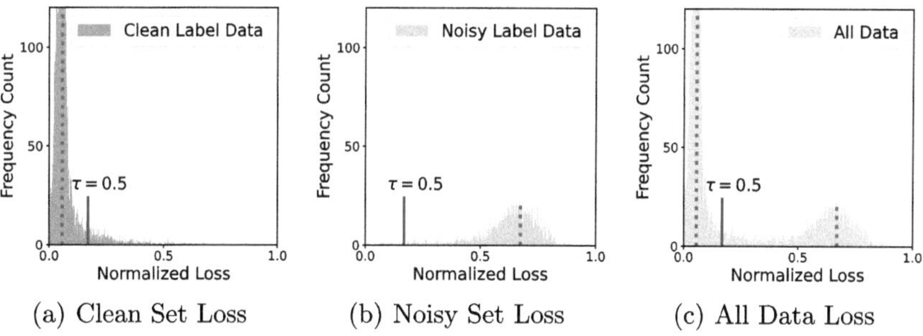

(a) Clean Set Loss (b) Noisy Set Loss (c) All Data Loss

Fig. 3. The loss distribution of SEU-QUIC2022 with 30% label noise after 30 epochs warm up. The blue dotted line represents the center of the Gaussian distribution. The purple short line represents the division threshold τ that has a 50% probability belong to clean label distribution. (Color figure online)

the training data as the ground truth, including the noisy labels. As the number of epochs increases, the model will gradually overfit on noisy labels. Therefore, we set a small number of training epochs for warm-up, ensuring that the model reaches a good convergence before overfitting. In the training process of warm-up, we use the method in Sect. 3.2.1 to get feature representation x_g. We perform the class prediction of x_g via the classification head and thus calculate its CE Loss [19] with label smoothing.

After the warm-up phase, we train the model using the complete label-noise fine-tuning strategy for the remaining epochs. Firstly, we use all labels as ground truth and obtain the standard cross-entropy loss values for all samples. Arpit et al. [2] shows that when datasets have label noise, deep learning networks learn clean samples faster than noisy samples. This results in clean samples commonly have a lower loss.

$$\ell(\theta) = \{\ell_i\}_{i=1}^{N} = \{-\sum_{c=1}^{C} y_i^c \log\left(\mathrm{p}_{\text{model}}^{\text{c}}\ (x_i;\theta)\right)\}_{i=1}^{N} \tag{3}$$

Suppose $\mathcal{D} = \{(x_i, y_i)\}_{i=1}^{N}$ represent the training set, the losses of samples $\mathcal{D}$ will form two Gaussian distributions with different centers, as shown in Fig. 3. We use the bimodal Gaussian mixture model (GMM) [21] to fit the loss distributions of clean samples and noisy samples. The samples with a smaller center value is considered the clean set, while the samples with a bigger center value is considered the noisy set. Furthermore, we can express the two sets of samples in the form of Eqs. (4) and (5), where $\mathcal{X} \subseteq \mathcal{D}$ denotes the set of clean samples, $\mathcal{U} \subseteq \mathcal{D}$ denotes the set of noisy samples. We use p to represent the probability that whether $(\mathbf{x}_i, \mathbf{y}_i)$ is clean sample, where ℓ_i denotes the loss value, γ denotes the GMM parameters, τ denotes clustering threshold. Usually, τ is set to 0.5, it means that if a sample's loss value has a probability of more than 50% belonging to the clean set distribution, then this sample is considered to have a clean label.

$$\mathcal{X} = \{(\mathbf{x}_i, \mathbf{y}_i) : p(x_i = \text{clean} \mid \ell_i, \gamma) \geq \tau\} \tag{4}$$

$$\mathcal{U} = \{(\mathbf{x}_i, \mathbf{y}_i) : p(x_i = \text{clean} \mid \ell_i, \gamma) < \tau\} \tag{5}$$

As mentioned earlier, we train two networks simultaneously for mutual supervision. We use one network to divide the noisy training dataset into $\mathcal{X}$ and $\mathcal{U}$. The other network will use this partitioning result in its LNL module. This method avoids the confirmation bias of self-training where the model accumulates errors.

3.2.3 Label-Noise Learning Module

We introduce the training method of the label-noise learning (LNL) module, which mainly includes the loss value calculation strategies adopted respectively for sets $\mathcal{X}$ and $\mathcal{U}$. In noisy set $\mathcal{U}$, the correctness of the original labels is very low. So we can regard $\mathcal{X}$ as the labeled dataset while regarding $\mathcal{U}$ as the unlabeled dataset. Referring to MixMatch [3], we propose an LNL module suitable for traffic data. Its innovations are demonstrated in the following three aspects. Firstly, to avoid the damage caused by the traditional image augmentation method, we propose a traffic matrix augmentation method. It is to randomly mask the patches on traffic images. The patches have 2 pixels length and width. For each patch, it has a 20% probability of being masked. We use this method in the LNL module to improve model generalization and perform feature contrastive training. Secondly, we remove the MixUp step. Because each pixel in the traffic matrix represents real traffic bytes, performing the MixUP operation on the traffic matrix will severely damage the original semantic information. We find that MixUP will lead to approximately 5% performance degradation. Thirdly, we propose a new loss function design for the unlabeled traffic data set, the specific process will be introduced below.

For the sample (x_i, y_i) in $\mathcal{X}$, we use $w_i = p$ in Eq. (4) to represent the confidence of origin label y_i. We obtain (x_i^1, x_i^2) through data augmentation and use the network to predict its new labels (p_i^1, p_i^2). We add the two together and take the average to get $\bar{p_i}$. After that, we use w_i to perform a weighted sum between y_i and $\bar{p_i}$. Finally, we perform sharpening on the result to obtain pseudo-label $\bar{y}_i$.

$$\begin{aligned}
(x_i^1, x_i^2) &= Augmentation(x_i), \\
(p_i^1, p_i^2) &= \mathrm{p}_{\mathrm{model}}^{\mathrm{c}}\left((x_i^1, x_i^2); \theta\right), \\
\bar{p_i} &= (p_i^1 + p_i^2)/2, \\
\bar{y}_i &= w_i y_i + (1 - w_i)\,\bar{p_i}, \\
\hat{y}_i &= \bar{y}_i^{c\frac{1}{T}} / \sum_{c=1}^{C} \bar{y}_i^{c\frac{1}{T}}, \text{ for } c = 1, 2, \ldots, C
\end{aligned} \tag{6}$$

For the sample x_i in $\mathcal{U}$, due to the absence of the original label, the quality of the generated pseudo-label is poor. We add unsupervised contrastive learning loss and confidence-based cross-entropy loss to improve pseudo-label quality. We first perform data augmentation twice to x_i to obtain x_i^1 and x_i^2. After that, we use the Mamba encoder to obtain features z_i^1 and z_i^2. We calculate the contrastive learning loss $\mathcal{L}_{CL}$ using the loss function in SimCLR [5]. As shown in Eqs. (7) and (8):

$$\mathcal{L}_{CL} = -\frac{1}{2N} \cdot \sum_{i=1}^{N} [l(z_i^1, z_i^2) + l(z_i^2, z_i^1)], \tag{7}$$

$$l(n,m) = -\log \frac{\exp(z_n \cdot z_m/\delta)}{\sum_{k \in 2N, n \neq k} \exp(z_n \cdot z_k/\delta)} \tag{8}$$

Here, $l(n,m)$ indicates the similarity score between the input z_n and z_m, N indicates the number of samples in a minibatch, and we use δ to sharpen the product of feature similarity, we fix it at 0.025. By adding the contrastive loss, we utilize all the noisy set data, ensuring that the model always learns toward the feature center of x_i, which reduces the bias caused by incorrect pseudo-labels.

Next, we generate the pseudo-label for $x_i \in \mathcal{U}$. We use the two networks to predict x_i^1, x_i^2 separately. After that, we take the average of the four results and perform sharpening to obtain pseudo-label $\bar{y}_i$. Since pseudo-labels with incorrect predictions can negatively impact model performance, we set a confidence threshold to filter out pseudo-labels with low confidence. We apply softmax to $\bar{y}_i$ and check whether its maximum value is greater than 0.5, i.e., the pseudo-label confidence exceeds 50%. We only calculate the loss for $\bar{y}_i$ with a confidence higher than 50%. This design allows us to avoid the cumulative training errors caused by incorrect pseudo-labels. Combined with the $\mathcal{L}_{CL}$ used earlier, we can fully utilize every data point in the noisy set while significantly mitigating the impact of label prediction errors.

Correspondingly, we denote $\mathcal{X}$ and $\mathcal{U}$ with the pseudo-labels as $\hat{\mathcal{X}}$ and $\hat{\mathcal{U}}$, and calculate the cross-entropy loss $\mathcal{L}_{CE}$ for them. A regularization term $\mathcal{L}_{\text{reg}}$ is added to prevent the network from assigning all samples to a single class under a high noise ratio [1]. This regularization term uses a uniform prior distribution π (i.e., $\pi_c = 1/C$) to regularize the model's average output of all samples in a mini-batch.

$$\mathcal{L}_{\text{reg}} = \sum_c \pi_c \log \left(\pi_c \Big/ \frac{1}{\left|\hat{\mathcal{X}}\right| + \left|\hat{\mathcal{U}}\right|} \sum_{\hat{x} \in \hat{\mathcal{X}} + \hat{\mathcal{U}}} \mathrm{p}_{\text{model}}^{\mathrm{c}}(\hat{x}; \theta) \right) \tag{9}$$

Finally, the total loss is:

$$\mathcal{L} = \mathcal{L}_{CL} + \mathcal{L}_{CE} + \mathcal{L}_{\text{reg}} \tag{10}$$

4 Performance Evaluations

In this section, we detail and dissect the outcomes of our experimental evaluations. Concretely, we tackle the following four key research inquiries:

- **RQ1:** How does our method perform compared to other approaches when dealing with label noise?
- **RQ2:** How well does each module contribute to our method?
- **RQ3:** How about the computational efficiency of our method?
- **RQ4:** How does our method perform in real-world and asymmetric label noise scenarios?

4.1 Experiment Setup

Our experiments are conducted on three public real-world encrypted traffic datasets: the Browser dataset [26], the SEU-QUIC2022 dataset [20] and the CICIoT2022 dataset [7]. We partition the datasets and set the number of samples between 10,000 and 13,000. The similar total data volume ensures the results of GMM clustering will not be affected by quantity difference between datasets. We set the ratio of the training set to the test set as 6:4 in all datasets. The detail is in the following way:

- **Browser** [26]**:** This is a browser traffic dataset, which includes traffic data of four different browsers. The classes are Chrome, Firefox, Samsung Internet, and UC Browser. We randomly extract 3,000 flows from each class to generate traffic matrices. There are a total of 12,000 samples.
- **SEU-QUIC2022** [20]**:** This is a video streaming traffic dataset, which includes 8 different classes such as Facebook and YouTube. We use all the flows to generate traffic matrices. There are a total of 12,995 samples.
- **CICIoT2022** [7]**:** This is an IoT device traffic dataset. We select 9 classes from the dataset and randomly extract 1,500 flows from each class. For classes with less than 1,500 flows, we use all the flows to generate traffic matrices. There are a total of 11,273 samples.

We compare our method with a range of baselines and state-of-the-art models to comprehensively evaluate our model, as listed below:

- **CNN** and **FS-Net** [18] are DL-based traffic classification methods, they use raw packet information for supervised learning.
- **PERT** [6], **ET-BERT** [17] and **YaTC** [31] use traffic data for pre-training, after that they use a small number of labels for supervised learning. They turn the traffic information into NLP task or CV task and perform well under no label noise scenarios.
- **CE** [4], **MixUp** [30] and **LSR** [19] are methods that use various different loss functions. They employ the same feature extraction method and Mamba backbone network in our classifier, but do not utilize the label-noise fine-tuning strategy.
- **UNICON** [13] and **DivideMix** [15] are methods that use semi-supervised learning framework to handle label-noise learning task. These methods are typically applied to object image datasets such as CIFAR [14], and their performance on traffic classification remains to be tested.

Table 1. Comparison of Accuracy (%) with Baselines on Three Real-World Traffic Datasets.

Method	Browser					SEU-QUIC2022					CICIoT2022				
	10%	20%	30%	40%	50%	10%	20%	30%	40%	50%	10%	20%	30%	40%	50%
CNN	76.5	67.6	58.0	49.3	43.4	82.8	76.6	66.5	56.7	44.7	85.0	77.9	69.5	60.6	52.4
FS-Net	46.1	43.3	41.3	36.5	36.3	86.4	80.3	78.3	76.1	75.5	77.1	76.0	74.8	71.4	70.3
PERT	64.1	60.8	53.9	43.7	37.5	87.1	83.2	73.3	65.0	53.2	84.0	76.9	75.0	58.0	49.0
ET-BERT	63.9	58.8	53.6	48.6	40.5	87.3	83.5	74.7	65.9	56.6	82.8	76.0	68.4	57.3	49.3
YaTC	89.3	82.4	74.1	58.5	46.9	95.8	92.3	86.5	78.9	66.1	89.6	83.8	76.1	67.6	56.6
CE	87.1	79.2	67.0	54.4	46.2	90.5	85.8	76.1	65.1	53.9	86.4	84.1	70.5	60.3	49.9
MixUP	85.4	77.8	66.9	55.8	46.4	91.3	85.5	77.9	67.6	54.1	87.9	81.8	71.7	62.8	53.0
LSR	88.3	77.3	65.0	55.2	45.1	90.5	85.7	76.6	66.0	54.5	87.4	84.5	80.9	61.9	51.5
UNICON	70.3	67.8	63.6	59.7	55.7	82.3	81.3	76.7	72.5	63.2	82.7	81.6	78.7	76.5	72.1
DivideMix	70.1	66.8	63.4	59.3	53.9	92.4	89.0	83.2	78.3	68.6	87.3	85.2	81.8	75.3	68.6
TCNL (Ours)	**93.4**	**92.9**	**92.0**	**91.2**	**87.8**	**96.2**	**95.0**	**93.1**	**91.1**	**86.3**	**90.7**	**90.0**	**88.5**	**85.9**	**80.8**

All the evaluations are conducted in Python 3.10 with the PyTorch framework of version 2.1.2 and running on the PC with Intel® Core™ i9-11900K@3.50 GHz, 64 GB RAM, and an NVIDIA GeForce RTX3090 GPU. In the pre-processing stage, the batch size is 128 and the total step is 150,000. We set the base learning rate to 1×10^{-3} and use the linear learning rate scaling rule with the AdamW optimizer. We randomly mask 90% tokens. In the label-noise fine-tuning stage, we use the AdamW optimizer for 200 epochs, where the base learning rate is set to 2×10^{-3}, batch size is 64 and warm up epoch is 30.

4.2 Comparison with State-of-the-Art Methods (to RQ1)

Table 1 presents the results of the traffic classification performance under different label noise ratios. In our experiments, we introduce symmetric (i.e. uniformly random) label noise and set the noise ratios to 10%, 20%, 30%, 40%, and 50% respectively. Meanwhile, Browser is a partitioned balanced dataset, while the other two datasets are imbalanced. This setup also examines the impact of sample quantity distribution on the model.

Experimental results show that our method achieves the best performance under various noise ratios for the three datasets. It is obvious that traditional DL-based methods such as CNN and FS-Net have rather limited classification capabilities. As the noise ratio increases, their classification ability drops rapidly.

PERT, ET-BERT, and YaTC all employ pre-training to enhance the classification ability of the models. Meanwhile, they all use the Transformer backbone to learn the internal relationships of traffic data. It can be noted that these models show better classification performance than traditional DL models when the label noise ratio is low. However, as the noise ratio rises, the classification performance of these models also declines rapidly.

Table 2. Ablation Study of Accuracy (%) on Three Real-World Traffic Datasets. The abbreviations are explained as follows: HFE: hierarchical feature extraction structure, CT: 50% confidence threshold, CL: contrastive learning loss.

Method	Browser					SEU-QUIC2022					CICIoT2022				
	10%	20%	30%	40%	50%	10%	20%	30%	40%	50%	10%	20%	30%	40%	50%
TCNL (Ours)	**93.4**	**92.9**	**92.0**	**91.2**	**87.8**	**96.2**	**95.0**	**93.1**	**91.1**	**86.3**	**90.7**	**90.0**	**88.5**	**85.9**	**80.8**
w/o pretrain	91.8	91.5	90.7	77.1	74.8	93.6	91.8	91.0	87.7	85.8	84.9	81.7	83.2	81.1	75.4
w/o HFE	93.0	92.0	89.1	82.8	74.9	95.3	93.7	91.0	85.3	82.7	90.2	82.1	86.3	81.7	75.2
w/o CT&CL	93.4	92.6	91.1	88.6	83.3	95.8	94.8	92.0	86.7	83.6	90.4	89.9	87.4	84.8	79.1
w/o Mamba	92.9	91.7	89.4	82.7	75.4	95.5	94.8	93.0	89.9	86.2	90.5	89.2	87.9	85.2	78.0

CE, MixUP, and LSR use the traffic hierarchical feature extraction structure and Mamba backbone designed by us, but without label-noise fine-tuning strategy. It can be seen that when using different loss functions, the performance degradation is still quite obvious under high-noise conditions. MixUP and LSR can slightly improve the classification performance of models. When the dataset is more imbalanced or the noise level is higher, the performance improvement will be more significant.

DivideMix and UNICON use a SSL framework. We replace the origin data augmentation method with the traffic data augmentation method mentioned in this paper. The experimental results show that DivideMix has significant advantages in label noise scenarios. However, due to its lack of feature processing for traffic data, its overall performance is inferior to our method. UNICON performs slightly better than DivideMix on Browser dataset, but it performs worse in most cases on the other datasets. It demonstrates better performance under higher noise ratio and on more balanced dataset.

Our method TCNL leverages a LNL framework and designs Mamba traffic classifier. It can effectively mitigate the impact of high noise ratio. As can be seen, under the noise level of 50%, the performance of our model is significantly higher than other methods. At the same time, when the noise ratio is low, our model also demonstrates excellent classification performance. This is because our method employs more advanced feature extraction methods and backbone network design, so it remains an excellent traffic classifier even under low noise conditions.

4.3 Ablation Study on Performance (to RQ2)

To further examine the level of benefit that each component of our TCNL framework brings to the performance, we conduct an ablation study on three baseline datasets. The evaluation results are reported in Table 2.

Experimental results show that performing pre-training can enhance the model's classification ability. Unsupervised pre-training makes better use of general features especially when the samples are balanced and sufficient. In the

Browser dataset, pretraining brings a performance improvement of more than 10% under high noise levels. Meanwhile, in the other two imbalanced datasets, there is still an improvement more than 3%. During the experiment, we also find that the pretrained model can use fewer epochs in the warm up phase and has a higher best accuracy.

Furthermore, our hierarchical feature extraction structure (HFE) also works effectively in noisy scenarios. In ablation experiment, we directly input x_0 in Sect. 3.2.1 into Mamba encoder. Experimental results show that HFE can improve test accuracy, and the improvement is more significant under high noise ratio conditions. Without HFE, model is more prone to produce NaN values during training process. It often requires smaller learning rate, i.e., 1×10^{-4} and longer training time. In contrast, model with HFE is robust even when using larger learning rate, i.e., 1×10^{-3}. It shows that our design also improves training stability.

The ablation experiment also shows that the loss funtion design of LNL module have positive result. In ablation experiment, we adopt the original loss function in MixMatch [3], which means applying cross-entropy loss to $\hat{\mathcal{X}}$ and mean squared error (MSE) loss to $\hat{\mathcal{U}}$. It removes confidence threshold (CT) and contrastive learning loss (CL). In this case, the model is more likely to learn low-quality pseudo-labels. Experimental results show that this ablation can bring a 1%-3% performance drop. This confirms the effectiveness of our design.

4.4 Ablation Study on Efficiency (to RQ3)

We also evaluate the compute efficiency between Transformer and Mamba by replace the Mamba blocks in the model with Transformer blocks while keeping other conditions unchanged. The experiments are conducted with a batch size of 64. The result in Table 2 last line shows that Mamba achieve the same classification performance and even better. At the same time, Mamba outperforms the Transformer in many computational performance metics. As shown in Fig. 4, we test the memory usage of the model during the label-noise fine-tuning stage. It can be seen that Mamba only uses 68% of the GPU memory to achieve the same classification performance. Moreover, with linear time complexity of $O(n)$, Mamba only use 59.0% parameters. Finally, we test the throughput under the same GPU memory occupancy, Mamba is also superior to Transformer. This implies that Mamba has a faster processing speed. It is important in real-time tasks such as intrusion detection.

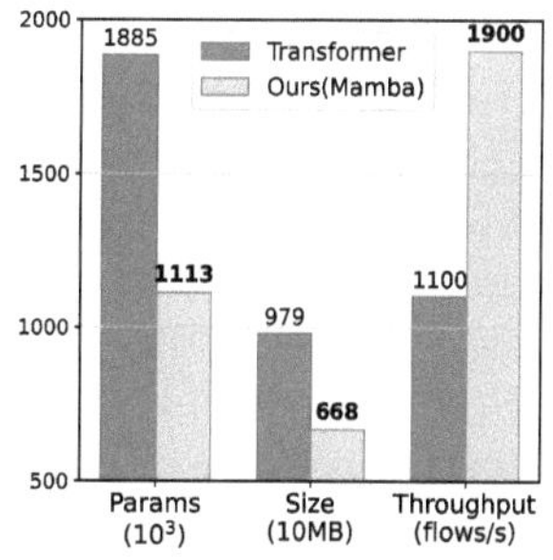

Fig. 4. The efficiency and computational performance of the backbone network.

Table 3. Precision and Recall (%) of Divide Process on Three Real-World Traffic Datasets.

Label Type	Metrics	Browser					SEU-QUIC2022					CICIoT2022				
		10%	20%	30%	40%	50%	10%	20%	30%	40%	50%	10%	20%	30%	40%	50%
Noise	Precision	79.0	88.1	92.2	94.8	97.2	84.2	91.5	94.3	96.6	96.4	65.9	82.1	89.1	91.1	91.4
	Recall	96.2	94.2	93.4	92.1	87.2	96.1	92.9	90.0	89.3	88.4	92.3	92.2	90.2	90.1	87.3
Clean	Precision	99.6	98.6	97.2	94.9	88.5	99.6	98.3	95.9	93.3	89.1	99.1	98.0	95.8	93.5	87.9
	Recall	97.1	96.9	96.7	96.7	97.6	98.0	97.9	97.8	98.0	94.0	94.5	95.0	95.3	94.2	91.8

Table 4. Statistics of Noisy Labels in the CICIDS2017 dataset. The abbreviations are explained as follows: NN: original noisy label divided into noise, NC: original noisy label divided into clean.

Class	Count	NN	NC	Precision (%)	Recall (%)
BENIGN	16,593	15,827	766	99.8	95.4
Bot	490	0	490	0.0	0.0
PortScan	466	208	258	81.6	44.6
DDos	112	60	52	10.4	53.6
FTP Patator	11	0	11	0.0	0.0
Total	**17,672**	**16,095**	**1,577**	**96.4**	**91.1**

4.5 Real-World Evaluation (to RQ4)

In this section, we test our framework in real-world label noise scenarios. Firstly, we verify the ability of our method to divide the clean sample set $\mathcal{X}$ and the noisy sample set $\mathcal{U}$ on the three baseline datasets. As shown in Table 3, we tested the precision and recall rate of the division results. It can be seen that as label noise ratio increases, dividing the clean sample set $\mathcal{X}$ shows a downward trend precision, while the noisy sample set $\mathcal{U}$ keeps a rising precision. This phenomenon is in line with statistical laws. As the number of samples with label noise increases, it becomes easier to find the noisy samples, while it becomes more difficult to find the clean samples. By observing the recall rate, we find that it remains stable at a relatively high level. This indicates that our model can correctly divide out the label noise samples and resist the impact of the increase in the noise proportion.

Next, we test our method on real-world label noise. Engelen et al. [9] discover that CICIDS2017 [24] dataset has issues such as misunderstandings of the TCP mechanism and mislabeling malicious traffic as benign, resulting in a large number of noisy labels. They provide a better labeled dataset using origin data. There are a total of 261,216 traffic flows, among which 17,672 traffic flows have incorrect labels, accounting for 6.8% of the total, as shown in Table 4. Since it is difficult for us to know the true labels of the noisy data in the real-world label noise scenario, we test the ability of our model to find label noise samples.

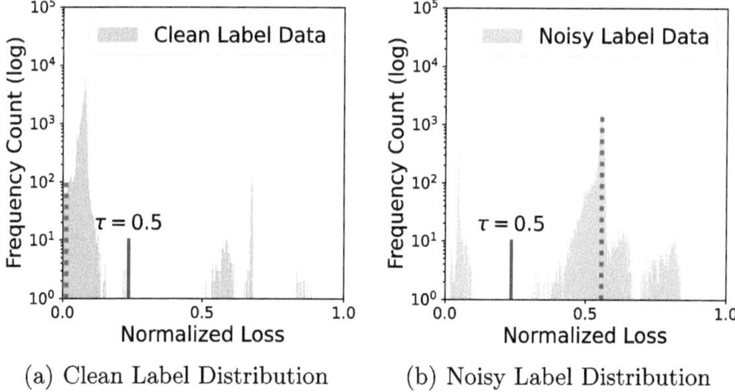

(a) Clean Label Distribution (b) Noisy Label Distribution

Fig. 5. The loss value distribution after 60 epochs of training on the CICIDS2017 dataset. The blue dashed line represents the clustering center of each set. The purple line represents the position where the model divides the data according to a 50% clean set clustering probability. (Color figure online)

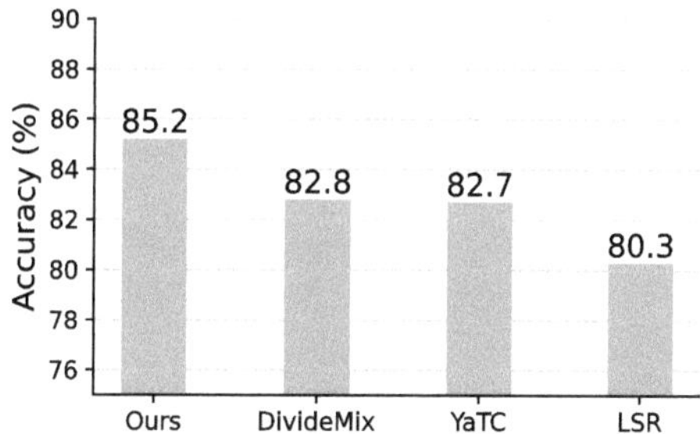

Fig. 6. Asymmetric noise experiment results on SEU-QUIC2022 dataset.

We set the batch size to 200 without pre-training, and carried out a warm up for 30 epochs. When the training reaches 60 epochs, the division accuracy of noisy labels has reached more than 96%. The division result is showed in Fig. 5. According to the research of Engelen et al. [9], a large number of BENIGN traffic in the original CICIDS2017 dataset are judged as noise. As shown in Table 4, our method successfully detected the vast majority of noisy labels in the BENIGN class, and also had an effective detection result on classes with fewer samples. This proves that our model can very effectively find label noise in real-world scenario, which further inspires us to use our method to efficiently discover potential noisy labels in other traffic datasets.

4.6 Evaluation Under Asymmetric Label Noise (to RQ4)

In an asymmetric noise environment, two types of similar data are often assigned the same label. For example, in an animal image dataset, a cat may be labeled as a dog, or a cow may be labeled as a horse. This can cause the network to overfit during the warm-up stage, thereby affecting the ability of the GMM to distinguish the loss distribution [15].

In order to verify the effectiveness of our method in an asymmetric noise environment, we selected 4 traffic types from the SEU-QUIC2022 dataset and mapped them to other specified categories to introduce asymmetric noise. We set the noise ratio to 40% and conduct tests using the best methods of each category shown in Table 1. The experimental results are shown in Fig. 6. Under the condition of asymmetric noise, our method still surpasses other methods. This indicates that our method remains effective in asymmetric label noise scenario, which also inspires us to conduct further exploration of the potential applicable label noise scenarios in the future.

5 Conclusion

In this paper, we propose TCNL, a two-stage training framework for multi-class traffic classification under noisy labels. In the first stage, we introduce a Mamba-based encoder for traffic feature encoding and perform self-supervised pre-training on unlabeled traffic to obtain general representations. In the second stage, we fine-tune the pre-processed encoder to build a robust classifier under noisy labels via hierarchical feature extraction, clean-and-noisy data division, and the label-noise learning module. Experiments on three real-world datasets demonstrate that TCNL consistently outperforms strong baselines across noise levels from 10% to 50%, with accuracies remaining above 80% even under the highest noise ratio. In addition, TCNL is also efficient, requiring about 68% GPU memory and 59% parameters of the Transformer classifier while delivering higher throughput. These results show that robust and efficient traffic classification can be achieved under noisy labels, providing a new solution to this real-world challenge in traffic analysis.

Acknowledgments. This work was supported in part by the Basic Research Program of Jiangsu under Grant BK20251353; in part by the National Natural Science Foundation of China under Grant 62502089; and in part by SJTU-QI'ANXIN Joint Lab of Information System Security. Ruijie Zhao is the project lead for this work.

References

1. Arazo, E., Ortego, D., Albert, P., O'Connor, N., McGuinness, K.: Unsupervised label noise modeling and loss correction. In: International Conference on Machine Learning, pp. 312–321 (2019)
2. Arpit, D., et al.: A closer look at memorization in deep networks. In: International Conference on Machine Learning, pp. 233–242. PMLR (2017)
3. Berthelot, D., Carlini, N., Goodfellow, I., Papernot, N., Oliver, A., Raffel, C.A.: MixMatch: A holistic approach to semi-supervised learning. Adv. Neural Inf. Process. Syst. **32** (2019)

4. Burges, C.J.: A tutorial on support vector machines for pattern recognition. Data Min. Knowl. Disc. **2**(2), 121–167 (1998)
5. Chen, T., Kornblith, S., Norouzi, M., Hinton, G.: A simple framework for contrastive learning of visual representations. In: International Conference on Machine Learning, pp. 1597–1607. PMLR (2020)
6. Cui, Y., Yang, Z., Liu, T.: PERT: pre-training BERT with permuted language model. arXiv preprint arXiv:2203.06906 (2022)
7. Dadkhah, S., Mahdikhani, H., Danso, P.K., Zohourian, A., Truong, K.A., Ghorbani, A.A.: Towards the development of a realistic multidimensional IoT profiling dataset. In: 2022 19th Annual International Conference on Privacy, Security & Trust (PST), pp. 1–11 (2022)
8. Dosovitskiy, A., et al.: An image is worth 16x16 words: transformers for image recognition at scale. arXiv preprint arXiv:2010.11929 (2020)
9. Engelen, G., Rimmer, V., Joosen, W.: Troubleshooting an intrusion detection dataset: the cicids2017 case study. In: 2021 IEEE Security and Privacy Workshops (SPW), pp. 7–12 (2021)
10. Fooladgar, F., To, M.N.N., Mousavi, P., Abolmaesumi, P.: Manifold DivideMix: a semi-supervised contrastive learning framework for severe label noise. In: Proceedings of the IEEE/CVF Conference on Computer Vision and Pattern Recognition, pp. 4012–4021 (2024)
11. Gu, A., Dao, T.: Mamba: linear-time sequence modeling with selective state spaces. arXiv preprint arXiv:2312.00752 (2023)
12. Guerra, J.L., Catania, C., Veas, E.: Datasets are not enough: challenges in labeling network traffic. Comput. Secur. **120**, 102810 (2022)
13. Karim, N., Rizve, M.N., Rahnavard, N., Mian, A., Shah, M.: UNICON: combating label noise through uniform selection and contrastive learning. In: Proceedings of the IEEE/CVF Conference on Computer Vision and Pattern Recognition, pp. 9676–9686 (2022)
14. Krizhevsky, A., Hinton, G.: Learning multiple layers of features from tiny images. In: Handbook of Systemic Autoimmune Diseases, vol. 1 (2009)
15. Li, J., Socher, R., Hoi, S.C.: DivideMix: learning with noisy labels as semi-supervised learning. arXiv preprint arXiv:2002.07394 (2020)
16. Lin, K., Xu, X., Gao, H.: TSCRNN: a novel classification scheme of encrypted traffic based on flow spatiotemporal features for efficient management of IIoT. Comput. Netw. **190**, 107974 (2021)
17. Lin, X., Xiong, G., Gou, G., Li, Z., Shi, J., Yu, J.: ET-BERT: a contextualized datagram representation with pre-training transformers for encrypted traffic classification. In: Proceedings of the ACM Web Conference 2022, pp. 633–642 (2022)
18. Liu, C., He, L., Xiong, G., Cao, Z., Li, Z.: FS-Net: a flow sequence network for encrypted traffic classification. In: IEEE Conference on Computer Communications, IEEE INFOCOM 2019, pp. 1171–1179 (2019)
19. Lukasik, M., Bhojanapalli, S., Menon, A., Kumar, S.: Does label smoothing mitigate label noise? In: International Conference on Machine Learning, pp. 6448–6458 (2020)
20. Niu, D., Cheng, G., Chen, Z., Qiu, X.: Video stalling identification for web live streaming under HTTP-FLV. Comput. Netw. **254**, 110714 (2024)
21. Permuter, H., Francos, J., Jermyn, I.: A study of Gaussian mixture models of color and texture features for image classification and segmentation. Pattern Recogn. **39**, 695–706 (2006)
22. Qing, Y., et al.: Low-quality training data only? A robust framework for detecting encrypted malicious network traffic. arXiv preprint arXiv:2309.04798 (2023)

23. Sachdeva, R., Cordeiro, F.R., Belagiannis, V., Reid, I., Carneiro, G.: EvidentialMix: learning with combined open-set and closed-set noisy labels. In: Proceedings of the IEEE/CVF Winter Conference on Applications of Computer Vision, pp. 3607–3615 (2021)
24. Sharafaldin, I., Lashkari, A.H., Ghorbani, A.A., et al.: Toward generating a new intrusion detection dataset and intrusion traffic characterization. In: ICISSp, vol. 1, pp. 108–116 (2018)
25. Taylor, V.F., Spolaor, R., Conti, M., Martinovic, I.: AppScanner: automatic fingerprinting of smartphone apps from encrypted network traffic. In: 2016 IEEE European Symposium on Security and Privacy (EuroS&P), pp. 439–454 (2016)
26. Van Ede, T., et al.: FlowPrint: semi-supervised mobile-app fingerprinting on encrypted network traffic. In: Network and Distributed System Security Symposium (NDSS), vol. 27 (2020)
27. Van Gansbeke, W., Vandenhende, S., Georgoulis, S., Proesmans, M., Van Gool, L.: SCAN: learning to classify images without labels. In: European Conference on Computer Vision, pp. 268–285 (2020)
28. Wang, W., Zhu, M., Zeng, X., Ye, X., Sheng, Y.: Malware traffic classification using convolutional neural network for representation learning. In: 2017 International Conference on Information Networking (ICOIN), pp. 712–717 (2017)
29. Xu, J., Li, Y., Deng, R.H.: Differential training: a generic framework to reduce label noises for Android malware detection. In: Proceedings 2021 Network and Distributed System Security Symposium (2021)
30. Zhang, H., Cisse, M., Dauphin, Y.N., Lopez-Paz, D.: mixup: beyond empirical risk minimization. arXiv preprint arXiv:1710.09412 (2017)
31. Zhao, R., et al.: Yet another traffic classifier: a masked autoencoder based traffic transformer with multi-level flow representation. In: Proceedings of the AAAI Conference on Artificial Intelligence, pp. 5420–5427 (2023)
32. Zhu, L., Liao, B., Zhang, Q., Wang, X., Liu, W., Wang, X.: Vision Mamba: efficient visual representation learning with bidirectional state space model. In: International Conference on Machine Learning, pp. 62429–62442 (2024)

A Multimodal Asynchronous Federated Learning Approach for Encrypted Traffic Classification

Xiangbin Wang[1,2], Qingjun Yuan[1,2(✉)], Yongjuan Wang[1,2(✉)], Yu Yan[1,2], Xiangyu Wang[1,2], and Chunxiang Gu[1,2]

[1] Henan Key Laboratory of Network Cryptography Technology, Information Engineering University, Zhengzhou 450001, Henan, China
gcxyuan@outlook.com, pinkywyj@163.com

[2] Key Laboratory of Cyberspace Security, Ministry of Education, Zhengzhou 450001, Henan, China

Abstract. With the widespread application of encryption technology in network traffic, traditional traffic classification methods face significant challenges when dealing with encrypted communications. Moreover, the effectiveness of machine learning-based classification approaches is often hindered by data isolation across different organizations and the scarcity of labeled traffic samples. To address these challenges, an encrypted traffic classification method based on multimodal asynchronous federated learning is proposed in this paper, named MaFT. This approach leverages federated learning to enable collaborative model training across distributed organizations without sharing sensitive raw data, thereby overcoming data isolation while preserving data locality requirements. The method employs multimodal learning to fully utilize different types of traffic features, including raw bytes and packet length sequences, through Deep Canonical Correlation Autoencoders that can handle both single-modal and multi-modal clients with varying data capabilities. MaFT adopts a semi-supervised training strategy, conducting unsupervised autoencoder training on the client side to reduce reliance on labeled data, while performing supervised fine-tuning on the server side to complete the traffic classification task. Additionally, an asynchronous update mechanism with staleness tolerance is introduced, combining exponential temporal decay weighting and modal importance differentiation to handle delayed model updates, thereby improving training efficiency without requiring strict synchronization. Experiments conducted on the publicly available dataset demonstrate that MaFT achieves superior performance compared to baseline methods, with accuracy reaching 98.14%, indicating the effectiveness of multimodal federated learning in addressing practical challenges of distributed traffic classification.

Keywords: Cybersecurity · Encrypted traffic classification · Federated learning · Multimodal learning · Asynchronous update

R. Chen et al. (Eds.): Inscrypt 2025, LNCS 16409, pp. 467–486, 2026.
https://doi.org/10.1007/978-981-95-6203-9_25

1 Introduction

With the rapid development of Internet technology, the scale and complexity of network traffic continue to grow, making encrypted traffic classification increasingly critical for network management and security. Encrypted traffic classification refers to the identification and categorization of different types of network applications and services based on traffic characteristics, even when the payload is encrypted, and is widely used in fields such as network monitoring, quality of service management, security analysis, and traffic engineering. Traditional traffic classification methods mainly rely on signature-based detection or machine learning approaches, but these methods often have certain limitations when facing increasingly sophisticated encryption techniques and diverse application behaviors. Especially with the widespread adoption of encryption protocols like TLS, traditional deep packet inspection techniques become ineffective, requiring new approaches that can analyze encrypted traffic patterns [1–3].

In recent years, machine learning and deep learning-based encrypted traffic classification methods have shown promising results [4–8]. However, these approaches face a fundamental challenge: the effectiveness of classification models heavily depends on the availability of large-scale, high-quality labeled datasets. In practice, network traffic data and application samples are often distributed across different organizations, such as enterprises, internet service providers, and security vendors. Each organization typically maintains its own network infrastructure and collects traffic data independently, leading to data isolation that prevents effective collaboration. This fragmentation results in several critical issues: individual organizations may have insufficient data to train robust classification models, certain types of applications may only be observed by specific organizations, and the diversity of traffic patterns across different network environments cannot be fully captured by any single entity [9].

To address the challenge of data isolation while respecting data locality requirements, federated learning has emerged as a promising solution [10]. Federated learning enables multiple organizations to collaboratively train machine learning models without directly sharing their sensitive raw data. Instead of centralizing data collection, federated learning allows each participant to train models locally and share only model parameters or updates, thereby maintaining data sovereignty while benefiting from collective knowledge. This approach is particularly valuable in the network management domain, where organizations are often reluctant to share detailed network traffic information due to privacy concerns, regulatory compliance requirements, and competitive considerations. By leveraging federated learning, organizations can collectively build more robust traffic classification models that benefit from diverse application patterns and network characteristics observed across different environments.

At the same time, the characteristics of network traffic are highly diverse, and traditional classification methods based on single features (such as packet size, protocol type, etc.) often cannot effectively cope with complex application scenarios. The integration of multimodal learning has become an important direction for better identifying and distinguishing different types of network applications [11–15]. Multimodal learning can comprehensively characterize network traffic by combining information from different modalities, such as raw byte sequences and packet length patterns, thereby improving the performance of classification models [16]. In federated learning environments, however, different organizations may have varying capabilities to extract and provide different types of features. Client heterogeneity manifests in: (1) computational resources (computing power, memory capacity), (2) network conditions (bandwidth, latency, connectivity), and (3) data processing capabilities (feature extraction infrastructure and regulatory constraints). Some participants might only be able to contribute one type of feature due to computational constraints or data processing limitations, while others can provide multiple modalities. This heterogeneity in feature availability presents both challenges and opportunities for collaborative traffic classification.

Furthermore, in large-scale distributed systems, multiple participants may experience synchronization issues during the training process due to differences in computing power, network bandwidth, or local data volume. Traditional federated learning methods use synchronous mechanisms where all participants must complete local training and upload updates before the next round begins. As the number of participants increases, synchronization waiting can lead to significant time delays and reduced overall efficiency. To overcome this bottleneck, asynchronous mechanisms that allow participants to update independently without waiting for others have become increasingly important. However, asynchronous updates introduce the challenge of handling "stale" model parameters that are based on outdated global models, requiring careful design to maintain model convergence and performance.

To address these challenges, this paper proposes a novel **M**ultimodal **a**synchronous **F**ederated Learning approach for Encrypted **T**raffic Classification, named MaFT. The main contributions of this work include:

1. **Multimodal Federated Framework for Heterogeneous Clients**: We design a federated learning architecture that accommodates both single-modal and multi-modal clients through Deep Canonical Correlation Autoencoders, enabling effective collaboration between organizations with different feature extraction capabilities while addressing data isolation challenges.
2. **Semi-supervised Learning Strategy**: By employing unsupervised autoencoder training on the client side and supervised fine-tuning on the server side, we reduce dependence on labeled traffic samples while maintaining classification performance, which is particularly important given the scarcity of labeled traffic data.
3. **Asynchronous Aggregation with Staleness Tolerance**: We implement an asynchronous update mechanism that combines exponential temporal decay weighting with modal importance differentiation, allowing the system to effectively utilize delayed model updates without requiring strict synchronization, thereby improving training efficiency in distributed environments.

2 Related Work

2.1 Network Traffic Analysis Methods

Network traffic analysis has evolved significantly over the past decades, progressing from simple rule-based approaches to sophisticated machine learning techniques. This evolution reflects the ongoing challenges posed by increasing application complexity, encryption adoption, and the need for more accurate traffic understanding in diverse network environments.

Traditional Rule-Based and Statistical Approaches: Early traffic analysis methods relied on explicit identifiers and predefined rules [17]. Port-based classification [18,19] assumes applications use specific port numbers, but became less effective as applications adopted dynamic ports and obfuscation techniques. Payload-based methods utilized deep packet inspection (DPI) to examine packet content for application signatures [20], which face challenges with encrypted communications. Statistical approaches [21,22] extracted flow-level features such as packet sizes, inter-arrival times, and flow duration, demonstrating notable effectiveness even in encrypted environments since these features remain observable regardless of payload encryption. However, these methods remained limited by their reliance on manually engineered features and predefined patterns, which may not capture the full complexity of modern traffic behaviors.

Machine Learning and Deep Learning Approaches: The introduction of machine learning enabled automatic feature learning and improved adaptability. Early ML methods employed SVM, Decision Trees, and clustering algorithms with statistical features. Deep learning [23] brought more dramatic advances: Convolutional Neural Network (CNNs) [4,24,25] proved effective for processing raw packet data, Recurrent Neural Networks (RNNs) and Long Short-Term Memory (LSTM) networks excelled at modeling temporal dependencies [26,27], and Transformer architectures [28,29] demonstrated capabilities in capturing long-range patterns. Graph Neural Networks (GNNs) have been employed to capture relational features and model non-Euclidean data structures in network traffic, enabling analysis of flow correlations, host-to-host relationships, and complex network interaction patterns [30,31]. Autoencoder-based approaches [32] have proven valuable for anomaly detection and scenarios with limited labeled data.

Multimodal Deep Learning Approaches: Recent advances have applied multimodal learning to encrypted traffic classification by integrating complementary information from multiple data sources. Early approaches include App-Net [11] and MIMETIC [12], which combine raw packet bytes and packet length sequences using CNNs and recurrent networks (LSTM, GRU) with simple fusion techniques like concatenation. DISTILLER [13] extended these methods to multi-task frameworks for joint classification across multiple traffic attributes. More recently, PEAN [14] leverages Transformer encoders and bidirectional LSTM to jointly model byte sequences and packet length dynamics. Advanced approaches like AN-Net [33] introduce robustness considerations through probability masking and mutual information estimation to enhance feature-level representations and filter noisy modalities before fusion.

2.2 Federated Learning for Distributed Network Traffic Analysis

Federated learning has emerged as a promising approach for distributed traffic analysis, enabling collaborative model training across multiple organizations without sharing raw data. This paradigm addresses the critical challenge of data isolation in cybersecurity scenarios where organizations need to benefit from collective knowledge while maintaining data privacy and regulatory compliance.

Semi-supervised Federated Approaches: Given the scarcity of labeled traffic data, several works have explored semi-supervised federated learning [34,35]. FLUIDS [36] employs unsupervised autoencoder training on clients followed by local supervised fine-tuning, while FSSL [37] performs server-side supervised learning after client-side unsupervised training. Wang et al. [38] developed a framework for smart home networks with DPI-based traffic labeling. These approaches demonstrate the potential of leveraging abundant unlabeled traffic data in federated settings.

Advanced Federated Architectures: Recent work has explored more sophisticated federated learning designs. FS-GAN [39] employs distributed GANs for self-supervised learning and unknown traffic detection. SFML [40] integrates split learning and mutual learning to address client resource limitations. Li et al. [41] proposed dynamic weighted aggregation for traffic classification, while Sun et al. [42] incorporated blockchain consensus for IoT scenarios.

While existing federated learning approaches have made significant contributions to distributed traffic analysis, there remain several areas for further exploration and improvement: (1) **Participant heterogeneity handling** - most current methods assume participants can provide similar data modalities, while real-world scenarios often involve organizations with varying data processing capabilities; (2) **Training efficiency optimization** - existing approaches typically employ synchronous aggregation, which may face challenges when participants have different computational resources and network conditions; (3) **Multimodal feature utilization** - while multimodal learning [12,14] and federated learning [36,37] have been studied separately, there is potential for further exploring their integration in distributed traffic analysis scenarios. Building upon these existing works, our MaFT framework explores solutions for participant heterogeneity through adaptive multimodal learning, investigates asynchronous aggregation mechanisms to improve training efficiency, and examines the integration of multimodal approaches with federated learning for traffic classification applications.

3 Methodology

This section presents the architecture and design components of the MaFT model, as illustrated in Fig. 1. The figure shows three types of clients with different modal capabilities, demonstrating the framework's ability to accommodate diverse organizational needs. MaFT consists of four main components: traffic preprocessing, client-side local model training, server-side asynchronous model update, and global model distribution. Our framework adopts a semi-supervised learning approach where autoencoders perform unsupervised training on the client side to learn traffic representations, while supervised fine-tuning occurs on the server side to complete the traffic classification task. The following subsections first formalize the problem definition and objectives, then detail each technical component of our framework.

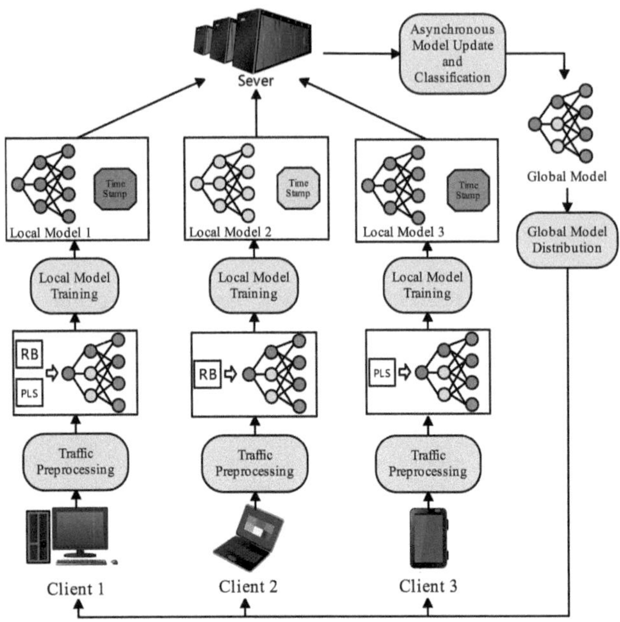

Fig. 1. Framework of MaFT. RB: Raw Byte; PLS: Packet Length Sequence.

The complete MaFT algorithm workflow is presented in Algorithm 1. This algorithm integrates all key components including client-side training, server-side asynchronous aggregation, and the staleness tolerance mechanism.

3.1 Problem Definition and Objectives

Consider a federated learning system with K participants and one central server for collaborative traffic classification. Each participant $k \in \{1, 2, ..., K\}$ possesses local encrypted traffic dataset $\mathcal{D}_k$ but cannot share raw data due to privacy and regulatory constraints. Participants have heterogeneous capabilities: multimodal participants can provide both raw byte sequences and packet length patterns, while unimodal participants can only contribute one feature type due to computational or processing limitations.

Our objective is to collaboratively learn a global traffic classification model $f(\cdot; \theta)$ that: (1) preserves data locality without sharing raw traffic data, (2) effectively integrates contributions from heterogeneous participants, (3) leverages

Algorithm 1. MaFT Algorithm Workflow

Require: Global model θ_0, client datasets $\{\mathcal{D}_k\}_{k=1}^{K}$, aggregation interval Δt
Ensure: Trained global model θ_{global}
Initialize global DCCA encoder parameters θ_0, set $t = 0$
while not converged **do**
  Client Training (Parallel):
  for each client k **do**
    Download θ_{global}, preprocess local data $\mathcal{D}_k$
    if multimodal client **then**
      Train DCCA: $\mathcal{L}_{\text{MC}} = \mathcal{L}_{\text{recon1}} + \mathcal{L}_{\text{recon2}} + \lambda \mathcal{L}_{\text{CCA}}$
    else
      Train autoencoder: $\mathcal{L}_{\text{recon}}$
    end if
    Upload (θ_k, t_k) asynchronously
  end for
  Server Aggregation: $t = t + \Delta t$
  for each update (θ_i, t_i) **do**
    Compute weights: $w_{final}(i) = w_{time}(t, t_i) \times w_{modal}(i)$
  end for
  Aggregate: $\theta_{global} = \frac{\sum_i w_{final}(i)\theta_i}{\sum_i w_{final}(i)}$
  Server Fine-tuning:
  Train MLP classifier, fine-tune encoders, broadcast θ_{global}
end while

multimodal information when available, and (4) reduces dependency on scarce labeled traffic samples. Formally, we minimize:

$$\min_{\theta} \sum_{k=1}^{K} \frac{|\mathcal{D}_k|}{|\mathcal{D}|} \mathcal{L}_k(\theta), \tag{1}$$

where $\mathcal{L}_k(\theta)$ is the local loss function for participant k.

3.2 Traffic Preprocessing

Considering the varying computational capabilities of different participants, we assume that network traffic feature modalities provided by participants may differ. As illustrated in Fig. 1, some participants can provide multiple feature types while others contribute only single modalities. In our experiments, we use network flows as the basic classification unit, utilizing raw bytes and packet length sequences as features.

Traffic is segmented into flows based on the quintuple source IP, destination IP, source port, destination port, protocol. We filter out certain traffic types with limited relevance for traffic classification, including unsuccessful TCP handshakes, DNS queries, and LLMNR protocol traffic, as these typically represent background noise rather than meaningful application behaviors. Additionally, we remove explicit identifiers such as IP addresses, port numbers, and certificates to improve model generalizability.

To address variability in packet sizes within flows, we standardize packet representation by selecting the first N packets from each flow, setting header length to L_h bytes and payload length to L_p bytes. Packets exceeding these lengths are truncated while shorter packets are padded, generating a sequence of $L_b = N \times (L_h + L_p)$ bytes represented as $[b_1, b_2, ..., b_{L_b}]$. To compensate for structural information lost during standardization, we extract the original packet length sequence from the first M packets as a complementary modality. This dual-modal approach enables comprehensive traffic characterization while maintaining computational efficiency.

3.3 Client-Side Local Model Training

To address the difficulty of obtaining labeled data locally on the client side, we employ autoencoders for unsupervised training to learn effective traffic data representations. Considering the heterogeneous capabilities of different clients, we utilize two types of autoencoder models: classic autoencoders for unimodal clients and Deep Canonical Correlation Autoencoders (DCCAs) for multimodal clients.

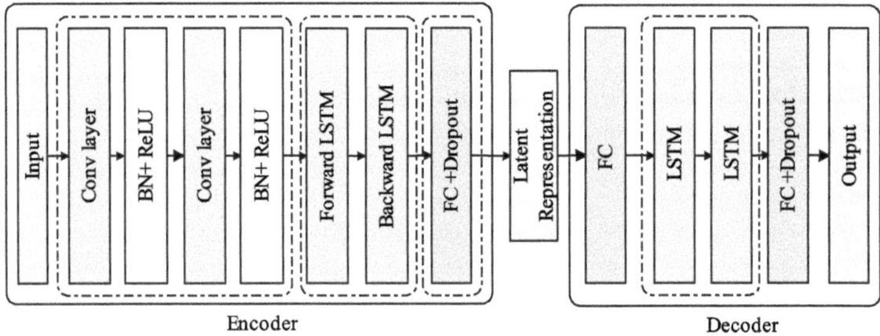

Fig. 2. The structure of the Autoencoder.

Unimodal Client Architecture: For clients providing single modalities, our autoencoder architecture is illustrated in Fig. 2. The encoder consists of three main components: (1) a CNN module with two layers of 1D convolution, each followed by batch normalization and ReLU activation, for extracting local features from input sequences; (2) a bidirectional LSTM module with two layers capable of capturing both forward and backward dependencies, outputting hidden states at each time step; (3) a fully connected layer that maps the final LSTM output to a low-dimensional latent space, with dropout applied for regularization. The decoder reconstructs the original traffic data from the latent representation using a reverse architecture with LSTM layers and fully connected mapping. The reconstruction loss is calculated using Mean Squared Error:

$$\mathcal{L}_{\text{recon}} = \frac{1}{N}\sum_{i=1}^{N}(x_i - \hat{x}_i)^2. \quad (2)$$

Multimodal Client Architecture: For clients capable of providing multiple feature modalities, we employ DCCA as shown in Fig. 3. DCCA integrates two autoencoders (following the architecture described above) with Canonical Correlation Analysis to learn shared latent representations from correlated data modalities. The key innovation lies in maximizing the correlation between latent representations of different modalities while preserving individual reconstruction capabilities. The canonical correlation ρ for latent representations z_1 and z_2 is calculated as:

$$\rho = \max_{w_1, w_2} \frac{w_1^T \Sigma_{12} w_2}{\sqrt{w_1^T \Sigma_{11} w_1 \cdot w_2^T \Sigma_{22} w_2}}, \quad (3)$$

where Σ_{11}, Σ_{22} are covariance matrices and Σ_{12} is the cross-covariance matrix. The canonical correlation loss is defined as:

$$\mathcal{L}_{\text{CCA}} = -\log(\rho). \quad (4)$$

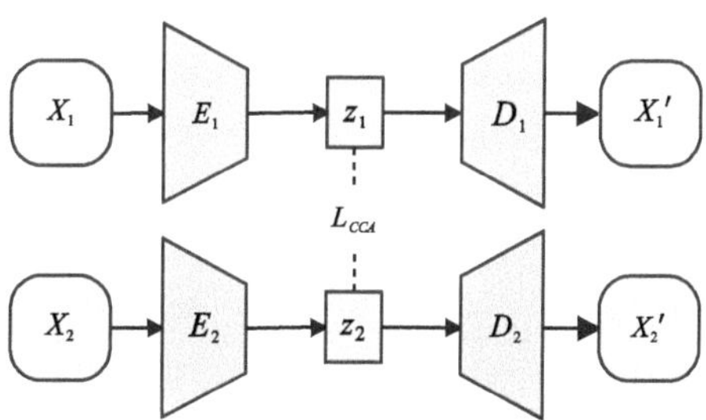

Fig. 3. The structure of the Deep Canonical Correlation Autoencoder.

The total loss for multimodal clients combines reconstruction losses and canonical correlation:

$$\mathcal{L}_{\text{MC}} = \mathcal{L}_{\text{recon1}} + \mathcal{L}_{\text{recon2}} + \lambda \mathcal{L}_{\text{CCA}}, \quad (5)$$

where λ is a weighting parameter that balances the reconstruction and correlation terms.

Training Strategy: When the server distributes updated global model parameters, it provides complete DCCA encoder parameters to all clients. Unimodal clients utilize only the autoencoder corresponding to their available modality, freezing parameters of the other autoencoder and excluding canonical correlation loss computation. Multimodal clients train the complete DCCA framework. Upon training completion, clients upload updated encoder parameters along with timestamps to the server for asynchronous aggregation.

3.4 Server-Side Asynchronous Model Update

On the server side, to enhance the efficiency of training, we adopt an asynchronous update approach, where each client (or node) updates the global model independently at different time points rather than simultaneously. This means that clients can continue their own learning and model updates while waiting for feedback from other clients, thereby accelerating the training process and improving the system's efficiency and responsiveness. Even if some clients experience delays or occasional offline status, the system can still proceed without being affected by the overall progress. Moreover, asynchronous updates better utilize resources and reduce bottlenecks caused by synchronization issues.

During asynchronous updates, some clients may upload parameters that are not based on the latest global model, meaning there are partially "stale" models. Here, "staleness" refers to the temporal delay $(t-t_i)$ between current aggregation time t and client i's update timestamp t_i, arising from network latency or varying computational speeds. Discarding these model parameters by the server would result in a waste of resources. Therefore, we introduce a staleness tolerance mechanism.

For the aggregation process at time point t, the base time weight for client i is defined as:

$$w_{time}(t, t_i) = \begin{cases} \exp(-\alpha(t-t_i)), & \text{if } t - t_i < \tau_{max} \\ 0, & \text{if } t - t_i \geq \tau_{max} \end{cases} \quad (6)$$

where t is the current time, t_i is the update timestamp of client$i$, α is the time decay factor controlling the rate at which the update weight decays with staleness time—the larger the α, the faster the decay; and τ_{max} is the maximum staleness time, i.e., the threshold beyond which the update weight is zero.

Additionally, when aggregating local models, we assign different weights to multimodal clients (β) and unimodal clients (γ) to reflect their different contributions.

Typically, multimodal clients are assigned more weight because they play a crucial role in adjusting both modalities, which helps single-modal clients benefit from the data of the other modality.

The final weight is calculated as:

$$w_{final}(i) = w_{time}(t, t_i) \times w_{modal}(i). \quad (7)$$

At each aggregation time point t, the model aggregation can be described as:

$$\theta_{global} = \frac{\sum_{i=1}^{N} w_{final}(i)\theta_i}{\sum_{i=1}^{N} w_{final}(i)}. \quad (8)$$

Parameters uploaded by multimodal clients are used to update the encoders of the entire DCCA, while parameters uploaded by unimodal clients only update the encoder corresponding to their modality.

After the server completes the aggregation of the encoders, it can utilize the encoders to generate latent representations of the two modalities of the traffic data. Subsequently, a late-fusion approach is employed to obtain the joint representation of the modalities, which is then fed into a Multilayer Perceptron (MLP) containing two fully connected layers to serve as the classifier for completing the classification. Each fully connected layer in the MLP is followed by a batch normalization layer, with ReLU used as the activation function, and Dropout is applied to prevent overfitting.

In the classification task, supervised learning is employed. As a service provider, the server can offer a set of auxiliary datasets with labels, which are generated based on expert knowledge of the service tasks. The loss function used for the classification task is the cross-entropy loss function.

During the training process, the encoder of the DCCA is fine-tuned to ensure that the features it extracts are more suitable for the classification task. The fine-tuned encoder is then distributed as the new global model to the clients.

4 Evaluation

4.1 Experimental Setup

Dataset. We performed experiments on a real-world public traffic dataset Malicious_TLS [43] to evaluate our model's performance. The dataset includes 22 distinct types of active malware traffic, along with corresponding benign traffic. All traffic is encrypted using TLS, causing different traffic types to appear similar, which makes differentiation challenging. The dataset is split into training, testing, and validation sets in an 8:1:1 ratio, and the data is evenly distributed across all clients and the server.

Baseline. To assess the performance strengths and weaknesses of the proposed MaFT model, we chose seven existing models for comparison. The descriptions of these methods are as follows:

1D CNN [24]: This model is an end-to-end classification approach that first converts byte sequences into grayscale image values. It then employs a one-dimensional convolutional neural network (1D CNN) to classify network traffic, leveraging the spatial hierarchy in data for effective feature extraction and classification.

ACID [44]: This model focuses on clustering encrypted network traffic. The ACID model is specially designed to handle the complexities of encrypted data flows, providing robust classification capabilities in secure communication environments.

FSSL [37]: This model employs a CNN-based classification model to implement semi-supervised learning within the framework of federated learning.

FLUIDS [36]: This model is based on semi-supervised learning and federated learning. It employs an autoencoder model for local training, utilizing unlabeled samples for training. After global aggregation, it fine-tunes the model using locally labeled samples.

FLAECNN [38]: This model is a semi-supervised federated learning model, which directly utilizes labeled data for semi-supervised learning on the sub-nodes.

Environment Settings. The proposed model is implemented using PyTorch 2.5.1 and python 3.10.14, with all experiments conducted on a Ubuntu 22.04 server equipped with CPU of Intel(R) Xeon(R) Gold 5218R @ 2.10GHz, GPU of NVIDIA TESLA V100 32GB.

Evaluation Metrics. The performance of the model was evaluated using four key metrics: accuracy, macro-precision, macro-recall, and macro-F1-score. These metrics were computed in a macro-averaged manner to ensure that each class contributes equally to the final score, which is particularly important in multi-class classification tasks with potential class imbalance.

For each class i, we first compute the individual precision, recall, and F1-score using the standard definitions based on true positives (TP), false positives (FP), true negatives (TN), and false negatives (FN). Then, the macro-averaged metrics are obtained by taking the arithmetic mean of the per-class scores across all C classes.

The overall accuracy is calculated as:

$$\text{Accuracy} = \frac{\sum_{i=1}^{C} TP_i}{\sum_{i=1}^{C} (TP_i + FP_i + TN_i + FN_i)}, \tag{9}$$

Macro-precision is defined as:

$$\text{Macro-Precision} = \frac{1}{C} \sum_{i=1}^{C} \frac{TP_i}{TP_i + FP_i}, \tag{10}$$

Macro-recall is defined as:

$$\text{Macro-Recall} = \frac{1}{C} \sum_{i=1}^{C} \frac{TP_i}{TP_i + FN_i}, \tag{11}$$

The macro-F1-score is the harmonic mean of macro-precision and macro-recall:

$$\text{Macro-F}_1 = \frac{1}{C} \sum_{i=1}^{C} 2 \cdot \frac{\text{Precision}_i \cdot \text{Recall}_i}{\text{Precision}_i + \text{Recall}_i}, \tag{12}$$

where TP_i, FP_i, TN_i, and FN_i denote the true positives, false positives, true negatives, and false negatives for class i, respectively, and C is the total number of classes.

Experimental Parameters. The key parameter settings are provided as follows:

- Traffic preprocessing: $N = 5$, $L_h = 80$, $L_p = 240$, $L_b = 1600$, $M = 30$
- DCCA loss weighting: $\lambda = 0.5$ (Formula 5)
- Staleness mechanism: $\alpha = 0.1$, $\tau_{max} = 5$ (Formula 6)
- Client weights: $\beta = 1.0$ (multimodal), $\gamma = 0.7$ (unimodal)
- Local training: learning rate 0.001, batch size 64

The staleness threshold $\tau_{max} = 5$ was determined via sensitivity analysis (Sect. 4.3) to optimally balance delayed update utilization and model quality.

4.2 Comparison of Classification Results

In this section, we conducted classification experiments on the Malicious_TLS dataset, selecting six types of traffic for evaluation. The results are presented in Table 1.

Table 1. Comparison experimental results (%).

	Method	Accuracy	Recall	Precision	F1
Non-FL	1D CNN	91.84	91.76	91.31	90.86
	ACID	92.23	92.51	91.68	91.74
FL	FSSL	96.90	95.09	95.98	95.51
	FLUIDS	96.37	94.73	95.29	94.98
	FLAECNN	96.37	94.53	94.95	94.72
	MaFT	98.14	97.25	97.83	96.98

The experimental results demonstrate that the MaFT model outperforms other federated learning (FL) methods, achieving an accuracy of 98.14%, a recall of 97.25%, a precision of 96.98%, and an F1 score of 97.83%. These metrics are superior to both other FL methods and non-federated learning approaches.

Among the non-federated learning methods, we compared two typical models: 1D CNN [24] and ACID [44]. The 1D CNN model shows strong performance across all metrics, with a slightly higher recall compared to precision. However, the F1 score is relatively lower than the other methods, indicating that there may be a slight trade-off between recall and precision. Despite this, the model achieves a solid accuracy of 91.84%. ACID outperforms the 1D CNN model in all metrics, particularly in recall (92.51%) and F1 score (91.74%). This indicates that ACID is better at correctly identifying positive samples, as well as maintaining a balance between recall and precision. The increase in accuracy (92.23%) and the improvement in recall suggests that ACID may have better generalization capabilities compared to the 1D CNN.

Among the baseline federated learning models, FSSL [37] stands out as the strongest performer, achieving an accuracy of 96.90%, a recall of 95.09%, a precision of 95.98%, and an F1 score of 95.51%. Compared to non-federated learning models, FSSL's accuracy improves by approximately 4.5%, demonstrating significant performance enhancement. Notably, FSSL maintains a good balance between recall and precision, indicating its ability to identify most malicious traffic while reducing misclassifications.

The results of FLAECNN [38] are similar to those of FLUIDS [36]. The higher recall and lower precision of FLAECNN suggest that it is more sensitive to detected malicious traffic, capable of identifying more potential malicious behaviors. FLUIDS performs slightly worse than FSSL but still outperforms non-federated learning methods, particularly in maintaining a balance between recall and precision. FLUIDS may achieve stable results across different learning tasks through more efficient feature fusion or optimization strategies. This model is robust and suitable for application in highly dynamic network environments.

Overall, federated learning models outperform non-federated learning models, likely due to their distributed nature. MaFT's superior performance (98.14% accuracy) results from three design components: (1) multimodal DCCA integration (1.24% improvement over FSSL), (2) semi-supervised learning strategy enabling effective unlabeled data utilization, and (3) staleness-tolerant asynchronous mechanism with optimal $\tau_{max} = 5$ setting. Furthermore, by comparing the MaFT model with other federated learning models, the results indicate that multimodal learning effectively enhances classification performance. MaFT leverages multimodal learning to integrate information from multiple feature sources. This approach not only improves classification accuracy but also significantly boosts the F1 score, fully demonstrating the powerful potential of multimodal learning in handling complex traffic data.

4.3 Ablation Study

To further examine the impact of multimodal learning on model performance, we conducted ablation experiments on the Malicious_TLS dataset in this section. We considered the following variables:

1. Excluding raw byte: All clients and the server used only packet length sequences as model inputs for training.
2. Excluding packet length: All clients and the server used only raw bytes as model inputs for training.

The experimental results are presented in Table 2.

The first ablation experiment, "Removing Packet Length Sequences", aimed to test the model's performance without using packet length sequence features. The results show that removing this feature led to a slight decline in performance. This indicates that packet length sequences play a significant role in capturing malicious traffic characteristics. Although the performance remains relatively high without this feature, there is a noticeable decline compared to the full

Table 2. Experimental results of ablation on Malicious_TLS(%).

Method	Accuracy	Recall	Precision	F1
w/o packet length sequence	92.27	91.23	91.81	91.54
w/o raw byte	93.64	92.52	93.17	92.79
MaFT	98.14	97.25	97.83	96.98

model. This suggests that packet length sequences provide critical information that helps the model better identify malicious behavior. In contrast, when the model excludes raw byte data, the overall performance decline is less pronounced. This phenomenon suggests that raw byte data may introduce noise or irrelevant information, which slightly weakens the model's classification capability.

The results of the ablation experiments demonstrate that both packet length sequences and raw bytes play significant roles in malicious traffic classification using multimodal learning. Removing packet length sequences causes a 5.87% accuracy drop (98.14% to 92.27%), while removing raw bytes leads to a 4.50% decline (to 93.64%), validating our DCCA's ability to effectively fuse both modalities. Removing either feature leads to a decline in performance. This indicates that they are complementary in the model's decision-making process, especially when used together, as the model's classification performance improves significantly. This highlights the advantages of multimodal methods in detecting malicious traffic behavior.

4.4 Sensitivity Analysis

In this section, we primarily discuss the impact of the maximum tolerance time in the staleness tolerance mechanism on the model's performance. We set different values for the maximum tolerance timeτ_{max}: 1, 5, and 10, representing low tolerance, moderate tolerance, and excessive tolerance, respectively, for the server's acceptance of "stale" model parameters uploaded by clients during global model updates. We ran the model under these three parameter conditions for the same duration and recorded the changes in training loss. The experimental results are illustrated in the Fig. 4.

According to the experimental results, when $\tau_{max} = 1$, the model's loss converges slowly and exhibits fluctuations, with the final loss being the highest among the three scenarios. This is because, under low tolerance, the server utilizes fewer asynchronous updates from client model parameters, discarding a significant portion of them, which slows down the update process. When $\tau_{max} = 5$, the server adopts a moderate tolerance strategy, resulting in a noticeable improvement in convergence speed and reduced fluctuations compared to the low-tolerance scenario. This is due to the increased utilization of updates by the server, enhancing the frequency of model updates and reducing the gap between iterations. Additionally, the final loss decreases as the client parameter updates are better utilized. When $\tau_{max} = 10$, the model's performance lies

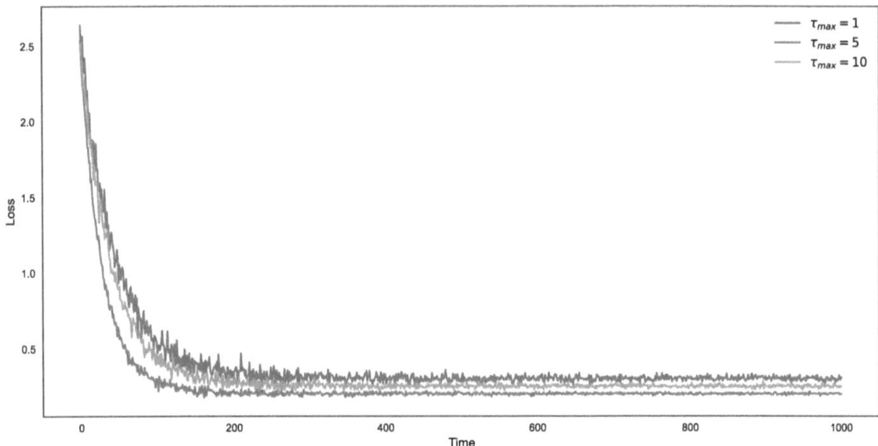

Fig. 4. Comparison Results of Different Maximum Tolerance Times.

between the previous two cases but exhibits more pronounced fluctuations. This is caused by the server's excessive tolerance, which incorporates client updates that differ significantly from the current model.

Therefore, when using the staleness tolerance mechanism, it is crucial to select a moderate value for the maximum tolerance time. Both excessively large and small maximum tolerance times can adversely affect the model's final performance.

5 Discussion

While federated learning provides significant privacy advantages over traditional centralized approaches by avoiding direct data sharing, recent research has identified potential privacy risks that warrant consideration. Theoretical studies have shown that under certain adversarial conditions, sophisticated attackers might potentially extract limited information about training data from shared model parameters through techniques such as gradient inversion or membership inference attacks [45]. In the context of our MaFT framework, these theoretical risks could include exposure of certain network characteristics or timing correlations, particularly given the asynchronous nature of our approach. However, it is important to note that such attacks typically require specific conditions and sophisticated adversaries, and federated learning still provides substantially better privacy protection compared to centralized data collection and processing approaches.

To further enhance privacy protection, future work could explore the integration of additional privacy-preserving mechanisms, with differential privacy being a particularly promising direction [46]. This can be achieved by adding calibrated noise to model updates before transmission to provide mathematical privacy guarantees. Other potential enhancements include secure aggregation protocols, local differential privacy mechanisms, and homomorphic encryption techniques. The primary focus of this work is to explore the feasibility of combining multimodal learning with federated learning for addressing data isolation challenges in distributed traffic classification. Our experimental results demonstrate that this approach can maintain reasonable classification performance while enabling collaborative learning across distributed organizations, though significant opportunities remain for enhancing privacy protection and evaluating the framework's performance in more diverse real-world deployment scenarios.

6 Conclusion

In this paper, we explore the challenges of data privacy, reliance on labeled data, and feature utilization in the task of encrypted traffic classification within the field of network management. We propose MaFT, an innovative multimodal asynchronous federated learning classification framework that combines multimodal learning and federated learning to achieve distributed encrypted traffic classification. Multimodal learning effectively leverages different features of encrypted traffic to enhance classification performance. The framework adopts a semi-supervised training approach, reducing dependency on labeled data. Additionally, the introduction of asynchronous updates and a staleness tolerance mechanism improves training speed. Experimental results demonstrate that MaFT outperforms existing methods, highlighting the potential of multimodal federated learning in addressing the challenges of encrypted traffic classification.

Acknowledgments. This work was supported by the National Key Research and Development Program of China (No. 2023YFB2705000), and the Natural Science Foundation of Henan (No. 252300420992).

References

1. Akbari, I., Salahuddin, M.A., Ven, L., Limam, N., Tuffin, S.: A look behind the curtain: traffic classification in an increasingly encrypted web. In: Proceedings of the ACM on Measurement and Analysis of Computing Systems 5(1), pp. 1–26 (2021)
2. Shiqian, X., Geng, G.-G., Jin, X., Liu, D., Weng, J.: Seeing traffic paths: encrypted traffic classification with path signature features. IEEE Trans. Inf. Forensics Secur. **17**, 2166–2181 (2022)
3. Meng, Q., et al.: IIT: accurate decentralized application identification through mining intra- and inter-flow relationships. IEEE Trans. Netw. Serv. Manage. **22**(1), 394–408 (2025)
4. Lotfollahi, M., Zade, R.S.H., Siavoshani, M.J., Saberian, M.: Deep packet: a novel approach for encrypted traffic classification using deep learning. Soft. Comput. **24**, 1999–2012 (2020)

5. Lin, X., Xiong, G., Gou, G., Li, Z., Shi, J., Yu, J.: ET-BERT: a contextualized datagram representation with pre-training transformers for encrypted traffic classification. In: WWW: Proceedings of the ACM Web Conference, pp. 633–642 (2022)
6. Lin, X., et al.: Respond to change with constancy: instruction-tuning with LLM for Non-IID network traffic classification. IEEE Trans. Inf. Foren. Security **20**, 5758–5773 (2025)
7. Malekghaini, N., et al.: Deep learning for encrypted traffic classification in the face of data drift: an empirical study. Comput. Netw. **225**, 109648 (2023)
8. Yuan, Q., et al.: Multi-agent for network security monitoring and warning: a generative AI solution. IEEE Network. https://doi.org/10.1109/MNET.2025.3579001
9. Zhang, J., Liang, S., Ye, F., Hu, Q., Qian, Y.: Towards detection of zero-day botnet attack in iot networks using federated learning. In: ICC-IEEE International Conference on Communications, pp. 7–12. IEEE, Rome (2023). https://doi.org/10.1109/ICC45041.2023.10279423
10. Zhou, X., et al.: Federated distillation and blockchain empowered secure knowledge sharing for Internet of medical Things. Inf. Sci. **662**, 120217 (2024)
11. Wang, X., Chen, S., Su, J.: App-Net: a hybrid neural network for encrypted mobile traffic classification In: IEEE INFOCOM 2020 - IEEE Conference on Computer Communications Workshops (INFOCOM WKSHPS), pp. 424–429. IEEE, Rome (2020). https://doi.org/10.1109/INFOCOMWKSHPS50562.2020.9162891
12. Aceto, G., Ciuonzo, D., Montieri, A., Pescapé, A.: MIMETIC: mobile encrypted traffic classification using multimodal deep learning. Comput. Networks **165**, 106944.1–106944.12 (2019)
13. Aceto, G., Ciuonzo, D., Montieri, A., Pescapé, A.: DISTILLER: encrypted traffic classification via multimodal multitask deep learning. J. Netw. Comput. Appl. **183–184**, 102985 (2021)
14. Lin, P., Ye, K., Yishen, H., Lin, Y., Chengzhong, X.: A novel multimodal deep learning framework for encrypted traffic classification. IEEE/ACM Trans. Networking **31**(3), 1369–1384 (2023)
15. Wang, X., et al.: Entropy-regulated cross-modal generative fusion for multimodal network intrusion detection. Inf. Fusion **126**, Part: A, 103581 (2026)
16. Peng, X., Zhu, X., Clifton, D.A.: Multimodal learning with transformers: a survey. IEEE Trans. Pattern Anal. Mach. Intell. **45**, 12113–12132 (2022)
17. Karagiannis, T., Papagiannaki, K., Faloutsos, M.: BLINC: multilevel traffic classification in the dark. ACM SIGCOMM Comput. Commun. Rev. **35**(4), 229–240 (2005)
18. Zejdl, P., Ubik, S., Macek, V., Oslebo, A.: Traffic classification for portable applications with hardware support. In: International Workshop on Intelligent Solutions in Embedded Systems, pp. 1–9. IEEE, Regensburg (2008). https://doi.org/10.1109/WISES.2008.4623292
19. Yoon, S.-H., Park, J.-W., Park, J.-S., Oh, Y.-S., Kim, M.-S.: Internet application traffic classification using fixed IP-Port. In: Management Enabling the Future Internet for Changing Business and New Computing Services (APNOMS), pp. 21–30, Springer, Heidelberg (2009)
20. Park, J.-S., Yoon, S.-H., Kim, M.-S.: Performance improvement of payload signature-based traffic classification system using application traffic temporal locality. In: 15th Asia-Pacific Network Operations and Management Symposium (APNOMS), pp. 1–6, Hiroshima, Japan (2013)
21. Moore, A.W., Zuev, D.: Internet traffic classification using bayesian analysis techniques. In: Proceedings of the 2005 ACM SIGMETRICS international conference

on Measurement and modeling of computer systems (SIGMETRICS), pp. 50–60. ACM, Banff, Alberta, Canada (2005)
22. Crotti, M., Dusi, M., Gringoli, F., Salgarelli, L.: Traffic classification through simple statistical fingerprinting. Acm Sigcomm Comput. Commun. Rev. **37**(1), 5–16 (2007)
23. Bovenzi, G., Nascita, A., Yang, L., Finamore, A., Aceto, G., Ciuonzo, D., Pescapé, A., Rossi, D.: Benchmarking class incremental learning in deep learning traffic classification. IEEE/ACM Trans. Networking **21**(1), 51–69 (2024)
24. Wang, W., Zhu, M., Wang, J., Zeng, X., Yang, Z.: End-to-end encrypted traffic classification with one-dimensional convolution neural networks. In: IEEE International Conference on Intelligence and Security Informatics (ISI), pp. 43-48. IEEE, Beijing (2017). https://doi.org/10.1109/ISI.2017.8004872
25. Wang, Z., Ma, B., Zeng, Y., Lin, X., Shi, K., Wang, Z.: End-to-end encrypted traffic classification with one-dimensional convolution neural networks. In: International Conference on Networking and Network Applications (NaNA), pp. 220–225. IEEE, Beijing (2022). https://doi.org/10.1109/NaNA56854.2022.00044
26. Ren, X., Huaxi, G., Wei, W.: Tree-RNN: tree structural recurrent neural network for network traffic classification. Expert Syst. Appl. **167**, 114363 (2021)
27. Yao, H., Liu, C., Zhang, P., Wu, S., Jiang, C., Yu, S.: Identification of encrypted traffic through attention mechanism based long short term memory. IEEE Trans. Big Data **8**(1), 241–252 (2022)
28. Yang, L., Guo, S., Liu, D., Zeng, Y., Jiao, X., Zhou, Y.: ConViTML: a convolutional vision transformer-based meta-learning framework for real-time edge network traffic classification. IEEE Trans. Netw. Serv. Manage. **21**(3), 3344–3357 (2024)
29. Yang, J., Jiang, X., Lei, Y., Liang, W., Ma, Z., Li, S.: MTSecurity: privacy-preserving malicious traffic classification using graph neural network and transformer. IEEE Trans. Netw. Serv. Manage. **21**(3), 3583–3597 (2024)
30. Han, X., et al.: DE-GNN: Dual embedding with graph neural network for fine-grained encrypted traffic classification. Comput. Netw. **245**, 110372 (2024)
31. Hu, G., Xiao, X., Shen, M., Zhang, B., Yan, X., Liu, Y.: TCGNN: packet-grained network traffic classification via graph neural networks. Eng. Appl. Artif. Intell. **123**, Part C, 106531 (2023)
32. Telikani, A., Gandomi, A.H., Choo, K.-K.R., Shen, J.: A cost-sensitive deep learning-based approach for network traffic classification. IEEE Trans. Netw. Serv. Manage. **19**(1), 661–670 (2022)
33. Deng, X., Wang, Y., Xue, Z.: AN-Net: an anti-noise network for anonymous traffic classification. In: Proceedings of the ACM Web Conference (WWW), pp. 4417–4428. ACM, Singapore (2024). https://doi.org/10.1145/3589334.3645691
34. Zejdl, P., Ubik, S., Macek, V., Oslebo, A.: A distributed traffic classification model based on Federated Learning. In: 7th International Conference on Big Data Computing and Communications (BigCom), pp. 75-81. IEEE, Deqing (2021). https://doi.org/10.1109/BigCom53800.2021.00022
35. Guo, Y., Wang, D.: FEAT: a federated approach for privacy-preserving network traffic classification in heterogeneous environments. IEEE Internet Things J. **10**(2), 1274–1285 (2023)
36. Aouedi, O., Piamrat, K., Muller, G., Singh, K.: FLUIDS: federated learning with semi-supervised approach for intrusion detection system. In: IEEE 19th Annual Consumer Communications & Networking Conference, pp. 523-524. IEEE, Las Vegas, NV (2022). https://doi.org/10.1109/CCNC49033.2022.9700632

37. Jin, Z., Liang, Z., He, M., Peng, Y., Xue, H., Wang, Yu.: A federated semi-supervised learning approach for network traffic classification. Int. J. Network Manage **333**, 1–13 (2023)
38. Wang, Z.X., Li, Z.Y., MengYi, F., Ye, Y.C., Wang, P.: Network traffic classification based on federated semi-supervised learning. J. Syst. Architect. **149**, 103091 (2024)
39. Xiao, Y., et al.: Distributed traffic synthesis and classification in edge networks: a federated self-supervised learning approach. IEEE Trans. Mob. Comput. **23**(2), 1815–1829 (2024)
40. Xia, J., Meng, W., Li, P.: SFML: A personalized, efficient, and privacy-preserving collaborative traffic classification architecture based on split learning and mutual learning. Futur. Gener. Comput. Syst. **162**, 107487 (2025)
41. Li, J., Tong, X., Liu, J., Cheng, L.: An efficient federated learning system for network intrusion detection. IEEE Syst. J. **17**(2), 2455–2464 (2023)
42. Sun, N., Wang, W., Tong, Y., Liu, K.: Blockchain based federated learning for intrusion detection for Internet of Things. Front. Comput. Sci. **18**, 185328 (2024)
43. Yuan, Q., et al.: BoAu: Malicious traffic detection with noise labels based on boundary augmentation. Comput. Secur. **131**, 103300 (2023)
44. Diallo, A.F., Patras, P.: Adaptive clustering-based malicious traffic classification at the network edge. In: IEEE INFOCOM 2021 - IEEE Conference on Computer Communications, pp. 1–10. IEEE, Vancouver, BC (2021). https://doi.org/10.1109/INFOCOM42981.2021.9488690
45. Geiping, J., Bauermeister, H., Dröge, H., Moeller, M.: Inverting Gradients – How easy is it to break privacy in federated learning? In: Advances in Neural Information Processing Systems (NeurIPS), pp. 16937–16947. Curran Associates, Inc., Virtual (2020)
46. Cui, J., Xiao, J., Zhong, H., Jing Zhang, L., Wei, I.B., He, D.: LH-IDS: lightweight hybrid intrusion detection system based on differential privacy in VANETs. IEEE Trans. Mob. Comput. **23**(12), 12195–12210 (2024). https://doi.org/10.1109/TMC.2024.3407709

Correction to: An Early Detection of Risky Crowd Dynamics Scheme Based on Motion Entropy and Scene Semantics

Sourabh Choudhary, Chunqiang Hu, Syed Murtoza Mushrul Pasha, MD Tanvir Islam, Rashedin Islam, and Arnob Barua Himo

Correction to: Chapter 12 in: R. Chen et al. (Eds.): *Information Security and Cryptology*, LNCS 16409, https://doi.org/10.1007/978-981-95-6203-9_12

The original version of Chapter 12 was inadvertently published with incorrect figure. The chapter has been updated with the correct figure 1 as:

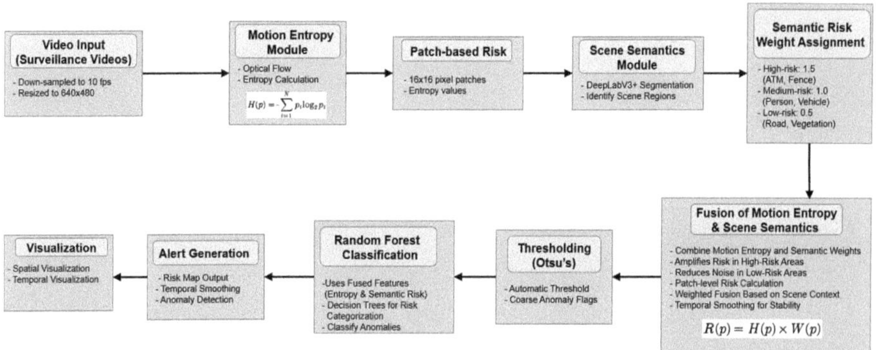

Fig. 1. System architecture of the proposed framework. Video frames are processed through the motion entropy module to compute optical flow and entropy heatmaps, then fused with semantic information to produce frame-level risk scores. The alert generation stage outputs visual heatmaps and logs, enabling real-time monitoring and decision-making.

The updated version of this chapter can be found at https://doi.org/10.1007/978-981-95-6203-9_12

R. Chen et al. (Eds.): Inscrypt 2025, LNCS 16409, p. C1, 2026.
https://doi.org/10.1007/978-981-95-6203-9_26

Author Index

R. Chen et al. (Eds.): Inscrypt 2025, LNCS 16409, pp. 487–488, 2026.
https://doi.org/10.1007/978-981-95-6203-9

MIX
Papier aus verantwortungsvollen Quellen
Paper from responsible sources
FSC® C105338

If you have any concerns about our products,
you can contact us on
ProductSafety@springernature.com

In case Publisher is established outside the EU,
the EU authorized representative is:
Springer Nature Customer Service Center GmbH
Europaplatz 3, 69115 Heidelberg, Germany

Printed by Libri Plureos GmbH
in Hamburg, Germany